外教社跨文化交际丛书 15

跨文化交际
—— 东西方对话

INTERCULTURAL COMMUNICATION
East and West

Editors:
Bates Hoffer
Jia Yuxin（贾玉新）
Honna Nobuyuki
Song Li（宋 莉）

上海外语教育出版社
外教社 SHANGHAI FOREIGN LANGUAGE EDUCATION PRESS

图书在版编目（CIP）数据

跨文化交际：东西方对话 /（美）贝茨·霍弗，贾玉新，（日）本名信行，宋莉主编.
—上海：上海外语教育出版社，2014（2019重印）
（外教社跨文化交际丛书）
ISBN 978-7-5446-3483-0

Ⅰ.①跨… Ⅱ.①霍弗…②贾…③本名…④宋… Ⅲ.①东西文化－文化交流－文集
Ⅳ.①G04-53

中国版本图书馆CIP数据核字（2013）第237177号

出版发行：**上海外语教育出版社**
　　　　　（上海外国语大学内）　邮编：200083
电　　话：021-65425300（总机）
电子邮箱：bookinfo@sflep.com.cn
网　　址：http://www.sflep.com
责任编辑：李健儿

印　　刷：上海信老印刷厂
开　　本：787×965　1/16　印张 36.75　字数 897 千字
版　　次：2014 年 4 月第 1 版　2019 年 8 月第 3 次印刷
印　　数：1 000 册

书　　号：ISBN 978-7-5446-3483-0 / G・1071
定　　价：70.00 元

本版图书如有印装质量问题，可向本社调换
质量服务热线：4008-213-263　电子邮箱：editorial@sflep.com

"外教社跨文化交际丛书"编委会

主　任：
胡文仲（北京外国语大学）
贾玉新（哈尔滨工业大学）

副主任：
Bates Hoffer（三一大学）
Nobuyuki Honna（青山学院大学）
Steve Kulich（上海外国语大学）
陈　凌（香港浸会大学）
高一虹（北京大学）

委　员：
Andy Kirkpatrick（科廷大学）
Michael Byram（杜伦大学）
Michael Prosser（上海外国语大学）
Richard Wiseman（加州州立大学福勒顿分校）
Robert N. St. Clair（路易斯维尔大学）
陈国明（罗得岛大学）
顾嘉祖（南京师范大学）
林大津（福建师范大学）
申惠中（悉尼大学）
宋　莉（哈尔滨工业大学）
孙有中（北京外国语大学）
许力生（浙江大学）
张红玲（上海外国语大学）
张惠晶（伊利诺大学芝加哥分校）
庄恩平（上海大学）
庄智象（上海外国语大学）

总　　序

　　跨文化交际学是一门在传播学等学科理论的基础上,与人类学、心理学、语言学、文化学以及社会学等相互交叉而发展起来的学科。其实,不同文化间的交流古已有之,但是真正将文化交流进行理论研究进而发展成"跨文化交际学",还只是近四五十年间的事情。想要深入探究这门学科,我们首先要了解它的起源。

　　20世纪60年代是信息技术和交通技术高度发展的年代。随着科技的进步,空间距离大大缩短,各种文化间的交流日益频繁。但是空间距离的缩小并不意味着人们之间的文化距离或是心理距离可以瞬间缩短。与之相反的是,人们不能再用旧有的文化观念和思维方式来理解和解释日新月异的世界里出现的各种新问题。同时,文化差异滋生众多的交际失误、矛盾和冲突,反而使人们的心理距离加大。矛盾和冲突的背后不仅仅是利益或者领土的争夺,也不仅仅是政治和意识形态的分歧,而更多的是文化和价值观念上的巨大隔阂——正是这些隔阂使"地球村"中的人们虽然身在"咫尺"之间,却有如隔天涯之感。

　　美国作为一个多民族、多种族的国家自然而然成为跨文化交际研究的兴起之地,其中以美国人类学家Edward T. Hall为代表的一些学者在前人研究成果的基础上提出了跨文化交际的理论,现在学界也一致将他的著作 *The Silent Language*(Anchor Books,1959)当作是这一学科的奠基之作。

　　到了20世纪70、80年代,学者们把研究重点逐渐从对比和分析不同文化交际(Cross-cultural Communication)中的差异转到研究跨文化交际(Intercultural Communication)动态多变的过程中去。以此为基点,William B. Gudykunst等一批学者建构了动态的跨文化交际理论。理论的突破带来了学科的快速发展,跨文化交际研究所涉及的学科越来越多,研究的内容更加丰富,研究方法日益科学。学科的发展引起了世界各国学者空前广泛的关注,跨文化交际学被引进大学课堂,相关的研究学会和专业学刊相继出现,各种国际学术研讨会也定期举行。现在只要在网上简单查询一下相关书目,我们就会发现此类专著多达几百种,在刊物上发表的论文更是不胜枚举。William B. Gudykunst 曾在其著作 *Cross-cultural and Intercultural*

Communication（Sage Publications，2003）一书中总结了 15 种不同的跨文化交际理论。理论研究和探索上的巨大进步标志着跨文化交际学的学科发展日臻成熟。

进入新世纪，"地球村"每个角落的每个公民都不同程度地被卷入了经济一体化和全球化的浪潮。同时，人们清楚地意识到全球化不等于一元化。在多元文化并存的时代中，个人之间、社会全体之间、民族之间乃至国家之间，无不存在着文化差异甚至文化沟壑。培养对文化差异的敏感性，缩短文化距离，发展跨文化交际能力，已经成为新时代的迫切需求。由此，我们不难预见到跨文化交际研究会在 21 世纪被逐步推向高潮。

在关注国际学科发展趋势的同时，让我们把目光转向中国。虽然我国历史上早有注重语言与文化、语言与社会研究的传统，但是现代的跨文化交际研究在我国的起步还要追溯至上世纪的 80 年代。当时随着国内学界对于语言学和文化研究的不断重视，在"文化热"和"反思热"的影响下，语言研究人文化成为新的热点，这无疑为跨文化交际研究的兴起奠定了基础。改革开放繁荣了国际学术交往，外语界的学者和教师成为国内首先接触到跨文化交际研究的一批人，他们理所当然地成为这一学科的研究主力。我们可以这么说：上世纪 80 年代是跨文化交际学诞生、成长和发展的关键十年。一方面，海外归来的学者把西方有关跨文化交际理论、研究方法和教学实践介绍和引进到中国；另一方面，国内研究者在学习和借鉴的同时，在继承前人成果的基础上，结合中国实际，多方位、多角度地探索和开发我国跨文化交际的学科外延，开创了初步繁荣的研究局面。

外语教师和对外汉语教师是我国跨文化交际研究领域的主力军。他们在教学的过程中认识到跨文化交际能力的培养应当成为外语教育的重要内容，外语教学必须与文化相结合。在上世纪 80 年代末，国内一部分外语院校首先推出了跨文化交际学课程。时至今日，我国已有几十所大学的外语院系开设了这门课程。

1995 年，首届中国跨文化交际国际研讨会在哈尔滨召开，来自世界 20 多个国家和地区的几百名学者进行了学术交流与探讨。中国跨文化交际研究会也在这次会议中正式成立——这标志着跨文化交际研究在中国迎来了一个新纪元。自学会成立以来，已定期组织了 6 次国际研讨会。同时有些院校也多次组织大型研讨会，广泛开展国内不同地区间和国际间的学术交流，跨文化交际研究得到了空前迅速的发展。

广大教师、语言学者们兼收并蓄，著书立说，撰写论文，编写教材。据不完全统计，目前出版的专著和教材多达几十本，发表的论文也有 2000 篇以上。他们研究和探讨的内容丰富多样，涵盖范围广泛；有些学者和教师的研究更是对西方学者的某些理论提出质疑，提出了自己的视角独特的观点。

由于学科性质所决定，跨文化交际研究比其他学科更需要不同文化间的交流。实际上，中国跨文化交际研究会已成为国际大家庭的一部分，并为推动跨文化交际研究在世界范围上的发展做出了应有的贡献。我们的研究会中有不少教师学者同时也是国际学会会员，他们或在国际学会组织和国际学刊中承担重要工作，或是经常受邀参加在海外举行的学术会议，在会上交流论文。不少论文受到国际学界的好评，并在国际学刊上发表。我国的跨文化交际研究学者也在国外出版他们的专著，传播中国在这一领域的研究成果。

回顾这20余年的学科发展，我们也应清楚地意识到前进路上存在着的诸多问题。首先，在理论研究方面，正如王宗炎先生所指出，"收集采购之功多，提炼转化之功少"，我们还没有形成具有中国文化特点的理论。William B. Gudykunst教授也曾指出亚洲学者需要创建适合自己文化的交际理论。只有学习和借鉴而没有发展和改造，没有结合自己文化特点的理论，是不可能把跨文化交际研究建成一门适合中国国情的学科的。其次，由于理论指导不足，我们的研究多集中在文化对比方面，对动态多变的交际过程的研究和探讨不够，在研究方法和研究内容上尚需要更多的探索和拓展，这些都影响了我们在这一领域的进一步发展。

在新的世纪，我们需要进一步开阔视野，发展我国的跨文化交际研究，推动此领域的学科建设，加强此领域的教学和教材建设，以满足广大教师、研究生以及各方面读者的需要。上海外语教育出版社出于推动我国跨文化交际研究的考虑，决定推出"外教社跨文化交际丛书"。丛书既引进国外权威力作，也出版我国学者的著述，还有中外专家的合力之作。我国读者可以通过这套丛书学习和借鉴来自不同文化背景的学者的真知灼见，在领略我国学者和专家的新思维和新成果的同时，还可以欣赏各种文化交流的结晶。我们相信"外教社跨文化交际丛书"对于今后我国跨文化交际学的发展将会起到极为重要的作用。在此，我们代表丛书编委会对上海外语教育出版社的大力支持表示诚挚的谢意。

胡文仲
北京外国语大学
贾玉新
哈尔滨工业大学
2006年4月

Table of Contents

Foreword   *xiii*

OVERVIEW: PROBLEMS AND PERSPECTIVES

1. The Future of Cross Cultural Communication: Perspective of 20 years of the IAICS   3
   L. Brooks HILL
2. China's Intercultural Communication Studies: Its Current status and problems   30
   HU Wenzhong

THEORY

3. Towards a Comprehensive Perspective for Intercultural Communication Study   45
   L. Brooks HILL & Eric FAULK
4. Discourse Identity, Social Identity, and Confusion in Intercultural Communication   66
   Ron SCOLLON
5. The Framework of Cultural Space   81
   Robert N. St. CLAIR & Ana C. T. WILLIAMS
6. Sociolinguistic Approach to Intercultural Communication   98
   JIA Yuxin
7. Cultural Identification, Cultural Identity and Communication   130
   CHEN Ling & PAN Shiwen
8. Hierarchical Manifestation in Intercultural Communication   139
   KIM Kun-ok
9. Intercultural Communication and Global Democracy: A De-weyan perspective   149
   SUN Youzhong

Ethno-relativity and Multiculturalism

10. On the Multiculturalism of Asian Englishes   *163*
    Nobuyuki HONNA
11. On Chinese Indirectness: A multi-dimensional exploration   *172*
    CHANG Hui-Ching
12. Changes in the Cultural Arguments of Chinese Political Leaders   *196*
    D. Ray HEISEY
13. Politeness Phenomena in Japanese Intercultural Business Communication   *207*
    Helen MARRIOTT
14. Reconstructing Eastern Paradigms of Discourse Studies   *228*
    SHI Xu
15. A Contrastive Study of Requests in Chinese and American Cultures   *252*
    JIA Xuerui & HUANG Furong

Intercultural Communicative Competencies

16. Intercultural Nonverbal Communication (In)competence   *273*
    Bates L. HOFFER
17. When Shyness Is Not Incompetence: A case of Thai communication competence   *301*
    Suwichit Sean CHAIDAROON
18. A Contrastive Analysis of Chinese and American Views about Silence and Debate   *315*
    GU Xiaole
19. Understanding Strategic Competence for Intercultural Communication   *331*
    XU Lisheng
20. Multimodal Manifestation of Conceptual Metaphors in Multimedia Communication   *345*
    Ning YU
21. Intercultural Communication Between Japanese and Thais Through Discrepancies in Images   *358*
    Yuko TAKESHITA

Management of Conflict

22. Analyzing an Intercultural Conflict Case Study: Application of a social ecological perspective   *381*
    Ruifang ZHANG & Stella TING-TOOMEY
23. Intercultural Sensitivity and Conflict Management Styles in

     Cross-Cultural Organizational Situations   *406*
                              Yu Tong & Chen Guo-Ming

24. Dealing with Chinese Negotiating Partners: A cross-cultural co-operation strategy   *422*
                                    Alexander Thomas

25. How to Avoid Language Conflict in Europe in the Third Millennium   *448*
                                         Peter H. Nelde

26. Reporting on Sino-Japan Conflicts in *The New York Times*: A critical discourse analysis   *462*
                                         Chen Xiaoxiao

The Educational Context

27. Intercultural Dialogicality Between LC1 and LC2 in the EFL/ESL Classroom   *487*
                                           Song Li

28. Covert Culture in the Foreign Language Classroom: Confronting contrast in target and base mindsets   *503*
                                        Eleanor H. Jorden

29. An Analysis of Language Use and Topic Management in Business Decision-making Meeting   *514*
                                        Bertha Du-Babcock

30. Do They Tell Stories Differently?: Discourse marker use by Chinese native speakers and nonnative speakers   *535*
                                      Xiaoshi Li & Jia Xuerui

31. Intercultural Communication Education and Foreign Language Education: Shared precedents, procedures, and prospects   *558*
                                         Warren B. Roby

后记   *571*

FOREWORD

Groups of people from different cultures with different languages have been communicating for centuries during such activities as trading, religious missions, diplomacy and so on. As these groups increased in numbers and geographical spread, the problems inherent in intercultural communication increased as well. Intercultural communication conflict could take many forms. An example of this conflict involves the situation in which captured peoples interacted with their conquerors. As the Roman Empire and its language Latin expanded their boundaries from about 44 BC through AD 1453, they came in contact and conflict with many dozens of languages and cultures across Europe and parts of the Middle East and North Africa.

The 19th and 20th century inventions of radio and television and the World-Wide Web both helped and hindered communication. For the most part, the ability to communicate quickly around the world with people from different cultures was helpful. While this ability facilitated communication, so miscommunication was also facilitated. As the saying goes, "the age of instant communication is also the age of instant miscommunication." In many if not most cases miscommunications are eventually corrected, but when they not are corrected the results can be negative, or even very negative in terms of intercultural interaction.

The underlying cultural and linguistic problems that both aid intercultural communication and cause miscommunication have been under study by scholars in many fields for several decades. Many of the general basic studies have been done and many of the problems that arise in the use of the major languages across cultures have been studied as well. The resulting articles, books, DVDs, college courses, and training programs have multiplied and they help solve the inevitable communication problems that arise in cross-cultural contact.

Several organizations are devoted to the study of intercultural communication. One such organization is the International Association for Intercultural Communication Studies (IAICS). From its origin in 1985, IAICS has been a multicultural organization. The three founders and original Board of Directors members were from Korea, Japan, and the USA. Soon after its founding, Chinese scholars were included on the Executive Board and among the Presidents.

The IAICS conferences have attracted scholars from the continents of Africa, Asia, Australia, Europe, North America, and South America. Generally the conferences alternate each year from the Eastern hemisphere to the Western hemisphere.

The IAICS journal that began in 1991 is titled *Intercultural Communication Studies* (*ICS*). The articles in the journal are usually first presented to one the organization's conferences and then re-written for publication. *ICS* has published works by scholars from some twenty countries around the world. The editors have selected for this volume thirty-one articles, most of which were written by contributors to *ICS*. The final versions of the papers both present a wide range of intercultural communication topics and explore in depth some of the topics in the field that were under close investigation during the late 20th century and in the first decade of the 21st century. The contents of this volume provide a foundation for the exciting research results that we can anticipate during the remainder of the 21st century.

The Editors

Bates HOFFER
Trinity University, USA
JIA Yuxin
Harbin Institute of Technology, China
Nobuyuki HONNA
Aoyama Gakuin University, Japan
SONG Li
Harbin Institute of Technology, China

Overview: Problems and Perspectives

1

The Future of Cross-Cultural Communication: Perspective of 20 years of the IAICS

L. Brooks Hill
Trinity University, USA

Abstract: During my forty-three years in the profession and especially during the last two decades in IAICS, I have contributed to the field while observing some of the areas of cross-cultural communication that need more careful research. Based on this lifetime commitment, the following article will channel my experience into suggestions for the future. The sections of this article will address a cluster of closely related ideas that form three major challenges for our future. The first section assumes a more theoretical perspective and identifies several specific concerns that we must confront to unify our collective efforts and direct them with more synergy toward greater scholarly and practical achievements. The second section serves as a serious caution about the uncritical acceptance of technological innovation as a means of teaching and otherwise applying our knowledge. The third and final section turns our attention to ethnic relations. Throughout the world, poor ethnic relations are causing the disintegration of society. We must apply our knowledge more carefully to the resolution of these concerns. Overall, this article will synthesize my experience into three general directions for improvement of the study and practice of cross-cultural relations. Its central theme will address the primary question of this anthology: How can we better pull together our collective efforts and thereby synergize our potential for a better world?

For the last forty years I have worked in the intersecting fields of intercultural, international, and development communication, and have spent my career devoted to these challenging areas of study (Honna &

Hoffer, 2003). Over twenty-three years ago I arrived at Trinity University and was recruited into a new interdisciplinary organization devoted to all of my language related interests. Since that time I have served for two terms as President of the International Association for Intercultural Communication Studies (IAICS), served on the Board of Directors for several years, served as the General Editor of the IAICS journal *Intercultural Communication Studies*, and now serve on the Editorial Board. During these forty-three years in the profession and especially during the last two decades in IAICS, I have contributed to the field while observing some of the areas of cross cultural communication that need more careful research. Based on this lifetime commitment, the following article will channel my experience into suggestions for the future.

Perspectives for Scholars and Scholarship[①]

The studies of intercultural, international, and development communication emerged from slightly different traditions with different emphases. Despite ancient origins of intuitive and general considerations of these subjects, they seemed to have originated as areas of systematic study during the twentieth century with the growth of the social sciences, media technology, and world organizations devoted to global concerns. More specifically, intercultural communication emerged from a more interpersonal orientation, fostered in significant ways by the work of Edward T. Hall and his re-orientation of the United States Foreign Service Institute programs after World War II (Leeds-Hurwitz, 1998). Finding an academic home within speech and applied anthropology, it tended to focus on the mutual negotiation of social reality among participants. In contrast, international communication seemed to originate in political science with emphasis on international relations and the new developments in media technology. While these two separate academic disciplines followed somewhat independent paths, they have come closer together with the more extensive and rapid expansion of media technology as a central focus in globalization. The growth of cultural studies over the last three decades has brought these disciplines even closer. The vast area of development communication perhaps originated with attention to the problems with the diffusion of agricultural and public health information. Because of the communication aspects of these problem areas people from applied anthropology and sociology drew to them contributors from communication studies who were interested in the overlapping topics of organizational

---

[①] An earlier version of this section appeared in Hill, L. B., Dixon, L. D. & Goss, L. B. (2000). Intercultural communication: Trends, problems, and prospects. *Intercultural Communication Studies*, 10 (1), 189–194.

communication, campaigning and movement studies. Intercultural, international, and development communication are rich sources of information about cross-cultural problems, but instead of benefiting from symbiotic relationships, they have progressed in relatively independent directions with often separate literatures, academic disciplines, and unfortunately rare integration of resources.

The varied development of interests in cross-cultural questions is further Balkanized by the patterns of humanistic studies. The studies of literature, linguistics, and additional areas of anthropology represent substantive considerations of intercultural, international, and development communication, but they are often not well integrated into the more social scientific traditions represented in the preceding paragraph. As a result, many scholars who treat the processes of communication ignore treatments of the artifactual products of the cultures and nations they engage. Granted that the specific interests of each scholar are important in their own right, they deserve some broader and synergistic integration. My background was primarily in the arts and humanities, but I saw the overlap of my interests with the social sciences and attempted to take a position with a foot in both camps. This has enriched my experience and expanded the perspective of my students. The motivation that encouraged me to make the IAICS my primary professional organization was the attraction of diverse scholars from all over the world to our collective work. Within this framework I came to some useful definitions that honor the differences of these primary areas, but also consider the shared emphases.

We seriously need to settle on some shared definitions that can serve as points of departure to realize more of our collective potential. By keeping these definitions simple and general, they can chart our work together, as well as sustain our relative independence: **Communication** may be defined as the process of symbolically eliciting meaningful responses that facilitate understanding and/or the fulfillment of other purposes. In other words, communication involves the creation, adaptation, and transmission of messages that can facilitate mutual understanding or other possible results. Culture is another process that overlaps, and often coincides, with communication. **Culture** may be defined as the process of (a) knowing and behaving in a manner acceptable to persons who are members of a culture; (b) developing the semantic or cognitive framework to facilitate appropriate knowledge and behavior; and (c) transmitting and / or perpetuating this knowledge, framework, and behavior. Because communication is a sine qua non of society, and society is a major dimension of culture, these three interrelated constructs form an essential dimension of our humanity.

The term **cross-cultural communication** has two general uses: In one sense the term refers to any interaction among people from different cultures. In a much more specific sense the term is used in reference to a more methodological concern called comparative perspectives wherein we compare similar phenomena within two different cultures and derive generalizations that exceed the limits of one culture. While the latter has specific use for research methods, the more general term may be even more useful as a vehicle for integrating all of our mutual concerns. **Intercultural communication** comes primarily out of an interpersonal orientation and addresses the mutual negotiation of social reality among participants. Because of the necessity and reality of interpersonal aspects of our globalization, we can no longer neglect these aspects of any communication among peoples around the world, whatever problems we may be addressing. **International communication** comes out of a mass media and political orientation; it addresses information flow between and among nations and other large groups of people. While these areas are constantly in the news and represent the more visible issues confronting us, we must recognize that these concerns subsume the more personal aspects of interpersonal communication. Finally, **development communication** is the use of all means of communication to assist with the development or social improvements of nations and cultures in need. This may well be the bridge that completes the interconnections between interpersonal communication, international communication, and globalization. We cannot continue as a world community without spreading our achievements more equitably so that good, rather than evil, dominates the diverse peoples of the world. Our collective success on planet earth will depend on how well we can understand why we communicate interculturally and replace the tendencies to exploit each other with progress for the common good of us all.

Beyond the broad definitional level of our need for closer collaboration, a few serious limitations of our work also encourage attention. Breadth and diversity are the cornerstones and most distinctive features of IAICS, as we have from its inception tried to pull together people from many disciplines and interests into a single organization dedicated to the improvement of cultural understanding and intercultural relations. Anyone who hears our convention programs and reads our journal should be excited by the diversity of our subject and the methods of our research. Examination of these materials will not only generate excitement, but also some concerns. From our conference programs and my work on the editorial board, I have identified two general categories of concerns; one is methodological and the other substantive. These reactions focus on the work of scholars in IAICS, but these general observations apply more widely.

> (1) The rigor of our methods and the quality of our critical assessments are sometimes weak. We need to establish and present more explicit criteria for research quality, and then meet them; this will reveal our commitment to high standards and

provide a better basis for comparing and integrating our studies with those of others.
(2) We sometimes neglect theoretical and conceptual concerns. Whenever we can make our theoretical framework explicit we should do so. We should never forget that knowledge is cumulative, and the building blocks are clear concepts. Here again, more explicit treatment of our theoretical foundations and conceptual clarity will facilitate comparison and integration of our work with that of others.
(3) We tend to be excessively anecdotal, sometimes relying too much on the idiosyncratic. Greater attention to the two preceding concerns should correct this tendency.
(4) We are sometimes overly cynical in our work with far more attention to deconstruction, rather than to something more constructive. Essentially, we need to restore a more critical attitude about our methods with greater precision, carefulness, thoroughness, and rigor in our approach to research and its report. Too much of our literature attempts to correct social imbalances by privileging the minority voice; while some of this approach may be desirable as thought pieces, we should not confuse more careful research with elaborated anecdotes.

Regarding the substance of our work, I applaud the increased integration of perspectives and how the scholars of IAICS are filling the gaps created by more rigid academic compartmentalization. Despite these achievements, my reviews of our programs and journal submissions reveal three serious concerns:

(1) We infrequently address real social problems, escaping instead into the cleanliness of academic scholarship. We need to use what we know to help us understand and possibly resolve social concerns. As noted in my 1997 IAICS presidential address, we can certainly help with our understanding of ethnic or co-cultural problems within our own national cultures.
(2) As noted as a more general problem above, we tend to separate international and intercultural concerns. Granted these two areas emerged within different traditions and sets of issues, the realities of our current world strongly encourage us to bring them back together. In our consideration of these interrelated problems we are not filling the gap effectively.
(3) Especially those of us from the developed nations are ignoring the downside of technological innovation. We cannot and should not permit our economic advantages to worsen the distance between peoples around the world. We must not ignore the subtle ways that technology can seductively generate counterproductive

ethnocentrism. Overall, these concerns reinforce a serious need to remember a major concern of IAICS: to increase the applicability of our work to genuine improvement of the human condition for all peoples.

A primary goal of this first section is an exhortation to those of us who work in the overlapping areas of intercultural, international and development communications, in one or another of the widely divergent possibilities, to formulate a more interdependent agenda for future study. As we reflect on this challenge, several procedural implications for our organization emerge: IAICS can provide a direction for solutions to real social problems. Alone we scholars may be "voices in the wilderness," but together we comprise a set of influential teachers and scholars who can potentially impact our world. Within this sort of mission statement, we must continually work to bring the diverse perspectives together to confront the overwhelming variability of cultures and challenges of intercultural relations. For our organization this means that we will need even more effective communication among our members. To this end we have initiated a new website, which has improved access to our journal, and facilitated the maximum use of our journal articles. We plan to create a "news and notes" section of both our website and journal to encourage greater familiarity among our membership and more collaborative, interdependent research. In addition the conferences that IAICS sponsors every year provide us an opportunity to renew our commitments and expand our potential to address the problems we confront. At each of our twelve conferences we have grown and advanced our collective cause.

Technological Questions for Intercultural Communication Study[①]

Permit me to begin this section with a hypothetical presumption significant to our concerns: How we recognize and treat differences between and among people is the heart, the core, of intercultural relations. If we accept this point of view, then the study of intercultural relations entails four interrelated goals: (1) the objective, non-judgmental detection of differences, (2) the understanding of the source(s) of differences, (3) the tolerant management of differences, and (4) the appreciation of differences in self and group fulfillment and growth. More specifically, intercultural communication addresses the tactics and strategies of message development, adaptation, and transmission as we use our knowledge of

---

[①] An earlier version of this section appeared in Hill, L. B. (1998). Technological enhancement of experiential learning for intercultural communication. *Cross-Cultural Communication East and West in the 90's* (pp. 15-22). San Antonio, TX: Institute for Cross-Cultural Research, Trinity University.

human differences to achieve some level of intercultural effectiveness. From my perspective nearly everyone reading these words is interested in intercultural relations, each of us comes to this concern with varied emphases, but whatever our professional label and identity our work contributes to one or more of the goals of intercultural relations. Mine is a very practical communication orientation.

Those of us who teach intercultural relations, from whatever vantage point, recognize the limitations of the traditional classroom context. No matter how hard we work at our instructional approach we cannot capture the vitality of the real intercultural experience. Thus, over the years we have developed several supplements for our traditional courses to provide what we have called experiential learning opportunities. Among these are study abroad, various exchange projects, international living dormitories, foreign language exclusive summer sessions, foreign travel, and even exposure to foreign teachers. These supplements are valuable, but often unavailable to many students. So, we have tried to enhance our somewhat static courses with technology. The possible alternatives lead us to the central question of this section: What are the prospects and liabilities for technological enhancement of experiential learning for intercultural effectiveness?

As with most topics of significance, this one also suffers definitional problems.

(1) The first definitional problem involves "instructional technology," which is the new label for the "instructional media" programs of yesteryear. But unlike prior circumstances, the responsibility for instructional technology is not being relegated primarily to our colleagues in colleges or departments of education. No longer are they expected to consolidate our equipment in a few rooms and cart it to our classes as needed. Instead, the prominence of computers and the need for very special facilities in the recent trends of instructional technology have introduced unusual demands on the subject area adaptation by disciplines; so, we now have many "cooks in the kitchen." But I fear that even with more, varied contributors, we are recreating some of the same problems encountered with the old instructional media centers.

(2) A second set of definitional problems involves our need to distinguish mass media from mediated interpersonal technology. The former typically includes such media as television, video, and film, while the mediated interpersonal technology includes innumerable computer-facilitated interpersonal connections and various other interactive, individualized media. Overall, however, the distinctions involved among these media are not

absolute and tend to range on a continuum of personal to impersonal to non-personal with the same media serving different functions at different points on the continuum. So, when we speak of technological enhancement, I am excluding no medium. In fact, I strongly support varied combinations of media. Perhaps most importantly, I am not equating technology with computers, because the tendency to confuse the two is a dangerous threat to contemporary efforts to use instructional technology more effectively. The "cyberspace craze" in the United States illustrates the naive infatuation of many Americans with the unbridled progression of technology. We hope this economically motivated wave of hysteria will soon reestablish strong roots in reality rather than the imaginary projections of virtual reality.

(3) A third and final set of definitional concerns forces us to focus our attention. At the broadest level of this subject area is a concern for the use of technology in any type of instruction; this certainly applies to our interests but is much broader. Current interest with experiential learning in several disciplines also exceeds, but is applicable to, our concerns (Kolb, 1984; Jackson & Caffarella, 1994; Lewis & Williams, 1994). We are very specifically interested in instructional technology in all possible combinations and applications as a potential enhancement of experiential learning of intercultural communication effectiveness (Jackson & MacIsaac, 1994). Were this a book-length project, we would need to examine instructional technology, experiential learning, intercultural communication effectiveness, and ultimately their interrelations. In this less expansive effort, I shall instead consider first some general uses of technology to enhance experiential learning of intercultural communication effectiveness, noting the several advantages of these prospects. Then, I will consider three current examples, and the preponderance of my discussion will consider the problems with our dependence on technology.

Many studies are now available that assess media appropriateness for intercultural communication and cross-cultural learning. These studies provide many examples of the effective use of video tapes, teleconferencing, freeze-frame telephone, facsimile, e-mail, and video conferencing, and others in teaching intercultural communication to students in varied parts of the world. Overall, the studies find the efforts successful and worth the time, energy, and money invested, but questions usually remain about the degree of success and costs. Whatever the results, the authors seem to believe that these technological enhancements foster student motivation and energize their subsequent study. Most of us have extensive anecdotal support to confirm these tendencies. At a very advanced level, simulation and virtual reality programming provide some fascinating prospects; adventure programs, video games, even music television or MTV are good prospects currently used. At a more basic level, we now are using e-mail in programs between all parts of the world, and cognitive mapping exercises serve to encourage more effective conceptual development of intercultural communication theory and research, as well as applications. A somewhat retrospective collection of efforts falls under the label "distance learning" which is using many of these techniques to reach audiences unable to come for classes at a central location (Lee & Caffarella, 1994).

These current uses of technology range from the fascinating to the mundane, vary widely in costs, and require a diversity of skills to use as instructor and/or student. They do, however, seem to provide some clear advantages. They maximize opportunities for students and teachers who cannot afford to travel or to spend large amounts of time away from home. These technological enhancements can certainly motivate and energize students to study cultural variability and intercultural relations. They further expand the number of cultures one can learn about and interact with. It seems without question that at the initial level of cultural sensitivity and intercultural relations, the technological enhancements are successful. What we lack is evidence of their longer term effectiveness, usefulness, and dangers (MacIsaac & Jackson, 1994; Bassett & Jackson, 1994).

Consider three examples of current technological techniques being used to facilitate an experiential approach to intercultural communication effectiveness. The first occurred in my undergraduate course in international communication. While browsing the "net," one of my students encountered a request for interpersonal contact with a student from an eastern European university. Through e-mail they began to discuss the problems with universities in eastern Europe following the end of communist rule and the collapse of the Soviet Union. This contact led my student to conduct his major project for the course on the topic of computers in higher education in eastern Europe. The results of this experience were exciting for all involved. My student learned first-hand about issues critical to education in another part of the world, developed a working relationship with a student in another culture, and they taught each other a lot about their respective cultures. Although the costs for my student were minimal, the monetary costs for his contact were comparatively large and virtually impossible to reimburse. From this assignment, my student also learned many of the inadequacies of this limited contact. The conclusion for my student and me, however, was that this was an exciting and extraordinary supplement to an otherwise typical university course, and the lessons learned from the foreign student significantly enhanced my student's learning experience. Subsequently, other students in my classes, and as I understand from colleagues around our country students from their classes as well, have used the internet and e-mail to expand their assignments well beyond the limits of regular courses and library constraints. The extent to which this approach serves to enrich the actual experience of another culture is questionable, however, because students are primarily using the technology to gather information, rather than to learn about or increase their skills for intercultural interaction with people from another culture. The simple act of dealing with someone from another culture, however, is a major step in the right direction, and I strongly urge you to encourage your students to work on projects through internet and e-mail with students from other countries if at all possible.

A second set of examples comes from colleagues at other universities in the southwestern and western United States. They have developed a network of interrelated courses at American and Mexican universities in which video conferencing, supplemented by e-mail, is a primary vehicle for teaching intercultural communication. Through prior arrangements, instructors of courses at American and Mexican universities develop common syllabi with designated sessions to be managed through video-conferencing and direct student interaction. Obviously, this is an expensive prospect with not only substantial monetary costs, but large demands on time to coordinate the activities. Through e-mail many of the logistics are addressed. Similar to other parallel efforts around the world, this project can in time become such a standard operating procedure that the logistical difficulties virtually disappear. If these projects can be supplemented by exchanges and other joint efforts, then the prospects become even more exciting. Here again, costs and logistics are major concerns, and these realities may constrain the potential.

A third and final illustration involves the exchange of video cassettes between students at an American and a Japanese university. Initiated primarily to secure examples of spoken English, these tapes were requested by a Japanese instructor eager to provide her students with opportunities to learn conversational American English. What soon evolved was a desire for these students to address questions and concerns that would encourage greater cultural sensitivity among both groups of students. Obviously, the products did not have to be of professional quality. So, what we did was simply to provide students a video camera, to set up an agenda of selected questions for discussion, and to turn the students loose to enjoy the filmed discussion. We then mailed the tape to the Japanese teacher who played it for her students, and her class reciprocated. The overall effect of this video exchange was the emergence of a very useful learning experience by both groups. We ultimately learned to send a list of questions which our group wanted the other group to discuss, and they would do likewise. In time the students came to know each other and to actually make comments to one of the foreign students during the discussions. This, too, suffered logistical difficulties, but in time we learned to overcome them. The constraints of completing a course during a limited time frame made these exercises less than integral to the course, but still very enjoyable. Current technology makes this sort of project even more feasible. Ultimately we made arrangements for groups of Japanese students to come to our university during their semester break (March) and to stay in the dorms with their counterparts, attend American classes, and simply "hang-out" with the American students. While this arrangement was more expensive, it was a wonderful success.

Most readers could add more cases perhaps with much greater creativity and even more on the cutting edge of technology. These examples serve my purpose, however, much better than a lengthier list of illustrations or more complex cases. From these examples, which in some combination or another are probably very common around the world, we can begin to see some of the problems and shortcomings of the use of technology as aids for experiential learning. No matter the downside, they do serve to energize and excite students, but unless they are carefully used they may create greater problems than they ever address. The popular and scholarly literature is currently replete with considerations of the pitfalls of technology (Wishnietsky, 1994). Because of our very specific focus and time at our disposal, I will summarize and abbreviate these concerns into three interrelated categories: (1) the more obvious problems which confound our use of technology; (2) the less conspicuous, though more insidious, problems, and (3) illustrations of central intercultural communication concepts which will suffer from technological intervention.

Obvious Problems

Perhaps most apparent is the simple lack of available technology and functional skills. Those of us in well-developed countries often fail to realize that most of the world does not have access to our technology, and this obviously renders its use for any type of education or training somewhat meaningless. So, whatever its potential value, we cannot expect in the near future to benefit from its use in much of the world. Because of the unavailability of technology, very few people are trained in its use or have even considered its potential. What we need at our conferences are sessions to discuss such technological innovations and their potential as a means of anticipating the time when these options do become available. Unfortunately, even those of us in intercultural relations sometimes forget the wide gap between the haves and the have-nots. While the gap may be diminishing, we must learn how to deal with people with and without technological enhancement.

A second obvious problem is similar to those of the old instructional media programs. We often lack systematic integration of our technology into an overall pedagogical approach. To integrate these innovative possibilities successfully will require re-conceptualization of our courses and major alterations of our instructional techniques (Caffarella & Barnett, 1994). Too often, technology is used in an ad hoc fashion, and the primary benefit may be its novelty. Perhaps we should reassess our approach to intercultural communication education, and for at least a major unit in a course, if not the entire course, we must concentrate on an experiential approach which builds on some of the current technology. In my own undergraduate course I currently use a "contact" paper as a term project (Javidi & Hill, 1987) in which students are to establish contact with a foreign student, conduct extensive interviews, and write about the problems of acculturation encountered by that student. How much more valuable that experience might become if a complementary, simultaneous project required contact with a student in another country through mediated interpersonal communication?

A third obvious problem anticipates some later considerations of the more insidious variety. Dependence on technology can lead students into deceptive oversimplification. No matter how carefully set up, the exercises are contrived and shallow. Despite the value of this contact, the likelihood of a deeper and more intense experience is compromised by the intrusion of the media and the class formalities. The greatest danger stems from the potential that students might think they really understand another culture because they have interacted well in this constrained situation. If we do use these teaching techniques, then we need to work carefully to overcome this potential hazard to intercultural effectiveness.

Growing out of the tendency to oversimplification is a threat to one of the major goals of education in intercultural communication. Reliance on technology can lead one to involvement with technology for its own sake. Not only will this infatuation confound our progress in intercultural communication, but it will also compromise another major reason for the study of intercultural relations, namely, its service as a voyage of self-discovery for the student. Just as the US Peace Corps may help other countries deal more effectively with certain real problems, the primary mission of the Peace Corps is not so much to help others, but to use this service opportunity to help the youth of our own country develop a better sensitivity to the world and to increase their level of cosmopolitanism. Similarly, coursework in intercultural communication should also be a journey of self discovery in that students learn about interaction with other cultures in order to learn more about themselves and their own coping behavior regardless of cultural context. Distractions by the media may compromise this critical goal of cultural self-discovery.

Insidious Problems

Much less obvious is what Professor Helen Harrington has called the "essence of technology" or what is happening to us and our students through the subtle use of technology (1993). In her discussion of this essence, Harrington addressed the "illusion of technological neutrality," and explained how nothing so socially pervasive is neutral and how educators must be especially sensitive to the implications of our pedagogical techniques. Among the possible effects are the ways technology can create a counterproductive orientation toward people and simultaneously distract us away from any realization of these consequences.

For example, technology invites a very functional and manipulative perspective. Especially with mediated interpersonal communication, one resolution of problems is simply to turn off the equipment, an option unavailable in the real world. Beyond this illustration, we should note that the mechanistic dimensions of technology invite further a manipulative sense of control over the variables involved, and this subtly developed orientation works counter to the genuine needs of sympathy and empathy which intercultural effectiveness entails. Finally, the real constraints of time and money on the use of technology also invite a strongly functional orientation. Even though these constraints may be minimized, they have become through our socialization somewhat engrained in our behavior and expectations.

When we examine closely the realities of intercultural communication, the experience is clearly dynamic, can only be grasped holistically, and is a very humane activity. In one way or another, each of these essential characteristics is compromised by technology. No matter how many permutations our machines may predict, the potential irrationality of human behavior and the infinite combination of behavioral possibilities cannot be captured. Were these purely human activities codifiable, robotics would be much further along than it is. As anyone from an individualistic culture can attest, dealing with someone from a collectivistic culture absolutely requires a holistic conceptualization of their behavior. Technology can provide us a slice of reality, but it can only assist us in capturing the many ingredients. Perhaps most important, technology can never integrate the personal touches, the nuances so critical to understanding the behavior of another person.

Problems with Intercultural Communication Concepts

As a final extension of the preceding discussion, several intercultural communication concepts are unusually difficult to address through technology. Some dimensions of culture fatigue and shock can surface through the use of technology, but the visceral aspects of symbolic disorientation and the individual reactions are lost in the illusion of understanding. Similarly, uncertainty and anxiety can be addressed through technology, but the intensity, the confusion, and the individualized adjustments are here again lost.

A subject which is difficult to address through any techniques is the synchronization of verbal and non-verbal behavior. Whereas technology may help identify aspects, it is inadequate. Closely related to the questions about dynamic, holistic, and humane dimensions of intercultural communication, technology also has trouble helping students to approach the aesthetic harmony and balance of another culture. Although technologically enhanced learning can provide a taste of these concepts, the danger of oversimplification and deception is a central problem.

As anyone who works with intercultural relations can attest, effective intercultural communication is hard work. It requires a constant reception, digestion, and effective utilization of huge amounts of information as we struggle to render explicit those innumerable "taken-for-granteds" of our daily existence, to decipher those qualities in another culture, and to adjust the two systems into a workable milieu. Success requires continual sensitivity and diligence as one functionally learns another culture. To succeed in the long haul will certainly require more than the immediate gratification of technology. No matter whether we are the student or the teacher, we must wrestle with the real complexities which technology often insidiously conceals.

As a teacher who is willing to use whatever works, I am strongly encouraged by the persuasive allure of current technology and do make frequent use of the possibilities. But I remain concerned with the less obvious pitfalls involved with more extensive dependence on technology. To conclude this section, I would like to provide some statements by three others who share these concerns. In her fascinating discussion of "Networlds: Networks as Social Space," Professor Linda Harasim raised two very penetrating questions: "How does the mediation of computer networks affect human interaction and communication? What are the salient properties of the technology and how do they impact on the communication?" (1993). Later in her discussion of these questions, she ventured a partial answer: "Global networks enrich our experience and knowledge options but also introduce new and complex issues. Cultural, linguistic, and political factors in global conversations can confound our ability to establish the meaningfulness of the discourse. Place-independence challenges many habits and customs of interpersonal and group communication" (Harasim, 1993). Consistent with her position, I seriously question the uncritical acceptance and utilization of technology for it may deceive more than enlighten us.

In a similar, yet more cynical, vein we all need to be skeptical about the brash claims currently made for technology. As Mander and Harrington remind us:

> Since most of what we are told about new technology comes from its proponents, be deeply skeptical of all claims. Assume all technology "guilty until proven innocent."
> Eschew the idea that technology is neutral or "value free."
> Every technology has inherent and identifiable social, political, and environmental consequences.
> In thinking about technology within the present climate of technological worship, emphasize the negative. This brings balance. Negative is positive. (Mander, 1991)

In her struggle with the implications of technology for her students and courses, Harrington prudently concludes, "... we may not know what we have lost until it is too late" (1993). For those of us working with intercultural communication the dangers may be profound, because effective intercultural relations requires personal contact, interaction with people of diverse cultures, and the preservation, as well as the overcoming, of differences. Technological interpositions can open prospects, may energize our students, and may enhance the prospects for learning, but, regardless of the attractive potential, technology cannot supplant the dynamic, holistic, humane personal contact.

The Centrality of Ethnic Relations[1]

Even a casual reader of any major newspaper or news magazine encounters a barrage of ethnic strife from throughout the world, as almost every continent is afflicted with these problems, and few nations enjoy ethnic peace and tranquility. For most of my professional career I have struggled both inside and outside of the classroom with these concerns. In retrospect, however, I must confess that I often escaped direct engagement of these serious problems by treating my subject abstractly or digging ever more deeply into "cleaner" research. Occasionally students would press or push me into the perplexing world of ethnic discord, but even then I tried to keep my distance. Motivated by the ravages of ethnic strife at home and abroad, I have begun within the last decade or so to alter my university courses to wrestle with the realities of disintegrating social life around our world. Because of the personal significance of this message to me and because of its potential for others, I would like initially to identify a catalyzing and precipitating factor which strongly motivated my present

---

[1] An earlier version of this section appeared in Hill, L. B. (1997). Ethnic relations and the decline of civility. *Intercultural Communication Studies*, 6 (2), 1–11.

course of action, and then provide an approach to culture that may better assist our analysis of ethnic problems. From these points of departure, I will introduce a position about the relevance of civility and what we can do to better our world on the basis of our skills, knowledge, and limited opportunities. Most importantly, and perhaps the primary purpose of this section is that I want everyone to develop an enhanced commitment to action; that is to say, I want us to realize that the vision of IAICS is to transcend limitations and to utilize what we know to make our world better for all groups whatever the basis of their differences.

Have you ever noticed the parallel between the chemical processes stimulated by a catalyst and the operations of our mind? We may have many ideas or chemicals floating around, and then something catalyzes intense activity. Such was my state of mind during the spring months of 1996 when Professor Hoffer gently nudged me to specify a title for an upcoming presidential address for IAICS. I drew upon some recent conversations about ethnic problems and our ineptitude at talking about them. So, I tossed him a title and thought that I would simply reflect on it for a while, gathering information from diverse sources as I formulated my position. And then, from a most unlikely source, a catalyst fell into my placid thoughts and energized them with tumultuous intensity. This chemical reaction so stirred my very person that it became the precipitating cause of my present course of action. Let me describe that catalyst for you.

In addition to national and international communication organizations, the USA has four regional associations dedicated to the study of human communication, with each providing an annual convention, a quarterly journal, and several other services. My home state of Texas is aligned with the Southern States Communication Association. With my membership, I receive the *Southern Communication Journal*. Summer, 1996, was the final issue for Editor Andrew King of Louisiana State University. In his last issue he provided a short editorial entitled "The Summing Up" (p. 363). Rarely do I read such notes, but fate provided me a few odd minutes before an appointment, and his title caught my eye for no other reason than retiring editors often conclude their tenure with many lessons learned.

King's comments shocked my perennial, yet complacent, optimism. "As I leave my editorship," he wrote, "my most vivid impression of our field's scholarship is of a somber humanism unfamiliarly mixed with nihilism. Perhaps it is only the fin *de siècle* sense of exhaustion, but the bulk of the manuscripts brought me to the margin of despair." To explain this emotional reaction, he identified two dominant characteristics of the submissions: "The first is that society achieves cohesion through victimage. Many articles featured the serial mugging of groups as the flywheel of social mobilization. Their point was that if Brutus could not destroy others he would destroy himself." The second characteristic was "the necessity and the impossibility of constructing new social visions. The common argument: our contemporary crisis of meaning demands the production and destruction of ideologies at an ever increasing rate. The weaker our social text, the more robust social analysis becomes." He concluded with an ominous warning from the German philosopher Spengler: "There is the dark moment when all concentric forces become eccentric and the dance macabre begins."

Because of their relevance, my reactions to King's editorial deserve a short chronicle. Initially I felt like one of the witches from Shakespeare's *Macbeth* as I stood before a cauldron of mixed ingredients stirring up some potential evil for my adversaries. Vicariously experiencing King's pain, I lashed out in my thoughts at the deconstructionists who had torn the text from our lives, rendering nothing permanent or sacred except the processes of interpretation. I wanted to thrash the scholars who had made unbridled relativism the ultimate rationalization for "do your own thing" and "anything goes." My critical acuity, as well as my blood pressure, reached a peak as I stirred, and stirred, and stirred my intolerant and unholy ideas. After a few days of this contemplative bitterness, I paused one morning while shaving. In a fleeting moment I perceived the social value of mirrors: the reflection permits us, if we open our eyes widely enough, to see ourselves as others see us. Just as I was looking to others for the causes of our social failures, I had neglected to see how others could similarly place me in this chain of blame. In what ways, I mused, am I in my own modest ways responsible for the disruption, if not destruction, of our social fabric?

The more I pondered my role, the clearer my vision became. With the world struggling with ethnic strife, I wanted to avoid the issues or at least avoid studying or writing about them from the standpoint of my scholarly expertise. I was so captured by a sense of political correctness and cultural sensitivity that I was unable to speak out, thus leaving the forum open to the extremists who never seem to suffer such reticence. With this frustration and momentum, I approached my topic with renewed vigor and an unanticipated eagerness. Even though my topic originated with dim light and little heat, my revitalized interpretation increased the light and heat, resulting in greater clarity and surging passion. With renewed energy, I broached the problem of ethnic discord. Armed only with the tools of scholarship, I launched into the fray.

Culture and Ethnic Relations

As scholars and many other problem solvers tend to do, I started at the most basic level by listing what I can safely assume about my subject: (1) Poor ethnic relations comprise a serious social problem throughout the world. (2) These problems seem to emerge from diverse causes and within widely different contexts. (3) People who address ethnic problems continually identify cultural variables at work, and some extend these problems to panoramic proportions. For example, American political scientist Samuel Huntington (1996) and his disciples argue that conflict among cultural diasporas is rapidly replacing the cold war and its conflict between superpowers as the context for future international relations. (4) Virtually every writer acknowledges more or less that language and communication are variously woven into ethnic conflicts. (5) As a professed expert in language and human communication, with special concern for intercultural communication, I should be able to help with these problems.

From these basic assumptions and observations, I asked, where can I turn? In other places I have written about what it means to assume an intercultural communication perspective toward a subject (1997), but some pieces of the puzzle are still missing. Even with the caveats, my intercultural perspective and inclinations compelled me to examine the cultural dimensions of these social problems more carefully and then to use those insights to help me better conceptualize ethnic discord. This rather personal series of steps have led me to revisit my conception of culture.

Like the notion of meaning, the concept of culture is pervasive and defined variously to fit nearly any and all circumstances. In fact, many scholars have abandoned both concepts as too expansive for theoretical use. I continue to use these two concepts and would draw on an insightful approach to meaning by American philosopher May Brodbeck for a more useful conceptualization of culture (1968, pp. 58-78). In her analysis Brodbeck differentiated levels or categories of meaning by a subscript with Meaning 1 indicating the object or idea referenced, Meaning 2 identifying significance or a lawful connection of one term to another, Meaning 3 referring to intentional meaning, and Meaning 4 signifying psychological meaning. Without digging into her distinctions, suffice it to say that she used these variations to facilitate use of the concept meaning in the development of theories and discussions about science, and to make far clearer exactly what she was specifying in her subsequent arguments. On a parallel with this line of analysis, I recommend that we differentiate levels of culture which may, in turn, enhance our efforts to conceptualize the problems of ethnic relations.

For many years I have recited to students my definition of culture as a three-part process of (1) knowing and behaving in a manner acceptable to persons who are members of the culture; (2) developing the semantic framework to facilitate appropriate knowledge and behavior, and (3) transmitting and/or perpetuating this knowledge, framework, and behavior. This abstract, behaviorally oriented, cognitive definition has provided a useful point of departure for my students of intercultural communication. Conveniently, I chose to omit "haute couture" and artifactual remains of culture as the business of others who are less concerned with the vicissitudes of culture in the functional, daily ways of life. I was also somewhat aloof from those who would merely list the many ingredients of culture, such as attitudes, values, beliefs, myths, folklore, and many others. My process orientation about culture meshed neatly with my concern for communication processes, and, in turn, permitted me to evade the content of culture. Addressing ethnic relations, however, forced me to confront both the processes and substance of culture, and especially the interrelationship of process and substance. My definition, therefore, needed expanded re-conceptualization, and Brodbeck's approach to meaning suggested a viable way.

As I have read about ethnic conflicts during the last few years, three prominent features of the commentaries have struck me: First, the underlying causes of the problems are varied, but seem to fall into general categories of economic, political, and religious value differences. Poverty, powerlessness, and spiritual deprivation are regular features of such analyses. Second, the writers regularly comment on the language and communication activities of the participants. Whether the varied expressions of position, the latest caption for their cause, or the stages of negotiations, the interactions of the different groups are variously discussed. Third, diagnoses usually address the clash among various dispositions and prejudices growing out of either the values or the interactions. Differences of attitudes, beliefs, misattributions or stereotypes often become the mediating variables between the value differences and actual behaviors. Based on these realistic commentaries, I was led to a three-part conception of culture similar in some ways to Brodbeck's approach to meaning, rather than to my convenient process orientation which seems to capture only a portion of the total concept.

This line of reasoning generated a three dimensional model. Culture with a subscript v (Cv) constitutes the first dimension and embraces core values. The second dimension is culture with a subscript p (Cp) which embraces the mediating predispositions, such as attitudes, beliefs, and stereotypes. The third dimension offers the behavioral operationalizations; here we have culture with a subscript o (Co), the space where language and communication interface with other aspects of culture most directly. To apprehend this three dimensional model, consider another icon in my life, the golf ball with its core, the surrounding rubber bands, and its cover. Just as golf balls have evolved, so too has our conception of culture evolved in that the core, its surrounding substance, and cover have become more unified into a single ball with far greater dynamics than prior versions.

Like most models, this one can help us analyze problems with the dynamic processes it embraces: Ethnic strife usually emerges from a history of suppression and unequal treatment by one or more groups. If everyone had equivalent resources, power, and spiritual freedom, then I suspect that we could eliminate ethnic strife. But such a circumstance is only a twinkle in the idealist's eye, and we will probably never achieve such equality on earth. Thus the economic, political, and religious causes will remain deeply centered in ethnic conflicts. Because most people acknowledge a more realistic world, the problems shift to the second dimension where value-rooted predispositions displace and complicate the lack of capital, power, and spirituality. Instead of simply asking for more assets, ethnic minorities make impassioned statements of their predispositions until they weave a fabric of injustice which they wear on appropriate occasions. Language and communication enable them to form these perceptions into tangible artifacts with a greater sense of permanence and illusory security until their vision is blurred and distorted. Thus we can use this model to generate questions about all three dimensions and possibly sort out the nature of an ethnic problem and directions for its resolution.

As a student of intercultural communication, my use of this model will emphasize rhetorical analysis, broadly defined as the systematic study of functional symbolic behavior. Within this methodological framework are many thoughtful procedures for the study of language and communication, and in one way or another most of the membership of IAICS conducts rhetorical analysis. More of us simply need to study the discourse of ethnic groups and the groups they engage, sort out the problems of basic cultural values (Cv), relate these problems to the predispositional matrix (Cp), and then study how ethnic groups, other co-cultures, and the overculture tactically and strategically pursue their goals (Co). In this fashion we can potentially identify the salient aspects of each dimension of the problem, and the enhanced conception of culture will keep us continually aware that all of the pieces ultimately integrate. This approach should enable us to present and examine the social fabric objectively, locate the agreements and disagreements, and build a diagnosis and prognosis accordingly. If this approach works as expected, the dialogue about the problem should improve. Unfortunately, no groups really enjoy the social value of mirrors and often resent the careful examination of their actions. In fact, ethnic groups are sometimes so engrossed with an immediate goal that they cannot see what they themselves are doing to thwart their long-term efforts. Our work with language and communication can provide a basis for clearer reflection and possibly more thoughtful dialogue.

We may lack the power to rectify problems in the cultural dimension of core values or Cv. We can, however, use language to aid with values clarification, and through our rhetorical analysis we can locate the motivational despair of social inequities. We may define the complaints, weigh their intensity, and determine their level of justification. For this dimension, I suggest four general patterns of value relations: (1) Convergence of values of different groups can lead to the disappearance of conflict and greater homogeneity. (2) Parallel development of differing values can stabilize differences with reasoned agreement to disagree, but with respect for the equity of positions. (3) Divergence of values can result in greater misunderstanding and lessened cooperation through increased separation and segregation. And (4) the denunciation of values of one group by another can deny the opportunity for resolution, contradict reason, and create revolting circumstances. Values clarification through rhetorical analysis of Cv can help us identify the relationship among sets representing different groups, and thus generate a basis for more reasonable approaches to the problems.

The next layer or dimension of ethnic problems concerns Cp, the collective predispositions of one group about other groups. If our initial values clarification at level Cv does not uncover sufficient motivational force for the strife, then predispositions may represent hardened categorizations which do not permit reasonable flexibility. At this level, rhetorical analysis will consider stereotypes of the groups and break them down through careful language analysis. How, for example, does the estranged group label and categorize the other ethnic groups, cocultures, and/or overculture? How are these labels combined or configured to create myths and storylines about their intergroup relations? Do these rhetorical categorizations generate subversive themes and chains of destructive characterizations? Are they susceptible to legitimate consideration or do they instantly enflame opposition? Answers to these questions may provide some control over abusive predispositions if we can bring them up for public scrutiny and objective consideration. If we are unable to subject them to legitimate scrutiny, then they will function as subversive stereotypes inimical to reasonable consideration and to improvements in intercultural relations. The central problem at this level is defensive unwillingness to examine in public our predispositions about other groups of people. More open consideration is prerequisite for checking the counterproductive outcomes of this dimension of culture.

The third and most encompassing dimension of culture is the behavioral operationalization or Co. Here the collective behaviors of the ethnic groups are formed into tactics and strategies for pursuit of their goals and objectives. If our values clarification is thorough, it should lead to clear coordination of goals and strategy. If the values analysis is ambiguous or vague, then the goals may float without a definite tethering point, or, worse yet, vary with the faddishness of more fickle predispositions. The latter scenario will result in tactics confused with strategies and no clear strategic development. In many ways this becomes a volatile, dangerous combination that is conducive to ready manipulation by articulate participants who for whatever reason thrive and often survive on confrontation. The Co level is most observable and any rhetorical analysis can piece together the patterns of action, but without the underlying causes from Cv and Cp, the determination of strategic possibilities is weakened. Whatever anyone does to correct the situation exclusively at the Co level will likely fail, but through this analysis the grounds for addressing problems at Cv or Cp can develop. What our scholarship must achieve is realistic depiction of these rhetorical behaviors and the opportunity to break down the conflict into manageable proportions.

Throughout this profile of cultural analysis emerges a central argument: culture, language, and/or communication are rarely the cause of ethnic problems. They are all, however, concomitant manifestations of human difficulty, and, as such, become a vital source of data for the analysis of these problems. Just as they are not a primary cause of ethnic conflict, they are also not a solution, but because of their concomitance they become essential propaedeutics for problem solution. In other words, our rhetorical analysis can help us describe and analyze ethnic problems and create a perspective which will permit us to contribute toward the healing of this social disease. We should never, however, imagine that our approach is the answer. We can best serve to elucidate and frame the problems for those people with greater social power to resolve them. Our greatest value may well center on identification of the dimensions of the problems and the interrelationships among the various levels of rhetorical behaviors. To achieve our potential contribution, we must develop ways to call more attention to our analyses.

Ethnic Relations and Civility

During a presentation at Trinity University (2/21/97), David Maybury-Lewis, the prominent American anthropologist and internationally renowned cultural activist, accented the importance of addressing ethnic relations. "If ethnicity is not accommodated in modern society," he argued, "it will poison it." Drawing upon his personal experiences, he noted the "growing tendency to recognize ethnic legitimacy" as "countries throughout Latin America are classifying themselves as pluri-ethnic rather than mestizo" and governments are shifting away from policies of killing off these ethnic groups through genocide or total assimilation to programs of recognition and inclusion. This shift, he explained, seems based on the realization that "ethnic conflict does not come from expression of ethnicity, but rather from the suppression of ethnicity."

In other parts of the world, ethnicity is not only recognized, but variously celebrated. Yet, even at this more positive end of the continuum of ethnic viability, relations among ethnic groups and with the dominant over-culture are problematic. In these situations, such as the USA now represents, ethnicity has become more than a matter of recognition and respect for one's diversity. It has become a political instrument for social engineering as groups employ their ethnicity to secure whatever they may from the existing power structure. Unfortunately, in the process of this legitimate employment of ethnic identity our ineptitude at discussing the issues and rhetoric of this ethnic gamesmanship is diminishing the constructive vitality of ethnic diversity and exacerbating the problems of ethnic conflict (Hill & Lujan, 1983 and 1984). Somewhere between the genocidal policies toward ethnic groups and the rampant abuse of ethnicity lies a more reasonable approach to the positive development of ethnic identity and relationships among all groups. Creating an environment where we may achieve such balance is where civility and our potential intervene.

In another speech at Trinity University, former US Senator Bill Bradley examined what he perceived as the primary political issues facing our nation (3/4/97). Among these was our problem with ethnic relations. He offered a very simple solution, or at least a first step toward solution of this problem: "We've got to talk to each other," he observed, and then he extended this simple idea into a number of challenges. He made quite clear that the USA, as the remaining superpower on the stage of global politics, cannot lead the world without moral quality; so, we must treat each other equitably and fairly and thus set a model for other countries. How can we hope to guide the world, I was stimulated to wonder, when we are so tongue-tied in dealing with our own circumstances? As some of you probably know, the US Congress has actually held retreats to address the decline of civility in the operation of our own government. They seemed to recognize that restoration of civility was a first step in overcoming the gridlock of ineptitude undermining reasoned discourse about our national policies and agenda.

As scholars and teachers we are in positions to advance the cause of civility which may permit us to open perspectives about ethnic problems and to create opportunities for their resolution. To realize this prospect requires us to examine the concept of civility, what it entails, how we can nurture it, and how on the basis of its revitalization we can advance our rhetorical/cultural approach to ethnic discord. For help with this task, and quite predictably, I turned to a colleague for help. Colin Wells, a distinguished British professor of Classical Studies, guided me through the historical evolution of the Latin concept of civility: In his biography of the Emperor Claudius, Seutonious noted how being restrained and unassuming (*civilis*) Claudius refused the title of Emperor; that is, he refused to be so-called, preferring to be called first citizen (*princeps*). *The Oxford Latin Dictionary* quotes this passage and translates *civilis* here as "suitable to a private citizen, unassuming, unpretentious." Focusing on this idea of *civilis princeps*, British classicist Andrew Wallace-Hadrihl discusses *civilitas* or civility, and defines the concept as "the conduct of a citizen among citizens" or the politeness and consideration due to one's social equals (1982). He further noted that "... it is not until the second century A. D. that an abstract noun is formed: the ideal can be described as *civilitas*" (p. 43). From this historical vantage point, we can understand how civility came to imply a set of behaviors which make a leader good or bad in relation to the people governed.

On the contemporary scene, we understand the concept to embrace these two ancient dimensions, but it has become generalized beyond the behavior of emperors to include the populace as well. On the one hand, the concept refers to the performance of our duties as citizens, and, on the other hand, to an ethical code of behavior appropriate to good citizenship. Thus civility refers to our assumption of citizenship and behaving toward each other in a civil manner which translates as affable, courteous, differential, gracious, polite, and respectful. If we further translate these synonyms for civil behavior, they collectively imply avoidance of rudeness toward others, the observance of social requirements, and a positive, dignified, sincere, and thoughtful consideration of others (*Random House Dictionary*). As we incorporate these qualities into codes of habituated behavior, we refer to civilized people forming themselves into civilizations. Obviously, civility is closely related to the reasonable consideration of problems between groups of people.

Because civility is expressed symbolically, our rhetorical analyses can become indispensable for the operationalization of guidelines. Simply reflect on the expanding literature about the idea of "face" and how people in different cultures engage in face-saving interactions that create more civil situations for the resolution of personal concerns. What we need to do with this example and hundreds of others which come from our research is to teach our students the relevance of such principles for effective citizenship and the use of these guidelines in the actual treatment of ethnic problems. At no time in our history is this task more compelling; we must prepare our students for lives of civility and give them the instruments of respect, rather than the weapons of destruction which come from the neglect of civility. To meet this challenge would only require modest alterations of our scholarship and teaching strategies. We can easily shift our attention to the broader implications of our work for enhanced intercultural communication and more cooperative ethnic relations.

When I began research on the topic of this section, I had a genuine, but somewhat modest, commitment to this subject. The despair reflected in an editor's postscript catalyzed my behavior well beyond what I expected to do on this occasion. For the past few months I have been unable to extricate myself from this topic. I sincerely hope that my comments will serve to catalyze each of you to transcend the boundaries among our disciplines and nations and join in the vision of IAICS to use our skills and knowledge to make our world a better place for all groups of people. What began for me as a sojourn into an interesting subject has passed the point of no return. My work with intercultural communication has attained a new focus which will help my students and me to become more civilized in a world of interdependent people.

As we enter a new century on Western calendars and reflect on the lessons learned from the past, I hope that we will see the importance of pulling together the best of the East and West in a broader remedy for the diseases of social disintegration. Among the possibilities are two prominent schools of thought. From the West and our individualistic orientation come the concepts of dialogue and self worth. From the East and their collectivistic orientation come the concepts of social order and community. If we can integrate these two orientations, we will have the basis for a new millennium created from the strengths of our different orientations. One of the greatest pitfalls along this integrative path will be ethnic instability. If we can use our potential for rhetorical analysis, perhaps we can enhance our leadership in describing the problems more usefully and creating approaches which foster reasoned consideration of the confounding differences. My suggestions may not be the answer, but they may stimulate some of you or some of your students to improve on these ideas and determine ways to enhance our role in the analysis and resolution of these problems. Unlike the manuscripts of the editor I mentioned, I have a vision of a better future, a vision that transcends the boundaries of our disciplines and nations and that includes our collective scholarship in making this a better world. Will you join IAICS and me in this challenge?

Conclusion

I was honored by the invitation to contribute to this book. Having spent my entire professional career in the study and application of intercultural, international, and development communication, I sincerely believe that I have something valuable to contribute for those who hold the future in their hands. As the preceding sections indicate, we have three major challenges that we must ultimately address: (1) We need to pull together the widely varied groups of people who work in these areas and concentrate on better systemization of our collective work. With this improved synergy, we can generate a much more powerful influence. (2) We need to be cautious about excessive commitment to technology, rather than personal interaction, as we deal with the "people problems" of our world. We should never neglect the downside of any technology in human affairs. (3) Finally, we need to focus our attention on ways to resolve the most threatening social disease we have ever confronted. As our world grows in population and technology brings us closer together, we must be constantly vigilant about the threats of poor ethnic relations. We can valuably contribute to the dialogue about these problems and the results of improved dialogue may bring our collective work into better focus. Overall, better synergy of our efforts will lead to greater potential for the use of our ideas and research in coping with the serious problems that confront our world.

References

Bassett, D. & Jackson, L. (1994). Applying the model to a variety of adult learning situations. In L. Jackson & R. Caffarella (Eds.), *Experiential learning: A new Approach. New directions for adult and continuing education*, No. 62, summer. San Francisco, CA: Jossey-Bass.

Bradley, B.. (3/4/97). "America: the path ahead." Speech delivered at Trinity University, San Antonio TX.

Brodbeck, M. (1968). Meaning and action. In May Brodbeck (Ed.), *Readings in the philosophy of the social sciences* (pp. 58–79). London, England: Collier-Macmillan.

Caffarella, R. & Barnett, B. (1994). Characteristics of adult learners and foundations of experiential learning. In L. Jackson & R. Caffarella (Eds.), *Experiential learning: A new approach. New directions for adult and continuing education*, No. 62, summer. San Francisco, CA: Jossey-Bass.

Harasim, L. M. (Ed.). (1993) *Global networks: Computers and international communication*. Cambridge, MA: MIT Press.

Harasim, L. M. (1993). Networlds: Networks as social space. In L. M. Harasim (Ed.), *Global networks: Computers and international communication*. Cambridge, MA: MIT Press.

Harrington, H. L. (1993). The essence of technology and the education of teachers. *Journal of Teacher Education*, 44 (1).

Hill, L. B., Long L., & Cupach, W. (1997). Aging and the Elders from a cross-cultural communication perspective. In Hana S. Noor Al-Deen (Ed.), *Cross-Cultural Communication and Aging in America* (pp. 5–22). Hillsdale, NJ: Erlbaum.

Hill, L. B. & Lujan, P. (1983). The Mississippi Choctaw: A case study of intercultural games. *American Indian Culture and Research Journal*, 7, 29–42.

Hill, L. B. & Lujan, P. (1984). Symbolicity among native Americans. *Journal of Thought*, 19 (3), 109–121.

Honna, N. & Hoffer, B. L. (2003). L. Brooks Hill — A professional overview. *Intercultural Communication Studies*, 12 (2), 181–185.

Huntington, S. (1996). *The clash of civilizations and the remaking of world order*. Old Tapper, NJ: Simon and Schuster.

Jackson, L. & Caffarella, R. (Eds.), (1994). Experiential learning: A new approach. *New directions for adult and continuing education*, No, 62, summer. San Francisco, CA: Jossey-Bass.

Jackson, L. & MacIsaac, D. (1994). Introduction to a new approach to experiential learning. In L. Jackson & R. Caffarella (Eds.), *Experiential learning. A new approach. New directions for adult and continuing education*, No. 62, summer. San Francisco, CA: Jossey-Bass.

Javidi, M. & Hill, L. B. (1987). International students and intercultural communication instruction. *Journal of Thought*, 22 (4).

King, A. (1996). The summing up. *The Southern Communication Journal*, 41. 363.

Kolb, D. (1984). *Experiential learning: Experience as the source of learning and development.* Englewood Cliffs, NJ: Prentice Hall.

Lee, P. & Caffarella, R. (1994). Methods and techniques for engaging learners in experiential learning activities. In L. Jackson and R. Caffarella (Eds.), *Experiential learning: A new approach. New directions for adult and Continuing education*, No. 62, summer. San Francisco, CA: Jossey-Bass.

Leeds-Hurwitz, W. (1990). Notes in the history of intercultural communication: The foreign service institute and the mandate for intercultural training. *The Quarterly Journal of Speech*, 76, 262–281.

Lewis, L. & Williams, C. (1994). Experiential learning: Past and present. In L. Jackson & R. Caffarella (Eds.), *Experiential learning: A new approach. New directions for adult and continuing education*, No. 62, summer. San Francisco, CA: Jossey-Bass.

MacIsaac, D. & Jackson, L. (1994). Assessment processes and outcomes: Portfolio construction. In L. Jackson & R. Caffarella (Eds.), *Experiential learning: A new approach. New directions for adult and continuing education*, No. 62, summer. San Francisco, CA: Jossey-Bass.

Mander, J. (1991). *In the absence of the Sacred: The failure of technology and the survival of the Indian nations.* San Francisco, CA: Sierra Club Books.

Maybury-Lewis, D. (2/21/1997). "Indigenous peoples and the 21st Century." Speech delivered at Trinity University, San Antonio TX.

Random House Dictionary. (1967). "Civility," "Civil," "Civilized," and "Civilization." *The Random House Dictionary of the English Language* (The Unabridged Edition). New York, NY: Random House.

Wallace-Hadrill, A. (1982). Civilis princeps: Between citizen and king. *Journal of Roman Studies*, 72, 32–48.

Wishnietsky, D. (Ed.). (1994). *Assessing the role of technology in education.* Bloomington, IN: Phi Delta Kappa.

2

China's Intercultural Communication Studies: Its Current Status and Problems[*]

Hu Wenzhong
Beijing Foreign Studies University, China

Abstract: This paper first reviews the beginning, growth and landmarks of China's intercultural communication (ICC) studies. Then it discusses its special features in the past decade: 1) the publication of articles and books on ICC has increased rapidly; 2) the scope of research has widened and a diversified approach is beginning to emerge; 3) research in international communication has broadened and inter-ethnic communication has also become a topic of research; and 4) a number of intercultural communication classics have been reprinted in Chinese mainland. The limitations of China's ICC studies mainly lie in two aspects: Most of those engaged in ICC research are foreign language professors, who are not well-equipped with theories of communication and psychology and have not had systematic training in ICC research methodologies; and secondly, the scope of research is still too limited and the approach often is not multi-disciplinary.

The writer holds that an analogy may be drawn between linguistic studies and ICC studies in China. While the situation of linguistic studies was much the same as what ICC studies is like today, remarkable progress has been scored in China's linguistic studies in the past two decades because of the measures taken over the years. The writer recommends that the strengthening of graduate programs and the training of teachers and scholars in ICC theoretical and methodological issues should be top priority. Plans should also be made to work on syllabus design, course development and teaching resources.

---

[*] This is an address made on June 11, 2010 at the Chinese Intercultural Disciplinary Development Symposium held at Shanghai International Studies University.

It is my great pleasure to be invited to this symposium, for it has given me a chance to meet so many distinguished intercultural communication scholars from Germany, the UK, the United States, China and other countries. I am especially pleased to see pioneers of intercultural communication studies like Professor Michael Prosser and Professor Dan Landis are here with us. I am sure we all feel indebted to Shanghai International Studies University for hosting this symposium and for bringing together scholars from all over China. I believe this symposium will be an impetus to China's intercultural communication teaching and research and to furthering the collaboration between Chinese scholars and scholars from overseas.

Before we delve into the history of China's intercultural communication, there is one important concept we have to clear up first. This is the translation of the English word "communication." In English this word covers interpersonal communication as well as mass communication. Thus under International Communication Association (ICA) there are such divisions as Interpersonal Communication, Intercultural Communication, Global Communication and Social Change, Journalism Studies, Mass Communication, Language and Social Interaction, Organizational Communication, Information Systems and some others. When intercultural communication was first introduced in China, it had five or six different versions of translation①. After about ten years we now settle for two terms: *kuàwénhuà jiāojì*（跨文化交际）and *kuàwénhuà chuánbō*（跨文化传播）. The former is used by scholars often with a foreign language teaching background while the latter is used by scholars with a media studies background. When the former group holds conferences, those in the latter (*chuánbō*) group sometimes join. But foreign language professors as a rule do not attend conferences of the other group. When you use the English word "communication", you may understand it in either its broader or narrower sense. But when it comes to Chinese, you have to decide what you mean before you choose the right word. This dual translation reflects the way China's intercultural communication has developed.

Roughly speaking, China's intercultural communication studies started in the early 1980s. This was at a time when China first opened its door to the outside world and everything from the West appeared new and alien to the Chinese. Those who went overseas to study noticed that in addition to language obstacles there were cultural hurdles in communicating with foreigners. Teachers of foreign languages were among the first to recognize the importance of culture in teaching languages and they started to introduce culture in their language courses. It was against this background that intercultural communication was first introduced to the

---

① They include 跨文化传通, 跨文化交流, 跨文化交际, 跨文化传播, and 跨文化沟通.

Chinese. Professor Xu Guozhang published "Culturally-loaded words and English language teaching" in 1982, thus ushering in the study of language and culture in foreign language teaching circles (Xu, 1982). He Daokuan introduced the discipline of intercultural communication in an article he wrote in 1983 (He, 1983). In 1988 the first collection of papers on intercultural communication was published under the title of *Intercultural Communication: What It Means to Chinese Learners of English* (Hu, 1988) and two years later the first reader of intercultural communication was published by the Hunan Education Press (Hu, 1990). In 1991 Edward Hall's *The Silent Language* was published in translation by the Shanghai People's Publishing House (Hall 1991). Articles about how to handle cultural differences in communication appeared in journals and magazines in increasing numbers, but the total number of articles published at the time was still very small. According to the Chinese Journal Full Text Database (CNKI), in 1989 only 11 articles on intercultural communication were published in Chinese journals. The breakdown of these articles is as follows:

Interpersonal communication	3
Translation	2
Linguistics	2
Language teaching	1
Theory	1
Miscellaneous	2

From the above we can see that articles on language study make up about half of the total. This is a trend that has persisted throughout the history of China's intercultural communication studies. These articles deal with such topics as the cultural connotation of words, pragmatic failures, discourse patterns, and problems involved in translation.

It was during this period that some universities started offering intercultural communication as a course at undergraduate and graduate levels. These include Peking University, Beijing Foreign Studies University, Shanghai International Studies University, Harbin Institute of Technology, Zhejiang University, Fujian Normal University and some other universities. At present there must be over a hundred universities in China where one or more courses in intercultural communication are offered. A few universities offer graduate programmes in intercultural communication at both masters' and doctoral levels.

The year of 1995 marks a turning point in China's intercultural communication history. Two things deserve our mention here. It was in August 1995 that China's first conference on intercultural communication was held at Harbin Institute of Technology. This was held in conjunction with the 5th International Conference on Cross-cultural Communication. Attending the conference were over 270 participants and about 120 of them came from overseas. The topic areas include theories of intercultural communication, verbal communication, nonverbal communication, literature and culture, information science, culture and media, and bilingualism. It was during the conference that the China Association for Intercultural Communication came into being. The standing council of the association decided that a conference be held biennially. Since then seven national conferences on intercultural communication have been organized in China and because of the national association and the conferences it organized the influence of intercultural communication grew quickly in academic circles. Up till this year 14 intercultural studies centres have been set up in this country. The close collaboration between Chinese and overseas scholars in this area has been a special feature of China's intercultural communication and some of the conferences were jointly organized. Secondly, it was also in 1995 that the first intercultural communication monograph written by a Chinese scholar was published. This is Guan Shijie's *Intercultural Communication: An Area of Study to Improve Skills in Communicating with Foreigners* (Guan, 1995). In that book Guan made a comprehensive study of intercultural communication and unlike other works published in China he laid emphasis on media studies and international politics. The following year saw the publication of Lin Dajin's *Intercultural Communication Studies: A Guide to Communicating with Britons and Americans* and Wang Hongyin's *Intercultural Communication: How to Interact with Foreigners* (Lin, 1996; Wang, 1996). In 1997 Jia Yuxin published his *Intercultural Communication*, which adopts a sociolinguistic approach to the study of this subject (Jia, 1997). Other works on intercultural communication were published soon after and most of them were written by professors of foreign languages. And most deal with how culture impacts foreign language learning including the teaching of Chinese as a foreign language and how intercultural communication competence is to be acquired.

Since the beginning of this century intercultural communication in China has taken on some new characteristics. Firstly, the number of publications has increased rapidly. According to the Chinese Journal Full-text Database, in 1999 573 articles were published in Chinese journals. In 2000 it jumped to 859 and in 2009 the total number of articles reached 5,812. What follows is a table showing the fast growth of published articles on intercultural communication in Chinese journals.

Table 1: Number of articles in Chinese journals on intercultural communication 2000–2009

Year	Number of articles	Percentage growth over past year (%)	Year	Number of articles	Percentage growth over past year (%)
2000	859		2005	2,748	25.7
2001	1,151	34.0	2006	3,596	30.8
2002	1,584	37.6	2007	4,895	36.1
2003	1,831	15.6	2008	5,693	16.3
2004	2,185	19.3	2009	5,812	2.0

We should note here that the database has as its source 6,642 journals, of which only 37% (2,460) are classified as core or important journals. So a big proportion of the articles included here are what we may call general discussion articles published in less important journals.

The number of books published on intercultural communication has also grown. The catalogue of the National Library of China shows that the number of monographs and textbooks written or compiled by Chinese scholars on intercultural communication has increased steadily in the past decade.

Table 2: Number of books published between 2000–2009 on intercultural communication

Year	Number of books	Year	Number of books
2000	4	2005	6
2001	5	2006	10
2002	5	2007	15
2003	8	2008	13
2004	7	2009	21

Secondly, the scope of research has widened and a diversified approach to the study of intercultural communication has emerged. We pointed out earlier on that foreign language teaching takes up a predominant position in China's intercultural communication research. This situation at present is undergoing a change. For instance, in 1999 articles related to FL teaching account for 44.6% of the total number of articles published while in 2009 they take up only 29.16%.① While FL teaching-related articles have dropped in ratio, articles related to other branches of study begin to assume bigger proportions. According to Peng Shirong, between 1994 and 2003 a total of 1,109 articles were published in 564 Chinese journals. FL teaching and contrastive study of languages take up 35.89%, economics and management 11.81% and culture and media 9.47% (Peng, 2005). A survey of the catalogue of the National Library shows that in 2009 monographs written on cross-cultural studies by Chinese writers totaled 53②. Textbooks and general introduction account for about a quarter of the total. Language, culture, literature and translation take up about 17%; economics and management about 15%. It is amazing to find that almost 10 percent of the monographs deal with religious beliefs in intercultural communication. The percentage taken up by film and drama in relation to intercultural communication is also relatively high compared with past record.

Table 3: Content classification of monographs on cross-cultural studies published in 2009

Area of study	Number of books	Percentage of total (%)
Textbook and general introduction	13	24.53
Language, culture, literature and translation	9	16.98
Economics and management	8	15.09
Religion	5	9.44
Film and drama	4	7.55
Theory	3	5.66
Science and technology	2	3.77
Psychology	2	3.77
Media	2	3.77
Other areas	5	9.44
Total	53	100

---

① According to the CNKI database, the total number of articles published in 2009 on intercultural communication related to language and communication is 1,695 while in 1999 the number is 256. The total number of articles published on ICC in general in 2009 is 5,812 while the total number in 1999 is 573.
② This is the result of the search using "kuàwénhuà (跨文化)" instead of "kuàwénhuà jiāojì (跨文化交际)".

Here are some of the titles of the monographs:

- *Traditional Chinese Theatre in Cross-cultural Context* by Cao Lin
- *Japanese Corporate Culture and Intercultural Communication* by Wang Xiuwen
- *Cross-cultural Business Communication* by Yu Wenlei
- *Cross-cultural Management* by Chen Xiaoping
- *Cross-cultural Interpretation of American Films* by Hua Mingda
- *Psychology of Cross-cultural Communication* by Peng Kaiping
- *A Study of Cross-cultural Adaptation Problems of Foreign Students in China* by Yang Junhong

Many of these books should be of interest to researchers both at home and overseas, but since they are all written in Chinese, their circulation is limited to the home market only. Theoretical explorations are under way, and this is manifested in publications (Hu, 2005; Lin & Xie, 2005). The topics of doctoral and MA theses have also diversified. Here is a list of the thesis topics of the graduating MA students of Shanghai International Studies University in 2010:

- Advertising Appeals as a Mirror of Cultural Values: A Comparison Content Analysis of Video Beer Advertising in the U.S. and China
- A Qualitative Study of How Business Context Impacts Intercultural Conflicts — Examining the Localization of Top Managers in MNCs in Shanghai
- The Interrelated Factors of Chinese Students' Adaptation in France: Emotion Regulation, Social Support & Acculturative Stress
- The Effects of Personality on the Adjustment of American Sojourners and Settlers in Shanghai
- A Qualitative Study Investigating the Cross-Cultural Adaptation of Taiwanese Working in Shanghai
- Test of an Intercultural Framework of Measuring Web Design Differences — Strategies to Internationalize English Version of Qingpu District Government Website
- Structural Equivalence of Values Domains in China: Values among Migrant Workers and Local Permanent Residents in Shanghai
- A Qualitative Study of Intercultural Contact on Campus — Perspectives from Host Chinese Students at Fudan University

Thirdly, research in international communication has broadened to include Sino-Japanese, Sino-Russian, Sino-German and Sino-French communication in addition to Sino-American communication and inter-ethnic communication has also attracted increasing attention among researchers. In the early stage Chinese researchers focused on communication between Chinese and Americans and most of the articles discussed differences in communication style, behaviour pattern and cultural values between them. Gradually they shifted their attention to communication between Chinese on the one hand and Japanese, Russians, Germans, and the French on the other. Inter-ethnic communication has not been a research area until recent years. Following is a list of some of the articles published in Chinese journals on inter-ethnic communication and the problems involved.

- Ding Liyan. (2002). Interethnic cultural differences and foreign language teaching today. *Journal of Jiamusi University (Social Sciences)*, *1*.
- Tan Houfeng. (2002). On the language and culture of the Dongs and translation. *Journal of Guizhou Institute of Nationalities, 5*.
- Pan Qixu. (2002). A comparative study of the thought patterns of the Zhuangs and the Hans as revealed by the word order they use. *Guangxi Nationalities Research, 2*.
- Yan Liping. (2003). On the taboos in the verbal and nonverbal communication of the Hans and the Uighurs. *Journal of Xinjiang Normal University (Social Sciences), 3*.
- Li Qiang. (2006). On pragmatic differences between English-speaking people and minority nationalities in Yunnan. *Journal of Yunnan University of Nationalities. 1.*
- Zhao Juan. (2008). An investigation and study of ethnic minority students' pragmatic competence. *Journal of Southwest Nationalities University, 4.*

Lastly, a number of intercultural communication classics have been reprinted in Chinese mainland and these include Gudykunst and Kim's *Communicating with Strangers: An Approach to Intercultural Communication*, Samovar and Porter's 10th edition of *Intercultural Communication: A Reader*, Hofstede's *Culture's Consequences: Comparing Values, Behaviors, Institutions and Organizations across Nations*, Ting-Toomey's *Communicating across Cultures*, Spencer-Oatey's *Culturally Speaking: Managing Rapport through Talk across Cultures* and other titles. They are now widely used by both researchers and graduate students. This series of ten titles was published in 2006 by the Shanghai Foreign Language Education Press. Other publishers such as Peking University Press and Foreign Language Teaching and Research Press have also bought copyright for the reprint of other ICC titles.

While we list the achievements in China's intercultural communication studies, we are not oblivious of the problems facing us.

First, although there is widespread interest in intercultural communication studies in China, those who have had a good grounding in communication studies theory, cross-cultural psychology and research methodologies are small in number. Only a few have had the chance to do doctoral work in communication studies at home or overseas. Most of the scholars can only catch up in their reading of related works while they engage in teaching and research. So compared with our overseas counterpart intercultural communication scholars in China taken as a whole are relatively weak in theoretical and methodological preparation. This is why it is sometimes difficult to adopt a multi-disciplinary approach to the study of intercultural issues, for not too many are equipped with theories of social psychology, sociology or communication studies. Concerned scholars have stressed the need for empirical research at conferences and in journal articles (Peng, 2005), and we are pleased to find that in recent years there is an obvious increase in papers based on empirical research. But there is still a large number of articles in journals that are of a general discussion nature and some of them are repetitive.

Secondly, because of the special circumstances in which China's intercultural communication studies was initiated and developed, all along foreign language teaching looms large and assumes a disproportionately big role. In publications topics related to foreign language teaching and language and culture form the bulk of articles, papers and monographs published. Intercultural communication conferences are mostly attended by foreign language professors and graduate students. This situation is gradually changing with more and more scholars from other disciplines joining the ranks. We are pleased to see this symposium has drawn media studies scholars, psychologists, and sociologists in addition to foreign language scholars. In anthologies published in recent years on intercultural communication we find contributions not only from foreign language professors, but also from scholars in other fields including media studies, economics and trade, ICC training and other branches of study. It is only natural that the path intercultural communication takes in each country varies and the point of emphasis in research differs from country to country. For instance, in the United States the influence of psychology is greater than some other disciplines and the issues dealt with by ICC researchers cover a wide range including interracial relations, immigrants, foreign students, multi-national companies, bilingual education, gender differences and many others. In Germany the teaching of German overseas (intercultural German Studies), economic collaboration and trade across nations seem to be the focus of attention of ICC researchers. In Russia the teaching of Russian to foreigners was given primary attention and many academic works were published on how Russian culture could be combined with the teaching of the Russian language. In the UK the teaching of culture in conjunction with language has been given much attention. In China foreign language education is of great importance to its modernization and collaboration with other countries and it is exactly for this reason that intercultural communication lays emphasis on it. Nonetheless, the scope of research still seems to be too narrow and limited and the approach often is not multi-disciplinary. There are many issues in

China we need to address such as interracial and inter-ethnic relations, inter-regional communication problems, cultural clashes in transnational companies, the adaptation of foreign students in China, migrant workers in the cities, bilingual education and many others. We need to broaden our scope of research and adopt a multi-disciplinary approach to the study of these intercultural issues.

Now I would like to make some recommendations on our ICC studies from the perspective of disciplinary development. Steve Kulich and Chi Ruobing in their article on developing intercultural communication as a discipline (Kulich & Chi, 2009) have given us a comprehensive review of the state of the art and laid out a roadmap for further development. I agree with their general assessment and future plans and will not repeat what they said. But I would like to draw an analogy between ICC studies and applied linguistics in China. In the 1980s and the early 1990s China's linguistic studies was much the same as what we experience in ICC today. Foreign language teachers mostly had not received systematic training in theories of linguistics and research methodologies. Journal articles were mostly introductions or elaborations of Western theories and practices and empirical research was scarce. Textbooks and teaching resources were hard to obtain and it was under fairly difficult circumstances that graduate students were trained. But twenty years later the situation has changed significantly. Many teachers have now obtained MA or doctoral degrees in linguistics either at home universities or at universities overseas. Those who have not had a chance to go through graduate studies engage in in-service training. Now the general level of teaching and research in linguistics and applied linguistics at our universities has risen to a new level. In the core journals articles based on empirical research are the mainstream while general discussions have dropped significantly in ratio. Publishers have reprinted hundreds of books written by Western linguists and textbooks written by Chinese scholars are also in plentiful supply. Masters and doctoral programmes have graduated a large number of young scholars equipped with linguistic theories and research methodologies. What has been achieved in linguistic studies in China provides much food for thought and we need to reflect on this to determine what we should do with ICC studies.

In disciplinary development there is a number of factors we need to consider including teacher training, syllabus design, course development, textbook compilation, provision of resource material, journal publication, research and international collaboration. Of these teacher training is the most important, for only with the right people can we do the rest. I suggest that graduate programmes in ICC studies should be strengthened and that the universities that offer Masters and doctoral programmes in ICC studies expand their enrolment. Where possible, scholars well-trained in ICC theories and research methodologies should be drawn into our ranks. Training courses should also be organized during vacations to provide in-service teachers with training in basic ICC theories and research methodologies. Syllabus design and course development should also be given adequate attention. As far as I know, the Intercultural Institute of Shanghai International Studies University offers the largest number of ICC courses in this country. On the basis of the ICC courses offered at SISU we can draw up a list of compulsory and elective courses to be offered at graduate level. As for textbooks, we now have at least half a dozen to choose from. I suggest that the national association make recommendations as to which ones are suitable for what level. We do not yet have a journal specializing in ICC studies, but we are pleased to see the publication of Volume One of *Intercultural Communication Research* edited by Professors Jia Yuxin, Guo-Ming Chen, Sun Youzhong and Ray Heisey (Jia et al., 2009). This is an important publishing outlet for ICC research and we hope more volumes will be forthcoming. International collaboration is extremely important for us today, for we need to familiarize ourselves with the latest developments in ICC studies overseas. The growth of China Association for Intercultural Communication and the achievements of the Intercultural Centre at Shanghai International Studies University are outstanding examples of international collaboration in the ICC field. This symposium is another example of such collaboration. When all the steps mentioned above are taken and followed through, we are sure that ICC teaching and research in China will make remarkable progress.

References

Guan, S. J. (1995). *Intercultural communication: An area of study to improve skills in communicating with foreigners*. Beijing: Peking University Press.
Hall, E. (1991). *The silent language*. (J. R. Liu, Trans.). Shanghai: Shanghai People's Publishing House.
He, D. K. (1983). Introducing a new discipline — Intercultural Communication. *Waiguo Yuwen Jiaoxue (Foreign Language Teaching)*, 2.
Hu, W. Z. (Ed.). (1988). *Intercultural communication: What it means to Chinese learners of English*. Shanghai: Shanghai Translation Publishing House.
Hu, W. Z. (Ed). (1990). *Selected readings in intercultural communication*. Changsha: Hunan Education Press.
Hu, C. (2005). *Intercultural communication: Paradigms of the E-age and competency building*. Beijing: China Social Sciences Press.
Jia, Y. X. (1997). *Intercultural communication*. Shanghai: Shanghai Foreign Language Education Press.
Jia, Y. X. et al. (Eds.). (2009). *Intercultural Communication Research Vol. 1*. Beijing: Higher Education Press.
Lin, D. J. (1996). *Intercultural communication studies: A guide to communicating with Britons and Americans*. Fuzhou, Fujian: Fujian People's Publishing House.
Lin, D. J. & Xie, C. Q. (2005). *Intercultural communication: Theory and practice*. Fuzhou: Fujian People's Publishing House.

Kulich, S. & Chi, R. B. (2009). Developing intercultural communication as a discipline in China. In Y. X. Jia et al. (Eds.), *Intercultural Communication Research Vol. 1, 48-74*. Beijing: Higher Education Press.

Peng, S. Y. (2005). Intercultural communication studies in China: Status quo, problems and suggestions. *Journal of Hunan University (Social Sciences Edition)*, 4, 86-91.

Wang, H. Y. (1996). *Intercultural communication: How to interact with foreigners*. Beijing: Beijing Language Institute Press.

Xu, G. Z. (1982). Culturally-loaded words and English language teaching. *Xiandai Waiyu (Modern Languages)*, 4. pp. 19-25

THEORY

3

Towards a Comprehensive Perspective for Intercultural Communication Study[*]

L. Brooks Hill[**]
Trinity University, San Antonio TX

Eric Faulk[**]
University of Texas, Austin TX

Abstract: Intercultural communication is a broad and challenging area of study primarily because it represents the confluence of so many different disciplines of traditional study, forces us into the gaps that separate these diverse disciplines, and pushes us into the somewhat a-theoretical world of nearly chaotic change with some very fuzzy concepts. Theories about intercultural communication tend to originate within one or another of the more traditional disciplines and typically suffer the consequences of a narrowed perspective. Whereas these positions are useful for certain purposes, they often fail to provide a broad base for the synthesis of the widely varied work under the umbrella of intercultural studies. Thus, the purpose of this paper is to provide a comprehensive perspective about intercultural communication study that integrates more limited approaches and builds around the shared dimensions of human behavior. This expanded position will emphasize six primary and interdependent dimensions of human behavior: physicality, personality, sociality, politicality, symbolicity, and spirituality. After setting some general guidelines for this paradigm, separate sections will explain each of the six dimensions and identify distinctive contributions for each. A final section will project the utility of this comprehensive perspective for the future of intercultural communication study.

---

[*] Revised and expanded version of an article that appeared in the journal *Intercultural Communication Studies*, XIV, No. 2 (2005), 38–52.
[**] L. Brooks Hill (Ph.D., University of Illinois, 1968) is Professor of Human Communication, Department of Human Communication and Theater, Trinity University, San Antonio TX, USA. Eric Faulk (B.A., Trinity University, 2003) is a Master of Public Affairs candidate at the University of Texas, Austin TX, USA.

Introduction

During a graduate seminar several years ago, the senior author was pressed, if not pushed, by his students to generate a broad-based framework for the integration of diverse perspectives about intercultural relations. Shared or universal features of homo sapiens became the point of departure. Every human being, he reasoned, is minimally a physical entity with a psychological, social, and political orientation. Facilitating the interaction of these major components and the application of them in real contexts is the symbol-using capability. The students wrestled with this interdependent set of systems and added a more ethereal sixth dimension of spirituality. Because of the widely diverse, if not infinite, manifestations and permutations of these six sub-systems, this paradigm served primarily as a pedagogical framework for organizing class discussions. Stimulated by another class discussion several years later, the junior author decided to advance this position with emphasis on spirituality as it works with symbolicity to integrate the several parts. This renewed interest compelled both of the authors to reconsider the potential of this broad perspective. With renewed incentive they found its potential as an organizational schema that can provide a perspective for integrating diverse traditional disciplinary approaches to the study of intercultural communication.

The recurring suffix for all six dimensions is more than coincidence. The suffix "-ity" is typically "used to form abstract nouns expressing state or condition" (Random House Dictionary, 1987). For each of these categories we are identifying a state or condition and the tendencies of an individual to demonstrate what is involved in this dimension. Thus we identified (1) physicality, (2) personality, (3) sociality, (4) politicality, (5) symbolicity, and (6) spirituality. These features generally categorize the most prominent aspects of homo-sapiens and even more loosely identify areas of study within the scholarly community that study these aspects. One problem that this re-conceptualization was intended to correct was the somewhat random growth of traditional disciplines that study one or more of these dimensions. Sociology, for example, may study aspects of behavior embraced by sociality and politicality with occasional forays into symbolicity and spirituality. Likewise, psychology and political science treat varied aspects, but the specialists within those disciplines often work in isolation from specialists in other areas. One of the attractive features of intercultural communication study is the necessary interaction of scholars from all disciplines. An outgrowth of this paper should be a roadmap that can help us coordinate and synthesize the results of our collective studies more effectively. In no way should this article be interpreted as an indictment or denigration of anyone's scholarship. That is certainly not the intent. Instead, we are proposing an alternative schema for integrating this wide diversity according to some universal categories less burdened by academic constraints.

If all six of these dimensions are represented in each of us as states, conditions, and tendencies with infinite permutations, then we need some sort of model that can pull them together. In his work about leadership Brooks Hill located such an analogy with Chinese fretted balls (1999). Using this model the six dimensions are related to a ball within a ball with physicality at the center and other more encompassing balls up to spirituality that becomes indistinguishable from the outer context within which each of us resides and which works with symbolicity to facilitate the expression of the other dimensions. Imagine for a moment these fretted balls and their parallel dimensions within the human being. Each ball is relatively independent, but exists as interrelated with the other balls. For example, we can certainly study the physiology of the human being, but in terms of interaction with other people these physical qualities become important as they impact on one's personality, social relations, and so forth. We also need to recognize that these balls move around within the other balls, permitting amazing diversity of interaction potential as they are variously closer or further from the encompassing balls and are more stable or mobile in different situations. Each ball is variously perforated, often with intricate and distinctive designs, to permit us to see the balls within, as well as to permit permeable movement of influence between and among the balls. Ultimately, the collection of fretted balls is suspended in some sort of environment or context that can serve in widely variable ways to cause the balls to move, to stabilize, or otherwise reconfigure. Ultimately, each of us is represented by a set of fretted balls and as we move among diverse contexts we see the similar and dissimilar features among the sets of balls.

As a point of departure for this re-conceptualization, some central definitions may help to frame our approach constructively. We define culture as a process, rather than a product, with three distinctive areas of concern: (1) it involves knowing and behaving in a manner acceptable to persons who are members of the culture; (2) developing the semantic or cognitive framework to facilitate appropriate knowledge and behavior; and (3) transmitting and perpetuating this knowledge, framework, and behavior. Thus the process of culture embraces behavioral, cognitive, and social concerns. We also define communication as a process of symbolically eliciting meaningful responses, which facilitate understanding and / or fulfillment of other purposes. Although important, intention is not a definitional aspect of communication, because any of us may be "giving off" information about our selves whenever we are the object of attention, whether we intend to "give" that information or not (Goffman, 1959; Watzlawick, Beavin, & Jackson, 1967). Intercultural communication then becomes the process of generating or negotiating a shared sense of social reality in which people of different cultural perspectives attempt to create sufficient rapport to facilitate understanding and / or fulfillment of other purposes.

The study of intercultural communication is perhaps one of the most expansive and varied of all areas of human study. Even a cursory examination of any intercultural studies journal reveals a wide array of topics, reflects numerous disciplines, and underscores the creative potential of our diversity. This breadth and variety is at once a source of our strength, but is also a source of weakness if our efforts are not integrated in some fashion. The value of this comprehensive perspective is to organize our thinking, to determine how and where what we do individually fits within our system, and to use this collective effort to locate those questions we need to address. Perhaps most importantly, thinking so broadly will help us recognize that nothing we do is isolated from the work of others and trying to maximize the potential of our work requires us to collaborate ever more effectively. What follows is a brief consideration of the first five dimensions, a more detailed consideration of the sixth dimension, and a final projection of the potential of this approach for the future study of intercultural communication.

Physicality

As with each of our six dimensions, the central questions for this section are what is involved and how does physicality relate on the one hand to culture and to human communication on the other? For physicality, the inherent notion of "physiology" demands explanation and qualification. The common meaning of "physiology" is "the organic processes or functions in an organism or in any of its parts" (Random House Dictionary, 1987). Obviously this area of study is a primary concern of all biological and medical sciences. Those of us who focus our attention on the behavioral manifestations of prior physiological conditions are likely to lose some of the distinctive contributions of this area, as they become blurred in the interrelationship with psychological and sociological aspects of our behavior. Therefore, this area of physicality is treated independently of personality only in an artificial and heuristic fashion in order to call attention to some questions and variables from biological sciences which may get neglected or unwisely subsumed under more general psychological notions.

To treat the area of physicality independently involves some assumptions regarding homo-sapiens. First, the species significant characteristic for homo sapiens is assumed to be a chemical compound, perhaps related to DNA or RNA. Second, outgrowths or developments of this chemical constitution lead to neurological development necessary for those aspects of homo-sapiens often thought to be species significant, namely, our symbolic ability and abstract reasoning, among others. Third, members of our species are genetically unique, generally similar, and follow varied development, which fosters differential cultivation of genetic potential. The variation of our species over time may be attributable to environmental demands, such as diet and climate, and results in varied features such as differential stature, pigmentation, gait, and other variables. Fourth, this variation of development leads to varied patterns of perception, reasoning, and other more observable behavioral patterns as the sensorium differs according to these patterns and their usage. Finally, we can reasonably assume that evolution and selectivity operate at the physical level over time and therefore contribute to this varied development.

The resulting patterns of this varied development create a reciprocal relationship between physiology and culture. Depending on the relative isolation of the group, this relationship may be modal or configurational. Whatever the patterned tendency, the result is some physiological commonality that influences the development of culture. For example, similarity of stature may lead to commonality of living quarters, similarity of gait may lead to concepts of mobility, skin pigmentation may lead to conceptions of what a god looks like, and other similar physiological patterns may lead to a widely varied development of myths and myth structures. As in most cases we can locate exceptions, but patterned physiological tendencies do become foundational elements of cultural features. Conversely, culture can also lead to physiological patterns. Consider, for example, how the use of drugs and other chemicals can alter our life style and corresponding physiological tendencies; antibiotics, artificial sweeteners, illegal drugs, and other chemicals can have invasive consequences for our development. Similarly, more socially derived conditions can also affect our physiological development; consider, for example, pollution, sun bathing, dieting, birthing, and child feeding techniques.

These physiologically based cultural patterns do, in turn, influence our actual communication behaviors. Examples abound in several major areas of contemporary research, such as neural linguistics, sociobiology, and communico-biology. The most recent research in communico-biology reports the physiological foundations of many communication behaviors. Consider some examples from these lines of research as they directly effect communication variables: Our labeling and abstracting, our grammatical functions of language, and our varied use of speech and language reveal the operations of our physiologically based perceptions, reasoning, and symbolic activities. As the work of Walter Ong (1967), Marshal McLuhan (1964), and their many followers reveals, our media capabilities are strongly influenced by receptions in our sensorium. How we conceive of the person will seriously impact our self-perceptions, as well as our interpersonal relations. Consider the recent discussions of whether stereotyping may have physiological roots in our defensive reactions to differences among people (Wartik, 2004). We can also point to examinations of the basal ganglia's role discerning stimuli in the brain (Lieberman, Chang, Chiao, Bookheimer, & Knowlton, 2004) to show the vital role physicality plays in every aspect of communication from receptivity to delivery.

The connection to other spheres of human behavior cannot be ignored either as physicality plays a facilitator to a human's personality, sociality, politicality, symbolicity, and spirituality. Note, for example, the fairly recent phenomena of instant worldwide communication in today's global community and the "extensible self" (Adams, 2005) required to reach from one's local station to another continent; one's physicality is the engine motoring locally while one exchanges globally. The body with its continuous heartbeat and many neurological functions makes it possible for the other five universal human capacities to become effectively integrated for intercultural communication through telephone, videoconference, or electronic letter. The work of Lieberman and Rosenthal (2001) further illustrates the close integration of physicality and personality in the nonverbal decoding between humans with introverted and extroverted personalities.

Many other examples abound, but these will suffice as illustrations of the fundamental relations among physicality, culture, communication, and the other universal spheres of human behavior. We might debate for many years exactly what these relations are, how they should be weighted, and exactly how they impact our specific behaviors, but we know the relations are there. Ours is the task to sort and sift the evidence and determine what questions deserve our attention. Regardless of the answers, a lot of work by scholars of intercultural communication has linkages to physicality, and these connections should be acknowledged and expanded to create the total mosaic of intercultural relations.

Personality

The progression from the core dimension of physicality to the next dimension of personality raises several questions that have long troubled the behavioral and social sciences. Essentially, can concepts and principles in these broader dimensions be explained in terms of more core concepts? Labeled "reductionism" by philosophers of social science, the varied positions on this topic fit on a continuum ranging from a strict reductionism on one end to an anti-reduction position anchoring the other end. The latter argument would conclude that some concepts and principles relating them are distinctive to the more encompassing dimension and cannot be explained by reduction to more basic ingredients. The ultimate resolution of these questions will depend on the advancement of our knowledge, but meanwhile this paper presumes a middle ground between the anchors, a flexible position reflected in the perforations and movement of the fretted balls of our over-arching model. To wit, some aspects of homo sapiens we might label personality cannot be reduced to physical components, and yet, others may now or at some point in time be so reduced; the parallel of this position extends to sociality and politicality as well. The final two dimensions symbolicity and spirituality serve to integrate and synthesize the other dimensions, thus constraining the applicability of questions about reductionism in their regard.

The notion of personality demands some basic explanation and qualification. Drawing upon the common denotation, "personality" may be defined as the "sum total of the physical, mental, emotional, and social characteristics of an individual; ... the organized patterns of behavioral characteristics of the individual" (Random House, 1987). As with the other dimensions, personality is treated independently of its closest neighbors, physicality and sociality, only in an artificial and heuristic fashion. Ultimately and realistically these three dimensions are interdependent and feed each other directly and indirectly. The origins of personality are found in the unique development of the person within its physical and social context. The physical and physiological contexts frame the self-environmental connection that leads to varied influences in development. Similarly the social context adds concomitant influence on the emergent self-concept and self-other relationships. As the child progresses it learns about the relative value of the pieces of influence and its relative status and roles in the social system of which it is becoming a part. Granted that this statement overly simplifies the personality and recognizes the potential of subsequent social changes, these emergent characteristics certainly constitute the formative aspects of one's personality.

Many basic textbooks in the discipline of psychology identify the host of ingredients that variously comprise one's personality. Consider a few of the possible ingredients: The development of perceptional patterns is central to our personality, and these perceptions form the foundation of selectivity patterns that lead to how we subsequently perceive, interpret, and respond to our world. From this basis numerous authors have addressed how we form and change impressions, how these impressions develop into cognitive structures or constructs, and how these are variously influenced by interaction patterns with other members of our society. Less precisely behavioral, but certainly influential, is the assignment of relative values to our emergent attitudes, beliefs, and other predispositions. These values permeate the emergent frame of reference, a unique result of our cognitive and behavioral inclinations. As our next dimension will address, out of these learned tendencies we come to appreciate our social groups as a source of protection, both defensive and supportive. Close examination of these collective personality features reveals the rudiments of our reasoning processes and worldview. Lest we forget, however, many of these aspects and their tendencies emerge from inherent physiological conditions and become operational only in the social context.

One of the most provocative treatments of how personality and culture are reciprocally related comes from a classic work by Anthony F. C. Wallace. His *Culture and Personality* (1961) builds simplistically on the number of individuals involved and the number of behavioral categories to create a grid-work that moves from a simple habit or response by one person to a modal configuration of personality types that constitute the basic cultural framework of a people. Within the development of his position emerges a central concept that relates personality at the individual level to culture, namely, the concept of "mazeway." Summarizing his position, mazeway may be compared to a map of a gigantic maze with an elaborate key or legend and many insets. The three primary sets of ingredients are (1) the goals or values we might seek, (2) the objects, including self, that we will encounter, and (3) the techniques or ways to manipulate objects to realize end states. Whereas these elements may be combined in an almost infinite variety of imagined sequences, to the individual all of these phenomena normally constitute one integrated dynamic system of perceptual assemblages or a cultural framework. As Wallace presents his position, he relates this broadened concept to most areas that touch in one way or another with the dimension of personality.

Personality based cultural patterns are also reciprocally related to communication behaviors. Consider, for example, the implications on our symbol and code systems of the Sapir-Whorf hypothesis for perceptual patterns (Whorf, 1957), the work of Basil Bernstein for socio-economic class behaviors (1964), and the relevance of various other information-processing positions. Regarding the communication channels and media, notice the further relevance of work by Walter Ong and Marshal McLuhan for the function of our sensorium and the implications of media violence, transportation speed, and computerization for our children as compared to the older generations. The communication source and receiver relationships help create self-concept, self-esteem, self-disclosure patterns, identity formation, as well as our general social attitudes toward interpersonal communication tactics and strategies. Our individual personality and the modal personality reflective of culture and sub-cultures directly effect our development, adaptation, and transmission of messages. Collectively, personality based cultural patterns in one way or another impact directly or indirectly on all parts of the communication process.

Sociality

The so-called "herding instinct" of humans reflects a basic tendency to form groups in order to facilitate survival. Sociality addresses this social nature or tendency to group and includes the actions on the part of individuals to associate together for varied purposes. The central problem with this dimension is its relationship with the word "society," a term that encompasses the products of sociality, as well as politicality. When we use the word "society" it will be in this dual sense, referring to both the formation of groups or to the broader collections of groups into organizations and institutions. This third dimension of the human condition is treated independently of physicality, personality, and politicality in an artificial and heuristic fashion, as, once again, this fretted ball is strongly influenced by its core and encompassing dimensions. Whether sociality can be reduced to the personality and physicality elements is unclear, but it certainly has clear roots in our gregariousness, tendencies to empathize, and the defensive networks we establish for our survival. The environment in which the individual develops leads to specific group functions as it mediates the personality and social tendencies. As groups form and evolve, they assume distinctive features that emanate from the development of social norms, power structures, leadership needs, and the status and role systems. These and many other group phenomena reinforce the crucial nature of sociality and point to politicality where inter-group relations form some of the grandest structures in government and religious organizations.

Whereas society and culture in general conversation are more obviously related, the exact relationship is confusing for no other reason than the dual use of the word "society" in reference to groups emerging from sociality and inter-group developments emerging from politicality. For the immediate purposes, if we refer to society as a product of group development, then the relationship is more clearly part to whole, as culture would be a broader set of concerns comprised of diverse intra-cultural groups and groupings. Even so, this simplistic conception is in reality far more complicated as groups may overlap cultural boundaries, may comprise sub- or co-cultures within or across cultural boundaries, and may mix up the reciprocal relations among these socio-cultural components in confusing patterns. Regardless of the somewhat imprecise conceptualization of society and culture and the highly variable representation of these phenomena in real situations, one is not possible without the other; both are inextricably tied to the interaction patterns of people and form matrices of interaction responsibilities. If we look to its core neighbor personality, rather than to its broader more encompassing potential, we can manage it more reasonably. As Wallace's personality grid revealed, we can allow anyone of these human dimensions to expand and incrementally morph into a perspective about culture. If, however, we focus on the distinctiveness we can heuristically perceive the relative independence of each dimension, as well as its interaction with the other dimensions.

Socially-based cultural patterns are reciprocally related to communication patterns and behaviors. As a point of departure, whenever sociality and society exist, communication is a concomitant, if not a sine qua non. In fact the symbolic interactionists suggest that society is a communication matrix, i.e., a pattern or mold that grows out of human interaction. The channels of communication constitute patterns of dependence and interdependence that lead to roles and role systems that, in turn, form the foundation of society. As societies initially form to assist coping and survival skills, communication is the means by which decisions are reached and implemented. The intrapersonal and interpersonal communication patterns comprise the individual decision-making networks, but they also pattern to form the essentials of social norms, rules, and laws. Changes in one side of this equation will result in changes on the other side. For example, whether a society uses force, persuasion, or small groups to reach decisions, the communication patterns will similarly shift. Whether the mediated communication overwhelms the face-to-face interaction will also create change in society. These changes may be quick or slow, gradual and unnoticed or quick and alarming, but they reinforce the reciprocal relations among communication, sociality, and culture.

Beyond the broader level of communication and society as general systems, sociality manifests its influence directly on specific communication variables. Consider, for example, how jargon and dialectical variability reveal group patterns and the centrality of these socio-linguistic trends to the formation and dissolution of cultural units. Notice further how conceptions of the source and receiver, as well as their interactions, grow out of socially influenced development of self-concept and matters of self-esteem, and how the roles, norms, and power structures regulate communication interaction. The implications for communication channels and media are so prevalent today that they are regularly topics of conversation. Who can ignore the social dependence on media technology and the concerns for diverse social issues? Just as social groups influence our viewpoints, they further alter the function of our perceptual patterns and worldview. Message variability is also impacted, as much of what we talk about and the ways we talk about them grow out of our social concerns, and the strategies and tactics we employ as we adapt to each other result from group norms and rules of propriety and tolerance. We all realize the dangers of social violations and the consequent punishment. Our communication behavior reflects our sensitivity, or lack thereof, to these social concerns.

Politicality

As sociality refers to the human tendency to form groups, politicality recognizes the need for inter-group relations. Parallel with the prior three dimensions of the human condition, politicality requires explanation and qualification as it is treated independently of sociality, personality, and physicality in an artificial and heuristic fashion. As indicated in the preceding section, politicality is an aspect of society broadly conceived. We define politicality as the tendencies shown in organizing or institutionalizing relations and interactions between and among groups. "Organize" refers to the actions used to form into a whole the interdependent or coordinated parts or groups. Politicality has evolved with environmental complexity as increased population, transportation efficiency, and technology generally have created social changes for mating, trade, conflict resolution, and other features of survival. The potential structure of government and religion represent the grandest achievements of social differentiation among power and role structures, as well as systems for conflict resolution, economic transactions, and military engagement. The results of these political efforts are the states, religions, and countries that uniquely reflect our culture and sub-cultural systems. Just as groups develop to permit coordinated efforts that exceed the potential of any individual, political entities exist to permit coordinated efforts that exceed the potential of any single group.

Political systems or institutions, by whatever name, and politicality are reciprocally related to culture. In Wallace's aforementioned grid, political institutions are to some extent reflections of the modal personality that, in turn, constitute the basic features of social groupings. How society relates to political systems is a matter of definition, but society or societies become at the multi-group level the components of political institutions. Perhaps the simplest way to sort these confusing relations is to point to possible ways that political systems relate to culture: The geometric options are part to whole, whole to part, concomitant, concentric, or overlapping. In fact all of these possibilities are available in the constellation of current states, governments, non-governmental organizations (NGOs), and religions. The reciprocal influence between culture and these political institutions is readily apparent when we observe that changes in either result in changes in the other.

The politically based aspects of culture are reciprocally related to communication phenomena. Consider first the symbol system, as the architecture we construct reflects the cultural interaction with political institutions, the rituals of power groups with their specialized norms and roles reveal the values assigned to such varied groupings, and the metaphors and myths associated with our religions often are inseparable from cultural phenomena. The channels and media influence strike at the heart of politics, which we might define as the system for allocation of power and scarce resources. Through the media we conduct campaigns to assume power and secure the resources. Social power reveals further the conception of source and receiver as the political units work to preserve the integrity or suppress the individuality of their members, individually or as groups. For example, the individual-collective distinction drawn for cultural differentiation is directly and indirectly reflected in the host governments and religions. Finally, message variability, both in content and in form, reflects the political features of our culture. The diverse coalitions will influence the basic arguments used, and the strategies and tactics for preservation of power will impact the acceptable modes of interaction. Compare the use of education, persuasion, and force among political institutions as indicators of cultural patterns. In his classic work *The Symbolic Uses of Politics*, Murray Edelman urged political scientists to reconsider many of the symbolic and other communication aspects of politics and political institutions (1964; also see 1971).

Symbolicity

The symbol-using capacity of the human being is often considered a species identifier that distinguishes us from other creatures in our world. Personally, we use symbols to label and organize the diverse world we occupy, and socially we use symbols to communicate with others for coping with this diverse world. We develop our symbols into systematic sets we call languages, both verbal and non-verbal. Essentially all languages have four components: the symbols, such as sounds and gestures, that signify phenomena in our world; the categories of symbols, such as nouns and verbs, that permit us to differentiate objects from actions and other relationships among the worldly phenomena; the logic, such as verbal syntax, that permits us to make reasonable statements about how the symbolic categories and phenomena within them may relate to each other, and the idiomatic and creative deviation from our language rules that allow us to expand our language and creatively deal with the diversity of our world. The origins of our symbolicity are deeply woven into the four prior dimensions of the human condition, as our symbol-producing capacity is rooted in the chemical and neurological aspects of our physicality, the psychological uses of symbols so central to our emergent personalities and world organization system, and the social uses that grow out of our sociality and politicality. The broadest level of spirituality builds upon the integration of the prior dimensions through symbolicity.

Symbolicity and culture are at least reciprocally related, if not, according to some authors, indistinguishable. To anthropologist Edward T. Hall culture is communication and vice versa (1959); to anthropological linguist Dell Hymes communication processes provide a comprehensive entry point for the discovery of culture (1964). If we wish to approach culture as a symbolic process, then we can draw upon the work of a broad spectrum of research to reinforce our perspective. Semanticists and the recent derivative of cultural studies demonstrate how all aspects of reality grow from our symbolic constructions and the interpretation / application of them. The grammarians provide us a structural framework from both the logic and psycho-logic of language. The studies of metaphor, myth, and folklore from literary scholars and anthropologists such as Levi-Strauss (1963) add features to our study of symbols that accent the potential for religiosity and spirituality. From a socio-logical perspective, such as symbolic interaction and ordinary language philosophy, we encounter symbolicity as the interaction matrix that forms the foundation of sociality and politicality. Any issue of an intercultural studies journal will clearly indicate the varied relevance of symbolicity to the multiple dimensions of our humanity.

Because symbols are the sine qua non of communication as we know it, we will not pursue the parallel reciprocity between the two areas as we did with the four prior dimensions, but instead will offer a position that forms the basis for our expanded treatment of spirituality. Let us first return to our model of the Chinese fretted balls. Symbolicity represents the fifth ball within which are the preceding core dimensions. Recall that each ball is perforated with various designs reflecting the variety of learned behaviors within varied cultures. Through these perforated designs light can pass and touch any aspect of whatever is within. This transparency is crucial for symbolicity that permeates all of the dimensions like the passage of light, thus potentially enabling the individual to identify, specify, and relate to all aspects of its being. In this fashion our symbol using capacity does become the gelatin that gives stability and order to the entire model. Without this lubricating and consolidating potential the fretted balls would be too loose and inaccurately reflect the stability of the human condition they are designed to indicate. To examine how this works, one needs only to consider how language and its symbols serve us. As we label in different languages, we simultaneously illuminate or shade certain aspects of the phenomena we are specifying. As we link these pieces of reality we simultaneously reflect the logic or psycho-logic of how pieces of reality may be connected. As we creatively expand our perspective, we use our metaphors and myths to create new visions and stimulate our imaginations.

Spirituality

The final innate dimension of our humanity is modeled by the fretted ball that connects each of us to the broadest aspects of our world and to the preceding core dimensions. For some individuals spirituality is deeply seated in religious institutions, but for others less interested in the political features of their spirituality this may simply entail the quest for our fit or position in the natural or metaphysical world. Wherever it may take us, this search for the meaning of life recognizes broader questions than the prior dimensions, forcing us to look outward from the most encompassing fretted ball to the ultimate source of light that integrates the many dimensions of our lives. The major professor of the senior author of this article was someone who believed deeply in the unity of our universe whether apparently irrational or not. In truly Aristotelian fashion he sought the basic categories and analogies that might unify our world. Such a quest for the ultimate theory of knowledge certainly motivated the present study, but the model and particulars are uniquely the products of the authors, and as we turn toward spirituality we may have located the containing dimension of our humanity. We are, therefore, like the graduate students in the seminar mentioned at the outset of this article convinced that spirituality is an essential dimension of the human condition that ultimately, both individually and socially, provides the light that enables us to see how the other dimensions of our humanity relate to each other.

Perhaps the best definition of spirituality for our use is a multifaceted conception by Ken Wilber. He lays out four "major meanings" of the word "spiritual" used in both scholarly and lay approaches, underscoring that clear definitions are crucial when talking about spirituality: "... we absolutely MUST identify which [definition] we mean, or the conversation goes nowhere fast, with the added burden that one thinks ground has actually been covered" (2006, p. 100). His first aspect of "spirituality involves the highest levels of any series of developmental lines" (1998, p. 561). For instance, the universal capacities of physicality, personality, sociality, politicality, and symbolicity each develop along a certain path or line over time in a particular human's growth. One could almost imagine a graph where the individual lines run parallel and surpass or fall behind one another, mostly developing, sometimes into a spiritual turquoise zone. When one's personality, for example, reaches a very high level of development (the turquoise zone) this capacity begins to operate at a spiritual level of development. These developmental lines may be divided into pre-conventional, conventional, post-conventional, and post-post-conventional stages of development with the post-post conventional level being the spiritual. Thus, in one sense "spirituality is the sum total of the highest levels of any series of developmental lines" (1998, p. 562). One could be at the post-post-conventional level of both sociality and politicality, and the level of spirituality would be the total of those two lines developed to the spiritual levels. Thus, in this sense, spirituality is *"the highest levels in any of the lines"* (2006, p. 101), a concept that parallels closely Maslow's (1973) realized self actualization in the highest stages of human development.

Another prospect is the potential that "spirituality is itself a separate developmental line" (1998, p. 562). As spirituality is an innate human dimension in and of itself, this capacity may unfold along its own path. This line develops as states of conscious awareness unfold. When levels of awareness begin to emerge at what Wilber calls the "transpersonal stages," the individual approaches the spiritual levels of conscious awareness. These stages may be achieved through spiritual practices, such as meditation or prayer, and are most easily described by the work of Evelyn Underhill who "divides spirituality into three broad hierarchical stages (with numerous substages), which she calls *nature mysticism* (a lateral expansion of consciousness to embrace the stream of life), *metaphysical mysticism* (culminating in formless cessation), and *divine mysticism* (which she divides into dark night and union)" (cited in Wilber, 1998, p. 565). Each of these states transcends the previous one in depth, creating different levels of spiritual awareness within the development of one's spirituality.

According to Wilber, spirituality may also be "a *special attitude* that can be present at *any* stage or state: perhaps love, or compassion, or wisdom ... " (2006, p. 101). As "probably the most popular and common definition" (1998, p. 565), it often involves aspects of the other definitions and relies upon levels or lines of development, and it describes spirituality as an emotion or realization of, for example, compassion that a human may have toward the world or other humans. This attitude involves a transcendence of the ego or self to embrace a socio-centric or world-centric perspective in which love and openness to all peoples and the entire universe follows. Closely correlated with "spirituality as attitude" is Wilber's idea that "spirituality basically involves peak experiences" (1998, p. 566). These peak experiences are direct apprehensions of spiritual realities and may or may not develop along any lines or within specifiable stages. For example, during the states of meditation or prayer, one may realize one's self in complete unity with the universe or God. These are temporary experiences like moving in and out of a room; they are entered and then exited by human consciousness and may happen spontaneously or at more advanced levels of spiritual development.

Spirituality can be a mix of all or some of these aspects or definitions, a mix of developmental lines, a combination of these lines, a line unto itself, a realized attitude of love or openness, or apprehensions of peak spiritual experiences. With all of these spiritual realities, at some point it becomes necessary for the person to communicate this spirituality with other people. This is where symbolicity interacts with spirituality. As one operates from spiritual or post-post-conventional levels in their developmental lines, experiences love or openness, or has peak spiritual experiences, a new set of referents emerges, spiritual referents that can be communicated through spiritual symbols. Through the innate human capacity for symbolicity, whole vocabularies of spiritual symbols may be created to communicate between two people or within a culture of people who have the spiritual referents from their spiritual experiences. As Wilber explains, "If a Zen master says 'Emptiness,' and you've had that experience, you will know exactly what is meant." He adds, "Zen masters talk about Emptiness all the time! And they know exactly what they mean by the words, and the words are perfectly adequate to convey what they mean, *if* you have had the experience (for what they mean can only be disclosed in the shared praxis of zazen, or meditation practice)" (1995, p. 271). But if one has not experienced the referent for "emptiness," then this aspect slips into the shadows of our fretted ball analogy and is lost to the spiritually inexperienced. Just like the child is unable to comprehend "as if" statements, someone who has not developed to a spiritual point in their lines of development, or has not had the spiritual experience symbolized, will not apprehend or comprehend that spiritual experience.

To grasp the relationship between spirituality and the other dimensions of our humanity, we can examine the human being within our over-arching model of fretted balls with each sphere functioning from its own level along a developmental line. A person's physicality is, as the term suggests, the purely self or body and the physiological action the body takes. A person's body grows and develops naturally over the course of a lifetime, but this growth is not the only development that occurs. The body's overall health and well being may improve or diminish as an individual ingests food or engages in exercise. Physicality's developmental line is contingent upon the level to which one nourishes one's body and engages in physical practice, and whereas a pre-conventional level of development along this line would be the result of a disability or basic neglect of one's body, the post-conventional level of development would be the apex of healthful nourishment and activity, wherein the body is at a maximum level of health.

The body's nourishment and activity are heavily contingent upon the person's personality. Carl Jung's (1971) psychological types help us to relate spirituality to personality; it provides us with a framework within which to analyze personality and apply it to developmental lines. In Jung's system, a person deals with the world through a combination of being either introverted or extroverted, sensing or intuitive, thinking or feeling, and judging or perceptive. Sixteen personality types are possible. For example, a person can be extroverted, sensing, thinking, and judging

(ESTJ) or introverted, intuitive, feeling, and perceptive (INFP), to list only two of the sixteen different personality possibilities which an individual may use to gather and evaluate information. In this model, a person is only functional in so far as he or she integrates the opposing preferences — extroversion with introversion, thinking and feeling, and so forth. One can imagine the trouble a person would face if he or she were completely introverted; the introverted individual cannot function independently without exercising some degree of extroversion, just like a completely extroverted person would not be safe without some introverted, contemplative thought before acting. Developmentally, at a pre-conventional level, an individual's personality functions solely at one end of the spectrum for each of the four dualities-a pre-conventional ENTP would solely function with extroversion, intuition, thinking, and perception, with no inclination towards the other ways of dealing with the world. Ideally, a post-post-conventional level of personality development, within the framework of Jung's typology, would operate with all four dualities completely integrated so that there is no tendency either way; feeling tendencies would be balanced with thought, for instance, so that a person could love as well as reason when the individual interacted with the world and other people. Of course, each person is an individual in and of them selves and can never be strictly labeled or pigeonholed, but Jung's system is a very useful tool for seeing how people own various personalities and how those personalities may be disintegrated at a pre-conventional level or fully integrated at a post-post conventional level of development, experiencing peak spiritual experiences as they engage the world.

A person brings their personality or self to a group, socially and politically. Sociality and politicality relate to spirituality in the domain of community. That the words community and communication are so similar is no coincidence. While engaging in sociality, individuals are operating with their physicality, taking in information from their environments with their personality, and communicating with other individuals through sociality. The pre-conventional level along sociality's developmental line would be a person's incapability to interact and communicate with other individuals who were engaging in sociality, while the post-conventional level would represent the human being as a complete integration into a social situation, with a mastery of communication and interaction with other individuals. As these communities are institutionalized and organized, individuals begin to communicate between different institutions and organizations as representatives of their respective groups. Wilber explains, "They exist in intricate networks of relational exchange with [concentric spheres] at the same level of structural organization" (1995, p. 91). Politicality's function is contingent upon levels of organization; this is where developmental lines become apparent. Similar to sociality, the pre-conventional level of politicality along its developmental line would find a group unable to integrate into an institution or organization. On the other hand, an individual functioning at a post-conventional level of development within this sphere of politicality would fully organize, institutionalize, and integrate into a community, and thus the person or group would represent the organization or institution effectively at a level of communication and interaction with other representatives.

Nearly all people interact primarily in the final two spheres of symbolicity and spirituality that facilitate interaction like a binding social and political force. These spheres provide a sea of mind and spirit in which all people, physically, personally, socially and politically, swim. Wilber calls this the "noosphere," the realm of socio-cultural reality. This reality includes "... symbols and tools that both [create] and [depend] upon new levels of social holons in which the users of symbols and tools ... exist and reproduce themselves, but the reproduction [is] now the reproduction of culture through symbolic communication and not just the reproduction of bodies through sexuality. Kinship [gives] way to 'cultureship' ... " (1995, p. 100). Culture is formed using the universal function of symbolicity. Humans create a mental reality, an environment in which they are free to engage in sociality and politicality, using their physicality and personality. As frequently suggested, people are like fish, swimming in the cultural waters of symbolicity, i.e., Wilber's "noosphere" that includes transcendent spirituality. As spirituality is the transcendent, or post-post-conventional, aspect of all levels of development and also includes love and openness, love and spirituality is shared between people as they reside in the noosphere. Not only can people transcend themselves and share love, they can communicate these experiences with one another through symbolicity in a culture of shared experience.

When one says to another, "I love you," love is between the two people, transcending each person and "flowing" between each one in the noosphere. Here we see symbolicity and spirituality's symbiotic relationship in intercultural communication. As intercultural communication is people, representing various cultures, communicating and overcoming their cultural differences, symbolicity and spirituality are the facilitating factors in this process. Through symbolicity, two people communicate, and through spirituality, people may transcend themselves and connect with others through openness and love. The two cultural representatives are free to interact and engage each other, communicating interculturally, overcoming their differences, through shared symbolicity and love for one another. In this fashion Wilber's noosphere and the better known concept of community become the vehicles for a better synchronized and harmonious world.

Conclusion and Projections

Originating many years ago, the central message of this paper is a set of six interrelated and interdependent dimensions common to all people: physicality, personality, sociality, politicality, symbolicity, and spirituality. Over the last thirty to forty years, a rapidly expanding literature has encouraged us to reconfigure our study of human behavior around this less contaminated set of universal characteristics. Many scholars bemoan the constraints experienced as their questions fall into the breech between and among the established domains of our educational system. The value of this alternative results from shaking up the traditional categories derived from independent disciplines and returning to the basics of our humanity (cf. Koestler, 1964). The study of intercultural communication is a remarkably propitious point of departure to launch this re-orientation.

The senior author has served as an officer in the International Association for Intercultural Studies (IAICS) since it origination in 1996. He has served as a reader and / or editor for the journal *Intercultural Communication Studies* (ICS) since its inception in 1991. This extensive and intensive work provides a foundation for projecting a vision of intercultural studies for the future. In reflection about the fellow members of IAICS and contributors to ICS, specialists in all six dimensions of the position taken in this article are active, and our conversations continually address the interaction about the dimensions of this paradigm from diverse cultural vantage points. What remain for this paper are some suggestions about how to realize the potential of this invigorating vision for one intercultural organization and one journal, but that vision can expand in parallel fashion to other organizations and their journals. In this collective endeavor we might create a synthesis otherwise impossible to achieve.

One way to align our work consonant with this vision is through our journal and related publications. The articles printed in each issue of ICS consider a wide variety of topics that are often merely fragments of the proposed system. What if we developed a set of basic questions and asked each author to address the relevant questions in a projection section at the end of the article? These questions would seek the author's identification of how the topic relates to this alternative system, what contribution does the article potentially make to what dimension, and what are the implications for the relationship between or among the dimensions? We should restrict the length of this response to no more than five hundred words, but even such a short commentary would invite the authors to fit their work into a shared perspective. At the end of each volume, one of the editorial board members could synthesize these short commentaries into a reflection of where we are and where we see gaps for the expansion of our collective vision.

We can and should use our conferences to synthesize our work more effectively. One way would be to set up panels of papers around these dimensions and to create dialogue sessions that consider the implications of our current work for the advancement of our vision. Even a quick examination of our work indicates a predominant emphasis on symbolicity, but more careful study of our work indicates serious questions that are beneath the surface of our topic about the relation of this work to other dimensions of our humanity. What is most likely is that we simply have not considered more completely the implications of our work. Because we can so easily read the results of our work in the journal, I would like to see us talk much more at our conferences about the implications of our work. Sometimes the missing key to unlock far greater potential of our work can come from someone who is far removed from our specialty and yet who shares our broader vision. We need, therefore, to re-examine the potential of our annual meetings.

Perhaps the most important concern addressed by this paper is largely implicit. Despite the amazing proliferation of research and publications about human behavior we continue to constrain rather than expand our potential. As disciplines compete at universities for scarce resources they build and solidify their base of success at the expense of greater enlightenment and vision. The breadth necessary to address intercultural communication study compels us to escape those constraints. Because so many of us can recount unfortunate experiences that have reduced our initiative and momentum, we seriously wish that we could wave a wand and terminate these counterproductive developments of a political sort, but we cannot. What we can do is follow the advice of the mariners in Booker T. Washington's famous Atlanta Exposition Address in the nineteenth century: "Cast down your bucket where you are" (1895/1954, p. 462) and thereby gain the sustenance we need for the future. Let us use this occasion to launch an alternative perspective framed around the distinctive features of our humanity. Let us use IAICS and its journal and conferences to re-envision a more promising future for world community through better intercultural communication.

References

Adams, P. C. (2005). *The boundless self: Communication in physical and virtual spaces*. Syracuse, NY: Syracuse University Press.

Bernstein, B. (1964). Elaborated and restricted codes: Their social origins and some consequences. *American Anthropologist, 66*, 35–65.

Edelman, M. (1964). *The symbolic uses of politics*. Urbana IL: University of Illinois.

Edelman, M. (1971). *Politics as symbolic action: Mass arousal and quiescence*. New

York NY: Academic Press.

Goffman, E. (1959). *The presentation of self in everyday life*. Garden City, NY: Doubleday.

Hall, E. T. (1959). *The silent language*. Greenwich, CN: Fawcett.

Hill, L. B. (1999). Leadership. In W. G. Christ (Ed.), *Leadership in times of change*. Mahwah, NJ: Lawrence Erlbaum. Pp. 199–225.

Hymes, D. (1964). Introduction: Toward ethnographies of communication. *American Anthropologist*. 66, 1–35.

Jung, C. (1971). *Psychological types*. Princeton, NJ: Princeton University Press.

Koestler, A. (1964). *The act of creation*. New York, NY: Macmillan.

Lieberman, M. D., & R. Rosenthal. (2001). Why introverts can't always tell who likes them: Multitasking and nonverbal decoding. *Journal of Personality and Social Psychology, 80*, No. 2, 294–310.

Lieberman, M. D., G. Y. Chang, J. Chiao, S. Y. Bookheimer, & B. J. Knowlton. (2004). An event-related fMRI Study of artificial grammar learning in a balanced chunk strength design. *Journal of Cognitive Neuroscience, 16*, no. 3, 427–438.

Levi-Strauss, C. (1963). *Structural anthropology*. Garden City, NY: Doubleday.

Maslow, A. H. (1973). *On dominance, self-esteem, and self-actualization: Germinal papers of A. H. Maslow*. Edited by R. J. Lowry. Monterey, CA: Brooks/Cole.

McLuhan, M. (1964). *Understanding media: The extensions of Man*. New York, NY: McGraw-Hill.

Ong, W. J. (1967). *The presence of the word*. New Haven CT: Yale University.

The Random House Dictionary of the English Language. 2nd Edition, Unabridged. New York, NY: Random House, 1987.

Wallace, A. F. C. (1964). *Culture and personality*. New York, NY: Random House.

Wartik, N. (April 20, 2004). Hard-wired for prejudice? Experts examine human response to outsiders. *New York Times*. P. D5, cols. 1–5.

Washington, B. T. (1895/1954). Atlanta Exposition Address. In W. M. Parrish and M. Hochmuth (Eds.), *American speeches*. New York, NY: Longmans, Green and Co.

Watzlawick, P., J. H. Beavin, & D. D. Jackson. (1967). *Pragmatics of human communication*. New York, NY: W. W. Norton.

Whorf, B. L. (1957). *Language, thought, and reality: Selected writings of Benjamin Lee Whorf*. Edited by J. B. Carroll. Cambridge, MA: The M. I. T. Press

Wilber. K. (1998). *The eye of the spirit: An integral vision for a world gone slightly mad*. Boston, MA: Shambala.

Wilber, K. (2006). *Integral spirituality: A startling new role for religion in the modern and postmodern world*. Boston, MA: Integral Books.

Wilber, K. (1995). *Sex, ecology, spirituality: The spirit of evolution*. Boston, MA: Shambala.

4

Discourse Identity, Social Identity, and Confusion in Intercultural Communication

Ron SCOLLON
City University of Hong Kong, China

Abstract: Identity in discourse is a complex issue which goes beyond the question of either the social or personal identities of the participants. Intercultural communication as a field has long recognized that while individual participants may work with the best of intentions, because of culturally structured differences in discursive frames, participants in a discourse may not successfully interpret the intentions of others. News reports of international negotiations, for example, often say that talks have broken down because one side has accused the other of insincerity. Similarly business negotiations across international or cultural boundaries are often halted or delayed because each side believes the other side cannot be trusted. While such accusations are often unfortunately true, in many cases of intercultural communication the mistrust and feelings of insincerity are unintentional. They are the result of misinterpretations of the real intentions of the other side brought about by differences in the ways speakers and writers relate themselves to their discourses. In this paper I report on an ethnographic study of public discourse in Hong Kong which shows that within any discourse there are specific discourse identities which are expected to be taken up by the participants in the discourse.

Discourse Identity in Intercultural Communication

The specific identities that appear in discourse are not the same as the social identities of the persons who are participants in the discourse. Within any cultural group or discourse system (Scollon & Scollon 1995) there are preferred discourse identities which tend to be matched with particular social identities. Furthermore, within every group, divergences of matched discourse identity from social identity may be taken as expressions or demonstrations of insincerity, deviance, or dishonesty. That is, clear communication relies on successfully matching the discourse identity and one's expected social identity. To put it more directly: In any discourse you are expected to be the person you present yourself to be.

One paradoxical issue is that when one does successfully adapt to the discourse identity — social identity combinations expected in other languages or by other groups, one feels disconnected. That is, one feels that one is falsifying one's own identity. Similarly, when one unconsciously 'exports' one's preferred discourse identity — social identity matches to other languages or other groups, one may take on unacceptable discourse identities which may be perceived as either unacceptable social identities or as insincerity and dishonesty.

The result of this is that speakers and writers in intercultural communication may be accused of the social faults of insincerity or dishonesty when the social identity they project is perceived to be at variance with their discourse identity: This source of intercultural miscommunication can be alleviated with a clearer understanding of the concept of discourse identity and of cultural differences in the way it is constructed within each discourse.

The Structure of Discourse Identity: Production / reception roles

The ways in which a person can enter into a discourse have been shown to be extremely complex (Goffman 1974, 1981). Other analysts have also indicated the polyvocal (Uspensky 1973) or dialogic (Bakhtin 1981 [1934-35 original]) nature of discourse. For my purposes, Goffman's analysis is most directly useful. He indicates, for example three 'production format' roles, animator, author, and principal, which may be analyzed in virtually any act of communication (Goffman 1981).

We normally take it for granted that these three roles are unified in a single person who enters into a discourse. For example, in a conversation with a friend I make up the wording for the concepts I wish to convey (author), I also speak them with my own voice (animation), and furthermore, except when I quote other people, I take responsibility for what I say (principal). On the other hand, when I write a memorandum and ask a secretary to type it for me, I have separated the role of animation (the mechanical production of the message by typing) from authorship and principalship which I retain.

More extreme cases are not hard to imagine either. A department head might ask me to draft up (author) a letter which is typed (animated) by a secretary, and signed by him (principal) as the person who takes responsibility for the discourse. Presidents of nations often have speech writers (authors) who prepare their addresses which the presidents then animate themselves and for which they also take the responsibility of principal.

Of course in considering various forms of public discourse we should not think that any one of these roles is restricted to a single person. There are a large number of people who are involved in the production of a newspaper (animators), for example, and a president of a nation may have a number of speech writers who jointly author his speeches. Beyond that, in many discourses the responsibility lies with a committee or even a government as when a government employee drafts (authors) and others produce (animate) communications which represent the government (principal).

While Goffman develops these production roles with considerable sophistication, like much other work in interpersonal communication, there is an unbalanced focus on the production of communication with a rather attenuated interest in how communications are received. I argue that a parallel set of receptive roles can be identified which parallel the three production roles. The animator role, for example, focuses on the mechanical or physical production of the signals of communication. The animator is the speaker, the typist, the word processor, the printing press and the people who run it, the microphones and loudspeakers, and all the rest of the mechanical means of communicative production from the lungs and larynx right through to the new spring and sound-waves. That is to say, Goffman's animation focuses on mechanical or physical matters.

I argue that these mechanical matters are paralleled in reception. Thus a person might hear and be able to pass on a message without in any way understanding or interpreting it. This is, indeed, what a linguist or a secretary might be doing in taking down phonetic dictation to be analyzed and interpreted later. It is also what an answering machine and a tape or video recorder do even more accurately and mechanically than the person who operates them. I call this role the *receptor* role.

Analogously we could say that the author role in Goffman's scheme is a rhetorical one. The author strategizes the communication, chooses the words and the forms it will take. In reception I argue there is an interpreter role which is the interpretation of the rhetorical aspects of the communication. Thus a person might not only hear or read a message (receptor), but also develop a rhetorical interpretation-still staying short of taking any particular action. A secretary might say, for example, 'Ms Smith called and said you might call back (receptor) but I think she meant you ought to call immediately (interpreter)'. It seems natural to call this role the *interpreter* role.

Finally, the principal role is that of taking responsibility and I believe it is paralleled in a receptive role as what we might call the *judge* role, though I am not particular happy with that term. My meaning is to indicate that one might hear a communication (receptor), and interpret its rhetorical intent (interpreter), but it still remains to accept *responsibility* for undertaking a response.

Adding these three reception roles to Goffman's three production roles we can form the six following production/reception roles:

Productive		Receptive
animator	*mechanical*	receptor
author	*rhetorical*	interpreter
principal	*responsible*	judge

A secretary who receives a telephone call for his or her employer will often simply receive the message, write it down, and pass it on. In this case only a mechanical reception is involved, often without interpretation. In other cases, one might overhear someone asking another to tell him the time. In this case one has received the message in the most basic sense of hearing it, one has also interpreted it accurately, but as it was someone else of which this was asked, the overhearer has no responsibility to respond. That is, he or she has no need to make a judgment about what is the best way to answer the other person in the discourse.

The Structure of Discourse Identity: Social/interactive roles

Walking along a street, riding on a bus, or watching people in a cafe, a university lecture, or at a ball game we frequently notice that several people are together and set themselves off from others around them. Goffman observed this characteristic of face-to-face social interaction and called these little groupings 'withs' (1971). A with[①] as Goffman defines it is as follows:

> A with is a party of more than one whose members are perceived to be 'together' (p. 19).

The characteristics which he describes are that the with will show ecological proximity, that is they will stand, sit, or otherwise orient

---

[①] I will keep to Goffman's practice of not indicating the nominal usage of this word with single quotation marks hereafter, even though I recognize that from time to time this usage requires giving a sentence a second reading. I will adopt the same practice below in regard to the term 'watch'. This latter term has a long established nominal form.

themselves toward each other within a relatively small space.① They will display what he calls 'civil inattention', that is, they will disregard the sounds and sights of other people immediately within their perceptive field. Among the members of the with there will be special rights to initiate talk and other communications, and there will be special ritual practices for joining and withdrawing. Other researchers (Goodwin 1986, 1995) have added to this list that withs will show their communicative status with eye gaze directed toward or among each other.

Many studies of discourse have focused on this sort of small group or even dyadic social interaction in face-to-face situations. So much is this the case that one finds that the with has often been taken to represent all forms of discourse. This has led to an unfortunate split between discourse studies which focus upon spoken or oral discourse on the one hand and, on the other, those which focus upon written or mediated discourse even though a series of studies have argued against this dichotomous conceptual division from Tannen's (1982, 1984) early critique to the very recent set of papers edited by Quasthoff (1995).

Recently I have argued that there is an intermediate ground upon which we can establish a further elaboration of social-interactive roles. In a set of studies of television and newspaper discourse (Scollon 1996) I argued that the primary *social interactions* are, in fact, among journalists with television viewers and readers watching them as spectators. When a presenter reads the evening news, the producer, the people in the studio handling the cameras and microphones, and even the other presenters form the withs within which the news is read.

The social-interactive relationship between the presenter and the viewer must be seen to be of a different order of social interaction (Ang, 1996). Thus, in the home, we might find a with consisting of a couple, husband and wife, who are watching the news. Their primary social interaction is with each other as a Goffman-defined with. Their relationship with the television presenter is what I would call a 'watch'. I define a watch as

> any person or group of people who are perceived to have attention to some spectacle as the central focus of their (social) activity. The spectacle together with its watchers constitutes the watch (Scollon, 1996).

This difference in social-interactive status in the case of a television broadcast or a newspaper has typically been characterized as there being no possibility of feedback among participants, but I believe that characterization is rather limited. In a football game, for example, the spectators as observers watch the spectacle, the game. The primary social

---

① Non-hearing withs are an exception to this principle since a direct line of sight is the crucial necessity to direct sign-language communication.

interaction among the players is that of a with-they react to each other, adjust their movements to the movements of each other, they have particular, often ritualistic means of joining or withdrawing from the action, and show all the other signs of attention which indicate that they are engaged in the same social interaction.

At the same time, however, there is a kind of social interaction between the players of the game and the spectators watching the game. There are cheers from the crowd and there are gestures from the players toward the crowd. This is also a kind of social interaction, but one which is highly restricted on both ends and with specialized player and spectator rights and obligations.

Players, for example, are expected to direct their attention to performing the game and to make only the most minimal of gestures toward the spectators. In American football players may even be fined for excessive spectator-directed displays. Spectators on the other hand have the right to highly critical and judgmental commentary and observation. What they may not do is enter into the game.

It is worth noting in this respect that these rights and obligations are maintained even when physically violated. For example, the crowd of spectators may swarm down onto the playing field and in doing so disrupt the primary social interaction, but they may not in doing so enter into the primary social interaction. That is, the spectators may enter the playing field, and perhaps even kick the ball into the goal, but they cannot score a goal. ①

The distinction between a with and a watch, then, is that in the former the primary social interaction is based upon more or less reciprocal rights and obligations to maintain the focus of the interaction, but in the latter the rights and obligations are rather asymmetrical-the participants in the spectacle (players in the ball game or television presenters) have extremely limited rights of interaction with the watchers who have limited rights of involvement but may exercise rather loosely constrained rights to criticism and judgment.

The distinction between withs and watches characterizes the difference between the primary 'players' in face-to-face interaction and those who are only observers or spectators, but there is at least one more form of social interaction which must be considered. To return to the

---

① The earlier case where an English football player was convicted in court for kicking a spectator shows how seriously the division between player and observer is maintained. While the spectator was said to have overstepped his critical and judgmental rights by making racial comments, the football player exceeded his rights to territory by jumping into the stands and kicking the spectator. Had the spectator restricted his negative comments to the quality of the football player's game it is quite unlikely that the event of crossing the boundary of the two types of social interaction would have occurred.

football game analogy, there are the umpires, referees, police, league organizers, team owners, and sporting associations who set the larger frame upon the interaction. Players do not play the game without a set of rules which are set out by the sporting association and enforced upon the field by the referees and linesmen. I call this rather large group of participants in the discourse the 'framers' of the discourse. They do not enter directly into the play, nor are they often actual observers (though they may be observers as well), but they do set the frames within which play takes place.

I have mentioned such framers of the discourse in the case of a football match as the referees or owners. In other forms of discourse such as the production of the daily newspaper the role of framer is played by a range of people including the owners, or the organizations which sponsor the paper, the upper-level editorial staff, and even in some cases the advertisers when they set restrictions upon what forms of discourse may or may not be performed within the boundaries of their financial support.

Using these three perspectives on social interaction, then, I would like to distinguish at least three social-interactive roles as follows:

framers: have overriding rights to define communicative events
players: form 'withs' with focal attention upon maintaining the discourse
observers: neither define the events nor participate as withs, but have heightened observational rights

Discourse Identity

I am now in the position to define discourse identity as follows:

> Discourse identity is the persona along with the degree or range of power a particular person can claim in a specific discourse. It consists of the range of production/reception format roles intersecting with the social-interactive roles over which one has the power, right, or obligation to enact in any particular discourse.

This definition, of course, reflects the normative notion of the identity one is <u>expected</u> to claim which raises further difficulties of answering by whom these expectations are held. It also raises the problem of contested identities and falsified identities. My purpose in using such a normative definition is to be able to show that, in fact, there are often rather serious departures from these norms, but because these norms are held, the interpretations which arise from departures are themselves the grounds for misinterpretation of intentions or even hostilities. It is to these departures from expected discourse identity to which I turn in the following section.

Negotiated Identities

The concept of intercultural communication relies heavily upon the idea of culture itself-that broad groups of human organization can be analyzed which are distinct enough in their internal characteristics that members of these groups differ significantly from members of other cultural groups. While this has been a very useful idea in some areas of anthropology and sociology, the concept of culture is often problematical in studies of discourse and communication. If one wants to speak of cultural differences between 'Chinese' and 'Westerners' one is rather easily led into simple stereotypical descriptions which, in fact, fit none of the members of either group in any realistic way.

Carbaugh (1994) gives a striking example from the point of view of stereotypical characterizations of 'Western' behavior. At Oxford in England he, an American, had a conversation with a British scholar in which each failed to understand the basis of the other's position. The British scholar asked him something like, 'What brings you to Oxford?' Carbaugh answered that he was there to study some particular research issue, but that answer completely failed to satisfy the British questioner who in several attempts repeated his question.

The problem as Carbaugh describes it is that from an American point of view, one operates as an individual scholar whose own research interests and problems are the dominant ones and therefore the question of why he had gone to Oxford was taken by him to be a question about his personal interests and motives. What he learned was that for the British scholar at Oxford, the most important single issue is to which part of the Oxford social and institutional structure is one attached. This is the fundamental basis for all other social interaction. The question, 'What brings you here?' means something like 'What is your social position? Are you a student, a lecturer, a professor, a visitor? If you are attached to Oxford, to which college are you attached?' Only within that institutional position can his research interests then be pursued.

To phrase Carbaugh's example in terms of discourse identity and social identity, Carbaugh, as an American, took it that his primary social identity was as an independent research scholar. Furthermore, as an American it was his independent and individualistic position which gave him the right to author, animate, and to be the principal of what he said about his own research interests. And beyond that, he felt that he could exercise the right to speak freely both as a player in this discourse and as the framer of the overall discourse itself. In other words, Carbaugh's assumption was that within academic discourse, the individual scholar is both framer and player and that these two social-interactive roles grant to him the right to freely take on all production / reception roles.

The British scholar's assumption, as Carbaugh describes it, is that the institutions of academic discourse — particularly those of Oxford University — are granted the primary framing role. Those institutions frame academic discourse so that only those to whom the institutions have granted the right to become players can engage in mutual academic exchanges. Within that frame, of course, the exchanges are much like those of the American scholar — the individual may take on all three production/reception roles and thus, within the proper frame American and British scholars look quite similar to each other.

Where Carbaugh and his British counterpart had gone wrong was that the British scholar was asking quite indirectly, 'What institution here frames your position in the discourse as a player?' His answer, again quite indirectly, was to ignore that aspect of the question and therefore to answer, 'No institution has the right to frame my position in this discourse.' That is an answer that was unintelligible to his British counterpart. From Carbaugh's point of view the British scholar's insistence upon repeating his question about why he was in Oxford was equally unintelligible.

This is a simple case of two scholars who are in many respects quite similar and from quite similar 'Western' cultural groups but who belong to rather different discourse systems and therefore cannot successfully interpret each other. Their inability to interpret each other is tied directly to the fact that each was taking up a discourse identity which was different from that expected by the other.

But is this a 'cultural' issue? That is to say, have I only refined the definition of 'Western culture' a bit by making a distinction between 'American culture' and 'British culture'? Together with my colleague Suzanne Scollon we have argued (Scollon & Scollon 1995) that it might be more useful to speak of *systems of discourse* than of cultures and therefore to speak of *interdiscourse system communication* instead of intercultural communication.

I used this example of the British and the American scholar in a lecture last year and although I described Carbaugh as an American male, I made no reference to the gender of the British scholar. A woman, herself British and from Oxford, commented to me later that she was certain, although I had not said so, that the British scholar was a male. She was, of course, correct in this supposition. Although I can only speculate in this case, what I would suggest is that what Carbaugh describes more broadly as a difference between American and British assumptions might better be narrowed to the intersection among British and American academic discourse systems and a trans-cultural gender discourse system. That is to say, this conversation might have been very different had the participants been an American woman scholar and an Oxford woman scholar.

In developing the idea of discourse systems we have argued that in any particular situation there are multiple discourse systems operating and that a major aspect in any communication is an ongoing negotiation of a person's discourse identity within several discourse systems. Thus as a man or a woman, a person participates within a gender discourse system. At the same time as a member of a particular generation or class — I belong, for example, to an American class / generation formed within the Great Depression and the Second World War among immigrant factory workers — one shares many characteristics with other members of that same generation. One's place of employment often forms another type of occupational or professional discourse system with its own internal forms of discourse, assumptions about proper relationships among its members and between its members and outsiders, and ways of socializing new members.

Any person simultaneously must negotiate a position among all of the discourse systems to which one belongs as a crucial aspect of one's ability to communicate. To use the terminology I am developing here, one's discourse identity in any particular discourse is an identity negotiated among all of the potential discourse identities defined by the discourse systems of which one is a member.

Discourse Identity in News Discourse

Intellectual copyright is an issue between nations over which we have recently seen intensive and sometimes acrimonious negotiations. Furthermore, within academic domains there have been a growing number of cases in which the issue of plagiarism has been seen to be compounded by 'cultural' differences in assumptions about when and where it is appropriate to cite references to the texts of others. I would like to argue that in addition to the fundamental issues of ownership and theft involved there may also be problems of differences in discourse identity at issue in these cases.

In a series of studies of news discourse in Hong Kong we have found that across newspapers there are major differences in patterns of bylining, the major means by which newspapers identify the writers of news stories and in patterns of quotation (Li *et al*. 1993; Yung 1995). For example, in comparing a story about a tragic accident on New Year's Day 1993 we found that the English newspaper, the *South China Morning Post*, gave the story under the name of a bylined author, Tommy Lewis. The story about the same event in the Chinese newspaper, *Ming Pao*, appeared with no indication of authorship.

When one compares these two stories with many others which appear in these two newspapers one finds that regularly the *South China Morning Post* and *Ming Pao* display this difference in pattern which is further supported by another practice-that of quotation. One finds that it is much more common to find the words of newsmakers cited as direct quotations in the *South China Morning Post* than *Ming Pao*. As we argued in our report on this contrastive study (Li *et al*. 1993), what one hears in *Ming Pao* stories is the editorial voice, but in *South China Morning Post* it is the reporter's and the newsmaker's voices one hears.

To contrast these two newspapers in terms of discourse identity and social roles, one could say that same social role — the newspaper reporter — is expected to display different discourse identities. The *South China Morning Post* the framers of the discourse — the owners and editors — delegate principalship and authorship to reporters in almost all instances other than on the editorial page. In turn, reporters may delegate some degrees of both authorship and principalship to newsmakers through quotation.

That is to say, the framers of the discourse set the major editorial policies but then retire from sight giving the appearance at least that reporters are taking direct responsibility for what they write.

We know, of course, that the various sub-editors who prepare the headlines and leads and who also control other matters of layout take on a very significant authorship role (Bell 1991), but they present themselves as having no authorial voice; they remain anonymous. The reporters are the ones who are expected to display the discourse identity of the named author and principal of the stories.

In the case of the stories in *Ming Pao* we find that reporters take on the role of authors but principalship remains firmly in the hands of the editorial staff, the framers of the discourse. Furthermore, as there are very few quotations, it seems that since the reporters themselves have not been delegated the discourse identity of a named author / principal, they themselves do not have the power to further delegate these roles to the newsmakers about which they write. In other words, the major difference between these two newspapers in the question of discourse identity is that the reporters in the *South China Morning Post* are framed as players with rights to both authorship and principalship and further with the right to delegate those production format roles to newsmakers; in *Ming Pao* the reporters are framed as very restricted players with only authorship rights — they are not delegated the right to take on responsibility through being named in a byline.

It is clear that the social roles of newspaper reporters are substantially the same in both cases. At news conferences, for example, all reporters from whatever sources must display press cards to be allowed into the conference, they frequently associate with each other at other events, and socially associate with each other as well. In other words, the differences we see on the pages of the newspaper (the discourse identity) are not paralleled by differences in the social role of newspaper reporter, they are differences within that particular discourse. We can outline these discourse identities as follows:

	SOUTH CHINA MORNING POST	MING PAO
Framers		
editors	principal	principal
Players		
reporters	principal, author	author
newsmakers	principal, author	—
publication staff	animation	animation

There is a systematic difference in the discourse identities taken on by news reporters in these two Hong Kong newspapers. These two newspapers differ in language and so one might be tempted to leap to conclusions about linguistic or cultural differences. If all one were to look at were other English language newspapers, one would see that the *South China Morning Post* uses bylining and quotation much like almost all other English newspapers in Asia, North American, Europe, and Australia. Further, one finds almost no newspapers which display the discourse identity for reporters of the *Ming Pao*.

Nevertheless, one must be careful. The very widely published British English language periodical *The Economist* does not give bylines to its reporters and thus we see that while there may be a difference in practices across genres-newspapers and magazines-we cannot claim any clear linguistic or cultural difference in practices. Also, and more to the point, other Chinese newspapers in Hong Kong as well as major Chinese newspapers in Chinese mainland practice very careful and rigorous bylining practices. For example, one finds very few news items in *Renmin Ribao* (i.e. *the People's Daily*) or *Guangzhou Daily* without very specific identification of the reporters by name and news organization.

Within this example of newspaper discourse I have described two different patterns of discourse identity, one in which the social role of the reporter is expected to take on both authorship in writing the article and principalship through the display of his or her name in the byline and another in which this same social role is expected to take on only authorship. I have shown that there is no simple means of ascribing these two different discourse patterns to cultural or linguistic differences since not all of the newspapers in Chinese mainland nor all of the newspapers in Hong Kong expect their reporters to take on the same discourse identity.

Consequences of Mis-matching Social and Discourse Identities

The question I want to raise, finally, is what happens when one expects one pattern and finds the other? In interviews where I ask the question: 'Why does the English language newspaper (*South China Morning Post*) have bylines and the Chinese language newspaper (*Ming Pao*) not have them?' I am told that this is because in Western culture there is an emphasis on the individual and putting the byline on a writer's story gives him or her credit for his or her original creative contribution. On the other hand, I am told that Chinese are collectivistic and prefer not to let the individual stand out or to take on distinctive individualistic identity. Thus, I am told, these two patterns of bylining reflect primary cultural differences between Chinese culture and Western culture by marking the difference between collective social organization and individualistic social organization.

When I then introduce the second question, 'Why, then, in the Chinese newspapers from the People's Republic of China are the reporters fully credited with bylines?' a frequent response is that this must be wrong, am I really sure? In other words, it does not fit the explanation of East-West cultural difference and so the respondents doubt the data rather than their explanation. Another answer I frequently get, however, is that this is because in China there is no freedom of expression and anything written in the newspaper must be carefully attached to a particular writer so that if something goes wrong the responsibility can be directed at that person. In other words, I am told that one and the same discourse identity in 'the West' reflects a free society which values individuality and creative expression but in China the same discourse identity represents just the opposite, a collective society in which individual expression must be watched carefully.

Many years ago at the height of the Cold War in the 1950s I read an article in the *Saturday Review of Literature*.① School children in the United States were shown photographs of trees along a country road which they were told was in Kansas and then were asked the question, 'Why have trees been planted along the roadside?' The answer they gave was that this was to protect the soil on the fields from erosion or to beautify the landscape. Another group of children were shown the same photograph but told that the picture was taken in Russia and were then asked the same question. The answer they gave was that the Russians had planted those trees to hide what was going on behind them — probably some military installation or some other military secret.

Conclusion

We draw inferences based upon our assumptions about the nature of the

---

① I apologize for not being able to locate a reference to this article. It appeared sometime in the period of 1956–1958, the period during which I regularly read that magazine.

world. This is no less true in intercultural discourse. When we have an expectation for the match-up between a social role and a discourse identity, we then use that expectation to interpret any deviations from that match-up. If we expect reporters to have bylines, we then need to find an interpretation for cases in which they do not. On the other hand, if we expect the voice of the reporter to be hidden behind the voice of the editor, we need to find an interpretation for the cases in which the reporter is clearly identified.

This research shows that often those interpretations about mis-matches will call upon stereotypical and often negative perceptions of the people involved in the mis-matched discourse identities. The role of culture in this process is more likely to be as a source of unexamined ideological and stereotypical assumptions made about expected matches of social identities and discourse identities than in the structure of those identities themselves. The concept of discourse identity, by increasing our awareness of the complexity of the roles we take on in discourse including production / reception format roles as well as social-interactive roles, will increase our awareness of the dangers of drawing overly hasty inferences about people who are different from each other.

References

Ang, I. (1996). *Living room wars: Rethinking media audiences for a postmodern world*. London: Routledge.
Bakhtin, M. M. (1981). *The dialogic imagination*. Austin: University of Texas Press. (Originally published in 1934–1935).
Bell, A. (1991). *The language of the news media*. Oxford: Basil Blackwell.
Carbaugh, D. (1994). Cultures in conversation: Prospects for new world communities. In: D. Marsh & L. Salo-Lee (Eds.) *Europe on the move: Fusion or fission?* Jyväskylä: SIETAR EUROPA 94 Proceedings. 24–34.
Goffman, E. (1981). *Forms of talk*. Philadelphia: University of Pennsylvania Press.
Goffman, E. (1974). *Frame analysis*. New York: Harper and Row.
Goffman, E. (1971). *Relations in public*. New York: Harper and Row.
Goodwin, C. (1986). Gestures as a resource for the organization of mutual orientation. *Semiotica* 62 (1/2):29–49.
Goodwin, C. (1995). Sentence construction within interaction. In U. M. Quasthoff (Ed.) *Aspects of oral communication* (pp. 198–219). Berlin: Walter de Gruyter.
Li, Chor Shing David, Poon Lau Woon Yee Wanda, M. Rogerson-Revell Pamela, R. Scollon, S. Scollon, Yu Shiu Kwong Bartholomew, and V. Yung Kit Yee. (1993). Contrastive discourse in English and Cantonese news stories: A preliminary analysis of newspaper, radio, and television versions of the Lan Kwai Fong news story. Department of English, City Polytechnic of Hong Kong, Research Report, No. 29.
Quasthoff, U. M. (1995). *Aspects of oral communication*. Berlin: Walter de Gruyter.
Scollon, R. (1996). The depicted watch: cross-cultural variation in media pictures

of people watching others in Hong Kong and China. Paper presented at the Conference on Communication and Culture: China and the World entering the 21st Century, Beijing, August 13-16, 1996.

Scollon, R. & S. W. Scollon. (1995). *Intercultural communication: A discourse approach*. Oxford: Basil Blackwell.

Tannen, D. (1984). *Coherence in spoken and written discourse*. Norwood, N.J.: Ablex Publishing Corporation.

Tannen, D. (1982). Oral and literate strategies in spoken and written narratives. *Language*, 58.1:1-21.

Uspensky, B. (1973). *A poetics of composition*. Berkeley: University of California Press.

Yung, V. (1995). The presentation of voice in Chinese and English newspapers in Hong Kong. *Perspectives, Working Papers of the Department of English, City University of Hong Kong* 8(1):64-96.

5

The Framework of Cultural Space

Robert N. St. CLAIR
University of Louisville, USA

Ana C. T. WILLIAMS
Northwestern University, USA

Abstract: The metaphor of time is both linear and spatial. It places temporal events into the disparate categories of the past, present, and the future. This static model of time cannot account for the dynamics of cultural space. A better model of time and space can be found in the writings of Michel Foucault. In The archeology of knowledge, Foucault proposes that the relationship of time to space is uniquely connected. Layers of space accrue over time resulting in a laminated or stratified space. The model presented in this essay takes this metaphor one step further. It argues that time is embedded in space; the present is embedded in the past. In the sociology of everyday life, one understands the present because it is embedded in the past. There are rituals, social scenarios, and social practices that constitute the practical knowledge that underlies everyday social interaction. The present and the past encounter each other in the co-present. It is here where one accepts the past in the context of the present and reformulates it into the new-past. Similarly, it is in the co-present that one modifies, redefines, or re-interprets the past as the new-present. Newly-emergent realities may also develop in the co-present and these form the basis for the future as the future is embedded in the new-present. What is important about this theory of the stratification of cultural time and space is that it provides a structural analysis of changes taking place within a cultural space.

Introduction

Time and Space are always theoretically linked because space grows and develops in time. In the model of linear time, this linkage is based on the linear movement of time over space (St. Clair, 2006). What is missing from this temporal linear model is how cultural space changes over time. A resolution to this problem can be found in the insightful theories in the work of Foucault. In *The Archeology of Knowledge* (Foucault, 1969), Foucault presents cultural space as the sedimentation of layers over time. A modification of this metaphor provides the foundations for this essay in which the sedimentation theory of time in space envisions time as the accumulation of social practices layered in cultural space. In other words, it differs from the linear model of time in that it argues that time is embedded in space: the present is embedded in the cultural past and the future is embedded in the cultural present. What is important about this framework of the sedimentation of time is that it accounts for many contemporary cultural constructs, among them globalization and modernization. This investigation explains how culture functions within spatial contexts of colonialism, cultural habitus (Bourdeiu, 1977, 1984), global expansions, modernization, social scripts (St. Clair, Thomé-Williams, & Su, 2005), social structuration (Giddens, 1984), and mass media culture as the new-social-reality (Mehan & Wood, 1975). In essence, it claims that cultural change involves the retaining of some cultural practices along with the modification, revision, and re-invention of events in the co-present. Just as the present is embedded in the past, the future is embedded in the present.

Linear Time	*Sedimentary Time*
Time is based on movement over space.	Time is embedded into strata of previous time. The present is embedded in the past; the future is embedded in the present.
Space does not change; only time changes.	Both space and time change and are evidenced as vertical strata.
There are four possible models of linear time. In two of them, time moves in space (the future approaches the present); in the others people move in space and time remains immobile (one approaches the future)..	Time is associated with cultural space. The present is embedded in the past; the future is embedded in the present.

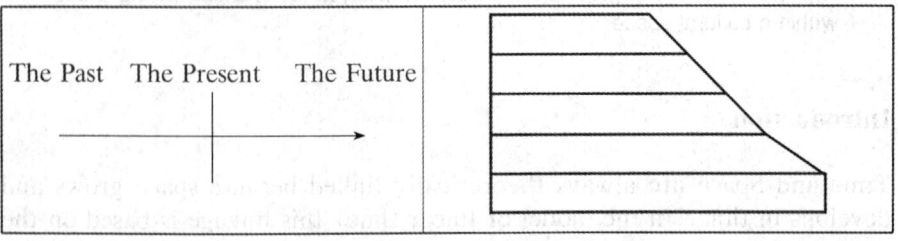

Linear Time: The linear movement of time over space.	Archeological Time: The deposition of layers of space over time.
Space remains the same and it is time that changes.	Space changes over time; both time and space undergo change.

The Sedimentation of Cultural Space

Defining culture is a difficult task because it brings into play so many different perspectives and one of the greatest dynamics has to do with change, which is the theoretical concern of this essay. There are many models of change, but one of the most influential models of change can be found in the work of Thomas Kuhn (1962, 1971). In this work, he argued that theoretical models of physics undergo structural changes from normal science to revolutionary science. Although this model of change accounts for the motivation of change in the natural sciences, viz., problem solving, it does not provide much insight into other aspects of the phenomena of change, especially cultural change.

It is in the context of this model that the concept of cultural emergence is investigated and discussed. It is argued that the present is constantly being socially constructed to make sense of a plethora of daily routines that constitute the sociology of everyday life. These routines are integrated into the sociology of everyday life by individuals and this integration results in a sense of being centered and connected to the world. Many daily routines function as recipes for daily living. They are not always fully integrated into the global structure of social life and are often left unresolved.

It is argued that in the context of the emerging-present (co-present), new levels of consciousness are raised and this leads to the creation of new perspectives and new forms of knowledge. This information is integrated into the emerging-present of those who share in these new experiences. When they are integrated into the daily experiences of individuals, they are also socially enforced by maintenance rituals and centered through meaningful social interactions involving symbolic maintenance.

The Co-Present

When the present is emerging into a new level of consciousness, the co-present, it comes into conflict with many of the more established patterns of the past. These conflicts must be resolved. They are usually accommodated by redefining the past in order for it to make sense in the cultural present. The redefinition of the past is part of Kuhn's theory of scientific revolutions. After the new revolutionary science develops as the new reigning paradigm for a scientific community, the old patterns of thought are redefined in the context of this new framework. The past is re-presented into a new model of the present. It is taken out of its old context and placed into a new one. The result is a structured form of historical anachronism, a historical discontinuity.

Why is the study of cultural emergence important? It is important because cultural change is a constantly occurring phenomenon. The study of culture is not an established pronouncement of what happened in the past. It is not a body of knowledge that has been defined by cultural experts as a super-organic entity. Culture is dynamic. It has to do with sets of practices that change and redefine themselves from one generation to the next. It creates a new future (new-present) while redefining its past (old-present). This new future is a directional marker. It merely identifies the new forces that are taking place in the present and that will continue to take place in the future. In order to make a transition into this new future, the old past has to be redefined. It must be broken down and reorganized so that it can be understood in the cultural present.

In order to explain the nature of the cultural dynamics outlined above, there are several concepts that need to be introduced and developed within the context of cultural emergence. These concepts include the archeology of knowledge, the concepts of presentation and re-presentation, the structure of scientific revolutions, zones of proximal development, structuration, and the process of revising the past in order to make sense of the present.

Explaining the Dynamics of Cultural Change

The traditional way of explaining change can be found in linguistic structuralism. It is assumed within that framework that change occurs when one steady-state of knowledge is replaced by a new steady-state. Examples of this approach can be found in historical linguistics where a steady-state of the later past, Old English, developed into a steady-state of the more recent past, Middle English. This is followed by the steady-state of the present, Modern English (Lehman, 1962). How does the movement from one state to the other take place? The answer to this question is described *ex post facto* by describing the sound changes that took place within the transition from one steady-state to the other. These laws are presented as the reason for the changes that occurred. The problem with this account is that it omits a discussion of the many epistemic ruptures (Foucault, 1969) that motivated those changes.

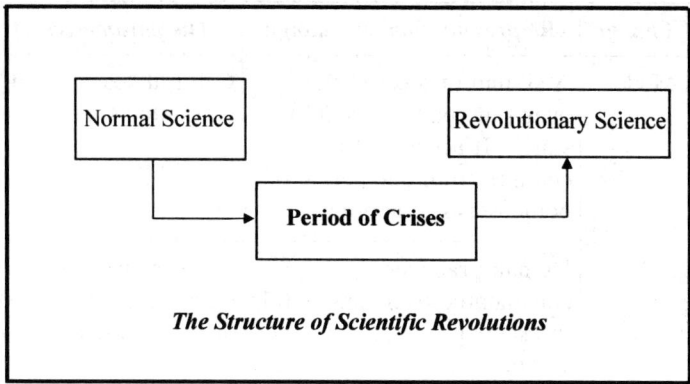

The Structure of Scientific Revolutions

As noted earlier, Kuhn (1962) developed a theory of scientific revolutions within the natural sciences. Once again, his model of change is based on paradigm shifts from one steady-state (normal science) to another (revolutionary science) Kuhn argues that problem-solving is the rationale for scientific change. When certain anomalies occur within a scientific discipline, this prompts the scientific community to engage in a quest to resolve those problems. There is a period of open discussion and debate (a period of crises) followed by the discovery of a workable solution in which a new paradigm emerges (period of scientific revolution). Within the historiography of the discipline, these transitions are seen as scientific events and are treated as historical discontinuities. Foucault (1969) considered these periods of events to be distortions of the historical record.

Within the humanities, models of structural change are not met with favor. There are several reasons for this. Although scientific paradigms may go unchanged for decades, events within modern culture are undergoing rapid change. The cultural present is immersed in a wide range of social, economic, and technical changes. The old method of defining a culture by containing it within the borders of a nation-state no longer holds. Modern technology has enabled cultural events to readily transcend national boarders. Many modern cultures are involved in the process of global exchange and this has resulted in complex patterns of cultural hybridity (Nederveen Pieterse, 2004). Not only are cultural patterns and belief systems exchanged, borrowed, or incorporated within each nation-state, but large masses of individuals have entered into an economic diaspora where they live and work in other countries as expatriates. Hence, culture can no longer be envisioned as a steady-state phenomenon defined over time. It is far more dynamic. It is constantly being redefined by a plethora of social and cultural forces within a cultural space. The forces of modernization have transcended local borders (Wallerstein, 2005). All countries are either engaged in or influenced by a capitalist world-economic system (Wallerstein, 1974, 1980, 1989).

Models of Change	Re-presentation of Change	The parameters of Space
Structural Model	A system of ideas change over time but the model is static. It accounts for changes from one period of homeostasis to another.	Cultural space is not accounted for.
Archeological Model	Human practices are documented over time within the same geographical space.	Modern space is superimposed over older layers of space over time.
Sedimentation Model	The layers of the past are not separated from the layers of the present. They are connected within the collective consciousness of those living in the co-present.	Many layers of the past remain in the present. The past never dies. It is redefined, modified, or reinvented to fit the contexts of the co-present.

Newly-Emergent Realities

How do newly-emergent realties emerge from within a steady-state model? For example, how did these emergent structures arise from normal science within a scientific discipline? These mechanisms of change occur within the period of crises. What is important about the transition from normal science to revolutionary science is the fact that new structures emerge from the process of one paradigm shift to another. These structures are either a recombination of old structures or a re-presentation of old structures. This means that the past never dies. It can and does undergo one of several changes; while undergoing these changes, the past is embedded within a new context where it is restructured, re-presented, or reinvented. This means that after the new paradigm of revolutionary science is established, the older form of normal science is re-written from the perspective of the new paradigm. This is not a radical phenomenon. Scientific textbooks also revise history and present information from the perspective of the new paradigm (Kuhn, 1962). The old structures undergo a transformation. They are elements of an embedded past that are reconstructed into a new component within the newer paradigm. Once these redefined units are introduced into the realm of revolutionary science, they come to designate a different level of consciousness within the present. They become part of the new-present.

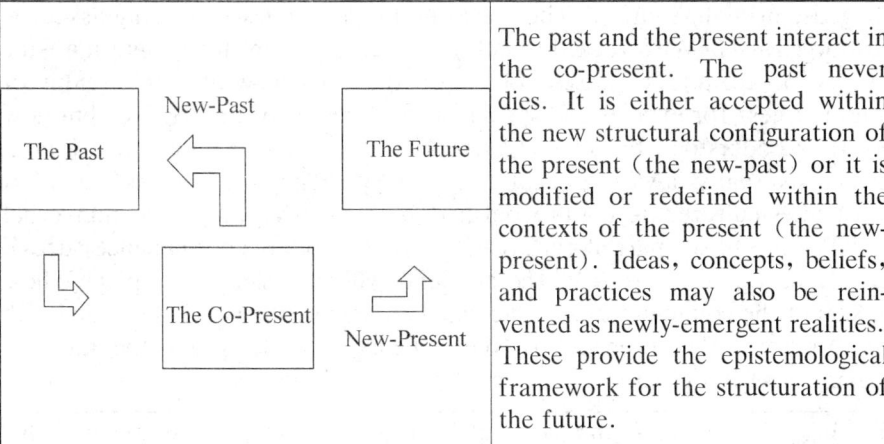

The co-present contains the habitus of the past and the newly-emergent realities of the future. The co-present is where the phenomenon of change takes place. It is where the older structures are re-presented into new entities: the new-past and the new-present. Why does the past need to be restructured into different entities? It is because the contexts characteristically associated with the past have changed. When the present is embedded within the past, it brings into play new connotations and new associations that have to do with the co-present. The past has been re-contextualized. These re-presentations are important when they have been connected in a different way with the newly-deposited layer of the co-present. In this case they are associated in the context of a new level of consciousness. In the process of creating a co-present reality of structures within a paradigmatic shift, these re-presentations of the past may undergo further change. They are either brought into the co-present as an unmodified structure (the past) and remain within the habitus of the co-present realm or they are endowed with such a heightened level of change that its presence demands that the past be redefined (the new-past).

The fact that the past is always undergoing redefinition raises an important question for scientific research. What is the past? This is the question that Foucault (1969) sought to address. Why are such vagrant examples of historical anachronism allowed within a scientific enterprise? Why are historical discontinuities created in the historiography of a discipline? Can historical accounts of the past really be trusted? Do they have authenticity? Are primary sources just reconstructions of other allegedly primary sources? These are the kinds of questions being asked by postmodernists. With regard to culture, the co-present may contain a wide variety of cultural artifacts. Some of these exist within the realm of consciousness for experts and specialists as domains of knowledge, but how are they understood by others? Outside of the cultural sciences, are non-specialists really aware of cultural theory? Can they articulate what constitutes culture? Is culture defined by what they do? Are nonverbal social scripts also a part of culture? If culture is to have permanence, does it have to be a part of the past? The problem: whose version of the past? Whose version of the co-present defines the past? For many, the past is associated with new-originals. The co-present is where the past is ending and the future is beginning. It is a place of transition. It is the world in flux.

The Past	This is the past that belongs to an older paradigm. It is the past that is associated with what happened before it was brought into contact with the co-present. It is also the past associated with the unconsciousness.
The Old-Past	The past is taken out of one context and placed into another. The new context is the co-present. It is where the past is re-evaluated in terms of the present. When one speaks of the past in the co-present, they are referring to the old-past.
The New-Present	When the old-past is restructured, redefined, or reinvented, it becomes a part of the new present. Sometimes new vocabularies are created to reflect these changes, but often they are not. The old worlds are used with the new meanings, resulting in polysemy.
The Co-Present	This is where change takes place within the consciousness of the presence of everyday life. This is where the events of the past and the present collide. The retaining of old events in the present is the old-past. The revision of the past (restructuring, redefining, or reinventing) results in the new-present.
The Newly-Emergent Reality	Within sedimentation theory, a new layer of practices may develop into a newer stratum of cultural space over the older strata. This new layer provides the basis for replacing older concepts, objects, and events with newer ones. They become the newly-emergent realities. The painting of Mona Lisa is the original; the replica or simulacrum of the painting in popular culture becomes the newly-emergent reality. It is called the newly-emergent reality because the newer generation within the co-present is not aware of the historiography of that object in the past, old-past, and the new-past.

Constructing a Sedimentation Theory of Culture

There are several viable concepts that come together to constitute a model of cultural change. One of them is the concept of re-presentation that Foucault (1966) introduced in *The Order of Things*. He noted that the Middle Ages went through a time when the old idea of imitating nature was replaced by one in which the events of the present were re-presented and this meant that they were cast in a different code and possessed different social and cultural values. The way in which people think changed during this period of time. Instead of seeing art as copies of an original, the originals were re-presented and made into new entities. In this sedimentation theory, these new entities are called the newly-emergent realities. These developments occur within the co-present in the framework of a "contextualized emergence" in which some elements of the past are retained while others are modified or replaced with newer concepts. In terms of Foucault's sedimentation model of time, the layer of the present is placed onto the previous layer of the past. Hence, the present is embedded into the past. Those aspects of the past that undergo change come to represent the newest layer of sedimentation: the new-present or the makings of the future.

The implications of this investigation is that language is used to re-present the social construction of reality and in doing so it redefines the past in terms of the relevancy of the present. As Kuhn (1962) noted in his model of the Structure of Scientific Revolutions, the past is rewritten to reflect the new paradigm. This phenomenon is not limited to the natural sciences but is endemic in daily social interaction involving language. The idea that scientific revolutions lead to new paradigms and new models of normal science is what Foucault (1969) sees as historical discontinuities. These models of the emergence of new knowledge frameworks is the by-product of a process that begins with the anomies discovered in normal science, the attempts to correct them during the period of crisis, and the successful implementation of a new scientific paradigm during the period of scientific revolution. This is how natural and social scientists argue for a model of change. What they are revising and reconstructing is a system of thought; an old paradigm is replaced with a new one.

Towards a Theory of Cultural Change

Within the theory of the sedimentation of cultural time and space, it is argued that cultural consciousness plays an important role in the co-present, the place where the present is embedded in the past. It is in the co-present where the new-past is established and where traditions are redefined and given attributes that concur with its new contextual frame. It can be argued that the meaning of the present comes from the past. Old traditions provide road signs to the present. Old patterns of behavior provide social structures that legitimate the present. These patterns may not be fully obvious to the individuals functioning within the co-present. In such a case, the past becomes the new-past. However, where individuals are conscious of these transformations, the past becomes the new-present. They represent the newest layer of cultural space that is placed upon the co-present. This new layer will eventually form the old past for future generations of people inhabiting that cultural space.

Future	Newly-Emergent Realities New-Past Reinvented		
Present	Old-Past	New-Past Redefined	New-Past Modified
	The Co-Present		
Past	The Past		

It is also in the co-present where the new-present is created. This is because the future is embedded in the present. It is the place where human projections are created and where hopes and desires are developed and contextualized. Changes in the new-present are most obvious across generations within a social setting. A clear case of this can be found in the generation gap that has occurred among baby boomers from 1946–1964. Jones (1981), a demographer, studied this period in American culture and documented how the social construction of reality of the children of this generation differed substantially from those of their parents. There were several factors that led to this difference. It was during this time that people moved from the inner city to live in the suburbs. The automobile became a dominant means of transportation and television the dominant means of entertainment. A plethora of new patterns of socialization led to the creation of a new mind set, an entirely new cultural consciousness. The new-present of the children of this era differed significantly from the new-present of their parents. What the parents called new-present and the newly-emergent realities, their children viewed the same phenomena as the present.

Making the Present Coherent through Habitus

Living in the co-present means that one inhabits a world that is in a state of flux. However, individuals who live in the co-present do not experience the sociology of everyday life as an unstructured and constantly changing world. Why is that? The answer can be found in the concept of *habitus* (Bourdieu, 1977, 1984; Bourdieu & Wacquaint, 1992). The structures that underlie everyday life are the routines, habits, beliefs, and patterns of behavior that one acquires by living within a cultural complex known as one's social and cultural habitus. Life is embedded in this habitus. Without this habitus, life would undergo constant scrutiny. One would ask some very basic questions about the daily routines in life. What must one do when entering a restaurant? How does one go about ordering a meal? Life is full of these nonverbal social scenarios. They are learned by living and participating in a cultural complex. Life makes sense because these routines provide daily activities and actions with a semblance of order. When others share the same social scripts, the result is a sense of social order. Primary and secondary socialization formed the training ground for the creation of this social order. Television programs also provide information on what is available for the purchase in the common market. These programs also contain examples of social behavior in the form of soap operas, movies, and documentaries. Much of what constitutes culture exists in the form of tacit knowledge. It can be found in the cultural habitus of daily living.

The Manner of Time in Space

In the linear model of time, not only is time used as a metaphor of space, but time is also modified. There are different manners of time which linguists refer to as aspect-markers (St. Clair, 2002, 2006).

Not only do layers of space (cultural strata) encounter changes over time, but these changes in time continue from the past into the co-present and from the present into the future. In linguistics, this modification of the manner of time is called *aspect*.

The transition from the past into the present may be part of duration or iteration. This means that the past continues into the co-present as a prior event.

Linguistic Time	Concepts	Comments
Semantic Time	The past, present, and the future are semantic entities. They function as temporal concepts.	There are languages that use time words to define time, but they have no tense. They have the concept of time but no linguistic markers of time.

(to be continued)

Linguistic Time	Concepts	Comments
Linguistic Tense	Many languages have grammatical markers of time. These linguistic markers are called tense.	Tense is a linguistic marker of time. These may occur as the present tense, the past tense, or the future tense.
Aspect Markers	Aspect has to do with how time is modified. Time may occur as durations, cycles, iterations, inceptives (beginnings), terminatives (endings), etc.	Duration is a length of time that may begin in the past, endure, and end in the past. The markers for duration in English are have + verb + en: I had eaten. I have eaten. I will have eaten. I would have eaten.

Aspect	Linguistic Markers	Commentary
Duration	**Had+V+en**, John had eaten. **Has+V+en**, John has eaten. **Will have+V+en**, John will have eaten.	An event begins in time, endures, and ends later in time.
Iteration	**Was+V+ing**, John was eating. **Is+V+ing**, John is eating. **Will be + V + ing**, John will be eating.	An event repeats itself. It begins at one point in time and repeats itself. It concludes at a later point in time.
Inceptive	**Start**, John started to sing. **Begin**, John began to sing.	This marks the beginning of an event.
Terminative	**Finish**, John finished the book. **End**, John ended the project.	This marks the end of an event.

Re-Inventing the Cultural Past

Globalization is the new label that has replaced the concept of multiculturalism. It has been chosen as a new term for several reasons. In globalization the *terra firma* of a cultural space is overlaid with new earth. The mores (the ways of life) of other cultures invade the cultural spaces of new regions in the present. The co-present is a mixture of not only new and old cultures, but also disparate cultures. There is another reason why globalization has been a more significant concept in modern times and this has to do with large movements of human beings going across international boundaries to resettle in new lands. The old concept of culture was defined by nation-states. In this context, the political entity of a nation-state constituted its cultural framework. Once an individual leaves his country or nation-state, he enters into a new culture. The mixture of different cultures was referred to as multiculturalism. With globalization such a definition of multiculturalism no longer holds. People are transported *en masse* in new cultures where they become hybrid citizens. In the old country, the present was embedded in the past. In the new host country, however, the cultural past is different. This means that their cultural identity has been compromised. They want to be participants in the new culture and yet remain favorable to their cultural past. This problem is resolved by transporting components of the cultural past and relocating it in the new home land. Those who reside outside of this phenomenon have labeled such communities as ghettos, barrios, or Chinatowns. It is wrong to treat these groups as marginalized citizens. They are not marginalized communities. Their experiences have more to do with the making of a hybrid culture. They are engaged in the making of a new cultural space. Within the Foucault model of the archeology of knowledge, earth from the old country is brought into the new country and mixed with its new cultural space.

For those who are being bombarded with modernization in the form of new styles of architecture, new products, new languages, and new ways of thinking, the opposite is true.

Their cultural past has taken on a new stratum of co-existence which allows new forms of earth to be placed on its *terra firma*. It also constitutes a hybrid culture but of a different kind.

Emergent Realities and the Social Construction of Culture

One aspect of socialization that has not been fully addressed so far comes from the uses of mass media. This use of media comes in many forms and is directed to cultural niches. What one sees on television becomes a part of the conscious co-present. Those who share the same media use it as a way of reaffirming their social construction of reality. The soap operas, movies, and situation comedies they watch are comparable to other forms of socialization except that the participation is passive and the messages may be tacit. Years after a certain event took place on television individuals may invoke them in conversations and role playing. These invents are part of their virtual memory and form a part of their virtual culture. They function, in part, as a collective memory that has been distributed individually to individuals and these persons invoke the same memory at the same time in a public setting. They have become the newly-emergent realities. One can ascertain after a short conversation, for example, if another person subscribes to cable and what programs he or she watches on television. These forms of virtual memory become social markers of group coherence with regard to one event. It is as if there are niche cultures that can be invoked and used to unite disparate individuals by means of one event.

Sociologists do not want to deal with the concept of collective memory. They find it too mystical. This concept, it should be noted, was introduced by Durkheim (1951), one of the founders of sociology. Durkheim (1964, 1970) argued that individuals are bound together in society in two ways. Societies share their lives with others in a communal setting (*Gemeinschaft*) or they are bound together by institutions, laws, and regulations (*Gesellschaft*). Those who see life as a community share the same religion, the same hope, fears, and aspirations. Those who are bound by rules and regulations belong to a group but they do not feel bonded to the group. With the advent of television and the creation of the consumer culture, the kinds of bonding that occur in mass society have many of the elements associated with the primal communities that Durkheim discussed. Virtual cultures share virtual memories. They are bonded by virtual events. They have the same kind of deep emotional connection over events that earlier societal types encounter. They are part of the phenomenon of secondary orality (Ong, 1982). If there ever was a time when a case could be made for the existence of fragments of a virtual memory distributed over a wide range of niche cultures, it is in the co-present world of television, the internet, blogospheres, and other forms of mediated communication.

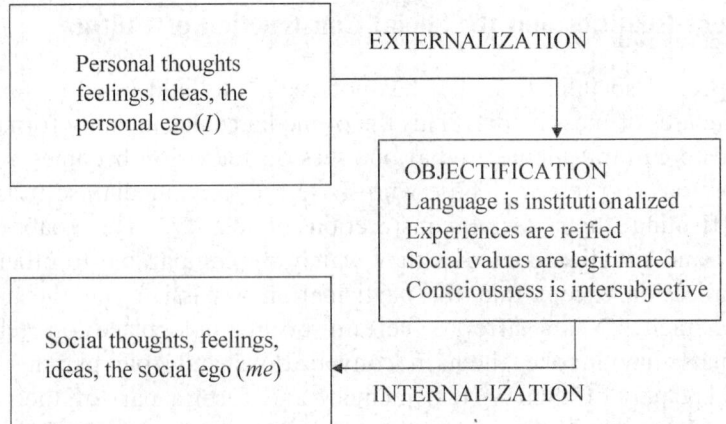

Conclusion

The concept of culture as a unit of knowledge shared by all individuals within a nation-state can no longer be maintained. Just as economic groups transcend national borders in order to do business, mass media transcend these same borders in order to market goods. What was once a simple matter of defining the mores of a tribal unit or a nation-state has emerged into a calculus of cultural artifacts that play a role in the co-present worlds of numerous consumer societies. How does one begin to explain this new form of cultural diffusion? How does one begin to define the forces behind these infusions of cultural symbols (Debord, 1995)? How does one deal with the spectacle of life (Baudrillard, 1973; Debord, 1995)? One could liken this overflow of information to a cultural flood over the old terrains of the nation-states. What happens in this cultural flood is that some of the cultural artifacts remain and take hold on the old cultural space and some of the cultural artifacts are washed away and deposited elsewhere. Those cultural artifacts that remain are either accepted, revised, or re-invented. Those that are accepted become part of the new-past. Those that are revised are taken to be a part of the new-present and those that are re-invented are treated as newly-emergent realities. At some point, the new-present becomes a part of the old-past only to be reintroduced within the new co-present as the new-past.

It was argued earlier in this investigation that Kuhn's theory of scientific revolutions provides a basis for the discussion of change within the cultural fabric of a society. Emphasis was placed on the period of crises where the social construction of reality is questioned and new potential paradigms emerge. It was argued that this locale is not the present (normal science) but the co-present (the period of crises), the place where the past and the present encounter each other. It is where the present is embedded in the habitus of the past. It is also where the future (revolutionary science) is being created by means of new levels of consciousness-raising and new re-presentations of the artifacts of the past. It is here that the rationale for change takes place. It is from this context that cultural changes emerge. Some of these function as newly-emergent realities. Others just remain as the new-present.

What the structuralists propose as a framework for the study of culture is that culture is a steady-state phenomenon. It accounts for the dynamics of change by claiming that time moves along a linear space. It progresses by moving from one linear moment of frozen time to another. Such a model cannot account for the phenomena of modernity or the complexity of globalization. If modernity had to do with steady-state phenomena of the past and postmodernism has to do with the state of flux between steady-states, the question that needs to be asked is how did this shift from one steady-state to another occur?

The Old-Past never dies. It is redefined or modified
Into the New-past in the Co-Present

		New-Past-3 New-Configuration-3	Old-past-3 Old-configuration-3
	New-Past-2 New-configuration-2	Old-Past-2 Old-configuration-2	
Old-Past-1 Old-configuration-1			

The claim that time is embedded in a cultural space provides an interesting model of social and cultural change. It recognizes, for example, that the present is not separated from past. The past provides the network of meanings that gives meaning to the present. The present belongs to a different cultural configuration. It takes elements from the past and reinterprets them within the context of the situation demanded by the present. Hence, the past is processed in the co-present and this results in parts of the past being seen as the old-past. Other aspects of the past may be re-contextualized and seen in a new framework as part of the new-present. The present can also provide the past with a new interpretation of events resulting in the redefined-past or the reinterpreted-past. Finally, new concepts may emerge as newly-emergent realities. These contain the seeds of cultural change associated with the future. What this model of laminated cultural space claims is that there is a structure of cultural change and that most dynamic aspects of this model occur in the co-present where the present and the past encounter one another in the sociology of everyday life. Hence, the concept of cultural space is presented as part of that new paradigm.

References

Baudrillard, J. (1973). *The mirror of production*. St. Louis, MO: Telos Press.
Baudrillard, J. (1995). *Simulacra and simulation*. Ann Arbor, MI: University of Michigan.
Bourdieu, P. (1977). *Outline of a theory of practice*. Cambridge University Press.
Bourdieu, P. (1984). *The logic of practice*. Stanford, CA: Stanford University Press.
Bourdieu, P. (1986). The forms of capital. In J. G. Richardson (Ed.), *Handbook for theory and research for the sociology of education* (pp. 241-258). New York: Greenwood Press.
Bourdieu, P. (1991). *Language and symbolic power*. Cambridge University Press.
Bourdieu, P., & Wacquant, L. (1992). *An invitation to reflexive sociology*. Chicago, IL: University of Chicago Press.
Debord, G. (1995). *The society of the spectacle*. Cambridge, MA: Zone Books.

Durkheim, E. (1951). *The elementary forms of religious life*. New York: The Free Press.
Durkheim, E. (1964). *The division of labor in society*. New York: The Free Press.
Durkheim, E. (1970). *The rules of sociological method*. London: Routledge and Kegan Paul.
Foucault, M. (1966). *Les mots et les choses* [The order of things]. Paris, France: Editions Gallimard.
Foucault, M. (1969). *L'archéologie du savoir* [The archeology of knowledge]. Paris, France: Editions Gallimard.
Foucault, M. (1971). *L'ordre du discours* [The order of speech]. Paris, France: Editions Gallimard.
Foucault, M. (1982). *Ceci n'est pas une pipe* [This is not a pipe]. Paris, France: Editions Gallimard.
Giddens, A. (1979). *Central problems in social theory: Action, structure and contradiction in social analysis*. London: Macmillan.
Giddens, A. (1984). *The constitution of society: Outline of the theory of structuration*. Cambridge, MA: Polity Press.
Giddens, A. (1991). *Modernity and self-identity: Self and society in the late modern age*. Cambridge, MA: Polity Press.
Jones, L. Y. (1981). *Great expectations: America and the baby boom generation*. New York: Ballantine.
Kuhn, T. S. (1962). *The structure of scientific revolutions*. Chicago, IL: University of Chicago Press.
Kuhn, T. S. (1971). *The Copernican revolution: Planetary astronomy in the development of western thought*. Cambridge: Harvard University Press.
Lehmann, W. P. (1962). *Historical linguistics: An introduction*. New York: Holt. Retrieved February 10, 2007, from http://dl.media.mit.edu/viral/
Mehan, H., & Wood, H. (1975). *The reality of ethno-methodology*. New York: John Wiley and Sons.
Nederveen Pieterse, J. (2004). *Globalization and culture: Global mélange*. New York: Roman & Littlefield.
Ong, Q. J. (1982). *Orality and literacy: The technologizing of the word*. London: Methuen.
St. Clair, R. N. (2002). *The major metaphors of European thought — Growth, game, language, drama, machine, time and space*. New York: Edwin Mellen Press.
St. Clair, R. N. (2006). *The sociology of knowledge as a model for language theory: Language as a social science*. NY: Edwin Mellen Press.
St. Clair, R. N., Thomé-Williams, A. C., & Su, L. (2005). The role of social script theory in cognitive blending. In M. F. Medina & L. Wagner (Eds.), *Special issue of intercultural communication studies* XI. V
Wallerstein, I. (1974). *The modern world-system I: Capitalist agriculture and the origins of the European world-economy in the sixteenth century*. New York: Academic Press.
Wallerstein, I. (1980). *The modern world-system II: Mercantilism and the consolidation of the European world-economy, 1600–1750*. New York: Academic Press.
Wallerstein, I. (1989). *The modern world-system III: The second era of great expansion of the capitalist world-economy, 1730–1849*. New York: Academic Press.
Wallerstein, I. (2005). *World-systems analysis: An introduction*. Durham, NC: Duke University Press.

6

Sociolinguistic Approach to Intercultural Communication*

JIA Yuxin
Harbin Institute of Technology, China

Abstract: This paper introduces the sociolinguistic approach to the study of intercultural communication. However, this approach is different from the traditional sociolinguistic approach in the sense that it takes the position that cultural and social identities are largely *communicatively* produced. That is, people in the globalizing world are using appropriation of linguistic resources to produce and reproduce their right, style, and cultural and social identities. Therefore, to understand issues of social reality, social change, and social and cultural identities and how they affect and are affected by cultural, social, political, and ethnic divisions we need to gain insights into the communicative processes by which they arise. This paper seeks to present and develop an interpretive sociolinguistic approach to interpret and explain intercultural communication, and the communication behavior in the Chinese context, hoping to uncover the role language behavior plays in the production and reproduction of cultural and social identities and realities.

Introduction

The study of the theories of intercultural communication has made tremendous progress in recent years. The theories in this field include

---

* This paper was based on the author's presentation at the Second World Forum on China Studies sponsored by Shanghai Academy of Social Sciences, September 21–22, 2006 and published in Jia Yuxin (Ed.), *Intercultural Communication — Research and Exploration* (pp. 1–29). Harbin: Harbin Institute of Technology Press, 2007.

many aspects of research on culture and communication, which can generally be summed up within the broad rubric of communication across cultures *at the cultural level and individual level* (Gudykunst, 2003). In the growth of the study in this field, we have also found some other approaches, from which the study of intercultural communication has gained insightful ideas both in theory building and communication practice. Among these perspectives, is the sociolinguistic approach which studies the interplay of language, communication, culture and society. This sociolinguistic perspective has made unique contributions to the study of cross-cultural communication, especially in terms of language behavior. This paper introduces the sociolinguistic approach to the study of intercultural communication. However, the sociolinguistic approach is different from the traditional sociolinguistic study in the sense that it takes the position that cultural and social reality, social identities are largely communicatively produced. That is, people in the globalizing world are using linguistic resources to produce and reproduce their cultural and social identities. In fact, the use of language is constitutive of social reality. "Where the communicative conventions and symbols of social identity differ, the social reality itself becomes subject to question. On the other hand, however, both talk and social reality are part of and serve to maintain an ideology which takes on a historical life of its own" (J. J. Gumperz, 1982). We can hardly claim that language determines social reality or vice versa, social reality determines language. We just want to say that, to understand issues of social reality, social change, and social and cultural identity and language, we need to gain insights into the communicative processes in which they interact. This paper seeks to present and develop an interpretive sociolinguistic approach to account for intercultural communication — and in particular, the communication phenomenon in the Chinese context. By doing so, the author hopes to uncover how ideology enters into face-to-face communication to create an interactional or intercultural space in which the subconscious and automatic sociolinguistic processes of interpretation and inference can generate a variety of outcomes and make interpretations subject to question (Gumperz, 1982, p.3).

1. Sociolinguistic Approach to Intercultural Communication

Sociolinguistics as a study of language use related to social and cultural reality is of fundamental importance to the study of intercultural communication. Language is not merely a system of sounds, grammar, and meaning. It is social behavior and it is influenced and conditioned by social and cultural norms, rules, and values. It is the differences in these factors between cultures that lead to misunderstandings and even worse outcomes in intercultural interactions. Inevitably, knowledge about these factors as well as the cultural variations in these aspects should be the main concern of intercultural communication at the cultural and individual levels. The development of knowledge and intuitive sensitivity to the sociolinguistic or socio-cultural differences engenders deep interest and scholarly research into this new field.

The sociolinguistic approach to the study of intercultural communication is important but the systematic study of it is hitherto under-discussed. Scholars have been doing contrastive research on speech acts and interactional principles both at the cultural level and individual level. They have explored situations of communication between cultural groups in today's world. Even though the research work has been based on scratches and instances of everyday interactions and case studies, we may seek to develop interpretative sociolinguistic approach to interactions out of these scratches and instances. We can start from scratches, stick them together and combine them into a systematic and coherent framework. This framework also includes those theories, concepts, and propositions that appear in other approaches. These may just as well fall into our sociolinguistic scope.

1.1 The Basic Premises and Guiding Principle for the Sociolinguistic Approach

1.1.1 The Role of Communication: Communication as Social and Cultural Identities

The assumption that social and cultural identities are communicatively produced constitutes the premise of the sociolinguistic approach. This premise is grounded in Gumperz' statement regarding language and communication of identity (1982): "social processes are symbolic processes but that symbols have meaning only in relation to the forces which control the utilization and allocation of environmental resources." Gumperz further points out that traditionally, we used to regard gender, ethnicity, class etc. as given parameters and boundaries within which we create our own social identities. However, in today's world which is shrinking into a global village, the ever increasing intercultural contacts demonstrate that these parameters are not constants that can be taken for granted but are communicatively produced. The role of communication in social interactions today has become the resources of individuals' social and cultural identity. "Communicative resources thus form an integral part of an individual's symbolic and social capital, and ... this form of capital can be every bit essential as real property resources were once considered to be" (Bourdieu, 1973). "Therefore to understand issues of identity and how they affect and are affected by social, political, and ethnic divisions we need to gain insights into the communicative processes by which they arise" (Gumperz, 1982).

> Symbolic processes are social processes. But symbols or communication does not exist in isolation. They should be analyzed in relation to its social and cultural environments, including people who are using them. The most important characteristic of the social and cultural environments in which we live and in which we use symbols to communicate is the intense and ever increasing cultural and ethnic diversity, which is best characterized as cultural pluralism or globalization. What distinguishes today's world from the world of yesterday is "the modes of interaction among subgroups and the ways in which individuals of different backgrounds must relate to each other and to the system by which they are governed have changed" (Gumperz, 1982).

Nowadays there is a widely shared — almost taken for granted — view that globalization is taking place throughout almost all aspects of social life. As a result, intercultural contact is increasing rapidly and dramatically. Cultures, economies, and politics appear to merge across the globe through the rapid exchange of information, ideas, knowledge, and investment. However, in spite of this, recent experience has shown that physical closeness and economic interconnectedness between and among people from different cultures cannot automatically guarantee effective communication and friendly interpersonal relationship. Greater intercultural contact may actually reinforce cultural and social distinctions and create separation. The experience of increasing global contact has made us realize that intercultural contact, though inevitable, is not always successful. It is the diversity of communicative behavior of different cultures that always creates miscommunication and misunderstanding. The different behavior can be strange and, at times, even bizarre as it often fails to meet our usual expectations. Even when the natural barrier of a foreign language is dissolved, we may still fail to understand and make ourselves understood due to the differences in communication mechanism: the subconscious processes of inference that result from situational factors, social presuppositions and sociolinguistic or discourse conventions or norms.

All this suggests that talk or communication itself constitutes cultural and social identity. Just as Gumperz points out, "Where communicative conventions and symbols of social identity differ, the social reality itself comes subject to question. On the other hand, however, both talk and social reality are part of and serve to maintain an ideology which takes on a historical life of its own." Communication in today's world plays a role that it has never played before. The role of communication in social interactions today has become the resources of individuals' social and cultural identities.

1.1.2 Sociolinguistic Relativity as the Guiding Principle for Sociolinguistic Approach

We assume that the concept of sociolinguistic relativity serves as the guiding principle for the sociolinguistic approach to the study of intercultural communication.

The concept of sociolinguistic relativity was introduced by Nassa Wolfson in her *Perspectives: Sociolinguistics and TESOL* (1989). Sociolinguistic conventions or norms can be defined as culturally and socially shared expectations of appropriate behaviors (Gudykunst and Kim 1992;贾玉新, 1997). Wolfson considers this concept to be relevant to the studies of communication across societies and cultures. According to Wolfson, sociolinguistic relativity refers to the phenomenon that the norms that inform speakers' knowledge as to what is appropriate to say to whom, and under which conditions show considerable variation from community to community around the world, not only from one language group to another but within language groups as well.

The concept of sociolinguistic relativity can in fact be regarded as an extension of cultural relativity, which is proposed in opposition to the concept of linguistic relativity. The concept of cultural relativity, according to many communication scholars, usually refers to the phenomenon that human behavior, including language use, as well as way of thinking and so on are culturally related. That is, culture influences human behavior, thinking, and so on. And as a result, when people from different cultural backgrounds encounter each other, they tend to judge and evaluate each other's behavior according to their own value systems.

Sociolinguistic relativity refers to the phenomenon that each culture has its own unique value systems and as a result each culture has its own conventions or norms for its language use. Stated differently, sociolinguistic conventions or norms that influence the way people speak and write in a given culture differ from culture to culture. However, the differences between culturally related sociolinguistic conventions are not a matter of better or worse — it is just a matter of being different or a matter of emphasis.

Conventions or norms for language use are far from universal. Different cultures have different sociolinguistic conventions or norms for the use of interaction and discourse conventions and the differences in values and conventions exist in great intensity and with a wide variety of language behavior. This is what is called sociolinguistic diversity. The intensity of pragmatic conventions or norms calls for our great attention because of this lack of the knowledge of the pragmatic diversity, people from different cultural backgrounds often misunderstand each other. They misinterpret and misunderstand the intent of the speakers because they tend to interpret and judge the behavior of people from a different cultural background with their own cultural standard and values.

Related to the concepts of sociolinguistic relativity and diversity is the concept of pragmatic transfer which means the use of conventions or norms from one's own culture when interacting with people from a different culture. And in fact it is not uncommon that people tend to subconsciously and automatically transfer many of the mechanisms of their native speech and written discourse conventions to the use of a different language when they come to interact with people from different cultures. This phenomenon, is referred to as interference or transfer, which was early recognized as bilingualism by such researchers as Uriel Weinreich, who says that those instances of deviation from the norms of either language which occur in the speech of bilinguals as a result of their familiarity with more than one languages, i.e. as a result of language contact, will be referred to as interference phenomena (Weinreich, 1953). Later, this phenomenon has been widely taken into consideration and gained wide currency in recent years through the research of applied linguists who have focused on foreign or second language learning and teaching. It is in recent years that this phenomenon is introduced into the studies of cross-cultural communication. The adoption of such a point of view, we hope, will help us reduce the negative results of the sorts of misunderstandings which are bound to arise when people interact between cultures.

1.1.3 The Role of Culture: Culture as Explanatory Variable for Communication Behavior

The sociolinguistic approach requires incorporating culture in communication theory and treating culture as a theoretical explanatory variable. Only when culture is treated as a theoretical variable, can differences in language behavior including interaction and discourse organization styles be well described and explained.

We believe that differences in language behavior are very likely to lead us to the thought that it is necessary to consider the differences at the level of culture in the first place. When we encounter the differences in the speech behavior between cultures, for example, we resort to culture for help for reasons behind the differences. Culture is the first and the most important factor that programs the way we behave and explains why we do so.

Communication is culture specific and at the same time, there are systematic similarities and differences between cultures. According to many scholars, the similarities and differences can be explained and predicted theoretically by using culture as a variable. When culture is treated as a theoretical variable, differences in language behavior including interaction and discourse organization styles can well be accounted for.

Culture is manifested at different layers of depth, ranging from inner core values, through outer core conventions and norms, to the surface level communication behavior including interaction and discourse styles.

A diagrammatic representation of the different layers of culture could be as follows:

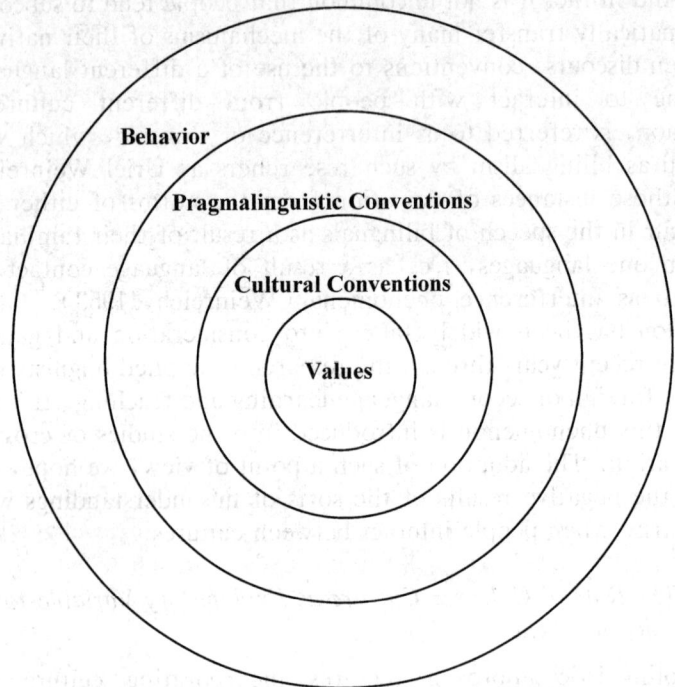

It is difficult to conceptualize culture. According to Kroeber and Kluckhohn, (1952) there are 164 definitions of culture. Despite the problems in defining culture, we adopt Spencer-Oatey's definition in this dissertation as it fits our way of looking at the relationship between culture and language use:

> Culture is a fuzzy set of attitudes, beliefs, behavioral conventions, and values that are shared by a group of people, and that influence each member's behavior and his/her interpretations of the 'meaning' of other people's behavior. (1999: 2)

From this figure, we can easily see that values, the inner core, are the essential determining factor that shapes conventions or norms, which in turn shape communicative behavior including language behavior in a given situation. In this light, we regard conventions and norms as part of or the outer-manifestation of values in a given culture. Conventions or norms, as mentioned earlier, are culturally and socially shared expectations of appropriate behaviors (Gudykunst and Kim 1992; Lustig and Koester

1999;贾玉新 1997). Stated differently, they are guidelines for expected and accepted behaviors in a society.

We may also regard language behavior, the surface level of culture, as the outer-manifestation of values and conventions or norms.

Language behavior or language use is part of cultural values and conventions or norms and cultural values and conventions or norms, do enter into face-to-face (intercultural) communication to create "an interactional space in which the subconscious and automatic sociolinguistic processes of interpretation and inference can generate a variety of outcomes" (Gumperz 1982) and a variety of interpretations. In such an interactional encounter, our most cherished expectations, assumptions, and ways of thinking cannot travel across cultural boundaries. What is customarily expected and understood becomes incomprehensible in a diverse culture. Cultural values form the basic principles that program the way we think and behave. They set the background criteria for how we should communicate appropriately with others, say, with people from different cultures. "They set the emotional tone for how we interpret and evaluate cultural strangers' behavior" (Ting-Toomey 1999). They influence our overall self-conception, and our self-conception, in turn, influences our behavior.

In this light, language use, including interaction and discourse organization styles, can be defined as a cultural construct because it is not only influenced by but also acts on cultural values in one way or another. Stated differently, the differing cultural values impose different conventions or norms upon the use of language including interaction and discourse organization styles. The values are enacted in a variety of manners of communication. Values in this way can be used as variables for explaining and interpreting the similarities and differences in communication between cultures.

According to Gudykunst (2003) and many others, we need to treat cultures as theoretical variables. On the basis of these variables, there are different dimensions on which a culture can be employed to explain communication between cultures (Kluckhohn and Strodtbeck 1961; Hall 1976; Hofstede 1980). These dimensions of cultural variabilities have been used to different extents by communication scholars for years in explaining cultural differences and similarities in communication between cultures.

2. Overview of Sociolinguistic and Discourse Conventions

Although people in the world may have similar communicative tasks to accomplish or problems to solve in order to survive and to get along with each other, the realizations of these tasks and the resolutions of these problems as social practice are culture specific. The variation can be analyzed from several different perspectives:

1) People from different cultural background may have different cultural assumptions about the situational and other contextual factors that influence communication as well as appropriate behavior and intentions within it.

2) People from different cultural background may have different pragmalinguistic conventions or norms for selecting strategies and interpreting their use in given contexts (Helen Spencer-Oatey, 1999).

3) People from different cultural background may hold differing principles conditioning and programming their interaction in given contexts (Helen Spencer-Oatey, 1999).

2.1 Investigation of Spoken Interaction and Discourse Conventions

2.1.1 Sociolinguistic and Discourse Conventions as Culture-Specific

Despite differences in language use between cultures, scholars have made many efforts to design universal principles, maxims, or conventions, such as Grice's Cooperative Principle (1975), Leech's Politeness Principle (1983), Searle's Speech Acts (1975), Brown and Levinson's Face Theory (1987), and so on and so forth. The generalizations proposed in these works provide useful insights into the mechanisms of language use. However, these universal principles, maxims or conventions should not be seen as absolutely true. For example, according to Lim (2003), Searle's assertion that ordinary conversational requirements of politeness normally make it awkward to issue flat imperative sentences and explicit performatives and that politeness is the chief motivation for indirectness is only an illusion and simple manifestations of Anglo-Saxon cultural values. Matsumoto (1988) criticized Brown and Levinson, saying that they have ignored the interpersonal or social perspective on face and they have over-emphasized the notion of individual freedom and autonomy. Gu (1998) points out that it is not that concerns about autonomy, imposition, and so on do not exist in Eastern cultures, but rather that they are not regarded as face concern. Grice's principle of cooperation, the four maxims of conversation, and the implicature-generating mechanisms are also specific to the North American culture. Asians are not likely to presuppose these principles or maxims to trigger implicatures, as evidenced by Chinese, Japanese and Korean conventions. According to He Zhaoxiong (何兆熊, 2000), Grice's principle does not explain why people may violate cooperative principle and communicate with each other in an implicit and indirect way (2000: 167). Brown and Levinson's universal Face Theory (1987) also received criticism for the claimed universality of their theory. Even though it was based on a dozen languages from all over the world, the theory reveals a strong Anglocentric bias. Anglocentrism allows English-speaking scholars to make cross-cultural generalizations of their ethnographic knowledge with examinations of some isolated examples from other languages. Evidence shows that scholars have been greeted by culture-specific differences (Blum-Kulka, House, & Kasper 1989). Pragmatics and cross-cultural communication should concentrate on the studies on specific uses of language or should be more sensitive to cultural relativity and diversity.

Even if there do exist universal principles, to some extent, the maxims included in these principles may vary in importance and emphasis from culture to culture. In sociolinguistics as well as in the studies of intercultural communication, one of the ways of 'unpackaging' culture is by drawing on Leech's Politeness Principle (1983), which consists of six maxims dealing with interpersonal and social relationship. The maxims claimed by Leech in fact reflect the sociopragmatic conventions people seem to follow in managing interpersonal and social relationship. Leech argues that people are often far more indirect than the Grice's Cooperative Principle suggests. Leech maintains that Japanese culture attaches greater weight to the Modesty Maxim than British culture does, and that conversely the Agreement Maxim is more important in Britain than in Japan. He maintains that such differences can thereby explain why the Japanese typically respond to compliments with greater modesty than the British do. Likewise, according to some scholars, Modesty Maxim is much more favored in China and some other Asian countries than in European countries.

The maxims put forward by Grice, Leech and others in the West, are in general based on verbalized interactions or verbalized meanings. Preciseness, clarity, expressiveness, brevity, disambiguity, explicitness, directness, assertiveness, and so on, are the conventions in many of the Western countries. However, these may not represent the Chinese communication. The ways in which the Chinese communicate, the ways in which they generate implicature, for example, fall outside the scope of Grice's theory. One of Grice's maxims for cooperative conversation is manner, which suggests that the speaker should avoid obscurity of expression and ambiguity (1975). This direct style of communication is a convention or norm in North America despite the extensive use of indirect communication. Grice's principle would not be accepted as a convention or norm, however, in East Asia. In Chinese culture which is collectivism and relationship oriented, for example, it seems that the traditional rule of communication which does not advocate demanding, rejecting, asserting oneself, or criticizing the listener straightforwardly, is much more a dominant sociopragmatic convention than Grice's maxim of manner. For the Chinese and Japanese, to understand the real intention in communication, what needs to be employed on many occasions may not be the knowledge of conversational maxims and contextual information but pure intuition obtained through long time of contact with others or what is called Kan by the Japanese scholar Tae-Seop Lim (2003: 65). This point has been examined and verified by many scholars. Koreans, according to Lim (1996), have to develop noon-chi to figure out the intention, desire, mood, and attitude of the speaker from the ambiguous message.

Indeed, there is hardly anything universal about the conventions or norms of speaking and writing. In the communication of the Chinese cultural context, conventions and norms are unique and it is these culture specific conventions or norms that dictate the way the Chinese speak and write.

2.1.2 Pragmalinguistic Conventions as Culture Specific

Pragmalinguistic conventions or norms refer to the fact that different cultures or communities have different sets of norms or conventions operating in the process of selecting strategies and interpreting their use in a given context. This phenomenon is related to speech act in particular, such as requesting, refusing, complimenting, and apologizing. Although different cultures or communities may share similar acts or functions of language, the conventions of strategies performing these functions or acts may vary with cultures. Although much research remains to be done in this area, a fruitful beginning has been made. Empirical analysis of speech or pragmalinguistic behavior have been centered around forms of address, apology, greeting, request, compliment, invitation, and so on.

To uncover the specific Chinese conventions or norms of speech behavior, empirical studies were conducted by Jia W. S. (1997) on apology-making as well as the behavior of compliment, among university students, in which the most distinctive features of apology and compliment behavior and the socio-cultural variables that influence the selection of apology strategies in Chinese context are examined.

The examination and analysis of the case study of the behavior of request in Chinese and American cultures (Jia, X. R., 2006) also prove that Chinese culture largely prefer pragmalinguistic conventions unique to its own culture.

Differences in the speech behavior of request between Chinese and American cultures lie in the semantic sequence or order of the components that make up a request or in the use of supportive moves, as well as in the way a request is stated. It is especially the case when politeness is observed. For example, the Chinese very often prefer to embed their requests in the supportive moves, such as lengthy explanations, or facework and justifications which are often placed at the beginning while Americans may place request at the very beginning and if they do use supportive moves, such as reasons or justifications for their request, they are very likely to place them after the request.

We tentatively call the lengthy explanatory and preliminary remarks, or supportive moves *frame*, the purpose of which is to set up a shared background or an atmosphere in which sort of good relationship or connection is hopefully to be set up.

The indirect style in Chinese culture and the direct style in American culture may differ in the extent to which communicators reveal their intention through the implicitness or explicitness of their content messages. The indirect style in Chinese culture may find expression in the implicit statement of the speaker's intention while the direct style may find expression in the explicit statement of the speaker's intention.

The implicit request is often used, in Chinese culture between people who are friends and acquaintances, or at least, who have had personal contact with each other for a long time and hence share a good understanding of each other's condition for needs and wants, the condition for request, for example. The speaker adopting the implicit style is likely to avoid verbalizing their intention straightforwardly and hence the interpretation of the intention requires the listener to discern the cues from the speaker. It is not uncommon that the listeners would most probably rely on tacit understanding or intuition that is based on years of contact with the person who makes the request. The explicit request is used both in Chinese and American cultures, however, the Americans are inclined to lay more emphasis on verbal performance than the Chinese, paying much attention to grammatical structure, lexical and phrasal selection, subjunctive mood and conditional moods, etc. Even when the Americans attempt to express their intention implicitly, their intention can be less difficult to discern from the context. On the Chinese side, communication is often listener oriented, in the sense that it is the listener who is responsible for discerning the meaning through tacit understanding or intuition or for reading the speaker's mind from the contextual cues whereas on the American side, it is the speaker who is responsible for stating his or her intention clearly and logically so that the listener can get or deduce the meaning forthrightly.

Obviously, misunderstanding and miscommunication are inevitable when the Chinese and the Americans meet in many request situations as each side may act intuitively and unconsciously according its own cultural standard and conventions. The Americans may complain about the Chinese for their "beating about the bush" in their request and ask them to say what they mean. By being implicit, the Chinese may leave the impression of being 'insincere' and 'untrustworthy' on the Americans. The Americans may leave no better impression on the Chinese — the Chinese may complain about the Americans for their being too forthright and straightforward in their request. The Americans may leave the impression of being blunt, impolite, and even rude on the Chinese.

2.1.3 Sociopragmatic Conventions as Culture Specific

As mentioned earlier, the so called universal principle proposed by the

Western scholars may not operate in the interaction of the Chinese cultural context. For example, One of Grice's sociopragmatic conventions or maxims for cooperative conversation is *manner* which suggests that the speaker should avoid obscurity of expression and ambiguity (Grice, 1975). This direct communication is a norm in North America, despite the extensive use of indirect communication. Grice's principle, however would not be accepted as a norm in Chinese culture, which prescribes not to demand, reject, assert yourself, or criticize the listener straightforwardly. In fact, going indirectly or in a roundabout way in demanding, rejecting, asserting oneself or criticize others in many situations is much more dominant than Grice's maxim of manner.

Sociolinguistic conventions or norms are cultural conventions. They are the outward manifestations of values and beliefs. They are socially shared expectations of appropriate behaviors in a given situation or context. In this light, cultural conventions or norms are themselves sociolinguistic conventions or norms and language use is their main concern. Conventions or norms vary with cultures in terms of their importance and intensity. Unlike values, however, conventions or norms can change over a period of time, whereas values are much more enduring. Different cultures, may have different range of options of sociolinguistic conventions, either indirect, implicit, covert, or direct, explicit, and overt in their management of social relationship in everyday interactions. Even if people from different cultural backgrounds speak the same language, say, English, the English they speak may be characterized by different sociolinguistic conventions. We tend to assume that it is the attitude and meaning that are conveyed through one set of conventions and interpreted through another rather than the differences in accents or in grammatical structure that often bring about breakdowns of communication.

Traditionally, sociopragmatic norms or conventions have been addressed by many scholars in China such as Chinese principle of politeness, and so on. Nowadays, some scholars such as Gu Yueguo (1998) and professor He Zhaoxiong (2000) have addressed the issue of politeness in Chinese culture from the sociolinguistic or pragmatic perspective. In the study of this area we should especially mention the theories related to sociopragmatic conventions such as the Updated Face and Face-Negotiation theory contributed by Stella Ting-Toomei, and similar theories which are Chinese culture specific by Jia Wensheng and Huang Guangguo, and Jia Yuxin.

Many scholars have written on Chinese communication, but one of the most recent and comprehensive publications on this is Gao and Ting-Toomey's *Communicating Effectively with the Chinese* (1998). They have listed four features to represent the communication in Chinese culture: *hánxù*（含蓄）, *tīnghuà* （听话）, *kèqi*（客气）and the *insider effect on communication*. By *hánxù*, they mean "one does not spell out everything but leaves the 'unspoken' to the listeners" (1998: 17). In communicating with others the Chinese prefer to be implicit rather than explicit. In other words, one does not bring everything out into the open. Something is left unsaid and the listener is expected to read the speakers' mind or to bet the message from the situation or the context. *Tīnghuà* is listening-centeredness, which means the Chinese pay a lot of attention to listening in communication and hierarchy plays a part in who is supposed to talk and who is supposed to listen. By *kèqi*, they mean that people should be polite. However, this does not mean the use of polite expressions alone. It implies the value of reserve, humility, and modesty and the use of appropriate expressions to show one's reserve, humility, and modesty. Finally, by the *insider effect on communication* they mean that there is in general a clear distinction between their in-group and out-group and tend to be involved with their in-group but are reluctant to interact with strangers.

3. Indirectness Resources as Individual's Social Capital in the Chinese Culture

Indirective interaction style as a communicative resource in the Chinese context in facts form an integral part of an individual's symbolic and social capital (Gumperz 1982) and in today's China this form of capital can be every bit as essential as real property resources were once considered to be (Bourdieu 1973). Chinese indirect interaction style serves as an important sociopragmatic convention for people to manage communication and interpersonal relationship, or to manipulate people, in the term of Chang Hui-Ching (1995).

Chang Hui-Ching, when talking about Chinese preference of indirect interaction style, points out that manipulating interpersonal interactions, whether through verbal or other means has always been an important topic in Chinese philosophical and political thinking. The complexity of Chinese social and interpersonal relationship creates the need for interactants to negotiate and managing relational positioning via exchange of verbal messages, whether with good intentions or under the guise of superficial harmonious interaction (Chang, 2005). Interaction skills function as a lubricant to the interpersonal system. Appropriate use of such skills, will help one create a desirable social network and bring personal advantage to those who employ them, particularly in a world that emphasizes relationship, favor or human emotions (*rénqíng*); and face needs. To achieve personal or individual's goals, one can use a variety of indirect linguistic forms, ambiguous expressions, indirect speech act, hidden words, and so on. Anyway, whether one is sincere in taking care of the needs of participants or merely interested in gaining advantage or power, knowing how to talk appropriately with people from different social positions so as not to spoil seemingly pleasant, harmonious situations is highly valued in Chinese culture.

Linda Wailing Young (1982), on the basis of the data derived from a variety of formal speech encounters, including an academic conference and a number of business meetings involving Chinese speakers of English as active participants, argued that Chinese in the main in discourses such as explaining, justifying and persuading, the organization of the discourse mirrors the order presented in the topic-comment utterance. The relationship of the main point to the rest of the discourse is in the order of the semantic relationship of topic to comment. According to her, in most cases, the Chinese discourse patterns seem to be the inverse of English discourse conventions in that definitive summary statements of main arguments are delayed till the end.

According to Jia Xuerui's empirical study and investigation, in fact, the indirect — direct dichotomy in spoken interaction finds a parallel in written discourse across Chinese and American cultures. It seems that the differences in preference of interaction styles like these across these two cultures are in no way incidental. It is systematic. The examples and facts in both spoken and written discourses provided in her dissertation provide evidence to the fact that there is a Chinese preference for the steady unraveling and build-up of information before arriving at the important message. All this boils down to the point that indirect interaction style in fact is the preference of the Chinese. They prefer the conventions of frame-main sequence or what is called the inductive / indirect style while the Americans prefer the conventions of the main-frame sequence or what is called the deductive / direct style. The differences in preference of interaction styles like these across these two cultures are in no way incidental. It is systematic.

To prove the hypothesis of Chinese preference of indirect / inductive convention, Jia Xuerui conducted examinations and made analysis of data derived from a considerable Prize Essays by non-English majors, model essays by English majors of Peking University, essays written by American speakers, and hundreds of abstracts of papers presented at 2005 Symposium on Intercultural Communication in China, as well as paper abstracts published in American journal, (written by native US American scholars) and the conclusion reinforced the assumption that in Chinese writing in English the indirectness or inductive approach is a general preference, and therefore dictating Chinese cultural identity in their communication. As some of the data and case study are based upon academic writings, the conclusion may, relatively speaking, sound more convincing. The convention reached in the discussion may be more representative of Chinese English writing discourse and the authors tend to think that Chinese preference towards the orientation of harmonious social and interpersonal relationship can be traced to culture specific notion of acceptable discourse conventions.

Actually both of these indirect or inductive style and direct or deductive style are found in both spoken and written discourses in Chinese and American cultures. That is to say, there is nothing inherently Chinese or American about these styles. Nevertheless, Jia Xuerui argues that there is great probability that the Chinese tend to prefer indirect or inductive style in more situations than the Americans.

Up to now, a very large amount of work from different perspectives and different disciplines has been done on the Eastern indirectness vs. Western directness difference of both spoken and written discourses as well as the factors that bring about the difference. Each perspective and discipline has provided insight into this area.

The indirect interaction and discourse conventions in Chinese culture vs. the direct interaction and discourse conventions in American culture are demonstrated in the following table. (Jia, Y. X., & Jia, X. R. 2008)

3.1 The Concept of Face and Facework as Culture Specific

Table 1   Face and Facework in Chinese and American Cultures

Contents Compared	Chinese Culture	American Culture
Relation Orientation	Harmony	Autonomy
	Interdependence	Independence
Interaction Style	Indirect	Direct
Semantic Sequence	Frame-Main Sequencing	Main-Frame Sequencing
Request	Facework-Justification/ Reason-Request	Request-Justification/ Reason
	Implicit; Contextualized	Explicit; Verbalized
Conflict Negotiation and Resolution	Indirect facework strategies	Direct facework strategies
	Third Party	Confrontation
	Tacit Understanding, intuition	Verbal Context-based Understanding
	Low Degree of Illocutionary Clarity	High Degree of Illocutionary Clarity
Written Discourse	Inductive/Indirect	Deductive/Direct
	Frame-Main (Subordinate-Main)	Main-Frame Main-Subordinate

3.1.1 The Concept of Face as Cultural Product

The concept of face plays an important role in human interaction. It is important to recognize that face and facework serve as essential sociopragmatic conventions or norms operating in the management of human interaction and interpersonal relationship.

In essence, the concept of face is not only social in nature. It is at the same time a psychological and cultural product. As social and cultural product, face entails both cultural-universal and culture specific aspects (Ting-Toomey & Cocroft, 1994). However, the scholars in the West have over-emphasized the universal aspect and paid inadequate attention to the cultural aspect of it.

Erving Goffman (1967) in his seminal work takes a sociological approach in describing face regarding face as a means of managing impression for human being in their social interpersonal interactions in the society. Goffman metaphorically describe people as performers on the stage, presenting and projecting various kinds of face or one's self-identity.

Brown and Levinson (1987) in a classic monograph, extended Goffman's concept of face and took a sociolinguistic approach in describing face and associated strategies. They regarded face as the public self-image every individual desires for himself or herself. They developed a rich theory of linguistic politeness around Goffman's concept of face. They proposed the dual concepts of positive and negative face as the basic wants of any individual in the social interactions. The positive face refers to the self image to be affirmed, appreciated, and approved of. The negative face refers to an individual's freedom to act and freedom from imposition. (Brown and Levinson, 1987). Both the positive and negatives face serve as social mechanism regulating interpersonal relationship in terms of linguistic expressions.

Goffman, Brown, and Levinson all argue that the claim or desire for face is a universal phenomenon underlying interpersonal relationship and interactions. The etic approach undertaken by Goffman, Brown, and Levinson is an attempt to discover a general theory that underlies human interaction and communication. However, this approach does not pay adequate attention to the cultural factors that influence the concept of face and facework, and therefore inevitably invite criticism.

Cross-culturally speaking, for example, what is a polite behavior for another person in the interaction in a given culture may very likely be very impolite in a different culture. What constitutes positive face may become negative face. "I am having a party this weekend. Come if you *want*." Is a polite invitation in a given situation in the United States. It however can be a face threatening act in a similar situation in the Chinese cultural context. In American society, this kind of way of invitation demonstrates the addresser's concern for the addressee's time and freedom of action. In Chinese society, however, it can be very impolite as it in no way takes the feelings of the other person into account, especially when this interaction occurs between friends. Likewise, compliment is considered an important strategy or a typical face-lauding act as it is often intended to have a positive effect on the addressee especially in the Western cultural context. However, it can have negative effect on the addressor as it may make the complimentee feel uncomfortable in the Chinese context.

As a cultural product, face may differ from one culture to another in terms of concept, nature, and functions. So much so that the so called universal theory regarding the concept of face advocated by Goffman, Brown and Levinson, etc. may not be adequately enough to account for the concept of face underlying interpersonal relationships and interpersonal interactions in the context of the Chinese culture as well as many others, as the universal theories are mainly based upon the Western self-oriented and individualistic cultures.

Scollon & Scollon argue that there are three factors in communication that bring about differences in the concept of face between the people in the East and West. They include the relative emphasis given to information and relationship, the hierarchical nature of interpersonal roles and, the contrast between negotiation and ratification of such roles.

Hu (1944), Scollon and Scollon (1995), and Jia W. S. (1997) argue that, contrary to the Western view of face, which is largely transactional, the Eastern view of face is fundamentally moral in nature. In the Chinese way of thinking, the concept of face includes two aspects, namely, lián (脸) and miànzi (面子) and there should be a clear distinction between these two. The former refers to an individual's inner qualities or the inner sense of character while the latter refers to an individual's outer sense of self in terms of the reputation one has achieved. However, the Westerners lay emphasis on the aspect of outer sense of face or miànzi rather than lian. Obviously, this aspect of the conception of face is transactional in nature as opposed to the concept of lian which is moral in nature. "Lian is the primary carrier of moral codes" (Jia, W. S., 1997). And the loss of face may function as "a condemnation by the group for immoral or socially disagreeable behavior" (1997). Obviously, the quality of manhood or character-based concept of face is out of the favor of the Western scholars. Hu also offers the distinction of inside and outside in terms of interpersonal relationship. In this way, the loss or gaining of an individual's face may be connected with the loss or lauding of the face of his or her in-group members.

Chang & Holt (1994), Gu (1998), Matsumoto (1998), and Ting-Toomey (1988) etc. argue that Brown and Levinson's theory of politeness is highly rational model rather than a relational one as the conceptions of positive face and negative face are mainly based on the individualistic cultural framework or self-oriented (Jia, W. S., 1997). The self-oriented or individualistic orientation-based concept of positive and negative face naturally results in the idea of face as impression management in interpersonal interaction which reflects individualistic orientation of the western culture. This may run counter to the concept of face in Eastern culture.

Many scholars tend to agree that China, Japan, and many cultures in the East are collectivism oriented while the United States, Canada and many others in North America and Europe are individualism oriented. Obviously, the individualism-collectivism can be used as important cultural variables to explain the cultural differences between these countries in face negotiations and the management of conflict. Following this individualism-collectivism dimension, experiment data seem to prove that the cultural differences lie in the fact that the collectivism oriented cultures such as Japan and China may favor interdependent face while individualism oriented cultures such as the U.S.A. and other Western cultures seem to favor independent face in their social interactions.

In the West, people tend to be an independent, autonomous, isolated, and unique self. Geertz (1975) describes, a Westerner "as a bounded, unique, more or less integrated motivational and cognitive universe, a dynamic center of awareness, emotion, judgment, and action organized into a distinctive whole and set contrastively both against other such wholes and against a social and natural background". Western individualism oriented culture requires "construing oneself as an individual whose behavior is organized and made meaningful primarily by reference to one's own internal repertoire of thoughts, feelings, and action, rather than by reference to the thoughts, feelings, and actions of others" (Markus and Kitayama (1991).

According to Markus and Kitayama (1991), the interdependent face predominates the Eastern cultures and some collectivism oriented cultures in the West, because the self is intersects with others. Or the self exists in the intersections of overlapping selves or in relation with others. In social interaction, it is not the independent self but the interdependent self that most likely underlie the people's behavior. It is the self-in-relation or self-in-context that serves as social mechanism regulating people's behavior in their interpersonal relationship.

Many research data highlight the fact that where interdependent face or self-construal predominates, conformity will be more emphasized and where independent face or self-construal predominates, conformity will be less emphasized. Jia Yuxin and his colleagues found that the Chinese are very much concerned with social appropriateness. Whether their behavior is appropriate or not to the situation in their speaking and writing is regarded as most important in their social interaction. And more often than not they prefer indirectness in their communications in their daily interaction. In contrast, Americans often prefer direct and confrontational style of speaking and writing.

In the collectivism oriented Chinese cultural context, face serves both as an end and means in realizing or building up harmonious relationship, which is the ultimate goal of the society. As an end, it stands as a moral code for the accomplishment of virtue of man and woman, which each member of the society strives for so as to become a person of complete virtue. In this way, *miànzi* or face is the ideal goal for each member in the society to reach in the cultivation of manhood and womanhood. Therefore, people fear the losing face (丢脸) as it may likely lead to the loss of, in different degrees, the quality of manhood or womanhood (丢人). As a means, it serves as reward or sanction or simply as "*a substitute for strict legislation regarding duties and rights and obligations among men*" (Cheng; 1986). In this sense, *miànzi* or face, helps people to build up good character and establish good interpersonal relationship, which in turn leads to social harmony. In whatever sense, face in the Chinese context is moral, relational and social.

3.1.2 The Chinese Indirect Facework Strategies vs. Americans' Direct Facework Strategies in Conflict Negotiation and Resolution

Conflict is a well-nigh inevitable part of relationships in our lives. All of us experience conflict in our lives one kind or another. It occurs in intimate and non-intimate relationships. We all probably know clearly that conflict is an emotionally laden, face-threatening experience. However, seldom do we know that conflict negotiation and resolution in different cultures involves different face-saving, face-enhancing and face-attacking strategies and in managing and resolving conflict, though both indirect and subtle and direct and explicit facework strategies are used, some cultures may emphasize indirect facework strategies and some cultures may emphasize direct facework strategies. We tend to assume that, like the concept of face, faceword strategies adopted by Chinese and American cultures in negotiating and resolving emotional and relational conflict also differ.

According to Jia Xuerui's case studies, the differences in face negotiation in negotiating and resolving conflict may in general be illustrated in the following diagram.

Table 2 Differences in Negotiation and Resolving of Conflicts in Chinese and American Cultures (Jia, X.R. 2008, p.114)

	Chinese Culture	*American Culture*
Cultural Orientation	Collectivistic / Relational	Individualistic
Face Orientation	Other face and mutual face concern	Self-face concern

(to be continued)

	Chinese Culture	*American Culture*
Attitude to Conflict	A threat to relationship	Involvement with others
Relationship	Interdependent	Independent
Facework Strategies	Indirect face strategy	Direct face strategy
	Implicit, third person's help, process oriented, (rhetorical) question	Explicit, outcome-oriented
	Non-verbal nuances and subtleties to signal meaning	Fewer non-verbal behavior to signal meaning
	low illocutionary clarity (intuition and tacit understanding)	High illocutionary clarity
	Forbearance, avoiding, obliging conflict style	Competitive, dominating, aggressive, challenging conflict style

The clear distinction in negotiating and resolving conflict between the Chinese and Americans seem to have to do with the differences that exist in their cultural attitude towards conflict.

The Chinese who are harmony or relationship or connection oriented in general hold a negative attitude towards conflict. To the Chinese, conflict is a threat to interpersonal rapport and interpersonal relationship or connections. Being in conflict means one's relationship or rapport and affiliation are facing danger. Hence, conflict should be avoided at all costs. Once conflict, or dispute, occurs, it should be settled, preferably, without direct confrontation.

To many Americans, conflict may not necessarily be the opposite of rapport or affiliation. According to Tannen (1990: 291–292), being in conflict may mean being involved with each other. Although it is true that many of them are more comfortable using language to express rapport, many of them are more comfortable using it for self-display. The situation is really more complicated than that, because self-display, when it becomes part of a mutual struggle, is also a kind of involvement or bonding. Conflict may be valued as a way of creating involvement with others. So, to many Americans conflict is not a threat to relationship or connections. It is the necessary means by which relationship can be negotiated, so much so that it is to be accepted and may even be *sought, embraced, and enjoyed* (Tannen 1990: 150). As a result, direct facework strategies, even confrontation and aggression are often preferred.

4. China English as Cultural Identity and Carrier of Chinese Cultural Value

4.1 China English as Carrier of Chinese Cultural Values

Social processes are symbolic processes but that symbols have meaning only in relation to cultural and social context. Our point is cultural and social identities are largely established and maintained through communication. Therefore, to understand issues of social reality, social change, and social and cultural identity and how they affect and are affected by cultural, social, political, and ethnic boundaries or division we need to gain insights into the communicative processes by which they arise. Gumperz (1982) argues that "Where communicative conventions and symbols of social identity differ, the social reality itself comes subject to question. On the other hand, however, both talk and social reality are part of and serve to maintain an ideology which takes on a historical life of its own."

The situation at present is that Anglo-American English has been considered as standard English. However, this so called standard language "hides an underlying diversity in values and discourse conventions" and "these conventions have long been dismissed as nonstandard language practices" (Gumperz, 1982). Today's world situation is changing and in the present world linguistic, interactional, and discourse conventions which persist are facing pressure to standardize, and they have in fact forced a reevaluation of their cultural, social and legitimate communicative significance. After all, they act out the cultural values and identities of the speakers and they constitute social and cultural reality.

Up to now, a considerable number of papers have explored the rules, norms or conventions that underlie the use of English as a lingua franca in the Chinese cultural context. These papers provide evidence for the fact that the rules, norms, and conventions that operate in the use of English in many situations in the Chinese cultural context are to different degrees different from those that operate in interactions in the western cultures and they hence may serve as markers of the Chinese social realities, as well as social and cultural identity.

This variety of English used by the Chinese is generally called *China English*, which develops from both internationalization and indigenization of Anglo-American English. It has the native-speaker based world English as its core system but integrates with Chinese symbolic systems that underpinned with the Chinese cultural values, hence distinguishing itself from Anglo-American English with its unique Chineseness at the linguistic level such as the phonetic, lexical, syntactic as well as pragmatic level such as pragmalinguistic, sociopragmatic, discourse conventions, and stylistic modes of communications and so on.

China English is a standard variety of English used by competent Chinese speakers of English and serves both linguistic and socio-cultural functions for communications between the Chinese and the world community at large.

Culture nurtures language and no language is able to survive if taken out of its cultural environment. China English is no exception. As carrier of Chinese culture and a hybrid of internationalization and nativization of English, China English is a highly productive carrier of Chinese culture and society. Symbolic process is fact is a social process as mentioned earlier, looked at in this light, in general, the China English both as symbolic and social process largely bears or carries the following cultural values and social meanings (Jin Huikang, 2003; Song Li & Jin Huikang, 2006):

(1) geographic references
(2) historical references
(3) social and institutional references
(4) political references
(5) ideological references
(6) folk culture references

As can be seen from the above rather limited list of descriptive terms, English is used for every aspect of life in China. This is of great significance for both China and the international community, because China and the world need to enter one another's world in their pursuit of peace and further development. Without China English, communication between China and the world is almost impossible today.

4.2 Sociolinguistic Conventions of China English as Cultural Identity

Symbolic processes are social processes, people use linguistic symbols to create sociolinguistic or pragmatic conventions or norms in their social or communicative processes. The conventions or norms are signals of interpersonal relationship and they are in fact signals of membership or cultural identity. We tentatively imply here where communicative conventions (including interaction and discourse conventions) differ, the social and cultural realities themselves become subject to question. That is, communicative conventions are social and cultural reality. They are part of and serve to maintain the ideology that makes the cultural identity of a person.

The Chineseness of China English is not only exhibited in what it represents but also in how it represents cultural and social processes. And what is more, cultural identity relies on linguistic symbols to establish (sociolinguistic or pragmatic) conventions that are significantly distinct. Although built on an educated variety of English, China English has proved to be distinctively different at many levels of the symbolic system, including phonetic lexical, and syntactic phenomenon at the linguistic level and sociolinguistic or pragmatic and discoursal conventions or what is called the level of language use. The Chinese speakers of English are first and foremost socio-cultural beings. Whatever language they use, they will think and behave like Chinese. The Chinese language and conventions and values that are encoded in the language that they have acquired early in their socialization process will stubbornly persist when they come to speak English or other languages.

Sociolinguistically or pragmatically speaking, China English represents Chinese social conventions, cultural values and identity. The pragmalinguistic and sociopragmatic performances of Chinese English speakers are often found to be different from those of other English speakers. This fact is, more often than not, a socio-cultural matter rather than a pure linguistic one.

Sociolinguistic or pragmatic rules are defined by cultural conventions or norms which are underpinned by cultural values and they in turn reflect those constraint values and norms. In this sense, sociolinguistic or pragmatic performances in interpersonal communication are social realities, cultural and social identities, as well as the enactment of values. As people from the same culture have a shared knowledge of social norms for proper conduct, many cultural stereotypes are based on how a cultural group realize their speech behavior.

What identifies a group of English speaking people as American or Chinese, British or Australian, is not only the accent, choice of word, but also the way these people use words to realize everyday speech or pragmatic functions. In other words, sociolinguistic behavior is one of the significant markers of the speakers' cultural identity. Among members of a culture, there are shared rules of conduct in realizing speech behavior. In spite of the fact that many Chinese English learners can speak English fluently, it is, however, unavoidable and inevitable that they tend to transfer Chinese sociolinguistic and pragmatic conventions or rules to the use of English in face-to-face interaction. The fact is that "transferred behaviors" are even recurrent among competent Chinese English speakers including advanced learners, teachers, and professors. The discussion in this paper that deals with pragmatic and sociolinguistic use is not limited to spoken language or oral communication. The rules and norms that regulate oral communication also define how written messages are produced and interpreted.

5. The Emergence and Construction of Individualistic Identity through Communication in China today

Fortunately, today, some scholars have successfully studied from sociolinguistic perspective how a great number of people, particularly the young people have constructed their new cultural and social identity and their style through active appropriation of linguistic resources since the economic reform and open-door policy were adopted in China.

Jia Xuelai and Jia Yuxin followed throughout four years the steps of a famous Chinese soccer star in his journey towards the establishing and construction of a new individualistic identity in China.

This study, applying a sociolinguistic approach to the study of intercultural communication, examines and analyzes the emergence and construction of the individualistic identity in today's China. It examines and analyzes how the newly emerging ideological discourse which makes up the component of the individualistic identity enters into a space of intercultural or intracultural communication in the process of which the emerging individualistic identity mobilizes linguistic resources in its competition and negotiation with the traditional ideology to assert and reassert and claim its right, entitlement, and identity and eventually establish itself.

The data analysis of this paper concludes with the following points:

1) The author agrees with and reinforces the idea that identity derives from cultural and social context and is established by self and others. Identity constitutes an integral part of communication. It emerges, and is developed, established, and constructed through communication.

2) The individualistic identity is emerging and developing in today's China due to economic globalization and the establishment of the free market, and the Western influence, etc. in China. The emergence and establishment of the individualistic identity is accomplished through long years of dialogue and negotiation with the well-established traditional discourse.

3) The individual identity may be similar to the individualistic identity. However, it may also be different in many aspects from the individualistic identity in the West.

4) The newly emerging individualistic identity may adopt sort of communication patterns unique to its culture and at the same time it may adopt what is called universal cultural patterns across cultures.

The point that new identities are constructed through linguistic resources China today also finds expressions in Zhang Qing's PhD dissertation "Chinese Yuppies" (unpublished).

In her dissertation, Zhang Qing successfully studies how Chinese yuppies, a new professional group working for foreign businesses that has emerged since the economic reform and open-door policy of Chinese Mainland in the late 1970s, construct their style and social identity through active appropriation of linguistic resources. She journeys through various theories in sociolinguistic variation, gender-related variation, linguistic market, style and identity while giving critiques of the existing theories and past studies, which leads to her new approach of thinking about and analyzing linguistic variation data. Gender differences are also considered and discussed in the analysis of Chinese yuppies' linguistic variation data with elucidation of social history of linguistic variables and social identities.

Her initial hypothesis that "patterns of linguistic variation are related to the interaction between the various constraints and opportunities which the yuppies face in the international business sector and their active appropriation of linguistic resources to construct a Chinese yuppie style and identity" is successfully proved. She finds out that the yuppies use Beijing Mandarin variants significantly less than the state professionals and that they adopt the full tone from non-Mainland varieties, which she dubs as a "deterritorialized" variety of Mandarin. Another finding is that gender difference is mild among the state professionals but dramatic among the yuppies. Female yuppies overwhelmingly lead in the use of the new Mandarin variety.

6. Differences in Concept of Self and Self-Expressions in Chinese and American Cultures

As mentioned earlier, in our sociolinguistic framework, culture is used as an explanatory variable to account for why people in different cultures behave the way they do. In the following we just use the concept of self and self expression in Chinese and American cultures as a variable to explain why differences in interaction occur.

Philosophically speaking, among others, the Chinese and Americans' sociolinguistic conventions or norms are also consistent with the concept of self in terms of interpersonal relationship in these two cultures. Cross-culturally speaking, the differences in interaction and discourse organization styles and self-expressions can be attributed to the differences in the concepts of the Eastern self and the Western self and their self-expressions.

The concept of self is not something we are born with. It doesn't develop in a vacuum, either. It is not until we begin to interact with others that we achieve any sense of self at all. Self is part of the social world which we live in. It is not only something we have but also something given to us by society. The self cannot be differentiated from the nexus of social relationship in which the individual participates. We become aware of who we are, based on our relationships with others.

The Chinese or Confucian self is different from the Western view of self as it is basically conceptualized in relation to others in society. It is social and relational in nature and it is just this relational and interdependent self that lies underneath the Chinese behavior including face behavior and renders it just as relational and interdependent. In essence, the Chinese self is more a self in relationships and less a self in isolation than that in American culture (Scollon 1991). Asians are therefore more or less considered to be seeking harmonious relations, in which self is downplayed or depreciated.

In the Chinese context, "人" or a human being is perceived as a social being, firmly rooted in the nexus of relationship. Relationship is inseparably an aspect of the self. The ideal of manhood or of the fine quality of a human being is defined in the Chinese character as "仁" (BENEVOLENCE), which is a homophone of the word "人" (HUMAN BEING), which, etymologically the combination of the Chinese ideographic characters of "人" and "二" (meaning TWO), literally means two persons. In fact the Chinese culture is embedded in the way Chinese characters are formed. Deducing from the formation of the character "仁", we may have the following ideological ideas underlying the Chinese concept of self.

The Chinese characters (the written forms of the Chinese language) are believed to be a conceptual systems as each of the basic Chinese characters indicates the basic cultural and philosophical meaning. The most important and fundamental concept is *characterized* by the character 仁 (*rén*) which is composed of the graph for human being and that for the number TWO. This throws light on the social nature of human being. We may have the following interpretations of this concept:

- Self is conceptualized as in relationship of two interdependent persons or a collective self.
- Self is identified in relation to others or as relational, focusing less on the isolated self and more on the relational self, less autonomous and more obliging and accommodating to others. Stated differently, relationship is part of self or self is part of relationship. Or simply, self exists in relations.
- Self cultivation and establishment is accomplished in the realization of benevolence, which stands for the ideal manhood specified on the basis of (kinship) relationship. The achievement of good relationship / harmony is the ultimate goal of self-cultivation and establishment. However, the individual self can never achieve the ideal personhood alone as 仁 stands for the relationship between two interdependent persons.
- Self or an individual resides and survives in the nexus of social relationships, in the judgment and approval or disapproval of others. Therefore, the Chinese are very particularly sensitive to situations and what to say and how to say in the society.
- Others or the group one belongs to in social interaction are often more important than the individual self. On many occasions, what one says seems to be less important than who says to whom and how.

The notions suggested by the formation of this Chinese character has a profound implication for cross-cultural communication. It is not only the hierarchical power relationships that operate in interpersonal interactions. According to Scollon and Scollon (1995), the most crucial point for the Chinese is that Confucian self consists of participation in these (and many other) social relationships. One is oneself to the extent one enacts his or her part of such relationships. In the Confucian or Chinese sense of self, one is more a self in human relationships, and less a self in isolation. Godwin Chu notes, "A self of this nature is not highly assertive, but seeks to accommodate (and oblige too, the author) others and in return receives enduring social support" (1985: 259, quoted in Scollon and Scollon and Kirkpatrick 2000: 144). Influenced by Confucian ideologies such as 仁, 义, 恕, etc., the concept of persons is defined in terms of context. In Jia Yuxin's paper (unpublished), he starts with the explanation of the concept 义 to trace back how the Chinese traditionally conceptualize *self* and how the concept *self* is connected to the concept 仁 or 人 (human beings) as a whole. He considers that the Chinese concept of human beings is a process of self-realization, a process starting with self-cultivation to the realization of moral integrity, which is what 仁 all about.

This social nature of the conception of human beings as a whole, as well as the conception of self results in contextual orientation in social interaction in Chinese culture. And this orientation distinguishes the Chinese communication from the Western communication in many ways. For example, to establish harmony, the Chinese tend to be other-oriented and prefer to be obliging and accommodating to others in their communication. This leads to, for example, the use of appropriate words and speech and the ability to adjust to various situations and relational positioning is a gift to a person. Confucius taught people to be prudent and cautious in speaking as he believed that "what a man of complete virtue cherishes is cautiousness of every action." Confucius also advised his disciples to be sensitive, obliging, and empathetic to audience and to be modest in speaking and behavior as well as in appearance. Speaking skills function as a lubricant to the interpersonal system. Appropriate use of such skills will help one create a desirable social network and bring personal advantage to those who employ them in Chinese culture which emphasizes relationships, human emotion (rénqíng), and face needs. Such a preference for skilled speaking certainly paved the way for Chinese indirectness and implicitness in communication, since it requires one to have the ability to use words effectively to create desirable situations and achieve harmonious relationships. So much so that the self-expression in Chinese culture is the expression which is not part of the self but the relationship with others. That is, self-expression is the enaction of his/her part of relationship with others.

7. Further Study

In general, in the study mentioned above, more attention is paid to the examination and analysis of communication at the cultural level. According to Schwartz, (1994) and Bond, et al., (1999), more attentions should be paid to beliefs, attitudes, and behavior that are related to individual differences in values priorities. At the same time, when proposing culture as the construct of situations, we should further study the relationship between interactional conventions and situational factors and how they operate in the process of communication in given situations. On the whole, more work and efforts are needed to bring together the notions of values, maxims, situation, script, communicative conventions in order to provide a coherent approach to the study of (intercultural) communication (Bond, et al, 1999).

References

Blum-Kulka, S. & House, J. (1989). Cross-cultural and situational variation in requesting behavior. In S. Blum-Kulka, J. House & G. Kasper (Eds.), *Cross-cultural Pragmatics: Requests and Apologies* (pp. 123–154). Norwood: Ablex Publishing Corporation.

Blum-Kulka, S., House, J. & Kasper, G. (1989). (Eds.). *Cross-Cultural Pragmatics: Requests and Apologies*. Norwood: Ablex Publishing Corporation.

Bond, M. H. (1988). Finding universal dimensions of individual variation in multicultural studies of values: the Rokeach and Chinese value surveys. *Journal of Personality & Social Psychology* 55: 1009–1015.

Bond, M. H., Zegarac, V. & Spencer-Oatey, H. (1999). Culture as an explanatory variable: problems and possibilities. In H. Spencer-Oatey (Ed.). *Culturally Speaking: Managing Rapport through Talk across Cultures* (pp. 27–40). London: Cassell Academic.

Bourdieu, P. (1973). Cultural reproduction and social production. In *Knowledge, Education and Cultural Change*. R. Brown, (Eds.). London: Tavistock.

Brown, P. & Levinson, S. C. (1987). *Politeness. Some Universals in Language Usage*. Cambridge: Cambridge University Press. Originally published as *Universals in Language Usage: Politeness Phenomena*. In E. Goody (Ed.) (1978). *Questions and Politeness: Strategies in Social Interaction*. New York: Cambridge University Press.

Chang, H. C. (2005). On Chinese indirectness: a multi-dimensional exploration. Paper presented at the International Conference on Language, Culture, and EFL Teaching, Harbin, China.

Chang, H. C. & R. Holt. (1994). A Chinese perspective on face as inter-relational concern. In S. Ting-Toomy (Ed.). *The Challenge of Facework: Cross-Cultural and Interpersonal Issues* (pp. 95–132). New York: State University of New York Press.

Chu, G. (1985). The changing concept of self in contemporary China. In Marsella, Anthony J. George DeVos & Francis L. K. Hsu (Eds.). *Culture and Self: Asian and Western Perspectives*. New York: Tavistock Publications.

Gao, G. & Ting-Toomey, S. (1998). *Communicating Effectively with the Chinese*. Thousand Oaks, CA: Sage Publications.

Geertz, C. (1975. On the nature of anthropological understanding. *American Scientist* 63: 47–53.

Goffman, E. (1967). *Interaction Ritual: Essays in Face-to-Face Behavior*. New York: Anchor Books.

Grice, H. P. (1975). Logic and conversation. In P. Cole & J. Morgan (Eds.). *Speech Acts*, Vol. 3 of *Syntax and Semantics*. New York: Academic Press.

Gu, Y. (1998). Politeness and Chinese face. Lecture given in the Department of Linguistics, University of Luton, Summer 1998.

Gudykunst, W. B. (Ed.) (2003). *Cross-cultural and Intercultural Communication*. Thousand Oaks: Sage Publications.

Gudykunst, W. B. (2003). Cross-cultural communication: Introduction. In W. B. Gudykunst (Ed.), *Cross-cultural and Intercultural Communication* (pp. 1–5). Thousand Oaks: Sage Publications.

Gudykunst, W. B.. L. Stewart & S. Ting-Toomey. (1985). (Eds.). *Communication, Culture, and Organizational Processes*. Beverley Hills, CA: Sage Publications.

Gumperz, J. J. (1982). (Ed.) *Language and Social Identity* (p. 3). Cambridge: Cambridge University Press.

Hall, E. T. (1976). *Beyond Culture*. New York: Doubleday.

He, Z. X. (2000). A New Edition of Pragmatics. Shanghai Foreign Languages Publication Press.

Hofstede, G. (1980). *Culture's consequences: International differences in work-related values*. Beverly Hills, CA: Sage.

Honna N. (2005). *English as an International Language*. Tokyo: コンテンツワークス株式会社.

Hsu, F. (1981). *Americans and Chinese: Passage to Difference*. Honolulu: University of Hawaii Press.

Hu, H. C. (1944). The Chinese Concept of Face. *American Anthropologist*. 46, 45–64.

Jia, Y. X. (2005). The Chinese concept of face and face negotiation involved in conflict resolution. In N. Honna (Ed.). *English as an International Language (pp. 251-271)*. Tokyo: コンテンツワークス株式会社.

Jia, X. R. (2006). *The Chinese Indirectness. Americans' Direct Interaction and Discourse Organization Styles: A Contrastive Study of Communication Conventions in the Management of Relationship*. (Doctoral Dissertation, unpublished).

Jia, X.R. (2008). *A Comparative Study of Chinese and American Communication Styles*. Harbin Institute Publication Press.

Jia, W.S. (1997). Facework as a Chinese conflict-preventive mechanism: a cultural discourse analysis. *Intercultural Communication Studies* 7:1 43–62.

Jin, H.K. (2003). *China English*. Foreign Language Teaching and Research Press.

Kim, Y. Y. & W. B. Gudykunst. (1975). (Eds.). *Theories in Intercultural Communication*. Newbury Park, CA: Sage.

Kroeber, A. L. & Kluckhohn, C. (1952). *Culture: A Critical Review of Concepts and Definitions* (Vol. 47, No. 1). Cambridge, MA: Peabody Museum.

Leech, G. N. (1983). *Principles of Pragmatics*. London: Longman.

Li, X. S. & Jia, X. R. (2004). Face negotiation in conflict resolution in the Chinese context. M *Intercultural Communication Studies 13* (1): 29–35.

Li, X. S. & Jia, X. R. (2006). Why don't you speak up?: East Asian students' participation patterns in American and Chinese ESL classrooms. *Intercultural Communication Studies* 15 (1): 192–206.

Lim, T. S. (1994). The structure of face and the determinants of face needs in Korea. *Korean Journal of Journalism and Communication Studies 32*: 207–247.
Lim, T. S. (1994). Facework and interpersonal relationships. In S. Ting-Toomy. (1994). (Ed.). *The Challenge of Facework: Cross-Cultural and Interpersonal Issues* (pp. 209–229). New York: State University of New York Press.
Lim, T. S. (2003). Language and verbal communication across cultures. In W. B. Gudykunst (Ed.). *Cross-Cultural and Intercultural Communication* (pp. 53–71). Thousand Oaks: Sage Publications.
Lustig, M. W. & Koester, J. (1999). *Intercultural Competence: Interpersonal Communication across Cultures*. New York: Addison Wesley Longman, Inc.
Markus, H. R. & Kitayama, S. (1991). Culture and the self: implications for cognition, emotion, and motivation. *Psychological Review 98*: 224–253.
Matsumoto, Y. (1988). Reexamination of the universality of face: politeness phenomena in Japanese. *Journal of Pragmatics 12*: 403–426.
Schwartz, S. H. (1994). Beyond individualism / collectivism. New cultural dimensions of values. In U. Kim, H. C. Triandis, C. Kagitcibasi, S. C. Choi & G. Yoon. (Eds.). *Individualism and Collectivism: Theory, Method, and Applications* (pp. 85–119). Newbury Park, CA: Sage.
Scollon, R. (1991). Eight legs and one elbow. Stance and structure in Chinese English compositions. Paper presented at International Reading Association, Second North American Conference on Adult and Adolescent Literacy, Banff.
Scollon, R. & Scollon, S. W. (1995). *Intercultural Communication: A Discourse Approach*. Cambridge: Blackwell Publishers.
Scollon, R., Scollon, S. W. & Kirkpatrick, A. (2000). *Contrastive Discourse in Chinese and English — a Critical Appraisal*. Beijing: Foreign Language Teaching and Research Press.
Song, L. & Jin, H. K. (2006). China English, *Asian Englishes*. N. 2, 2006.
Spencer-Oatey, H. (1999). (Ed.). *Culturally Speaking: Managing Rapport through Talk across Cultures*. London: Cassell Academic.
Spencer-Oatey, H. (1999). Introduction: Language, culture and rapport management. In H. Spencer-Oatey. (Ed.). *Culturally Speaking: Managing Rapport through Talk across Cultures*. (pp. 1–5). London: Cassell Academic.
Spencer-Oatey, H. (1999). Rapport management: A framework for analysis. In H. Spencer-Oatey. (Ed.). *Culturally Speaking: Managing Rapport through Talk across Cultures*. (pp. 7–26). London: Cassell Academic.
Tannen, D. (1990.) *You Just Don't Understand*. New York: Ballantine Books.
Ting-Toomey, S. (1985.) Toward a theory of conflict and culture. In W. B. Gudykunst, L. Stewart & S. Ting-Toomey (Eds.). *Communication, Culture, and Organizational Processes*. (pp. 71–86). Beverley Hills, CA: Sage Publications.
Ting-Toomey, S. (1988). Intercultural conflict styles: A face-negotiation theory. In Y. Y. Kim & W. B. Gudykunst. (Eds.). *Theories in Intercultural Communication*. (pp. 213–238). Newbury Park, CA: Sage.
Ting-Toomey, S. (1999). *Communicating across Cultures*. New York: The Guilford Press.
Ting-Toomey, S. & Cocroft, B. A. (1994). Face and facework: Theoretical and research issues. In S. Ting-Toomy (Ed.). *The Challenge of Facework: CrossCultural and Interpersonal Issues*. (pp. 307–339). New York: State University of New York Press.
Weinreich, Uriel. (1953). *Languages in Contact: Findings and Problems*. New York: Linguistic Circle of New York.
Wolfson, N. (1989). *Perspectives: Sociolinguistics and TESOL*. Cambridge: Newbury House Publishers.

Young, L. W. L. (1982). Inscrutability revisited. In J. J. Gumperz. (Ed.). *Language and Social Identity*. (pp. 72–84). Cambridge: Cambridge University Press.
Zhang, Q. (2004). Chinese Yupies. (Ph. D. Dissertation) Unpublished.
何兆熊. 2000. 新编语用学概要. 上海：上海外语教育出版社.
何兆熊主编. 2003. 语用学文献选读. 上海：上海外语教育出版社.
胡文仲主编. 1999. 跨文化交际面面观. 北京:外语教学与研究出版社.
贾雪睿、李晓石. 2001. 汉英语篇逻辑模式对比分析.《外语学刊》第4期.
贾玉新. 1997. 跨文化交际学. 上海：上海外语教育出版社.
金惠康. 2004. 中国英语. 外语教育与研究出版社
孔宪倬主编. 2002. 北京大学英语专业学生优秀作文选. 北京:北京大学出版社.
束定芳主编. 2001. 中国语用学研究论文精选. 上海：上海外语教育出版社.
孙骊评析. 2000. 全国大学生英语作文竞赛获奖作文集. 上海：上海外语教育出版社.
王本华. 2002. 实用现代汉语修辞. 北京:知识出版社.
王秋海主编.1999. 美国大学生作文选. 北京:世界知识出版社

7

Cultural Identification, Cultural Identity and Communication

CHEN Ling
Hong Kong Baptist University, China

PAN Shiwen
Guangxi Normal University, China

Abstract: Cultural identification and cultural identity describe two different but related concepts. The concepts refer to two interrelated sociopsychological processes constructed and manifested through communication. In this essay, we discuss the interrelation and distinction between the cultural identification and cultural identity. The focus is on their construction, expression, or communication.

Cultural Identification

As a type of identification, cultural identification is internal to an individual. From a sociopsychological point of view, identification is a phenomenon where one cannot separate oneself as an entity from the environment or from part of it. The environment may be another individual, a collective of individuals, a physical location, or a combination of any or all of these or just the idea of them. One entity is identifying with another when boundaries between the two become blurred or indistinct. This ambiguity of boundaries may be between two entities, between attributes or properties of two entities or between one entity and attributes/properties of another. Identification with another is not necessarily in totality or entirety and, yet, no less intense, nor is the object of identification necessarily something substantive. Indeed, identification can be "grounded in fantasy, in projection and idealization" (Hall, 1996, p. 3) and be the stronger because of this.

Similarly for cultural identification, when a person identifies with a culture, there is boundary ambiguity between this individual and a particular cultural environment, or between this individual and some parts of that cultural environment. The individual is bound to this culture and is part of it. Thus, cultural identification is characterized by a conscious or not so conscious state of mind or, rather, a state of heart, whereby there is a strong, insuppressible desire or wish to be recognized and accepted as a member by a target culture. There is also a feeling of belonging to that target culture and, thus, being part of what that culture represents. To identify with a culture is to resonate with the culture, in part and / or in whole, to be emotionally, almost involuntarily and inextricably attached to that culture.

Cultures differ in the degree to which there are boundaries between an individual and the environment he or she is in. Still, a culture stipulates how to draw the lines between self and others. This, however, is a topic for another time. What we discuss next is expression or manifestation of cultural identification.

Expression of Cultural Identification

Being an internal state of affairs, cultural identification is rather personal and private, and subjective, which may be shared to become intersubjective and public, and be recognized, acknowledged and identified. This transformation of the internal state to an external one is communicative in nature and necessary for it to be a social process. Some even argue that cultural identification is a discursive process of construction (e.g. Hall, 1996). Communication of cultural identification displays the internal state in verbal or nonverbal ways and takes many forms. A most common expression of cultural identification is for one to hold oneself in such a way as to be deemed behaving as a member of a culture in question by others who are members of that culture. Cultural identification is the communicative process in which individuals or groups behave in ways that mark them out as belonging to a certain target culture. One walks, talks, and holds oneself in ways that are expected of everyone in the culture under the circumstance. In other words, one does not stand out, or attract notice by other members, as behaving differently. Cultural identification, in a sense, expresses in social conformity at the most mundane and fundamental levels. All the routines that one performs in a day, getting up at certain hours, dressing and feeding in certain ways, going to work and exchanging greetings with those one encounters, addressing certain others in certain ways, all are expressions of one's identification with a target culture rather than with some other culture. These routines are communicated to and also understood as such by others inside and outside the target culture.

Cultural identification may be seen in demanding others to also behave in culturally appropriate ways. When deviation in behavior by others evokes displeasure, resentment or an urge to correct and / or sanction the deviant, such feelings are often driven by cultural identification. This reaction is because deviation communicates difference and separation of identity, which contradicts what cultural identification is, or the feeling of being part of a culture. At the same time, the displeasure, resentment, and the desire of rectifying the deviation express and communicate a desire to belong to and be part of an integral culture. To maintain integrity of one's culture and, thus, the oneness of oneself by association, one needs to keep the culture the way one thinks it should be. One does so by correcting the deviation and by drawing the line between what is and what is not one's culture. Seen in this light, such matters as the request for using the native language properly, the sense of social propriety, and the like are all individual or collective expressions of cultural identification. This is the same force that is behind the demand for cultural adaptation of prospective members, such as immigrants. Cultural identification, then, is a phenomenon propelled by a force for cultural convergence, for homogeneity and for similarity. It involves a relationship between a part and a whole, the longing of a part toward the whole concurrent with the demand by the whole on the parts.

Cultural Identification and Cultural Membership

Although cultural identification is often a natural outcome of the individual's socialization, i.e., one naturally identifies with one's native culture, it may also be a product of conscious choice. The latter is seen in those who, for one reason or another, turn their back on their native culture and adopt another culture as their own (Kim, 1996). There are also circumstances when individuals embrace and identify with more than one culture with equal or varied intensity. Regardless, expression of cultural identification often corresponds to the individual's cultural membership status. Put it another way, it is reflection of the stage of socialization or acculturation. For nonmembers or new members of a culture, who are not or not yet completely socialized or acculturated, cultural identification is more often expressed in behavioral terms in more ostensive ways. When one has an interest in learning the language of the target culture, in interacting with native cultural members, in knowing about the cultural rituals, in getting involved in local social events, in keeping up with the domestic current affairs and community activities, one is communicating cultural identification. These and many similar expressions, each on its own, may indicate a simple curiosity or a personal interest, but combine to express an unmistakable desire to be accepted and to belong. However, the sincerity of the desire is a different matter, while the presence of such a desire is not a necessary condition.

For members native to a culture or to seasoned members who are well socialized or acculturated, cultural identification may be more of a matter of emotional reaction. To cultural members in this category, behavioral aspects are a matter of routine completely taken for granted. Behavioral practice is part of their personhood as an unquestioned cultural member, who knows the cultural way and who, in a way, represents the culture. These members are so totally at one with the culture that the culture is firmly rooted in their identity as part of whom they are. The feeling of being inextricably connected to one's culture, to its past, its present and its future, and to the honor and disgrace it experiences even when it does not concern one personally, is the ultimate expression of cultural identification. Cultural identification is expressed when one is proud of the achievements of fellow countrymen, outraged by the wrongs done to them, frustrated at the potential social harms that follow as consequences of their actions, and saddened by their losses or setbacks. It is communicated when one joins in the cheers, participates in protests, goes to demonstrations, and signs petitions, all in the name of one's culture or cultural group. Communication of cultural identification, as mentioned above, is communication of a relationship between the individual and a culture in the context of the culture in question.

Cultural Identity

A closely related concept of cultural identification is cultural identity, referring to a process against the background of cultural identification. The two are related in such a way that there is no cultural identity without cultural identification. On the one hand, unlike cultural identification, cultural identity involves placement of an individual, in comparison to others, in the map of cultures, by the individual himself or herself or by others. As such it involves a relationship of the individual with self or, in the latter case, a relationship of the individual with the society, i.e., social ascription. On the other hand, like cultural identification, cultural identity is also an internal affair (Devo, 1993). It is one of the many identities that constitute the core of the individual, the essence of what makes one who one is. Also like cultural identification, cultural identity is, thus, in need of an external outlet, to be expressed or communicated, be known, and be recognized, or accepted.

As cultural identity may originate from the individual concerned or others around, it involves two parties and is a more complicated process than is cultural identification, which involves only the individual in question. To make matters more complicated still, the second party in the process may be from one's own culture or from other cultures, while the ascribed cultural identity may or may not correspond with the cultural identity that one avows. The complication is significant, in a communicative sense, if not a sociopsychological sense, for it deals with intercultural matters, directly or indirectly (Belay, 1996). When the ascription is inconsistent with the avowed identity, negotiation or contestation follows until one version is recognized and confirmed. Communication of cultural identity, including presentation, negation, and contestation, may also take many forms and be done in many ways. Choice and use of language and paralanguage in communication are common nonverbal ways of cultural identity expression. Choice and use of terms and vocabulary, and of conversational topics, are important verbal means to communicate cultural identity.

Language and Cultural Identity

Each language carries identity traits of the speakers. It enables people to obtain information common to a particular social group. This is especially true about a minority language that has had little contact with other languages. A language can thus serve as an identity marker that differentiates one group from the rest and may evoke identity stereotypes of those who have come in contact with this group. These cultural stereotypes are cultural identity information that is ethnical, territorial, socio-economical or professional. The linguistic features pertaining to a particular variety of the language significantly help people to identify its speakers. For instance, a conversation in French on a New York Street may inform passers-by of visitors from French-speaking Quebec or France. Shanghainese heard on the streets of Beijing informs passers-by that the speakers originally came from Shanghai or its neighboring counties. Other identity information associated with the social group is then evoked.

However, a more prestigious language, like English, may entertain a vast population with diverse cultural backgrounds, and the linguistic cues themselves may not portray cultural identities of its speakers as accurately as those of a minority ethnic language does. The greater the size of this membership group, the greater the difficulty in associating the language with the identities of all its speakers. As a 'favored' language is normally widely used and learned as a second language or used as a lingua franca in a multi-lingual society, it cannot define a clear geographical border to confine its increasing number of speakers. The influx of new members from other cultural and linguistic groups has made each language less pure than it used to be. The cultural identities of its speakers could be so complex that they are not readily reflected by the language itself. Under this circumstance, other linguistic and extralinguistic sources may help present the identities of the speaker.

Identifying through Language Choice

Individuals in various cultures are in a constant struggle to identify themselves in different social contexts. In reality, the society has given an individual a variety of identities and he or she may simultaneously belong to social groups of different cultural heritage. An individual's sense of cultural identity could be so complex that he or she may assume each of the identities at different times.

Language sometimes is an effective means to convey cultural messages and people learn to portray themselves by using languages at their disposal. One common strategy employed by individuals is that they consciously alternate or choose languages appropriate to portray themselves in a particular social context.

In a dominant but hostile culture, to favorably identify oneself is a necessity that is decided by situation rather than personal free will. An ethnic identity could be a stigma in one culture while a source of pride in another. For example, the identity of a Mainland Chinese used to be stigmatic in Hong Kong society, thus a Chinese multilingual would normally speak Cantonese or English instead of Putonghua, the latter being associated with negative stereotypes of poverty, ignorance, ill-mannered, etc. However, inside China, where the negative stereotypes are non-existing, the same speaker may choose Putonghua for better communication and appropriate identification. The languages thus mirror individuals' varied self-images in different settings.

In a society where a minority identity does not normally bring up the benefits to its members that a dominant one does, individuals who strive for positive social identities to enhance their self-esteem may intentionally choose to give up the minority identity and language. In the long run, the migration of speakers from the minority cultural groups to the dominant cultural and linguistic group threatens the very existence of the minority culture and language.

However, not all minority cultures and languages are so ill-fated. In places where ethnicity and diversity are valued, or where programs are underway to revitalize minority cultures and languages, people are not so eager to assimilate to the mainstream culture and language. In Hawaii, the language immersion programs have attracted both natives and outsiders to rehabilitate the Hawaiian Polynesian culture. In Norway and Finland, speakers of the minority languages of Sami and Kven think it an advantage to show their ethnic identities. Speakers of these minority languages do not need to intentionally cover up their identity traits, but instead they feel proud to identify themselves as cultural and linguistic minorities (Fishman, 1999).

Speech Accommodation as an Identifying Process

Speech accommodation is another strategy that a speaker employs to show identification and to achieve communication efficiency. Speech accommodation is a social psychological process in which an individual negotiates a cultural identity by emphasizing linguistic and stylistic similarities or differences. By doing so, the individual either departs from or draws near to the target group. The range of strategies can be discussed mainly in terms of convergence and divergence.

Speech convergence has been discussed as an effort to accentuate linguistic similarity between the speaker and listeners when the speaker seeks to be identified as an in-group member. This linguistic similarity could be phonological, lexical, rhythmic, syntactic, and stylistic. Convergence usually occurs in one direction, yet it could also be bi-directional; i.e., speakers may accommodate to each other at the same time that they both like to show closeness to or esteem of their interlocutor. When two people meet, they tend to sound more alike in their language, accents, and style (Giles, 1977). In New York City, speakers of the two major Mandarin varieties, i.e., Putonghua and Taiwanese Guoyu, show a tendency to converge to the other variety of Mandarin. The more willingness one shows to understand and accept the speakers of the other Mandarin variety, the more linguistic changes he or she is likely to make towards the other variety of Mandarin.

When linguistic modification occurs, value and status connotation of the speaker is thus betrayed. Convergence to the other's speech style is a direct result of the speaker's favorable and cooperative sentiment toward the receiver. It enables the receiver to perceive an optimal sociolinguistic distance from his or her own speech patterns.

Language divergence, on the other hand, stresses an identity difference from the listener whose cultural identity the speaker does not like to associate with. Divergence may be considered as a relatively rare tactic employed by a speaker. A speaker of a dominant language and culture tends to differentiate linguistically from the listeners who have a relatively lower social or cultural status. In Beijing, for instance, indigenous Mandarin speakers rarely compromise standard Putonghua to any other Mandarin varieties nor do the average Beijing residents have the same zest to learn another Chinese dialect as other speakers do to converge to standard Putonghua.

Divergence may be employed by speakers of a minority language and its culture. There are occasions on which a speaker of a minority language may dissociate from his or her receivers by accentuating identity differences. The speaker could belong to a less privileged social group that has been taken advantage of politically or economically by the receiver group in the past. The speaker may either realize his or her speech convergence is not welcome or want to manifest the identity gap with the receiver.

Identity Crisis and Language Death

The last century witnessed vigorous nationalist movements and advances of science and technology, especially communication technology. All this has greatly helped the rapid spread of a few chosen standard languages and cultures in various countries and regions. Cultural dominance has caused heavy damage to ethnic minorities whose members became assimilated to the dominant culture by giving up their traditional cultural and linguistic heritage. This identity crisis is vividly described in an account of the Ugong speakers in Thailand:

> When David Bradley, the language researcher, went in search of this endangered Tibeto-Burman language in western Thailand, a number of Ugong speakers he encountered felt so shamed to admit to being able to speak Ugong, but they claimed Thai identity instead. He was then directed by them to villages where other Ugong descendents were living, but there the regular Ugong speakers refused to speak Ugong to him as they also claimed Thai identity (Fishman 1999).

Great majorities of human languages are spoken by relatively small numbers of people and have no official status. They receive little institutional support for maintenance and development. The past century recorded the greatest number of these languages disappearing from the Earth. The endangered languages in the world nowadays are encountering a bleaker prospect for their mere existence in the new century that glorifies IT (Internet Technology) and globalization. Each year, dozens of endangered minority languages are dying out when their last speaker passes away. Opportunities go mainly to speakers of the national language standard; people from a minority group normally do not want to admit their minority background nor do they want to stick to their mother tongue.

China has faced similar challenges ever since Mandarin was officially promoted as the language standard last century. The popularization of Putonghua has virtually changed the majority of younger generations of Chinese minorities into bilinguals of Putonghua. As Putonghua has been successfully made the lingua franca of the nation, many of the regional minority language variations have gradually lost speakers or disappeared totally. Take Tungusic language varieties in northern China, for example; about half a dozen of these languages are currently hanging on the edge of extinction. With new generations from these languages joining the mainstream Han culture, their speaking populations have shrunk to sizes from a few dozen thousand to a few thousand. It is doubted that this group of minority languages, together with many others in other parts of China, will have the luck to survive in this new century.

Conclusion

Cultural identification and cultural identity, in conclusion, are processes in which members of cultures interact and communicate among themselves and with one another in efforts to orient themselves, position themselves, and find a footing for themselves in the cultural space. Every encounter activates anew the same processes, as occasions of intra- and intercultural communication. It is contestation and negotiation of identity and brings something different and something new to the individual member and to the collective of members that constitute the cultures involved.

References

Belay, G. (1996). The (Re)construction and negotiation of cultural identities in the age of globalization. In H. Mokros (Ed.), *Interaction & Identity* (pp. 437–456). New Brunswick, N.J.: Transaction Publishers.

Devo, G. A. (1993). A psychocultural approach to ethnic interaction in contemporary research. In M. E. Bernal, & G. P. Knight (Eds.), *Ethnic Identity: Formation and Transmission among Hispanics and Other Minorities* (pp. 235–270). Albany, NY: SUNY Press.

Fishman, J. A. (1999). *Handbook of Language and Ethnic Identity*. New York & Oxford: Oxford University Press.

Giles, H. (1977). *Language and Social Identity*. Cambridge: Cambridge University Press.

Hall, S. (1996). Introduction: Who needs identity? In S. Hall & P. du Gay. (Eds.) *Questions Of Cultural Identity* (pp. 1–17). London: Sage.

Kim, Y. Y. (1996). Identity development: from cultural to intercultural. In H. Mokros (Ed.), *Interaction & Identity* (pp. 457–469). New Brunswick, N. J.: Transaction Publishers.

8

Hierarchical Manifestation in Intercultural Communication*

KIM Kun-ok
Chung-Ang University, Korea

Abstract: Korean culture is shaped around the concept of hierarchy. Cultural values and belief systems in interpersonal relations, and language behavior, are heavily on the side of hierarchical emphases rather than horizontal equality. Entities, animate or inanimate, abstract or concrete are stratified into a more-or-less prestigious hierarchy. Confucianism and its emphasis on hierarchy in Korean culture have produced unique intercultural language behavior. Koreans distorted use of English results from their conceptualization (conception) of this prestige hierarchy. In this study, Koreans' misapplication of hierarchy-conscious language behavior to their use of English is explored at the phonological, morphological, syntactic, and semantic levels.

Introduction

Humans in any society belong to several different social groups and thus play different roles assigned to them. As they interact in different roles, their status changes to some extent from one group to another social group. For each role they play, not only do they ascertain their status, in most cases without any dispute or conflict, but also they act on the norms that are considered as appropriate within a given socio-cultural context. However, some of these status-roles that are institutionally assigned to them can be more or less prestigious in the hierarchical structure of a

---

* This research was supported, in part, by The Chung-Ang University Research Fund.

particular social group.

No society has ever had an entirely egalitarian social structure. Inequality and injustice have always been present, although their forms and degrees vary considerably from one society to another. In the case of Korean society, one of the most salient cultural aspects pertains to the hierarchy of relationships, which is omnipresent in almost every sector of the society. The interconnections between norms for social behavior and the hierarchy of relationships are so highly institutionalized and conventionalized that their aftermath in most circumstances is taken for granted.

Hierarchical Structures

An individual's stand in the social structure (system) of a hierarchy is determined by complex criteria. Major factors that categorize roles and status into hierarchical structures are sex, age, rank, position / location, and direction. Consequently, in any given socio-cultural context, those involved must classify self and others using those factors in selecting appropriate social and linguistic behavior. For example, there is a strict hierarchy. Males are higher in the hierarchy than females. Consequently, sons, especially first-born sons, have the privilege of a better and a higher education. They will inherit a greater portion of the family's fortune, despite the fact that it is illegal in a court of law. Korean parents believe that sons are name-bearers and they are assigned to perform the rituals dedicated to their deceased ancestors. In earlier times, it was a common practice for Korean girls to toil in order to support their older brothers through higher education. The female is often taken for someone who brings bad luck, one finds that restaurants or taxis in Korea would not let in a female as their first customer (Lee, 1987).

There exists a hierarchy among parts of the body. The head, the highest part of the body, is the highest point in the hierarchy and consequently, it is treated with the utmost concern. Consequently, such gestures as snatching someone's hat or slapping someone's face would be considered far more offensive and insulting than any other form of physical assault. Given this hierarchical framework, the foot is regarded as a degraded object. Therefore, for a wife to wash her husband's feet is still considered as the foremost service that a wife can give her husband after a long day's work. In earlier times, a servant would warm his master's rubber shoes on his chest until the master showed up (Lee, 1987).

Among the parts of the head, the hair is given special status and is regarded as a personal and sacred domain. Consequently, most females do not have their hair cut until death. Understandably, having one's hair cut by force is still regarded as the worst offence and shame one could endure in Korean culture. During the military regime in the 1970s wearing long hair for males was condemned as anti-Korean and unethical. In those days young men with long hair had to go through the ordeal of having their hair cut on the street by the police. Hence, Koreans get their head shaved in order to protest or to demonstrate dissension. The practice is also very popular among Korean congressmen, college students, and athletes. Recently, one hundred and eleven actors in Korea had their heads shaved to show disagreement against the government's policy on the screen quota system.

A prestige hierarchy applies even to the hands. The right hand is the higher on a hierarchy than the left and it is reserved for sacred work, whereas the left had is assigned meager tasks and dirty work. On this basis, most Korean parents do not tolerate left-handedness among their children. Therefore, foreigners would find it rare to encounter Koreans who write with the left hand. A hierarchy also exists among the fingers: the thumb is the highest in this hierarchy and is assigned the privilege of being Number One.

A hierarchical structure even exists among geographical directions. The east is given higher status than the west. The morpheme meaning 'east' is used to indicate righteousness, fairness, prestige, and honor; while it is natural for the term 'west' to be used as an indication of degradation.

Koreans' imposing importance on the head and the right hand is described in the story of Park Jiwon's *Yulkhaiki*. In the story, Yulkhaiki's servants met an unexpected storm. To avoid impending embarrassment, they all took off their clothes to cover their hats, which covered their precious heads. The scene is unimaginable: they started running in all directions, stark naked, as their precious right hands were holding their hats on their heads, while their left hands were down below covering the disgraceful (unmentionable) parts of the body.

When a seat is offered to Koreans, most of them would avoid sitting down in the middle since the center seats are reserved for the ones that are superior in the hierarchical system. In a study on the efficiency of using three-seat benches in the park, it was found that a person would always sit on one of the sides, leaving a space in the middle. When another person shares the seat, he or she always takes the other side, leaving the space in the middle vacant. Consequently, the author of this study argues that three-seat benches do not serve an optimal purpose for Koreans and, therefore, urges its discontinuation and proposes the manufacture of two-seat benches instead (Lee, 1995a, b, c).

Nonetheless, some of the norms by which Koreans play roles can be viewed as archaic and groundless from the standpoint of contemporary Korean youth. Some of them are regarded as radical with respect to traditional hierarchies and they react against existing social norms and order. However, there is only limited evidence that this kind of reaction occurs.

Notwithstanding the viewpoints of contemporary Korean youth, the concept of a prestige hierarchy has been to a large extent cherished and nurtured in the Korean social and linguistic context that spans a cultural history of five millennia, a remarkable and breathtaking gesture of sustained cultural and language behavior.

It is argued in this study that the grammatical structure of a language tells us a great deal about the ways in which speakers view and experience the world. At the same time, the ways in which they view the world are also mirrored in the use of language.

In the following section, reflections of Koreans and their concept of hierarchy when using English are explored at the phonological, morphological, semantic, and syntactic levels.

Phonological Level

In English, the initial consonant or consonant clusters of a syllable or word are variable; however, to speakers of Korean, sounds or phonological segments have a hierarchical structure. They are inclined to categorize the consonants in a higher position in the hierarchy than vowels. As a result, Koreans are likely to phonologically restructure a polysyllabic word with a consonant. That is, given a choice, Koreans place a syllable boundary beginning with an initial consonant for each syllable, as can be seen in the following examples of nativization: *television* > te-le-vi-sion and *secondary* > se-con-da-ry.

The emphasis on the initial consonant of a syllable, in some cases, creates syllables lacking codas. For example, when followed by syllable with onsets. Koreans are likely to say [aulet] for *outlet* and [nan nau] for *not now*.

When a Korean polysyllabic word is spoken in isolation, each syllable of the word receives an equal amount of stress. In principle, it can be argued that no hierarchy of stress exists among the parts of speech. That is, stress, such as word, phrase and sentential stress syllable is not a phonemic property in Korean but rather an emphatic feature of the language. In English, in most usage, a noun phrase such as *a very pretty lady* can have four levels of stress.①. The word *lady* receives the primary stress, the adjective *pretty* the secondary stress, the adverb *very* the tertiary stress, and the article *a* no stress. However, when the Korean counterpart of this phrase is simply read or recited, no discernable stress differences can be detected. In a conversational setting, though, Koreans

---

① The author acknowledges that any part or word within an English sentence can be stressed, especially in spoken English.

place stress in a reversed order. The primary stress is on the word *very*, the secondary stress is on the word *pretty*, and the tertiary stress is on *lady*. This reversed order of stress pattern can be explained in two ways: the position of a word, and the novelty of its information.

In the Korean socio-cultural context, 'position' is a very significant barometer of the hierarchical structure. The front or the top is in a higher place in the hierarchy than the rear or the bottom. In the case of a noun phrase, which consists of an adverb, an adjective, and a noun in that order, for instance, the word in the fronting (leading, initial) position receives the primary stress, second word the secondary stress, and the third word the tertiary or not stress at all. To be more specific, in the process of nativization whatever comes first, that is, whatever is in the leading position receives focal stress.

Most English sentences have the order of agent-action-object. Contrary to English, Korean sentences have the order of agent-object-action. This can be interpreted that new information precedes old / given information in the Korean sentence structure. For example, in the phrase *a very pretty lady* (remember that the use of indefinite articles is not a common practice) Koreans regard the word *lady* as the oldest information, whereas the word *very* is the newest information. That is, the word with focal stress or a phrase containing such stress conveys the new information, while the rest of the sentence conveys the given information. Hence, in the Korean language structure, the word that intensifies or modifies is given higher status within the hierarchy than the word modified, and thus receives the focal stress.

Once I watched a movie entitled *2 Die 4* on television and wondered what the original title was. It took me a while to figure out that the original tittle was *To Die For*. This hilarious misrepresentation may have resulted from Koreans' placing stress on the first word, followed by non-stressed 'Die' and then another-stressed word 'For.' This 'first come first serve' language attitude beguile Koreans into producing *Miss Communication* for *miscommunication*, *PRESIDENT Kim* for *President Kim*, and *Inn accessible* for *inaccessible*. Instead of *Thank you very MUCH*, Koreans will *thank you VERY much*.

Morphological and Lexical Level

Korea's hierarchy-conscious culture is best reflected in the kinship terms that are classified with reference to categories such as sex and hierarchy of relationship. Kinship terms in the Korean language are especially interesting on two accounts. In the first place, many of them indicate not only the hierarchy of relationships, but also the gender of the person concerned. In the second place, and as a result, certain equivalent generic kinship terms such as *parents* in English cannot be found in the Korean vocabulary.

English kinship terms, such as *parents*, *grandparents or siblings*, do not indicate sex or hierarchy of relationships. They are merely terms for people in those categories. However, in the Korean language, there are no generic terms for *parents*, *grandparents*, *brother* or *sister*. These kinship terms in Korean require specification of hierarchy as well as sex. Therefore, the term parents in the Korean lexicon is spelled out as either *father-mother* (and always in that order) or *father and mother*. By the same token, brother and sister relationships in Korean are bound up not only with differences in gender but also with the birth-order of the person involved. For example, if two girls are sisters, one is the elder sister and the other is the younger sister. Naturally, there exist kinship terms indicating *older brother*, *younger brother*, *older sister*, and *younger sister*, respectively, in the Korean lexicon.

Thus, factors such as gender and hierarchy of relationships of the people involved must be indicated in most of the kinship terms in Korean. For example, males precede females even in linguistic contexts. As a consequence, a term such as *mother-father* is neither a legitimate nor permissible word in the Korean lexicon. When Koreans are asked how many members there are in the family, they are most likely to replay, *I have father-mother, one older brother, one younger brother, one older sister, and one younger sister*; whereas speakers of English simply say, *I have both parents, two brothers and two sisters*.

In addition, speakers of Korean employ kinship terms for use as address forms. For example, Korean speakers address adult males and adult females as *uncle* and *aunt*, respectively, even though they are total strangers to them.

A hierarchical structure at the morphological level is best illustrated in the nativization of English by Koreans. The following examples show how Koreans apply their hierarchy-conscious language practices to the coinage of English words and phrases, by clipping, shortening, abbreviating, and blending, irrespective of the internal structure of the English words. The results are outrageously unique amalgamations of Korea's hierarchical tradition and foreign-loan words.

As presented earlier, rules for the nativization of English are quite simple. Koreans have a disposition to create syllabic structures with initial consonants, and they take an initial syllable or the beginning of a word as the nucleus of a given word or phrase. The following are examples of how English words are nativized by Koreans:

> running shorts > running; permanent > perma; air conditioner > air con; supermarket > super; bargain sale > bargain; apartment > apart; stainless steel > stain; television > teli; captain > cap; Seoul Grand Park > Seoul Grand P; headphone > head; (Burberry's) trench coat > burberry; General Electric Company > general; pineapple juice > pine juice; night club > night; frying pan > fry pan; ball-point pen > ball pen;

after-sale service > after service; white-out (correction fluid) > white; sharp pencil > sharp; skin softener > skin; contact; handy phone > hand phone; remote control > remocon.

Syntactic Level

As the association between sentence structure and semantics becomes closer, it will be almost impossible to draw a clear-cut distinction between them. Thus, the points that are made in the following syntactic and semantic levels intersect and overlap each other.

In Korean, nouns assume a morphological shape according to their roles in the sentence. Roles are manifested in the grammatical case suffixes of the noun. For example, the subject takes a suffix indicating the nominative case, and the object takes a suffix indicating either the accusative or the dative case. Since Korean has suffices indicating cases, such as instrument, possession, causative, source, etc., Koreans are likely to say, *With what did you write* instead of *What did you write with?*

In the case of the English language, a word can be negated by prefixing a negative prefix to the word, as in *unattractive*, or by adding a negative particle or modifier word, as in *not attractive* or *hardly attractive*. However, in the Korean language, the negative counterpart is added to the end of the word forms. Thus, the negating element is most likely followed by the affirmative part. As a consequence, Koreans generally prefer *I think that he is not telling the truth* rather than *I don't think he is telling the truth*.

Generally speaking, the doer or the agent is higher in the hierarchy than the recipient or patient in the Korean social context. The English sentence *My mother is looked after by a social worker* is both grammatically and semantically legitimate. However, Koreans are most likely to avoid a passive construction and use the active voice, as in *A social worker looks after my mother*. In the paucity of the passive, the subject does not reflect the relative status of the person concerned.

In contrast, 'the one that undergoes' an action, in some linguistic contexts, is higher in the hierarchy than 'the one who performs the action. In conjunction with the paucity of the passive, Koreans are inclined to say *My baby changed the diaper*, *I cut my hair*, *I repaired my car* and *I dry-cleaned my mink coat* rather than their English counterparts — *My baby got her diaper changed*, *I had my hair cut*, *I had my car repaired*, and *I got my mink coat dry-cleaned*.

In Korean culture 'means' are regarded as a higher virtue than 'ends.' Consequently, in the structure of the Korean language, the conditional clause precedes the main clause. A majority of Koreans would say *If it rains I'll stay*, or *If I were rich I'd buy you a car*. The English sentence such as *I will not do it if it rains* carries a nuance of insolence for Koreans, since the negative conclusion comes before the condition.

In the cultural context of the hierarchy concept, it may sound implausible that Koreans do not syntactically mark the degree of remoteness in time or in reality. There are no distinct grammatical structures for real and unreal conditionals. Koreans would say *If I have money, I'll buy you a car* conveying the message, either *If I have money, I will buy you a car* or *If I had money, I would buy you a car*. The English sentences *If I have money, I will buy you a car* and *If I had money, I would buy you a car* carry approximately the same degree of remoteness in reality.

Based on the foregoing, it can be argued that the temporal point of an event is in a higher part of the hierarchy than the state or outcome of the event. That is, what is important for Koreans is whether the particular event occurred or not. Consequently, the temporal point of an event or an occurrence plays an important role in the conception of tense. For example, in terms of tense, the reference to 'death' of a particular person can only occur in the past tense. The literal translation of the English sentence *My grandfather is dead* is anomalous semantically as well as syntactically. Koreans would say either *My father was dead* or *My father died*.

Semantic Level

Korean culture is often referred to as a "culture of self-effacing." In the self-effacing culture, "I" is rarely recognized as an individual, but is mostly identified and appreciated as a member of a certain social group. Therefore, Koreans avoid referring to himself or herself or the first person singular pronoun. This results in constructions such as *Would you like to meet our wife* instead of *Would you like to meet my wife* (Kim, 1991).

Korean culture, in which males are in a higher place of status within the hierarchy than females, has yielded unique language practice that places males before females. This practice is observed only in a high-profile context. Consequently the Korean *Gentleman and Ladies* when addressing an audience corresponds to *Ladies and Gentlemen* in English.

The Korean language has very interesting deictics (deixis) involving directions. Take, for example, the pair of verbs *come* and *go* which is direction specific in English. The verb come is restricted in a way that it indicates direction toward the speaker and go indicates direction toward anyone or anything other than the speaker. Similarly, the pair of verbs *bring* and *take* function in exactly the same way. As a result, Koreans would say *I'll go and see you soon* instead of *I'll come and see you soon*.

Since the declarative is in the hierarchy higher than the imperative, Koreans might opt to take the imperative as an offense or insult. Visitors to Korea can easily find notices such as *Let's keep off the grass* and *We would appreciate it very much if you do not smoke here, since this is a public place* instead of *Keep off the Grass* and *No Smoking*. Therefore, the sentence *It would be wiser for you if you would take a leave at this moment* perfectly conveys a message of urgency in nativized Korean English.

The English language has a number of relational opposites that exhibit the reversal of a relationship between items. There are pairs of words in English, such as *put on* and *take off* or *turn on* and *turn off*, that are in a symmetric hierarchy, both semantically and syntactically. However, in the Korean culture, *to add* is in a higher hierarchy than *to subtract* or *to take off*. In the Korean lexicon, for example, the verbs *to wear* or *to put on* is expressed by different words depending on which part of the body is involved. For examples, *to wear a hat*, *to wear glasses*, *to wear clothes*, *to wear mittens*, *to wear a belt*, *to wear shoes* all have different verbs equivalents to the English forms for *wearing*. However, there is only one verb in Korean that serves the act of taking off. Instead of *I am now wearing my gloves*, Koreans would *say I am now putting my gloves onto my hands*. It may sound absurd, but Koreans do use expressions like *to put my gloves onto my hands*.

As stated earlier, Korean sentences have the order of agent-object-action. That is, the object precedes the verb. The Korean expression equivalent to the English SOS is 'saram salyo.' The word 'Saram' means "person as an object" and 'salryo' is a verb form meaning "to save." Thereby, the one-to-one translation of this sentence is "person save," which should be interpreted as either *Save me*! or *Rescue me*! The following episode expresses the essence of the Korean concept of hierarchy;

A Korean man was drowning in the water and he was shouting for help at the top of his lungs. When a passerby stopped and asked him "What?" The drowning man had the time and breadth, only enough for a two-syllable word. So when he surfaced on the water, he answered "saram," since the word "saram" (indicating me) precedes the verb "salyo" (meaning *save*). The exchange between the passerby and the drowning man was carried out three times and finally the drowning man gave up and said "get lost!" and drowned. In retrospect, the passerby murmured "*Gee! Wasn't he supposed to say 'salryo' instead of 'saram'?*," and continued on his journey.

Conclusion

In modern times, the state of technology may be taken for granted. Another thing that is taken for granted is the emergence of the global village and the lessening of geographical distances that separate us. The global village, it is argued, no longer poses a barrier to intercultural understanding. However, intercultural communication should not aim at the convergence of cultural and linguistic divergences, but rather their divergence. What we need to do is recognize different cultures and in the process come to appreciate and understand them. This attitude towards cultural diversity should be nourished and allowed to co-exist harmoniously. For these reasons, We must foster an understanding of why cultural miscommunication occurs. Only by understanding diversity can we achieve the ultimate goal of successful intercultural communication.

References

Kim, K-O. (1991). What causes communication problems between English speakers and Korean speakers? *Intercultural Communication Studies I*: 2, 117–136.
Lee, K-T. (1987). *Consciousness Structure of Koreans*, Volumes 1–4. Seoul: Shinwonmoonwhasa.
Lee, K-T. (1995a). *Consciousness Structure of Koreans*, Volumes 1–4. Seoul: Shinwonmoonwhasa.
Lee, K-T. (1995b). *Consciousness Structure of the Common People*. Seoul: Shinwonmoonwhasa.
Lee, K-T. (1995c). *Consciousness Structure of the Scholar*. Seoul: Shinwonmoonwhasa.

9

Intercultural Communication and Global Democracy: A Deweyan Perspective

SUN Youzhong
Beijing Foreign Studies University, China

Abstract: Understanding intercultural communication as the exchange of information between individuals of different cultural backgrounds, theorists of this field are primarily concerned with mapping the patterns of cultural similarities and differences, revealing the effects of cultural factors on the process of intercultural communication, sorting the components of intercultural communication competence, and seeking the formulas to remove misunderstandings and breakdowns in intercultural communication. By contrast, American philosopher John Dewey takes a moral approach to define communication as individually distinctive members of a community sharing experiences, participating in joint activities, cooperating in free social inquiry and the distribution of its conclusions, transforming habits, and ultimately making life rich and varied in meanings. This Deweyan moralist perspective can be applied to situate intercultural communication studies in the context of a globalizing world where global democracy, though far from playing any noticeable role in regulating international relations at present, should ultimately rule if humankind is to have a future and continue to thrive. From a Deweyan perspective, the construction of a global public in a global democratic community is the foundation or precondition of global democracy. This is where intercultural communication, understood not only as practical means to satisfy immediate individual, organizational and national needs in intercultural contexts, but also as consummate ends or an intercultural democratic way of life, could make its unique contribution.

It is generally agreed that we live in an age of globalization. But when did it begin? Some historians might point at October 24, 1946, when the first grainy, black-and-white photos of our earth were taken from an altitude of 65 miles by a 35-millimeter motion picture camera riding on a V-2 missile launched from the New Mexico dessert. Clyde Holliday, the engineer who developed the camera, wrote in *National Geographic* in 1950, the V-2 photos showed for the first time "how our Earth would look to visitors from another planet coming in on a space ship." That was the first time human beings saw with their own eyes their habitats on separate continents as one globe. Other historians would trace further back to the late 19th century when the second industrialization coupled with Western imperialism incorporated all the countries of the globe into one world market system. But that first stage of modern globalization slowed down during the period from the start of the First World War until the third quarter of the twentieth century. According to the official observation of the United Nations (2002), the advanced stage of globalization emerged during the fourth quarter of the twentieth century. Another historical point of time in the development of globalization might be August 6, 1991, when British scientist Berners-Lee posted a short summary of the World Wide Web project on the alt. hypertext newsgroup, marking the debut of the Internet age.

Obviously it is futile to try to pin down a particular date as the beginning of globalization because it did not take place within one day or one year or even one decade. It was, according to David Held (2000), "a set of processes which shift the spatial form of human organization and activity to transcontinental or inter-regional patterns of activity, interaction and the exercise of power" (p. 19). Viewed historically, globalization has undergone an accelerating evolution process over centuries on three dimensions: "1) the extensiveness of networks and connections; 2) the intensity of flows and levels of activity within these networks; and 3) the impact of these phenomena on particular bounded communities" (p. 19).

The first two dimensions indicate the growing interconnectedness of the peoples and their activities across national borders. Economically, a rising number of giant multinational corporations has led to the rapid expansion of international trade reaching unprecedented levels; at the same time, global financial flows have also grown tremendously, creating a more integrated financial system than has ever been known. Culturally, the inexorable spreading of English as the dominant language of the global society, the vigorous prosperity of international tourism, the rapid escalation of mass communication across national borders launched by the dramatic globalization of telecommunications and the booming success of international multimedia conglomerates have ushered in the birth of a global village, for good or bad. Environmentally, for the first time in world history, human beings spread in different zones of the globe have found themselves confronting a myriad of serious common problems such as global warming, transboundary pollution, desertification, resource over-consumption, etc. Institutionally and legally, the behavior of nation-states of the world is more and more constrained and regulated by various international organizations and laws (Held, pp. 20-26).

The "stretching" and "deepening" of the interactions among nations and peoples of the world have exerted far-reaching impact on the local communities and individuals around the globe. As McGrew (1997) commented:

> ... in the context of intense global and regional interconnectedness, the very idea of political community as an exclusive territorially delimited unit is at best unconvincing and at worst anachronistic. In a world in which global warming connects the long-term fate of many Pacific islands to the actions of tens of millions of private motorists across the globe, the conventional territorial conception of political community appears profoundly inadequate. Globalization weaves together, in highly complex and abstract systems, the fate of households, communities and peoples in distant regions of the globe. (p. 237)

Faced with this growing tendency of global interconnectedness, theorists of globalization have proposed various scenarios, among which five major ones are worthy of examination here, namely benevolent imperialism, nationalism, multilateralism, localism and global democracy. Benevolent imperialism advocates the use of power for the United States to shape the world according to its values. Nationalism or realism maintains that all states use their power in pursuit of their national interests, that balance-of-power politics is not only a descriptive, but also a prescriptive view of the world, that it is the duty of national government officials to defend national interests, and that accepting international constraints on the exercise of power is not only undesirable, but also dangerous. Multilateralism, sometimes called liberal internationalism, subscribes to the existing international institutions within which nation states solve global problems and resolve conflicts among their respective national interests. Localism is strongly committed to the fulfillment of human rights throughout the world, yet insists that sustainable economic development and ambitious global objectives could be achieved through national or local decision making (Jacobs, 2007, pp. 69-93).

The globalization scenario, which is the most idealistic (not necessarily utopian), most morally justified and worthy of our utmost devotion, is global democracy or cosmopolitan democracy.

Didier Jacobs (2007) defines it as "the application of key concepts of liberal representative democracy to the global level of government, which would happen incrementally over several decades by developing institutional innovations already adopted by some international institutions" (p. 94).

Daniele Archibugi (1998) defines it as "an ambitious project whose aim is to achieve a world order based on the rule of law and democracy" (p. 198). He accepts David Beetham's definition of democracy as "a mode of decision-making about collectively-binding rules and policies over which the people exercise control, and the most democratic arrangement to be that where all members of the collectivity enjoy effective equal rights to take part in such decision-making directly" (Archibugi, 1998, p. 199). He stresses the need of developing democracy within nations, among states and at the global level simultaneously (p. 216).

For David Held (2000), global democracy or cosmopolitan democracy is "a double-sided process" involving "not just the deepening of democracy within a national community, but also the extension of democratic processes across territorial borders" (p. 30). He writes, "In a world where transnational actors and forces cut across the boundaries of national communities in diverse ways, and where powerful states make decisions not just for their peoples but for others as well, the question of who should be accountable to whom, and on what basis, do not easily resolve themselves" (Held, 1998, p. 22). Therefore, in order for democracy to function in a world of "overlapping communities of fate" (Held, 1998, p. 22), new institutions and mechanisms of accountability need to be established.

For Richard Falk (1998), global democracy, just like domestic democracy, means "the accountability of those with the power of decision, participation by those who are subject to governance structures, transparency of governance operations, adherence to established procedures and rules with means for redress in the event of perceived deviance, and the advocacy of non-violence as a core value with respect to security and development policy" (p. 328).

The above normative prescriptions have set beautiful goals for global democracy; the remaining question is: how can we get there from here? Theorists have offered various road maps for democratizing globalization, for example, encouraging nation-states to extend internal democracy, reforming the United Nations, creating a global parliament, establishing an effective, accountable, international army, developing interconnected global legal system, strengthening the European Union and other regional organizations, fostering the growth of civil society, etc.[1] These solutions almost exclusively concentrate on applying democratic principles in transforming existing institutions or creating new mechanisms, ignoring the possibility that all these positive changes could never happen unless

---

[1] See Held's and Archibugi's detailed proposals in Daniele Archibugi et al., eds. *Reimagining Political Community: Studies in Cosmopolitan Democracy*, p. 25, and pp. 219–222.

something more fundamental is ready, that is, "the creation of a global perspective and values in the depths of people's hearts and minds" (Sakamoto, 1991, p.122). In the same light, David Held (1998) mentions in passing the following two "general conditions" among five as essential for the establishment of global democracy:

1) Recognition by growing numbers of peoples of increasing interconnectedness of political communities in diverse domains including the social, cultural, economic and environmental;
2) Development of an understanding of overlapping "collective fortunes" which require collective democratic solutions — locally, nationally, regionally and globally. (p.26)

The major concern of this paper is: How can we bring about this shared "recognition" and "understanding" among citizens of the world? My answer from a Deweyan perspective, to put it briefly, is: **intercultural communication**.

Why intercultural communication then? Because if we do not choose intercultural communication, we have only two other worse options, imposing or drifting. With the former, we can imagine a superpower that wields its overwhelming influence, economic, cultural and military, to impose on the citizens of the world, for hidden national interests, its provincial values often in the name of promoting universal values of democracy, human rights, peace and free trade. This imposing way of globalizing democracy goes against democratic principles and is doomed to fail democracy in the end. With the latter option of drifting, human beings submit to determinism, believing that without any human efforts to give direction and guidance, globalization will work its way out of chaos one day for the miraculous realization of global democracy. This drifting way of laissez-faire globalization has already proved ineffective and dangerous economically, environmentally and politically.

The last resort seems to be intercultural communication.

Understanding intercultural communication as the exchange of information between individuals and groups of different cultural backgrounds, theorists of this field are currently preoccupied, justifiably, with mapping the patterns of cultural similarities and differences, revealing the effects of cultural factors on the process of intercultural communication, sorting the components of intercultural communication competence, and seeking the formulas to remove misunderstandings and breakdowns in intercultural communication. By contrast, American philosopher John Dewey takes a moral approach to define communication as individually distinctive members of a community sharing experiences, participating in joint activities, cooperating in free social inquiry and the distribution of its conclusions, transforming habits, and ultimately making life rich and varied in meanings. This Deweyan moralist perspective can be applied to situate intercultural communication studies in the context of a globalizing world where global democracy, though far from playing any noticeable role in regulating international relations at present, should ultimately rule if humankind is to have a future and continue to thrive. Unlike the leading theorists of global democracy who define it as mostly a decision-making mechanism among nation-states of the world, this paper stresses, from a Deweyan perspective, the construction of a global public in a democratic global community as the foundation or precondition of global democracy. And this is where intercultural communication, understood not only as practical means to satisfy immediate individual, organizational and national needs in intercultural contexts, but also as consummate ends or an intercultural democratic way of life, could make its unique contribution.

What follows is a redefinition from a Deweyan perspective of intercultural communication in the context of a globalizing world where democracy is pursued as an ultimate good.

(1) Intercultural communication is a transactional process of knowing involving individuals and groups of different cultural backgrounds.

Epistemologically, intercultural communication can be understood as a distinctive method of knowing that requires the cooperation among individuals and groups of different cultural backgrounds. Stressing the "transactional" nature of communication, John Dewey writes, "The transactional is in fact that point of view which systematically proceeds upon the ground that knowing is cooperative and as such is integral with communication" (Dewey, LW 16: 5)[①]. Put in an intercultural context, this statement means that the involved parties of intercultural communication should respect each other as unique and equal partners undertaking a common cause of inquiry into problems concerning their common interests. It also means valuing the unique contribution each party might make to the process of inquiry. And for that reason, intercultural communication that is transactional requires the involved parties to be ready to "give and take" in the reciprocal exchanging of information and views.

In addition, the transactional nature of communication prescribes the cooperative knowing as an open-ended process. Dewey argues, "By its own processes it is allied with the postulational. It demands that statements be made as descriptions of events in terms of durations in time and areas in space. It excludes assertions of fixity and attempts to impose them. It

---

[①] References to Dewey's writings are from the collected works published by Southern Illinois University Press under the editorship of J. A. Boydston. The standard way of citing pieces in this collection is by citing the sub-collection first (i.e., *EW* for *Early Works* [1882–1898]; *MW* for *Middle Works* [1899–1924]; and *LW* for *Later Works* [1925–1953]), followed by the volume and page numbers.

installs openness and flexibility in the very process of knowing. It treats knowledge as itself inquiry — as a goal within inquiry, not as a terminus outside or beyond inquiry" (Dewey, LW 16: 5). Following this principle of "openness" and "flexibility" would help rid intercultural communication of ethnocentrism, absolutism and fundamentalism that often reduce intercultural communication into intercultural confrontation and antagonism. When intercultural communication becomes transactional, global problems of any kind blocking the way of global democracy can be investigated cooperatively and experimentally by individuals and groups of different cultural backgrounds so that rich resources of the world's myriad of cultures are pooled together and exploited to the fullest extent and various possible solutions are tried experimentally and conditions are ameliorated gradually.

(2) *Intercultural communication transforms the hardened habits of individuals and groups of different cultural backgrounds, ultimately generating one dynamic heterogeneous world culture.*

As individuals learn to adapt to their environment, they form habits. The habits thus formed may set a limit on their further learning, preconditioning what to learn as well as how to learn. This, however, happens only when individuals are isolated from communicating with one another, resulting in "a non-communicating habit" (Dewey, LW 1: 215). According to Dewey, "Communication not only increases the number and variety of habits, but tends to link them subtly together, and eventually to subject habit-forming in a particular case to the habit of recognizing that new modes of association will exact a new use of it. Thus habit is formed in view of possible future changes and does not harden so readily" (Dewey, LW 1: 215).

It is the same case with culture. When cultures are isolated and prevented from communicating with one another, they tend to ossify. By contrast, intercultural communication creates opportunities for various cultures to interact with and learn from each other, expanding the horizons of individual cultures and introducing novel cultural resources for cultural reconstruction and innovation. The increasing frequency of individual cultures interacting with each other accelerated by globalization will gradually lead to one cohesive world culture that is at the same time heterogeneous and dynamic.

(3) *Intercultural communication contributes to the forming of a global democratic community where sharing and participation are made possible for individuals and groups of different cultural backgrounds.*

Throughout his life from late 19th century to the middle of the 20th century, Dewey was never satisfied with the existing American democracy model consisting of two major parties competing against each other. He argues, "[D]emocracy is much broader than a special political form ... . It is ... a way of life, social and individual. The keynote of democracy as a way of life may be expressed ... as the necessity for the participation of every mature human being in formation of the values that regulate the living of men together: which is necessary from the standpoint of both the general social welfare and the full development of human beings as individuals" (Dewey, 1946, p.57). To be more particular, Dewey (1916) upholds two criteria to measure democracy:

> The two elements in our criterion both point to democracy. The first signifies not only more numerous and more varied points of shared common interest, but greater reliance upon the recognition of mutual interests as a factor in social control. The second means not only freer interaction between social groups ... but change in social habit — its continuous readjustment through meeting the new situations produced by varied intercourse. And these two traits are precisely what characterize the democratically constituted society. (p.101)

For Dewey, the most secure foundation of democracy is a democratic community in which social inquiry is cooperatively conducted, its conclusions freely distributed, and social institutions flexibly readjusted accordingly.

But how to bring about such a democratic community? Dewey writes, "Communication can alone create a great community. Our Babel is not one of tongues but of the signs and symbols without which shared experience is impossible" (Dewey, LW 2: 324). For one thing, communication enables individuals to share experiences and recognize common interests; for another, as Dewey put it, "Communication, sharing, joint participation are the only actual ways of universalizing the moral law and end" (Dewey, MW 12: 198). Through communication, Dewey believes, a self-conscious public is formed that would devote itself to the constant amelioration of the democratic community.

This is also true of global democracy. As some theorists point out, cosmopolitan citizens with a shared set of global values and due recognition of common global interests have to be present so that global democracy could function. The most effective way of creating such cosmopolitan identities lies in, most probably, the creation and expansion of a global public sphere or a global civil society where free communication among the global public or world citizens across cultures is guaranteed. As Dewey writes, "[Democracy] will have its consummation when free social inquiry is indissolubly wedded to the art of full and moving communication" (Dewey, LW 2: 351). The growing numbers of well-organized international conferences are good examples of such communicating communities. Other examples include nongovernmental organizations or civil society groups organized for some global public purpose. To accelerate this trend, intercultural communication research and education in the universities worldwide plays an especially significant role in inculcating in the minds and hearts of future world citizens a human identity, "multiple citizenships" (Holden, 2000, p.30) and a core set of cosmopolitan norms, laying a solid foundation for global democracy.

(4) Intercultural communication is both means and ends of global democracy.

If global democracy can be understood as a democratic community in which individuals and groups of various cultural backgrounds share interests, cooperate to solve the problems facing them, and enrich the meanings of each other's life, then intercultural communication and its "congenial objects" are objects "ultimately worthy of awe, admiration, and loyal appreciation" (Dewey, LW 1: 160-1). Dewey writes, "They are worthy as means, because they are the only means that make life rich and varied in meanings. They are worthy as ends, because in such ends man is lifted from his immediate isolation and shares in a communion of meanings." In this sense, global democracy and democratic intercultural communication are interchangeable terms.

As such, global democracy is not to be achieved within a short period of time through undemocratic means that claim to be immediately effective. Dewey maintains, "[D]emocratic ends demand democratic methods for their realization. ... [D]emocracy can be served only by the slow day by day adoption and contagious diffusion in every phase of our common life of methods that are identical with the ends to be reached ...." (Dewey, LW 13: 188) Global democracy is, therefore, an open-ended process in which intercultural communication is operated democratically on a daily basis.

(5) Intercultural communication through mass media is liable to manipulation and malfunction at the expense of public sphere.

In the early years of mass production, Dewey was far-sighted to detect the potential negative impact of mass media. According to his observation, media technologies produced by modern science had multiplied the means of modifying the dispositions of the mass of the population, which, in conjunction with economic centralization, had enabled mass opinion to be mass-produced like physical goods (Dewey, LW 13: 91). He further points out, "Aside from the fact that the press may distract with trivialities or be an agent of a faction, or be an instrument of inculcating ideas in support of the hidden interest of a group or class (all in the name of public interest), the wide-world present scene is such that individuals are overwhelmed and emotionally confused by publicized reverberation of isolated events" (Dewey, LW 13: 93). With the evolution of mass communication expanding into every corner of the globe today, all these problems of media manipulation and malfunction that Dewey was concerned about have worsened rather than disappeared. In the globalization context, international mass media have more often than not hindered the constructive communication between different cultures.

To offset the negative effects of mass communication, Dewey advocates a return to face-to-face communication. He writes, "Vital and thorough attachments are bred only in the intimacy of an intercourse which is of necessity restricted in range .... (Dewey, LW 2: 367-8)" He believes that "[d]emocracy must begin at home, and its home is the neighborly community" (Dewey, LW 2: 367-8). Unfortunately, Dewey did not live to see the birth of various kinds of new media that have the potential to increase the opportunity of "face-to-face" communication in the "virtual neighborhood." It remains a question how we can use mass media, old and new, intelligently to better promote intercultural communication and global democracy.

In conclusion, this paper has attempted to formulate a Deweyan normative version of intercultural communication conducive to the growth of global democracy. Skeptics of global democracy might simply deride it as utopian, but I share Raffaeld Marchetti's (2008) not entirely unfounded optimism:

> [G]lobal democracy is no more unrealistic today than national democracy was 200 years ago, or women's enfranchisement fifty years ago, or blacks voting in the US south just a few decades ago, or the end of the apartheid system in South Africa even more recently, if we assume the correct normative perspective. (p. 174)

References

Archibugi, Daniele. (1998). Principles of Cosmopolitan Democracy. In Daniele Archibugi et al., (Eds.), *Re-imagining Political Community: Studies in Cosmopolitan Democracy* (p. 198). Cambridge: Polity Press.
Dewey, John. (1916). *Democracy and Education*. New York: Macmillan.
Dewey, John. (1946). *Problems of Man*. New York: Philosophical Library.
Falk, Richard. (1998). The UN and Cosmopolitan Democracy. In Daniele Archibugi et al., (Eds.). *Re-imagining Political Community: Studies in Cosmopolitan Democracy* (p. 328). Cambridge: Polity Press.
Held, David. (1998). "Democracy and Globalization," In Daniele Archibugi et al., (Eds.). *Re-imagining Political Community: Studies in Cosmopolitan Democracy* (p. 26). Cambridge: Polity Press.
Held David. (2000). The Changing contours political community: Rethinking democracy in the context of globalization. In Barry Holden (Ed.). *Global Democracy: Key debates* (p. 19). London and New York: Routledge.
Holden, Barry. (2000). *Global Democracy: Key Debates*, (Ed.). London: Routledge.
Jacobs, Didier. (2007). *Global Democracy: The Struggle for Political and Civil*

Rights in the 21st Century. Nashville: Vanderbilt University Press.

Marchetti, Raffaeld. (2008). *Global Democracy: For and Against*. London and New York: Routledge.

McGrew, A. G. (1997). Democracy beyond borders?: Globalization and the reconstruction of democratic theory and politics. In A. G. McGrew (Ed.). *The Transformation of Democracy* (p.237). Cambridge: Polity Press.

Sakamoto, Yoshikazu. (1991) Introduction: The Global Context of Democratization. *Alternatives*, 16, 119–128.

United Nations Economic and Social Commission for Western Asia. (2002). Summary of the Annual Review of Developments in Globalization and Regional Integration in the Countries of the ESCWA Region.

Ethno-relativity and Multiculturalism

10

On the Multiculturalism of Asian Englishes

Nobuyuki HONNA
Aoyama Gakuin University, Japan

Abstract: English now is said to be an international language or a global language. When we say this, do we really understand what it means? Actually, it seems extremely difficult to comprehend various sorts of logical deductions stemming from the current state of the English language. As a part of its global spread, English is now here to stay as an Asian language. Asian speakers are taking advantage of this additional language and exploring new dimensions of English use, phonetically, lexically, syntactically, semantically, and of course pragmatically. This paper explores issues involved in recognizing English as a multicultural language and using it as an international language in Asian contexts. The task is challenging because we have to find ways of achieving mutual understanding while promoting intercultural differences, not eliminating them.

Introduction

English now is said to be an international language or a global language. When we say this, do we really understand what it means? This is a profoundly important question we have to ask ourselves in Japan now when the nation's 24,000 public primary schools are preparing to introduce English language teaching to their pupils of grades 5 and 6 in 2011. Actually, it seems extremely difficult to comprehend various sorts of logical deductions stemming from the current state of the English language.

English today is a unique language, formally and functionally quite different from other languages of the world. For one thing, a sizable number of countries designate it as their national, official, or working language. The concomitant result of this is that English is bound to reflect a diversity of disparate cultures. English is a multinational language and therefore a multicultural language.

Thus, from a Japanese point of view, English is not the language for us to use only with Americans, the British, or any other native speakers. Rather, English is the language for us to use with Koreans, Chinese, Thais, Indonesians, Singaporeans, and other Asians. It is the language for us to use with Europeans, Africans, Arabians, South Americans, and many others. That English has become an international language means that it has become a language for multinational and multicultural communication.

Another characteristic that is peculiar to English now is that, as the spread of English progresses, non-native speakers outnumber native speakers. There are more non-native speakers using English with other non-native speakers than native speakers using English with other native speakers or non-native speakers. Conspicuously, non-native speakers are taking advantage of this additional language and are exploring new dimensions of English usage, structurally and pragmatically. Since no language is used to its fullest extent by its native speakers, there is always much room left for non-native speakers to exploit it in their unique ways. As a matter of fact, they are using English in non-Anglo-American cultural contexts.

When Japanese speak English with Singaporeans, there is no room for American or British culture. It would be clumsy if the Japanese had to represent American ways of behavior and the Singaporeans the British version while speaking English to each other. The case is true with English conversations between Turks and Brazilians, French and Finnish people, or any other interactions that may occur on the global stage. What actually happens is that Japanese behave like Japanese and speak English in Japanese ways, and so do Thais, Malaysians, Arabians, Pakistanis, and many others respectively. This demonstrates that English now is a variegated language.

Diffusion and Adaptation

In order to grasp this English language trend, it is important that we fully understand the relation of diffusion and adaptation. If things are to spread, they must most normally mutate. For example, Italian food we enjoy in Japan is locally adjusted to attract a large clientele. Should it have happened that Italians objected to Japanese ways of serving spaghetti, this Italian cuisine would never have been as popular as it is now. We simply cannot internationalize things and ideas without having them accommodated to the customs of people who are supposed to use them for their own purposes.

This principle apparently applies to language, too. The fact is that the internationalization of English has prompted the diversification of English. The diversification is the cost of the internationalization of English. Here, it is important to recognize that English has become an international common language simply because it is being created as a culturally diverse language.

People might imagine that a common language should be a uniform language. But this is not true. A common language is a diverse language. A lot of allowances have to be made, and differences accepted. If American English standards, for example, were imposed upon all users of English, English would never become an international common language.

Many non-native speakers are learning English as an additional language. In addition to their native tongue, they want to acquire a working command of English for their own purposes. They are free to use it in their own ways. It is important to note that for most non-native speakers, the use of English is limited to a certain set of roles or domains. For native speakers, English is used in a wide range of fields in their social lives. But for non-native speakers, the situation is simply different. We use English partially in acts related to our jobs, interactions, enlightenment, entertainment, research, overseas studies, and the like. It is just one means to accomplish our objectives. We are happy if we get something done in English.

Non-native speakers generally are not expected to acquire native-speaker proficiency in English. We use our native language in our intranational domains of life. If we acquire a certain amount of English proficiency, we can significantly achieve a lot of things in our jobs or human relation acts. This means that English not only incorporates a variety of structural differences but also contains a multitude of functions. English is a multiformal language as well as a multifunctional language. In this sense, more attention should be paid to teaching English for specific purposes (ESP).

English in Asia

As such, the spread of English as a language for multinational and multicultural communication employed by an enormous number of non-native speakers shows that English is becoming more and more de-Anglo-Americanized all over the world. This creates a new role English can play in the contemporary world.

People of the 3rd World first worried invariably that if they chose English as their official language after independence, they might retain some destructive remnants of Anglo-American colonialism. Yet, while they continued using English in their own social, cultural, and linguistic contexts, they discovered that they could solve this anxiety. They have created their own varieties of English best fit for their intranational and interethnic communication.

As a matter of fact, English has become a very important language in Asia. It is a working language for intranational and international communication in many parts of the region. According to a *Newsweek* report (October 28, 1998), 350 million people speak English for various purposes in Asia, a number that is more than the combined populations of the United States and Britain, where English is a native tongue for many citizens.

In much of Asia, English is no longer a colonial import. Throughout the region, English is the language of education, culture, business and, above all, regional cooperation. English-speaking Asians claim English as their own language. Filipino poet Gemino Abad once said, "The English language is now ours. We have colonized it, too." (*Newsweek*, October 28, 1998)

This is not a political statement. This is simply a descriptive remark concerning the current state of the English language in this part of the world. Thus, students are becoming more and more aware that English is an indispensable Asian language. The likelihood of using English with other Asians motivates an increasing number of students to learn the language better.

For English language training, Vietnam, Laos, and Cambodia send their diplomats and other professionals to the Regional Language Center (RELC) of the South East Asian Ministers of Education Organization (SEAMEO) based in Singapore. These countries are preparing to play a larger role in the Association of South East Asian Nations, where English is considered the sole official language.

English schools in Singapore or the Philippines attract a huge number of students from Asia. England and America used to be the places to go to in order to learn English. But now this urge has comparatively weakened. "The best way to learn English is to go to a country where English is spoken." This is an expression Japanese students learn in the classroom. Some Asian countries are now added to a list of their destinations.

The Multiculturalism of Asian Englishes

Asian Englishes are diverse, however, with different social roles attached to the adopted language. Each country has used the language in its traditional cultural and linguistic contexts, thereby producing a distinct variety characterized by unique structural and functional features.

Proficiency levels also differ with English-as-a-second-language countries generally producing more skillful speakers than English-as-a-foreign-language counterparts.

As most Asian countries recognize English as an indispensable language for intranational or international communication, they are increasingly committed to strengthening and improving English language teaching (ELT). Most prominently, they start teaching English at the elementary school level. While primary school English is common in ESL countries, many EFL countries are following suit.

In parts of Asia where English serves as an official language and ELT expands and succeeds, people start speaking English among themselves. Wherever this happens, a set of indigenous patterns develop, a kind of patterns people find easier to handle.

The notion of one language as an independent system is only an imaginary creation. As languages come into contact, they get mingled in many interesting ways. This has become increasingly obvious in Asian English studies, where multilingual analysis is a key to significant exploration.

As such, the forms and uses of English in Asia are enormously influenced by other Asian languages. While the influence is visible in lexical borrowing, it often gets blurred in syntactic superposition. Thus, deep insight is called upon to reveal the intrusion of Chinese, Malay, and probably Tamil in the reduplication phenomenon in Singaporean English and some other varieties. Here are some examples I heard on the street in Singapore. Ho (1998) describes many aspects of these syntactic patterns:

(1) If you go to Seiyu, everything is cheap-cheap. (Taxi driver)
(2) Saturday can-can. (Reservation clerk at a restaurant)
(3) I like to wear big-big. (T-shirt vendor referring to her XL size)
(4) Play-play, no money; work-work, no leisure. Combination is better. (Taxi driver)
(5) My friend from China, she likes (to) shop-shop. (Shop clerk)
(6) Choose-choose-choose-choose-choose, but no buy. (Shop clerk referring to recent Japanese tourists)

I have another example, which was downloaded from an Internet page in Singapore:

Under the ang mo, we all live happily together, no complain.
Malaysia & Singapore is one big family in our brains.
One moment like brothers, can give and take.
Next moment we kena kicked out by the leg.
Everybody know we water no enough.
They turn off tap only we all cannot last.
They threaten us with water supply and shout "Cut! Cut! Cut!"
Aiyoh! They all think the water is one big ketupat.

But their own economy now all go bust.
Got to sell water otherwise money no enough.
I think hor maybe they don't understand us very well.
That's why relationship sometimes like heaven sometimes like hell.
I think hor, Singapore is like chili padi in a pot.

Glossary:

ang mo	red hair (referring to the British)
kena	to get
Aiyoh! :	Oh!
ketupat	boiled rice cake wrapped in a banana leaf;
hor:	particle of familiarity

In this connection, it is important to note that teachers do not teach local varieties of English in the school. They teach Standard British English in the classroom in Singapore. Singaporean English is the result of the ELT in Singapore. If people are compelled or encouraged to speak English, they do so only in the way best fit for them. The same thing can happen in countries where English is taught as an international language if we encourage our students to speak it, as we must for various good reasons. For example, Japanese speakers might begin to say:

A. 1. He has a wide face (is well known).
   2. He has a black belly (is roguish).
   3. He has a tall nose (is boastful).

It would be illogical to turn down these expressions as incorrect because these are non-native. Above all things, most Japanese learners are non-native speakers, encouraged to speak English by taking full advantage of the repertory they have, however limited it might be. It would also be hard to accept that A sentences above are incorrect while B sentences below are correct simply because they are native-based.

B. 1. He has a bitter tongue.
   2. He has a sweet tooth.
   3. He has green fingers.

Language Awareness as a Measure of Diversity Management

With this much said, I would like to address one important issue, that is diversity management. In order to enrich the multiculturalism of Asian Englishes and to ensure their mutual intelligibility and communicability, it is important we develop internationally coordinated educational programs. Most effective is the introduction of language awareness training into school curriculums of Asian countries. Teaching language awareness in Britain and Europe has proved useful for students to become conscious of the function of language in multilingual and multicultural settings. This is witnessed in papers in *Language Awareness*, a journal devoted to the issues involved, published by Multilingual Matters in the UK. In Asian countries, we should cooperate to work for similar goals in an attempt to overcome, for example, the possible inconveniences to be caused by the spread of English as a multicultural language in this part of the world.

One thing that should be included in these programs is the study of metaphors. A cognitive and expressive device human beings are generally equipped with, the metaphor relates concept X to concept Y. Human beings have a propensity to use basic and concrete experiences to understand and express profound and abstract affairs. Yet, in many countries in Asia, metaphor is considered as a technical term for literary criticism, a tool limited to analyze fiction and poetry. It is essential that we understand that *metaphoring* is an operation ordinary people employ in all domains of their daily lives based on their perception of similarities in an array of natural and social phenomena.

The body-part lexicon is a good example. People use it to refer to various affairs associated with body parts. For instance, Japanese extend the head, chest (or heart), and belly as containers, each intended for a different type of contents. Thus, the head is a container of knowledge ("He crammed everything into the head."), the chest of romantic thoughts ("He has his love for her hidden in the chest.") and the belly of emotions ("He decided to contain this conversation in his belly.").

If people are aware of the structure and the function of metaphors, they should not be confounded to hear Japanese say in English: "He is a kind of person who does not reveal his belly to his subordinates," or "I can't read his belly." If people see what metaphors are involved here, they would not have difficulty making sense of these expressions: the belly is a container the content of which this guy does not show easily for the first sentence and the belly is a container his message wherein is too obscure for me to read for the second sentence.

Incidentally, *Time* (March 22, 1999) quoted Monica Lewinsky as saying: "I know he (Bill Clinton) had remarked to me that we both had fire in our belly." If fire signifies passion in American English, as Monica reportedly said after this remark, Japanese speakers would have it in the chest (or heart), not in the belly. But if metaphorically aware, they could easily understand the difference and interpret the expression appropriately.

The story of metonymies should also be included in the study of metaphors. The knowledge of metonymies can save a lot of mis- or non-communication among speakers of different varieties of English. Japanese train conductors might say: "Don't put your face out of the window." Or Japanese housewives might say: "I am putting my neck into teaching Japanese as an international language." If the face and the neck were understood as representing the head in these cases, these expressions might be unlikely to appear incorrect, nonsensical, or illogical.

For the concepts of Asian Englishes to be put into practice, it is essential that we coordinate educational efforts on a regional scale. If we establish a basis for international cooperation and develop enlightening curriculums for language awareness in various language-related subjects, we will be able to better use English as a language for international and intercultural communication while enjoying its multicultural values.

Conformism is not a plausible way of accommodating the multiculturalism of Asian Englishes. What is needed for mutual intelligibility is intercultural literacy, of which language awareness constitutes a fundamental component.

ELT in Asia as an ODA Project

I have one more ramification to add here. If English is recognized as an Asian language, Japanese people, for example, may find themselves in a position to promote it as such in their regional cooperation efforts. There is a lot to be done to improve the socio-pedagogical environment of English communication in Asia. English language teaching in Asian contexts can legitimately be listed, for example, for official development assistance (ODA) of the Japanese Government.

I recently had a talk with an executive officer of the Japan International Cooperation Agency (JICA) over English in Asia as a possible ODA project. He first said that JICA could not concern itself with ELT in Asia because English is a British or an American language. After I explained our idea of English as an Asian language, he saw the relevance right away and expressed his willingness to consider proposals if made appropriately.

In spite of the increasing demand for English language teaching in Asian countries, the lack of qualified teachers is chronic. Can Japanese ODA funds be used for supporting teacher training programs in Asia? How about for developing better teaching / learning materials? How about for distance education? How about for use of multimedia and information / communication technologies? Japanese tax payers would agree to these expenditures only if they had a clear understanding of English as an Asian language.

Right now, there are a considerable number of Japanese volunteer teachers of English in Laos, Vietnam, or Cambodia. Most of them are dispatched there by the non-government and non-profit organizations to which they belong. According to reports, they are deeply impressed by the extent to which their students, mostly children, devote themselves to learning this language of better opportunities under the difficult circumstances of scarce textbooks and other resources.

If English is an Asian language, it becomes appropriate that Japanese and other Asian nationals take responsibility for the language, which many of us are learning as well as enriching as a means of wider communication. As I described elsewhere (Honna & Takeshita 1998), the concept of English as an Asian language is still new in Japanese educational quarters. Yet, it gets smoothly accepted into the business sectors.

Japanese business people use English as an international language in Asia more and more frequently these days. Once they recognize the legitimacy of the Asian varieties of English, they become interested in learning why Asian people speak English the way they do. To meet these demands for linguistic and cultural information, further stimulated by an ever-increasing number of inquisitive Japanese tourists visiting Asian cities, Tokyo's major publisher endorsed a project on a Japanese dictionary of Asian Englishes. Another prestigious publisher supports the international journal of *Asian Englishes* that is 14 years old now. A change in attitudes toward English among its most frequent users should very likely lend impetus to an imminent readjustment in Japan's English language teaching practice.

References

Ho, M. L. (1998). Forms and functions of reduplication in colloquial Singaporean English. *Asian Englishes 1*, No. 2.

Honna, N. & Y. Takeshita. (1998). On Japan' propensity for native speaker English: A change in sight. *Asian Englishes 1*, No. 1.

11

On Chinese Indirectness:
A multi-dimensional exploration*

CHANG Hui-Ching
University of Illinois at Chicago, USA

Abstract: The pervasiveness of the "collectivism" metaphor leads many scholars to treat Chinese indirectness as constraints imposed by relational hierarchy. While informative, this view fails to take into account Chinese cultural resources and historical background and is severely limited, as indirectness involves far more than just inhibiting one's talk. It encompass manifold forms of expression (such as analogies, poetry, and paradoxical language); performs multiple functions (such as politeness; mediating or usurping relational structure; expressing artistry; stimulating the mind); appears in mundane as well as spiritually elevated contexts; and so on. This paper analyzes Chinese indirectness from three vantage points. First, as a means of manipulation, one can use indirect language to elevate oneself by communicating competition, boastfulness, and other messages, while appearing kind and sincere. Second, encapsulated in the concept of *hánxù* are gestures of humility and respect for others, in which Chinese choose not to outspeak others and the universe. Third, as acts of linguistic artistry, Chinese engage life through critical commentary at the expense of others by means of expressive forms such as poems, matched couplets, *chengyu*, doggerel, and so on. Each facet taps a unique aspect of Chinese indirectness that can coexist, be in conflict with, or be integrated into various patterns.

---

* An earlier draft of this paper was presented at the International Conference on Language, Culture, and EFL Teaching, Harbin, China, Jan. 6–7, 2004.

Introduction

Ethnography of communication has long established that to be able to communicate effectively, one needs to have not just linguistic competence, but also know the rules of speaking as espoused by the cultural contexts in which one communicates. However, although much research has been conducted in Chinese communication (see G. Chen, 2008), scholars still fall short of in-depth understanding of their indirect communicative activities. With the pervasiveness of the "collectivism" metaphor ascribed to the Chinese, many scholars in cross-cultural communication treat Chinese indirectness as the result of the constraints imposed by social hierarchy and interpersonal connections, which consequently makes it difficult for individuals to express themselves directly and honestly. With an ultimate goal of reaching social harmony, Chinese prefer a high-context, indirect communication (G. Chen, 2001; Ding, 2006; Gao & Ting-Toomey, 1998; Samovar, Porter, & McDaniel, 2007). This view of Chinese indirectness, while informative which fails to take into account Chinese cultural resources and their historical background, is severely limited, if not distorted (Chang, 2001, 2003, in press).

Indirectness appears to be a characteristic feature of Chinese interpersonal life, and it involves far more than just inhibiting one's talk due to relational constraint. It encompasses manifold forms of expression (such as analogies, metaphors, poetry, paradoxical language), forming a genre (Bakhtin, 1986) of its own; performs multiple functions (such as politeness, mediating or usurping relational structure, expressing artistry, stimulating the mind); appears in mundane as well as spiritually elevated contexts; and so on. To give a few examples, Ma (1996) proposes four categories of "contrary-to-the-face-value" communication (CFVC), based upon internal motivation (whether the speaker aims at serving self or other) and external speech (whether the speaker says "yes" for "no," or says "no" for "yes"). Chang (2001) also points out that Chinese sense of "harmony" may only be played out at a surface level, with turbulent undercurrents — including aspersions cast on interactants, elevating oneself, and so on, all through verbal play — underneath an apparently peaceful façade. More specifically, Wang (2000) notes the profound recognition of indirection in Chan Buddhism: Applying the principle of "never tell too plainly," the Chan master uses languages that are sensibly and flexibly tailored to the needs of the situation, to evoke thought and inspire students to enlightenment.

While there are many possible routes to capture the richness of such a diverse range of indirect expression, in the following I analyze Chinese indirectness from three vantage points: as a means of manipulation; as gestures of humility and respect for others; and as acts of linguistic artistry

(Chang, in press). In addition to consulting a wide range of literature, selected real-life examples collected in Taiwan are also included to give an in-depth reading. Before we analyze these phenomena, an exploration of Chinese cultural foundations is in order.

Some Cultural Foundations

Pervasiveness of Indirectness

The pervasiveness of indirect communication can be observed from a variety of Chinese words[①]. For individual characters, there is, for example, *fěng* (讽, to satirize or to deride). For compound characters, there is *yǐngshè* (影射, use shadows to project); *fěngcì* (讽刺, to convey criticisms through veiled messages); *wākǔ* (挖苦, to criticize the other indirectly and mercilessly); or *hánxù* (含蓄, reserved). These words describe the situation, give advice, or outline attitudes, and all point toward Chinese tendency not to be straightforward in expressing what is on their mind. Between expression and concealment, such evasive expressions are used to mask what one does not want to express, while paradoxically, the mask informs others what it actually hides (Anolli, Cicert, & Giaeleinfantino, 2002a, 2002b).

A quick look at *chéngyǔ* (成语, stylized expressions that usually contain four characters) and common sayings also point to the Chinese inconsistencies between the surface and what lies beneath. In the *Book of Thirty-Six Stratagems*, for example, the sixth stratagem *shēngdōngjīxī* (声东击西, sounding the East while hitting the West) aims to divert an opponent's attention to the wrong thing. The tenth stratagem *xiàolǐcángdāo* (笑里藏刀, hiding a knife behind a pleasant smile) is used to communicate unkind messages while on the surface making their speaker appears pleasant and cooperative. The sixteenth stratagem, *yùqínggùzòng* (欲擒故纵, to capture, one must first set free) refers to the idea of retreating to advance. The twenty-sixth stratagem, *zhǐsāngmàhuái* (指桑骂槐, pointing to the mulberry tree and scolding the locust tree) is used to communicate less pleasant messages while protecting the face of interactants (von Senger, 1988).

In addition, other *chéngyǔ* such as *pángqiāocèjī* (旁敲侧击, knocking

---

[①] Here I use Chinese "words" as a general term to designate various expressions, including *zì* (individual character or 字); *cí* (word that usually combines two characters to form a complete meaning system, or 词); and phrases. While a "character" has only one syllable, a "word," as a unit of speech, may have more than one syllable and hence more than one character. A character may form a word, or it may be part of a word, particularly since some characters do not occur independently (J. Liu, 1962).

and hitting on the side); *xiánwàizhīyīn* (弦外之音, sound beyond the string); *kǒumìfùjiàn* (口蜜腹剑, mouth sweet and knife in the stomach); *yìyǔshuāngguān* (一语双关, one word with two meanings); *kǒushìxīnfēi* (口是心非, mouth "yes" heart "no"); *dáfēisuǒwèn* (答非所问, answers not relating to the question); and so on (cf. Z. Chen, 1996) aptly describe Chinese indirect styles of interaction. Even phrases such as *jìn zài bù yán zhōng* (尽在不言中, mutual understanding without words uttered) reveals the lingering feeling of something not yet finished, something that cannot be spelled out directly but must be contemplated.

Cultural and Philosophical Reasons

Chinese indirectness can also be observed from its cultural foundations. Their tendency to use linguistic forms such as metaphor, euphemism, irony, analogy, hidden words, and sarcasm, as well as convoluted styles of expression, is intimately connected to their philosophical and ontological contemplation of human life. Their preference for skilled speaking is coupled with their philosophical contemplation of reversion and further aided by the unique construction of the Chinese language — together they pave the way for Chinese indirectness. First, contrary to the widespread belief that Chinese are slow at speaking, being gifted at speech is seldom criticized and even preferred. Skilled speaking allows one to use words effectively to create desirable situations, whether for spiritual or mundane reasons, particularly in a complex interpersonal world. For example, "language," or "words," is one of the four central areas of study in the Confucian school (Legge, 1985; Mao, 1988). Confucius saw appropriate speech and the ability to adjust to various situations and relational positioning as a gift, so long as such talk does not go astray from the speaker's internal spiritual foundation and humanity (Chang, 1997).

Indeed, while the Confucian ideal is related to the refinement of one's mind, manipulating interpersonal interactions, whether through verbal or other means, has always been an important topic in Chinese philosophical and political thinking (see He, 1991; Garrett, 1993; Lu, 1998; Raphals, 1992). This focus can be observed in various Chinese philosophical texts, classics, records of history, novels, folktales, legends, drama, and literary texts, with the majority recorded about people in the Spring-Autumn period (722-481 B.C.); the Warring States period (403-221 B.C.); and to a lesser extent, the Three Kingdoms period (220-280 A.D.) (see Chan, 1963b; Fung, 1983). Due to turbulence in political environments, this period produced many great speakers and provided numerous examples of eloquence. Times were chaotic, so that they spoke and wrote during a period when "the rulers [got] carried away with the eloquence of *yan* speech, discourse," when the society as a whole synonymized wisdom with "subtlety in discourse" (*Han Feizi* XIX.49.3) ... (Y. Liu, 1996b, p. 40)

Given the omnipotence of emperors and warlords, a single individual, based on his words, might either rescue a nation or be executed. At times, one might need to be direct, roundabout, striking, or remonstrating. Because they served a ruler who controlled whether they would live or die, many subjects had to be especially clever with words so they could successfully accomplish their goals without putting their lives in jeopardy. They thus had to walk a fine line between expression and concealment and were able to do so only if they could fashion messages that implied, rather than directly communicated, criticism of their ruler's actions (S. Chen, 1998).

According to *Han Feizi*, for example, the difficulty of giving advice to a superior lies not in having knowledge, nor in expressing it verbally, nor in having the courage to speak out. Rather, it lies in having the ability to read the mind of one's target and incorporate one's words accordingly (Shou, 1994, p.70). More specifically, that which the other is proud of, you should praise. That of which the other is ashamed, you should avoid ... When the other is selfish and dares not take action, you should use grand reasons to strengthen his will. If he already knows what he does is useless but cannot stop doing it, you should tell him that what he does is not bad and there is no need to stop. If the other has ideals, but incurs too heavy a burden, you should tell him that it is not workable, and advise him to give it up soon. To give advice to the leader to prevent him from continuing to pursue dangerous activities, you should tell him that such actions will destroy his personal reputation, giving him hints that there is nothing for him to gain personally. (p.71)

Designing indirect messages requires one to focus on situational, psychological, and interpersonal factors. Uncrafted straightforwardness that fails to take into account the other parties involved in the situation is considered simplistic and superficial. Zeng (1992) uses the analogy "broken glass" (p.241) to describe people who simply plunge blindly ahead without considering the needs for smoothness in social situations. Direct speech is as coarse as the broken glass whose sharp edges injure those with whom one interacts.

Realized at the more mundane level, being good at using words to get to the right balance is highly valued by Chinese. Concepts such as *zuòrén* (做人); *yuántōng* (圆通); *yuánhuá* (圆滑); *bāmiànlínglóng* (八面玲珑); and so on, point to "smoothness" as a central quality in managing interpersonal situations (Zeng, 1992). Such smoothness is mainly dependent upon one's skill in speaking effectively. One should be *yuántōng*, that is, not only *yuán* (round), but also *tōng* (able to move freely or to let pass without hindrance); more often than not indirect communication is needed to accomplish such goals since straight language is likely to impair rather than assist in smoothing the situation. Zeng notes that Chinese see human beings as embraced by the universe, within which they must be "square inside and round outside" (*nèifāng wàiyuán*) (p.246) —

i.e., insisting on one's own principles while expressing them skillfully with all involved. To mediate this seeming contradiction, one must learn to employ various stratagems (especially indirect verbal tactics), similar to the "push, drag, and pull" actions one sees in the rhythmic movement of Chinese shadow boxing, tàijíquán.

The complexity of Chinese interpersonal ties often creates the need for interactants to negotiate relational positioning via exchange of verbal messages, often under the guise of superficial harmonious interaction (Chang, 1999, 2001). Speaking skills function as a lubricant to the interpersonal system. Appropriate use of such skills will help one create a desirable social network and bring personal advantage to those who employ them, particularly in a world that emphasizes connections (guānxì); human emotion (rénqíng); and face needs (miànzi). To achieve one's goals, one can use a variety of indirect linguistic forms, such as hidden words, irony, and sarcasm, as well as metaphors and analogies (see He, 1991), choose the right context to convey messages, or even utilize mediators as one's conduit to facilitate interaction.

Thus, while the complexity of Chinese relational configurations may have constrained speakers from expressing directly what is on their minds, it at the same time refines and provides a challenge to a speaker's perception and ability to assess diverse situations and levels of relationships, thus making speakers more, not less, clever with words. Maintaining or even augmenting face needs; showing emotional concern; balancing interpersonal debts; and so on, can be accomplished either by using cleverly crafted expressions and quick words; going through the right person; or maneuvering one's utterances through using a more opaque, indirect, and circumscribed manner of communication.

Whether one is sincere in taking care of the needs of participants or merely interested in gaining power, knowing how to talk appropriately with different people so as not to spoil seemingly pleasant, harmonious situations is highly valued in Chinese cultures. If one can view communication as a dance, the dance can continue, and the dancer can avoid stepping on a lot of toes, only if he or she develops more elaborate and skillful steps to maneuver around different partners and thereby successfully carry out the performance (Chang, in press).

Second, the notion of reversion and relativistic positioning permeates Chinese philosophy and serves as the foundation, albeit seemingly remote, of indirect talk. As Chapter 36 of *Daodejing* puts it, "In order to contract, it is necessary first to expand. In order to weaken, it is necessary first to strengthen. In order to destroy, it is necessary first to promote. In order to grasp, it is necessary first to give" (Chan, 1963a). What seems empty is actually full, what seems straight is actually crooked, and what seems weak is actually strong. These beliefs also find expression in the common saying, "fullness invites decrease, whereas humbleness brings advantages" (mǎn *zhāo sǔn, qiān shòu yì*), a notion which propounds, as a natural law of the universe, the principle that any extreme leads automatically to its reverse. Following the same logic, indirectness, while seemingly opaque, is in fact quite appropriate as a means of communication, as it is not as obscure as it may seem.

X. Xiao (1998) notes that *dào*, with all its paradoxes and ambiguities, is the most sacred and authoritative concept to Chinese. It held a central position in Chinese political, social, moral, and spiritual life, and serves as the key discursive topic for philosophers, religious practitioners, moralists, and politicians in ancient China. Those who wanted to rise to political power had to master *dao*-discourse. They had to seek a balance point between discourse on *dào* as emptiness and *dào* as solid, material manifestation, through combining clear everyday language with ambiguous metaphysical language. Moreover, they had to use various forms of rhetoric to prove that the connection they discovered was the best route toward unlocking the mystery of *dào*, the blurred, dark complex from which the universe originated (X. Xiao, 1998).

In expressions such as "the Way that is no way" or "use of no use," which render expression drastically more dynamic (Wu, 1989, p.239), we find the seeming contradiction that pervades much of Chinese writing. Language, therefore, can only capture the ephemeral world through such relativistic means. Indeed, the most language can do is to outline a relativistic and dualistic world-concept via compound words such as "long-shortness," instead of just "long" or "short"; "high-lowness," rather than just "high" or "low"; and so on (J. Liu, 1962, p. 48). The Chinese language, according to Hansen (1989), is a system composed of contrasting features. Chinese philosophers treat language as essentially social, since people are taught to make distinctions with words, and learning any term entails learning its complement or converse.

If indeed language possesses no absolute truth but meaning must be inferred from, and go beyond, various contrasts, then understanding can be accomplished only through indirect communication. This idea also finds expression in Chan Buddhism's realization of enlightenment. Chan masters help students avoid the trap of language's duality and fixity, using "living words" to awaken Chan in the heart. Chan masters use language to go beyond the control of language — they play at the boundaries of language by using paradoxical language, tautological language, and poetry (Wang, 2000). The perspective taken toward reversion, and the keen insight in going beyond the artificiality of linguistic confinement, makes Chinese especially fond of indirect expression, as it is part of life and its contemplation.

Third and finally, the unique construction of the Chinese language also helps shape the Chinese tendency toward indirection. What is unique about such indirectness is that it must include not just forms of expression, but the symbols for expression themselves — i.e., words can be used to indirectly signify something other than what it originally represents.

Unlike some other languages, characters in Chinese (numbering more than 56,000) are monosyllabic, each single-syllable character encoding one sound and one meaning (P. Chen, 1999). With more characters than the number of syllables, a great many Chinese characters are homophonous (P. Chen, 1999). These unusual linguistic qualities may be one major reason for the high frequency in Chinese common literature of homophone-based verbal games (K. Chen, 1995, p. 18). The diverse meanings associated with the same sound opens up opportunities to create meaningful puns or double-entendres, greatly expanding the possibilities for being indirect (Chang, 2003).

Moreover, written Chinese does not indicate through formal marking such concepts as number, time, or person-orientation, nor are there inflectional markings for sentential roles. In fact, depending on word order, almost every word can serve as either noun, verb, adjective, or adverb (K. Chen, 1995; Hansen, 1989; Xiang, 1993/1966). As Wu (1989) puts it, "The Chinese language has no grammar that irrevocably fixes and categorizes; that is, it has no parts of speech, number, gender, tense, declension, and so on" (p. 247). Chinese sentences may omit the subject or other parts of the sentence and gender, number, tense, mood, and so on may remain unspecified (Mair, 1994, p. xxviii).

The concision with which Chinese can be expressed rests largely on its status as an uninflected language uninhibited by cases, genders, moods, tenses, and so on. The fluidity of a "part of speech" (J. Liu, 1962, p. 45), as when a noun is used as a verb allows the writer to retain the implications and associations of the word; in addition, fluidity also makes it possible to render descriptions more concretely (Chang, 2003).

It is also impossible to avoid ambiguity. That there is no subject in a sentence, for example, creates an impersonal and universal quality in literary forms such as poetry. Rather than being restricted in space and time, as in the phrase "I wandered lonely as a cloud," one might find in Chinese, "wandered as cloud" (J. Liu, 1962, p. 41). Because it does not focus on what parts of sentences do and how they are composed, the Chinese language does not overtly signal relations between sentence parts (Hansen, 1985). These qualities increase the potential for indirectness, since the interpretation and understanding of a given sentence based upon its context is often left to readers of Chinese:

> ... for these ambiguities not only act to shatter the narrow sense of the words; they establish another relation between the words. Breaking the linearity of unitary meaning in the sentence, they introduce a process of reversibility or of reciprocal becoming between the subject and object, between here and elsewhere, and finally, between what is said and what is unsaid. (F. Cheng, 1986, p. 40)

To summarize, Chinese culture has laid a solid foundation for them to use indirect language to contemplate cosmological order, as well as to create and mediate smooth interpersonal encounters. Their philosophical belief in reversion and in interdependence of the material world, further cast the entire scheme in terms of contrast and change, rendering definitive communication impossible. Finally, the unique construction of the written Chinese language further makes it possible to utilize a system that allows for flexibility and ambiguity in sentence construction and interpretation. Meanings are thus always beyond what is referred to in words, and Chinese indulge themselves in indirect forms of communication.

The Three Vantage Points

These cultural ideals and conceptions concerning indirectness are realized in people's everyday life, to compete and reflect, as well as entertain. In the following, I examine Chinese indirectness through three vantage points to explore its diverse forms of expression: the manipulator, the humble truth-seeker, and the artist. Each facet taps a unique aspect of Chinese indirectness that can coexist, be in conflict, or be integrated into various patterns.

The Manipulator

Cleverness in using language is of course not unique to Chinese. However, the Chinese cultural foundation does make this process particularly powerful and omnipresent. Such cleverness can often be successfully accomplished through various indirect forms of expression, with the primary goal of benefitting oneself. If one knows how to talk skillfully, one may communicate competition, flattery, cruelty, boastfulness, and a host of other possible messages, all the while appearing kind, sincere, and smooth. The inconsistency between the surface and what goes below is not only tolerated but oftentimes expected and even encouraged. Behaviors which appear to be passive, selfless, peace-loving, soft, and nonviolent, can in fact be quite manipulative (Chang, 2003; Ma, 2000). Even the well-known Daoist teaching about "withdrawing as a way of advancing" (yǐtuìwéijìn) can turn out the opposite of what it at first seems: one can withdraw, not to advance the status of others, but to reduce resistance and pave the way for a future personal advance.

For example, Li's sarcastic treaties, *The Thick and the Black*, satirize and ridicule authorities in position. Z. Li (1994 [orig. 1912])[1] addressed

---

[1] Z. Li's *Studies of the Thick and Black* (1994) was initially written for *Chengdu Public Opinion Daily* in 1912, and the first book volume was published in 1934 (publisher unknown).

a subject he called "studies of the thick and black," "thick" meaning "thick-faced" (that is, shameless), and "black" meaning "black-hearted" (that is, cruel and immoral). Among Li's six kinds of essence for acquiring positions and getting promoted, three — boasting, flattery, and coercion-deal with verbal skills. Li explains how it is possible to both flatter and at the same time coerce one's superior in order to get promoted through cunningly managing a discrepancy between the surface meaning and intended meaning:

> One should be able to integrate the tactics of flattery and coercion. Someone who is good at coercion knows to incorporate coercion within flattery. Those who observe can only see his flattery and support, when in fact his/her words are able to hit his/her superior's "sore spots." The superior listens to his/her words and sweats. Someone who is good at flattery knows to incorporate flattery within coercion. Those who observe can only see his dignity and self-assurance, as if every word of his criticizes his/her superior, when in fact the superior is overjoyed with what he/she says. (p. 18)

Such skills in talk, of course, are not limited to people getting promoted. Chinese employ a repertoire of effective, indirect verbal strategies that they use to mediate, redefine, or even relieve interpersonal obligations. In people's everyday encounters, for example, using inappropriate address terms can also upset the balance of a given relationship. Naming practice functions as an effective indirect strategy, particularly given the Chinese focus on relational connectedness and hierarchy. Much like using kinship terms to bring the tie closer, using higher- or lower-status forms of address can serve as ways to manipulate others. Blum (1997) notes, "In China as elsewhere, one can disparage people by calling them by a lesser term than expected; or one can try to oblige others by calling them by an 'undeserved' higher term" (p. 366). One can also flatter others, as well as bolster one's own position without doing so overtly. Again, "... names are one element to be deployed in strategies of giving, withholding, and exchanging face ... naming practices reveal distinctions among what may be said, what may not be said, and what must be said, in monitoring the delicate balance of self and world" (p. 372).

Aside from issues concerning relational structure and formality, substance is also subject to manipulation via indirectness. A good example concerns the norm of reciprocity. While the strong ingroup ties may compel Chinese to help each other, the need to repay is also enforced to ensure equitable exchange. As a result, no matter how humble and reserved Chinese may be, they are seldom shy about negotiating the amount of "credit" they feel that they accumulated in any interpersonal transaction (Chang & Holt, 1994) through elaborate displays of indirectness. They may use euphemism, opaque expression, analogies, or communicate through an intermediary, either to ask for the repayment of a debt (if they are creditors), or to tell the other party that they feel that they have repaid more "human feeling debt" than is required (if they are debtors).

Many of my informants told me how some people are particularly good at "asking for (the repayment of) debts of human feeling" (Chang & Holt, 1994). For example, they constantly remind their targets how much they have helped them either by hinting or — so they won't appear too calculating — by communicating "reminders" through an intermediary. Such "claiming of credit" can also be channeled through a third party: "I don't mean to claim the credit, but about this matter [I handled for him/her], if not for my *guānxì*, it will never get done!" The Chinese *chéngyŭ*, *kŏushìxīnfēi* ("mouth yes, hearts no," meaning what is said outwardly is opposite of what one feels inside), summarizes this situation perfectly. In turn, the third party is likely to become the representer and convey the message to one's target.

On the other hand, some gift-givers are so good with words that they can make even a small gift seem expensive or at least make it seem that they have gone to a great deal of trouble. People who know how to talk can claim credit through their words, rather than their actions, as in the following example:

> You know, this pen is really good. They don't make pens like this any more. I was lucky to get the last one. You know what, my daughter asked me to give it to her, and I told her that this is a special gift for your aunt, not for you. (Chang, in press)

These seemingly ambiguous messages allow Chinese considerable flexibility in negotiating relational positioning and role behavior within the confines of relational systems. Elsewhere (Chang, 1999) I have described this social mechanism as "indeterminate linguistic space." By using the indeterminate linguistic space skillfully, speakers can get around interpersonal constraints through active calculation and maneuvering. This flexibility is made possible, since in indirect communication, it may lighten as well as intensify the indirect aspect of the utterance, depending upon how listeners choose to interpret the message (Anolli et al., 2002a).

If one knows how to "get back at others" through indirect modes of talk, one can gain the upper hand over relational superiors. In one example, a woman (A) is looking for a job where one of her acquaintances (B) works, though in a lower position. Learning A will be invited for an interview, B called her and said, "*I am so glad that you applied for the position. We extended two offers to two candidates previously and neither of them took the offer. It'd be great if you can come.*"

This insult is effective due to clever, indirect language, since A would be seeking a position that was rejected by not just one, but two candidates.

Moreover, if A did not get an offer after the interview, it would mean that A is so unqualified as to be unable to get a position rejected by others. By casting the position as undesirable, the fact that B is in a lower position is no longer of any significance.

Examples of innuendo and sarcasm are not limited to interpersonal contexts. Even in public domains, particularly politics, one frequently encounters such verbal games. As an example, consider the title of Li Ang's (1997) book, "The Incense Burner in Beigang that Everyone Wants to Put Incense In" (*Běigǎng Xiānglú Rénrén Chā*). On the surface, it refers to a very common Taiwanese cultural artifact — an incense burner in a temple — in Beigang, a town in the middle Taiwan famous for its authentic folk arts. The cultural custom is for the worshipper, following worship, to "stick" (*chā*) his or her incense into a burner filled with sand. However, the image was said to imply (*yǐngshè*, "use shadows to project") a controversial female politician, Chen Wen-Qian, for not being chaste. Much as everyone "sticks" (*chā*) his or her incense into the burner, she is reputed to have been receptive to many male organs. Confronted with this interpretation, the writer denied having made it.

Whether or not it is due to the manipulation of others, such interpretation is made possible because of the Chinese tendency to use metaphor, irony, and analogy as forms of communication. Hints and indirection allow one to mitigate a threat to the speaker's face and image by appearing to adhere to cultural norms and expectations, so the speaker does not need to be responsible for his or her words, thus permitting strategic retreat by providing ambiguous messages (Anolli et al., 2002a; Young, 1994).

The Humble Truth-Seeker

Quite different from their interest in manipulating others through indirect words, a different side of Chinese interaction is that of humbleness. In the interpersonal realm, they prefer not to outspeak others, but rather remain humble. A similar posture also holds for their interaction with the universe: they prefer not to outspeak fate.

This inclination can be discerned in the Chinese concept of *hánxù*. As Gao and Ting-Toomey (1998) put it, "The Chinese phrase *hánxù* refers to a mode of communication (both verbal and nonverbal) which is contained, reserved, implicit, and indirect …. To be *hánxù*, one does not spell out everything, but leaves the 'unspoken' to the listener" (pp. 283-284). J. Liu (1986) notes that *hánxù* has been variously translated as "conservation," "the pregnant mode," "reserve," and "potentiality," among which "reserve" is the best translation, since it means both "holding back" (*hán*) and "storing up" (*xù*). To elaborate: by being "reserved" in words one could build up a "reserve" of meaning. (p.67)

Rather than pinning a point down by specifying its meaning,

indirection allows an issue to be contemplated from many angles and at many layers, thus inviting fuller, broader, and deeper understanding. For these reasons, "reserve makes for depth and restraint makes for strength" (Young, 1994, p. 123).

The propensity of Chinese to avoid pushing things too far — such as by using aggressive, straightforward expression — is also aimed at avoiding hurting the other's feelings and allowing oneself and the other some room to function (as in the concept of *hòudào*, "the way of being 'thick'", meaning to be kind to others). L. Xiao's (1981) famous novel, *Where there is water, there is a reflected moon*, recounts a heart-warming story of how some Chinese avoid direct confrontation. A farmer's neighbor tried to steal some cucumbers from his field. The farmer saw the thief in the act of stealing while coming back to his farm. Instead of calling the neighbor a thief and confronting him directly, the farmer stayed hidden, since he knew his neighbor's thievery was due not to simple greed, but to the neighbor's sorrowful and difficult life. The farmer's *hòudào* illustrates the generous aspect of Chinese culture.

This sense of concern, the willingness to allow interactants room to back away from overt conflict, underlies much of the Chinese indirectness. A person who cultivates him- or herself internally shows respect for others, and avoids criticizing them or putting them in embarrassing positions. Such a gentle person (*wēnhé*), one who is rational, ordered, and polite (*kèqi*), can be described as calm and peaceful (*xīnpíngqìhé*) (Silin, 1976). As Confucius said, "Love of straightforwardness without a love to learn finds itself obscured by warped judgment" (XVI, 8). Indirect communication helps create a strong bond, and build a harmonious society (Ding, 2006).

To avoid imposing on or hurting others, or overly asserting one's own position at the expense of others, Chinese often find it necessary to use hinting to convey negative messages and avoid harsh language. This way, not only can the target party be better protected, but the message will more likely lead to constructive results. For example, one respondent told me that sometimes he is absent-minded about managing affairs. His teacher, attempting to tell him that he should be more careful about how he treats matters and people, told him, "*Don't be like mail without a stamp. Who is going to deliver the letter [for you]?*". Based on the cultural focus of self-cultivation, the "sound beyond the string" (*xiánwàizhīyīn*) can be expected to be interpreted accurately. Such indirection can be accomplished by metaphor and analogy, which the target must examine in order to figure out the lesson for him- or herself (Chang, in press).

The analogy, "mail without a stamp," aptly captures the absent-mindedness the respondent seems to be exhibiting. Although the mail is ready to be sent, if one forgets to put the stamp on, the mail will never be delivered. If one is not careful to "follow through," all the effort one spends is wasted. Without directly drawing attention to the student's shortcomings, this veiled criticism allows the student to become aware of the problem through self-inspection, an attitude that reminds us of Confucian and Buddhist teachings. Practically speaking, one's face and self-image is also properly maintained.

On a more pragmatic level, "The Chinese say that when there are things left to be said, there is room for 'free advances and retreat'" (Gao & Ting-Toomey, 1998, p.284). The common expression, "give someone a ladder to back off the stage" (*gěi rén táijiē xià*) illustrates this cultural predilection. Young (1994) notes that, rather than push a point to completion, the Chinese speaker avoids the risk of appearing assertively egotistic or unduly interfering with the natural course of another's understanding; a communicator takes the role of a guide, one who skillfully employs stimuli to suggest and to evoke. (p.119)

This is similar to the spirit of the Chan Buddhist master, whose words evoke and inspire rather than to convey established messages to the students. The content of the talk is less important than how it is said (Wang, 2000). The teacher is meant to guide rather than to specify the direction, and the lesson must be deduced by the student / listener him- or herself.

Using a more circuitous means such as indirect communication, rather than resorting to more forceful means such as argument, reprimand, or bringing issues out into the open, is also in line with the Chinese distinction between *wén* (nonviolent, civil means) and *wǔ* (martial practices, force) (see Ferguson, 1998). *Wén*, while originally referring to those who had been decorated or adorned, has been extended to signify order, elegance, and ceremony, as well as culture (Ferguson, 1998, p.38). Indirectness, when expressed through the sincerity of a speaker's heart, can be said to observe this *wén* principle, that is, it is an attempt to regulate human relationships through refinement. Such refinement brings more contentment to all the parties involved. Indirectness comes about when one is cultured. In line with the Chinese sense of humility, in many situations indirectness is not considered evasive but rather a careful effort to beautify situations and make them more smooth and comfortable for all involved.

Aside from commenting upon others' conduct, when turning down another's request, indirectness can also be useful. Saying "no" directly to one's acquaintances always invites a feeling of *bùhǎo yìsī*, embarrassment; for this reason, many Chinese turn down requests by not responding or responding with noncommittal words such as, "Let me think about it." Alternatively, they can make up excuses to politely refuse a request. Many times, informants mentioned to me they were "embarrassed to say 'no' directly"; therefore, coming up with an excuse appears to be an effective way to resolve the problem while protecting the other's feelings.

Of course, making up excuses for not being able to do certain things is by no means specific to Chinese culture. However, the uniqueness lies in the degree of discomfort one feels when one must turn down another's request, for whatever reason. Liao and Lü-Shih (1993) note that for Chinese refusal is a dispreferred response to a request, and if indeed it does happen, it is likely to be embedded within a sustained interaction, that is, it will occur after several turns have been exchanged (quoted in Bresnahan, Cai, & Rivers, 1994). This orientation is clearly revealed in the prevalence of the expression that often accompanies one's refusal — bùhǎo yìsī.

Alternatively, one can simply make a noncommittal response, such as, "let me think about it." In other words, there has been no real response to the request — indirect, indeed! — which the requester can nevertheless take as a "no." Liao and Lü-Shih's observation is in line with what I have heard and seen in Taiwan Province. As many respondents put it, "I just pretend I did not hear anything, and the matter is dropped and never mentioned again!" By abandoning the matter without a trace, both parties' feelings are protected; there is then little need to "sit down and talk." As Chinese humbly pursue their interpersonal lives, they nevertheless decide to smooth unnecessarily sharp edges, thereby making everyone's life a little more endurable.

Although indirect messages are used to avoid hurting the other's feelings when communicating less pleasant information, they can also be useful when expressing more positive emotions. Traditionally, Chinese seldom utter words such as "I love you" to express their emotions for each other. Rather, the deep feelings one has for another are oftentimes expressed through, for example, a letter that makes no statements about emotion, but inquires about the other's day-to-day living. Matters related to one's personal, private life, as Xiang (1993/1966) notes, are to be expressed by indirect, hinting methods that are, in fact, deeper modes of expression (p.50). We can recall the earlier discussion on the paradox of language. Given that language is an imperfect means of communication, saying less may actually allow one to communicate more, since being succinct embraces more than being verbose and leaving things implicit is more persuasive than spelling things out (J. Liu, 1986, p.64). This is one reason why metaphors, analogies, hidden language, opposite statements, and so on, are so frequently employed by Chinese.

Still, humility is not only shown to others, but also to the universe. Showing humility toward the universe not only reflects spirituality but practicality, two realms that, in the Chinese view, are inseparable. Chinese try to avoid outspeaking fate, believing that human beings are part of the universe, rather than its masters. They try to avoid being "mouth hard" (zuǐ yìng), that is, to say something boldly, without modesty or restraint. Just as one could never predict or dictate the future by using words, insisting upon one's words through being "mouth hard" is contrary to the functioning of the universe.

If such words must be uttered, an alternate word could be used to assist in the situation, thus further contributing to the Chinese tendency toward indirectness. The contents of taboo words, which manifest as bad omens, concern unpredictable, accidental future fate that is unfortunate or evil, including death, losing money, becoming poor, or being subject to other unfortunate circumstances (K. Chen, 1995; Sung, 1979). People hope they will be able to manipulate such hapless occurrences by avoiding uttering words which share the same pronunciation as words with inauspicious meanings, a cultural tendency well served by Chinese literary tradition and the large number of homonymic words in the Chinese language.

Since death always brings sadness, as well as fear and aversion, people are reluctant to utter the word, particularly around those close to them. For this reason, a large number of euphemistic replacements have been made available. K. Chen (1995) noted that there were more than 40 replacement terms recorded in the early *Kangxi Dictionary*. In Taiwan Province, for example, replacement words include more literary expressions, such as passing this lifetime (*guòshì*, *císhì*, or *xièshì*), arriving at the ever-happy land (*dào jílèshìjiè*), and sleeping for a long time (*chángmián*); as well as more colloquial phrases, such as *qiàobiànzi*.

Of course, the availability of multiple euphemisms for death is a feature of many cultures and languages. However, the Chinese culture is somewhat unique in that, apart from the specific contents of such euphemisms, it also relies on homonyms. In this respect, perhaps the most commonly avoided word is the "four" (*sì*) which shares the same sound as "die" (*sǐ*) except that the two words are pronounced using different tones. The word "four," as a homonym of the word "die," is to be avoided in many situations. For example, on visiting a patient, one avoids giving gifts that contain four of something, since this would remind, or lead to the pronouncing of the word *sǐ* (death). Similarly, the visitor should not bring a peach to give to the patient, since "peach" (*lí*) is pronounced the same as the word for "separation."

On the other hand, objects that have auspicious names, or statements that reflect auspicious circumstances (lucky words, *jílìhuà* or *jíxiánghuà*), are used on various happy occasions such as the Lunar New Year, weddings, the birth of a child, or other occasions which convey good news in various ways. These words are for the most part either homophonic or rhymed with each other (Sung, 1979), allowing indirection to add further color to the situation. At the New Year, for example, oranges (*jú*) are often served, since the sound of the word *jú* is very close to the sound of the word for "lucky" (*jí*). Also, on such occasions banquets should include fish dishes, since the word for fish, *yú*, is homophonous with the word meaning to have a surplus (Blum, 1997; Sung, 1979).

The Artistic

Apart from grand reasons such as persuading rulers or cultivating minds, indirect messages can be used to entertain people, enabling them to enjoy life and refine their spirit, engage in critical commentary at the expense of others, or exhibit less humane treatment of others. Among all different forms of expression, stylized and otherwise, such as poems, matched couplets, *chéngyǔ*, common sayings and proverbs, metaphor, irony, doggerel (*dǎyóushī*), enigmatic folk similes (*xiēhòuyǔ*), and so on, we are able to trace Chinese artistic and philosophical inclinations through their indirect expressions[①].

From a historical perspective, we can note that Chinese rhetoricians are highly aware of indirectness as a rhetorical strategy. This orientation is found in the focus of compositional suggestiveness (*hánxù*), as expressed in Gui Youguang's distaste for *zhí* [直], directness, and the value Liu Dakui places on *yuǎn* [远], distantness or remoteness (Y. Liu, 1996a). More specifically, being subtle or using subtle words (微言 [*wēi yán*]) with hidden meaning can be traced back to Confucius (see Harbsmeier, 1990). For example, in the *Book of Songs*, indirectness manifests itself in

> Understatement flourishes with shrewd and humorous innuendo. It attracts skilled hands where nuances and implications are generally discovered more congenial to the true spirit of poetry than rational statement or moral assertion. (Wells, 1971, p. 65)

As Y. Liu (1996a) puts it, Chinese rhetoricians are concerned "about the need to avoid the kind of overtness that leaves nothing subtextually" (p. 330). By leaving things hidden subtextually, communication becomes inherently negotiable and indeterminate (Chang, 1999) since meaning must be worked out between interactants. This invitation through indirectness is, indeed, a display of artistry in expression.

Again, discourse concerning *dào* (see X. Xiao, 1998) gives us some clue about Chinese tendency toward indirection. As the generating force underlying all existence, *dào* transcends all being, names, and forms (Chan, 1963a) and cannot be named or even spoken about. For the Chinese, the origin of the universe was a blurred, dark complex (混沌 [*hùndùn*] or 太极 [*tàijí*], "The Great Ultimate") that can never be known. While it embraces this world, it also carries the characteristics of another world. Since *dào* is beyond logical comprehension and defies description of human language, perhaps ancient Chinese felt they could only use vague and ambiguous language to describe the mysterious *dào* (X. Xiao, 1998). Confucius' famous statement about *dào* gives us the

---

① For a more detailed analysis of how the construction of Chinese language and the long development history of Chinese literature has led to indirect expression, see Chang (2003, in press).

evidence: "The four seasons proceed by it, the hundred things [i.e., the sensible universe] are generated by it. Does Heaven speak?" (Graham, 1989, p.18).

Another good example of artistic indirection is the old-fashioned stylized form of *bāgǔwén* ("eight-legged essay"), whose details were specified around 1487. The "eight legs" are: the breaking open of the title; accepting the title; introductory discourse; introductory corollary; the middle pair; the architectonic technique of the parallel structure design; and two last "legs" to wind up the entire composition (Ch'ën, 1961, p.505). With four parts (*qǐ*, introduction of the theme or topical statement; *chéng*, elaboration of the thesis or lateral elaboration; *zhuǎn*, transition to another perspective, and excursions into tangential and oblique dimensions; and *hé*, summary or convergence) (Y. Liu, 1996a, p.331), the essay contains approximately six hundred words.

Such compositions run contrary to the Western ideal of rhetoric, in which arguments are brought to closure; instead, this form of expression relies on related images, balanced against each other, resulting in a conceptually complete entity (Young, 1984). The various techniques of expression make writing *bāgǔwén* a word game which discourages creativity. Although it has been blamed as an example of demerit in Chinese intellectual history (Ch'ën, 1961), its impact on Chinese orientation toward indirection is nevertheless quite obvious.

Chinese artistry in indirect communication is also influenced by attention to how situational differences give rise to unique patterns of interaction. On the one hand, this reflects the Chinese cultural emphasis on hierarchies and power differentials. Earlier I mentioned the one-person persuasive tradition cultivated during the Warring States period in ancient Chinese history. Rhetorical strategies of indirection became imperative for a speaker to operate successfully within the constraints imposed by the power imbalance between the speaker and his ruler (the target of persuasion) (Chang, 2003). These indirect strategies, based upon unique circumstances, include "hiddens" (*yǐn* [隐]), which were enigmatic opening lines used to gain an audience (such as "a big fish in the sea!"); *fěng* [讽], a form of veiled criticism through riddles and allusions; and "progressive analogies," which approached a sensitive conclusion through a series of increasingly close comparisons (Garrett, 1991, p.299).

On the other hand, the Chinese view of the universe as interlocking, and interdependent among all its different manifestations, also contributes to their sensitivity toward situational differences and hence the need for indirection. If the universe cannot be held constant even for a moment, then the language used to describe and represent it must also be fluid and flexible. Without being direct and being definitive, indirectness allows one to transcend the binary opposition within which language has long imprisoned communicators (cf. Wang, 2000). Such an attitude is itself literary as well as artistic.

The semiotic order sought by Chinese in the universe, in conjunction with a refined mind cultivated through contemplating nature, predispose Chinese toward indirectness. Indirection resonates with the need to step back, withholding aggressiveness while allowing oneself to freely enjoy what the universe has to offer. Words, as a means of representation, may be close to and intersect with "reality," but they never actually parallel. Being witty and playful with words has always been the signature feature of Chinese communication. Throughout *Analects*, Confucius uses irony, self-irony, sarcasm, satire, teasing remarks, and subtle words (*wēi yán*), such as jocular remarks, colloquialisms, and emphatic forms of speech. Indeed, from the material in *Analects*, one can see the intellectual mode as poetic and impulsive (Harbsmeier, 1990, p. 144), "a mild, subtle and very communicative form of humor which is certainly not inconsistent with mild irony, or with deep moral conviction①" (p.161).

For another example, the poem, "Drinking Wine," by Tao Qian, uses a homonym to create a double effect: "Within this there is true meaning (*cí zhōng yǒu zhēn yì*), about to discuss it, I've already forgotten words (*yù biàn yǐ wàng yán*)." Here the word 辩 [*biàn*], which means "to articulate or argue," shares the same sound as 辨 [*biàn*], which means "to make distinctions." What is particularly interesting, as J. Liu (1986) notes, is the double meaning in the word *biàn*, with which Tao is playing a homophonic game.

Metaphors are also a common literary device that allows Chinese to express their ideas indirectly. Mencius, for example, employed various rhetorical strategies such as similes and metaphors to defend Confucianism during the chaotic Warring States period. One example is water, which on the one hand symbolizes a major source of power for a benevolent leader while on the other hand a negative force which the leader must overcome (Ma, 2000). We may also recall a comment recorded in *Zhuangzi*: "One does not think well of a dog because it is good at barking nor of a man because he is good at talking" — an effective analogy that makes the unreliable activity of talking all the more conspicuous by comparing human beings with dogs (Harbsmeier, 1989). Aside from this humorous analogy, Wang (2004) notes *Zhuangzi* holds a negative attitude toward straightforward words and discourse, with denegation (paradoxical speech) and paradox (absurd speech) occupying important positions in his strategy of indirect communication.

Chinese common literature is also filled with language games using homophones, allowing meanings to be expressed indirectly. For example, the diverse characters associated with the same sound enables speakers to

---

① For an example examining Confucius from an argumentative mode, see Y. Liu (1996a).

create meaningful puns or double-entendres. Take the enigmatic folk expression, "a monk holding an umbrella — no hair and no sky (*wúfǎ-wútiān*)." Since the word "hair" (*fǎ*, 发) and "law" (*fǎ*, 法) share the same sound, whereas "sky" (*tiān*, 天) in Chinese represents moral principles endowed by heaven, the literal description of what happens when a monk holds an umbrella is cleverly used to denote someone who has no respect for law or the universe.

These literary aspirations persist even in modern times. In many public restrooms in Taipei, for example, there is often an poetic statement posted on the door: *biànhòu suí chōngshuǐ, chūnní liǎo wúhén* [便后随冲水，春泥了无痕] (flush the toilet right after [your] use, and the spring dust will have no trace). Thanks to the practice of indirectness, human excretion can be described as "spring dust." In a slightly different fashion, Kaohsiung's Cultural Center deliberately inscribes literary phrases to make restrooms artistic, again, through poetic indirection. These phrases came from poet Lu Hanxiu's writing: "How could it be, all writing is gone with the water?"; "There is one song that only oneself could hear"; "Coming here, I don't have any other wishes than to calmly inspect my heart"; "Let it go is the best way to meet clarity [of mind]"; and so on. Although these phrases are not originally intended for such personal activities, their implied messages seem quite appropriate (Xu, 2007), given Chinese practice of indirect communication and their ability to "read music beyond the strings" (Chang, in press).

From an artistic perspective, indirectness invokes pleasurable feelings associated with the knowledge that one's words are indefinitely interpretable, so that meaning will permeate deep into the minds of one's conversants (Young, 1994). Augmented by their poetic sensibility, the analogical nature of the Chinese language, and great literary traditions (Wang, 2000), the Chinese literary transaction, to use Hernadi's (2001) metaphor, is not so much production leading to consumption but seduction leading to consummation. Subtlety, from this perspective, can be seen as a way of handling the boundaries between self and other.

The Chinese philosophy of language makes it possible for them to enjoy life with words; through a variety of artistic yet indirect expressions, the meaning of life as situated within the unknown universe, is contemplated, reaffirmed, and understood by the heart. This artistic inclination has been inculcated through their unique linguistic features and literary aspirations, as well as rhetorical traditions, making one's life more colorful, enjoyable, and worth living.

Conclusion

From the outset of their philosophical thought, speaking has been held by

Chinese to be part of the principles of the universe. Paradoxically, though it is futile for humans to try to capture the essence of the cosmos through words, speaking at the same time represents and constitutes the universe. Much like their preference for remaining in the middle, that is, at neither extreme, the Chinese use of more indirect forms of talk reflects this basic cultural orientation. Such subtlety in linguistic expression reflects and at the same time actualizes Chinese cultural values, orchestrating a complex social life unique to the Chinese people, whether it done is for sake of manipulation; for sake of artistry; or for sake of politeness and humanity.

Aside from the Chinese view of the universe and the "reality" indexed in literary commentary, politics and history also shapes Chinese interest in taking an indirect, artistic attitude toward verbal or written expression in their management of everyday encounters. If we observe the Chinese philosophical perspective as situating forms within substance, we can appreciate how the selection of words, or how feelings and experiences are embraced and intertwined into unique forms of expression, can both enlighten and richly entertain us.

As mentioned earlier, the long-accepted scholarly dichotomy between direct and indirect communication appears over-simplified, since the so-called "indirect" message, for Chinese, represents a speech genre of its own, with individual messages differing according to their layers of implication. Indeed, the category of "hidden words" (*yǐnyǔ*) includes formats such as avoiding key words; implication by using similar meaning; implication by using words of similar sounds; metaphors; opposite words; ambiguous statements; and so on. All of these forms of expression allow meaning to go beyond what is conveyed on the surface by words (He, 1991). Through these indirect expressions, Chinese are able to manipulate others, to play with words artistically, and to show their humility toward others. Indirectness, for Chinese, represents a genre in itself, and this article is only a beginning attempt to explore its richness.

References

Anolli, L., Cicert, R., & Giaeleinfantino, M. (2002a). Behind dark glasses: Irony as a strategy for indirect communication. *Genetic, Social, and General Psychology Monographs, 128* (1), 76–95.

Anolli, L., Cicert, R., & Giaeleinfantino, M. (2002b). From "blame by praise" to "praise by blame": Analysis of vocal patterns in ironic communication. *International Journal of Psychology, 37* (5), 266–276.

Bakhtin, M. M. (1986). The problem of speech genres. In C. Emerson & M. Holquist (Eds., V. W. McGee, Trans.), *Speech Genres and Other Late Essays* (pp. 60–102). Austin, TX: University of Texas Press.

Blum, S. D. (1997). Naming practices and the power of words in China. *Language in Society, 26*(1), 357–379.

Bresnahan, M., Cai, D. A., & Rivers, A. (1994). Saying no in Chinese and

English: Cultural similarities and differences in strategies of refusal. *Asian Journal of Communication*, 4(1), 52–76.
Chan, W.-t. (1963a). *The Way of Lao Tzu (Tao-te ching)*. Indianapolis, IN: Bobbs-Merrill.
Chan, W.-t. (1963b). *A Source Book in Chinese Philosophy*. Princeton, NJ: Princeton University Press.
Chang, H.-c. (1997). Language and words — Communication in the *Analects* of Confucius. *Journal of Language and Social Psychology*, 16(2), 107–131.
Chang, H.-c. (1999). The "well-defined" is "ambiguous": Indeterminacy in Chinese conversation. *Journal of Pragmatics*, 31, 535–556.
Chang, H.-c. (2001). Harmony as performance: The turbulence under Chinese interpersonal communication. *Discourse Studies*, 3(2), 155–179.
Chang, H.-c. (2003). Serious play: Chinese artistry in verbal communication. *Journal of Asian Pacific Communication*.
Chang, H.-c. (In press). *Clever, Creative, Modest: The Chinese Language Game*. Shanghai, China: Shanghai Foreign Language Press.
Chang, H.-c., & Holt, G. R. (1994). Debt-repaying mechanism in Chinese relationships: An exploration of the folk concepts of *pao* and human emotional debt. *Research on Language and Social Interaction*, 27(4), 351–387.
Chen, G. M. (2001). Toward transcultural understanding: A harmony theory of Chinese communication. In V. H. Milhouse, M. K. Asante, and P. O. Nwosu (Eds.), *Transcultural Realities: Interdisciplinary Perspectives on Cross-Cultural Relations* (pp. 55–70). Thousand Oaks, CA: Sage.
Chen, G.-m. (2008). Intercultural communication studies by ACCS scholars on the Chinese: An updated bibliography. *China Media Research*, 4(2), 102–113.
Chen, K. (1995). *Zhongguoren shuohua de suqu* [The folk fun of Chinese talk]. Taipei: Bai-Guan Publishing Company.
Chen, P. (1999). *Modern Chinese: History and Sociolinguistics*. Cambridge: Cambridge University Press.
Chen, S.-j. (1998). Introduction: The art of negotiation that changes danger to peace, and transfers failure to success. In S.-j. Chen, *Wei-ji tanpan* [Crisis negotiation] (pp. 1–11). Taipei: Yuan-Liou Publishing Company.
Chen, Z.-r. (1996). *Jizhi duitan 72: Lishi renwu de koutou yuyan meili* [Witty conversation 72: The charm of verbal language of historical figures]. Taipei: Yuan-Liou Publishing Company.
Ch'ën, S.-Y. (1961). *Chinese Literature: A Historical Introduction*. New York: The Ronald Press Company.
Cheng, F. (Trans. by S. Owen). (1986). Some reflections on Chinese poetic language and its relation to Chinese cosmology. In S.-f. Lin & S. Owen (Eds.), *The Vitality of the Lyric Voice* (pp. 32–48). Princeton, NJ: Princeton University Press.
Ding, D. D. (2006). An indirect style in business communication. *Journal of Business and Technical Communication*, 20(1), 87–100.
Ferguson, R. J. (1998). Inclusive strategies for restraining aggression — lessons from classical Chinese culture. *Asian Philosophy*, 8(1), 31–45.
Fung, Y.-l. (1983). (Trans., D. Bodde). *A History of Chinese Philosophy (Vol. 1: The period of the philosphers)*. Princeton, NJ: Princeton University Press.
Gao, G., & Ting-Toomey, S. (1998). *Communicating Effectively with the Chinese*. Thousand Oaks, CA: Sage Publications.
Garrett, M. (1991). Asian challenge. In S. K. Foss, K. A. Foss, & R. Trapp (Eds.), *Contemporary Perspectives on Rhetoric* (2nd ed.) (pp. 295–306 & 311–314). Prospect Heights, IL: Waveland Press, Inc.

Garrett, M. M. (1993). *Pathos* reconsidered from the perspective of classical Chinese rhetorics. *Quarterly Journal of Speech, 79*, 19–39.

Graham, A. C. (1989). *Disputers of the Tao (Philosophical argument in ancient China)*. La Salle, IL: Open Court Publishing Company.

Hansen, C. (1985). Chinese language, Chinese philosophy, and "truth." *Journal of Asian Studies, XLIV*(3), 491–519.

Hansen, C. (1989). Language in the heart-mind. In R. E. Allinson (Ed.), *Understanding the Chinese Mind: The philosophical roots* (pp. 75–123). Hong Kong: Oxford University Press.

Harbsmeier, C. (1989). Humor in ancient Chinese philosophy. *Philosophy East and West, 39*(3), 289–310.

Harbsmeier, C. (1990). *Confucius Ridens*: Humor in the *Analects*. *Harvard Journal of Asiatic Studies, 50*(1), 131–161.

He, D.-z. (1991). *Yuyan yishu yu renji guanxi* [Language arts and interpersonal relationships]. Taipei: Asia-Pacific Press.

Hernadi, P. (2001). Literature and evolution. *Substance, 30*(1), 55–71.

Legge, J. (Ed. & Trans.). (1985). *The Four Books: A Chinese-English Version*. Taipei: Culture Book Co.

Li, A. (1997). *Beigang xianglu renren cha* [The incense burner in Bei-Gang that everyone wants to put incense in]. Taipei: Mai-Tian Publishing Company.

Li, Z.-w. (1994). *Hou hei xue* [Studies of the thick and black]. Taipei: Xin-Ruei Publishing Company.

Liao, C., & Lü-Shih, Y. E. (1993). Refusal in Mandarin Chinese. Paper presented at the Fourth International Pragmatics Conference, Shian Women's University, Kobe, Japan, July 25–30.

Liu, J. J. Y. (1962). *The Art of Chinese Poetry*. Chicago, IL: The University of Chicago Press.

Liu, J. J. Y. (1986). The paradox of poetics and the poetics of paradox. In S.-f. Lin & S. Owen (Eds.), *The Vitality of the Lyric Voice* (pp. 49–70). Princeton, NJ: Princeton University Press.

Liu, Y. (1996a). To capture the essence of Chinese rhetoric: An anatomy of a paradigm in comparative rhetoric. *Rhetoric Review, 14*(2), 318–334.

Liu, Y. (1996b). Three issues in argumentative conception of early Chinese discourse. *Philosophy East and West, 46*(1), 33–58.

Lu, X. (1998). *Rhetoric in Ancient China, Fifth to Third century B.C.E.* Columbia SC: University of South Carolina Press.

Ma, R. (1996). Saying "yes" for "no" and "no" for "yes": A Chinese rule. *Journal of Pragmatics, 25*, 257–266.

Ma, R. (2000). Water-related figurative language in the rhetoric of Mencius. In A. Gonzalez & D. V. Tanno (Eds.), *Rhetoric in Intercultural Contexts* (pp. 119–129). Thousand Oaks, CA: Sage Publications, Inc.

Mair, V. H. (Ed.). (1994). *The Columbia Anthology of Traditional Chinese Literature*. New York: Columbia University Press.

Mao, Z.-s. (Ed. & Trans.). (1988). *Luenyu jin zhu jin yi* [*Analects*: Commentary and interpretation of the present day]. Taipei, Taiwan: Taiwan Sun-Wu Publishing Company.

Raphals, L. (1992). *Knowing Words: Wisdom and Cunning in the Classical Traditions of China and Greece*. Ithaca, NY: Cornell University Press.

Samovar, L. A., Porter, R. E., & McDaniel, E. R. (2007). *Communication between Cultures*. CA: Wadsworth/Thomson Learning.

Shou, W.-y. (1994). (Ed. & Trans., X. Zhong). *Zhongkuo li dai renji molue baodian* [The treasure book of studies on historical Chinese interpersonal plotting]. Taipei: Shi-Cau Publishing Company.

Silin, R. H. (1976). *Leadership and Values: The Organization of Large-scale Taiwanese Enterprises*. Cambridge, MA: Harvard University Press.

Sung, M. M. Y. (1979). Chinese language and culture: A study of homonyms, lucky words, and taboos. *Journal of Chinese Linguistics, 7*, 15–30.

von Senger, H. (1988). (M. B. Gubitz, Trans.). *The Book of Stratagems: Tactics for Triumph and Survival*. New York: Viking Penguin.

Wang, Y. (2000). The pragmatics of 'never tell too plainly': Indirect communication in Chan Buddhism. *Asian Philosophy, 10*(1), 7–31.

Wang, Y. (2004). The strategies of "goblet words": Indirect communication in the Zhuangzi. *Journal of Chinese Philosophy, 31*(2), 195–218.

Wu, K.-m. (1989). Chinese aesthetics. In R. E. Allinson (Ed.), *Understanding the Chinese Mind* (pp.236–264). Hong Kong: Oxford University Press.

Xiang, T.-j. (1993/1966). *Zhongguo minzuxing yanjiu* [*A study of the Chinese people*]. Taipei: Shangwu Books, Inc.

Xiao, L.-h. (1981). *Qian jiang you shui qian jiang yue* [Where there is water, there is reflected a moon]. Taipei: United Newspaper.

Xiao, X.-s. (1998). "*Daoyu*" *de chuanli youxi* [The power game of "Dao-discourse"]. Paper presented at the Annual Convention of the Chinese Communication Society, Taipei, Taiwan.

Xu, R.-y. (2007, Nov. 21). *Wenhua zhongxin ruce zengjia tian "shi" yi* [Female restrooms in Cultural Center add poetic feelings]. *United News*. Retrieved Jan. 10, 2008, from udndata.com.

Young, L. W. L. (1994). *Crosstalk and Culture in Sino-American Communication*. New York, NY: Cambridge University Press.

Zeng, S.-q. (1992). *Yuantong de renji guanxi guanli fa* [Smooth management of interpersonal relationships]. Taipei: Fang-Zhi Publishing Company.

12

Changes in the Cultural Arguments of Chinese Political Leaders*

D. Ray HEISEY
Kent State University, USA

Abstract: The paper examines selected speeches of Chinese political leaders on domestic and international issues to determine the nature of the arguments used over time, from Sun Yat-sen to President Hu Jintao. Though the Chinese argument grounded in the five principles of international relations has not changed over time, as all contemporary leaders have used the five principles in their speeches, the casting of the cultural argument for China's position in the world, seen as a narrative, has changed in its emphasis. The argument, with its attending metaphor, shifts from Sun Yat-sen's rising up against oppression and restoring nationalism, to Mao Zedong's standing up for Chinese independence from feudalism and imperialism in an ideological struggle, to Deng Xiaoping's establishing a Chinese strategic economic pragmatism by groping the stones in measured self-reliance, to Jiang Zemin's creating a Chinese constructive strategic partnership while following its own path of national development, to Hu Jintao's creating a constructive and cooperative relationship in mutual dialogue. Each leader, constructing his version of the narrative argument, draws upon the unique history and conditions of China at the time, to move from independence to cooperation.

---

* A revision of a paper presented at the National Communication Association convention, November 21–24, 2002, New Orleans, LA, and published in *Human Communication*, Vol. 6, No. 1, (Spring/Summer), 2003, pp. 1–11 which granted permission for a revision of its article to be published.

Introduction

One of the characteristics of the Chinese culture has been its ability to adapt, whether to the behavioral demands of its foreign invaders or to the challenges of its leaders or to the threats of its neighbors. Adaptation, of course, is one of the hallmarks of political success as well as rhetorical success. When the audience makes demands on a speaker or leader, the skill of responding with appropriate adaptation signals the success or failure of the communicator. Deng Xiaoping has been acknowledged as a master of adaptation. In his speech to the leading comrades of the central propaganda department in 1981, he said, "The policy of 'letting a hundred flowers bloom, a hundred schools of thought contend' cannot be separated from the practice of criticism and self-criticism. In criticizing, we must be democratic and reason things out, but criticism should never be dismissed offhand as using the 'big stick'. We must get clear on this whole question of criticism and self-criticism, for it is important in bringing along the next generation" (Deng, 1984, p.370). The study of how leaders use language to bring their people along to their points of view and to their interpretation of reality enables one to advance in understanding the interaction between thought and behavior.

The purpose of the present study is to examine the language of selected Chinese political leaders to determine how the changes or adaptations in their use of language have enabled the leaders to conform to the cultural expectations of their society. Throughout the decades since the New China in 1949, how have the cultural arguments of the leaders changed for viewing the role of China in their world?

The plan is to look at speeches of the political leaders from Mao, Deng, Jiang, to Hu to compare their terminology, in translation, of course, in describing what it was that China was about. This is an overview, broad stroke attempt, to see what kinds of changes in rhetorical construction have taken place over the years, as one leader comes and goes and another takes his place.

When I use the term cultural argument I mean a claim made that grows out of what is understood as the thinking and experience of a people. When President Bush, for example, argues that the U.S. needs to go after Saddam Hussein because of the threat that he can supply the international terrorists with weapons of mass destruction, he is drawing upon the common understanding and experience of the American people on September 11. September 11 has become a uniquely American argument that presumably needs no explanation. Similar to an earlier study (Heisey, 1993) in which I examined the use of narrative structure and metaphoric language of international leaders in their interventionist rhetoric, in this Chinese case study I will look at the use of narrative and the use of metaphor to assist our understanding of how these leaders changed in their cultural arguments. By narrative I mean Fisher's notion of "a story conceived as a discrete sequence of thought and / or action" that holds "good reasons" (Fisher, 1985, p. 349). By metaphor I mean what Fernandez calls the strategic use of language to make a "shift in feeling tone — by adornment" that moves the listener's thinking "along a dimension" to "domains" with positive cultural meanings (Fernandez, 1986, p. 12).

There are two central arguments to be made, based on this examination. One is that in one sense, there has been no change in the primary cultural argument that China's role in the world is governed by the five principles of peaceful coexistence in international relations. This argument is historical and cultural. The other is that the casting of the argument as to what China is trying to do has changed in its emphasis to reflect the changing conditions of the inner and outer worlds in which China finds itself.

This is consistent with Mao's dictum that the essence of the revolution was, as he emphasized in his famous speech at Yan'an, to "Seek truth from facts" (Deng, 1984, p. 141). Deng illustrates this truism by explaining that Mao's strategy was to begin the revolution in the countryside, where the enemy was weak, and then encircle the cities, something he claims had never been tried before, even by Marx or Lenin, but it was "the specific road for the revolution in China's concrete conditions" (Deng, 1984, p. 141). The essence of Mao Zedong Thought, said Deng, was that "we must always proceed from current reality when handling questions of principle and policy" (Deng, 1984, p. 142). This provides the political, philosophical, and rhetorical underpinning for how China describes its role in the world and how it will proceed to practice that role.

Sun Yat-sen (1866–1925)

Before taking up Mao Zedong, however, I would like to go back to Sun Yat-sen, because there is in him a foreshadowing of the Chinese revolution carried out by Mao in terms of the language used to describe China's role and what it needed to do. In leading the revolution of 1911, and in the years following, Sun argued that China needed to go back to its cultural heritage and revive its cultural emphasis on family and clan and conceive the nation in terms of clan-ism, so that it would be proud of its language and religion and philosophy. In his well-known speech on "The Three Principles of the People" (Sun, 1981), given many times during 1924, Sun created a narrative of how China had allowed itself to be taken over by the Manchu dynasty from within and by the imperial powers from outside and needed now to throw off oppression at every hand, both internal and external, and build "a Chinese nation."

Sun was arguing a nascent nationalism where the people would be willing to fight for their own nation against the oppression that was ruining them. Sun asked his people to look back to their own historical roots and to their own cultural ways and be independent of the "road which the Great Powers are traveling" (Sun, 1981, p. 37). The metaphor that he used was an image of the nation itself "rising up to power," "restoring its national standing," and "lifting up the fall" of other nations, in short, a restoration of its once international upright position (p. 37).

This could best be done not by emulating the West, but by restoring the principles of Confucius, and reemphasizing the language, religion, and customs of the Chinese people. He asked the new Republic to practice non-cooperation and resistance to Western powers and instead practice what is from their own history and culture.

Sun is the one political leader that both the nationalists and the socialists of the Chinese communities can subscribe to and honor with glowing accolades. His picture is displayed in the most prominent position at Tiananmen Square and his leadership in calling for China as a nation to become a modern nation in the 20th century is heralded by all Chinese, whether on the Mainland or in Taiwan.

Mao Zedong (1893–1976)

Mao brought to China a revolution that made it a New country because of the way he stood up for Chinese independence from feudalism from within and from imperialism from without. In using this two-pronged approach with his argument he was similar to Sun. Mao's narrative was a story that demonstrated how an "imperial political system" engaged in a program that "subjected the farming and working class to the relentless coercion and exploitation of the few feudal lords"(Wang, 1999, pp. 266, 267).

The second part of his story was that "China was a wounded dragon subject to the ceaseless onslaughts of foreign powers" and after 1949 had as its main enemy the Western powers. (p. 267). Imperialism both from within and from without was Mao's obsession.

The end of Mao's narrative was the achievement of independence. The key rhetorical construction that Mao delivered was the concept that China once again could enjoy "independence." He needed to get the people to rise up and stand up with him against the oppressors, so that China could build itself into a nation that had the answers to its own problems. In this sense Mao was heralding what Sun had advocated a generation earlier. The feudal system within had to go and the enemy without had to be defeated so the language used was total and absolute. There could be no compromise. Independence was the whole game.

The metaphor used in Mao's argument for achieving independence was "struggle." It was a struggle to gain independence and it was a struggle to maintain independence from imperialist forces. In his famous *Talks at Yenan* in 1942 he said, "In our struggle for the liberation of the Chinese people there are various fronts, among which there are the fronts of the pen and of the gun, the cultural and the military fronts" (Quoted in Wang, 2000, p.189). He wanted to enlist artists and literary leaders, as well as soldiers in his struggle for liberation. In this he was successful.

Following Mao's successful "standing up" of the nation in 1949, and two decades later, Mao brought onto the landscape another struggle for maintaining liberation. In his analysis of Mao's Cultural Revolution Movement in the 1960s, Huang (2000) argues, "The movement was started with a 'sharp class struggle' on 'the ideological and cultural front,'" and had as its objective "to change people's subjective world while changing the objective world." In this struggle for change, Mao established that the "three dimensions of transformation of people — cognitive, attitudinal, and behavioral — were gained through mass participation in the movement" (Huang, p.209). Mao viewed his revolution for independence from imperialism both from within and from without, as a human, but more importantly, a class struggle.

The controversial impact of Mao's struggle for liberation is characterized by Wang (2000) as constituting "two equally incredible feats": "Beginning with a fragmented party and a decimated army, he succeeded in unifying China and bringing the nation out of a century of chaos and disorder; and second, more than once after 1949, he plunged the country into economic and political turmoil either for power consolidation or for ideological purification, culminating in the disastrous Cultural Revolution" (p.179).

Deng Xiaoping (1904–1997)

When Deng came into the picture with personal impact after obtaining power in 1978, he had the difficult task of making a transition from Mao's political revolution of achieving independence to his own economic revolution using strategic pragmatism. At first, he wasn't as interested in the struggle for independence from imperialist forces, as that was no longer needed, so much as in building self-reliance in the absence of outside help.

He wanted later on, however, to build a narrative that included a China who had a peaceful coexistence with other nations so that he, as China's leader, could build his own economic stability within and thus have a chance to develop his country in transition into a modern state. Though he wanted to remain faithful to Mao's principles, he could strategically accomplish this by interpreting what he was doing as being "socialism with Chinese characteristics."

> "To accomplish modernization of a Chinese type," he told a forum in 1979, "we must proceed from China's special characteristics" (Deng, 1984, p. 172). Later in the same speech, he said that it is following Mao's thought to have a type of democracy that is under the guidance of "centralism." He continued, "Under this system, personal interests must be subordinated to collective ones, the interests of the part to those of the whole, and immediate to long-term interests" (Deng, 1984, p. 183).

These interests were viewed as national interests and, according to Wang (1999), "national interest, not political ideology, guided China's foreign policy, a subtle change from Mao's thinking on international relations" (p. 273). This principle of conforming to national interests rather than political ideology is shown in the essay by Heisey (1999) in the way China's leaders, in the Gulf War and in the decade following, constructed "a rhetoric of socialization" (p. 234) by identifying with the interests of the UN and of other nations and in so doing achieved China's own international interests.

Deng's reform movement was based upon experimentation, as he moved ahead little by little. He began in designated zones only at first to see how the economic changes would go and the nature of the changes was also experimental. He liked to use the metaphor of "groping the stones," in reference to finding one's way across the stream by feeling for one stone after another. Qiu (2000) associates groping the stones with the term "hybridized nature of strategic pragmatism in particularism in experimentation" (p. 255).

His emphasis on flexibility and ambiguity in both language and policy allowed Deng to move away from Mao's oppression to a more open development of thought and behavior in economic matters, so long as they were directed by the overarching framework of Chinese characteristics. Thus Sun's call for the people to rise up with their own "Chineseness" was being answered and Mao's "struggle" for liberation and independence was still being followed in principle, for China was now transforming itself into a nation that was opening up to the outside world while at the same time was being true to its own historical and cultural integrity.

Jiang Zemin (b. 1926)

Deng's successor came to power in 1993 and continued in the presidency until 2003. His ten years in office represent a different generation from that of Deng's. He was brought up as a technocrat but carefully continued Deng's opening up and economic reform measures with an emphasis on

Chinese characteristics. He went even further in international relations, especially with the United States. In 1997 he made an important visit to the US to meet President Clinton and other leaders and took the opportunity to create a story for the world to hear in what he said at major speech events, such as at Harvard, and in the way he debated about issues with Clinton at press conferences and with his American listeners.

His narrative was one of how China was building, not just an economic reform, as Deng had done, but a "comprehensive reform" that included all aspects of living, whether economic, cultural, or political (Jiang, 1997, p.4). This comprehensive reform picture was based, Jiang emphasized, not on another nation's conception of what freedom is or is not or what rights are or are not, but on China's own peculiar circumstances, on the current situation, and "based on reality and history," (p.4) or, as he was fond of reminding his listeners, on what the Chinese socialists claim is "truth from facts."

Jiang's narrative of comprehensive reform was a broader and more complete story of what is happening in China than what Deng had built. What was being built from within China and, from without, by the plan of cooperating in a "strategic partnership" (p. 3) with the West, and especially the United States, was highlighted by the metaphor of following its own "path of development" (p.3) within this partnership.

This enabled Jiang to identify with the West in the desire for making progress in terms of world standards, such as joining the WTO, but also to claim that China's path of development must be uniquely guided by its own history and culture, as it has always done, except for the century when it was under imperialistic domination. The unique or special circumstance Jiang referred to, of course, was the need for political stability within his nation. As the largest developing country in the world, it has a responsibility, Jiang argued, to maintain and safeguard stability within its large borders so that it can protect the economic development that it has been able to build in the last 20 years.

Hu Jintao (*b.* 1942)

President Hu Jintao, being elected in 2003, increased in visibility as he was groomed to succeed President Jiang Zemin. In April and May of 2002 he made a visit to the United States and met with President Bush and other American leaders to discuss China-U.S. relations. He was invited by Vice President Cheney and made a major address on May 1 to representatives of 8 major organizations, such as the Council on Foreign Relations and the U.S. Chamber of Commerce.

An analysis of this address suggests that Hu (2002) has modified the language used in describing the relationship with the West, and in particular, the United States. The theme of the address is an "enhanced mutual understanding and trust towards a constructive and cooperative relationship between China and the United States" (p.1). Hu's narrative to his American audience is a story of how in the past decades, since Nixon went to China and since China has opened up to the outside world, China and the U.S. have been gradually building a "constructive and cooperative relationship" (p.3). There have been "many twists and turns" (p.4), as he acknowledges, but overall the two countries have been developing cooperative bilateral relations built upon "trust" and "strategic far-sightedness" (p.3).

Throughout the address Hu uses the terms "cooperative" or "cooperation" (pp. 1-4) a total of 18 times, more than any other major theme. He identifies the major areas where China and the U.S. have been cooperating, such as in "economic development" (p.2), "exchanges" (p.2), "trade" (p.2), fighting "terrorism" (p.4), preventing "proliferation of weapons of mass destruction" (p.4), and working together on "peace and stability" issues on "the Korean Peninsula, South Asia, and the Middle East" (p.4). From Hu's perspective, building a constructive and cooperative relationship is his story of the two countries.

What is the metaphor that Hu uses? The image he tries to construct is one of "dialogue." He says that he has had "candid and constructive dialogue" (p.1) with President Bush and other U.S. leaders since he arrived here. He argues further that "dialogues and exchanges are playing an irreplaceable role in enhancing mutual understanding and trust and developing constructive and cooperative bilateral relations" (p.3). He wants to see "high-level strategic dialogues" stepped up between the two sides in the future (p.3).

Especially in the areas where there is disagreement between the two nations, Hu advocates that the way to achieve greater understanding is through dialogue. For example, on the Taiwan issue, "the most important and most sensitive issue at the heart of China-U.S. relations," Hu says that "we can, through dialogue on an equal footing, increase our understanding, expand our areas of agreement and gradually reduce our differences" (p.4). In areas of world peace important to both countries, Hu refers to solid achievement where China and the U.S. "have conducted effective dialogue" (p.4).

Zhu Rongji, China's former premier, in reference as to what is needed between the U.S. and China, underscored the metaphor of dialogue when he said on China Central Television, "There must be a shift from threat to dialogue across the Pacific Ocean" (aired on C-SPAN, Mar. 15, 2000). Dialogue, implying the element of equality, or, "equal footing," as Hu put it, as a national behavior with the United States, is a shift in thinking as compared to following one's own path of development within a strategic partnership, as Jiang argued.

Conclusion

The paper has presented the argument that, though the major Chinese political leaders have been consistent in their argument that China has subscribed to the five principles of peaceful coexistence since the founding of the New China, changes have occurred in the casting of their cultural arguments as each succeeding generation of leaders assumed responsibility for guiding the country.

The narratives built by these leaders were first, by Sun, that China was the victim of imperialism and needed to rise up and become a nation once again. The metaphor he used to convey the essence of this story was "to restore its national standing." Second, Mao again emphasized the narrative of China's throwing off imperialism and achieving independence. The metaphor he used was "struggle," against the Nationalists, the imperialists and then to maintain the revolution, against the "rightists" of the 1960s in the Cultural Revolution.

Third, Deng created a narrative of China's peaceful coexistence in order to develop economic reform, not to insist on political ideology. Deng's metaphor of choice was "groping the stones" in experimentation in economic reform. China was no longer struggling, but experimenting. Fourth, Jiang constructed a narrative of comprehensive reform, more than economic, within the context of a strategic partnership with the U.S. His metaphor was a path of development, meaning that China was no longer needing to experiment because it had found its own way and was following its own enlightened pathway of Chinese characteristics, to use one of Deng's phrases to keep everything on course.

Fifth, Hu now is talking about, not so much a strategic partnership where one nation needs to be engaged with another in order to meets its needs, as a constructive and cooperative relationship where there is a recognized equality and mutuality. The metaphor Hu uses is dialogue. This creates a vision of two people engaging in dialogic communication which acknowledges the mutuality and equality of the two in the relationship. A relationship suggests a stronger connection, a longer connection, and a larger connection than an economic partnership. A dialogue suggests a much more powerful image of constructing a relationship than going down one's own path which may or may not be consonant with the pathways of others in the partnership.

We have seen in the course of this overview examination that considerable shifting has taken place in the nature of the narratives being constructed as to where China was coming from, and in the use of metaphors to describe what China's goal was. In each case, however, the rhetor kept secured to the basic Chineseness of their history and culture. This is to be expected of a national leader representing his/her people to other nations in the international community. The Chinese leaders have moved from telling a story of victimage from imperialism, the need to move from imperialistic domination to independence, the need to establish peaceful coexistence in order to secure an opening up and economic reform, the need for building a comprehensive reform at home and a strategic partnership abroad, and the need to build a constructive and cooperative relationship.

At the level of key metaphors used in telling the story, the Chinese leaders have resorted to the rhetorical terms of restoring their national standing, struggling to keep standing up, groping the stones to find their way across, following their own path of development, and engaging in the equalizing interaction of dialogue.

The limitations of this examination need to be noted, as well, which automatically suggest additional lines of research that could be advocated. First, the language looked at is in translation. This means subtle nuances of meaning are lost and could be very important to my interest in understanding shifts of meaning from one generation to another. Second, this has been an admittedly broad-stroke attempt to examine arguments that have been reduced to abbreviated language. Many more implications may be involved in a more detailed review of the texts. Third, the perspective has been from a Western point of view. The use of narrative, metaphor, argument, and rhetoric is strictly a Western notion. What might a Chinese perspective be that examines the texts of these leaders? Fourth, there has been no attempt to review the reaction to these speeches from the audiences to determine what their perceptions might be to the meaning of these texts given by these leaders in these contexts.

My argument has been that the major addresses of Chinese leaders throughout the twentieth century reveal a shift in emphasis from Sun to Mao to Deng to Jiang to Hu that is based upon the Chinese perception of its reality at the time and with the prevailing conditions in which the leader finds himself. This shift in the tone and feeling of the argument is understandable, based upon the progress the country has been making in its own development and in its relations with the international community. If we accept this shift in the cultural argument as to what China is doing in the world, we can make a prediction as to what might be the next stage on the argument's continuum. Following the stage of dialogue between what is claimed as two who have an "equal footing," could well come the stage of exerting a leadership role in the world as China becomes more powerful economically and politically, if indeed, that is what happens.

Much and more pervasive change will necessarily be required for this to take place. But if it does, Sun will have proven himself to be prescient 100 years ago when he argued not only should China rise up and restore its national standing, but it should go the next step in carrying out its worldwide responsibility and "rescue the weak and lift up the fallen." He said only then "will we be carrying out the divine obligation of our nation. We must aid the weaker and smaller peoples and oppose the great powers of the world" (Sun, 1981, p. 37). This attitude suggests a strong sense of exerting world leadership as a world power, not just engaging in dialogue in a mutual and cooperative relationship with the world's only superpower.

References

Deng Xiaoping, 1984. *Selected Works* (1975-1982). Beijing: Beijing Foreign Languages Press.
Fernandez, J. W. (1986). *Persuasion and Performances. The Play of Tropes in Culture*. Bloomington: Indiana University Press.
Fisher, W. R. (1985). The narrative paradigm: An elaboration. *Communication Monographs*, 52, 340-355.
Heisey, D. R. (1993). The strategy of narrative and metaphor in interventionist rhetoric: International case studies. In D. Zarefsky (Ed.), *Rhetorical Movement: Essays in Honor of Leland M. Griffin* (pp. 186-209, 253-256). Evanston: Northwestern University Press.
Heisey, D. R. (1999). China's rhetoric of socialization in its international civic discourse. In R. Kluver & J. H. Powers (Eds.), *Civic Discourse, Civil society, and Chinese Communities* (pp. 221-236). Stamford, CT: Ablex.
Hu Jintao. (2002). Enhanced mutual understanding and trust towards a constructive and cooperative relationship between China and the United States. May 1. www.china-embassy.org/eng, (pp. 1-4).
Huang, S. (2000). Power to the masses in a mass movement: An analysis of Mao's rhetorical strategies during China's Cultural Revolution Movement. In D. R. Heisey (Ed.), *Chinese Perspectives in Rhetoric and Communication* (pp. 207-221). Stamford, CT: Ablex.
Jiang Zemin. (1997, November 4). Enhance mutual understanding and build stronger ties of friendship and co-operation. *China Daily*, pp. 1-8.
Qiu, J. L. (2000). Interpreting the Dengist rhetoric of building socialism with Chinese characteristics. In D. R. Heisey (Ed.), *Chinese Perspectives in Rhetoric and Communication* (pp. 249-264). Stamford, CT: Ablex.
Sun Y-S. (1981). *The Three Principles of the People*. Abridged from the translation by F. W. Price. Taipei: China Cultural Service.
Wang, M. T. (1999). Civic discourse in China-U.S. relations: Great leaps forward and backward. In R. Kluver & J. H. Powers (Eds.). *Civic Discourse, Civil Society, and Chinese Communities* (pp. 265-277). Stamford, CT: Ablex.
Zhu R. J. (2000, March 15). Press conference. CCTV via C-SPAN.

13

Politeness Phenomena in Japanese Intercultural Business Communication

Helen MARRIOTT
Monash University, Australia

Abstract: This paper is concerned with the communication of politeness in intercultural business situations involving Japanese and Australian participants. Much lively debate on politeness phenomena in general has occurred in recent years and has included some thought-provoking critiques of existing theoretical approaches to the study of politeness, together with a variety of new empirical and descriptive studies.[1] Nevertheless, the communication of politeness in natural intercultural situations is an area where descriptive and empirical research, although not non-existent, remains insufficient (cf. Gumperz 1982; Thomas 1983; Neustupny 1986b; Stalpers 1992; Wolfson 1989). Furthermore, much of the research on politeness to date has concentrated on the linguistic dimension of politeness. In seeking to address the problem, this paper highlights some non-linguistic forms of politeness behaviour — specifically sociolinguistic and sociocultural forms as they are found in natural situations involving participants from different cultural communities.

In a 1968 paper on the structure of the politeness system, further expanded in 1974 and translated in 1978, Neustupny proposed the existence of three principal sub-systems of politeness — the Honorific system, Respect

---

[1] Brown and Levinson's revised version in 1987 of their 1978 publication contains an extensive bibliography listing research in the area of politeness. Certain journals have devoted special issues to politeness: *International Journal of the Sociology of Language* 27, 1981 and 92, 1991; *Multilingua* 7, 4, 1988 and 8, 2/3, 1989; *Journal of Pragmatics* 14, 1990.

Speech / Speech Rules and the Courtesy System.

(1) In this categorisation the **Honorific System** centres upon the linguistic code and is found only in some languages, Japanese being one of these.

(2) Second are the speech patterns which constitute the system of **Respect (Polite) Speech / Speech Rules**. The focus of most analyses of the English politeness system to date is upon this level, though few have covered as full a spectrum of behaviour as Neustupny's framework allows, which includes communicative rules on paralinguistics, topic, network, variety and message.

(3) The final sub-system of politeness, labeled the **Courtesy or Etiquette System**, covers non-verbal communicative behaviour which includes rules of precedence at social occasions, certain gift-giving patterns, dress rules, table manners and ritualised events such as weddings and funerals. Business luncheons also belong in this category.

In the examination of politeness to follow, the main interest centres not only upon the generative behaviour of participants but also upon their evaluative behaviour. Hitherto, much of the work in linguistics and the study of communication has been concerned with generation, leaving the important component of evaluation frequently untreated. Neustupny has made a substantial contribution in this regard by demonstrating the importance of the evaluative behaviour of participants in any communicative situation. He has shown that participants of intercultural contact situations frequently deviate from norms and he argues that the ways in which these deviations are evaluated are important processes for attention (Neustupny 1985a, 1985b, 1988). Consequently, apart from identifying the actual behaviour of individuals in naturally occurring situations, it is also necessary to understand which norms one considered appropriate by participants in each context (Marriott 1991a).

In studying evaluative behaviour, use is made of the concept of norm (cf. Bartsch 1987), that is, expected behaviour, the assumption being that norms account for the whole process of evaluation. Of course, one of the principal difficulties of an intercultural contact situation is to identify which norms are considered "correct". Much work conducted on Australian-Japanese contact situations shows that, regardless of the base language code selected in any interactive encounter, a mixture of norms exist (Neustupny 1985a, 1985b; Asaoka 1987; Marriott 1991a, 1991b). Behaviour is effected by norms which arise from either the Australian English or the Japanese systems, but, in addition, some behaviour is caused by the processes of pidginization which may involve a loss of rules (Neustupny 1985a) or "interculture" (an extension of the concept of interlanguage) (cf. Marriott 1991a, forthcoming a).

In relation to the study of politeness, only a few writers have attempted to systematically treat politeness deviations which are committed by non-native speakers in intercultural communicative situations. Similar to Kasper's category of unmotivated rudeness — "violations of the norms of polit behaviour due to ignorance" (Kasper 1990: 208) — the deviations treated in this paper encompass not only linguistic encodings, as considered by Kasper and others, but also deviations of a non-linguistic nature. It is argued that in the intercultural situation there is much norm dissonance which is caused by the co-occurrence of two disparate cultural systems — the Australian English and the Japanese systems, and, in addition, the processes of pidginization and interculture, as noted above. By showing which norms are judged by participants to be "correct" for the contact situation, we will attempt to identify the components of interaction where satisfactory resolutions can be reached and where, on the other hand, norm dissonance continues to persist. This approach carries important theoretical implications for politeness as well as for our understanding of the nature of the contact situation itself.

In order to examine the evaluative behaviour of interactants, this paper draws upon Neustupny's (1985a, 1985b, 1988) model of language management. This model allows us to examine deviations from norms and the ways in which these are treated, either by the participant who commits the deviation or by others in the situation. According to the theory, deviations can remain unnoted. If noted, they can attract a neutral evaluation, or, alternatively, a negative evaluation (which is also referred to as an inadequacy). On occasions, a positive rating may be given to norm deviations. Following noting, adjustment may occur at the next stage.

Although the concept of norm is crucial in the analysis presented here, the existence of individual variation in relation to politeness behaviour is also acknowledged. Given that the study of politeness is less advanced in comparison with many other components of the linguistic system, it will be necessary in the future to refine our analysis in order to cover individual and group norms as well as broader cultural norms.

In this examination, the study of politeness phenomena is organized around some of the principal rules of communication which were first delineated by Hymes (1962, 1964, 1972) and adapted by Neustupny (1973, 1987): spatial and temporal setting, personnel, frame, variety and content. Some reference will be made throughout the paper to certain processes found in intercultural contact situations, namely, transference or borrowing from the non-base system, pidginization and interculture.

Methodology

Data for this paper have been drawn from ten video tape-recordings of

Australian-Japanese business situations which were set in Australia. These included two negotiations, a management meeting, four other types of business meetings, a courtesy call and two business luncheons. This coverage enables us to deal with the central situations found in the business domain as well as peripheral situations like business luncheons. Business luncheons overlap with other domains but, nevertheless, are strongly in the domain of business and cannot be divorced from the central situations. The video tape-recorded data was principally of industries belonging in the tertiary sector and involved personnel from large Australian and Japanese corporations. These ten business encounters involved twenty-two (twenty male and two female) Australians and nineteen Japanese male participants. Except for one Japanese businessman, all the Japanese were sojourners (cf. Brislin 1981) in Australia, covering periods which ranged from one and a half months for one individual, to nearly ten years for another. The length and intensity of the Australians' contact with Japanese personnel varied: some had experienced extensive contact, others possessed no experience, while the contact of a further group was negligible. English was the language of communication in all the video tape-recorded data corpus.

In several cases the recordings of these ten situations were supplemented by follow-up interviews with the participants. In addition, I interviewed fifty-nine Australian and thirty-five Japanese business personnel in Australia and Japan on topics relating to their interaction in intercultural business situations. Apart from representatives of large Australian companies, personnel on the Australian side included those from medium and small enterprises, some of which belonged to the secondary sector of industry. Settings discussed in this paper thus cover Australia and Japan. Throughout, my focus was upon intercompany interaction, and apart from the management meeting, all the video tape-recorded situations fell within this category.

Setting Norms

Integral to all communicative situations is the feature of setting — both temporal and spatial (Hymes 1972: 60). In the data of situations involving Australian and Japanese businessmen various problems in politeness which relate to timing norms were identified. Where the problems involved deviations from the Australian norm, a negative evaluation was generally imposed by the Australians. Generally, Australian business personnel prefer mid-day business luncheons, whereas in Japan evening is the preferred time. This was so for all Australian participants in the two video-recorded luncheons. Through interviews it was established that Australian businessmen in Melbourne tend to negatively evaluate dinner invitations from Japanese businessmen. Negative evaluation also occurs if the invitation is issued just prior to the occasion, particularly for an evening encounter. This is so since in the Australian cultural system an invitation normally would be made well in advance. A7, for instance, who worked as an accountant, indicated his strong dislike of attending mid- to late-afternoon meetings at the offices of Japanese clients and then being asked to stay on and to join them for dinner, particularly when only social conversation would eventuate during the extended evening. To A7, such functions represented an imposition upon his personal time. Different Japanese cultural patterns for the temporal arrangement of a hospitality encounter, if applied in Australia, thus conflict with Australian politeness norms concerning timing.

Selection of the spatial setting also causes norm dissonance in the intercultural situation. This is conspicuous in the case of the venue for a hospitality encounter. Whereas in Japan a public setting such as a restaurant, hotel, bar or other location tends to be chosen (Sakajoo 1984: 219), both public and private venues are utilised in Australia. It has been claimed by Befu (1974a: 198) that Japanese home settings are restricted to certain intimate in-group members and, furthermore, that through the utilisation of public venues in Japan, "professional service" is available which is most suited to the hospitable treatment of a guest (Nissan 1984: 123). However, a contrary evaluation is applicable in the Australian culture: "home service" with all its personalised connotations is considered preferable to a de-personalised public setting. Australian business personnel report that it is not unusual for them to invite Japanese business guests on short-term visits to dinner, usually on weekends, at their home. A6a (in encounter 6) and A17 regularly extend such invitations to either Japanese sojourners in Melbourne or to visiting personnel from Japan. A8, A9, A13, A14, A16 and others also reported that they, too, on occasions, extend invitations incorporating meal engagements at their private residences to Japanese businessmen, usually those on short-term business assignments. As stated by A16: "I have a big entertainment budget, but it makes a better impression if you invite someone home, or take them out on the weekend". Notably, however, this pattern of utilising their private residence is generally relaxed for mid-week functions when public facilities are commonly used. It was clear from the interviews that although Australian businessmen are often aware of a different norm applying in Japan, they may assign an inadequacy marker when, in reciprocation for the numerous private invitations they initiate in Australia, they receive only invitations to public venues when visiting Japan on business. A17 reported that he feels disgruntled about never having been invited to a home in Japan, especially since he often invites Japanese business interactants to his home in Melbourne. On the other hand, the data do show that occasionally the Japanese utilize their own homes. A14, a young Australian businessman who was invited to three homes when in Japan for a period of six weeks on business, nevertheless evaluated three occasions as a small number, in view of the times he had invited Japanese businessmen to his home.

Norm discrepancy also occurs as a result of cross-cultural differences in the selection of spatial areas utilised for various types of business meetings. Data gathered in Japan and Australia show that Japanese settings for business meetings with participants from a different corporate network — irrespective of the geographical location — are of three types: a conference room, generally containing an elongated table; a meeting room with well-proportioned furnishings; or a meeting area located either within a large open-plan office or else incorporated within a superordinate's personal office. It was found that Japanese invariably transfer these spatial patterns to their overseas venues, with the only noticeable difference being an increase in the number of superordinate's personal offices which, in turn, incorporate a Japanese-style meeting area (Marriott forthcoming b). This form involves no compromise of their Japanese native norm, allowing the business host to treat his guest as a communication superior which accords with the Japanese system of politeness (Neustupny 1968: 414). On the other hand, Australian business hosts utilize a conference room in certain contexts, but where the number of visiting participants is small, not infrequently the host's own personal office is used. Of the eight business meetings in my data which were video tape-recorded in Melbourne, the Australian corporations provided the venue in three instances. In two cases, the business personnel utilised their own personal offices for the meeting venue, and a conference room equipped with an overhead projector was used for the third. On the other hand, Japanese corporations used a conference room for three business meetings, and a meeting room and a meeting area on another two occasions.

In relation to the expression of politeness, differences emerge in relation to the seating arrangements within the settings described above. Whereas the Japanese host treats his guest as a communicational superior and thus moves from his own territorial area to a neutral area, such as the meeting area in his office, an Australian host may continue to occupy a pivotal position at his personal desk. This was the case in the first tape-recorded encounter. In such contexts, this norm discrepancy may produce in the Japanese participant a negative evaluation which originates, of course, in his native system. Although most Japanese informants **report** that in their evaluative behaviour they become accustomed to the Australian norm, nowhere in the data are Japanese personnel seen to actually incorporate a similar pattern into their own behaviour.

For Australians, on the contrary, the sharing of their office with a guest is regarded positively, and contrasts with their negative attitude towards use of a de-personalised venue such as a conference room, as can be found in Japanese-initiated meetings. In certain cases like the settings of Australian companies in Tokyo where Australian businessmen are sometimes conscious of the discrepancy in the cultural norms concerning spatial arrangements, some adoption of the Japanese norm was observed. This involved either the use of separate conference and meeting rooms or the establishment of a meeting area within the superordinate's own office. At times such meeting areas contained furniture which frequently consisted of a sofa, matching armchairs and a coffee table which were placed according to the Japanese norm, with the low coffee table in between the other two pieces. However, despite attempts by the Australians to adopt the Japanese norm, the data reveal that actual arrangement of furniture did not always accord with the Japanese pattern and sometimes was more of an interculture pattern which was influenced by both Australian and Japanese spatial strategies. In certain Australian venues in Tokyo, the position of the furniture accorded with the regular Australian pattern of positioning against two walls. For example, at the company of A32 and A33, an Australian bank in Tokyo, Australian personnel had inappropriately positioned a sofa close to the entrance of a separate meeting room and, despite explicit criticism from a senior Japanese staff member, they did not undertake any reorganisation as they could not understand the inadequacy of their action.

What some of these examples of interaction reveal is that status meanings may be communicated in a different manner in different cultures, and that, furthermore, the communication of status meanings does not necessarily coincide with the status structure within the socioeconomic sphere (Neustupny 1968: 414). The position of guests in the Japanese politeness system is illustrative of this claim, for in the Japanese system a guest is treated as superior or at least as equal with regard to seating and some other expressions relating to precedence. This varies from the Australian system where, for example, the business guest is not usually awarded any superior position with regard to seating, nor is any attempt made to neutralise the positions assumed by either host or guest.

Significant cross-cultural variation in the procedures for initiating use of meeting venues also occurs. In Japan, or even on occasion in Japanese companies in Australia, due to the process of transference from the Japanese cultural system a business visitor is shown into an empty meeting room and waits there until joined by the Japanese host with whom he has established an appointment. It emerged from the interviews that a number of Australian businessmen interpret this as an extremely impolite act whereby the Japanese host asserts his superiority or even displeasure. It is not commonly understood that in the Japanese communicative system politeness is expressed by having the guest wait in the actual meeting area, rather than in a temporary waiting area as required by the Australian norm.

The rigidity of Japanese interpersonal seating arrangements represents another instance of norm discrepancy between the two cultures. In the Japanese communicative system politeness is displayed to the guest by awarding him the "highest" position, usually the side furthest from the door. This Japanese norm was unconsciously violated by a video technician in the second business meeting in the data corpus when he requested the Japanese host to sit on the farthest sofa. The reaction of the Japanese was one of complete surprise, and he confirmed with me after the encounter that he invariably allocates the far position to his visitor.

The data also show that intra-company hierarchy is evident in the seating order, with the superordinate either taking a central or a top position and all others seated in rank order. Australian businessmen familiar with the Japanese norm generally adjust to this norm when in Japan, though according to their reports, when acting as hosts in Australia they tend to expect the Japanese to adjust to the Australian pattern which is more flexible. For Japanese businessmen, violation of Japanese norms by Australians in contact situations can communicate impoliteness, not only *vis-à-vis* themselves as the interacting party, but in certain cases, also to senior members of the Australian corporate network.

Personnel Norms

Other important politeness norms are connected with personnel or participant rules which concern the nature of the individuals who participate in an interaction. Needless to say, various problems arise in the contact situation. Australian businessmen observe that Japanese personnel frequently outnumber them at a meeting and that, furthermore, there may be Japanese participants who only temporarily attend a portion of the meeting, and who leave prior to the conclusion of an encounter sometimes to make way for others to join. Such departure and entry during a meeting, while permissible in the Japanese culture, can be negatively evaluated by Australians as a violation of norms of politeness.

Participant rules also concern speaker prerogative and turn-taking. Although not particularly evident in the video tape-recorded business meetings, it was reported by some Australian informants that the Japanese superordinate generally exercises the prerogative of first and main speaker, a pattern which tends to be shared cross-culturally, but one which seems to be stronger in the case of the Japanese culture. (In business meetings variation does exist when a departmental representative assumes the role of a "temporary" pivot, but otherwise generally it is the superordinate who is awarded the pivotal position.) Furthermore, in the Japanese system, this prerogative also extends to hospitality situations and can include Japanese superordinates abruptly terminating an encounter. Such a pattern is not replicated in the Australian communicative system and is thus noted and sometimes marked as inadequate by Australians.

My data thus confirm the frequent claim that the communication of status relationships occurs more explicitly in the Japanese cultural system. As a result of this norm discrepancy, negative evaluations can be found in intercultural business situations. The Australian personnel note the over-attentiveness displayed by some Japanese subordinates to superordinates, particularly to the Japanese, but even on occasions to another Australian. On the other hand, the Japanese negatively evaluate the lack of focalisation by Australians upon their Japanese superordinate. Accommodation of such disparate norms is difficult in the contact situation, and often this dissonance remains unresolved.

The manner in which the expression of status occurs is of significance in any account of politeness. Examples provided above show that there are considerable differences in the surface expressions of politeness in the Japanese and Australian communicative systems. Differences in the input features are also found. Neustupny has characterised English as possessing a politeness system where stress is placed upon the communication of equality rather than upon superiority-inferiority type relations and he contrasts this with the Japanese system (Neustupny 1968: 415). It is noteworthy that several Japanese informants in the data considered the lack of appropriate expression of status towards senior Japanese to be the most serious inadequacy committed by Australians. This finding suggests that for the Japanese status expressions belong in the very centre of the politeness system, whereas for Australians these are less central and are manifested in different ways.

Differences in personnel roles are further seen in the conduct of Australian and Japanese personnel at business lunches and dinners. According to Australian norms of politeness, all participants of a small hospitality encounter should be involved in the selection of the meal, particularly those who belong on the guest side. The expression of this norm varies cross-culturally for, according to the Japanese norm, it is polite for the host to undertake the decision on behalf of participants (Befu 1974a: 199; Naotsuka et al. 1981: 32). In the two video tape-recorded business luncheons, the Japanese participants in each situation selected all the meal items; only in one instance (out of seven) in one luncheon, and four instances (out of five) in the other encounter did the Japanese permit the Australians to confirm the items pre-selected by themselves. This exclusion from the selection process received negative markings from the Australians (Marriott 1991a). Paradoxically, the Japanese were not even the hosts in one of these two luncheon situations, so a further violation of politeness was committed against the Australians.

Frame Norms

Frames refer to the way in which encounters are arranged, and can be dealt with at two levels. One is the arrangement of elements within a specific encounter; the other is the way in which encounters themselves form a part of the overall interaction. Greetings and introductions are essential components in the opening segments of encounters and perform an essential role in the expression of politeness. A handshake gesture is a normalised opening constituent of Australian business encounters and it is generally accompanied by greeting routines. All of the Japanese personnel in the video tape-recorded data engaged in handshaking activity, although some deviations from the Australian norm were noted. In encounter six, for instance, the handshake of J6a with the superordinate, A6a, seemed excessive and then the same interactant failed to shake hands with the Australian subordinate, A6b. Both of these actions constitute deviations from the Australian norm. Interviews with other informants confirmed that the Japanese do experience problems in generating this non-verbal expression of politeness: they engage in excessive handshaking, produce limp or weak handshakes or else avoid handshaking altogether. This act, which is highly communicative of politeness, is not necessarily easily adopted by Japanese businessmen even though most do consciously aim at its adoption.

The data also reveal that in contact situations with Japanese some Australians consciously avoid initiating a handshake because of their knowledge that handshaking is not an integral action within the Japanese internal system of communication. Interestingly, Australian informants, such as A8, report that this avoidance is triggered by their interpretation of politeness as it applies in the other cultural system. From interviews with Japanese, it is clear that the majority evaluate handshake activity in contact situations positively — even if they remain unconscious of problems with their own acquisition. Consequently, we can safely claim that handshaking is a "correct" norm in the Australian-Japanese contact situation. Any hesitation by Australians to continue implementation of this norm in the contact situation thus constitutes a form of norm deviation.

Transference of bowing from the Japanese cultural system is also evident in intercultural business situations. Both Australian and Japanese informants confirm that some Japanese continue to engage in bowing while some Australians adopt, almost involuntarily, the Japanese gesture of a bow. Bowing is, of course, an act of politeness and is used extensively in Japanese internal situations. However, in my data the bowing activity of Australians was sometimes observed to be pidginized, for they engaged in shortish, quick bows which represented deviations from the Japanese norm. For instance, in the closing segment of the business luncheon in encounter six, it was an Australian, not the Japanese, who initiated a deep bow as an expression of appreciation. The borrowing of such a norm from the non-base communicative system by the Australians may be due to an over-estimation of the position of bowing as a display of politeness in that culture. In the Australian cultural system bowing — even if highly restricted — is strongly marked behaviour, whereas in the Japanese system the regular bow is much more neutral and does not carry a high connotation of politeness (Neustupny 1987: 140). It is, nonetheless, a common component in the closing segment of a Japanese internal situation.

All informants confirm that the business card exchange is another Japanese norm which is widely borrowed by Australians. The exchange of business cards is an obligatory act in the introduction sequence of native Japanese situations and there appears to be an invariable expectation on the part of the Japanese that this act will also take place in contact situations. Australian businessmen who are experienced in interacting with the Japanese engage in the exchange of business cards as an obligatory component in introduction sequences, and they are often able to describe some of the ways in which the exchange differs from the Australian pattern. However, in the present data not all Australian businessmen were prepared to reciprocate and neither did they all follow Japanese politeness rules of exchange which the Japanese seem to automatically expect from both Japanese and non-Japanese business personnel. This claim applies to those Australians who lack familiarity with contact situation behaviour. Following an in-depth analysis of the six instances of business card exchanges in the video tape recordings (Marriott 1985, 1991b), it emerged that even those Australians who believed they had adopted the Japanese norm were observed to experience difficulty with the actual hand-to-hand presentation, and, in addition, they tended to supplement the exchange with a verbal expression of thanks, an obligatory verbal expression in this context in the Australian culture which has no parallel in the Japanese system.

As an expression of politeness toward their Japanese interactants, a new norm has arisen in Australian-Japanese business relations where many Australians print the reverse side of their business card in Japanese, often with their full Melbourne address transliterated into the Japanese script. Since no Japanese businessmen resident in Melbourne translates his address into Japanese in a similar manner, such behaviour on the part of the Australian side is clearly representative of the process of interculture. It is an attempt by the Australian to adopt a Japanese norm, but whereas the use of romanised equivalents on Japanese business cards is necessary in Japan for those who cannot read Japanese, the employment of a Japanese transliteration for an Australian address serves little functional purpose. Japanese personnel in interviews frequently indicted that they consider the use of such Japanese transliterations as unusual. When asked about the reasons for this action, Australians frequently report that it is "polite". Such folk interpretations of politeness are of interest. Firstly, it appears that the number of issues consciously identified for polite treatment by Australians is quite limited. Secondly, actions like the transliteration of a business card are not part of their normalised behaviour and perhaps, therefore, it is easily identified as an issue requiring action. Thirdly, the degree to which such behaviour is indeed polite remains questionable.

Another conspicuous feature in the contact situation is that many, though not all, Australians present the Japanese side of their business card, despite the fact that the shared spoken language is English. As in the above case, the reason the Australians give in interviews for such an action is that it is "polite". This interpretation of politeness is paradoxical, for the extent to which the Australian feels inclined to use the native language of his Japanese partner is often limited to a written version of his business card and perhaps to greetings and occasional expressions. The Australians remain unconscious that the presentation of the Japanese side of their card is negatively evaluated by some Japanese, even if for the majority the evaluation may be neutral. Several Japanese informants reported that it may communicate an evaluation by the Australian of deficiencies in the English competence of the recipients.

As noted above, the way in which different encounters are interlinked is also relevant to the frame component. In the intercultural situations in the data, courtesy visits constituted one discrete category of business encounter. In relation to courtesy visits norm discrepancy arises as a result of the application of native norms by both the Australian and Japanese businessmen respectively. Although courtesy visits are characteristically found in both cultures, in the case of Japanese internal situations, the first visit is generally, or at least sometimes, of this nature. While Australians temporarily resident in Tokyo acknowledge the existence of this norm, several reported that the heaviness of their schedule obliged them to discuss specific business tasks on the first visit in conscious violation of the Japanese norm. Regardless of being aware of the function of courtesy calls, A1 added: "they only usually talk about generalities but I haven't got time for this". Some Australian businessmen, like A16, describe the purpose of their visits to Japan as negotiations, or for "goodwill" or courtesy visits.

The periodic courtesy calls made by Japanese businessmen as a means of maintenance of contact with Australian personnel in Japan as well as in Australia represent another Japanese norm which is noted by Australians. In the Australian culture, such face-to-face contact is not carried out extensively as a means of network maintenance. On occasion, courtesy visits from Japanese are interpreted negatively, as involving a loss of time for the Australian. A13 explained that although he was now no longer involved in a particular joint company with a Japanese corporation, he continues to receive courtesy visits from the Japanese, an action which he believes is totally unnecessary.

A further difference in interaction occurs when a superordinate Japanese assumes a new position or, alternatively, leaves a position. On these occasions courtesy calls are made to important business interactants. Written communication of this event may be sent, as will be news of the change of an individual's status within an organisation or his move to another corporation. Japanese business personnel sometimes negatively evaluate the Australian's omission to provide information on personnel changes in this way. These instances which pertain to the establishment and maintenance of networks are significant for they indicate that a greater weighting is placed upon this component of interaction in the Japanese culture. The cause for such expression may be found in the stronger input of the feature of outgroup addressee in the Japanese communicative system (Neustupny 1972: 12). As the input of this feature is less strong in Australia, dissonance arises and it would seem that neither the Japanese nor the Australian party is comfortable with the behaviour of the other side.

Variety Norms

Variety norms, or the norms which determine the kind of language to be used is another principal component of communication. One of the most significant rules relating to variety or code in the contact situation concerns choice of language: English or Japanese. In the majority of instances English is the only shared language of Australian and Japanese business personnel, though the competence of the Japanese businessman in English varies from high to minimal. In certain circumstances, a third party interpreter or else a member of one of the networks, typically the Japanese side, assumes the role of interpreter. Although recently there has been a small increase in the number of young Australians temporarily resident in Japan who can competently conduct business communication in Japanese, within the range of the data presented here, invariably the base language is English, generally with or without interpretation.

Selection of the language to be used in a business encounter is of importance, as is maintenance of this language for the duration of that period. Australian informants report that extensive sequences of code-switching from English to Japanese sometimes occur in Australian-Japanese interaction. It can be argued that code-switching is a direct violation of English norms of politeness for it acts to exclude certain participants in the encounter from the ensuing discourse. In the business luncheons in the video tape-recorded data, all the sequences which contained the ordering of the meal items by the Japanese businessmen were encoded in Japanese, an act which was negatively evaluated by the Australians. In one long sequence covering the selection of three meal items, four instances of code-switching occurred. In response, one of the Australians pursued two types of actions. Firstly, he became involved in alternative activities such as examination of the label of the bottle near him, indicating his disengagement from the dialogue from which he was excluded. Secondly, he re-entered the discourse after each of three sets of switches to the Japanese code, thus simultaneously terminating the code-switch. In two of these turns he sought information about the message expressed in Japanese, yet was denied it. From the perspective of Australian rules of politeness, the exclusion of the Australian from the selection process in this context was highly impolite.

In the informant interviews, Australian businessmen disclosed a wide range of attitudes toward code-switching during business meetings. Some take a very lenient view in contexts where switching is seen as a corrective device to rectify inadequacies in English communication on the part of the Japanese interactant. Such a position seems to be representative of non-normative use of rules by the Australian participants (Neustupny 1985b: 166), since in internal situations they might be expected to reach a negative evaluation of this type of conduct. On the other hand, a strong marking of inadequacy is placed upon such communication by other Australian businessmen who view it as a violation of norms of politeness.

Another conspicuous deviation from English norms of address and reference occurs in contact situations when Australian speakers use the Japanese suffix -*san* in place of an English title such as Mr. In the video tape-recorded data Australian participants in six of the ten encounters employed this pattern in address or reference. Use of the suffix -*san* by Japanese speakers in the recorded data was exceptional, although numerous Australian informants report its use by the Japanese. Elsewhere it has been suggested that Australians readily adopt the Japanese norm as an avoidance measure for using an English title and surname — a pattern which in many contexts in Australian English communicates distance too strongly (Marriott 1991b). It emerged from the interview data that while Japanese business personnel neutrally evaluate the use of -*san* by Australians in most cases, they attach an inadequacy marking to it when used toward senior Japanese or toward personnel who are introduced for the first time. This instance thus parallels others where the status of outgroup addressee or superior referent are components in the input to politeness. Australians are unable to vary the norm pertaining to the use of -*san* and instead apply it rigidly, giving no consideration to the status of the referent involved (Neustupny 1985b: 165).

Apart from the use of -*san*, sometimes the phenomenon of mixing occurs in the discourse of Australians who employ Japanese greetings and other routine expressions (Middleton 1987). However, some Australians deviate from Japanese linguistic norms through their production of these expressions in pidginized forms; they exhibit rigidity in their usage, and are unable to adjust their discourse according to the addressee (Neustupny 1985b). My interviews revealed that Japanese informants negatively mark the use of Japanese language by Australian businessmen in introductions and greetings toward very senior Japanese and toward Japanese whom they meet for the first time (Marriott 1988: 10).

In some of the cases discussed above, it has been seen that politeness expressions receive maximum expression in any opening encounter involving outgroup addressee, and continuing expression where superior addressees are involved. The data confirm that Japanese transfer this norm to the contact situation where English is the language of communication, and where the behaviour of Australians does not accord with their interpretation, they mark such behaviour as inadequate.

Content Norms

Content norms constitute another main aspect of the communication of politeness. In much business interaction small talk is a category of content rules that appears to be shared cross-culturally as a component of opening segments. This category of discourse was observed in the opening position in the video tape-recorded data and its existence was furthermore confirmed by the informants.

Hospitality encounters within the business domain irrespective of the timing, also perform a significant role at the level of interaction as demonstrations of politeness. The characteristic feature of hospitality, which is the provision by a host of food and beverages, is an expression of politeness which is common to many cultural communities. Reports from both Australian and Japanese businessmen indicate that the frequency and lavishness which characterise Japanese-initiated displays of hospitality far exceed what is considered the norm in the Australian cultural system. Interestingly, Australian hosts not infrequently regard the type and frequency of their own hospitality towards the Japanese business guests as inadequate, when measured against the hospitality they receive from the Japanese.

With regard to content norms, a detailed analysis of the discourse topics in the two video tape-recorded business luncheons reveals a striking parallel in the type of discoursal themes found on both occasions: business or company topics, "regulation" (greetings, routines, ordering of meal, correction frames relating to eating), food consumption (meal and beverages), Japanese culture and personal experiences (Marriott 1991a). As business topics occupied a predominant position in the discourse of both situations, the finding is contrary to the general descriptive accounts found in the folk literature which proscribe business-related topics in intercultural hospitality situations (Sakajoo 1984: 58; Tanaka 1983: 104; Hall 1987: 109). The present data do not support the contention that business or task-oriented topics are avoided during a meal encounter. Furthermore, there seems to be no validity in the assertion that in either culture the selection of task-oriented topics is contrary to polite behaviour.

Nevertheless, certain topics that were preferred topics for Australian speakers during the business luncheons did not receive the same prominence in the discourse of the Japanese participants. Although there was some development of personalised topics by the Japanese businessmen, their participation was much weaker in comparison with the Australians. In contrast, there was a definite preference by Australian businessmen for topics of a personalised nature: these topics included holidays, overseas experiences and family. In English, the introduction of content of this nature is a means of expressing politeness because, in accordance with Australian rules of interaction, it reduces distance between participants at their first encounter.

Content norms also apply to the consumption of food and beverages in business situations. A detailed examination of the drinking norms applied in the two business lunches revealed that all four Japanese businessmen heavily transfer Japanese drinking norms to the intercultural setting: a "toast" was performed at the commencement of drinking activity; they poured drinks for others, usually for the interactant seated opposite; reciprocation occurred; an interactant often used the bottle of his recipient, in addition to his own when pouring another's drink; they did not acknowledge any pouring by the waitress; the Japanese held the glass in an upright position and commonly raised it above the table; furthermore, they held the glass up as a token gesture of receipt even after pouring commenced. Even so, there was considerable disparity between these norms and the ones exhibited by the Australians, despite the fact that two of the Australians believed they were employing Japanese drinking norms. Following Australian norms of behaviour, all four Australians held their beer glass slightly on a slant, they tended to employ a verbal expression of appreciation when a drink was poured for them, and furthermore, they revealed a preference to select their own bottle when pouring for another, rather than select the bottle of the recipient. The other two Australians who possessed little previous experience in Australian-Japanese contact situations did not apply any Japanese drinking norms and as a result of their failure to make reciprocal presentations, their conduct was marked as inadequate by the Japanese participants.

The inclusion of presentations of tea or coffee to visitors during business encounters is another means of displaying politeness, similar to the function of a hospitality encounter. The informants reported that in Japan, host companies invariably provide the business guest with tea or coffee, usually Japanese tea. This is essentially a politeness act on the part of the host and is supplied automatically. By contrast, in the Australian cultural system, it is polite, though not obligatory, to offer a guest a beverage, and in the case of acceptance, to generally provide a choice of tea or coffee, with or without milk and sugar accompaniments. That a beverage is delivered automatically in Japan, coupled with the fact that often no alternative is given, is not always positively evaluated by Australian participants. Contrariwise, some Japanese informants report that the enumeration of precise components in the Australian culture represents too strong an emphasis on individualisation.

Another significant content rule, which belongs in the courtesy sub-system and which causes norm discrepancy in the intercultural situation, is gift-giving. Gift-giving in business interaction has a long history in Japanese culture (Befu 1974b) and so it is not surprising that this pattern is commonly transferred to the intercultural context (Marriott 1988). Both Japanese and Australian informants confirm the general view that quite a few Japanese practise gift-giving in intercultural situations. For instance, A8, A9, A13 and A17 reported that Japanese businessmen visiting Australia bring gifts of varying quality and quantity. Similarly, A1, A3, A4, A6, A34 mentioned that the opening of an Australian office in Japan, the celebration of corporate anniversaries or the farewelling of an Australian are occasions when Japanese businessmen commonly presented gifts to them.

Not only are Australian business personnel unsure about the rules concerning receipt; rules of reciprocation are another target of intense concern. Some Australians are consciously reluctant to engage in giving gifts since it is not a feature of business relations in their own culture. Others, concerned not to violate a politeness norm in the intercultural situation, adjust to the Japanese pattern by engaging in some presentation of gifts, but understandably, the type of goods, timing and object of presentation remain as problems. The pattern of gift-giving is a complex one, at least partly due to the considerable amount of variation which actually occurs in Japanese culture itself, in addition to the diverse patterns occurring between Japanese and non-Japanese.

Finally, brief mention should be made of two other Etiquette system norms: dressing and posture. Many Australian informants commented on the formality and lack of variation in the dress of Japanese business personnel and some of them referred to their own attempts to adjust to the Japanese norm when on business assignments in Japan. They had thus evaluated their regular style of dress as being inappropriate in a contact situation — an interpretation which was proved correct in interviews with Japanese business personnel. Whereas dressing manners are more peripheral in the contemporary Australian politeness system, in the Japanese culture they remain of greater importance (Neustupny 1968: 414).

Posture, including sitting styles, is a further expression of politeness which is more central in the Japanese system. In the interviews some senior Japanese business personnel outlined the sitting style which they considered obligatory in formal business meetings to consist of an upright back with feet together and arms firmly placed at one's side. They marked as inadequate the crossing of legs, both in their own behaviour and in that of their Australian interactants. One senior Japanese participant (J10) related his overt correction of Australian businessmen with whom he worked in Tokyo for their habit of crossing their legs during formal business meetings. In the Japanese system, then, postural rules remain more central and are characterised by a set of prescriptions which do not apply to the same degree in the contemporary Australian cultural system.

Concluding Discussion

An investigation of politeness behaviour in naturally occurring contact situations throws light on the nature of such situations. The analysis has shown that norms from the Japanese system are often applied in contact situations, principally by Japanese personnel but also on occasion by Australians. We have also seen that sometimes deviations from the Australian norm occur on the part of the Japanese participant. Sometimes these deviations are not noted by either the Japanese or the Australian. There are also times when the presence of Japanese norms in the contact situation is positively rated by the Japanese or by the Australian participant or by both.

On the other hand, numerous illustrations have been provided to show that a wide range of norms which are applied in the contact situation by Japanese participants are evaluated negatively by Australians. Conversely, various examples were given providing evidence that Japanese business personnel mark as inadequate certain Australian norms of interaction. Such negative evaluations arise because of the application of native Japanese norms by members of that cultural system in the contact situation to their evaluation of the conduct of Australians.

It has also been argued that contact situations involve other processes of behaviour apart from the application of Japanese or Australian norms. Instances of the processes of interculture and pidginization were furnished, and it was argued that these too sometimes provide the basis for norm dissonance. The data of naturally occurring business situations and interviews where informants narrate actual incidents rather than provide attitudinal reports has thus permitted an examination of some of the norms of politeness which exist in specific Australian-Japanese contact situations. By focusing upon deviations from the norm we could highlight one significant feature, that of norm dissonance. Hopefully this study will confirm the importance of examining the ways in which participants of contact situations evaluate norm deviations, a dimension which has not frequently been awarded treatment in studies on intercultural contact.

Some attention was also given in this paper to the input features of politeness patterns. In this regard it was suggested that some differences are found in the Australian and Japanese systems of politeness. As this is a major underlying cause of norm dissonance in the intercultural situation, more empirical research is necessary. Various other tasks also await inquiry. An urgent undertaking is the establishment of scales of different degrees of inadequacy for different deviations from norms (cf. Neustupny 1990). Another concern is the interplay of the Respect Speech system with the Courtesy system and the effect of combined or multiple deviations from politeness norms. One important theoretical issue untouched in this paper concerns the effect on politeness behaviour of an individual such as a Japanese, who moves from a system which possesses three sub-systems of politeness — the Honorific system, Respect Speech system and the Etiquette system — to a system like English which has only two well-developed sub-systems, namely, Respect Speech and the Etiquette system. The effect which occurs upon individuals who move in the alternative direction is also of theoretical and empirical interest.

References

Asaoka, T. (1987). *Communication Problems between Japanese and Australian at a Dinner Party*. Working Papers of the Japanese Studies Centre, No. 3. Melbourne: Japanese Studies Centre.
Bartsch, T. (1987). *Norms of Language*. London: Longman.
Befu, H. (1974a). An Ethnography of Dinner Entertainment in Japan. *Arctic Anthropology 11* (supplement), 196-203.
Befu, H. (1974b). Gift-giving in a Modernising Japan. In T. S. Lebra and W. P. Lebra (eds.), *Japanese Culture and Behaviour* (pp. 208-221.). Honolulu: University Press of Hawaii.
Brislin, R. W. (1981). *Cross-cultural Encounters: Face to Face Interactions*, New York: Pergamon Press.
Brown, P. and C. L. Stephen. (1978). Universals in Language Usage: Politeness Phenomena. In Esther Goody (Ed.), *Questions and Politeness*. London University Press. pp. 56-289. Reprinted as *Politeness: Some Universals in Language Usage*, Studies in Interactional Sociolinguistics 4, Great Britain: Cambridge University Press.
Gumperz, J. (1982). *Discourse Strategies*. New York: Cambridge University Press.
Hall, E. T. (1987). *Hidden Differences: How to do Business with the Japanese*. USA: Anchor Press/Doubleday.
Hymes, D. H. (1962). The ethnography of speaking. In T. Gladwin and W. C. Sturtevant (Eds.), *Anthropology and Human Behaviour*. Washington: Anthropological Society of Washington. Reprinted in *Readings in the Sociology of Language*, Joshua A. Fishman (Ed.). The Hague: Mouton 1968, pp. 99-138.
Hymes, D. H. (1964). Introduction: toward ethnographies of communication. In *The Ethnography of Communication*, John Gumperz and Del Hymes (eds.), *American Anthropologist 66*, Special Publication, 6.2, 1-34.
Hymes, D. H. (1972). Models of the interaction of language and social life. In J. J. Gumperz and D. Hymes (Eds.), *Directions in Sociolinguistics*. New York: Holt, Rinehart and Winston, pp. 35-71.
Kasper, G. (1990). Linguistic politeness: current research issues. *Journal of Pragmatics 14*. 2. 193-218.
Marriott, H. E. (1984). *English Discourse of Japanese Women in Melbourne*, Papers of the Japanese Studies Centre, No. 14. Melbourne: Japanese Studies Centre.
Marriott, H. E. (1985) *Introductions in Australian-Japanese Contact Situations*, Working Papers of the Japanese Studies Centre, No. 4. Melbourne: Japanese Studies Centre.
Marriott, H. E. (1988) *Japanese Business and Social Etiquette*, Working Papers of the Japanese Study Centre, No. 13. Melbourne: Japanese Studies Centre.
Marriott, H. E. (1990a). Intercultural business negotiations: the problem of norm

discrepancy. *Australian Review of Applied Linguistics*, S.7. 33–65.

Marriott, H. E. (1990b). The development of Japanese business communication research. *Japanese Studies Association of Australia Newsletter 10*. 2, 17–31.

Marriott, H. E. (1991a). Etiquette in intercultural situations: a Japanese business luncheon. *Intercultural Communication Studies 1*. 1, 69–94.

Marriott, H. E. (1991b). Native speaker behaviour in Australian-Japanese business communication. *International Journal of the Sociology of Language 92*. 87–117.

Marriott, H. E. (n.d.) A note on interlanguage/interculture in Australian-Japanese business communication. *Journal of the Association of Teachers of Japanese*.

Marriott, H. E. (n.d.) Spatial arrangements in Australian-Japanese business communication. *Journal of Asian Pacific Communication*.

Middleton, J. (n.d.). *A Case Study of the Operations of an Australian Bank in Japan*. Unpublished Honours dissertation. Monash University, 1987.

Murie, A. (n.d.). *Communication Problems in Australia-Japan Business Relations*. Unpublished Honours dissertation. Monash University, 1976.

Naotsuka, R. and N. Sakomoto, et al. (1981). *Mutual Understanding of Different Cultures*. Tokyo: Taishuukan.

Neustupny, J. V. (1968). Politeness patterns in the system of communication. *Science Council of Japan Proceedings of VIIIth Congress of Anthropological and Ethnological Sciences III*, 412–419.

Neustupny, J. V. (1972). Remarks on Japanese honorifics. *Linguistic Communications 7*. 78–117.

Neustupny, J. V. (1973). Sociolinguistics and the language teacher. In M. Rado (Ed.), *Language Teaching: Problems and Solutions?* Bundoora: LaTrobe University. pp.31–66.

Neustupny, J. V. (1974). Keigo wa nihongo dake no mono dewa nai (Honorifics are not a special feature of Japanese). In S. Hayashi and F. Minami (Eds.), *Keigo Kooza* 8. Tokyo: Meiji shoin. pp.8–40.

Neustupny, J. V. (1978) *Post-structural Approaches to Language: Language Theory in a Japanese Context*. Tokyo: University of Tokyo Press.

Neustupny, J. V. (1982). *Gaikokujin to no komyunikeeshon* (Communication with foreigners). Tokyo: Iwanami shoten.

Neustupny, J. V. (1985a) Problems in Australian-Japanese contact situations. In J. B. Pride (Ed.), *Cross-cultural Encounters: Communication and Miscommunication*. Melbourne: River Seine. pp.44–64.

Neustupny, J. V. (985b). lLanguage norms in Australian-Japanese contact situations. In M. G. Clyne (Ed.), *Australia, Meeting Place of Languages*. Canberra: Pacific Linguistics. pp.161–170.

Neustupny, J. V. (1986a). *Foreigners and the Japanese*, Tokyo: Hokuseidoo Press.

Neustupny, J. V. (1986b). Language and society: the case of Japanese politeness. *The Fergusonion Impact* Vol. II., J. A. Fishman et al. (eds.). Berlin: Mouton de Gruyter. pp.59–71.

Neustupny, J. V. (1987). *Communicating with the Japanese*. Tokyo: The Japan Times.

Neustupny, J. V. (n.d.). Problems of English Contact Discourse and Language Planning. Unpublished paper presented at the Regional Seminar on Language Planning in a Multilingual Setting, University of Singapore, 1988.

Neustupny, J. V. (n.d.). Language planning and the testing of Japanese in Australia. Unpublished paper prepared for the International Working Group on Assessment of Proficiency Levels for Students of Japanese as Foreign Language, Canberra, 1990.

Nissan Motor Company. (1984) *Business Japanese 1: A Guide to Improved*

Communication. Tokyo: Bonjinsha.

Sakajoo, H. (1984). *Bijinesumanaa — 88 no Jooshiki* (88 points on business etiquette). Tokyo: PHP Kenkyuujo.

Stalpers, J. (1992). Between Matter-of-factness and Politeness. In R. J. Watts, S. Ide and K. Ehlich (Eds.), *Politeness in Language*. Berlin: Mouton de Gruyter. pp. 219–230.

Tanaka, S. (1983). *Bijinesuman no Sakusesu Manaa* (Successful etiquette for the businessman), Tokyo: Nagaoka.

Thomas, J. (1983). Cross-cultural Pragmatic Failure. *Applied Linguistics* 4.2, 91–112.

Wolfsan, N. (1989). *Perspectives: Sociolinguistics and TESOL*. Cambridge, MA: Newbury House.

14

Reconstructing Eastern Paradigms of Discourse Studies*

SHI Xu
Zhejiang University, China

Abstract: Current scholarship on language and communication has largely been culturally monological rather than dialogical and diversified. In this paper, I respond to this sorry state by arguing for the reconstruction of Eastern paradigms in favour of multiculturalism in discourse research. To that end, I first critique the ethnocentrism of Discourse Analysis, then point to the cultural realities of the Eastern discourses, i.e. the discourses of Asia, Africa and Latin America, and finally demonstrate the unique cultural legacies and intellectual accomplishments of the Eastern world useful for the study of their discourses. In conclusion, I outline the basic principles of the new paradigms and the corresponding action strategies for their reconstruction.

The Globalization of Ethnocentric Scholarship

The discipline of discourse studies, in spite of its international professional success, is by and large culturally monological, rather than dialogical and diversified. That is, if we take into account the imports and exports of

---

* This is an expanded version of a keynote speech made at 15th Congress of the International Association for Applied Linguistics (AILA), Essen, Germany, Aug 24–29, 2008. Further, Asian, African and Latin American scholars study less each other's languages and communication — if at all — than Western scholars do them. Nearly every institution has a department, college or other division on English or English-language-and-culture related subject; but there are far fewer programmes, departments or sections thereof that are devoted to Asian, African or Latino Studies.

books and textbooks, journals, websites, teaching programmes, international conferences and keynote speakers, etc., it is mainly the Western concepts, values, theories, methods and questions that occupy the centre stage and determine the research and teaching agenda. In that connection, it should be noted, too, that their representative and symbolically powerful writers, speakers, journal editors do not usually admit of any cultural bias but present their work strategically as etic, pancultural, universally applicable. Of course, the production and dissemination of this scholarly discourse cannot be divorced from the wider cultural web of global capitalism; they are encouraged, enabled and amplified by the almighty Western economic, political and cultural power in the form of institutional funding, the internet, and of course multinationals' publishing, advertising, marketing and distribution.

This discourse is not restricted to the Western world. Researchers based in the underdeveloped and developing societies of Asia (and the Middle East), Africa, Latin (Central and South) America and further afield, sometimes called the Third and Fourth Worlds, or the East or the South (but for convenience's sake, I will refer to these as the East) have a role to play as well, only it is a limited and dependent one. That is, they have to depend on the Western disciplinary discourse for carrying out their daily research and teaching tasks, including sometimes getting their works published internationally. Instead of using native ideas and techniques and addressing issues of the local people, more often than not they echo, emulate, and reproduce Western scholarship, completing the global circulation of the Western discourse thereby. ①

About such a global and globalised discourse of knowledge, one would of course ask what intellectual advancement it can bring and what political-policy implications it may have, and, here I wish to ask in particular, what they are in relation to the Eastern communities. It is my view that such cultural monologue will lead to anything but genuine intellectual innovation or intercultural understanding and solidarity. For one thing, this one-way "free" flow of communication and disproportionate expansion of Western interests and ideologies will leave native Eastern scholarships in neglect and decay and make Eastern scholars and students lose cultural identity and voice or as some authors would have it culturally "aphasic". For another, it will preclude opportunities for intercultural dialogue, critique and cross-fertilization. For still another, the culturally uninformed and locally irrelevant descriptions, explanations or judgements will only serve to

---

① Further, Asian, African and Latin American scholars study less each other's languages and communication — if at all — than Western scholars do them. Nearly every institution has a department, college or other division on English or English-language-and-culture related subject; but there are far fewer programmes, departments or sections thereof that are devoted to Asian, African or Latino Studies.

consolidate the existing misunderstandings and stereotypes of the Eastern World already ingrained in the Western mentality. As Bustamante (1997: 1) puts it when talking about the situation of Latino communication research: "International relations of power, language, and academic dissemination have added to the unjust marginalisation of the most important Latin American contributions."

More and more critics from both within the mainstream and other culturally divergent camps have questioned and tried to challenge the taken for granted truths and norms emanating from the Western centres (Caws 1994; Chesebro 1996; Bustamante 1997; Gordon 1999; Halloran 1998; Shi-xu 2005, 2006a, b). But for some, the plight of the international scholarship is but an incorrigible fact. For one thing, there is a century-old Western colonial and imperialist condition behind the contemporary scholarship (Said 1978). For another, the current state of affairs of the academia is not being less, but with the accelerated globalisation rather more under the sway of the West-centred hegemony (Lauf 2005; Shuter 2000). Is there really no way out of this cultural-intellectual plight? What could scholars and students in the Eastern world do? And what could the conscious, self-reflexive and critical intellectuals in the Western worlds do in order to redress the scholarly and power asymmetry and revitalise truly international scholarship?

The situation is grim, but not hopeless. So in this paper, what I shall do is to argue that it is not only urgently needed, but also rationally possible, for culturally critical students of discourse everywhere, but especially those based in underdeveloped and developing Asian, African and Latin societies, to transform this monological and Westcentric international scholarship by making concerted and informed efforts to reconstruct Eastern paradigms in co-existence and dialogue with the dominant Western counterparts. To that end, I shall show external reasons, internal basis and intellectual resources that will sustain my proposed reconstruction of new cultural paradigms of discourse research. Specifically, I shall identify the cultural peculiarities of the case of critical discourse analysis (CDA) from an Eastern perspective and its intellectual and cultural consequences. Then, as my central argument, I shall tease out the undeniable and irreducible shared characteristics of Eastern discourses in terms of their contexts and ways of speaking and, further, highlight the rich reservoir of Eastern language and communication scholarships that may shed new light on them. Finally, I shall sketch out the possible format of Eastern paradigms and the strategies of action to reconstructing an Eastern paradigm.

There have already been avowedly culture-specific approaches to language and communication being developed from Asian (Chen 2006; Dissanayake 1988, 2003; Miike 2006), African (Asante 1998; Prah 2002; Krog 2008) and Latin American (Bustamate 1997; Lenkersdorf 2006) perspectives. But these have remained in the margins of the international language and communication research arena. Part of the reason I think is that these have been concerned more with their respective issues and agendas rather than with their interrelations and so possible mutual enlightenment and support. In this paper, accordingly, I want to explore *shared* reasons and conditions and so *common* principles and strategies that will together make up a *collective* framework in relation to these on-going Asian, African and Latin American centred projects. So my purpose is not to replace these more culture-specific modes of research, or smooth over their respective distinctions, but *to provide a frame of reference that can not only act as one of the countervailing actors in response to and dialogue with the dominant Western scheme underlying its various paradigms, but also guide the reconstructive efforts on particular Eastern paradigms and conversely be modified by them*. (My use of the term PARADIGM here is more broadly conceived than the conventional one; here it refers to not only a research system consisting of ontology, epistemology, theory and method, but also the research goals, values and the practitioners involved in the research process.)

It is hoped that within the resulting new paradigms the culturally critical researchers will be more sensitive to and more reflexive upon local cultural discourses so as to help them become more successful in their own cultural milieu on the one side and on the other side to help the international communities to understand Eastern discourses better. It is hoped, too, that the new Eastern paradigms will enrich and re-invigorate the existing Western traditions. For, when culturally diversified forms of paradigms converse with, critique and learn from one another on an egalitarian and democratic basis, human intellectual and cultural horizons will be expanded and chances of genuine intellectual innovation and common cultural prosperity increased.

At this juncture, it may be necessary to insert some clarifications about the notions of "East" and "West" and related ones used in the present discussion. First and emphatically, the East and West and, for that matter, Eastern and Western paradigms, are understood not as dichotomised and homogenious entities, but rather as inter-related categories of *discourse* (i.e. units of text and context including communicators, culture and history), real or potential, amongst other possible discourses, each with external connections and internal differences, open to dialogue and subject to change. Thus, within such differentiated discourses, there may be individuals or groups who speak different or oppositional voices and turn into other discourses — effects of *yīn-yáng* in a Chinese dialectic perspective. By the same token, it may be pointed out that it is assumed that, within the envisaged Eastern paradigms, there may Asian, African and Latin American approaches and within an Asian approach, there may be further diverse types of approaches, say Chinese, Indian, Japanese, etc. Note Bene: in the present designation Eastern paradigms as alluded to above, the generic term "Eastern" on the one hand and plural form of "paradigm" on the other are coined precisely to highlight this dialectic of identity and diversity. This brings me to my second point.

Second, there has been a culture-nihilist argument in the social sciences which goes that since there is neither clear boundary nor fixed identity of the West, it simply doesn't exist; so, by the same token, the East is not there, either. What this argument does, I should like to point out, is effectively to erase or deny or explain away cultural hegemony and inequality in the international order. In the same stroke, it also writes off the disadvantages and marginalization of the non-Western world. So the cultural nihilism in the social sciences is merely a masquerade as postmodernist deconstruction, but in fact and crucially smoothes over the urgent and crucial issue of Western power and inequality in contemporary culture, ordinary and disciplinary. Therefore, I suggest that we should retain the notions and terms of East and West, Eastern and Western paradigms, not to homogenise or dichotomise, but as rhetorical ploys, close to Spivak's "strategic essentialism" (Donna & Gerald 1995) but locally grounded and globally minded, in order to highlight the existing cultural-political inequality, undermine the global universalisation of Western ideas and ideologies, and reclaim cultural identity and diversity of the underdeveloped and developing cultures.

Third, by implication, the Eastern paradigms are to be re-established as a new set of cultural-intellectual discourses, amongst other discourses, real or potential, not of domination and discrimination, but of cultural freedom, creativity and democracy, in co-existence and critical dialogue with the existing ones. Now if scholarship cannot be separated from cultural power and if the international discourse discipline has been culturally unequal or imperialised, then the proposed Eastern paradigms — and many others — should have been erected as equal but distinctive interlocutors at the international roundtable. To use still another metaphor, because the international and cultural order of the disciplinary discourse has been asymmetrical where the global hegemony threatens to become total, a call is made here for various, new paradigms to be erected to redress this cultural imbalance.

Deconstruction of Universalising Discourse

Now I want to look at the problem of scholarly imperialism in discourse analysis in a bit more detail by critically examining CDA as a particular case. I choose this partly because CDA is a typical exemplar of Discourse Analysis (DA) (e. g. both rests on the same linguistic-functionalist philosophy of language) and partly because it is being applied to discourses around the globe (there has been a bigger increase in the past 10 years of books, including textbooks and handbooks, journals as well as conferences and websites on CDA than on other sub-branches of discourse studies). A note of caution, though: CDA is itself internally differentiated, but my analysis here refers mainly to its dominant epistemological, theoretical and methodological stances, as well as its research outcomes which are fairly representative of CDA as a whole.

The globalized discourse scholarship emanating from the Western metropolitan centre as observed earlier is not merely part of economic activity, but, as a cultural commodity, it is linked with a supporting cultural ideology as well. CDA seems to appeal to the particular ideology of universalism as a ploy for globalization. For, it discusses neither possible cultural bias in its epistemological, axiological, theoretical or methodological perspectives, nor possible inappropriateness of its application to non-Western cultures. Rather, it indirectly or explicitly presents itself as universal, good, right and true, over and above other possible cultural approaches. That is why CDA practitioners, whether based in the East or West, do not normally reflect culturally-critically upon but only blindly apply CDA's concepts, values and models to their chosen phenomena and questions, whether or not they are situated in Asia, Africa, Latin America or elsewhere. That is why whatever data are chosen to be studied in a CDA framework are pre-destined to be proven wrong, bad and false. That is why local-cultural-and-historical definitions, claims, or explanations are ignored, denied or explained away by CDA's own model and worldview. And that is why the exercise of seeking out linguistic forms is the usual name of the game for proving and confirming pre-conceived, Westcentric definitions and judgements of non-Western situations: say, Uruguayan military's human right abuses (see Achugar 2007), Chinese hegemonic patriotism (see Flowerdue & Leong 2007), Islamic sexism and authoritarianism (see Al-ali 2006), Nigerian officials' illegitimate practices (see Mele & Bello 2007) and so on and so forth.

Truly plausibly universal approaches and intercultural consensus cannot emerge unless and until there is a mutual cultural respect and compassion in place and unless and until there is a diversity of cultural paradigms well accomplished. As Chen (2006: 5, 337) suggests of social science, "claims of universalism are premature in fact and what must be done is de-imperialisation and only then will we realise how extremely limited we are in knowledge" and "knowledge production is one of the important operational domains of imperialism and therefore critical intellectuals' *work of de-imperialisation must first be carried out in the domain of knowledge production* [emphasis original, translation mine]."

Issues of the cultural characteristics of the academic and commercial agents of CDA aside, let us look critically at the universality of some of the CDA's epistemological, theoretical and methodological positions. For this exercise, we shall not examine from within but take a culturally different, namely Eastern, and more particularly Chinese, perspective, because, as the Chinese saying goes, "you cannot see Mount Lushan when you are inside the mountain range".

Binarism vs. dialecticism

First, as a fundamental feature, CDA epistemologically tends to separate everything into two mutually exclusive categories, i.e. to polarise it: thus, subject vs object, discourse vs society, language vs cognition, text vs context; and, by extension to values, true vs false, good vs evil, right vs wrong. That is, it presumes an "either-or" nature of things. As a partial consequence of this, it has often to seek causal relations between the things it divides up for the sake of unity, hence descriptions of mechanical relations or causal explanations thereof (e.g. language and ideology, discourse and social structure, power relations and textual strategies). Such an approach to knowledge reflects the Cartesian separation of mind from body, in contradistinction to the Chinese dialectic approach to the understanding of the universe, i.e. seeing it as unity of interdependent, inter-penetrating and interchanging parts (*xiāngshēng xiāngkè*, *xiāngyi xiāngchì*); the latter tends to see the complex, "both-and" inter-relations of things. So when researchers proceed from a universalist position to examine Eastern discourses as object of criticism, they will automatically adjudicate the latter as bad, wrong and false. And now it is a particularly bad time for this to happen because the underdeveloped and developing societies are crying out for a fair social science that sees the more complex historical, cultural and global interconnections. In contrast, Chinese students would see contemporary discourses as interconnected with history on the one hand and with diverse cultures on the other hand and seek knowledge through critical dialogue with the object as subject and with other possible perspectives.

Self / Speaker-centred vs. Other / Listener-centred

Another noteworthy, related feature of CDA is that, theoretically, it proceeds from a functionalist view of language in which human beings use language as a social-institutional tool for achieving their purposes as speakers, the most important of which is to persuade others or get them under control.[①] In such a model, the speaker is a self-centred and

---

① The functionalist view of language can be traced, via M. A. K. Halliday, at least to Malinowsky, who believed that individuals have needs and social institutions develop to meet those needs.

calculating being and language activity basically an affair of speakers pursuing their own interests. That is why most of CDA work focuses on how speakers orient their language towards their goals, functions or ideologies. This functionalist view of language is obviously derived from classical Greek *rhetorica* and wider Western individualism. However, this understanding is in contradistinction with the Chinese traditional norm of communication, namely, to be, not self-centred, but social-Other-oriented, and more generally to create and maintain harmonious relationship (Chen 2004, 2006).

My point is not that human discourse is not purposeful. I do believe that it serves individual and social functions. At a general level, Hallidayan linguistic functionalism shares with, e.g. the classical (Confucian) Chinese understanding of language as serving purposes (and having social consequences). But the former differs from the latter at a more specific, fundamental — moral — level: the former, steeped in historically derived, Western ethos of individualism or individual self, assumes that language is used to serve the speaker's, not listener's or the Other's, purpose, ultimately, whereas the Chinese variant of linguistic functionalism, anchored in the wider Confucian culture exhorting social values such as *rén*, *héxié*, *qíjiā-zhìguó-píngtiānxià*, suggests that the most important value in Chinese communication is to attend to, not self-interest, but the Other's in the communicative event, and to maintain a harmonious relationship with the Other. Now, if one applies the Western theory to Chinese communicative phenomena, then one may miss the essential characteristics of Chinese discourse caring for others in speech. ①

Meaning-in-language vs. meaning-beyond-language

Another characteristic of CDA is that, methodologically, and not surprisingly, practitioners take written or spoken texts as the locus of, path to and matrix for meaning (and more particularly: truth) and consequently more often than not neglect their context. So, although they may recognise both text / talk and context, their overwhelming empirical attention is directed at the observable linguistic structures and rarely, if ever, is locally grounded and theoretically consistent language used to analyse context and its relation to the former. This is determined at least in

---

① But notice, I do not mean that every Westerner speaks only for him / herself and every Chinese speaks only for the other. There are individual differences and people usually speak for a variety of purposes but at morally different levels. Notice also that my stress is on the moral values or ideals of communication which are differentiated between the Westerners and Chinese. This means that people may break or "play with" their cultural rules.

part by the deep-rooted Western logocentric ideology① and perhaps also by the fact that European languages are grammatically analytic and low-context, in contrast to many Eastern languages such as Chinese which are synthetic and high-context. In the Chinese tradition, because it is understood that "all meaning is not expressed in and through language" (*yán bú jìn yì*) and because we should seek moral, imaginative, and dialogical meanings of language and life (e.g. *yìjīng* and *Dào*) are what we all should be seeking, language researchers have to resort to historical and cultural context and not just text, to personality and deeds and not just words, to intuition, imagination and moral values and not just apparent forms.

I am not saying these Western characteristics are all wrong and should be replaced, but rather that they are not universal as have been presupposed. The culturally different perspectives should be properly synthesised but the topic is rather for a separate treatment.

The Foundation of Eastern Paradigms

After considering the external reasons behind the proposed reconstruction of Eastern paradigms, I want to move now into the internal basis or conditions-in terms of the unique qualities of Eastern discourses, relevant cultural and intellectual resources, as well as contemporary research achievements.

The shared realities of Asian, African and Latin American discourses

Asian, African and Latin American discourses, while obviously interconnected with Western discourses, have their fundamental distinctions. There is a great urgency to learn about these now, not only because there has been little work on the commonalities of Eastern discourses from their own perspectives, but also because there has been no lack of stereotypes of and prejudice against them (Casmir 1974; Chomsky 1993; Cooks & Simpson 2007; Croteau & Hoynes 1994; Hawk 1992; Herman & Chomsky 1988; Pratt 1992; Said 1978, 1993; Tanno & Jandt 1994; van Dijk 1993). Unless the ignorance and misunderstanding of Eastern discourses are urgently addressed, the current accelerated globalisation will lead to, not less, but more intercultural conflict and alienation. As the African linguist Kinge'l (1999) has pointed out when

---

① Derrida uses this term frequently to refer to the western cultural way of understanding that, he argues, was instituted by Plato. Western logocentrism privileges language over nonverbal communication and speech over writing with a metaphysics of presence. (http://users.california.com/~rathbone/local4.htm accessed 042707)

speaking of African cultures, "If a researcher cannot understand the meaning and application of various oral forms (e.g. idioms, proverbs, popular sayings, tongue-twisters, idles, myths, legends, songs and poetry) in a given community, he or she may not fully understand the politics, economic activities, social organization and cultural values of that locality". Similarly, Brody (1994: 253) speaks of Western assumptions about South American speech, "Understanding local definitions and uses of genres has led to the realization that familiar Western distinctions between speech and song are no more relevant to South American oral traditions than the conventional Western distinction between prose and poetry is for North American oral traditions".

This may be seen from both contextual and textual perspectives. The picture would be quite complex in fact but I will only mention some of the more salient features of the two general categories of discourse, the contextual first and the textual second. (1) To begin with, the Eastern cultures of Asia, Africa and Latin America and their diasporas — have a shared past and present context of colonialism, cold war and imperialism since at least the 19th century, in which they were and continue to be dominated, exploited and excluded in social, political, economic, scientific, and various other spheres. (2) Under these circumstances, Eastern communities face common problems and challenges and hold similar concerns and aspirations: e.g. low-level industrialization, high-level illiteracy, poverty, famine, civil or tribal war, environmental disaster, birth control, economic and scientific dependency, sovereignty, self-determination, need for peace and development — in sum features of development and underdevelopment (Irogbe 2005; Lerner & Schramm 1967; Reeves 1993). (3) No less important, the USA-West-dominated international communication system (including the media, literature, education, social science, as well as everyday talk) has often portrayed Asia, Africa and Latin America as backward, repressive, totalitarian, corrupt, war-like, etc. as opposed to the modern, democratic, free, peace-loving West, which have tremendous consequences on the wellbeing and prospects of the underdeveloped and developing countries (Casmir 1974; Chomsky 1993; Cooks & Simpson 2007; Croteau & Hoynes 1994; Hawk 1992; Herman & Chomsky 1988; Pratt 1992; Said 1978, 1993; Tanno & Jandt 1994; van Dijk 1993). (4) Very importantly but far too often negated or ignored, Eastern cultures have their own traditional norms and values, in terms of age, kinship, gender, the state, etc. for human life in general and for linguistic communication in particular. For instance, Eastern societies traditionally take humane and communal consciousness and so harmony with others and with nature to be the highest principles of conduct and communication, in contrast to Western values of individual reason and control (Asante 1998, 2005; Beier & Sherzer 2002; Chen 2004, 2006; Fanon 1986; Freire 1985; Krog 2008; Orewere 1991;

56) and equilibrium is the watchword (see also Shi-xu 2007). ①(5) Finally, there are also dynamic differences and imbalances between and within societies of Asia, Africa and Latin America in political, economic and other spheres. This internal complexity and diversity must be grasped as well in the study of Eastern discourses.

The imperialised, subaltern and underdeveloped context is a crucial and critical background against which researchers of Eastern language and communication must reckon with (see e.g. Chasteen 1993; Gottlieb & La Belle 1990). Failing to do so, one may conveniently misinterpret their text and talk of, say, patriotism as fanatic nationalism, population control as abuse of human rights, selective reporting as propaganda or lying (for more information see also African Union: http://www. africa-union. org/; Latin America Integration Association: http://www. aladi. org; Association of Southeast Asian Nations: http://www. aseansec. org/; South Asian Association for Regional Cooperation (SAARC): http://www. saarc-sec. org/).

On the other side, in systematic inter-relation with that context, the Eastern communities also share a particular set of "family resemblances", as it were, in the production and interpretation of texts. (1) First and most obviously, the majority of the Asian, African and Latin American peoples do not speak English or other European languages as mother tongue in their daily life; as a legacy and result of the superimposed colonialism, they feel the European languages foreign and inadequate for their needs but at the same time their own native languages discriminated against at a national and international level (Basso 1990 Kinge'l 1999; Nodoba 2002; Orewere 1991; Prah 2002; Preuss 1989; Sherzer 1990; Urban 1991). This linguistic racism facing the Eastern world, or linguisticism as it is sometimes called, is an important point to notice particularly because international language and communication research is done largely in and often through English (Lauf 2005). (2) Secondly, Eastern discourses are

---

① Traditional Chinese discourse is required first and foremost to advance the moral-political project of the state and society ("ming bu zheng ze yan bu shun ...") and the particular nature of the requirement or principle is to achieve and maintain equilibrium in human society ("*zhìguó píngtiānxià*") (cf. Chen 2004; Lu 1998: 28–9). This highest principle may be seen as based on two lower-level values: the first is He, meaning harmony out of diversity (originally: harmony of different sounds and replying in conversation; "*jūnzǐ hé ér bùtóng*"); and the second Zhongyong (*zhōngyōng*), meaning moderation through choosing the middle point and / or keeping balance. This accounts, for example, for the fact that China increasingly resists to the American government's hegemonic practice of using "the human right issue" to contain China, on the one side, and, on the other side, tries to improve its human right situation at home, e.g. by writing the human right into law in 2004 and the party constitution in 2007, thereby keeping the international order of communication less unbalanced and at the same time the domestic situation of human rights more attended to.

characterised by shared patterns of speaking that are harmony- / other-oriented (e.g. Asante 1998; Brody 1994; Chen 2004; Urban 1991). In Asia, discourse can be harmony-oriented through affective linguistic expressions of *kèqi* (like politeness, Feng 2004; Gu 1990) and *miànzi* (like face, Jia 2001); in Africa the Shona is a language primarily of restoration of balance between people (Asante 1998: 193-6); In Latin America: "dialogicality" is a widespread feature of "positive acknowledgement of the other" in discourse (Urban 1991: 135). (3) Thirdly, Eastern discourses are characterised by rich and unique symbolic webs, modes and channels of communication (Cooke 1972). In Nigeria, for example, the indigenous and traditional community communication includes legends and myths, music and songs, steps and dances, tribal marks, pottery and wood carvings, birds and insects, to name but a few (Orewere 1991: 55-6). (4) Fourthly, in contrast to talk of identity, politeness, tourism, business and war on terror in the West, peoples in Asia, Africa and Latin America speak, as their topics of daily concern, of poverty, peace, development and self-determination (Duncan et al 2002). (5) Last but not least, Eastern discourses are comparatively poor in production, circulation and consumption, in information and efficacy, in both everyday and scientific spheres. Take their place in the international media for example: the overwhelming share of the international market and so media information are in the hands of the United States and other Western powers (Reeves 1993: 1-22; Shanbo 2004: 12). According to UNESCO, of every 100 titles of publications in the international circulation, 85 flow from the developed countries to Third World countries (Shanbo 2004: 12).

Eastern resources

Apart from the realities of Eastern discourses to be reckoned with, Eastern wisdoms in understanding the universe can also be mobilised for the paradigmatic reconstruction, for identity, creativity and authenticity.

There are many of them but I will mention two examples here. (1) On one hand, both Asian and African basic worldviews are *holistic and harmony-oriented*. That is, ontologically, they see all things in the universe, from nature to man, as One, i.e. as interconnected and unified whole; in close connection with that, axiologically, they take everything to be in Harmony and in Balance (Asante 1998; Ayisi 1972; Chen 2004, 2006). In Chinese philosophy, this worldview is expressed by such terms as *he* (unity in diversity) and *tianren heyi* (nature and man in one) (Zhang 2002) and in African philosophy by the Zulu word *ubuntu* (humanness through connections with others) (Bell 2002; Brand 2002; Krog 2008). The ontology and axiology of social and natural interconnection and harmony would compel one to strive for humaneness in relation with others and with the environment and for equilibrium in the human and natural world. If this worldview is adopted in discourse theory and research practice, then we will be able to see e.g. what the Asian, African and Latin American peoples are saying today and how they say it have to do not only with their histories and cultures, but also with what the Western world has said and done. Further, we can then evaluate communicative practices in terms of whether they are conducive to unity and harmony, or detrimental to them — precisely the kind of academic work that is badly needed in today's international culture of division and alienation.

(2) On the other hand, there is the typical Chinese dialectic approach to knowledge. That is, epistemologically, they tend to see things as a unity of two, or more, interdependent, interpenetrating and interchanging parts. Unlike the bi-polar way of thinking, as is crystalised in George W. Bush's statement that "in this war on terror, you are either with us or with the terrorists", Chinese would see the Other in the Self and the Self in the Other; they would see the fortunate in the disastrous, the possibility of overcoming the hard through the soft, and so on. If this epistemology is adopted in the methodology of discourse studies, then we will be able to go beyond the binary and hierarchical divisions between the general and the particular, the West and the Rest, the researcher and the researched, text and context, etc. and seek knowledge instead as a *continuous process of dialogue* between the researched as object and the researcher as subject, between the general and the particular, between Eastern and Western perspectives, and between understanding texts and understanding life.

Second, there are traditional Eastern concepts, theories and methods about linguistic communication research which can be excavated to garner their contemporary relevance and significance. While many are being forgotten amidst globalization, some continue to exert influence on contemporary research and others may offer broader and more sophisticated visions and techniques than what is available in the existing paradigms. Let me mention just a couple of these here.① One of the central and basic Chinese notions of linguistic communication is that all meaning is not expressed in and through language (*yán bú jìnyì*). It points to not only the limit of the form of language in relation to meaning, but also the need for new discovery, imagination and seeking of a broader meaning of life, hence such extra-linguistic meanings as *yìjìng*, *shényùn*, *xiánwài zhīyīn*, *Dào*, *tiān dào*, *rén dào* — all of them forms of imaginative, idealised and (speaker-listener, researched-researcher) dialogical meaning which is related to but beyond forms of language. In

---

① There are other unique categories in Chinese literary criticism such as *yìjìng*, *fēnggǔ*, *shényùn* and *wénqì*. Take *yìjìng* for example. It does not refer to cognitive or affective aspect of meaning of language, but to the indefinite and dynamic mixture of subjective feelings and objective circumstances, strategic alignment of absence and substance.

that connection, it should be added that the Chinese scholarly tradition emphasises the purposes of addressing societal needs and seeking meaning of life in researching language (Zhou 2002: 9). Because of the intractable, moral nature of language, the Chinese scholarly tradition contains such diverse forms of reproductive and interpretative techniques as resorting to classics, imagery (*xiàng*), reticence, combination of void and substance (*xūshí xiāngshēng*), illumination (*dùnwù*), meditation (*jìngsī*), praxis (*xíngdòng*), personality (*réngé*), the endless circle of understanding life through words (*jièwén tōngzhì*) and understanding words through life (*dézhì tōngwén*), etc. (Cao 2008; Qian 1999; Zhou 2002). Similarly, in India, there is the notion of *dhvani* from aesthetics and literary studies, first developed by Anandavardhana and later refined by Bhartrihari (Dissanayake this issue). The most important dimension or feature of this notion is that language is understood as pertaining to suggestive meaning or transfer of poetic meaning, involving active participation of the recipient. In order to achieve such suggestive meaning, methodologically, the reader has to resort to verbal resourcefulness, maturity of understanding and depth of imagination.

Third, there has already been an on-going and steadily growing body of contemporary research literature providing for the reconstruction. Until now the mainstream scholarly discourse has rendered this virtually invisible. To be sure, the academic output in the developing countries is still hampered by inadequate research resources, relatively restricted freedom of speech, low living conditions. Fortunately, this culturally critical work is helped by a group of scholars who live in between the East and West and identify with Eastern cultures and perspectives. (1) One branch of this, spearheaded by Bustamante 1997, Cesaire 1972, Fanon 1968, Halloran 1998, Irogbe 2005, McQuail 2005, Miike 2006, Pennycook 1998; Said 1978, 1993, etc. has deconstructed the colonialist, cold-war and imperialist scholarship on language and communication. It has shown that the Western research output has been ethnocentric in origin, substance and orientation and marginalises the Third World scholarship as part of the global capitalism. (2) Another strand, characterised by Cao 2008, Shi-xu 2005, outlines the principles for and methods of critical intercultural dialogue between the diverse communities of discourse research. Amongst the suggestions, it has been proposed that scholars must first and foremost respect and try to learn from different cultural traditions of research. (3) Still another line of substantive work, represented by Asante (1998), Basso (1990), Chen (2006), Dissanayake (1988, 2003), Ishii (2001), Kincaid (1987), Miike (2006), Sherzer & Urban (1986) and Urban (1991), has been painstakingly re-discovering and re-articulating the uniqueness and diversities of language and communication in Asia, Africa and Latin America, respectively. Here, notably, culture-specific, aboriginal notions of linguistic communication, such as *ming bian* (Lu

1998) and harmony as norm of speech (Chen 2004) in Asia, what is not said is often more important than what is in some African cultures (Medubi forthcoming), and the active role of the hearer / receiver (Bustamante 1997: 4; Lenkersdorf 2007; cf Fish 1980), ritual language (McDowell 1992) and double talk (Hill 1992) in Latin America have been found. (4) In addition and very importantly, there is an increasing amount of investigation into what might be called the "issue-discourses" of the Third World, as exemplified in Batibo 2005, Berardi 2001, Pardo 2008, Prah 1998, 2002, 2006, not from some external professional or cultural perspectives but from local, native perspectives, reflecting the problems, concerns, aspirations of the peoples themselves. For example, recurring themes in African language and communication research have been that preservation, harmonization and standardization of indigenous African languages across national boundaries demarcated by Europeans hold the key to African development, education, science and technology (Batibo 2005; Prah 1998, 2002, 2006), that the media must be tailored to the characteristics of Africans in order to serve the purpose of African development (Banda 2009), and that multilingualism and multiculturalism must be tolerated and respected before Africans can enjoy justice and peace (Verdoolaege 2008).

These and many others can serve as excellent starting points or even foundations for the proposed reconstructive work. For more details see (A of Asia):

> Asian Communication Research: http://www.asiancommunicationresearch.com/
> Asian Research Center: http://www.stjohn.ac.th/arc/01main.htm
> Southeast Asia Research Centre: http://www.cityu.edu.hk/searc/
> Asian Media Information and Communication Centre: http://www.amic.org.sg/
> Asian Mass Communication Research & Information Centre: http://sunsite.nus.edu.sg/amic/
> Asian Communication Resource Centre (ACRC): http://www.ntu.edu.sg/sci/research/acrc.html,
> Research Institute for Languages and Cultures of Asia and Africa: http://www.aa.tufs.ac.jp/index_e.html

(B of Africa):

> CODESRIA (Council for the Development of Social Science Research in Africa) : http://www.codesria.org/
> African Studies Quarterly: http://web.africa.ufl.edu/asq/v8/v8i2a15.htm
> South African Communications Association: <http://www.ukzn.ac.za/sacomm/>
> Africa-Communication- Syracuse University Library: http://library.syr.edu/research/internet/africa/generalia.html,
> African Studies : http://www.columbia.edu/cu/lweb/indiv/africa/cuvl/

langs. html

African Studies Center: http://www.africa.upenn.edu/About_African/ww_langsofw.html; and (C of Latin America):

Latin American Association of Linguistics and Philology: http://www.mundoalfal.org/, Inter-American Program: http://www.acdi-cida.gc.ca/CIDAWEB/acdicida.nsf/En/JUD-32712382-NPB).

Now it will be realised that there are not just factual grounds and real resources, but also culturally critical scholars and students of language and communication, especially those living and working in the underdeveloped and developing societies have the need, right, and duty, to re-articulate Eastern paradigms with cultural identity and equality in order, ultimately, for Eastern societies to communicate more effectively in the globalised world on the one hand and on the other for international communities to understand their discourses better.

Principles of the New Paradigms

The characteristics of Eastern discourses, their unique cultural wisdoms and contemporary intellectual achievements make up the fundamental basis and so justifications for the reconstruction of new Eastern Paradigms. But what would the envisaged Eastern Paradigms look like? What should they be able to do? Now if we agree the Eastern Paradigms are a necessary, feasible and worthwhile objective to pursue, then we ought to set the basic requirements which the new paradigms must meet, or principles they must follow.

1) The first principle is that the new paradigms should be locally grounded and globally minded, historically conscious and contemporarily helpful, and above all culturally inclusive and pluralistic, at all levels of discourse research. This implies that researchers should incorporate useful elements of Western approaches as well as those of different Eastern approaches. Underlying the present principle is the fundamental conviction that (a) diversity of cultures, including intellectual cultures, hence of research perspectives, is inevitable and good for humanity and yet (b) that all cultural-intellectual traditions should hold the same basic value of mutual respect and strive for common human wellbeing. This principle is somewhat idealistic but I think it represents a necessary ideal in the age of global capitalism, growing neo-colonialism and intensified international confrontation. I call this overarching principle the multiculturalist stance (Shi-xu 2006a).

2) The second principle is that Eastern paradigms should bear their own cultural-intellectual identities. This means that they should

reflect valued philosophical ideas, concepts, theories, methods, etc. of Asian, African or Latin American cultural-intellectual heritages. For, only paradigms capable of articulating their own cultural subjectivity, consciousness, experiences, aspirations can solve their own problems and moreover interact as Subject and Agent with dominant, mainstream Western paradigms. This is the essential condition for the desired cultural diversity and so dialogue in international discourse scholarship.

3) The third principle, in connection with the above point, is that Eastern paradigms should be mindful of, reflexive upon and helpful to the Eastern past experiences and present conditions. This means that the new paradigms should not be content with mere description or explanation, but equipped with tools that may help transform the repressive and stereotypic discourses and create new discourses useful to the Eastern communities and to the humanity as a whole. Thus, for example, they should deal with issues of subjugation, dependency and underdevelopment on the one hand and on the other hand aspirations for development and self-determination. In addition, such Eastern paradigms should be particularly concerned with indigenous discourses.

4) The fourth but not least important principle is that Eastern paradigms must be capable of conversing with the Western paradigms. This implies that they should be conceptualised, articulated and practised in ways that are *compatible with* Western paradigms, so that practitioners of Western approaches can understand, respond to and critique them and consequently both parties can learn from each other. For, one of the central purposes of re-creating Eastern paradigms is to enable East-West, or more broadly, equal intercultural diversity and dialogue. So for example, they might as well use the same or similar terminologies regarding the fundamental concepts from the Western paradigmatic discourse, like "discourse", "text", "context", and so on.

Needless to say, I do not mean that all Eastern paradigms should have the same properties; nor do I think researchers must follow the same set of procedures. But such collective standards are expected to coordinate the efforts of the Asian, African and Latin American scholars and students and so to consolidate the effects of their intellectual work in the local and global arenas.

Strategies for Reconstruction: A *to-do* list

How to reconstruct the Eastern paradigms? What must scholars of language and communication living and working in the Third World do specifically?

And what can those culturally critical and conscious scholars living and working in the developed world do?

But before considering the scholars themselves (including teachers and research students), I must make a few provisos. First, it is essential that governments, university institutions, enterprises must put in bigger investment and resources in Eastern language and communication studies. Second, more broadly, a general international context of teaching and research favouring cultural diversity and intercultural learning should be created, based on the understanding that multiculturalism is the recipe for genuine intellectual innovation.

1) Scholars and students should try to unlearn, uncover, and undermine any form of colonialism, ethnocentrism and imperialism, wherever they are, in not only research theory and practice but also research dissemination and application. In the same process, they must develop an attitude and willpower to break the pattern of cultural inferiority complex and dependency and rebuild their cultural confidence and self-esteem. Indeed I would maintain that, under the current historically derived conditions of intellectual colonialism and imperialism, great efforts have to be made to put the psychological and institutional decolonization high on the agenda of Eastern academia (cf Fanon 1986).

2) Having grasped the forms and substance of the Western discourses and continuing to engage with them, scholars and students should recover and reclaim their own cultural and intellectual heritages and articulate them in such a way that they are helpful for the study of contemporary languages, communication and discourses in their own cultures. For example they can trace in local culture similar, parallel or overlapping understandings of the world, notions of discourse, and associated methods of studying relevant phenomena. Further, they should find ways to reinterpret and reformulate relevant ideas and tools so that they become both useful for the contemporary realities and accessible to the mainstream scholars.

3) They should try to investigate into and make sense of Eastern discourses from local, indigenous and native perspectives. This would entail attention to the feelings, concerns, issues, aspirations as manifested in the local communities' own discourses. Equally, it would be necessary to observe and analyse the relevant local as well as global, international context in which the local people's texts and talk occur. To clearly understand and characterise such indigenous discourses, a culturally comparative approach may be helpful.

4) Very crucially, Asian, African and Latin American scholars and students should continue with the good old tradition of learning from and collaborating with one another in their common objectives. By the same token, they should tap into Black Studies, Women Studies, and Postcolonial Studies, etc. because the latter proceed from the same collective experience of oppression and exploitation, for enriching and deepening the multiculturalist drive in discourse studies. Critique of White, Western rationality and universalism may be equally applicable in the discipline of (Critical) Discourse Analysis.

5) Scholars and students should try to bring Eastern forms of discourse studies and research results into the international forum through all channels (the internet, conferences, journals, etc) and at all levels (e.g. teaching, research and publishing). Because the historically derived English-linguistic imperialism in international communication as a recent AILA Review (Carli & Ammon 2007) has so well demonstrated, it will be a long-term struggle but they should use all irons in the fire to make their cultural voices heard and interact with other cultural-intellectual communities as equal interlocutor. *Journal of Multicultural Discourses* is an international journal which is centrally and explicitly devoted to this purpose; tri-annual International Conference on Multicultural Discourses initiated in Hangzhou, China, is another forum for this intercultural dialogue and debate.

6) Given the heavy burden of history and formidable obstacles of contemporary culture both at home and abroad, Eastern scholars and students cannot accomplish this historic mission alone. They will need the culturally-conscious-and-critical intellectuals in the West to work with them. There are many things they can do: a) to end the one-way communication, education and investigation by learning from, listening to and conversing with Eastern researchers; b) to stimulate and encourage Eastern scholars and students to assume their own cultural-intellectual responsibility, identity and voice; and c) to help create the needs and conditions for cross-cultural dialogue and critique in theory and research practice.

Conclusion

In conclusion, let me reiterate the central themes of my paper: 1) the discourse of universal human discourse has been a universalisation of a culture-specific discourse and can only serve as a recipe for intellectual impoverishment and unending human conflict; it is high time for this to be de-imperialised; 2) as a response and solution, critical intellectuals, whether in the East or West, especially those who are familiar with and sympathetic to the developing societies, must begin in earnest to reconstruct culturally pluralist, dialogical and egalitarian paradigms in order for multicultural discourse studies to take place and for innovative and meaningful discourse scholarship to thrive; they have the reasons, responsibility and possibilities to do so; and finally 3) open to dialogue and subject to modification, the descriptions offered here of the textual and contextual realities of the Third World discourses, the principles of Eastern paradigms and the action strategies form the collective framework for the reconstruction of Asian, African and Latin American paradigms of discourse studies; at the same time, still other possible cultural paradigms should join at the multilingual and multicultural roundtable.

References

Achugar, M. (2007). Between remembering and forgetting: Uruguayan military discourse about human rights (1976–2004). *Discourse & Society*. *18*(5): 521–548.
Alexander, P. (1972). *An Introduction to Languages and Language in Africa*. London: Heinemann.
Asante, M. K. (1998). *The Afrocentric Idea*. Revised and expanded ed. Philadelphia: Temple University Press.
Asante, M. K. (2005). *Race, Rhetoric, and Identity: The Architecton of Soul*. Amherst, NY: Humanity Books.
Al-Ali, M. N. (2006). Religious Affiliations and masculine power in Jordanian wedding invitation genre. *Discourse and Society 17*: 691–714.
Ayisi, E. O. (1972). *An Introduction to the Study of African Culture*. London: Heinemann.
Banda, F. (2009). "What can we say when the English used has gone so high-tech?" Institutionalised Discourse and Interaction in Development Projects in a Rural Community in Kenya. *Journal of Multicultural Discourses*.
Basso, E. B. (Ed.). (1990). *Native Latin American Cultures through Their Discourse*. Bloomington: Folklore Institute, Indiana University.
Batibo, H. (2005). *Language Decline and Death in Africa: Causes, Consequences and Challenges*. Clevedon: Multilingual Matters Ltd.
Beier, M. & J. Sherzer. (2002). Discourse forms and processes in indigenous lowland South America: An areal-typological perspective. *Annual Review of Anthropology*. *31*: 121–145.
Bell, R. H. (2002). *Understanding African Philosophy: A Cross-Cultural Approach to Classical and Contemporary Issues*. London: Routledge.
Berardi, L. (2001). Globalization and poverty in Chile. *Discourse & Society*. *12*: 47–58.
Brady, A-M. (2002). Regimenting the public mind: the modernisation of propaganda in the PRC. *International Journal*. *57* (4): 563–578.
Brand, G. (2002). *Speaking of a Fabulous Ghost — In search of Theological Criteria, with Special Reference to the Debate on Salvation in African Christian Theology* (Contributions to Philosophical Theology Vol. 7) Frankfurt am main: Peter Lang.

Brody, J. (1994). Review: performance and discourse: transcribing Latin American languages and cultures. *Latin American Research Review*. 29(3): 249–256.

Bustamante, E. (1997). 'Limits' in Latin American communication analysis. *Media Development*. Vol. XLIV: 1–7.

Cao, S. Q. (2008). The discourse of Chinese literary theory and the dialogue between Western and Chinese literary theories. *Journal of Multicultural Discourses*. 3 (1): 1–15.

Canclini, N. G. (1988.) Culture and power : the state of the research. *Media, Culture and Society*. 10: 467–498.

Carli, A. & U. Ammon (Eds.) (2008). *Linguistic Inequality in Scientific Communication Today*. AILA Review (Special Issue) Volume 20.

Carey, J. W. (1992). *Communication as Culture: Essays on Media and Society*. New York: Routledge.

Casmir, F. L. (Ed.) (1974). *The International and Intercultural Communication Annual*. Vol. 1, New York: Speech Communication Association.

Caws, P. (1994). Identity: cultural, transcultural and multicultural. In T. D. Goldberg, *Multiculturalism*. Cambridge: Basil Blackwell, 371–387.

Césaire, A. (1972). *Discourse on Colonialism*, Trans. J. Pinkham. New York: Monthly Press.

Chasteen, J. C. (1993). Fighting words: the discourse of insurgency in Latin American history. *Latin American Research Review*. 28(3): 83–111.

Chen G. M. (2004). The two faces of Chinese communication. *Human Communication*. 7: 25–36.

Chen, G. M. (2006). Asian communication studies: what and where to now. *The Review of Communication*. 6 (4): 295–311.

Chen, G. M. & W. J. Starosta (2003). Asian approaches to human communication: a dialogue. *Intercultural Communication Studies*. XII (4): 1–15.

Chesebro, J. (1996). Unity in diversity: multiculturalism, guilt / victimage, and a new scholarly orientation. *Spectra*. 32 (12): 10–14.

Chomsky, N. (1993). *Year 501: The Conquest Continues*, Boston, MA: South End Press.

Chomsky, N. & E. Herman. (1988). *Manufacturing Consent: The Politics of the Mass Media*, New York: Pantheon Books.

Cooke, B. (1972). Nonverbal communication among Afro-Americans. In T. Kochman (Ed.), *Rappin' and Stylin' Out*. Urbana: University of Illinois: 170–186.

Cooks, L. M. & J. S. Simpson (Eds.) 2007. *Whiteness, Pedagogy, Performance*. Lanham, MD: Lexington Books.

Croteau, D. & W. Hoynes. (1994). *By Invitation Only: How the Media Limit Political Debate*, Monroe, ME: Common Courage Press.

Chu, L. L. (1989). In search of an Oriental communication perspective. In Christian Academy (Ed.), *Continuity and Change in Communications in Post-Industrial Society*. Seoul: Wooseok Publishing Co. Pp. 2–14.

Dissanayake, W. (Ed.). (1988). *Communication Theory: The Asian Perspective*. Singapore: Asian Mass Communication Research and Information Center.

Dissanayake, W. (2003). Asian approaches to human communication: retrospect and prospect. *Intercultural Communication Studies*. XII (4): 16–37.

Donna, L. & M. Gerald (Eds.) 1995. *The Spivak Reader*. London: Routledge.

Duncan, N., P. A. Gqola, M. Hofmey, T. Shefer, F. Malmga & M. Mashige. (Eds). (2002) *Discourses on Difference, Discourses on Oppression*. Cape Town: CASAS.

Fanon, F. (1968). *The Wretched of the Earth*. New York: Grove Press.

Fanon, F. (1986). *Black Skin, White Masks*. Trans. C. L. Markmann. London: Pluto Press.

Feng, H. R. (2004). *Keqi* and Chinese communication behaviours. In G. M. Chen (Ed.), *Theories and Principles of Chinese Communication*. Taipei, Taiwan: WuNan. Pp. 435–450.

Fish, S. (1980). *Is There a Text in This Class? The authority of interpretive communities*. Cambridge: Harvard University Press.

Flowerdue, J. & S. Leong (2007). Metaphors in the discursive construction of patriotism: the case of Hong Kong's constitutional reform debate. *Discourse & Society*. 18(3): 273–294.

Freire, P. (1985). *The Politics of Education: Culture, Power and Liberation*. London: Macmillan.

Gergen, K. (1999). *An Invitation to Social Construction*. London: Sage Publications.

Bottlieb, E. E. & T. J. La Belle (1990). Ethnographic contextualization of Freire's discourse: consciousness-raising, theory and practice. *Anthropology & Education Quarterly*. 21(1): 3–18.

Gordon, R. (1999). A spectrum of scholars: multicultural diversity and human communication theory. *Human Communication*. 2 (1): 1–8.

Gu, Y. G. (1990). Politeness phenomena in modern Chinese. *Journal of Pragmatics* 14: .237–257.

Halloran, J. D. (1998). Social science, communication research and the Third World. *Media Development* 2: 1–7.

Hinds Jr., H. E. & C. M. Tatum. 1987. *Handbook of Latin American Popular Culture*. Westport Conn: Greenwood Press

Hamelink, C. 1994. *The Politics of World Communication*. Thousand Oaks, CA: Sage.

Hawk, B. 1992. *African's Media Image*, NewYork: Praeger.

Heisey, D. R. (Ed.). 2000. *Chinese Perspectives in Rhetoric and Communication*. Stamford, CT: Ablex.

Hidalgo, M. (Ed.). (2006). *Mexican Indigenous Languages at the Dawn of the Twenty First Century*. Berlin: Mouton de Gruyter.

Hill, J. (1992). Myth, Music, and History: Poetic Transformations of Narrative Discourse. *Journal of Folklore Research*. 27 (1–2): 115–132.

Hornberger, N. H. (1996). (Ed.) *Indigenous Literacies in the Americas: Language Planning from the Bottom Up*. Berlin: Mouton de Gruyter.

Irogbe, K. 2005. Globalization and the development of underdevelopment of the Third World. *Journal of Third World Studies*. XXII (1): 41–68.

Ishii, S. 2001. An emerging rationale for Triworld communication studies from Buddhist perspectives. *Human Communication*. 4 (1): 1–10.

Jia, W. 2001. *The Remaking of the Chinese Character and Identity in the 21st Century: The Chinese Face Practices*. Westport, CT: Ablex.

Kincaid, D. L. (Ed.). 1987. *Communication Theory: Eastern and Western perspectives*. San Diego, CA: Academic Press.

Kinge'l, K. 2000. Language Development Research in 21st Century Africa. *African Studies Quarterly*. 3(3): 3. [online] (1999) http://web.africa.ufl.edu/asq/v3/v3i3a3.htm (June 1, 2008)

Krog, A. 2008. "... if it means he gets his humanity back ..." The worldview underpinning the South African Truth and Reconciliation Commission. *Journal of Multicultural Discourses*. 3(3) (Special Issue).

Lauf, E. 2005. National diversity of major international journals in the field of communication. *Journal of Communication* 55, No.1: 139–151.

Lenkersdorf, C. 2006. The Tojolabal language and their social sciences. *Journal of Multicultural Discourses*. 2, no.1: 1–15.

Lerner, D. & Schramm, W. (Eds.) (1967). *Communication and Change in the Developing Countries*. Honolulu: University Press of Hawaii.

Lin, A. N. 2001. The great firewall. http://www.cpj.org/Briefings/2001/China_jan01/Great_Firewall.pdf. Last accessed: 02/01/07.

Liu, Y. (1996). To capture the essence of Chinese rhetoric: Anatomy of a paradigm in comparative rhetoric. *Rhetoric Review*. 14 (1): 318–334.

Lu, X. (1998). *Rhetoric in Ancient China, Fifth to Third Century B. C. E: A Comparison with Classical Greek Rhetoric*. Columbia, SC: University of South Carolina Press.

Martin, J. N. & T. K. Nakayama. (2006). Communication as Raced. In G. J. Shepherd, J. St. John & T. Striphas (Eds), *Communication As — : Perspectives on Theory*. London: Sage Publications. Pp. 75–83.

Mattelart, A. 1978. *Multinationales et systèmes de communication, les appareils idéologiques de l'impérialisme (Multinational and Systematic Notise of Communication, Ideological Devices of Imperialism)*, Paris, Anthropos.

Mangena, M. 1995. Our black languages are being suffocated. *Pace Magazine*. Oct.: 49.

Mangena, M. 1996. *Quest for True Humanity: Selected speeches and writings*. Johannesburg: Bayakha Books.

McDowell, J. H. 1992. The Community-building Mission of Kamsá Ritual. Language. *Journal of Folklore Research*, 27(1–2): 67–84.

McDowell, J. H., J. Sherzer & E. B Basso (Eds.) 1990. *Native Latin American Cultures Through Their Discourse*. Bloomington: Folklore Institute / Indiana University.

McQuail, D. 2005. Communication theory and the Western bias. In Shi-xu, M. Kienpointner & J. Servaes (Eds.). *Read the Cultural Other: Forms of otherness in the discourses of Hong Kong's decolonization*. Berlin: Mouton de Gruyter. Pp. 21–32.

Medubi, O. 2009. A Cross-cultural study of silence in Nigeria: an ethnolinguistic approach. *Journal of Multicultural Discourses*.

Mele, M. L. & B. M. Bello. 2007. Coaxing and coercion in roadblock encounters on Nigerian highways. *Discourse & Society*. 18(4): 437–452.

Miike, Y. 2004. Rethinking humanity, culture, and communication: Asiacentric critiques and contributions. *Human Communication*. 7 (1): 69–82.

Miike, Y. 2006. Non-western theory in western research? An Asiacentric agenda for Asian communication studies. *The Review of Communication*. 6 (1/2): 4–31.

Nodoba, G. 2002. Many Languages, Different Cultures — Effects of Linguicism in a Changing Society. N. Duncan, P. A. Gqola, M. Hofmey, T. Shefer, F. Malmga & M. Mashige (Eds.). *Discourses on Difference, Discourses on Oppression*. Cape Town: CASAS. Pp. 331–357.

Orewere, B. 1991. Possible Implications of Modern Mass Media for Traditonal Communication in a Nigerian Rural Setting. *African Media Review*, Vol. 5 No. 3.

Pardo, M. L. 2008. Discourse as a tool for the diagnosis of psychosis: a linguistic and psychiatric study of communication decline. Plenary speech at Spanish in Society Conference 2008: Spanish at work. Swansea University, Wales, UK, 27 al 29 de abril del 2008.

Prah, K. K. (Ed.) 1998. *Between Distinction and Extinction: The Harmonization and Standardization of African Language*. Johannesburg Witwatersrand University Press.

Pennycook, A. 1998. *English and the discourses of colonialism*. London: Routledge.

Prah, K. K. (Ed.) 2002. *Rehabilitating African Languages*. Cape Town: The. Centre for Advanced Studies of African Society (CASAS).

Prah, K. K. 2006. *The African Nation: The State of the Nation*. Cape Town: The.

Centre for Advanced Studies of African Society (CASAS).
Pratt, M. L. 1992. *Imperial Eyes: Travel writing and transculturation*. London: Routledge.
Preuss, M. H. (Ed.). 1989. *"In Love and War: Hummingbird Lore" and Other Selected Papers from Laila / Alila's 1988 Symposium*. Culver City, California: Labyrinthos.
Qian,Z. S. 1999. *Guan Zhui Bian* (Book of Interpretation). Beijing: Zhonghua Shuju.
Reeves, G. 1993. *Communications and the 'Third World'*. London: Routledge.
Said, E. W. 1978. *Orientalism*. London: Routledge & Kegan Paul.
Said, E. W. 1993. *Culture and Imperialism*. New York: Alfred A. Knopf.
Shan, B. 2004. Xiandai Chuanmei Yu Shehui Wenhua Fazhan (Modern Media and Social Development). *Xiandai Chuanmei (Modern Media)* 1: 10–16.
Sherzer, J 1990. *Verbal Art in San Blas: Kuna Culture Through Its Discourse*. Cambridge: Cambridge University Press.
Sherzer, J. & G. Urban 1986. *Native South American Discourse*. New York: Mouton de Gruyter.
Shi-xu 2005. *A Cultural Approach to Discourse*. Houndmills / New York: Palgrave Macmillan.
Shi-xu 2006a. Editorial: researching multicultural discourses. *Journal of Multicultural Discourses*. 1(1): 1–5.
Shi-xu 2006b. A multiculturalist approach to discourse theory. *Semiotica*. 158 (1/4): 383–400.
Shi-xu. (Ed.). (2007). *Discourse as Cultural Struggle*. Hong Kong: Hong Kong University Press.
Shuter, R. 2000. Ethnics, culture, and communication: an intercultural perspective. In L. A. Samovar & R. E. Porter (Eds.), *Intercultural Communication: A Reader*. Belmont, CA: Wadsworth Publishing Company. Pp. 443–450.
Spivak, G. C. (1988). *In Other Words: Essays in Cultural Politics*. New York: Routledge.
Stratton, J. & I. Ang. (1996). On the impossibility of a global cultural studies: "British" cultural studies in an "international" frame. In D. Morley & K-H. Chen (eds), *Stuart Hall*. London: Routledge. Pp. 361–391.
Tanno, D. V. & Jandt, F. E. (1994). Redefining the'other'in multi-cultural research. *The Howard Journal of Communication*, 5, 36–45.
Thiong'o, N. Wa. (1981). *Writers in Politics*. London: Heinemann.
Unesco (1980). *Many Voices, One World*, Paris: Unesco. (Also known as the MacBride report, was a 1980 UNESCO publication written by the International Commission for the Study of Communication Problems, chaired by Irish Nobel laureate Seán MacBride.)
Urban, G. (1991). *A Discourse-Centered Approach to Culture: Native South American Myths and Rituals*. Austin: University of Texas Press.
Van Dijk, T. A. (1993). *Elite Discourse and Racism*. London: Sage Publications.
Verdoolaege, A. (2008). The South African Truth and Reconciliation Commission and Multicultural Discourse. *Journal of Multicultural Discourses*. 3(3) (Special Issue).
Zhang, D. N. (2002). *Key Concepts in Chinese Philosophy*. Trans. E. Ryden. Beijing: Foreign Languages Press.
Zhou G. Q. (2002). Zhongguo Gudian Jieshi Xue Daolun (Introduction to Chinese Classical *Hermeneutics*). Beijing: Zhonghua Shuju.

15

A Contrastive Study of Requests in Chinese and American Cultures

JIA Xuerui
Harbin Institute of Technology

HUANG Furong
Harbin Institute of Technology

Abstract: We make a contrastive study of the Chinese indirect and implicit and Americans' direct and explicit requests. We point out that the Chinese often prefer to delay their request until the end or after face-work and justifications or reasons while the Americans often prefer to place their request early or in general at the beginning and if they want to provide justifications or reasons for their request, they usually place them after the request.

Philosophically speaking, the Chinese indirect and implicit and American direct and explicit requests are consistent with the concept of self in terms of interpersonal relationship in these two cultures. In the Confucian or Chinese sense of self, one is more a self in human relationships, and less a self in isolation. To establish relationship or harmony, obliging and accommodating others are deemed to be the most important mechanism in interpersonal interactions. This necessarily leads to an indirect style in requests. Whereas, the Americans, who are autonomous-self-oriented, self-expression inherently becomes ideal and the inhibition of it is the biggest problem. And this leads to a direct style in requests.

Most cultures, if not all, have both direct and indirect requests. However, even though the direct and indirect requests seem to be universal, the degree to which they are employed varies from culture to culture. Some scholars maintain that the Euro-Americans prefer the direct requests, which is not preferred in a different cultural context, such as the Chinese cultural context.

Pragmatically speaking, differences in the speech behavior of request in Chinese and American cultures lie in the semantic sequence or order of the components that make up a request or in the use of supportive moves, as well as in the way a request is stated. For example, the Chinese very often prefer to embed their requests in the supportive moves, such as lengthy explanations, or face-work ("the actions taken to deal with the face-wants of one and the other") (Lim, 1994, p. 211) and justifications which are often placed at the beginning while the Americans may place request at the very beginning and if they use supportive moves, such as reasons or justifications for their request, they are very likely to place them after the request.

We tentatively call the lengthy explanatory and preliminary remarks, or supportive moves *frame*, the purpose of which is to set up a shared background or an atmosphere in which good relationship or connection is hopefully to be set up. According to Scollon and Scollon's investigation (Scollon, Scollon & Kirkpatrick, 2000), the Chinese generally prefer to follow a frame—main (the main refers to the main component or the main point, namely the request) semantic sequence in a request behavior while the Americans generally prefer to adopt a main—frame semantic sequence in making a request. In the Chinese culture, face-work is often included in the part of frame.

In this paper, the comparative study of the request centers around requesting people to do things and requesting people for something. First we will discuss the semantic sequence of requests, aiming to ask people to do things in both the Chinese culture and the American culture. In the Chinese culture, the frame consists of face-work and justification and the request follows a face-work / justification—request semantic sequence, while in the American culture, the request follows a request-justification sequence.

Indirect Requests in the Chinese Culture vs. Direct Requests in the American Culture

Requesting Others to Do Things: Face-work / Justification—Request Sequence vs. Request—Justification Sequence

According to Ron Scollon (1991) as well as our own experience and observation, in Chinese and many East Asian cultures, when requesting people to do things, people often prefer to follow a face-work / justification—request semantic sequence while in American and many European cultures, people prefer to follow request—justification semantic sequence. The Chinese prefer to delay their request until the end or after face-work and justifications or reason while the Americans prefer to place their request early or in general at the beginning and if they want to provide justifications or reasons for their request, they usually place them after the request.

Let us have a look at the following example from our own observations of a call of a middle-aged Chinese lady on her Chinese friend. She visited her friend to ask her to do something for her granddaughter.

Situation: A female (A, a retired worker, aged about 60) requests a female acquaintance (B, a retired teacher of English, aged about 60) to write a recommendation letter for her granddaughter who is applying to study in an American university.

> A: (*Knocks at the door*) Have you eaten /What are you doing? Long time no see.
> B: Oh, long time no see. What wind has brought you here (*A Chinese way of saying welcome to someone one hasn't seen for long*). Please come in. [*Face-work: face exchange*]
> A: Are you alone? You look so good. [*Face-work*]
> B: Yes, I am always alone during the day. They all go to work.
> A: Where are the kids? Are they OK? You've got lovely kids. [*Face-work*]
> B: My grandson has gone to school. He is very well.
> A: Your grandson is so cute. He must have grown very tall. [*Face-work*] (*A typical way of complimenting people: complimenting her through a third party.*) (*Lauding her face through praising her grandson*)
> B: You haven't seen him for long. He is a big guy now. He is almost as tall as I am. How time flies.
> A: How lucky you are! [*Face-work*]
> B: You look so good. How are you these days? [*Face-exchange*]
> A: You see I am not as lucky as you are. Nobody is as lucky as you are. By the way, how about your daughter and son-in-law? [*Face-work*]
> B: They are working at the university. Both are terribly busy.
> A: I really envy you. You have such a happy family. [*Face-work*]
> B: Just so-so. (*Being modest*)
> A: Oh, what I have come to see you to do is ... [*Prepare for request*]
> B: Out with it.
> A: You know my granddaughter wants to apply to study in America. She needs a letter of recommendation in English. You know I don't know English at all and your English is so good and you have been her teacher of English. You are the best person. Can you write the letter for her? [*Justification for the request*]
> B: Sure, sure. No problem at all. Just let her come and see me.
> A: I am sorry to give you such trouble. I know you are so busy every day. [*Apology*]
> B: You are so polite. It is no trouble at all. We are good friends you know ...
> A: I think I should be off now. You are so busy.

B: Why, we have so many things to talk about, you know.
A: I'll come again soon. See you.
B: See you. Take care.
A: I will. You too.

We may easily see that the presentation of the request or the purpose of the visit is delayed until the end of the interaction and is introduced only after a lengthy face-work or face-exchange and justification or reasons. Indirect communication in this way helps to prevent the embarrassment of rejection by the other person or disagreement among partners, leaving the relationship and each other's face intact.

Of course, things are not always like this. This may not be the case among friends, who would most probably feel entirely free to just use a direct way of request. And in cases such as buying a ticket or paying a bill or calling a taxi, a simple direct request without any preliminary remarks is quite enough.

If we look at similar activity of call on the phone between these two ladies, we may expect a similar semantic sequence (or what is called face-work—justification or reasons—request sequence) even though the interaction is much shorter.

The Americans in contrast prefer a direct communication style rather than an indirect one. They don't involve a third party to make a request for their benefit. They may make the request themselves.

So an American 'A' may have actually begun the interaction on his or her visit to his friend for a similar purpose in the following manner:

A: Hello. How are you doing?
B: Hi, I am doing fine.
A: Excuse me for ... You know, I need a recommendation letter. I want to study at XXX Department of XXX University. Could you possibly write it for me? [*Request—Justification / Reason*]. I think you are the right person to do it for me. [*Face-work*]
B: Ok. Would you come to see me in my office at two on Friday afternoon?
A: Yes, I will. See you then.
B: See you then.

The Americans tend to place the request at the very beginning. Even though they may have some face-work and justification or reasons, they tend to make them as short as possible. This kind of pragmatic conventions in the American culture is to give the other person some sort of autonomy or independence. By phrasing requests in this way, the Americans give the other person the opportunity to make their own decisions.

Requesting Something from People: Face-work—Justifications / Reasons—Request Sequence vs. Request—Justifications / Reasons Sequence

We have discussed the differences in requesting people to do things involved in the activities of calls or visits. In fact, similar semantic sequences are found in requests made by the Chinese and Americans for something. This is illustrated by the examples provided by Professor Andy Kirkpatrick in his study of the letters written by the Chinese to make requests (Scollon, Scollon & Kirkpatrick, 2000). In these letters the Chinese are found to follow the convention of face-work—justification / reasons—request sequence, which is obviously the result of the value of relationship. In a similar request, an American may possibly be found to follow a request—justification / reasons sequence, which obviously has nothing to do with relationship that is popular in the Chinese culture.

The following letters are written by a Chinese and an American respectively. The Chinese is a loyal listener to Radio Australia's English teaching programs and 'Songs You Like' and the American is a loyal listener to a French teaching program. Both the Chinese and the American are writing to request for something.

Now let us have a look at these two letters of request respectively.

The letter by the Chinese writer is a little bit modified. It goes as follows:

> Dear XXX,
>
> I have been a loyal listener to your English teaching program and 'Songs You Like' for several years. I consider the program to be extremely well produced.
>
> Let me describe myself a little: I am a university student. I am twenty years old and my home is in ... , a small border city. The cultural life really isn't too bad. Because I like listening to your English teaching program and 'Songs You Like,' I follow your program closely. But because the Central Broadcasting Station's English programs are rather abstruse, they are not really suitable for me and therefore I get all my practice in listening comprehension and dialogue from Radio Australia's English programs. This practice has been of great benefit. As I progress, step by step through the course, I am keenly aware that not having the teaching materials presents several difficulties. Because of this, I have taken time to write this letter to you, in the hope that I can obtain a set of Radio Australia's English program's teaching materials. Please let me know the cost of the materials.
>
> In addition, I hope to obtain a Radio Australia calendar.
>
> With best wishes.
>
> (Adapted from Scollon, Scollon & Kirkpatrick, 2000, p.81)

This is in fact a very common schema in letters of request in the Chinese cultural context. The first half of the letter is taken up with what is called facework, or the enhancement of the other's face. Then the writer introduces the reasons or justifications for a particular request and then, finally, makes the actual request.

What is interesting is the fact that this schema would not work well in an English request of an American. Given the same circumstances, an American writer would be very likely to omit all the face-work and make the request at the beginning of the letter. The letter of the American reads:

> Dear XXX,
>
> I am trying to learn French but find the local material I am using boring. I have heard your French lessons and wonder whether you could send me a copy of your teaching material. I will, of course, pay for them. If it's not too much trouble, I would also very much like a calendar.
>
> With best wishes.

Note that this letter provides the reasons or justifications for the request before the request is made. It would be quite possible, however, for the letter to begin with the actual request itself.

> Dear XXX,
>
> Could you please send me a copy of your French teaching materials: I will, of course, pay for them.
>
> Best regards.

The indirect request mentioned above is not uncommon in the Chinese culture. The request Jia Xuerui found in the lavatories at Hong Kong Baptist University in 2003 when she was attending an international conference may well support this point.

> Dear Users,
>
> First of all, thank you for keeping the lavatory clean and tidy.
>
> In our pursuit for a clean and healthy environment within the University Campus, your participation and involvement are necessary and must be welcomed.
>
> Therefore, should you have any opinion or suggestion on our cleaning service for the lavatories, please write or e-mail our office.
>
> Our e-mail address is eo@hkba.edu.hk
>
> Thank you for your attention.
>
> Estates Office
>
> Hong Kong Baptist University

What is more interesting is the fact that in this semantic sequence, the request is implicitly stated or understated — it is embedded in the salutation or the thank-you statement (or what is called face-work) and also implied in the statement that follows.

In this request, there is also a justification / reason—request semantic sequence, even though the part of justification / reason is shorter than that in the restrooms at Hong Kong Baptist University.

The Americans do use supportive moves or justification or reasons for request if necessary. They, however, prefer direct and brief request on most occasions.

The notice below is a posted at Dolphin Bay in the Sea World in San Diego, California. In it a number of requests are made of visitors. Obviously, it is extremely necessary and important as inappropriate behavior at Dolphin Bay may do harm not only to the visitors but also to the dolphins. Therefore, at the very beginning there are justifications and

---

In order to enhance your
experience & to ensure your
safety & the safety of the dolphins

P   L   E   A   S   E

Do not tease the dolphins.

Do not hold the fish in the air.

Cover your trays of fish with your hands at all times to protect them from the birds.

Do not sit, kneel or stand on the pool, wall or rocks.

Respect the dolphins and gently touch them with open palm while avoiding their mouths, blowhole and eyes.

Respect and follow the safety tips offered by the Animal Care and Education Staff.

We greatly appreciate your help and your time at Dolphin Bay.

reasons forewarning visitors to the Bay. However, the part providing the reasons or justifications for the requests at the top of the notice is short and brief and the printed words are much smaller in size than those for the requests which are considered more important and therefore are made most prominent.

In everyday conversation, the Americans may also make a request indirectly. They, however, prefer in general the direct approach. If you give, say, American friends, some reasons to justify your request, they may feel that you adopt a demanding attitude and they may feel unappreciated for what they are requested to do. According to John Gray's suggestion (1992, pp. 249-250), as a wife, when requesting your husband to help, you should try to avoid giving him a list of reasons why he should help you. Assume that he doesn't have to be convinced. The longer you explain, the more he will resist. Long explanations validating your request will make him feel as though you don't think that he will support you. He will start to feel manipulated instead of offering his support of his own accord. Long lists of reasons or explanations to justify the request do not make the request valid and therefore cannot motivate him. What a man hears is "this is why you have to do it". If he asks you "why?", then you can give your reasons — being cautiously brief and direct is the norm and indirect requests make a man feel unappreciated. Occasionally using indirect statements is certainly OK, but when they are repeatedly used, a man becomes resistant to giving his support.

Implicit vs. Explicit Requests

The concept of implicit request is here tentatively used by us to refer to the fact that the request often reveals the speaker's intention in a vague and roundabout way, that is, the speaker's intention is likely to be implied, hinted at, understated or even not verbalized. Very often the speaker's intention can only be guessed through intuition which is built up through years of personal contact between, say, friends.

The concept of explicit request, on the other hand, is used to refer to the fact that the request clearly reveals the speaker's intention. Speaker's intention is enunciated in a forthright tone of voice, that is, the speaker's intention is expressed explicitly and verbally.

The implicit request is often used, in the Chinese culture between people who are friends and acquaintances, or at least, who have had personal contact with each other for a long time and hence share a good understanding of each other's condition for needs and wants; the condition for request, for example. The speaker adopting the implicit style is likely to avoid verbalizing their intention straightforwardly and hence the interpretation of the intention requires the listener to discern the cues from the speaker. It is not uncommon that the listeners would most probably rely on tacit understanding or intuition that is based on years of contact with the person who makes the request. The explicit request is used both in Chinese and American cultures, however, the Americans are inclined to lay more emphasis on verbal performance than the Chinese, paying much attention to grammatical structure, lexical and phrasal selection, subjunctive mood and conditional moods, etc. Even when the Americans attempt to express their intention implicitly, their intention can be less difficult to discern from the context. On the Chinese side, communication is often listener oriented, in the sense that it is the listener who is responsible for discerning the meaning through tacit understanding or intuition or for reading the speaker's mind from the contextual cues whereas on the American side, it is the speaker who is responsible for stating his or her intention clearly and logically so that the listener can get or deduce the meaning forthrightly.

Obviously, misunderstanding and miscommunication are inevitable when the Chinese and Americans meet in many request situations as each side may act intuitively and unconsciously according to their own cultural standard and conventions. The Americans may complain about the Chinese for their "beating about the bush" in their request and ask them to say what they mean. By being implicit, the Chinese may leave the impression of being 'insincere' and 'untrustworthy' on the Americans. The Americans may leave no better impression on the Chinese — the Chinese may complain about the Americans for their being too forthright and straightforward in their request. The Americans may leave the impression of being blunt, impolite, and even rude on the Chinese.

The following five pairs of contrastive verbal request scenes of our observations when we were in the United States may well demonstrate the differences and conflicts between the implicit and explicit styles. These request scenes happen in sequence between two Chinese friends, a Chinese and her American friend, two American friends, a female Chinese student and her American friend, and two Chinese friends.

Scene 1

Both Xiao Wang and Min Chen were studying linguistics for Ph. D. in the United States. They came back to China to attend an International Conference on language and culture. They could stay at home for only about a week. In these seven days they were both busily engaged in the conference activities. So, they seldom stayed at home with their parents. This request dialogue happened between these two Chinese students.

Min Chen asked Xiao Wang to accompany her to go shopping. But Xiao Wang had just gone shopping the day before and right now she was busy preparing her paper which she was presenting at the forthcoming conference.

Min Chen: ... You know I have to buy a lot of things to take to the

	States. I am going shopping tomorrow. I think you must want to buy something too. [A conventionalized way of request or habitual hint for a request] (*I am giving her a hint, asking her to go shopping with me.*)
Xiao Wang:	(*She was asking me to accompany her to go shopping. I hope she would not as I have just done shopping and I would like to stay with my parents tomorrow.*) Well, I have bought a lot of things already. Things here are much cheaper. [Comment: a polite hint of rejection of the request]
Min Chen:	By the way, you may want to buy something else. [Comment: reasons to justify the request, again an implied hint of request]
Xiao Wang:	You know I have already bought a lot of things and I was shopping for the whole Sunday. [Comment: refusing to say 'no,' but giving reasons to justify her rejection] (*I hope she may understand why I don't want to go with her.*)
Min Chen:	But you may need something else. (*I hope she can understand that I need her company.*)
Xiao Wang:	(*It is rather frustrating, but I should give her face.*) ... Well ... O.K., I'll go with you ... [Comment: the Chinese are considerate for others or others' face]

Scene 2

A similar request dialogue occurred between Xiao Wang and Dr. Richard Patrick, an American professor of linguistics. He was invited as a keynote speaker for the conference. It happened on the evening, just when the conference was over. Xiao Wang had only one day left for her stay at home and was planning to have a party to say goodbye to her family and friends. Obviously, this day was precious and important for her. However, Richard came up to her during the intermission of the conference and asked if she would like to take him to go around places in the city the next day.

Dr. Patrick:	Hi, Xiao Wang, will you be free tomorrow? [Comment: a conventionalized way of request] [the illocutionary force is clear]
Xiao Wang:	(*Oh, my goodness. He is asking me to accompany him. I wish he would rather not.*) Well, have you ever been to Sophia Church? That is a very nice architecture. Many foreign friends would like to visit that place ...
Dr Patrick:	Good. I will go to see that place first. ... Would you accompany me then? I know you have just one day left before you go back to the States and time is very precious for you. (*She will say no if she cannot manage.*)
Xiao Wang:	(*Feeling frustrated. Why? That is the last thing I would expect to do as I am leaving the day after tomorrow. I have so many things to do and I am having a party tomorrow. But if I say no, it would be impolite to a foreign*

friend.) ... Well, it will be my pleasure. When shall we meet? [Comment: The American left an unfavorable impression of being inconsiderate to her and she would not say no or she thought he would lose face in that case. It is better to sustain good relationship.]

Dr. Patrick: How about ten in the morning in the Hotel Lobby?

Xiao Wang: (*Oh, dear me! Why not earlier. Another morning will be lost.*) OK. See you then. [Comment: she was disappointed. The American is not considerate enough.]

Scene 3

Let's look at what may happen when an American requests an American for a favor.

American 1: Hi, Bob, I am leaving the day after tomorrow. But I will be free tomorrow. I would like to go sightseeing the city a little bit. ... I may need a ride. Can you take us? (*He would say no directly if he doesn't want to*) [Direct request]

American 2: I am sorry I can't. I am going somewhere, too.

American 1: Oh, no problem. I may ask somebody else. Thank you just the same. [The American friend is not likely to be hurt as he understands that his friend means what he said.]

Scene 4

Now let's see what happens between a female Chinese student and her American friend in a similar situation.

Chinese: Hi, Linda, I am leaving the day after tomorrow. I will be free today. I would like to go sightseeing. Would you recommend me some places? [Comment: a conventionalized implied request and the request is well justified] (*She would most probably offer me a ride as she did last time as she knows that I don't have a car.*)

American: Wonderful. There are a lot of interesting places in this city. If I were you I would first go to the Flower Street. That's really a nice place. Then, you may visit the Roman Church. Very nice Roman style architecture. And then ... (*She would ask me for a ride if she wants to.*)

Chinese: (*Why didn't she offer to give me a ride? Perhaps she needs some more hints.*) Would you tell me how I can get to these places?

American: Why don't you get a Tour Guide? Things will be easier if you have one. (*It is funny. Why didn't she go and buy a Tour Guide?*)

Chinese: (*I have got a Tour Guide already. I am merely asking you for a ride.*) Oh, well. Thanks. Bye. [Comment: she was disappointed by her friend's inconsiderateness.]

American: Have fun. See you later. [Comment: the American did not know that she had hurt the feeling of her Chinese friend.]

Scene 5

Now let's see what may happen between two Chinese friends in a similar situation.

Chinese 1: We are going to New Orleans this weekend. [Comment: This is a conventionalized way of requesting for a ride as the speaker knows that her friend knows that she doesn't have a car and she had offered her several rides to the airport before. And what is more, they are good friends.] (*She knows that I am asking her for a ride.*)

Chinese 2: What fun! I wish we were going with you. How long are you going to be there?

Chinese 1: Three days. (*I hope she'll offer me a ride to the airport.*)

Chinese 2: (*She may want me to give her a ride.*) Do you need a ride to the airport? I'll take you. [She feels it is her obligation to help her friend. Chinese 1 feels that she has the right to ask her friend to offer herself a ride to the airport as they are good friends.]

Chinese 1: Are you sure it's not too much trouble? [A conventionalized Chinese formula of being polite and considerate. It is also a formula to enhance friendly relationship as she knows clearly that it will be no problem to use her friend's car.]

Chinese 2: It's no trouble at all.

(Note: The last dialogue is a modification of Ting-Toomey's example, 1999, p.104)

In these five verbal request situations, cultural differences are fully manifested. In Scene 1 Min Chen implied her request and re-request, which is a conventionalized way of making requests between acquaintances in the Chinese culture while Xiao Wang implied her refusals or stated her refusal implicitly. She didn't even say no. Min Chen, while understanding very well her friend's implicit rejection, requested her implicitly again. Xiao Wang, as a Chinese, avoided saying 'no.' Friends and well-acquainted people feel that they share reciprocal obligations to help each other. Besides, she had to give face to her friend so as to maintain a good relationship, therefore she suffered for offering help to her friend — spending a whole day accompanying her friend. As a result, her mother blamed her as she lost another day which she might have spent together with her at home. More often than not, the Chinese often adopt the indirect strategy both in requesting other people to do things and in rejecting others' request. They hate saying 'no' directly. The indirect style is an important mechanism for the Chinese to maintain harmonious or friendly relationship in the society.

In contrast, in Scene 2, Dr. Richard Patrick stated his request directly and forthrightly, thinking Xiao Wang would say no if she did not want to. Xiao Wang, however, did not expect such a request as she hoped that Richard would know it from the contextual cues (she was leaving the day after tomorrow and she would prefer to stay at home packing up and being together with her parents). And when requested, she could not but say yes as it would be very impolite to reject his request, especially to a foreign friend. She obviously acted according to Chinese cultural standard. As a result, she spent the whole morning with Richard and by doing so she had to give up some precious time during which she would have been together with her parents and friends at home. Some Chinese would regard the Americans' behavior as being inconsiderate and even blunt. We also have to remember that the Americans tend to believe what the Chinese say (the 'honest' norm), that is they tend to believe that the Chinese mean what they say, just as most Americans. They seldom know the Chinese may mean no when they say yes, just for being polite.

Scene 3 manifests the directness and forthrightness of the American way of requests and rejections to the requests and the fact that they take the rejection for granted which would otherwise strike the Chinese as impolite and inconsiderate, even rude in similar situations. Unlike the Chinese culture where friends and well-acquainted people are interdependent and hence they are mutually obligated to help each other just as the way brothers do, the American friends are independent and whether they mutually share obligations or not depends on their own wish. In the Chinese cultural context, request and accepting or rejecting request in similar situations is more a matter of rights and obligations than a matter of face concern. As Gu (1998) points out, it is not that concerns about autonomy, imposition, and so on do not exist in the Chinese culture, but rather that they are not regarded as face concerns. In the American cultural context, however, this act is not so much a matter of right and obligation. What one is obligated to do in the Chinese context may be regarded as sort of imposition on the individual autonomy and independent decision. It may, to different degrees, be related to what is generally called a negative face for the Americans. The Americans do not feel that they are obligated to do things for others in similar situations — they want to be unimpeded by others. They desire for autonomy and to be free to act.

Scene 4 is a very good example to demonstrate how the Chinese could implicitly and in a roundabout way state their request, thinking that the Americans would probably get their intention from the contextual cues or by intuition which was built through long time of personal contact. And when she failed to achieve her purpose, the Chinese even hinted her intention for a second time but she could not get her intention across the cultural barrier either. Are the Americans so impolite and inconsiderate? That is the impression left on the Chinese when asking a favor from their American friends and being rejected in such a way. In fact their feeling is often hurt. They are often disappointed by their American friends' behavior. The Americans simply lack what is called tacit understanding a good Chinese friend may share with his or her friends through years of contact. It has to do with what is called illocutionary clarity: the illocutionary meaning or pragmatic meaning is not clear to the American.

As mentioned earlier, the Chinese prefer to imply their requests or express them indirectly or implicitly so that they can save others' face and establish harmony between them, or at least they can prevent embarrassment of rejection or disagreement among individuals, hence leaving the relationship and the face of the other person intact (Yum, 1997). However, this requires the listener to guess the speaker's intention according to the contextual cues and then decide either to grant or reject the request. As a matter of fact, Chinese are mind readers (Jia Yuxin, 1997) and they are inclined to know what their friends may imply in what they say. And it is this mutual tacit understanding that helps them to effectively communicate with each other and maintain or further develop a harmonious relationship between / among them.

Scene 5 is an example of the most satisfying interaction between Chinese friends as the conversation results in not only the fulfillment of the request but the harmonious or friendly relationship is sustained or developed, which is the most important goal of communication. On many occasions, the Chinese regard the achievement of good relationship as more important than the achievement of their substantial need for help. So much so that, on many occasions of interaction, the form or style in which a request is issued is more important than the content. In contrast, the Americans in similar situations regard the fulfillment of the task or goal as more important than relationship and when their task is not accomplished for one reason or another, their feelings as well as their relationship will be in no way affected or damaged.

The following example taken from a Chinese professor's personal experience not only illustrates the differences but also the outcome due to the different interpretation of the same behavior.

The Chinese professor was elected president of the International Association for Intercultural Communication Studies in 2005. Once the general secretary presented a proposal concerning the publication of the association's journal, requesting for opinions and comments from the Board Directors, he received different responses. The responses are stated in different styles and the differences caused dramatic misunderstanding among the Board Directors. Now let us take a look at the request and responses.

Request for opinions from the general secretary of the association:
I have enclosed a detailed attachment in which I argue about the benefits for going online. The largest factor is financial. However, we could do color, pictures, even music on the online version. I would like us to

seriously consider the advantages of this suggestion. I welcome your comments. I think that I covered most of the concerns for and against both positions (the points for and against both positions are placed in the attached document).

Response from an American board director:
Just for the record, I strongly object to putting our journal online. This reduces drastically the value of the publication for the author(s), no matter what the Literature in computer science might tell us. I speak from the realities of Promotion and Tenure boards and the years of assessing resumes for faculty appointments. Frankly I could not care less about whether we have color, pictures, or music capability. Other journals, online or otherwise might be a better outlet for such enhancements. Please, let us put this issue to rest, at least for another five years until my retirement.

Response from the Chinese professor:
(*The Chinese professor talked about something else before he stated his opinion and he included his response to this request in his PS note*)
As for the proposal of the on-line publication of our journal, I have only one thing to say, the print form is more preferred in China. It seems the on-line publication is not regarded as formal as the print one.

To our amazement, the general secretary interpreted the Chinese professor's response as sort of agreement with some reserve while the American board director's response is clearly a straightforward "No". In fact, the Chinese professor's real intention, as he told us, is "No", too. He just stated his "No" in the most indirect and implicit way. He avoided saying 'no' and imbedded his opinion in the part of reasons. The reason behind is that he simply did not want to sound assertive, which he tends to think may hurt the general secretary's feeling. This understated comment needs tacit understanding between well-acquainted people in the Chinese cultural context. It is certainly something beyond the American's capacity to understand.

In fact, on most occasions, the Americans in contrast prefer syntactic, lexical and phrasal devices and intensifiers rather than the contextual cues like those mentioned in the Chinese context in requesting.

The Americans do use reasons/justifications and they sometimes do place them at the beginning of their request like the Chinese. They, however, still use sort of preparator to let the person being requested know they are being asked to do a favor to the requestor. The part of reason or justification or what is called supportive move is in general much shorter than those in the request of the Chinese. For example (Spencer-Oatey, 1999, p.12):

Do you mind if I ask you a big favor.　　[PREPARATORY]
I know you don't like lending your car,　　[SUPPORTIVE MOVE]

but I was wondering if I could possibly borrow it just for an hour or so on Tuesday afternoon,   [HEAD ACT]
if you're not using it then.   [SUPPORTIVE MOVE / IMPOSITION DOWN-GRADER]

This kind of sequence, however, according to our observation, is much less often used by the Americans. They generally prefer brief and direct request instead.

What merits our attention is that differences in expectations in any interactional situation may quite likely cause misunderstanding or even worse consequences. In some cases, the Chinese indirect approaches and the Americans' direct approaches often clash. Embarrassments are not uncommon when these two different approaches meet.

The Factors Leading to the Differences in Requests: Concepts of Self and Self-Expressions in Chinese and American Cultures

Philosophically speaking, among others, the Chinese indirect and implicit and Americans' direct and explicit requests are also consistent with the concept of self in terms of interpersonal relationship in these two cultures. Cross-culturally speaking, the differences in requests and self-expressions can be attributed to the differences in the concepts of the Eastern self and the Western self and their self-expressions.

The concept of self is not something we are born with. It doesn't develop in a vacuum, either. It is not until we begin to interact with others that we achieve any sense of self at all. Self is part of the social world which we live in. It is not only something we have but also something given to us by society. The self cannot be differentiated from the nexus of social relationship in which the individual participates. We become aware of who we are, based on our relationships with others.

The Chinese self is different from the Western view of self as it is basically conceptualized in relation to others. It is social and relational in nature and it is just this relational and interdependent self that lies underneath the Chinese behavior including face behavior and renders it just as relational and interdependent. In essence, the Chinese self is more a self in relationships and less a self in isolation than that in the American culture (Scollon, 1991). Asians are therefore more or less considered to be seeking harmonious relations, in which self is downplayed or depreciated.

In the Chinese context, "人" or a human being is perceived as a social being, firmly rooted in the nexus of relationship. Relationship is inseparably an aspect of the self. The ideal of manhood or of the fine quality of a human being is defined in the Chinese character as "仁" (*benevolence*), which is a homophone of the word "人" (*human being*), which, etymologically the combination of the Chinese ideographic characters of "人" and "二" (meaning *two*), literally means two persons.

In fact the Chinese culture is embedded in the way Chinese characters are formed. Deducing from the formation of the character "仁", we may have the following ideological ideas underlying the Chinese concept of self.

The structure of "仁" = 人 + 二 = 二人 / 人二

The literal translation: manhood = two persons, who are interdependent. From this we can draw the following implications about the nature of the Chinese self:

(1) Self is conceptualized as in relationship of two interdependent persons or a collective self.
(2) Self is identified in relation to others or as relational, focusing less on the isolated self and more on the relational self, less autonomous and more obliging and accommodating to others. Stated differently, relationship is part of self or self is part of relationship. Or simply, self exists in relations.
(3) Self actualization is the realization of benevolence, which stands for the ideal manhood specified on the basis of (kinship) relationship. The achievement of good relationship / harmony is the ultimate goal of self-actualization. However, the individual self can never achieve the ideal manhood alone as 仁 stands for the relationship between two interdependent persons.
(4) Self or an individual resides and survives in the nexus of social relationships, in the judgment and approval or disapproval of others. Therefore, the Chinese are very particularly sensitive to situations and what to say and how to say in the society.
(5) Others in social interaction are often more important than the individual self. On many occasions, what one says seems to be less important than who says to whom and how.

The notions suggested by the formation of this Chinese character has a profound implication for cross-cultural communication. It is not only the hierarchical power relationships that operate in interpersonal interactions. According to Scollon and Scollon (1995), the most crucial point for the Chinese is that Confucian self consists of participation in these (and many other) social relationships. One is oneself to the extent one enacts his or her part of such relationships. In the Confucian or Chinese sense of self, one is more a self in human relationships, and less a self in isolation. Godwin Chu notes, "A self of this nature is not highly assertive, but seeks to accommodate (and oblige too, the authors) others and in return receives enduring social support" (1985, p. 259, as cited in Scollon, Scollon & Kirkpatrick, 2000, p. 144). To establish harmonious relationship, obliging and accommodating others are deemed to be the most important mechanism in interpersonal interactions. This necessarily leads to an indirect style in requests. The Chinese often place their request after facework to laud the listener's face and establish harmonious relationship. They also rely on hints and contextual cues to let the listener figure out the implication. Thus embarrassment can be avoided when the request is rejected — each other's face is saved.

According to Confucius, the use of appropriate words and speech and the ability to adjust to various situations and relational positioning is a gift to a person. Confucius taught people to be prudent and cautious in speaking as he believed that "what a man of complete virtue cherishes is cautiousness of every action." Confucius also advised his disciples to be sensitive, obliging, and empathetic to audience and to be modest in speaking and behavior as well as in appearance. Speaking skills function as a lubricant to the interpersonal system. Appropriate use of such skills will help one create a desirable social network and bring personal advantage to those who employ them, particularly in a world that emphasizes relationships, human emotion (rénqíng), and face needs. Such a preference for skilled speaking certainly paved the way for Chinese indirectness and implicitness in requests, since it requires one to have the ability to use words effectively to create desirable situations and achieve harmonious relationships. So much so that the self-expression in the Chinese culture is the expression which is not part of the self but the relationship with others. That is, self-expression is the result of his / her part of relationship with others.

Whereas, the Americans, who are self and autonomy oriented, self-expression inherently becomes ideal and the inhibition of it is the biggest problem. And speaking and writing are considered to be the expression of the self, as well as the expression of independence and equality. And when speaking and writing becomes the expression of self, the true self should not be covered in whatever case — do not use a role to cover up your true self (Lanham, 1983), which necessarily leads to assertiveness and directness in requests for the Americans. The corollary is that directness is always to be preferred over indirectness (Scollon, Scollon & Kirkpatrick, 2000). Instead of giving hints, Americans clearly state their requests and place them before the justifications or reasons, which are usually much shorter than those given by the Chinese in the same situation.

Conclusion

Facts or incidents like these often occur in intercultural communication. To people who are perfectly competent in using and interpreting their own language and who can speak English but know little about the cultural interactional norms or conventions and the strategies to realize communication goals, these incidents may sometimes seem amusing, sometimes puzzling, but more often than not, they lead to misunderstandings. Even worse, misunderstandings may lead to unexpected emotional and practical consequences. In regard to what people should do to avoid these misunderstandings, Oliver gives his suggestion: "If we would communicate across cultural barriers, we must learn what to say and how to say it in terms of the expectations of those we want to listen" (1962, p. 154, quoted in Scollon, Scollon & Kirkpatrick, 2000, p. 74).

For the Chinese and Americans, to understand each other's requests, they need to be aware of the fact that the stance taken by the Americans in spoken and written communication is at odds with the sense of self generally held by the Chinese.

The more knowledge of the differences, the fewer the misunderstandings.

References

Chu, G. (1985). The changing concept of self in contemporary China. In A. J. Marsella, G. Devos, F. L. K. Hsu (Eds.), *Culture and Self: Asian and WesternPperspectives* (pp. 252–277). New York: Tavistock Publications.

Gray, J. (1992). *Men are from Mars, Women are from Venus*. New York: HarperCollins Publishers.

Gu, Y. (1998). *Politeness and Chinese Face*. Lecture given in the Department of Linguistics, University of Luton, Summer 1998.

Lanham, R. A. (1983). *Literacy and the Survival of Humanism*. New Haven: Yale University Press.

Lim, T. S. (1994). The structure of face and the determinants of face needs in Korea. *Korean Journal of Journalism and Communication Studies 32*, 207–247.

Oliver, R. (1962). *Culture and Communication: The Problem of Penetrating National and Cultural Boundaries*. Springfield, IL: Charles C Thomas.

Scollon, R. (1991). Eight legs and one elbow. Stance and structure in Chinese English compositions. Paper presented at International Reading Association, Second North American Conference on Adult and Adolescent Literacy, Banff.

Scollon, R., & Scollon, S. W. (1995). *Intercultural Communication: A Discourse Approach*. Cambridge: Blackwell Publishers.

Scollon, R., Scollon, S. W., & Kirkpatrick, A. (2000). *Contrastive Discourse in Chinese and English — a Critical Appraisal*. Beijing: Foreign Language Teaching and Research Press.

Ting-Toomey, S. (1999). *Communicating across Cultures*. New York: The Guilford Press.

Yum, J. O. (1997). The impact of Confucianism in interpersonal relationships and communication in East Asia. In L. A. Samovar & R. E. Porter (Eds.), *Intercultural Communication: A Reader* (pp. 78–88). Belmont: Wadsworth Publishing Company.

Jia, Yuxin. 贾玉新, (1997).《跨文化交际学》, 上海: 上海外语教育出版社.

Intercultural Communicative Competencies

16

Intercultural Nonverbal Communication (In)Competence

Bates L. HOFFER
Trinity University, USA

Abstract: Intercultural communication study includes a number of components, such as language competence (control of a language and its appropriate use), cultural competence (awareness of differences and difficulties), and nonverbal competence (awareness of the nonverbal systems and potential problems in intercultural communication). The language and the cultural components have been well studied and integrated into language classes and intercultural communication programs. Nonverbal competence, in contrast, has received less attention than it deserves in terms of the various potential negative impacts on intercultural communication.

Introduction

The field of intercultural communicative competence has progressed rapidly in the last several decades, although the progress has been more rapid in some areas that others. Languages, cultural studies, and nonverbal communication systems are three of the basic components of the field. The major languages have been well studied and the textbooks, visual aids, dictionaries and so on are much better than a century ago. In the USA, for example, Spanish, French, German, and Italian have had excellent textbooks and supporting materials. Those four languages account for over three-fourths of all language students: Spanish over 50%, French 13%, German 6%, and Italian 5%. Other modern languages that account for more than 1% of the total number of language students are Chinese,

Japanese, Russian and Arabic. Languages other than the major ones, especially the last four mentioned, are being studied and excellent materials are becoming more and more available.

The cultural awareness component of intercultural communication has also been studied well for the major languages and for many other languages as well. Cultural studies are usually integrated to some extent into language programs and intercultural communication programs.

The nonverbal communication (NVC) component studies have not been as well integrated for reasons discussed in this chapter. For all three of these areas, there is more study to do, but especially more so in nonverbal communication systems. In addition, the information needs to be better integrated into the language texts and language programs in general. A brief history of the study of nonverbal communication follows and then there is a section on some of the more problematic nonverbal communication behaviors that need to be included in the texts and programs.

History of the Study of Nonverbal Communication in the USA

In the 1950s, a seminal work appeared that became a basic source in the study of nonverbal communication in general. Edward T. Hall's *The Silent Language* in 1959 presented a wide theory of culture, one whose rules control people's daily lives. This work eventually led the general study into various related fields.

In the 1960's, his *The Hidden Dimension* (1966) dealt with the dimension of space in communication. Several other scholars carried the studies in various directions. Paul Ekman's work is crucial in some areas, for example, his 1969 work on the repertoire of nonverbal behaviors.

In the 1970's, other basic studies were produced by Birdwhistell in 1970, Knapp in 1972, Mehrabian in 1972, Ekman and Friesen in 1975, and others. An early book of readings on the topic is by Samovar and Porter in 1972. My own work on NVC began with work on the acquisition of some aspects of the field (1976).

By the 1980's studies were coming out on many different aspects of the field. A few examples include Ekman's major work *Emotion in the Human Face* (1982), Axtell (1985) on taboos to be avoided in cross-cultural communication, Leathers (1986) on *Nonverbal Communication Systems*, and Poyatos' edited collection (1988) on *Cross-Cultural Perspectives in Nonverbal Communication*. My own work included several studies on cross-cultural research. Examples include an article with Richard Santos on Anglo and Hispanic "clashes in kinesics" (1980), an edited book with R. St. Clair — who has an article in this volume — on *Developmental Kinesics* (1981) an article in Brunt and Enninger (1985) on cross-cultural (mis)communication, and an article on verbal and nonverbal communication across cultures in Koo and St. Clair (1986).

In the 1990's, the field continued expanding. Enninger wrote on the importance of understanding the use of silence as used in communication of other cultures (1991). Axtell (1991, 1998) extended his work on taboo behavior around the world and many other authors are represented in publications. Two examples are Kim (1992) who began working with various communication problems between Koreans and others and Akiyama (1993) who began working on facial expressions and potential mis-readings by outsiders and. My own work in this decade included one on the same problem including Americans, Japanese, and Koreans (Fendos, 1991), one on nonverbal phrases in prose and how they might not be understood or how they might not be recognized at all (1993), an article in 1994 with John Koo on communicative competence in Korean as based on our joint research trip to Korea, and a book edited with John Koo on intercultural communication East and West (1998).

Over the past 10 years, the field has continued to mushroom into many areas. The material below concentrates on nonverbal communicative competence, both the basic system that accompanies each language and the types of nonverbal communication and behavior that lead to a lack of understanding, that are misleading, that offend the native speaker, or that are considered repulsive or worse by the native speaker.

In addition and as an adjunct to this same topic, more attention to a related area of the nonverbal communication component of the field is needed. Briefly stated, more studies are needed of the appropriate communicative behavior that is appropriate for the non-native within the foreign context. A great deal of progress has been made over the last six decades, but there is more to be done to improve the textbooks and language programs for those who wish to interact well within a foreign culture.

The first section that follows treats components of nonverbal communication systems and the reader who is experienced in the field might prefer to skip to the second section below which presents some misunderstood or misused nonverbal behaviors that can have minor to serious to very serious results.

Nonverbal Communication

The nonverbal system of a culture includes several components, most of which are discussed below: facial expressions, gestures, gaze behavior, proxemics, haptics, and socializers. Following the description of the various components of a nonverbal system is a section that gives many examples of nonverbal behavior that may not be interpreted, may be interpreted incorrectly, may cause difficulties or distress, and may, in fact, lead to violence, arrest, and in rare cases death.

The particular motivation for including these potential errors involves language competence as well. A poor speaker of the foreign language among its native speakers is usually forgiven for offensive nonverbal behavior. A very good to excellent speaker is assumed to have intended the offensive behavior and is essentially never forgiven. ①

Facial Expressions

Facial expressions are a vital part of intercultural communicative competence because the face is usually the first thing noticed when conversing with another person. Although people tend to think that interpreting someone else's facial expression is easy and natural, they need to learn of the various differences across cultures — even in the facial expressions exhibiting basic emotions. Research has shown that the interpretation of even the basic facial expressions in a different culture is often wrong. These misinterpretations may have a significant impact and lead to miscommunication or partial communication.

Emotional expressions have received the most attention of all nonverbal behaviors. (Ekman 1982, Ekman & Friesen 1969, 1984; Ekman & Hoffer 2004) One area of research deals with the basic number of expressions that carry emotion and another area deals with those expressions that may be universal across cultures. There is some agreement that the basic set of expressions that carry emotional meaning consists of: happiness, sadness, anger, fear, surprise, and disgust. Research in many cultures around the world has found these emotions expressed. Posed pictures of these expressions made by Americans have been tested on people from America and other cultures. The accuracy rates vary somewhat, but the chart below which gives the percentage of accuracy indicates a general awareness of the emotion by natives. Also on the chart is the set of statistics for the same posed expressions being tested on people of different cultures.

	USA	*Argentinean*	*Brazilian*	*Chilean*	*Japanese*
Happiness	100%	94%	97%	90%	87%
Sadness	84	85	82	90	74
Anger	92	72	82	76	63
Fear	93	68	77	78	71
Surprise	86	93	82	88	87
Disgust	91	79	86	85	82

---

① This description of the result of a very good language speaker making an error in nonverbal behavior is called the "Fairbanks Rule", named for the long-time Cornell University Linguistics Professor Gordon Fairbanks.

The low accuracy for Japanese — and the even lower accuracy for a group from Africa who were tested later — may be a result of less awareness of the emotions when viewing another culture or it may be a result of translation difficulties in constructing the test.

The accuracy rates for the non-USA people indicate that the expressions are conveying information, but at a much lower accuracy rate than for pictures from the same culture. Posed pictures are used as one step in the research because they should be easier to recognize. If they prove difficult, spontaneous expressions that last only a short time would prove much more difficult. There is some evidence that training in awareness of facial expressions can increase the accuracy rate. Some early research reported an increase in accuracy of between 5 and 50 per cent or so. The current use of videos, CDs, DVDs, and other instructional media has improved this situation.

There is another important aspect to inaccurate awareness of expressions. The viewer may mistake Surprise for Disgust and misinterpret the other person's reaction to, for example, a new food or other item in the viewer's culture. The nonverbal communication may be taken as accurate and the miscommunication may cause difficulties in interpersonal interaction, such as trying to get the person to eat a food that he actually detests. This type of misreading or non-reading needs more research on specific pairs of cultures.

The study of cross-cultural recognition of basic facial expressions has been receiving much attention over the past few decades as interest in intercultural studies — especially intercultural communication — has grown. General attention has been drawn to the similarities and differences between cultures, including their nonverbal communication. The percentage of people with experience in other cultural settings has grown rapidly in the past 50 years. Jet travel, global TV coverage, and foreign films and TV programs are among the many ways people have "encountered" other cultures. They have seen both similar and dissimilar facial expressions and have reported a wide range of reactions. On the one hand, in some cases viewers report that they can see little difference in facial expressions. On the other hand, in some cases the viewers report bewilderment at their inability to understand the expressions. A major example of this difficulty in interpreting and understanding facial expressions in the target culture is in the use of smiling behavior.

The "smile" may be used as an example to show how much has been learned over the past few decades about facial behavior and emotion. For many decades writers reported that "smiles" could be signs of happiness, but they could also be used in situations where they feel contempt or incredulity or affection or so on. The word "smile," unfortunately, covers too many different facial expressions to be useful as a technical term. Ekman and Friesen (1975) distinguished many such smiling expressions which involve various different sets of muscles. If attention is only on the lip corners moving upwards, the research can go no further. By using close descriptions of facial muscle movements other than those that control the upward movement of the corners of the mouth, important distinctions can be made. Thus, there can be both muscle movements that are universal and other similar muscle movements that are used in different ways in various situations in different cultures.

Some of the programs that teach the interpretation of culture specific facial expressions have been doing a good job. Areas of facial expressions that the programs include are Dual and Masked Expressions and Display Rules.

Dual and Masked Expressions

Several researchers (e.g. Leathers 1986) have reported that facial expressions may show more than one emotion at a given moment. The facial muscles are sufficiently complex and independent for the discrete muscle patterns in different parts of the face to move in a pattern which presents the elements of two or more emotions. Some of these blended or **Dual Expressions** are observable even in still photographs. In the research, the combination of "Anger and Determination" seems to be the most recognizable of the dual expressions that people of the same culture viewed. Others that are less recognizable are "Anger and Surprise" and "Sadness and Determination." The level of complexity of the research into dual expressions dictates caution in drawing more than general conclusions.

The study of **Masked** expressions is to some extent related to the study of deceptive expressions. When a person attempts to mask a spontaneous expression such as Disgust so that an observer does not notice the basic expression, that person may use a smile or attempt to produce a different expression such as Interest. Native speakers seem to be much more accurate in interpreting the presence of masked expressions. Nonnative speakers are seldom accurate at such interpretation and often they see only the masking expression.

Display Rules

The basic facial expressions of emotion listed above are universal to the human species, but each culture develops "display rules" which govern the acceptable facial expressions that may be used (i.e. "**displayed**") on particular occasions. For example, in some cultures the Happiness facial expression would be considered rude and offensive at a wake or a funeral, but in other cultures a wake or a funeral is treated as a less solemn time. For another example, an expression of Disgust is considered highly offensive when offered a particular food by your host. Thus, the display rules suggest that the disgusted person should try to smile (masking behavior) and make a statement such as "Thank you. I'm not very hungry." Often some of these display rules are learned as part of the general etiquette of a group. Programs teaching intercultural communication should, as some do, include information about these display rules.

Gestures

The study of gestures ranges from body movements which intentionally convey precise information to other gestures which convey general information — intentionally or not — to body movements which can be interpreted by a trained observer such as a psychologist. Gestures carry their own communication or add information to the verbal communication. The study of gestures in the other culture should be an integral part of the study of the other language. This section is primarily concerned with two categories of gestures which have been studied for many but not all of the major cultural groups of the world: emblems and illustrators.

Emblems

Emblems are gestures that carry their own meaning. The use of body movement to convey information occurs in any situation where communication might be necessary. In a crowded and noisy room, a person on the far side of the room may use a hand signal that means "come here." An observer who is unsure of the intended meaning of the signal may point to his chest (or nose or whatever body part is appropriate as part of the emblem for "I" in that culture). The signaler may then use a signal such as pointing up with the index finger and quickly pointing it at the observer to mean "you got it!" ("Correct"). Here emblematic body movements have replaced a verbal exchange with precisely the same meaning. ("Come here." "Do you mean me?" "Yes.") Other examples include tapping the side of the forehead with the extended index finger to signal "smart" and a gesture with the thumb and forefinger forming an "O", meaning "OK." "OK" is an emblem which has become so widely used around the world that it is part of English as an International Language. The fact should be taught that the emblem can also have a much different meaning in some cultures and be offensive, as is discussed later.

The emblems presented below which are used in American English vary in their understandability. Many are perceived correctly by close to 100 per cent of the observers, others by less. None of the examples here was misunderstood by more than 10 per cent of the Americans tested. When people from a different culture are asked to interpret these gestures, the success ratio is lower to much lower. Of more importance is a gesture which a person from the other culture interprets as having the same meaning as a similar gesture in his own culture but actually his interpretation is wrong.

Emblem Meaning	Description of Gesture
OK	Thumb and forefinger form a circle, fingers up, palm sideways [This emblem has become almost universal, although it retains it original meaning as well in some cultures.]
Thumbs up	Thumb up and other fingers closed, palm flat, may be moved up or be moved up a down a few times
V for Victory	Index and middle finger pointing up, thumb and other fingers closed, flat palm toward viewer
Come here	Upright fingers or index finger alone, other fingers closed, with palm toward self, fingers moved back and forth in toward self; or hand at chest or waist level, fingers out pointing toward other person, palm down, fingers moved downward and back to flat one or more times
Goodbye	Hand at head level or higher, up with fingers and thumb spread, palm toward other person, then either the fingers alone or the whole hand moved downward and back a few times
Go away	Palm up toward other person, fingers erect, forearm moved toward other person one or more times, or forearm moved forward only a little and hand moves up and down, usually two or more times
Get lost, go away	Hand at waist level, extended fingers pointing downward, back of hand toward observer, either whole hand or fingers alone flipped up one or more times a few times
Go, Texas [aka "Hook 'em Horns"]	Index and little finger extended, thumb holding other two fingers down, hand up, hand perhaps moved up and down
Crazy	Index finger extended from closed fist, with finger pointed toward the temple area of the head, making small clockwise movements, usually three or more times

There are various emblems that with the same or similar meaning but which differ in emphasis. A raised index finger moved left and right a few times means for the viewer to avoid starting an action or to stop an action. An open hand, facing the other person, held chest high is more emphatic, especially if the hand is moved strongly forward. For even more emphasis, the emblem may move the open hand, palm down, quickly left to right just in front of the neck. This emblem is the one used by a film director to "cut" or stop the film that is being used at the time

The full set of emblems for each culture is still under investigation by several researchers. The examples above are in general use. Often small groups, such as those at a college, will create their own emblems — sometimes known as "slang" gestures — known only to that group. Emblems may then be borrowed in the same way slang and dialect forms spread from one group to another. Some may eventually enter the general emblem vocabulary of the language group. An example might be the emblem that seems to have come from Hawaii which means something like "everything's OK." In this emblem, only the thumb and the little finger are extended and the hand is rotated clockwise and back a few times. This emblem spread to California and then was used in television shows set in Hawaii and California. It has spread via television to the whole U.S.

Display Rules

The first step in learning about emblems in a language is that of being acquainted with the meaning of the most frequently used ones. Later in the process, the learner must learn the conditions under which an emblem is used and where it is not used. Those conditions define the display rules for the emblems in the language. Emblems and their use may vary with age, sex, ethnic background, social class, and so on. Some will be appropriate only in certain situations, such as in Church, and only if used by those in certain roles, such as the priest or preacher. Some are appropriate only for members of the group but not the outsider. One of the recurring problems in language learning is applicable to both emblems and illustrators. Learners whose language teachers are of the opposite sex may unconsciously — or consciously — imitate the gestures of the teacher when using the language later. In some cases the gestures are only appropriate to one sex and the native speaker's reaction to the inappropriate behavior may range from a polite ignoring of the behavior through humor to suspicions of the speaker's intelligence, sexual orientation, or so on.

For an example of the restriction on the use of emblems, the "shame on you" gesture may be used. In this case the signaler extends one index finger toward the other person, extends the other index finger and brushes it a few times from the base of the opposite index finger toward the other person, Ordinarily it is used to a youngster, although it may be used elsewhere in a humorous manner. It is inappropriate in any situation which is formal. For another example, there is an American emblem which seems limited to younger women: "heartthrob" or "he's a heartthrob." The fist is placed over the heart and lightly thumped against the chest as if the heart were beating faster. In this case "heartthrob" means that the young man or rock star or so on is attractive. A final example is the gesture above labeled "no, no" that should only be used by someone in authority, such as a parent, teacher, moderator, or so on. The extended index finger, pointed up, is moved slowly from side to side.

The display rules for emblems in a culture are still under investigation. For the language learner, there are further and often important restrictions which may apply to non-natives communicating in a language. For example, in the US very close friends or group members can use nasty language and crude gestures with each other, but no outsider would be allowed to do the same. Friends may put their hands on the other person's arm or shoulder or put their arm around the other person's shoulder, but non-group members should completely avoid such behaviors.

Illustrators

Illustrators are movements which are intimately tied to the content and/or flow of speech. Observation of speakers from various backgrounds usually shows that the speakers move their hands and heads at some points in their conversation. Closer study shows that some of those movements may relate directly to what is being said or correlate with the flow or rhythm of the conversations.

The use of the hands during conversation is so frequent in some cultures that there is a saying that Sicilians, for example, cannot talk if their hands are tied. Not all the hand movements are substitutes for words or phrases. Those body movements which are not emblems and which accompany speech are defined as Illustrators. Different cultures may have different types of illustrators, but those which seem well established in American English are presented below.

Different groups use different types of movements and with different frequencies. Listeners from a different culture are usually not familiar with the illustrators of the other culture and see only "meaningless" movements. They then may comment on the many "strange" hand motions made by the speaker. When they listen within their own culture, they do not usually take any special notice of a speaker's illustrators because the illustrators are a normal part of their spoken communication.

The inventory of types of illustrators which currently includes all those encountered in cultures of the world is the subject of this section. The list which follows included the illustrators, a brief definition, and a short example of each.

Deictics

Deictics are movements that point to referent. Deictics may have developed from reaching movements to movements which identified the object wanted or being spoken of. Most cultures use the fingers, hands, and/or arms for deictic movements, but other patterns have been found.

Among some Native American groups, the chin is used to point. In America, for example, display rules may prohibit pointing with the fingers or hands in formal occasions, so that the elbow, shoulder, or head is moved toward the referent. Americans point to their chest when they mean "I" but other cultures point to their nose or face.

Batons

Batons are movements that accent a particular word. Even as the voice can be changed in terms of loudness or pitch to call attention to a particular word, movements may provide the accent. Various movements have been observed which act as batons, such as a nod of the head or a shake of the fist or a widening of the eyes.

Spatials

Spatials are movements that depict a spatial relationship. These illustrators usually involve the hands or arms. The hands can be held apart to illustrate the relative distance between objects. The hands may also move to different locations in the air as if showing the observer places on a map.

Pictographs

Pictographs are movements that draw the shape of the referent in the air. These illustrators usually involve the hands, which trace in the air the outline of the object under discussion. The hand or hands draw a circle in the air for "ball", for example, or draw an upright rectangle for "refrigerator."

Kinetographs

Kinetographs are movements that depict a bodily action or a nonhuman action. A common example of this illustrator is used by children when they use their fingers to depict a walking action. Another frequent example is the use of the hands and fingers in the depiction of the jumping of a rabbit or kangaroo.

Rhythmics

Rhythmics are movements that depict the rhythm or spacing of an event. The head or hands may be moved at the same time interval being discussed, as with the frequency with which a telephone busy signal occurs when that is the subject of the conversation.

Underliners

Underlinder are movements that emphasize a phrase, clause, sentence or group of sentences. Batons seem to be learned at a fairly early age, whereas underliners seem to be acquired as one of the last illustrators used by a person. Movements of the body, such as the hands, may continue for as long as a verbal sequence is being produced. For example, the hands may depict a written underline by tracing a line in the air as if across a page. The fingers, usually the index and middle on both hands, may wiggle up and down to signal quotation marks around something being said.

Ideographs

Ideographs are movements that sketch the path or direction of thought. An example one ideograph treats past time as if physically behind the speaker and the future in front. "Yesterday" may be accompanied by a gesture pointing backward over the shoulder. Such a gesture is meaningless to those in whose culture there is no concept similar to past being "back" and future being "forward".

Editors

Editors are movements that "erase" the preceding word or words so that a replacement can be used. For example, just after an American mispronounces a word he may briefly shake his head and perhaps close his eyes before pronouncing the word correctly. Another example of editer — if a rare one — occurs when the speaker lifts his hand and "wipes" it left and right as if erasing a blackboard.

Gaze Behavior

Only two of the possible topics under this heading will be mentioned in this section. First is the reaction to staring. Children in the US are taught not to stare at another person. However, the display rule differs by area of the country. That is, in some areas a person may stare toward a second person as long as the second person is further than a certain distance away. In fact, that distance may be as short as 20 feet or so. In other parts of the country, 20 feet is still considered far too close for staring.

The second topic in Gaze Behavior is that of eye behavior in conversation (Samovar and Porter 1991; Leathers 1986). In one of the major gaze patterns in a dyadic conversation in general U.S. English, the speaker looks away from the addressee, makes brief eye contact every few to several seconds, and at the end of his turn makes and maintains eye contact. The addressee looks toward the speaker's eyes or face, with brief looks away, until his turn to speak. There are several variations of this scheme, up to and including the almost complete reversal of roles. For example, in one Black pattern, the speaker looks at the addressee who avoids most eye contact. In the intercultural situation, the pattern may interfere with ease of communication. The speaker of the first pattern looks toward a potential addressee of the second pattern and waits for the latter to make eye contact. That eye contact is the signal for the first speaker to begin. However, the second person is waiting for the first person to speak. If the second looks at the first person, it could signal that the second person should begin the conversation.

Proxemics

Proxemics derives from the Latin for "near, next." Two of the topics in this category are discussed here: the use of distance as used for human activity and the orientation of those involved. A major source is Hall (1959; 1966) in which he treats distances that people use in their culture for various purposes. A basic part of his analysis proxemics across cultures is as follows: "Space is organized differently in each culture. The associations and feelings that are released in a member of one culture almost invariably mean something else in the next. When we say that foreigners are 'pushy,' this may mean only that their handling of space releases this association in our minds."

The basic study, then, is the handling of space in each culture and then the results when an outsider "violates" the proxemic rules. A good place to start the topic of proxemics in an intercultural program is with the expected distances between speakers of the target culture. For Americans, Hall found four distance categories for personal space. The Intimate Distance is from 0–18 inches and is reserved for intimate friends or family and for very private conversations. The Personal Distance is from 18 inches to 4 feet and is the distance at which the people involved are comfortable with friends and acquaintances. The Social Distance is 4–12 feet and is used for nonpersonal business and for some role relations such as boss to worker, professor to student, or the like. The Public Distance is from 12–25 feet and is used in public ceremonies, public speaking, classroom instruction, and similar activities. The actual distance at which an individual is comfortable varies according to a number of factors: age, sex, formality / politeness of the situation, status of speakers, even the presence of an authority figure or outsider in or close to those involved in the conversation.

Along with the distance dimension in proxemics is the orientation of the body when speaking. For example, two people may feel comfortable when standing at 90 degrees to each other and another pair may prefer a face toward face stance. When person who prefers face to face coupled with a comfortable distance that is closer than the comfortable distance of the other, the latter can get very uncomfortable. In this situation the latter can turn 90 degrees to be more comfortable and the other then can step back in front with face to face. It is possible to see two people in this situation slowly turning and moving until their conversation is a yard or more away from its starting point.

Group distancing / orienting and the way to enter a group conversation without making the native speakers feel uncomfortable is another subject that needs to be included in the intercultural communication program. It should be noted that in some of the existing depictions of the learner within another culture, the learner begins to use the pattern of the native speakers right away. In some cultures the outsider who tries to act as if he is an integral part of the group is considered rude or boorish. In other cultures, of course, the native speakers are tolerant and inclusive at first. It is in the first of these two situations that appropriate instruction is especially required.

Haptics

Haptics derives from the Greek for "touch." In the field of nonverbal communication it refers to the study of humans making physical contact with one another such as in handshakes. Cultures differ (Samovar & Porter) in the types, durations, and frequencies of various touching behaviors. For a few examples, in greeting patterns some cultures use handshakes or hugs plus perhaps cheek touching or so on. Other cultures use a bow or other means to greet some one. In conversations, some cultures allow those involved to touch each other on the hand or arm while those from other cultures avoid contact. Often the Arab culture is used as an example of a high touch culture when two Arab men are conversing while the British are used as an example of a no-touch or rare touch culture. The variations between any two cultures are so many that such general rules are not often helpful. The learner should probably avoid any touching behavior unless explicitly taught to do so in a language or intercultural program.

Socializers

Socializers are a less studied part of the nonverbal communication system. Socializers are verbal / vocal / nonverbal features which "ease the friction" of social interaction (Hoffer 1976). The study of these features cuts across verbal / nonverbal and across other types of distinctions. The topic is a component of the study of intercultural communicative competence. Mistakes in using socializers in an intercultural context can cause difficulties. For example, in a situation where a person expects the listener to acknowledge what he is saying with a nod or eye contact or a vocalization, the lack of any such feedback or an incorrect feedback often makes the speaker feel uncomfortable. There have been cases where people who have experienced this lack of feedback are so uncomfortable that they prefer to avoid talking to those of the other cultural background completely.

In this section, the topics within the study of socializers that are covered are: channel markers, channel turn-takers, channel interrupters, channel changers, channel closers.

Channel Markers

Channel markers are nonverbal / vocal / verbal indications that the addressee is listening and is keeping the channel of communication open. In an American English conversation the addressee usually marks the listening channel every 5–10 seconds (varying with the pace of conversation) with a verbalization such as "yes" or "I see", a vocalization such as "uh huh", and/or a movement such as a head nod. This behavior is also called "back-channeling." Often this channel marking is done when the speaker makes eye contact, as if the eye contact is the cue for the channel marker. The channel marker may be more frequent if the speaker is speaking quickly and less frequent if the speaker is speaking slowly. There is a sort of conversational rhythm that is set up in such situations. In Japanese, by contrast, a channel marker such as the vocalization "ee ... ee" is usually made every 2 or 3 seconds on the phone and almost as frequently in some face-to-face interaction. The cue may be timing or rhythm, but another hypothesis is that the markers occur at grammatical junctures in the speaker's discourse. Again the contrast between English channel marking and Japanese channel marking is total in terms of timing. (It may be of interest to note that American scholars who have recently returned from Japan often maintain the much more frequent markers for a few days, yet upon questioning are unaware of their behavior.)

Channel Turn-Takers

Channel turn-takers are movements designed to let the addressee know when the speaker is ready for the listener to become the speaker. When a speaker who uses the first type of gaze behavior presented above is ready for the listener to take his turn as speaker, he usually looks at the listener as he stops talking. The listener, who has been looking at the speaker, then begins talking as he turns away.

This turn-taking behavior may be misused in various ways in the intercultural situation. In one type of misunderstanding, the non-native speaker looks at the listener for a few seconds as he is preparing his next utterance. The time gap may be long enough that the listener assumes it is his turn to speaker and takes over the channel of communication. This behavior may be misread as a rude interruption or other negative behavior.

Another type of misunderstanding may occur when the listener's channel markers are not a word or nod but are phrases or short comments on the speaker's words. It is not unusual for a listener in the USA to mark the channel by saying "Yes, I heard about that" or "That was too bad" or so on. The speaker may or may not pause for these longer channel markers. A non-native, however, may misread these long channel markers as turn-takers and stop talking. The resulting silence is a sign of the miscommunication and can be uncomfortable for those involved.

A subheading under Channel Turn-Taker is Channel Holder. An English speaker who does wish to end his turn may use a variety of methods to "hold the floor", i.e. continue his turn. He may continue to look away from the listener. He may utter a prolonged "uuuuhhhhh" or prolong a word such as "theeeeeennnnn." He may put up his hand in a "wait" gesture. He may use a combination of these three. If the listener tries to take a turn anyway, the speaker may raise the volume of his voice and continue.

Language learners should learn the simple channel markers and their timing in the target language early in the acquisition process. The more complicated situations can be described in the later textbooks and some examples of skillful use of longer channel markers can be presented on video or CD.

Channel Interrupters

Channel interrupters break the flow of communication so that the interrupter can begin talking. In causal conversations and in friendly conversations within a group, interruptions of a speaker may be frequent and expected. In other situations, interruptions of a speaker may be read as rude and offensive. Since interruptions may be offensive, young children in the USA are often taught various ways to avoid interrupting adult conversations (Hoffer & St. Clair 1983). The child may be taught that if he has a question, he may stand quietly alongside the conversationalists until he is recognized and "given the floor" to speak. If the reason for interrupting is sufficiently strong, the child may approach the adult from behind or the side and whisper the message into the adult's ear.

Adults acquire strategies for interrupting that do not cause negative reactions in most cases. A strategy may be as simple as saying, "Excuse me, but I'd like to ask you something about that." A nonverbal strategy uses a raised or slightly raised hand, perhaps with the index finger pointed up. The signal lets the speaker know that the gesturer would like to speak at the first opportunity.

The various strategies for use by natives and non-natives need careful research by scholars from both the native and the target culture. One goal of the research is a specification of the strategies that a non-native can use to cause no or little trouble when an interruption is appropriate or necessary (Hoffer 1994; Hoffer & Koo 1995).

Channel Changers

Channel Changers are verbal or nonverbal strategies to change the channel of conversation in terms of topic or formality or so on. The most direct way to change a topic is the verbal one of stating that the speaker is changing the topic, for example "But on another topic, ..." or "That reminds me of another thing." A simple strategy for a listener to change the topic at his turn is with a question about the new topic, for example "... Have you considered another possibility?" It may be considered rude to change the topic of conversation when the original speaker still has something to say about it. The question allows the speaker to continue the original topic, if he wishes, or to switch to the suggested topic. Changing the channel of conversation inappropriately is not necessarily a major problem. Even so, as noted several times above, a non-native that has communicative competence in Channel Changers causes the least amount of friction in the conversational flow.

Channel Closers

The strategies for closing a conversation are rather difficult to learn, at times even within one's own native language. Often in an intercultural conversation, the signals that a speaker uses to indicate a desire for closure are not read properly by the non-native. In such situations the conversation may become disjointed and uncomfortable. Even worse, the non-native may be misread as pushy, aggressive, insensitive or so on.

In a casual, friendly or informal situation, the strategies are rather simple. A simple announcement that the speaker must leave may be sufficient. In intercultural conversations where the speakers are worried about offending the other person, the strategies probably should be more subtle or should be more elaborate. For example, the simple announcement that one must leave could be embellished with apologies or excuses, as in "Well, I'm sorry to have to go, but perhaps we can continue this conversation some other time?"

Problematic Nonverbal Behaviors Across Cultures

The material on nonverbal communication systems across cultures contains many examples of those which cause difficulties of various kinds in intercultural communication, as discussed in this section. These types of problematic emblems, especially those that may have serious consequences, should be part of any language education and intercultural communication program. While the nonverbal system of a foreign language was rather poorly represented in the language textbooks of several decades ago, the good language textbooks now usually contain at least some of the most basic parts of the nonverbal communication system. Programs in intercultural communication have been integrating into their instruction parts of the target nonverbal system and the types of nonverbal behavior that should be avoided.

A misuse or misunderstanding of any nonverbal behavior may have some negative effect on the communication. In some cases the behavior is not interpreted as part of the communication. At other times it is misread. In either case at least one of those involved may feel uneasy or uncomfortable. In some such situations, the unease and "uncomfortableness" are strong enough that one person involved may want to walk away or to have no further contact.

Some misunderstandings cause trouble that ranges from simple misunderstanding to a sense of being upset or repulsed or outraged, and to even worse reactions. In the extreme cases, the nonverbal behavior may cause arrest, violence, injury, or even death.

Several examples of nonverbal behavior that may cause these negative reactions are given below. The topics are arranged from those that may cause discomfort or so on to those that may cause more serious results.

Emblem — *OK*

This near universal emblem still retains some original meanings in various countries. In France, it may mean "zero" or "nothing" and in Japan it may mean "money."

In Latin America the emblem my have a quite negative meaning. When President Nixon years ago was on a tour of Latin America, he got off the plane and made an "OK" gesture with both hands. The reaction was booing and the next day's newspapers reported that he had insulted them with their sign for "you assholes."

Similarly, the emblem is a curse in Saudi Arabia and should be avoided.

Emblems — *Hello and Come Back*

Americans wave hello and goodbye by holding the hand near the head, fingers extended, and the hand is moved left and right or somewhat up and down. When the hand is held with the palm almost horizontal and the hand moved up and down, the gesture is similar to the "come back" gesture in Japan. Elaborate misunderstandings have resulted such as happened to the American tourist on a Japanese bus tour. The driver signaled for the person to return to the bus. The American thought the signal was a friendly "hello there" and waved back. When he did not return to the bus, the driver thought he was wanted to stay and the driver drove away. Both thought communication had been achieved and that the other person was behaving strangely.

Editor — *Socializer*

Serious misunderstandings can occur when a simultaneous translator does not know the Editor illustrators. A famous example occurred several years ago when Richard Nixon was President of the US. His press secretary was asked by a group of reporters that included foreign correspondents about Nixon's awareness of the cause of some event. The press secretary said, "The president was ignorant, ['editor' illustrator here] was unaware of that cause." The press secretary had realized that "ignorant" might be misunderstood as "dumb, stupid" rather than the intended "unaware." Thus he "edited" the "ignorant" and replaced it with "unaware." A translator who did not know the editer illustrator translated the sequence into something like "the President was stupid and unaware of the cause." Needless to say, the international reaction was strongly negative. This example shows that even top level interpreters of the language need to know the nonverbal communication features of the other language very well.

Proxemics in General

There are many other components in the study of proxemics, but the appropriate distances for the learner to use in particular situations in a foreign setting is perhaps the highest priority. The other priority is learning the worst of the results of an outsider violating the appropriate distance. As noted above, standing too close can cause the native speaker to feel that the outsider is pushy or aggressive. Standing too far away can cause the native speaker to feel that the outsider is aloof and uninterested. Note that these feelings occur even when the native speaker is aware of the differences in distance behavior of the outsider. The reactions are automatic and can cause the native speaker to be uncomfortable even at times to the point of not wanting to talk to the other person.

Socializer — *Closer*

One type of difficult behavior is sometimes the Channel Closer Socializer, a category that can not only be different but may cause difficulty in communication. For example, when the Channel Closer used is less direct, the listener may not recognize it as a closer. One example (Hoffer 1976) that is treated in the literature follows. The situation is that a professor is talking to a graduate student from another culture.

Professor	"Well, I have a lot of papers to grade."
Student	"Yes. Professors are very busy, aren't they?"
[Pause]	
Professor	"It's getting a bit late, isn't it?"
Student	"Yes, the sun goes down early these days."

[Pause]   [and so on.]

The professor was using Channel Closers and the student misread the situation as a meandering and perhaps friendly conversation. Eventually the professor stood up, gathered up his books and papers, and walked toward the door of the office. Only at that point did the student realize that the conversation was ending.

Years later the two met and recalled that awkward situation. The exstudent, then a professor at an American University, indicated that he too had wanted to conclude that conversation but did not how to do so without offending his professor.

Socializer — *Channel Marker Nod (or vocalization such as "yes" or "uh huh")*

An American who uses Japanese channel markers at the slower American pace may be viewed by Japanese as aloof, uninterested in the subject or speaker, unable to understand, or so on. The Japanese who uses American markers at the Japanese pace, "uh huh . uh huh .. uh huh" rather than "uh huh ... ... uh huh ... ... uh huh," is often interpreted as wanting to take a turn to speak, since that is one way Americans signal they want to take a turn in the conversation. In other words, it is interpreted as a channel interrupter. Hearing the frequent channel markers from the Japanese, the American stops to allow the Japanese to take a turn. The subsequent silence is quite awkward and lends to the feeling of uncomfortableness in the intercultural situation. Perhaps this is an example of partial or "semi-" communication; in the sense that the content is clear yet the communication is prematurely interrupted and full communication is not achieved.

Facial Expression — *Masking Expression*

As noted earlier, masked expressions occur when the person does not want to offend the other person with an inappropriate expression, such as when offered a food of the culture. Bear's paw on a plate in China may provoke a feeling of disgust, sheep's eyes in Saudi Arabia may provoke revulsion, and cat or dog meat in various countries might provoke outrage in an American who may then try to mask the automatic expression with a smile.

There are cases in which the inability to recognize masked expressions may be more serious. For one example, some years ago there was a picture in many papers of an American diplomat talking with an Asian diplomat. The American had a slight smile on his face, but the rest of his face led 100% of three test groups of American college students to interpret the smile as a mask for very strong anger. When the same picture was shown to different Asian groups in Asian, 0% perceived the underlying expression of anger. The potential result of such a lack of reading is that the non-native

English speaker may think that the communication is proceeding well and that the two are agreeing, while the native is merely trying to be polite while disagreeing strongly with the other person.

Gaze Behavior in General

There are several variations of the eye behavior in conversation given earlier. One variation is the almost complete reversal of the gaze behaviors of the speaker and listener. For example, in one Black pattern, the speaker looks at the addressee who avoids most eye contact. In the intercultural situation, the pattern may interfere with ease of communication. The speaker of the first pattern looks toward a potential addressee of the second pattern and waits for the latter to make eye contact. That eye contact is the signal for the first speaker to begin. However, the second person is waiting for the first person to speak. If the second looks at the first person, it could signal that the second person should begin the conversation. This reversal of patterns at times causes difficulty in, for example, inner city schools in the USA where there is a large concentration of Black students. White teachers usually have only the first pattern and they tend to misread the students' gaze behavior as lack of attention or — even worse — lack of respect.

Usually inappropriate gaze behavior causes minor difficulties in communication. Inappropriate gazing, however, may cause miscommunication or discomfort.

First, there is the reaction to staring. Children in the US are taught not to stare at another person because it is considered rude and offensive. However, the display rule differs by area of the country. That is, in some areas a person may stare toward a second person as long as the second person is further than a certain distance away. That distance may be as short as 20 feet or so. In other parts of the country, 20 feet is still considered far too close for staring and is still offensive.

Another example is that Japanese have had a somewhat different conversational gaze behavior than those discussed earlier, at least through the older generation before so much foreign — especially Western — contact. Little eye contact is made; often the gaze is downward or, if the head is oriented away from the other, outward. Japanese children were taught to look, if at all, at the nose/mouth area of the other. The contrast here is totally different from the general U.S. English rule. The American system seems to be based on eye contact and the former on avoiding eye contact. The implications for semi- and mis-communication are rather clear. The American may be seen by the Japanese as trying to be very aggressive, powerful, assertive, and so on, all these being viewed quite negatively by the Japanese. The Japanese are too often misread by Americans as devious, or worse, since they avoid eye contact. The situation is sometimes worse when only a part of the basic rule is learned, as when a Japanese learning English is taught eye contact, then uses it without looking away often enough or at the appropriate times. This "staring" behavior is reported by Americans to be rather uncomfortable and causes some problems in intercultural communication.

A more serious example of Gaze Behavior problems illustrates the "culture shock" that someone might have in his own culture when confronted with the varying display rules. A female sociology professor from downtown New York City took a position in a major Southwestern US city. She began complaining about the aggression, the rudeness, and so on of the local people. She could be filling her car with gasoline, look up and see one or two men inside the store or gasoline station looking at her fixedly. She got so upset at times that she raised the gasoline nozzle and shook it at them. In their Gaze Behavior pattern, she was far outside the "no staring" zone. Although she had studied these differences in behavior across the US, she was unable to overcome the cultural differences that were causing her anguish, broke her contract with the university and retreated to the streets of New York City. Display rules can be known, but living with them might prove difficult.

Examples of More Serious Nonverbal Misunderstanding

The examples begin with some that cause a negative impact and continue with more and more serious impacts up to and including death.

Emblem — *Thumbs up*

The basic meaning is "OK" or "Good," but it may mean "one" in Germany and some other European nations and may mean "five" in Japan. The local ways of counting should always be part of the learner's education.

The emblem is a strong insult in Australia where it means "up yours." The gesture can start a brawl in pubs and elsewhere. The gesture is also a strong insult in other countries as varied as Bangladesh and Germany. An American couple in Germany were stopped by a policeman who decided not to give them a ticket. When the man driving the car started his car and gave the policeman the emblem for "OK," the policeman became enraged and arrested him.

In a related use of the thumb out gesture, a hitchhiker may signal for a ride with his thumb out, fingers closed, palm facing inward, and the hand moved right and left. The gesture is so insulting in Nigeria that some hitchhikers were beaten up by some people driving by.

Emblem — *V*

While the "V" emblem for peace or victory is common in, for

example, Britain and America, it is highly insulting in many countries if the palm faces the viewer. President Bush was photographed using this version when abroad and was castigated in the press.

If the wrong version of "V" is used in the wrong places, it can start an argument or fight. Basically it may mean "up yours" or "up yours and one for your mother, too."

If the hand is moved upward and the hand twisted at the same time, it is very taboo.

Emblem — *Hook 'em horns*

This emblem may be interpreted in its historically earlier meaning of "cuckold," i.e. "your wife is cheating on you." It is quite offensive.

As noted earlier this emblem is used by those supporting the University of Texas . When this emblem with its historical meaning of "cuckold" is used in the wrong places, it can be so offensive that it causes serious trouble. Some years ago some patrons at an Italian bar learned that other patrons were from Texas and signaled them with this emblem. The Italian waiters were so insulted that a brawl took place and people were injured.

Emblem — *Crazy*

The emblem as used in America may signal that someone is not making sense or is doing something without thinking about the potential results. The gesture used in other cultures is quite offensive. For example, it is considered so insulting in Germany that the person can be arrested.

Haptics — *Touching, Embracing, Kissing*

There are various touching behaviors that can be quite offensive in some cultures. For examples, patting the top of the head of a child is a common behavior in the US. Doing so in Some Far Eastern cultures and others is taboo.

Other touching behavior can have rather serious results. An example of a serious NVB difference occurred in Saudi Arabia some years ago. An American man was waiting in a car for an American woman. As she entered the car, she gave him a "greeting" nonverbal behavior by sliding along the seat and "pecking" ("kissing lightly and quickly") the man on the cheek. Such a behavior is appropriate and even common between males and females of certain groups in the USA, whether or not the two are related, married, engaged, or friends. Probably this "peck on the cheek" occurs hundreds of thousands of times a day in the USA.

This example, however, happened in Saudi Arabia where public displays of affection are strongly disliked or even forbidden. Such behavior would only be displayed in private and only done by married people. Marriage is sacrosanct in Saudi Arabia. An officer of the Saudi National

Guard saw the incident and demanded to see proof of their marriage. The two friends were married to other people. Thus, the woman was deported for her conduct. The man tried to argue about the situation and became so argumentative about it that he was thrown in jail.

Similar examples in Dubai were reported in the press early in 2010. Reports in English newspapers in March of 2010 covered the status of two different couples who were seen kissing. In Dubai, public kissing can land you in jail. In the first example, an Iranian-Italian couple in Dubai shared a kiss on the observation deck of world tallest building. A child witnessed the kiss and the couple was arrested. They faced a sentence of one month in jail.

In the other example, a 25-year-old woman was seen in a restaurant kissing a man who worked as a consultant for a marketing firm. The two insisted it was just a "peck on the cheek," but the judge did not agree and sentenced them to jail. At the time of the article, they were out on bail but banned from leaving the country. In court their lawyer had argued that they had no intention of breaking the law and that a peck / kiss on the cheek in their culture is used as a greeting, but the judge found them guilty.

A difference in appropriate cultural behavior is not a valid argument when the behavior breaks the local laws. People who plan to travel to any country should learn all they can about any laws that are different there. As in these cases, seemingly innocent behaviors can have serious consequences.

Illustrator — *Deictic*

Pointing with the index finger as done in the US is considered a social gaffe in some parts of the world and is a bit more offensive to very offensive in others. Pointing with the middle finger alone may be seen as a "screw you" emblem and be very offensive.

A much more serious result of a pointing gesture occurred in Los Angeles in 1988 at a Thai cabaret. A Laotian customer put his foot on a chair, perhaps to rest his leg muscles. The bottom of his shoe was visible to the Thai entertainer on stage. After the performance, the entertainer followed the customer outside and shot him to death. The entertainer was later convicted of second degree murder.

The motivation for the murder was the sole of the shoe. Showing the sole to someone is a seriously grievous insult among some Middle Easterners and some Southeast Asians, among other groups. In this case the Laotian may or may not have known that his nonverbal behavior would be interpreted as an insult. The example is an excellent illustration of the point that people who travel in places where certain nonverbal behaviors might be understood as insulting, whether seriously so or not, should try to learn about the appropriate nonverbal behavior of the country to which they will travel. This rule is especially important for all nonverbal behavior that may be considered quite negative.

Emblems — *Go away and Come Here / Come Closer*

The "Go away" emblem as used in America is with the flat hand, fingers out, held horizontally about the chest level, and the hand moved up and down a bit while the fingers go down and are raised rather quickly. As described here, the gesture is very close to the "Come here" or "Come closer" as explained above. The confusion of these two gestures had a drastic impact in Korea some years ago.

At an American military base near the demilitarized zone some years ago, when tensions were very high between North Korea and South Korea, some guards had been ordered to keep all non-official people 50 meters or more from the outer fences. The threat of bombings or other hostile activity was considered intense.

One evening two young Koreans seemed to be playing as they moved closer and closer to the fence. One American guard yelled at them in English to move away. The young Koreans did not seem to understand his English. When the guard then used the American "Go away" gesture, it is not surprising that the young Koreans approached even closer. The guard intensified the gesture, but they kept coming closer. The guard then followed his orders and shot the Koreans. Subsequently it was determined that the two were only playing and had no weapons or bombs. In this case the misreading of the emblem had a deadly result. There cannot be a worse consequence of a cross-cultural misunderstanding of a nonverbal behavior.

Conclusion

The nonverbal behaviors that cause reactions ranging from discomfort to violence and death may be quite numerous if all of them used in all cultures in the world were to be studied. A learner cannot learn all of these types of behaviors, but he can learn them as used in any of the well-studied cultures of the world. The etiquette patterns of his countries or countries of choice should be learned as well as the etiquette patterns that should be used by outsiders. It is, however, perhaps of more crucial importance to learn the nonverbal patterns that could have serious consequences if used inappropriately. Information about those patterns can be found in books and DVDs and so on that the learner can use alone, in intercultural training programs and courses, and to some extent in the experience of living within the other culture. In terms of the last item mentioned, it should be noted that many people have difficulty in acquiring nonverbal competence while living in the other culture because their own nonverbal patterns are automatic and therefore hard to bring to the level of conscious self-study and / or because they do not realize that certain behaviors they see have a meaning in the other culture or they do not realize that those behaviors have a completely different meaning. The best way for most people to learn about the nonverbal system of another culture is through the courses and programs explicitly designed for the target culture. Those courses and programs can be supplemented with texts on the subject, with books and visual materials, and with attendance at conferences devoted to the topic of intercultural communication.

The courses, programs, and materials have been improving over the past few decades. The research on language systems has helped improve language texts and language programs in general over the past several decades. Better and better language texts are produced regularly, but research on nonverbal communication systems has been improving at a much slower rate.

In terms of intercultural communicative competence, the research is more difficult, both because of the subtleties of intercultural communication and because of the numbers of pairs of languages that need to be studied. As more scholars across cultures collaborate on research and as their results enter the textbooks and the language learning programs, better and ever more useful intercultural communicative competence will be achieved. Researchers from both or all cultures involved who work together might be avoid their own potential misunderstandings and produce better research. ①

The new publications on intercultural communication that have appeared over the last few years provide avenues for publication of research on this topic that is directly useful for the language and culture learner and especially for the one interested in intercultural communication. A journal that is helpful is *Intercultural Communication Studies*, sponsored by the International Association for Intercultural Communication Studies. The association also holds conferences yearly in various countries, including China, Japan, the USA and Mexico, with other locations to be used in the future. Those conferences and the many other such conferences around the world that bring together scholars of different cultures to share information and plan joint research are good signs that great progress will be made over the next few decades in the area of intercultural communicative competence.

---

① For the Hoffer & Koo article (1994) we traveled to a small town in Southeast Korea and while Koo was talking to a small group of teachers I concentrated only on their NVC. Later it turned out that Koo had not noticed many of their hand gestures because they are natural for a Korean but foreign and therefore rather obvious to a non-native.

References

Akiyama, K. (1993). A study of Japanese TV commercials from socio-cultural perspectives: special attributes of nonverbal features and their effects. *Intercultural Communication Studies* III:2. pp. 87–114

Axtell, R. (1985). *Do's and Taboos around the World*. Elmsford NY: John Benjamin.

Axtell, R. (1991, 1998). *Gestures: the Do's and Taboos of Body Language around the World*. New York NY: John Wiley & Sons.

Birdwhistell, R. (1970). *Kinesics and Context*. Philadelphia PA: University of Pennsylvania Press.

Ekman, P. (1982). *Emotion in the Human Face*. New York NY: Cambridge University Press.

Ekman, P. & Friesen, W. V. (1969). The repertoire of nonverbal behavior: Categories, origins, usage, and coding. *Semiotica*, 1, 49–98.

Ekman, P. & Friesen, W. (1975). *Unmasking the Human Face*. Englewood Cliffs NJ: Prentice-Hall.

Enninger, W. (1991). Focus on silence across cultures. *Intercultural Communication Studies* I:1. pp. 1–38

Gans, H. (1962). *The Urban Villager: Group and Class in the Life of Italian-Americans*. Glencoe, New York NY: Free Press.

Hall, E. (1966). *The Hidden Dimension*. Garden City NY: Doubleday and Co.

Hall, E. (1959). *The Silent Language*. Greenwich, Ct: Fawcett.

Hoffer, B. (1976). The acquisition of non-referential verbal communication. *Neurolinguistics*, No. III.

Hoffer, B. (1986). Communication across cultures: Verbal and nonverbal. In J. Koo & R. St. Clair. (Eds.). *Cross-Cultural Communication: East and West*. Seoul, Korea: Samji Publishing Co.

Hoffer, B. (1998). (Mis-)Communication across Cultures. In B. Hoffer & J. Koo. (Eds.). *Intercultural Communication East and West in the 90's*. San Antonio TX: Institute for Cross-Cultural Research. pp. 1–5.

Hoffer, B. (1985). (Mis-) Communication in (cross-) cultural (mis-) communication. In R. Brunt & W. Enninger, (Eds.). *Interdisciplinary Perspectives at Cross-Cultural Communication*. Aachen, Germany: RaderVerlag. pp. 9–30.

Hoffer, B. (1993). Nonverbal phrases in prose. *Intercultural Communication Studies* III:2.73–86.

Hoffer, B. (1981). Patterns of kinesic development. In B. Hoffer & R. St. Clair (Eds.). *Developmental Kinesics: the Emerging Paradigm*. Baltimore MD: University Park Press.

Hoffer, B. (1991). Verbal and nonverbal communication: A cross-cultural project: American, Japanese, and Korean. In P. Fendos, (Ed.). *Cross-Cultural Communication: East and West*. Volume II. Tainan, Taiwan: T'ai Ch'eng Publishing Company. pp. 579–611.

Hoffer, B. & Koo, J. (1994). Communicative competence in Korean. *Korean Linguistics*. Vol. 8, pp. 85–96.

Hoffer, B. & Koo, J. (Eds.). (1998). *Intercultural Communication East and West in the 90's*. San Antonio TX: Institute for Cross-Cultural Research

Hoffer, B. & R. Santos. (1980). Cultural clashes in kinesics. In W. von Raffler-Engel (Ed.). *Aspects of Nonverbal Communication*. Amsterdam: Swets & Zeitlinger.

Hoffer, B. & St. Clair, R. (Eds.). (1981). *Developmental Kinesics: the Emerging Paradigm*. Baltimore: University Park Press.

Kim, K-O. (1992). What causes communication problems between English speakers and Korean speakers? *Intercultural Communication Studies I*.2. 103-116.

Knapp, M. (1972). *Nonverbal Communication in Human Interaction*. New York NY: MacMillan.

Koo, J. & St. Clair, R. (Eds.). (1986). *Cross-Cultural Communication: East and West*. Seoul, Korea: Samji Publishing Co.

Leathers. D. (1986). *Nonverbal Communication Systems*. Boston MA: Allyn & Bacon.

Mehrabian, A. (1972). *Nonverbal Communication*. Chicago IL: Aldine-Atherton.

Poyatos, F. (Ed.). (1988). *Cross-Cultural Perspectives in Nonverbal Communication*. Toronto: C. J. Hogrefe.

Samovar, L. & Porter, R. (Eds.). (1972). *Intercultural Communication: A reader*. Belmont CA: Wadsworth.

Von Raffler-Engel, W. (Ed.). (1980). *Aspects of Nonverbal Communication*. Amsterdam: Swets & Zeitlinger.

17

When Shyness Is *Not* Incompetence: A Case of Thai Communication Competence[*]

Suwichit Sean CHAIDAROON
University of Memphis, USA

Abstract: Following the framework of communication competence, which consists of motivation, cognition and performance, this paper argues that Thai communication competence differs from the American or Western counterparts in all three elements. Some Thai communication competence notions include shyness, reluctance to ask for favors, as well as knowledge and awareness of seniority, social links, and *Kreng Jai* (being extremely considerate). Instead of being assertive, appearing to be shy or reluctant to ask for favors, being humble, and not responding too quickly in interactions are strategic mode of communication to gain social respect and recognition in Thai society. Autoethnographic data and Thai proverbs are used to demonstrate those themes of Thai communication competence. The conclusion suggests that the notion of communication competence as motivation, cognition, and performance appears to be universal and the framework is heuristic in analyzing communication competence. However, ideology and behaviors that count as being competent vary from culture to culture. Therefore, there should be more attempts to employ an interpretive approach to study communication competence.

---

[*] I would like to express my sincerest gratitude to Professor Kazuo Nishiyama, my first teacher of intercultural communication, as well as Professor Guo-Ming Chen and Professor Yoshitaka Miike for their suggestions, support, and assistance.

Introduction

I first came to America in 1999. As a Thai student who had never been abroad before, I was excited to meet with people from other countries who look different from me and to live in a new environment. When looking back, I realize how little I knew at that time about the differences, not only in terms of the physical appearance but also the hidden assumptions about selves and lives, between other people and myself. When I was young, my parents taught me that to be *Kreng Jai*, or considerate, is the best strategy when dealing with people that I first meet or even with people that I know very well. If you show your consideration to others, they will reciprocate in the same manner. So, as a part of being *Kreng Jai*, I try not to speak up very often in hopes that other people I meet in America would consider that I am nice and sincere to them and that they would be nice in return and grant me a favor when I need. I have to admit that I am lucky to have met nice people who try to understand my behaviors. Usually, we communicate successfully but that is not always the case.

One day, my American classmate asked me to join the departmental soccer team as they needed people to sign up so that they could join the university's tournament. Even though this activity did not required a great skill and all my friends were studious students who barely knew how to play soccer, I really felt uncomfortable to join the team as I never played this kind of game before. At the same time, I did not want to refuse his wish because I was afraid that it would hurt his feeling. So I said to my friend, "I will try my best to show up at the game." The day after the game, my friend came to talk to me again and he seemed very upset. He asked me why I did not go to the game as promised. I was speechless as I thought he should have known that I was reluctant to accept his invitation in the first place.

This misunderstanding led me to question why my answer did not work in such a situation even though I had a good intention to maintain the relationship between my friend and me. I am certain that if I had said the same thing to Thai people, they would have known right away that I am refusing to play in the game. The effect of my communication strategy appeared to be one that I had not wished. My indirect answer did not seem to be an appropriate response to my friend. The effective communication strategy that I used while I was in Thailand did not work here at all. As a result of this incident, I start to be interested in investigating the differences between the notions of communication competence between Thai and Westerners.

In this paper, I will first review the literature on communication competence and approaches to study this concept. With this review, three main elements, i.e. cognition, performance and motivation, will be presented as a framework to analyze communication competence. Afterwards, the framework will be used to analyze shyness as a strategic communicative behavior. In this sense, shyness can be seen as a communicatively competent behavior among the Thai. This analysis will illustrate the heuristic framework of communication competence yet highlight the different notions of communication competence between the Thai and the Westerners. Finally, I will discuss the prospect of studying communication competence from an interpretive/ethnographic standpoint in order to expand the body of knowledge in this area.

Four Approaches on Communication Competence

Even though the study of communication competence can be traced back in the ancient times as far as the birth of rhetoric, communication scholars have seriously studied communication competence as a construct for more than two decades and the term first appeared in a communication journal in 1974 (Rubin, 1990). Since then, there have been debates and different perspectives on investigating communication competence. I found that communication scholars take four different perspectives to studying communication competence. The four approaches that appear in the literature consist of goal-oriented perspective, cognitive versus performance perspective, social and interpersonal perspective, and resources or skills based perspective. The goal-oriented, cognitive versus performance, and resources based perspectives have been conceptualized by Jablin and Sias (2001) while I found the social and interpersonal perspective emerging from my review of literature.

Communication competence from the goal-oriented approach focuses on the effectiveness or situations in which competent communicators interact to achieve the desired goals. Parks' (1994) definition of communication competence represents this approach, as he states:

> Communicative competence represents the degree to which individuals satisfy and perceive that they have satisfied their goals within the limits of a given social situation without jeopardizing their ability or opportunity to pursue their other subjectively more important goals (p. 595).

This definition places an emphasis on the goal achievement of a competent communicator which can be observed and/or perceived by the communicator. Communication competence from this perspective suggests that persuasion or control is the key element in communication effectiveness. Along with this perspective is the definition of communication competence offered by Phillips (1983) who states that "competence would refer to understanding of situations, skill in demonstration of necessary techniques, effectiveness to goal accomplishments all by a particular person in a given case" (p. 31). Even though both definitions focus on the goal achievement, Phillips' definition of competence differs from Parks' as it suggests that effective or competent behaviors must be demonstrated and observable while Parks focuses on the perception of communicators whether or not they achieve their goals. In addition, Phillips' definition of competence also implies that we should look at competence in a given situation and competence should not be viewed as a static trait of communicators across various cases.

The second approach to view communication competence focuses on the distinction of competence and performance. McCroskey (1982) is a major scholar who advocates that competence should be viewed separately from performance. Competence is the knowledge of behaviors while performance is the actual behavior one performs in an interaction. He argues that the "accomplishment of goals (effectiveness) is neither a necessary nor sufficient condition for a judgment of competence. One may be effective without being competent and one may be competent without being effective" (p. 3). This notion suggests that we need to look at motivation as another factor in studying competence. A competent communicator who has knowledge of effective communication behaviors may not be motivated to perform those behaviors in a given case. At the same time, a person who performs effective communication behaviors could be effective as a result of external factors, not his or her knowledge of communication competence. Therefore, "one may not infer competence from performance or project performance from competence. Neither is a necessary condition for the existence of the other" (McCroskey, 1984, p. 263).

The third approach of communication competence is based on interpersonal and social perspectives. Bochner and Kelly (1974) posit that communication competence is the ability to relate effectively to self and other. These scholars explicitly identify that their notion of competence focuses on interpersonal interactions. They suggest that communicators develop five skills to be interpersonally competent i.e. empathic communication, descriptiveness or giving feedback, owning feelings and thoughts, self-disclosure, and behavioral flexibility. Another definition of communication competence based on social and interpersonal perspective is offered by Littlejohn and Jabusch (1982). They propose that communication competence is "the ability and willingness of an individual to participate responsibly in a transaction in such a way as to maximize the outcome of shared meaning" (p. 29). Even though this definition sounds similar the to goal-oriented approach definition, it places an emphasis on shared meaning, implying that both interactants are engaging in a communication process to relate to each other. They also suggest further that competent communicators need to have understanding of communication processes and skills such as interpersonal sensitivity as well as ethical responsibility.

The last perspective on communication competence views the construct as resources of communication abilities. Jablin, Cude, House, Lee, and Roth (1994), for example, define competence as:

> [T]he set of ability (resources), which a communicator has available for use in the communication process. These resources are acquired via dynamic learning process and take the form of interrelated subjects of communication skills (capacities), and strategic knowledge appropriate communication behavior (p. 125).

This definition of competence places the emphasis on the practicality of certain communication skills and is mostly adopted by those who try to apply communication competence to workplace settings. Research from this perspective tries to provide catalogues of certain communication skills required in workplaces (Monge et al., 1981). However, this perspective is useful only when considering the minimum requirements of communication skills to get work accomplished while the superior quality of communication skills needs more investigation.

Three Main Elements of Communication Competence

Despite those debates and various perspectives on communication competence, there are three main elements that help explain the existence of communication competence from the approaches delineated above. These elements will serve as a framework for the later discussion on how Thai communication competence differs from the Western views on communication competence. First, competent communicators need to have the knowledge of competent behaviors. This includes the resources of effective behaviors as well as rules, norms, and ethics for choosing appropriate behavior. This element is referred to as cognition or competence. However, since the word competence itself may be misleading as communication competence actually requires more than just cognition, therefore I will use the term cognition to refer to the knowledge of effective communication strategy and competence as the overall communication competence for the remainder of this paper. Second, competent communicators must have the ability to perform certain behaviors. This is referred to as performance. Finally, the competent communicators must have motivation to mobilize their competence to performance, that is, they need to have a drive to perform what they know in a given situation. Cognition, performance and motivation provide a broad framework of communication competence that can be applied to analyze behaviors in various communication episodes.

The establishment and development of this communication competence framework is heavily influenced by communication scholars who primarily adopt the social scientific paradigm. I have noticed that the three elements are useful in explaining a communication phenomenon. The cognition and the performance, in particular, are instrumental in the teaching and learning of communication competence as they are observable and measurable. However, when encountering different cultural contexts, the same set of knowledge and behaviors may not be judged as competent. Therefore, we have to reconsider and examine if the sender's intention and motivation to communicate in that particular situation. Unfortunately, not much research has been conducted to investigate the situation when the sender is motivated to communicate but his or her repertoire of knowledge and abilities on communication competence do not fit in the context. In that case, we should take into our consideration not only the context of the situation but certain unobservable factors such as the sender's motivation or intention as well as the cultural value or ideology the interactants hold on to.

Chen and Starosta (1996) argue that with the technology development, globalization of the economy, widespread of migrations, development of multiculturalism, and de-emphasis on the nation-states, intercultural communication is inescapable and thus we need to re-conceptualize scholarly work on communication competence, particularly in intercultural interactions. These researchers define intercultural communication competence as "the ability to negotiate cultural meanings and to execute appropriately effective communication behaviors that recognize the interactants' multiple identities in a specific environment" (pp. 358–359). To understand intercultural communication competence, we certainly need to consider the affective, cognitive, and behavioral aspects of communication both of our cultures and the cultures of people we are interacting with. However, we need to investigate competence in different cultures more closely before moving on to the universal framework of competence.

In the following section, I will illustrate difficulties or misunderstandings as a result of different fundamental beliefs concerning communication competence of Thai people and that of the Westerners by analyzing my personal autoethnographic accounts. Even though this approach is subjective, it will allow Thai people to understand their own value, or at least for me, to investigate my personal cultural assumptions before attempting to understand other cultures. Moreover, it will shed lights on the notion of competence in one specific culture that may contribute to the understanding of universal communication competence in the long run. In so doing, I hope to call for an alternative approach to study or investigate communication competence.

Shyness as Thai Communication Competence

If we admit that communication competence varies from culture to culture, Thai communication competence is then different from the Western notion of competence. Sriussdaporn-Charoenngam and Jablin (1999), for example, conducted a survey to find out what Thai businesspeople perceive as communicatively competent behaviors. The researchers identified four issues in their study, i.e. knowing how to avoid conflict with others; controlling emotions; display respect, tactfulness, modesty, and politeness; and appropriate pronoun usages in addressing others. Among the Thai competent communicators, maintaining relationships with interlocutors will be the main concern even over task achievements (Komin, 1990). Relationships can be gained and maintained with subtle communication behaviors such as selecting appropriate terms of address for interlocutors (Palakornkul, 1975). The status of Thai interlocutors in a conversation can be displayed or honored by selecting appropriate personal pronouns, personal names, nominal reference terms such as kinship terms and occupational terms, the demonstrative this-that, or reference avoidance strategy. The level of formality in language use can also influence the Thai who communicate in English with their non-Thai colleagues.

All the studies cited above seem to identify competent behaviors without relating the behaviors to ideology, or cognitive knowledge, as well as the motivation of communicators and thus fall into the resource approach to studying competence as mentioned earlier. Viewing communication competence as a set of skills may be useful when we first conceptualize the notion but it isolates communication competence from its cultural context and disregard some hidden assumptions the communicators have in their minds. One example that illustrates the loophole of considering communication competence only from the observable elements is the way Thai people conceptualize and strategically choose to present themselves as shy persons.

Like many Asian cultures, Thai people tend not to speak up or appear to be assertive as in the Western sense. Fieg (1989) as well as Knutson, Komolsevin, Chatiketu, and Smith (2002), for example, describe Thai people as being shy, easy going, fun loving, polite, and kind, and reluctant to be in conflict or direct confrontation. If we adopt the value that being assertive or taking the opportunity to voice your opinions is always a trait of communication competence, then the characteristics of Thai people mentioned here will imply that Thai people are, for the most part, incompetent communicators. However, as a Thai person, I myself would argue that there are times when we, Thai people, deliberately appear to be shy in order to maintain social harmony. Shyness, for the Thai, is then a strategic performative behavior which is *not* a result of external factors or incompetent behavior per se.①

From the Western perspective, shyness is normally considered an unfavorable trait and is the opposite of assertiveness. I remember when I first started my graduate studies in America, I really felt uncomfortable participating in class discussions. It was not that I did not have any ideas to share with the classes but there were too many concerns going on in my head. I was not sure if I would appear to be rude to anyone, show off my knowledge too much, disrespect the teachers, waste the class time, etc. Generally speaking, I was not sure if speaking up would be considered a good thing at that time. As a result, I chose to be quiet. My quietness or shyness was not based on the fact that I did not want to communicate with others either but it was an intentional behavior that I chose to perform with the hopes to maintain good relationships with my teachers and classmates. That shyness may not lead to positive outcomes in interactions but it should not be considered a sign of incompetence.

Analyzing Thai Shyness from the Communication Competence Framework

As mentioned earlier, communication competence consists of three elements, i.e. cognition, performance, and motivation. This framework of communication competence can be used to illustrate that the Thai shyness is considered a communicatively competent behavior among Thai people. In the following section, I will discuss three specific behaviors that can be seen as parts of Thai shyness i.e. not asking for help, extreme humility, and not speaking up or not responding quickly. These three behaviors will be presented in relation to the ideology or cultural value that Thai people hold on to. The knowledge of this cultural ideology in this case serves as the cognition aspect of competence. Finally, the motivation to perform such shy behaviors will be analyzed.

Not Asking for Help and Not Refusing to Help

Without any relatives in America, graduate student classmates are the only group of people I mainly socialize with. Even though I believe I know some of them very well, I find it hard in several occasions to ask them to do me a favor as I feel uncomfortable to do so. One day, I walked into the graduate student lounge and chatted with my classmates as usual. I told them that I just moved into a new apartment and felt exhausted. A friend then asked me if I had had anybody to help me move. "No, I did it all by

---

① I also acknowledge that there are some situations when Thai people become shy or do not speak up due to the lack of knowledge or skills in those communication episodes. Sometimes, they may lack the motivation and intention to interact. In those situations, I consider Thai people really incompetent.

myself." Then, my friend said to me, "Why didn't you tell us? We were all free last week." Certainly, I was too shy to ask for help and that is not pragmatic in the American context. I recognized after that conversation that one American graduate student had asked others to help her move a semester before and I actually did help her. Asking for help is probably not considered rude if it is done right in among the American people. A person who is asked to help may or may not agree to do so as long as can justify his or her decision politely to the asking person. However, that is not the case that I have experienced as a Thai person when interacting with the Thais.

When considering this situation, I start to realize that I often feel uncomfortable asking for help from others no matter how well I know that person. You certainly feel uncomfortable asking for help from the people you don't know very well. For many Thai people, they also feel uncomfortable asking for help from people with whom they have close relationships. Asking your friends to help you in some way may jeopardize the interpersonal dynamics as that causes your friend an extra effort to help you. In that situation, you will be seen as inconsiderate. However, in a special case, if you are asked to help or grant someone a favor, you are not supposed to refuse even though you may feel uncomfortable in doing so. Refusing often hurts your interlocutors' feelings among Thai people. In short, there is a Thai saying that is taught and passed on for generations that we should "bring the others' hearts in to our hearts," meaning we should be sensitive to how other people feel or think. We have to realize automatically if our friends need help or not and offer them a favor instead of waiting for them to ask. At the same time, if we are asked to help we should try our best not to refuse. Not asking or not refusing does not mean Thai people are merely shy to do so but they do that to maintain the relationships.

The habit of not asking for help can be best explained by the Thai ideology, *Kreng Jai*. This concept is widely discussed as it is a unique characteristic of the Thais. Pornpitakpan (2000), for example, explained *Kreng Jai* as:

> diffidence; deference; consideration; sensitivity toward others; reluctance to impose on or interrupt others; reluctance to assert one's comments, wants, or disagreements, especially to one's superiors; reluctance to negotiate with or give instructions to superiors; complying with other's explicit or implicit wishes or requests, especially if those come from superiors; concealing negative feelings, such as anxiety, resentment, and anger, to avoid making others uncomfortable or lose face; and reluctance to demand one's own rights (a nonsmoker will patiently inhale the cigarette smoke from nearby smoker; a customer usually does not demand compensation for faulty products.) (p. 65).

Being *Kreng Jai* is a reciprocal process, that is, when you appear to be

Kreng Jai to someone, that person is obliged to become *Kreng Jai* to you in return. A *Kreng Jai* person does not exhibit the *Kreng Jai* trait only for presenting himself or herself as a socially admirable being in a Thai community but also performs *Kreng Jai* acts to create, maintain, honor, and / or rebuild the face of his or her interlocutor. *Kreng Jai*, thus, determines important communicative acts of the Thai including requesting and responding to request, conflict resolution, negotiation, giving criticism, group participation etc., where interlocutors are engaged in face-work (Goffman, 1967). This unique trait of Thai people is then a cultural knowledge that influences the Thais not to speak up or asking for help in various situations.

Extreme Humility

Another situation when Thai people seem to be shy is when someone acknowledges their achievements. People from different cultures employ different discourse strategies in responding to compliments. I have noticed that when I give compliments to my Thai friends such as when they did well on the exams or presentations, my Thai friends usually refer to their accomplishments as a result of luck, favorable factors in the situation, or assistance from others. On the other hand, my friends from other countries, particularly from the western hemisphere, usually refer to the effort they have put or how hard they have tried when they talk about their achievements. As for the Thais, speaking of one's own achievement or a good trait is considered bragging even though that person has concrete evidence or does not do it in a threatening manner. Thai people would rather be quiet and let the others appreciate their achievements without speaking of it themselves. Moreover, it is better to let others see your deeds from actions, rather than hear about them only from your words. This shyness to show off is a behavior that Thai people intentionally perform in order to maintain relationships with the others.

Being humble is a cultural knowledge that Thai people pass on to one another. Parents often refer to a proverb, "Don't lift your self up to threaten others" when teaching their children the concept of humility. Not putting one's self ahead of others' is what Thai people value (Vathanaprida, 1994). To maintain social harmony, it is better to put yourself in the same position as others. This can be done by not talking about your achievements. Another proverb that precipitates in the Thais' minds is "Stick a golden plate behind the Buddha image." One way the Thais make a religious merit is by sticking a golden plate on a Buddha image. If you stick the plate in front of the Buddha image, others will see it directly and people who do so may appear to have bad intention to get benefits back from their actions. Therefore, this proverb teaches Thai people not to overly expect benefits from their actions and not to show it off to other people. However, it is your responsibility to be sensitive to other Thais' achievements and acknowledge them as they are not supposed to speak on such things. This cultural knowledge is the reason why Thai people are shy to speak of their achievements in most situations.

Not Speaking Up and Not Responding Quickly

I once had a chance to teach Thai language at an American university. My American students often shared stories of misunderstandings they had with Thai people with me. One day, a female student told me how furious she was at a Thai restaurant. According to her, there was a mistake on the bill. She then talked to a Thai waitress to explain the situation. However, she said the Thai waitress just smiled back to her and that made her very angry.① After a while, the manager of the restaurant stepped in to solve the problem. I personally was not surprised with the waitress' response (or the lack of). When I taught in Thailand, I barely received any answers from my students when I asked them in class. These situations show that the Thai tend to be slow in responding in interactions or not speaking up at all.

Verbal prudence is highly valued among the Thais. We are taught to be conscientious in our behaviors and words. Thai parents often say to their children, "if you do something slowly and prudently, you will get two awards."②This passes on the value that you have to think carefully before actually doing or speaking something as it will lead to a better result. Therefore, it is common to see Thai people becoming slow in speaking up or responding in interactions even among people who are skillful communicators as they have to take time to think carefully before they interact. It is this cultural value that teaches them to be slow in responding. As a result, the Thai quietness in this case implies that the Thais are still engaging in the interaction cognitively while they are quiet and thus should not be seen as incompetent trait.

Motivation

Not asking for help, being humble, and slow responses are parts of behaviors that may cause people from other cultures to misunderstand Thai people and view the Thais as shy. However, these behaviors are influenced by the cultural knowledge that has been passed on to them. Actually, when not asking for help, appearing humble, or responding slowly, Thai people may intend to communicate with specific motives. As a high-context

---

① Thai smile is another research area that is worth looking into as there are several meanings of smile for Thai people. It is beyond the scope of this paper to discuss this issue extensively. In this situation, I would interpret that the waitress smiled to ease the tension and reduce the anxiety as she did not know what to do.
② A relevant proverb in Thai is *Cha Cha Dai Pra Song Lem Ngram*, which has a similar meaning to "slow but sure" in the English language.

culture (Knutson et. al., 2002), the three behaviors mentioned are strategic attempts of the Thais to gain respect or recognition from others without explicitly displaying them. The recognition or respect they try to create and maintain must be done with care while they desire to be accepted as a part of the community.

The interactions among the Thais may be subtle from the outsiders' perspective and I would also argue that Thai communication is heavily receiver-oriented. That is, the senders do not often show their actual motive explicitly in their interactions. They, for example, do not ask for help even when they need or do not speak of their achievements even when they are proud of them. It is the receivers' responsibility to be sensitive to their interlocutors' motives and respond accordingly. With the implicit strategies as a result of their cultural value, communication competence of the Thais then appears to be different from that of the Western. The implicit communication, or shyness in this case, is not a negative trait but a strategic choice of the Thais to gain respect and maintain social harmony.

Call for Alternative Approach to Researching Communication Competence

In this paper, I have argued that the Thai communication competence can also be explained by the framework of cognition, performance, and motivation and thus the framework is heuristic in analyzing competence from different cultures. However, the main research program in America is heavily influenced by the social scientific paradigm. Investigating competence from the observable and measurable aspects is beneficial for capturing the concreteness of communication episodes. Nevertheless, there are some intangible issues that influence our notions of competence.

More interpretive approaches will certainly help us make sense of competence by taking into considerations intangible factors such as cultural value, motivation, and underlying assumptions of communicators. These alternative ways of studying communication competence will also help explain the existing gap that social scientific research has found. For example, a recent study that employs the rhetorical sensitivity scale did not yield the results researchers have speculated (Knutson, Komolsevin, Chatketu, & Smith, 2003). Contrary to its hypothesis, the study found that US Americans display significantly higher levels of rhetorical sensitivity than the Thai. When I examined the instrument, I would guess that Thai subjects in the study did not rate themselves high on rhetorical sensitivity because all of items in that category are obviously positive traits. If they rated themselves high on those items, they would have been considered bragging which is against their value. So they may have tried to be humble in that study. When communication behaviors do not match with theories, such as Thai communication in this case, an interpretive viewpoint can provide a rich description and explanation why they do not work.

Conclusion

In this paper, I have illustrated that implicit communication behaviors of the Thai that non-Thai people may consider shyness are actually strategically performed by the Thais to maintain social harmony and gain recognition from others. Those behaviors, i.e. not asking for help, being humble, and slow response or not speaking up, are not necessarily viewed negative by Thais people. The communication competence which consists of cognition, performance, and competence, coupled with an interpretive approach are appropriate for explaining this phenomenon as it captures both tangible aspects of the Thai competence as well as the intangible factors such as cultural value and motivation. Therefore, more interpretive studies are needed to help us fully understand the notion of communication competence particularly when studying competence within different cultures.

References

Bochner, A., & C. Kelly. (1974). Interpersonal communication competence: Rationale, philosophy and implementation of a conceptual framework. *Speech Teacher*, *23*, 279–301.

Chen, G. M., & W. J. Starosta. (1996). Intercultural communication competence: A synthesis. In B. R. Burleson (Ed.), *Communication Yearbook 19* (pp. 353–383). Thousand Oaks, CA: Sage.

Fieg, J. P. (1989). *A Common Core: Thai and American* (E. Mortlock, Rev.). Yarmouth, ME. Intercultural Press.

Goffman, E. (1982). *Interaction Ritual: Essays on Face-to-face Behavior*. New York: Pantheon Books (Original work published in 1967).

Knutson, T. J., R. Komolsevin, P. Chatiketu. & V. R. Smith. (2002). A comparison of Thai and U.S. American willingness to communicate. *Journal of Intercultural Communication Research*, *31*, 3–12.

Knutson, T. J., R. Komolsevin, P. Chatiketu, & V. R. Smith. (2003). A cross-cultural comparison of Thai and US American rhetorical sensitivity: Implications for intercultural communication effectiveness. *International Journal of Intercultural Relations*, *27*, 63–78.

Littlejohn, S. W. & D. M. Jabusch. (1982). Communication competence: Model and application. *Journal of Applied Communication Research*, *10*(1), 29–37.

Jablin, F. M., & P. M. Sias. (2001). Communication competence. In F. M. Jablin & L. L Putnam (Eds.), *The New Handbook of Organizational Communication: Advances in Theory, Research, and Methods* (pp. 819–864). Thousand Oaks, CA: Sage.

Jablin, F. M., R. L. Cude, A. House, J. Lee, & N. L. Roth. (1994). Communication competence in organizations: A conceptualization and comparison across multiple levels of analysis. In L. Thayer & G. Barnett (Eds.), *Organization Communication: Vol. 4. Emerging Perspectives* (pp. 114–140). Norwood, NJ: Ablex.

Komin, S. (1990). *Psychology of the Thai people: Values and Behavioral Patterns*. Bangkok: Research Center, National Institute of Development Administration.

McCroskey, J. C. (1982). Communication competence and performance: A pedagogical perspective. *Communication Education*, *31*, 1–8.

McCroskey, J. C. (1984). Communication competence: The elusive construct. In R. N. Bostorm (Ed.), *Competence in Communication* (pp. 259–268). Beverly Hills, CA: Sage.

Monge, P. R., S. G. Bachman, J. P. Dillard, & E. M. Eisenberg. (1981). Communicator competence in the workplace: Model testing and scale development. In M. Burgoon (Ed.), *Communication Yearbook 5* (pp. 505–527). Beverly Hills, CA: Sage.

Palakornkul, A. (1975). A socio-linguistic study of pronominal usage in spoken Bangkok Thai. *International Journal of Sociology of Language*, *5*, 11–41.

Parks, M. R. (1994). Communicative competence and interpersonal control. In M. L. Knapp & G. R. Miller (Eds.), *Handbook of Interpersonal Communication* (2nd ed., pp. 589–620). Thousand Oaks, CA: Sage.

Phillips, G. M. (1983). A competent view of "competence." *Communication Education*, *32*, 25–36.

Pornpitakpan, C. (2000). Trade in Thailand: A three-way cultural comparison. *Business Horizon*, *43*(2), 61–70.

Rubin, R. B. (1990). Communication competence. In G. M. Phillips & J. T. Wood (Eds.), *Speech Communication: Essays to Commemorate the 75th Year of the Speech Communication Association* (pp. 94–129). Carbondale, IL: Southern Illinois University Press.

Sriussadaporn-Charoenngam, N., & F. M. Jablin. (1999). An exploratory study of communication competence in Thai organizations. *Journal of Business Communication*, *36*, 382–418.

Vathanaprida, S. (1994). *Thai Tales: Folktales of Thailand*. Englewood, CO: Libraries Limited.

18

A Contrastive Analysis of Chinese and American Views about Silence and Debate

Gu Xiaole
Harbin Institute of Technology, China

Abstract: As representatives of Eastern and Western cultures, China and America stand at the two extremes of the cultural continuum. People from the two cultures hold almost opposite views toward talk. We Chinese people always criticize the Americans being talkative and boastful, while the Americans blame the Chinese for their indifference to others' words and their lack of viewpoints. This paper attempts to show different beliefs about public speaking and debate between the Chinese and the Americans, and to analyze the reasons that lead to their differences. An analysis of the results of a survey of cultural members indicated four dimensions of contrastive cultural values between the Americans and the Chinese. Cultural values (e.g., the value of talk) and philosophical factors (e.g., Confucianism and Taoism versus the classical rhetoric of Ancient Greece and Rome) lead to differences in the views about silence and debate.

Introduction

We all admit the existence of sociolinguistic diversity, yet when an intercultural communication takes place, misunderstandings are almost unavoidable. This is something that always happens in the course of the communication between the Chinese and American people. One problem that always frustrates both the Chinese and Americans when they come across each other is that they seem to have difficulty in agreeing when a person should speak and how.

American teachers who teach in Chinese schools always complain that Chinese students don't participate in class at all. The teachers have thought that the Chinese students are not competent enough to comprehend what they have taught, but later, through the essays written by Chinese students, they find out that these students are very thoughtful. The Chinese people always criticize the Americans being talkative and boastful, while Americans blame the Chinese for their indifference to others' words and their lack of viewpoints. In the eyes of the Chinese people, the Americans display the national character of standing arrogantly over others, interfering others' affairs; while to the American people, China is such a mythic nation that will never be understood. These prejudices between two peoples have, too much extent, hinder the development of their relation, and the consequences brought by them can be far reaching.

The purpose of this paper is to study the different attitudes held by the Chinese and Americans toward silence and debate and to explore the reasons for these differences, with the hope that it can provide the two peoples necessary information about this issue so that misunderstandings between them can be avoided while cooperation be enhanced. In the first section, a questionnaire delivered to a number of Chinese speakers is described and its result is shown and briefly analyzed. In the third section, the paper focuses on several dimensions of contrastive values held by the Chinese and Americans, values that lead to their different views on silence and debate. The fourth section will examine the philosophical influence on their views on silence and debate.

Preliminary Study

In order to explore the Chinese and Americans' beliefs about public speaking and debate, I conducted a preliminary study on this issue. A questionnaire was distributed to different groups of the Chinese people and one group of American speakers. The Chinese speakers consist of a group of Ph. D. candidates (82), a group of teenagers (39), and a group of factory workers. To my surprise, I got quite similar results from the three groups of Chinese people despite their different family backgrounds, educational backgrounds, living and working surroundings, while the result given by the group of American speakers is quite the opposite. The questionnaire and its results are shown in the following table:

Factor analysis	Ph. D. candidates (82)		Teenagers (39)		Factory workers (32)		Americans (22)	
	N	Rates (%)	N	Rates	N	Rates	N	Rates
I consider myself a talker.	14	17.0	7	17.9	10	31.3	17	77.3
I feel comfortable initiating conversations with strangers.	15	18.2	5	12.8	8	25	18	81.8
I always voice my opinion voluntarily in a group discussion.	12	14.6	6	15.4	6	18.8	18	81.8
I feel comfortable to deliver a speech in a formal occasion.	10	12.2	4	10.3	6	18.8	15	68.2
I feel comfortable to voice my opinion in an informal occasion.	14	17.7	8	20.5	10	31.3	18	81.8
I believe that one always communicates most effectively through talking.	15	18.2	16	41.0	9	28.1	15	68.2
I feel comfortable to debate with others when I have different opinions with others.	17	20.7	10	28.2	8	25	17	77.3
Debates between my friends and me won't have negative effect on our friendship.	7	8.5	5	12.8	8	25	16	72.7
I have positive feeling toward people who talk a lot.	14	17.0	8	20.5	10	31.3	4	18.2
I think talkative people are annoying.	57	69.5	22	56.4	20	62.5	0	0
I feel comfortable with silences in a conversation.	52	63.4	24	61.5	18	56.3	2	9.1
If others try to persuade me, I would pretend to accept their opinions, while still sticking to my own in mind.	58	70.7	20	51.3	20	62.5	2	9.1
I'll try to find ways to break the ice during conversations.	22	26.8	10	25.6	8	25	20	90.9

The table shows that the rates among the three groups of the Chinese people are quite close. The answers given by the Chinese subjects show that most of them did not feel comfortable to talk a lot, especially to speak out their own ideas in public. Only a few liked to debate when they held different ideas with others, while most others preferred to keep silent while still sticking to their own opinions in order to keep harmonious relationships with others. The slight difference among the three groups of the Chinese subjects is due to the difference in sociability, knowledge storage, and social surrounding. Adults are more skilful at engaging conversations with strangers because of their rich social experiences, while children feel less uncomfortable to debate with others because they have only a vague sense of face. Ph. D. candidates do a little better in public speaking than factory workers because the former have more experiences in this aspect, while the latter feel more comfortable to carry out private conversations with friends.

On the other hand, the answers given by the American subjects are quite the opposite to those of their Chinese counterparts. Most of them regarded themselves as talkers and were willing to make contribution in-group discussions; almost all of them felt uncomfortable with silence; none of them considered being talkative a negative quality; most thought debates with friends would not affect their friendship.

Then what causes the differences in the view on silence and debate between the Chinese and Americans? This is just the issue we are going to deal with in the following sections. My focus will be on their contrastive cultural values and philosophical beliefs in silence and debate.

Contrastive Cultural Values in Talk

The different views between the Chinese and American people on silence and debate are a just reflection of a series of contrastive values held by the two groups of people. The following dimensions are selected to show how they have affected Chinese and American views on silence and debate.

High-Context Culture vs. Low-Context Culture

China and the United States are respectively a member of high-context culture and that of low-context culture. In high-context Chinese culture, communicators assume a great deal of commonality of knowledge and views, so that less is spelt out explicitly and much more is implicit or communicated in indirect ways. People depend on a number of paralinguistic factors, of which silence is of great significance, to decode the speaker's intension. In China, silence holds a strong contextual meaning, such as showing obedience to senior people, or being a sign of respect for the wisdom and expertise of others, or disagreement while avoiding direct confrontation, or a time interval for sorting out ideas, depending on the context of the time.

However, in America, which has a low-context culture, things are made explicit, and there is considerable dependence on what is actually said or written. People load as much information as possible in their words. Thus, their words must be adequate enough and not ambiguous, while silence can be perceived as an empty pause. There seems aversion to silence in that people find it awkward and embarrassing and silence tends to be interpreted variously as lack of interest; and unwillingness to communicate; a sign of hostility, rejection, or interpersonal incompatibility; anxiety or shyness; or lack of verbal skills. In low-context American culture, the responsibility for the meaning falls mainly to the speakers, whose job is to formulate ideas into clear language. Therefore, those who are good at expressing themselves with verbal languages are respected, and people are conscious to train themselves into competent speakers.

Thus, generally when Americans communicate with others, they verbally state what they are thinking, with very little need for non-verbal cues. The opposite can be said of the Chinese, who use body language, status, relationships, silence and many other factors to communicate meaning. As a result, it is of course difficult for an American to understand the words of a Chinese, because he has to not only master the Chinese language, but know the whole context behind the language as well.

Harmony vs. Confrontation

The silence of the Chinese can be linked to their propensity to seek harmony rather than confrontation. Chinese tradition appears to value reserving the harmony of the social group more highly than individual expression of one's inner thoughts and feelings. In Chinese eyes, taking opposite sides of an argument necessarily means becoming a personal rival and antagonist of the one who hold the other side. The more important concomitant of this idea is that if one does not wish to become a lifelong opponent of someone else, he will not venture contrary to the other's opinion in public. As a result, when the Chinese hold discussions, few people would like to voice their opinions voluntarily. Even when they do, their participation is never argumentative. They never openly express disagreement with others because it is considered to be aimed at the individual, thus will damage the long-nourished and established harmonious *guānxì* (i.e. social relationship), which has a very important position in Chinese society.

The Chinese word *guānxì* means relationships and it refers to the concept of establishing connections in order to secure favors in personal relations. It is a relational network that Chinese cultivate energetically and it contains implicit mutual obligation, assurance and understanding. It is very important for the Chinese to have harmonious relationships, since they consider good social relations as a symbol of personal ability and influence. Most Chinese are accustomed to keeping a different view to himself because they have been taught both at school and at home, since their early childhood, to agree with an opinion even if he does not like it in his heart.

Contrary to the Chinese preference for harmony, Americans will choose confrontation, i.e., honestly expressing his own ideas, defending his own opinions, and openly confront opposing ideas. To them, this is a better way to solve problems than avoiding conflicts. This means facing the facts, meeting the problem head on. Consistent with these tendencies, it is also desirable to face people directly, to debate with them, and to confront them. Confrontation is not necessarily rancorous, but it does involve reporting one's feelings honestly, expecting reciprocal honesty, and dealing directly with the person involved in the problem. The strategy of confrontation seems to call for a temporary neutralization of social relations to allow real facts of the case to emerge. At the root of the American confrontational style is the concept that adversaries can compete against each other and at the same time cooperate under the rules for interpersonal conflict. Even two intimate friends may often argue bitterly for their discrimination. However, they can still get on well afterwards as if nothing had happened.

Collectivism vs. Individualism

The Chinese and Americans' preference for silence or debate is also a reflection of their different views of collectivism and individualism. Chinese society values collectivism which expects people to identify with and work well in groups which protect them in exchange for loyalty and compliance. Contrary to this is Americans' individualism in which uniqueness and self-determination are valued. A person is more admirable if he is a 'self-made man' or 'makes up his own mind' or shows initiative or works well independently.

'Collectivism is, by its nature, an act of balancing the need of the individual against the need of society' (Stata@gw.home.vix.com). In China it is natural to look upon things as a part of something much bigger, where the will of one person is a part of the cooperative will. As a result, it's the responsibility of a group of people, not an individual person to reach decisions by consensus. Thus in a public occasion when a discussion is undergoing, it seems meaningless for one to speak out his unique ideas or argue with others for a final support because sooner or later, he has to join the majority by giving up his own standpoint (Wurzel, 1998). One is supposed to keep in accordant with the whole society and to know how to adjust him to the group when he has different idea in mind from the group.

Presenting the 'self' too obviously would give people the impression of being disrespectful of the community. Thus, it seems wise and also a customary thing for one to keep silence even though what he is thinking is quite contrary to others' views.

The identification of Americans' individualism can be dated back to about 150 years ago, when the French observer Alexis de Tocqueville described Americans as highly individualistic. He believed that this American individualism was inseparable from the new American concept of democracy (Scollon, 1995). To Americans, all individuals are different and unique, and everyone has a right to say what he considers right. The value of personal success, independence and the concept of 'pulling yourself up by the boot straps' are shared by common people. They think if one's view is different from others', then why not put it on the table and let everybody discuss it because everybody has the responsibility for the decision — making. After a heated discussion-presenting, defending, and opposing views — one will either persuade others or be persuaded by others while a problem will not be left unsolved.

Obedience vs. Aggression

The fact that Chinese people talk less is rooted in their cultural emphasis on obedience and social hierarchy, and a de-emphasis on aggression. In Confucian code, everyone should know their place in the social hierarchy and speak according to the norms required for him. This belief is deeply rooted in the Chinese minds because ever since they were born into their families — a kind of hierarchical institution — they have been brought up with the idea that one should behave within his own territory and should not cross the threshold. Some parents or grandparents tell the children explicitly that it is rude and disrespectful for children to take part in adult conversations.

At home, Chinese parents are intolerant of their children not treating them with respect and discourage fights between siblings. Chinese children are expected to accept whatever their parents ask them to do and are not supposed to question their parents' authority. Nor do they need to speak up to defend their action if they are to obey their parents. In addition, they don't have to verbalize their choices or decisions, which are often made for them by adults. Similarly, at school Chinese children are taught to respect and obey their superiors and are expected to listen to their teachers, take notes, and memorize. If they do not agree with something, they are trained to control this opposition and obey what the teacher says.

Because the Chinese are taught from a young age to avoid arguments, their performance on verbal tests is often lower than those of Westerners (Bond & Hwang, 1988, p. 217). They are weak in developing persuasive arguments and in their debating skills because they never get to practice it in real life (Bond & Hwang, 1988, p. 219). David Ho and his collaborators in Harvard University did a study comparing Chinese and Caucasian American infants and he came to a conclusion that the Chinese infants were less vocal, less active, and more apprehensive in social and separation situations; they were quieter, stayed closer to the mother, and played less when were with unfamiliar children or adults.

In the political field, the Chinese also practice this non-aggressive and obedient behavior. In Chinese culture, it is very important that the public respect the leader of the country. For example, in the ancient Chinese society, in a meeting with the leader about a certain program that was planning to be carried out, the subordinates must obey the leader and try to put their vision of truth aside. But if a difference in opinion occurred and could not be avoided, it was voiced privately through a third party. They would try to avoid a face-to-face confrontation but if it was unavoidable, the subordinate would use mild language to get the message through without offending the superior. Chinese often try to avoid direct confrontation if possible because they believe that arguing can lead to chaos.

In addition, the direct confrontation common to American style is ill-advised in the Chinese society where face is primary concern, since frequently the indirectness of statements masks feelings that, if stated, might cause embarrassment to both speaker and listener. A debate between friends may threaten their faces, and cause the breakage of their friendships. Thus, those who always argue with others will be thought too aggressive and won't be popular within a group. In short, Chinese prefer silence or agreement to bitter argument, even if the agreement is superficial. The language used by Americans in reference to communication, in the eyes of the Chinese, carries the feeling of adversarial confrontation and depersonalization.

Philosophical Influence on Silence and Debate

Religion and philosophy may be the most important factor that has affected the views toward speech and rhetoric of Chinese and American.

Confucian influence on Chinese views on silence and debate

Although there were several antagonistic schools of thought in ancient China, which have dominated the culture and philosophical scene in China since, they each held similarly negative views of speech and language. The two predominant schools are Confucianism and Taoism. Both Confucianism and Taoism promote social harmony, yet by different means. Confucianism has prescribed moral codes for both individuals and governments. Confucian virtues include *rén*, or benevolence; *yì*, or righteousness; and *lǐ*, or propriety. Taoism, on the other hand, sponsors a rhetoric emphasizing *wú-wéi* (the avoidance of action), *wú-xīn* (negation of mind), and *dé* (the principle of spontaneous functioning).

Confucius is often known as the father of Chinese philosophy and culture. His views had long been accepted as the official state philosophy of the Chinese empire ever since the Han Dynasty and are deeply rooted in common people's minds. Oliver (1971) states that 'The central theme of Confucianism was that ethical conduct creates conditions that result in just and harmonious human relations' (p. 124). Yum (1988) further argues that 'As a philosophy of humanism and social relations, Confucianism has left a strong impact on interpersonal relationships and on communication patterns.'

Central to Confucianism are three concepts: etiquette or propriety (*lǐ*, a term originally meaning 'ritual offering'), righteousness (*yì*, to behave with all moral qualities in every concrete situation), and benevolence (*rén*, to be kind to others). The first concept, *lǐ* (propriety), shows that everyone in society had to use certain etiquette suited to his rank to treat other people. Confucius urged people to adhere to the highest standards for five key role relationships: between ruler and subject, neighbor and neighbor, father and son, husband and wife, and brother and brother. The term *lǐ* could refer to many smaller 'ritualized' behavior patterns involved in day-to-day human interactions. This would include proper speech and body language according to status, age, and gender. In this sense, *lǐ* means any action *proper*, or appropriate to the situation. In the *Analects* (*Lúnyǔ*), *lǐ* is clearly defined in a relationship with humaneness, where humaneness is the inner, substantial goodness of the human being, and *lǐ* is the functioning of humaneness in the manifest world. That is to say, *lǐ* is filial piety, fraternal respect, familial affection, etc.

Based on this concept, common people were trained to exert obedience and loyalty to their superiors, filial piety to their ancestors, and virtue to society. As a result, in feudal society one was not supposed to question his rulers' authority or express too much of his own ideas in front of his superiors. People had learned to use a silent way to keep their thoughts to themselves. Although a few emperors had encouraged people to advise a higher authority frankly, yet few people would like to do so for the fear of being punished.

The second concept, *yì* (righteousness), exerts strong influence on the Chinese minds and behavior, although it is not quite as essential a concept as the other two. It refers to a strongly internalized human capacity. Being attuned to Righteousness allows people to do the proper thing in the proper situation, to give each person, place and thing its proper due. Therefore, respecting others in a quiet way and not raising any argument would be considered a right thing to do on most occasions.

The concept of *rén* (benevolence or humanness) was used to teach the

Chinese to keep a harmonious relationship with others and is the root of Chinese avoidance of confrontation with others during a discussion. According to Confucius, the purpose for communication was to make friends and exert benevolence. It was considered worthless to argue with others since if the interlocutors had different views then they would not cooperate with each other or be friends. Besides, arguing with another person was not something that should be conducted by *jūnzǐ*, a gentleman or superior man because, as Confucius said in the Analects, 'The Superior Man has nothing to compete for.' Any refined gentleman should embody the virtue of benevolence while maintaining traditional rites, customs, and filial piety toward his ancestors, family, and the gods.

Confucius established for China the ideal of the gentlemen, or 'superior man' — not necessarily someone from the upper classes, but one who has properly cultivated himself in virtue and righteousness. Confucius envisaged the ideal man in this way: 'The superior man is diligent in his work and careful in speech. The Superior Man desires to be hesitant in speech, but sharp in action.' Central to Confucius' philosophy was the principle that one's words should always be in accordance with that which one does, lives, and practices. He must always speak with discretion only of that which he is prepared to act upon to commit himself to. The superior man acts before speaking and speaks according to his action, and is ashamed of his words outstripping his deeds, since immodest statements are hard to live up to. Naturally, this principle manifested an antagonistic view towards bold or persuasive speech.

According to Confucius, some mistakes made by those who are of rank included: 'To speak when there is nothing to be said, this is imprudence; to speak without paying attention to the expression on the person's face, this is called blindness.' Of course, Confucius was aware that there were times when appropriate speech was indispensable, but for the most part, the verses in Analects manifest his reticence to speak, as we can see from his dialogue with one of his disciples:

> Someone said, 'Yung is a humane man, but he is not sharp enough with his tongue'
> Confucius said, 'Why does he need to be sharp with his tongue? If you deal with people by smooth talk, you will soon be disliked. I don't know if Yung is a humane man, but why should he have to be a clever speaker?'

In short, Confucius emphasis is continually on being humble and respectful, rather than bold, assertive, or innovative. As Confucian biographer Herlee Creel put it, 'Confucian was always markedly contemptuous of eloquence and of ornate language.' Confucius opposed eloquent and clever speech, advocating hesitancy over brilliance, and he grounded his criticism of speech deeply within his philosophy of the ideal man.

Taoist influence on Chinese views of silence and debate

Next to Confucianism, the most important stream in Chinese thought is Taoism. It was in large part a philosophy of retreat and withdrawal on the part of thinkers who were appalled by perpetual warfare, instability, and death and so turned away from the struggle for power, status, and wealth. Although the Taoists were interested in man's finding peace within himself and within nature, a view which is in contrast to the Confucian concerns with public behavior, etiquette, and politics, they also took an opponent position to speech and rhetoric.

The ancient school of Chinese Taoist philosophy is best represented by the *Tao Te Jing* of Laozi and by Zhuangzi. Tao, 'the Way,' is the ultimate reality of the universe, according to Taoism. The key to merging with the Tao is *wú-wéi* or 'doing nothing.' The Taoist goal brings the world back to the Way by means of quietism, nonintervention, and inaction. If left to itself, the universe proceeds smoothly according to its own harmonies. Man's efforts to change or improve nature only destroy these harmonies and produce chaos. By cultivating *wú-wéi*, a type of inaction characterized by humility and prudence, a person can participate in the simplicity and spontaneity of Tao. Striving to attain virtue or achievement is counterproductive and unnecessary. A man without ambitions could be beyond all harms and achieve tranquility, which is the highest level of human life. Laozi clearly expressed the importance of tranquility, as is stated by the following verse:

> The Way takes no action, but leaves nothing undone.
> When you accept this
> The world will flourish,
> In harmony with nature.
> Nature does not possess desire;
> Without desire, the heart becomes quiet;
> In this manner the whole world is made tranquil.

Arrays of Taoist sayings, such as 'To be always talking is against nature,' 'One who speaks does not know,' and so forth, provide some attitudinal and behavioral guidelines for the Chinese people to conduct their conversational lives. Because of the belief that meaning can be sensed out but not phrased, a talkative person is often considered showy or insincere, or even patronizing:

> 'Honest people use no rhetoric;
> Rhetoric is not honesty.'

Taoism values mystical contemplation, so the Taoists found it difficult to express their basic ideas in words. The Tao is founded on a nameless, formless 'Non-being' which is, in essence, the totality of the natural processes. The classic text of the *Tao Te Jing* advocates silence from the

beginning:
> Nature says only a few words:
> High wind does not last long,
> Nor does heavy rain.
> If nature's words do not last
> Why should those of man?

The Taoists also believed that 'Who understands does not preach; who preaches does not understand,' by which they argue that a knowledgeable person is cautious and modest in his words, while only those who do not know much are eager to show off in front of others. Thus, Taoists advocate:
> Reserve your judgments and words;
> Smooth differences and forgive disagreements.

Like Confucianism, Taoism also advocates harmony. Oliver Robert asserts in *The Rhetorical Implications of Taoism* that Chinese Taoists put much weight on such values as tolerance and harmony. As he says:
> They could not abide unnecessary conflict for it was too disruptive. They developed a high regard for tolerance. Their political ideal was less justice and equality than harmony. To them, justice was so complicated that the very effort to define it often led to disputes and conflict; and they thought that equality manifestly was not observable among human beings. For this reason, when a Chinese finds himself hold a different view from another interlocutor, he would most likely refrain from speaking it out directly for fearing a direct disagreement may hurt that person's feeling and thus may threaten their harmonious relationship. Instead, he will either choose a circumlocutory way or keep silent to maintain a rather strict reserve (Oliver, 1961).

The Tao Te Jing clearly states the importance of harmony:
> Cultivate harmony within yourself, and harmony becomes real;
> Cultivate harmony within your family, and harmony becomes fertile;
> Cultivate harmony within your community, and harmony becomes abundant;
> Cultivate harmony within your culture, and harmony becomes enduring;
> Cultivate harmony within the world, and harmony becomes ubiquitous.
> Who accepts harmony, becomes harmonious.
> Who accepts loss, becomes lost.
> For who accepts harmony, the Way harmonizes with him,
> And who accepts loss, the Way cannot find.

The Taoists believed that if one accepted what it was, then harmony was achieved and he could live with the world. In addition, language and precision are thought to be the root of contention and dissatisfaction, therefore a barrier to contentment and sagehood. While Taoism provides no solutions to social problems, it is thorough going in its rejection of both speech and communication.

The Influence of Greek and Roman rhetoric on American views of silence and talk

Since the Ancient Greeks, westerners have tended to celebrate talk and rhetoric, construing it as a vehicle for the discovery and expression of truth. The earliest known studies of rhetoric came from the Golden Age philosophers of Greece. They believed that rhetoric was the ancient art of argumentation and discourse, one of the most important functions of which was to persuade. One assumption implicit in the art of the Ancient Greek rhetoric was that people could disagree with each other. When disagreement became pronounced, there were only two results — either they began to fight, or they engaged in debate. Rhetoric removed disagreement from the arena of violence and turned it into debate — a healthy and necessary step in any democracy. When two persons have different views on an issue, they will directly speak out their opinions and try to solve the problem, instead of avoiding the conflicts. The Americans have inherited this belief.

Writers from the Ancient Greece, and from the Roman republic and empire, supply us with the largest store of early texts explicitly devoted to speech in public settings. The major objective of Athenian rhetoric at an early stage was to prepare members of the middle class (farmers, shopkeepers, tradespersons, etc.) for participation in public debate in competition with the traditional aristocracy of the city. The major Roman rhetoric, on the other hand, circulated chiefly among Latin politicians and lawyers who wanted tips on how to prevail in the Senate, before the popular assembly, and in the courts of law. Later, rhetoric became a tool for all common people to defend their ideas, to win others' support, and to protect their rights.

In addition, the Ancient Greek and Romans believed that democracy was linked to rhetoric in which citizens were free to address other members of the community who, in turn, were free to weigh and vote upon competing visions of truth. This tradition is still kept today. Modern Americans, affected by the Ancient Greek and Romans, think that government of, by, and for the people is a government based upon self-assertion. Democratic rule assumes that the best way to attain the good society is for self-interested individuals (read politicians) to pitch their claims to an audience which then decides among competing ideas.

A number of the Greek and Roman philosophers, who had promoted the development of classical rhetoric, taught many techniques for gaining influence and for winning over people. This kind of rhetoric was responsive to the desire of a free people to assert their own personal self interest.

Aristotle and Cicero shared the assumption that public speech was a tool available for use by self-interested persons seeking to win fortune and reputation. Aristotle's book, *The Rhetoric*, provided useful skills that practical speakers want. Aristotle identified the ways to make a good impression upon listeners, to find striking content for one's speech, and to make speech interesting by choosing the right words. One of Cicero's favorite practical techniques was a pictographic method of memory that allowed a person to demonstrate high competence by speaking with no notes or with a bare minimum of visible props. To Cicero, the survival of a free state depended on the ability of wise citizens to communicate effectively on matters that concerned the public. He was convinced that open deliberation and debate were vital for society, and he cautioned that 'mute and voiceless wisdom' could not advance humanity. Cicero saw a second danger when a society did not provide its public with a balanced education in rhetoric. Cicero recommended that a society should actively cultivate the eloquent habits of good speech. In this view, those who attained mature eloquence would 'obtain glory, honor and high esteem.' At the same time, society would benefit by fluent speech whenever, 'it is accompanied by wisdom.'

This sort of belief is deeply carved in western people's mind. Many philosophers or literate people have articulated the power of public speaking and debate, as is shown by the following typical examples:

> A sharp tongue is the only edge tool that grows keener by constant use.
>   (Washington Irving, in *Rip Van Winkle*.)
> Speech is civilization itself. The word, even the most contradictory word,
>   preserves contact — it is silence which isolates. (Thomas Mann)

Conclusion

In this paper, I attempted to show different beliefs in public speaking and debate between the Chinese and Americans, and to analyze the philosophical factors that lead to their differences. The Chinese see that public speaking is awkward and unnecessary. People will try to avoid debate when having different opinions because they value the harmony of social relationship far more highly than expressing one's inner thoughts, thus they think debates will have negative effect on their friendships. On the contrary, Americans see that public speaking is indispensable, while silence is awkward and embarrassing and is interpreted as lack of interest or verbal skills. They prefer to speak their own ideas out other than to keep them unknown. The traditional Confucian and Taoist codes imprinted in the Chinese minds have led to their preference to using silence to preserve harmonious relationships and stability, while the ancient Greek and Roman style of rhetoric as well as the Bible make them highly value public speaking.

However, people from these two cultures are always unaware the differences between their views about talk, thus often misunderstand each other when having interactions. This would especially be so when those involved are blissfully unaware of structural differences in their beliefs about debates, let alone complex intervening socio-structural, sociopsychological and sociolinguistic processes, often in flux, which determine their quite different styles of discourse over time. Therefore, this paper may provide some basic ideas for those who have chances to have interactions with people from the other nation but have little knowledge of the beliefs in silence and the debate held by their counterparts.

References

Analects of Confucius (Trans A. Waley). (1992). New York: Harper Collins Publishers.
Aristotle. (1926). *The Art of Rhetoric* (Trans. J. H. Freese). Cambridge, MA: Harvard University Press.
Birrell, A. (1993). *Chinese Mythology: An Introduction*. Baltimore: The Johns Hopkins University Press.
Bond, M. H., & Hwang, K. K. (1988). The social psychology of Chinese people. In M. H. Bond (Ed.), *The Cross-cultural Challenge to Social Psychology* (pp. 213–266). Newbury Park, CA: Sage.
Chan, W. (1953). *Religious Trends in Modern China*. New York: Columbia University Press.
Clerkin, K. (1988). *Intercultural communication: A reader*. Belmont, CA: Wadsworth Publishing Company.
Confucius and Confucianism (2003). Available at http://www.chinaknowledge.org.
Creel, H. (1953). *Thought from Confucius to Mao Tse-Tung*. Chicago: The University of Chicago Press.
Cua, A. S. (1985). *Ethical Argumentation*. Honolulu: University of Hawaii Press. Available at http://www.mhhe.com/socscience/comm/lucas/student/heritage/sproule.htm
Fleck, S. (1993). *Confucius on Jen*. Retrieved Oct 9th, 2006, from http://www.susanfleck.com/Philosophy/350_confucianism_w2w.htm
Hagen, K. (2010). *Confucian Key Terms*. Retrieved June 20th, 2010, from http://faculty.plattsburgh.edu/kurtis.hagen/keyterms_junzi.html
Is Speaking in Tongues the Evidence of the Baptism of the Holy Ghost? (2001). Los Angeles: Word of God Ministries, Inc. Available from http://www.wogm.com/
Legge, J. (1891). *Sacred Books of the East, Vol 39–40*. Oxford University Press.
Lau, D. C. (1963). *"Glossary" of Lao-Tzu: The Tao Te Ching*. New York: Penguin.
Majka, C. (n.d.) *Taoism and the Philosophy of Tai Chi Chuan*. Available at http://www.chebucto.ns.ca/Philosophy/Taichi/taoism.html
Oliver, R. T. (1961). The rhetorical implication of Taoism. *Quarterly Journal of Speech, 47*, 27–35.
Schafer, E. H. (1967). *Ancient China*. New York: Time Life Books.

Scollon, R., & Scollon, S. (2000). *Intercultural Communication: A Discourse Approach*. Beijing: Foreign Language Teaching and Research Press.

Sprunger, M. (n. d.). *An Introduction to Confucianism*. The Urantia Book Fellowship. Retrieved June 13th, 2008, from http://urantiabook.org/archive/readers/601_confucianism.htm

Sproule, J. M. (1998). *The Heritage of Rhetorical Theory*. New York: The McGraw/Hill Company.

Steward, E. (1991). *American Cultural Patterns*. Yarmouth, ME: Intercultural Press.

Valdes, J. (1986). *Cultural Bound*. Cambridge: Cambridge University Press.

Wurzel, J. S. (1998). Teaching reflective thinking, cultural constraints and cross cultural responses. *The Edge: The E-Journal of Intercultural Relations, 1(3)*.

19

Understanding Strategic Competence for Intercultural Communication

Xu Lisheng
Zhejiang University, China

Abstract: This paper is about the issue of strategic competence in relation to intercultural communication. It begins with a brief review of the development of the notion of communicative competence, and then it examines the relationship of its different components to culture, pointing out that strategic competence, unlike sociolinguistic or discourse competence, is not culture-specific and therefore is supposed to play a more crucial role in intercultural communication. Next the paper discusses research on strategic competence, particularly the contributions that it can make to our efforts to understand and improve intercultural communication. It also raises some questions that further research should address. Finally it stresses the special significance of exploring strategic competence to studying intercultural communication and indicates implications that the exploration may have for teaching a second or foreign language for intercultural communication.

Introduction

This paper discusses the issue of *strategic competence* in relation to intercultural communication, representing one of my research efforts on intercultural communicative competence, which has become one of the major research areas in intercultural communication studies.

Any discussion of strategic competence and intercultural communicative competence should begin with the notion of *communicative competence*, which was proposed by Hymes (1972) and some other scholars as a challenge to Chomsky's (1965) concept of *linguistic competence*, and has now become a primary theoretical construct in sociolinguistics and a number of related disciplines, especially for researching into the relationship of language use in communication to society and culture. Until recently, however, intercultural communication studies seemed to be more concerned with actual performance than with the competence underlying it. On the other hand, many researches on communicative competence were conducted without taking into consideration the real situations of intercultural communication, which, we can say, is already well on its way to becoming an everyday phenomenon the world over today. In recent years, there have already been more studies in which communicative competence is approached in intercultural perspective, but scholarly attention seems to have been exclusively on its sociolinguistic and discourse aspects. As for strategic competence, one of the four components of which the overall communicative competence is supposed to consist (Canale, 1983; Swain, 1984), research literature is still comparatively scant. However, this should not lead us to conclude that studying strategic competence is not as important as studying other components of communicative competence, though it may suggest that studying strategic competence is more difficult.

In this paper, I first review briefly the development of the notion of communicative competence and try to differentiate various components of communicative competence in their relation to culture, arguing that strategic competence, unlike sociolinguistic and discourse competencies, is not culture-specific and is supposed to play a particularly salient role in intercultural communication. Next, I discuss researches on strategic competence and point out what it can contribute to our efforts to understand and improve intercultural communication. Some questions are raised for further researches to address. In conclusion, I stress again the importance of researching into strategic competence to intercultural communication studies and indicate some implications the research may have for second- and foreign-language education.

Background

The notion of communicative competence was first introduced by Hymes in a 1966 paper later published in revised form in 1972. Other scholars, including Habermas (1970) and Campbell and Wales (1970), have also used the term, but Hymes' elaborated concept remains the most influential of all. Communicative competence defined by Hymes was actually a challenge to Chomsky's use of the term *competence* (1965). Chomsky, in order to delimit the area of his linguistic study, made a fundamental distinction between *competence* (the speaker's knowledge of his or her language) and *performance* (the actual use of language in concrete situations) and emphasized that linguists are concerned with the former, but not the latter. In his definition, linguistic competence is the tacit knowledge of language structure, the knowledge that is invariably possessed by the ideal speaker in a homogeneous speech community.

Hymes found Chomsky's concept very problematic. To him, this concept of competence was limited in that it included only grammatical competence and assumed uniform competence within the individual and the speech community. He argued that the notion of competence should be extended to include the 'rules of use' as well as the 'rules of grammar'. According to him, competence should describe the knowledge and ability of individuals for appropriate language use in the communicative events in which they find themselves in any particular speech community. Therefore, linguists' task should be not only the description of what a speaker knows about the grammar but also an accounting for what he or she knows about the appropriate use of the language. In a word, Hymes's notion of competence highlights its sociocultural dimensions.

In Hymes' model of communicative competence, there are four sectors that characterize the individual's underlying knowledge and ability for language use:

a) what is possible according to the individual's knowledge of the linguistic system in the speech community;
b) what is feasible in the psycholinguistic capacity of the individual, e.g. the individual's memory and perception;
c) what is appropriate in relation to the context of the communicative event;
d) what actually occurs or does not occur in language use.

After Hymes, there appeared a growing literature on communicative competence. Various aspects of communicative competence were further explored and new models were also proposed. In their attempt to offer a clear, all-embracing conception of what it means to know a language, Canale and Swain proposed a modular framework of three (Canale & Swain, 1980), and later four components (Canale, 1983; Swain, 1984), by which to describe communicative competence:

a) grammatical competence, including vocabulary, word formation, sentence formation, pronunciation, spelling and linguistic semantics;
b) sociolinguistic competence, addressing the extent to which utterances are produced and understood appropriately in different sociolinguistic contexts depending on contextual factors such as status of participants, purposes of the interaction, and norms or conventions of interaction;
c) discourse competence, concerning mastery of how to combine

grammatical forms and meanings to achieve a unified spoken or written text in different genres;
d) strategic competence, concerning mastery of verbal and non-verbal communication strategies that may be called into action to compensate for breakdowns in communication due to limiting conditions in actual situations or to insufficient competence in one or more of the other areas of communicative competence and to enhance the effectiveness of communication.

Canale and Swain's notion of communicative competence is obviously different form Hymes' in some aspects. For instance, they consider it unnecessary to include factors like memory and perception in one's model of communicative competence, for, to them, those factors are normally general psychological constraints on actual performance.

But the most significant difference between their model and Hymes' or many others', perhaps their most valuable contribution to communicative competence theory, is that they have integrated into their model communication strategies that people often employ to cope with the problems arising in the course of communication. According to them, such strategies are essentially part of communicative competence, i.e. strategic competence, which should be considered as no less important than grammatical or sociolinguistic competence. This extension of the notion of communicative competence, as I shall discuss in more detail later, has important implications for studying intercultural communication.

Unlike Chomsky or Hymes, who usually has the native speaker in mind in conceptualizing competence, Canale and Swain are more concerned with the non-native speaker learning and using a second or foreign language. That may be one of the reasons that they have extended the notion of communicative competence to include the ability of strategic use of language. Non-native speakers are generally supposed to have more problems when they try to use a second or foreign language to communicate with native speakers or with other non-native speakers. So the success of the communication often depends largely on their ability of employing communication strategies to deal with whatever problems that may arise in the course of communicating with people of different linguistic and cultural backgrounds.

Components of Communicative Competence and Culture

There is no doubt that communicative competence is shaped by social and cultural conventions of a particular speech community. Therefore, what is regarded as communicative competence in one speech community may be regarded as something else in another. In fact, the notion itself emerged to relate competence with the sociocultural contexts. To Hymes, communicative competence is actually part of cultural competence (Putz, 1992).

But it does not follow that we can assume that all the components of communicative competence have the same relationship with culture. On the contrary, it may actually be the case that some are very closely related to culture while others are not. So it is necessary for us to distinguish between what are culture-specific and what are not in the components of communicative competence. An examination of the relationships of the competencies to culture will reveal the differences existing between strategic competence and other competencies. As a result of such differences, the roles that various competencies can play in intercultural communication will be somewhat different from one another.

Whether grammatical competence is culture-specific or not is quite controversial. To advocators of Linguistic Relativity, the idea that a grammatical system is a specific way of organizing experience and ultimately a particular cultural practice, grammatical competence can hardly be viewed as separated from culture. Contrastively, proponents of Linguistic Universalism like Chomsky hold that grammar in its true sense has little to do with culture and should be regarded as something independent of the sociocultural environment in which language is used.

Though scholars disagree greatly in conceptualizing the relationship of grammar to culture, the history of second- and foreign-language teaching practice the world over seems to have suggested that the grammatical competence of a language can be acquired out of the sociocultural contexts of the community in which the language is used as the native tongue. We all know that in the world today there are so many people who are bilingual but not necessarily bicultural, and this may serve as an indication that grammar and culture, to some extent at least, are tow different things. Take speakers of English as an example. English as a world language used in communities of different cultures has become an undeniable fact. Speakers of English, whether they are American or British or Indian or Singaporean or South African, can be said to have almost the same grammatical competence of the language, though there are still some differences in the actual realization of the competence. That might also be one of the reasons that some scholars, when talking about language competence, prefer to give grammatical competence the same status as communicative competence and consider them complementary to each other instead of the latter subsuming the former.

Sociolinguistic competence is obviously very culture-specific. What lies in the centre of sociolinguistic competence is appropriateness, appropriateness of form as well as meaning in communication. Researches have shown that norms for the appropriate conduct of speech vary considerably from culture to culture. What is linguistically appropriate for a given speech situation in one culture may be completely inappropriate for the same speech situation in another culture. For instance, studies of the ways in which people compliment, apologize, complain, refuse and deny, etc. have all revealed great cultural differences in patterns of interaction and the underlying cultural values which are thus expressed. Sociolinguistic norms are actually part of culture and acquiring sociolinguistic competence of a language is, in a sense, acquiring the culture in which the language is used.

The knowledge of sociolinguistic norms of a particular culture, though crucial to successful interaction within the speech communities of that culture, will not often be of much help in intercultural communication, where participants may bring conflicting norms for appropriateness into play. There always exists a serious potential for communicative breakdowns when people from different cultural backgrounds and therefore with different sociolinguistic competence are involved in communication. In second- and foreign-language teaching, more emphasis is now placed on helping learners acquire the native-like sociolinguistic competence and it is expected that cultural differences in this aspect will be resolved and many communicative problems and breakdowns will be avoided as soon as non-native learners have acquired the native-like sociolinguistic competence.

However, this seems to be rather problematic. On the one hand the native-like sociolinguistic competence has proved to be far more difficult than grammatical competence for non-native learners to acquire unless they can actually get themselves into the associated sociocultural situations. On the other, since sociolinguistic norms are, by their very nature, reflective of the cultural values of the speech community, insisting on taking the norms of one culture, usually the native-speaker's culture, as norms for intercultural communication is sometimes found to be quite threatening to the cultural identity of participants from other cultures. Siegal's (1996) investigation of Western women learning Japanese discovers that the Westerners tend to resist the pressure of being totally appropriate in using Japanese because to them this means a change of their original cultural identity. To behave linguistically appropriately in Japanese, as has been pointed out, makes them feel that they are not allowed to be autonomous freely operating individuals, which Westerners usually value very much.

As Paulston (1992) has remarked, acquiring the native-like sociolinguistic competence can help, for example, a Chinese studying in the U.S.A. communicate appropriately with the British or the American, but it won't be much help for a Chinese communicating in English with an Indian or a South African. In the same way, it would be foolish for an American businessman in China using English to insist on only the sociolinguistic norms of American English. Imposing the norms and conventions for interaction of one culture on intercultural communication really involves the danger of may look like cultural imperialism. It is more likely that norms for intercultural communication are not based exclusively on one or the other cultural group's norms, but rather are negotiated and constructed out of both. What such intercultural norms will be like depends on the particular context in which the interaction takes place. In short, what is culturally appropriate may not be interculturally appropriate. Sociolinguistic competence acquired in any particular culture can hardly assure us of our behaving appropriately in intercultural communication.

Discourse competence is also culture-specific, though the way it is relate to culture is somewhat different from the way sociolinguistic competence is. Discourse patterns may not be confined to any particular speech situation, but they are often reflective of the mind-style as well as the values of a cultural group. Cultural differences in this aspect sometimes can be more difficult to discern and handle when people from different cultures are communicating with each other.

The research results from contrastive discourse analysis and contrastive rhetoric have indicated that discourse patterns and structures are often closely related to the cultural norms and meaning systems of the society using the language. A well-known research example is Kaplan's (1966) study of paragraph organization of several major language groups. His study, and many following him, has even in academic discourse. For instance, digressions are often found in German academic texts, while In English texts, such digressions can hardly occur, for they would be considered as unacceptable for lack of focus and cohesiveness (Clyne, 1981; 1987). Such cultural differences can also be found in spoken discourses. For example, Halmari's (1993) investigation of the business telephone conversations by Finns and Anglo-Americans has discovered that there are cultural differences in interruption behaviour and that the non-topical elements of the conversations tend to be lengthy for Finns than for Anglo-Americans.

Using the same language in communication does not reduce such differences to a minimum. Scollon and Wong Scollon (1991) have found that when East Asians are communicating with Westerners in English, there is a tendency for them to delay the introduction of topics, which is unexpected from the point if view of English-speaking Westerners and often leaves them confused about what the topic is. Conversely, Westerners' way of introducing topics early in a conversation strikes the Asian as abrupt or rude. The research of Young (1994), in which she examined the difficulties persistently marring Sino-American interactions, has shown us that the Chinese discourse patterns seem to be just the reverse of the English discourse conventions in that definitive summary statements of main arguments are delayed until the end. She explains that the Chinese discourse patterns persist even in the English of many Chinese because for the Chinese they are closely relate to the cultural concept of face, which lies at the very core of personal identity construction. In this sense, the discourse transfer as well as the sociolinguistic transfer in using a second or foreign language, which is usually considered as mistakes and may even lead to an impression of being unable to use the language properly, can sometimes be better understood as the speaker's efforts to assert his or her own cultural identity.

Unlike sociolinguistic or discourse competence, strategic competence may not be highly culture-specific. Though there has not been much research on the relationship of strategic competence to culture, available empirical results and anecdotal evidence have often seemed to confirm the assumption that strategic competence is greatly independent of the particular culture in which it is acquired. Paribakht (1985), supported by his analysis of the realization of communication strategies by different groups of English speakers, claims that strategic competence appears to develop in the speaker's first language with his or her increasing language experience, and to be freely transferable to his or second language. This transfer, unlike others such as sociolinguistic or discourse transfer has little to do with culture and therefore does not cause interference in communicating with native speakers or other non-native speakers of a different cultural group.

Perhaps the cultural background may have some influence on the individual's preference of certain communication strategies to others. For example, after comparing U.S. American and Japanese responses to embarrassing predicaments, Imahori and Cupach (1994) have reported that U.S. Americans used humor as a copying strategy more frequently than the Japanese, who relied heavily on remediation strategies. However, in spite of such differences, potentials of communication strategies are more likely to be shared cross-culturally, though their actual realization can be affected by some factors including the individual's cultural background.

To Canale and Swain (1980), all the components of communicative competence are equally crucial to successful communication. In theory this is probably true and, out of communicative context, we can hardly say which is more crucial than others. But, in reality, there are various types of communication and they are different in situations and conditions. Such differences may demand more or less of some abilities than others from the participants of communication. For instance, communication usually involves a degree of unpredictability. In intercultural communication, where there are more differences and less shared knowledge between participants, strategic competence often plays a more salient role. In many cases, communication strategies may be the only resources that the participants can draw on to cope with communicative problems, including the problems arising from a higher degree of unpredictability.

SC Research and Communication

Research on strategic competence is still somewhat recent. Though Selinker (1972) coined the term *communication strategy* in 1972 discussing 'strategies of second language communication' and there were a few studies in 1970s, the real 'career' of the research in this area started in the early 1980s, when Canale and Swain extended the notion communicative competence to include strategic competence as one of its primary components. In 1983, French and Kasper (1983) had an edited volume published, which contained many important papers on communication strategies. It was followed by increasing research interest and a growing number of publications since then. Most of the researches have focused on what strategic competence consists of, namely, communication strategies and their use in communication, particularly second language speakers' communication with native speakers.

Since there have been different approaches to strategic competence and communication strategies, it is not possible to make general comments on all the major issues of the research in this paper. For the purpose of the present discussion, two things are to be mentioned.

First, by its very definition, strategic competence, the mastery of communication strategies has got much to do with intercultural communication. It is true that there is no universally agreed definition of communication strategies, though Canale and Swain's concept of strategic competence seems to have been generally accepted. Of all the definitions that have been offered so far, the one given by Farech and Kasper (1983) is most extensively used. They defined communication strategies as 'potentially conscious plans for solving what to an individual presents itself as a problem in reach a particular goal'. The two criteria here are problem-orientedness and potential consciousness, of which only the first has widely considered as essential. Now most researchers in this field agree that the main purpose of communication strategies is to manage communication problems. Though Canale (1983) extended the scope of communications strategies to include effect-enhancing devices, many scholars prefer to treat them separately from problem-solving devices, which are regarded as the communication strategies proper. Since communication problems are more likely to occur in intercultural communication than in communication within the same cultural group, it naturally follows that a skilful use of communication strategies will be very crucial to success in intercultural communication.

Second, the developing of the research, Faerch and Kasper's original conceptualization of communication strategies, which concerned only one problem type, resource deficits — gaps in speakers' knowledge preventing them from verbalizing messages, has been duly extended to cover a much wider range of communication problems. This suggests that research on strategic competence can now make more contributions to studying intercultural communication. For example, in an extended taxonomy of problem-solving strategies recently proposed by Dornyei and Scott (1995), the strategies included are intended cope with four types of communications problems: a) resource deficits; b) processing time pressure; c) own-performance problems, whatever is problematic in one's own communicative performance; d) other-performance problems, whatever is problematic in the communicative performance of the other participant(s). Each type of problems is usually dealt with by using certain strategies. For instance, various negotiation strategies are often employed to deal with the problems of the third type. The strategies are classified according to the manner of problem-management, that is, how they contribute to resolving conflicts and achieving mutual understanding. There are three basic categories: direct, indirect, and interactional strategies. Most traditionally identified communication strategies are direct strategies, for they provide a means of solving the problems directly. Indirect strategies are intended to help create the conditions necessary for achieving communicative goals. For instance, feigning understanding is sometimes quite necessary because it can prevent breakdowns and keep the communication channel open so that the intended goals of the interaction can finally be achieved. Interactional strategies involve co-exchanges, the chief purpose of which is to solve the problems faced by both or all participants of the communication. Such a taxonomy of communication strategies is clearly more relevant to investigating intercultural communication situations.

Research on strategic competence itself is certainly not without problems. From the view point of studying intercultural communication, one of the problems is that the research focus has been too much upon the second or foreign language speakers, particularly learners, in their attempts to communicate with native speakers of the language. But the real situation of intercultural communication is that native speakers will also encounter some problems that they seldom do in intracultural communication and the responsibility of solving the communication problems has to be shared by both or all of the participants. It is therefore important to research into the strategic language use of native speakers in intercultural communication if we hope to have complete picture of communication strategies and their uses for achieving cross-cultural understanding and to form a well-grounded notion of strategic competence. For instance, Yule and Tarone (1990) have pointed out that strategic competence must involve the ability to access the relationship between one's own knowledge and the interlocutor's knowledge in an area, and then to use one's knowledge effectively in accordance with that assessment. Obviously, this ability is no less, if not more, essential for native speakers taking part in intercultural communication.

As a matter of fact, native speakers may often have to make no less use than non-native speakers of various strategies to prevent and solve communication problems in cross-cultural interactions. Those native speakers having stronger strategic competence and making better good use of strategies naturally stand great chances of communicating successfully with non-native speaker in intercultural communications. Unfortunately, there has been little research on the use of communication strategies by native speakers when they try to communicate cross-culturally with non-native speakers, except some study of what is called 'foreigner talk', concerned mainly with native speakers' coping with the problems caused by their non-native interlocutors' inadequate grammatical competence. It is now quite necessary to extend the research scope to include every aspect of language use — production as well as comprehension — of all the participants — native as well as non-native — in communication.

In order to gain a better understanding of strategic competence for intercultural communication, I think that there are still a few important questions that future research on strategic competence should address:

1) Are there any significant similarities and differences between the strategic use of language for intracultural communication and for intercultural communication? We have had some researches on communication strategies in the first language use, but the research focus has been almost exclusively on children, whose communication problems are mostly resource deficits.

2) What are the significant similarities differences between the strategic language use of the native speaker and that of the non-native speaker in intercultural communications? What effects the linguistic proficiency of an individual can have upon his or her strategic use of the language?

3) How and to what degrees the transfer of strategic competence from the first language to the second language is possible? And whether it is different and, if it is, how is it different from other language transfers?

4) Are there any substantial influences that the individual's cultural background may have upon their characteristic preference of some strategies over others in intercultural communications? If there are, what are the most salient cultural factors in this respect? To what extent does the cultural distance between the participants of the communication determine what strategies are employed and how much use they have to be made of?

Concluding Remarks

Intercultural communication studies should not be occupied only with investigating and analysing communicative problems, difficulties or breakdowns that have resulted from cultural differences. It is as important to study how people tackle problems, overcome difficulties and repair breakdowns. It has to be noted that while researches on sociolinguistic aspect of language use and the related cultural differences can help explain much of the failure and misunderstanding in intercultural communication, researches on SC and the use of communication strategies may account for many cases of communication in which cross-cultural understanding is achieved in spite of seemingly formidable difficulties and problems involved. In this sense, researching into the issues of strategic competence is really important to intercultural communication studies, the ultimate aim of which is to help improve our intercultural communication practice.

For teaching a second or foreign language for intercultural communication, researches on strategic competence will have some important implications. More importance should be attached to developing strategic competence of second and foreign-language learners. Whether communication strategies can explicitly taught or not is still controversial, but there is little doubt that learner's strategic competence often play an important role in their attempts to communicate cross-culturally. Yule and Tarone (1990) have pointed out that some people may not have proper strategic competence even in their use of the first language, so they will need much assistance in developing strategic competence when they are learning a second or foreign language. Many scholars and teachers now consider it necessary to incorporate developing learners' strategic competence into second- and foreign-language instruction though they still disagree on that are the proper and effective ways to do so. The methods suggested by some researches such as Chen (1990) and Dornyei and Thurrell (1991) to help facilitate learners' development of strategic competence have yet to be proved in teaching practice. But it seems necessary to mention that Chen (1990) even calls for a reform in syllabus design. In his opinions, most of the syllabuses we have had now are designed to prevent learners from running into problems and therefore contribute little to the development of their strategic competence. As a result, many learners, even some with fairly high linguistic proficiency, are often found quite incompetent in dealing with communicative problems, especially the problems arising in situations for which our teaching has not prepared them.

Strategic competence will also have to be included in our second- and foreign- language testing. As a matter of fact, what has been extensively tested so far is mostly learners' grammatical competence and, occasionally, their sociolinguistic and discourse competencies. Strategic competence seems to have never been included in our test. It should be recognized that our test cannot be truly reliable indicators of the learners' overall competence in the target language before we find a way to test their strategic competence. We all know that there often exist discrepancies between what is tested and what learners have actually acquired and are able to do in real situations of communication. Including strategic competence in our tests can, to some extent at least, reduce such a discrepancy. Of course, to find an effective way to test learners' strategic competence is not easy, but it is surely worth our greater efforts.

References

Berns, M. 1990. *Context of Competence: Social and Cultural Considerations in Communicative Language Teaching*. New York: Plenum Press.
Bialystok, E. 1990. *Communication Strategies*. Oxford: Blackwell.
Campbell, R. & Wales, R. 1970. The study of language acquisition. In J. Lyons (ed). *New Horizons in Linguistics* (pp. 242-260). London: Penguin.
Canale, M. 1983. From communicative competence to communicative language pedagogy. In J. C. Richards & R. W. Schmindt (eds) *Language and communication* (pp. 2-27). Harlow: Longman.
Canale, M. & Swain, M. 1980. Theoretical bases of communicative approaches to second language teaching and testing. *Applied linguistics*, 1, 1-47
Chen, S, Q. 1990. A study of communicative strategies in interlanguage production by Chinese EFL learners. *Language Learning*, 40, 155-187.
Chomsky, N. 1965. *Aspects of the Theory of Syntax*. Cambridge, MA: MIT Press.
Clyne, M, 1981. Cultural and discourse structure. *Journal of Pragmatics*, 5, 61-65
Clyne, M. 1987. Discourse structured and discourse expectations: Implications for Anglo-German academic communication in English. In L. E. Smith (ed) Discourse *Across Cultures: Strategies in World Englishes* (pp. 77-). Herfordshire: Prentice Hall
Dornyei, Z & Scott, M. L. 1995. Communication strategies: An empirical analysis with Annual Symposium of the Desert Language and Linguistics Society (pp. 155-168). Provo, UT: Brigham Young University.
Dornyei, Z & Thurrell, S. 1991. Strategic competence and how to teach it. *ELT*, 45, 16-23.
Faerch, C. & Kasper, N. G. 1983. *Strategies in Interlanguage Communication*. Harlow: Longman.
Habermas, J. 1970. Towards a theory of communicative competence. *Inquiry*, 13, 360-375.
Imahory, & Cupach, W. R. 1994. A cross-cultural comparison on the interpretation and management of face: U. S. American and Japanese responses to embarrassing predicaments. *International Journal of Intercultural Relations*, 18, 193-219.
Kaplan, R. 1966. Cultural thought patterns in inter-cultural education. *Language Learning*, 16, 1-20.
Paribakht, T. 1985. Strategic competence and language proficiency. *Applied Linguistics*, 6, 132-146.
Paulston, C. B. 1992. *Linguistic and Communicative Competence: Topics in ESL*. Clevedon: Multilingual Matters Ltd.
Putz, M. 1992. (ed.) *Thirty Years of Linguistic Evolutions*. Amsterdam: John Benjamins.
Scollon, R. & Wong-Scollon, S. 1991. Topic confusion in English-Asian discourse. *World English*, 10, 113-125.
Selinker, L. 1972. Interlanguage. *IRAL*, 10, 209-230.

Siegal, M. 1996. The role of learner subjectivity in second language sociolinguistic competency: Western women learning Japanese. *Applied Linguistics*, 17, 365–379.
Scarcella, R. C. et al. 1990. (Eds.) *Developing Communicative Competence in a Second language*. Philadelphia: Newbury House.
Swain, M. 1984. Large-scale communicative language testing: A case study. In S. J. Savingnon & M. S. Berns (eds.) *Initiatives in Communicative Language Teaching*. Reading, MA: Addison Wesley.
Tarone, E. & Yule, G. 1987. Communicative strategies in East-West interactions. In L. E. Smith (Ed.) *Discourse across Cultures: Strategies in World Englishes* (pp. 49–65). Hemel Hempstead, UK: Prentice Hall.
Young, L. W. L. 1994. *Crosstalk and Culture in Sino-American Communication*. Cambridge: Cambridge University Press.
Yule, G. & Tarone, E. 1990. Eliciting the performance of strategic competence. In R. C. Scarcella et al. (eds.) *Developing Communicative Competence in a Second Language* (pp, 179–194). New York: Newbury House.

20

Multimodal Manifestation of Conceptual Metaphors in Multimedia Communication

Ning Yu
University of Oklahoma, USA

Abstract: In the light of conceptual metaphor theory of cognitive linguistics, this paper discusses the multimodal manifestation of conceptual metaphors in TV advertising. It makes an in-depth analysis of an educational advertisement on "Chinese Virtues" screened on China Central Television Channel 4 (CCTV-4). It shows that this TV commercial is a "conceptual blend" constructed with visual and aural, as well as verbal, components, but at its core is a conceptual metaphor virtue is water. This metaphor finds its roots in the Laozi, from which one line of the verbal message is quoted: "True goodness is like water" (上善若水). Thus, the whole commercial unfolds on the images of water: the snow-capped mountains, drops of water dripping from the tips of icicles, streams of water running down the mountain, terraced and flat rice field submerged in water, dashing water of a river rushing down a waterfall, two branches of rivers merging into one main river course, and sea waves surging and rolling. It is argued that these visual images metaphorically reinforces the verbal message: Virtue originates in "drips" and "drops," "flows" from the "heart-field," harmonizes in communication ("cross-flowing"), and prospers in eternity (of the ocean and sea).

Introduction

During the past two decades, cognitive linguistic studies have shown that human minds are embodied in the cultural world, and thinking and reasoning are largely metaphorical and imaginative, shaped by bodily and cultural experiences (e.g., Gibbs, 1994, 2006; Johnson, 1987; Kövecses, 2002, 2005; Lakoff, 1987; Lakoff & Johnson, 1980, 1999). According to the conceptual metaphor theory of cognitive linguistics, metaphor is not merely a figure of speech, but also a figure of thought, giving rise to understanding one conceptual domain in terms of another conceptual domain. The rise of the cognitive linguistic theory of conceptual metaphor has seen an increasing interest in and necessity for the study of nonverbal and multimodal metaphors (e.g., Forceville, 1996, 2002, 2005, 2006; Yu, 2007c). If metaphor fundamentally characterizes thinking, and is only secondarily manifested in verbal form, it should be able to produce nonverbal manifestations as well as the purely verbal ones (Forceville, 2006).

In the light of conceptual metaphor theory of cognitive linguistics, this paper discusses the multimodal manifestation of conceptual metaphors in TV advertising. It makes an in-depth analysis of an educational advertisement on "Chinese Virtues" screened on China Central Television Channel 4 (CCTV-4). It shows that this TV advertisement is constructed with visual and aural, as well as verbal, components, but at its core is a conceptual metaphor VIRTUE IS WATER. This metaphor finds its roots in the *Laozi*, from which one line of the verbal message is quoted: "True goodness is like water"(上善若水). Thus, the whole advertisement unfolds on the moving images of water, accompanied by special musical effects: the snow-capped mountain, drops of water dripping from the tips of icicles, streams of water running down the mountain, terraced and flat rice fields submerged in water, dashing water of a river rushing down a waterfall, two branches of rivers merging into one main river course, and sea waves surging and rolling. These moving images, which show a long process of natural change from "drips and drops" to "seas and oceans," interact with and reinforce the verbal messages that speak of Chinese virtues in terms of a river with "a remote source" and "a long course" that "flows forever" into eternity.

In the remainder of this paper, I will first present a synopsis of the TV commercial in Section 2. I will then analyze the manifestation of the conceptual metaphor VIRTUE IS WATER in the interaction between the three modes in Section 3. I will reach a brief conclusion in Section 4.

Synopsis

The TV advertisement begins with a long shot of a snow-capped mountain that looks lofty and towering (Figure 1), when the audio track plays a symphonic music that starts light and slow, giving rise to a sense of "peace in solemnity" before the sunrise in the early morning. The long shot shifts into a close-up of a part of a tree coated in ice but the focus is on a few glittering icicles hanging from the twigs of the tree (Figure 2). The glistening of the hanging icicles and the ice coat against the black color of the tree branches and twigs over the blue background seems to suggest that the sun is emerging from the horizon. The shot now focuses on the very tip of one icicle as a drop of water is dripping from it and the music imitates the clear sound of the dripping drop hitting the water surface below. At the same time, the verbal message shows on the screen: "发于点滴 Originating in drips and drops" (Figure 3).

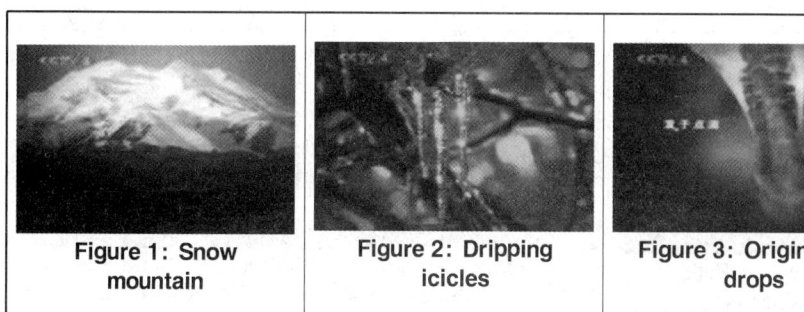

Figure 1: Snow mountain   Figure 2: Dripping icicles   Figure 3: Originate in drops

The next shot is a close-up showing a brook or stream running its course down the mountain, the descending water being separated by rocks and boulders here and there along the course (Figure 4). At this point the audio track also imitates the sound of running water. The screen then changes into a long shot from a high angle showing terraced fields, submerged under water, over green hills while white clouds are floating past (Figure 5). It is already broad day. The next scene is that of a bird's-eye view of rice fields over an expanse of flat land, as the verbal message shows in the middle of the screen: "行于心田 Moving / flowing in the 'heart-fields' (i.e. the heart)" (Figure 6).

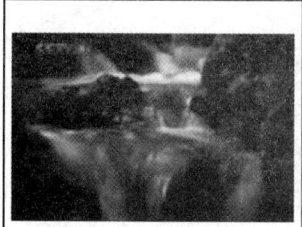  

Figure 4: Streams running   Figure 5: Terraced rice fields   Figure 6: Flow in heart-field

The rice fields then fades into dashing water (Figure 7), which then turns into water rushing by a huge rock (Figure 8). As the music of strings gives way to a peaceful melody of a flute, the close-up of rushing water fades into a long shot of a bird's-eye view of a river where two branches merge into the main course and the verbal message is shown: "融于交流 Fusing or harmonious in 'cross-flowing' (i.e. communication)" (Figure 9). The scene then changes into that of the blue sea where a surging wave strikes the coastal rocks sending gigantic white splashes high into the air (Figure 10). It then changes into a close-up of a high rolling wave (Figure 11). When the high wave fades into a vast expanse of sea water below the clouded sky, which seems to be getting dim and dark, the verbal message appears: "盛于久远 Flourishing in the 'long and far' (i.e. eternity)" (Figure 12).

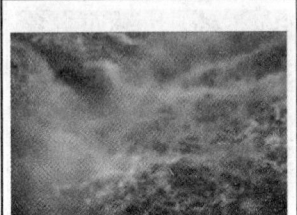
Figure 7: Falls dashing

Figure 8: River rushing

Figure 9: Harmonize in cross-flow

Figure 10: Sea surging

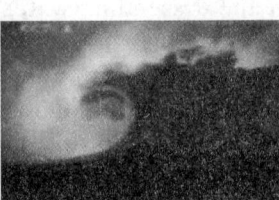
Figure 11: Sea rolling

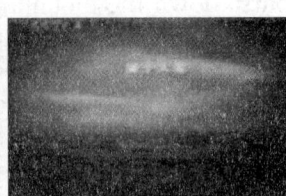
Figure 12: Flourish in long and far

The sky then becomes darkened with a full silver moon hanging against the black backdrop above the shining silvery water of a calm and peaceful ocean. Also against the dark sky appears the verbal message: "上善若水，厚德载物 True goodness is like water, with profound (lit. thick) virtue carrying (i.e. nurturing) all things" (Figure 13). The final scene, shot from a low camera angle, shows some huge dark rocks against the light gray sky across which clouds are flying. The scene is suggestive of the dawn of another day. On the biggest rock to the right side is the verbal message: "中华美德，源远流长 Chinese virtue has a remote source (i.e. a long history) and a long flow (i.e. it flows forever)" (Figure 14). As the verbal messages on Figures 13 and 14 are displayed on the screen, a male voice speaks them out, slowly and firmly, accompanied by the music. That is, the final verbal messages are presented both visually and aurally.

Figure 13: Moon over sea   Figure 14: Rocks against sky

Analysis

In this section, I analyze the multimodal manifestation of the central metaphor around which the TV advertisement revolves and unfolds. This central metaphor is VIRTUE IS WATER or, more specifically, CHINESE VIRTUE IS WATER, which is rooted deeply in traditional Chinese culture. In this Chinese TV advertisement for public good, the metaphor is manifested in both visual and aural modes, as well as verbal mode.

Visually, the advertisement displays a natural process of change as follows:

Snow/Ice → Drop → Stream → River → Ocean

That is, initially, it is a process of transformation from solid to liquid, and then it is a process of accumulation from drips and drops of water to the vast multitude of the sea and ocean. Along this process of accumulation are the following two processes of change:

Temporal: Daybreak → Day → Night → Dawn
Geographic: Mountain → Hill → Plain → Sea

The first process of change suggests the temporal cycle of day and night, which however can be interpreted metonymically (i.e. PART FOR WHOLE) as standing for the larger cycle in time, for instance, the four seasons of a year, and for the more abstract concept of eternity. For the second process of change, the geographic features characterize China, which, generally speaking, has higher altitude in its west, with plateaus and mountain ranges (including the world's highest mountain system the Himalaya and highest peak Mount Qomolangma), lower altitude in its east, with vast plains. That is why its two main rivers, the Yangtze River and the Yellow River, flow from west to east before they pour into the Pacific Ocean. In the audio track, the musical melody that imitates or accompanies the sounds of dripping water from icicles, a descending brook, dashing falls and torrents, calm merging of river courses, and surging and rolling sea, helps intensify the visual effect of a variety of water movements created by the moving images.

It is, however, the verbal messages shown on the screen that, step by step, surfaces the underlying conceptual metaphor VIRTUE IS WATER, by which the abstract concept of virtue is talked about, as well as visually presented, in terms of physical mass of water. The verbal messages, consisting of eight lines, are divided into two groups: the target concept of the metaphor, VIRTUE, is implicit in the first group of four lines, but explicitly expressed in the second group of four lines. Here are the four lines that compose the first group:

[1] Group One
    a. 发于点滴 'Originating in drips and drops' (Figure 3)
    b. 行于心田 'Functioning in the heart' (Figure 6)
    c. 融于交流 'Fusing in communication' (Figure 9)
    d. 盛于久远 'Flourishing in eternity' (Figure 12)

These four lines, all subjectless, are composed of an intransitive verb and a prepositional phrase indicating manner or location. Table 1 explicates the manifestation of the conceptual metaphor VIRTUE IS WATER in both verbal and visual modes.

As shown in the table, the visual images and at least the first line of the verbal message seem to dictate WATER as the subject here. However, WATER is but the source concept of VIRTUE, the target concept, as will become clear in the second group of verbal messages. Thanks to the help of visual images, the manifestation of this metaphor is then shown below in [2]:

[2] VIRTUE IS WATER
    a. which originates in drips and drops
    b. which flows in the (rice) fields
    c. which merges in cross-flowing
    d. which abounds in the sea and ocean

That is, virtue originates in small amounts, functions in the heart (lit. the heart-field), fuses in communication or exchange of ideas, and flourishes in eternity.

Table 1: Explication of the metaphor in verbal and visual modes

Metaphor			Verbal		Visual
Target	Source	Verb	Prepositional phrase		Images on the screen
VIRTUE	WATER	发 *fā* Start Originate	于点滴 *yú diǎn-dī* in drips and drops		a drop of water dripping from the tip of an icicle
VIRTUE	WATER	行 *xíng* Go Flow Function	于心田 *yú xīn-tián* (lit. in the heart-field) in the heart		an expanse of rice fields

(to be continued)

Metaphor		Verbal		Visual
Target	Source	Verb	Prepositional phrase	Images on the screen
VIRTUE	WATER	融 *róng* Merge Fuse Harmonize	于交流 *yú jiāo-liú* (lit. in cross-flowing) in communication	two branches of a river merging into one main course
VIRTUE	WATER	盛 *shèng* Abound Flourish	于久远 *yú jiǔ-yuǎn* (lit. in long-far) in eternity	a vast expanse of ocean

As shown in Table 1, the Chinese heart, which is culturally conceived of as the locus of moral sense and character in particular and the central faculty of cognition in general (Yu, 2007a, b), is sometimes called "heart-field", i.e. HEART IS A FIELD. It is a SOIL metaphor that often appears in combination with, for instance, the PLANT and WATER metaphors, which together fall in the source domain of agriculture. According to HYDCD (2000, p. 1128), 心田 *xin-tian* (heart-field) is originally a term in Buddhism referring to the heart. Buddhism maintains that the heart stores the seeds of good and evil that would grow under suitable circumstances, just like a field in which both crops and weeds would grow. It is said that the Buddha taught the disciples that the heart is a piece of land where you will get fruits in return for whatever seeds you have sowed. Here are some sentential examples.

[3] a. 我把环保种子播撒在他的心田里。
Wǒ bǎ huán-bǎo zhǒngzi bōsǎ zài tāde
I PRT environment-protection seeds sowed at his
xīn-tián li.
heart-field in
'I sowed the environment-protection seeds in his heart (lit. heart-field).'

b. 有时她那短暂的微笑,真会令我的心田开出温暖的花朵呢!
Yǒushí tā nà duǎnzàn de wēixiào, zhēn huì lìng
sometimes she that transient MOD smile really would make
wǒde **xīn-tián** *kāi-chū wēnnuǎn de huāduǒ ne!*
my heart-field bloom-with warm MOD flowers PRT
'Sometimes that transient smile of hers would really make my heart (lit. heart-field).'

c. 她那无助的感觉一波又一波地涌进我的心田。
Tā nà wú-zhù de gǎnjué yì bō yòu yì bō de
she that no-help MOD feeling one wave again one wave MOD
yǒng jìn wǒde **xīn-tián**.
surge into my heart-field

'That hopeless feeling of hers surged wave after wave into my heart (lit. heart-field).'

d. 如同泉涌的泪潮，畅快地洗涤着我的心田。
Rútóng quán yǒng de lèi-cháo, chàngkuài de xǐdí-zhe
like spring gushing MOD tear-flood free-happy MOD cleanse-DUR
wǒde **xīn-tián**.
my heart-field
'The flood of tears, like gushing spring water, is cleansing my heart (lit. heart-field) free from any inhibitions.'

e. 他的话似四月的惊雷，响彻了我封闭幽暗的心田。
Tāde huà sì sìyuè de jīng-léi, xiǎng chè le
his words like April MOD sudden-thunder reverberate across PER
wǒ fēngbì yōu'àn de **xīn-tián**.
my closed dark MOD heart-field
'His words, like a sudden clap of thunder in April, reverberated over that closed dark heart (lit. heart-field) of mine.'

As in [3a], ideas or thoughts are "seeds", and to communicate ideas or thoughts to other people, or to educate them, is to "sow the seeds" into their "heart-field". The seeds sowed into the "heart-field" will grow, blossom, and bear fruits (of earlier education). Thus, [3a] involves some metaphorical mappings from the source to the target: Sower → Educator; Seeds → Ideas / Thoughts; Sowing → Communicating / Educating; Field → Heart of the educated; Expected harvest → Expected result. In [3b], the heart is the seat of feelings or emotions. Happy and warm feelings are "flowers" grown out of the "heart-field". In Chinese, the idiom 心花怒放 xīnhuā nùfàng (heart-flowers wildly-blossom) is a common metaphorical expression of happiness (see Yu, 1998). In this case, the cause for the instant bloom of the "flowers", i.e. the "transient smile of hers", is the much-needed "nourishment" for the plants. Example [3c] describes the state of empathy, i.e., the sharing of one's feeling by another. Here, one person's feeling of helplessness is water that "surges" into the "heart-field" of another person. It shows that true understanding and sympathy are established upon the connection of the two hearts through which feelings and thoughts in one person's heart can "flow" into that of another. The example involves various metaphorical mappings: Field → Heart; Water → Feeling; Way of water moving → Way of feeling experienced; Force of water → Strength of feeling; Water flowing from one field into another → Empathy. The metaphor here is structured by multiple image schemas such as CONTAINERS, LINK, FORCE, and SOURCE-PATH-GOAL. In [3d], the narrator is crying, and the tears, like gushing spring water, are "purifying" his or her "heart-field". It can be expected that, in both [3c] and [3d], something positive will grow out of the "heart-field" being "irrigated". These examples may have deep roots in ancient Chinese thought, reminiscent of Mencius' similar metaphors for moral sense and character (see Yu, 2007a, 2007b). In [3e], it is clear that the "closed" container that is "dark" inside refers to the whole heart while the "heart-field" is but the "bottom" of that container. In this example, the narrator seems to have both heaven and earth in the heart, which is conceived of as microcosmic of the whole world (Yu, 2007a, 2007b).

Now, let us turn to the second group of verbal messages, which makes explicit the metaphor VIRTUE IS WATER or CHINESE VIRTUE IS WATER. The four lines are displayed on Figures 13 and 14, with two lines on each figure.

[4] a. 上善若水,厚德载物 (on Figure 13)
True (lit. upper) goodness is like water, with profound (lit. thick) virtue carrying (i.e. nurturing) all things.
b. 中华美德,源远流长 (on Figure 14)
Chinese virtue has a long history (lit. a remote source) and will flow forever (lit. for long).

As in (4a), 善 *shàn* and 德 *dé* are synonymous in this case. While *dé* is a noun meaning "virtue", *shàn* is primarily an adjective meaning "good" and "virtuous". In this case it means "being good" or "being virtuous". Both *shàn* and *dé* are qualified in terms of a spatial metaphor. Being good is being "up", namely GOOD IS UP. The dimensional adjective *hòu* 'thick' here indicates a great amount of virtue. At the same time, however, *hòu* 'thick' can mean "kind", "magnanimous", "generous", etc., which are apt modifiers of *dé* 'virtue', too. Although "True goodness is like water", strictly speaking, is a case of simile, this simile is embedded in the larger context of multimodal (primarily visual and verbal, and to some extent aural) manifestation of metaphorical mappings. These mappings are combined into a "complex metaphor" (Grady, 1997a, 1997b, 2005),

HISTORY OF CHINESE VIRTUE IS RIVER OF WATER:
[5] River of water → History of Chinese virtue
  a. River → History
  b. Water → Chinese virtue
  c. Source of river being far away → History beginning long ago
  d. Long course of river → Long course of history

At a more abstract level the complex metaphor HISTORY OF CHINESE VIRTUE IS RIVER OF WATER involves two "primary metaphors" (Grady, 1997a, 1997b, 2005): PASSING TIME IS MOVING OBJECT and ABSTRACT QUALITY IS PHYSICAL SUBSTANCE, with the mappings shown below:

[6] a. Moving object → Passing time
  b. Physical substance → Abstract quality

These two primary metaphors are widespread or even universal in nature. The image schema that structures the metaphor HISTORY OF CHINESE VIRTUE IS RIVER OF WATER is SOURCE-PATH-GOAL. Chinese virtue grows stronger and lasts forever, just like a river, which originates in drips and drops from melting ice and snow but, after a long process of merging and accumulating, would flow into the sea and ocean, which represent, metonymically and metaphorically, such abstract concepts of profundity and eternity. That is, Chinese virtue, with a long history of growth, will last forever in profundity and eternity.

As mentioned earlier, the metaphor CHINESE VIRTUE IS WATER is deeply rooted in Chinese culture. In fact, the verbal message 上善若水 'True goodness is like water' is cited from Chapter Eight of the *Laozi* or *Daode Jing* written by Laozi about two thousand and five hundred years ago. There, it goes:

[7] 上善若水。水善利万物而不争,处众人之所恶,故几于道。
    True goodness is like water. Water is good in that it benefits the ten thousand things but never vies for profits, and that it stays in the low places that all others find loathsome, and therefore it is close to the Way.

In other words, water is good and virtuous in that it nurtures all living things but never fights for its own profits. It stays humble in the "low" places that others dislike and do not care to be in. Because it is helpful, modest, and humble, water is close to the Way, which is, according to Daoism, the Law of Nature for the heaven and earth or the universe.

The metaphor CHINESE VIRTUE IS WATER, I argue, reflects the fundamental idea that has dominated Chinese thought from the dawn of its history, namely, "the unity of man and Heaven". Ancient Chinese philosophy advocated the ideas that man and nature are a unified one (天人合一 *tiān rén héyī*) and man and the universe correspond to each other (天人对应 *tiān rén duìyìng*). The words *nature* and *universe*, both used to translate the Chinese word *tiān* (天) that primarily refers to the sky or heaven, should be interpreted as to mean "the external world" (see, e.g., Zhang & Rose, 2001, Ch. 4). Thus, for instance, the Daoists conceived of the human body as "a microcosm of the universe" (p. 86). They "always tried to understand what was happening inside the body by comparing and contrasting it with what was happening outside in nature" (Chia & Chia, 1990, p. 14). To them, "The microcosm is a mirror image of the macrocosm", and "The universe within is the same as the universe without" (p. 15). Therefore, one can understand the entire universe by understanding one's own body and vice versa. In the metaphor CHINESE VIRTUE IS WATER under discussion, a quality of humans, virtue, is expressed visually and verbally in terms of water, one of the five elements (the remaining four being wood, fire, earth, and metal) of which the universe is composed according to ancient Chinese philosophy. The metaphor thus conceptually links human as the microcosm on the one hand and universe as the macrocosm on the other, and suggests the unity and correspondence between the two.

Conclusion

In this paper I have analyzed a specific example of multimodal manifestation of a conceptual metaphor, VIRTUE IS WATER, in TV advertising. As I have shown, the metaphor is manifested through the interaction between visual, aural and verbal discourse. The visual and aural modes initially interact with each other to present a long natural process in which drips and drops of water accumulate into vast multitude of seas and oceans. Their combination then interacts with the verbal mode to realize the multimodal manifestation of the conceptual metaphor VIRTUE IS WATER. The interaction between and combination of the three modes are summarized by Figure 15.

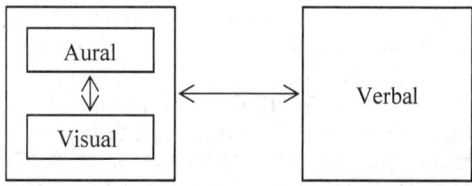

Figure 15. The interaction between and combination of the three modes

The visual discourse consists of a series of moving images involving water: drops of water dripping from icicles, a brook flowing descending the mountain, terraced and flat rice fields soaked in water, dashing water of falls and torrents, branches of rivers merging into one main river course, sea waves surging and rolling, and so on. However, the visual discourse, combined with aural discourse of music, which is either imitative or suggestive of various sound effects of water movements, only presents the source domain concept of WATER. Its mapping onto the target domain concept of VIRTUE is realized through the interaction between the visual and aural discourse on the one hand and the verbal discourse on the other. As in Figure 6, when the verbal message that literally means "Going / flowing in the heart-field" appears on top of the image of patches of rice fields, sensitive viewer should begin to realize that the subjectless verbal phrase refers to something more than just water because in Chinese "heart-field" (心田 xīntián) really refers to the heart or, more abstractly, the central faculty of cognition. As in Figure 9, when the verbal message that literally means "Merging in cross-flowing" appears on the scene where two branches of river merge into one main course, the viewer can tell that the subject of the verbal phrase is not water despite the images of the river because in Chinese "cross-flowing" (交流 jiāoliú), while a WATER metaphor, really means "communication", in which people's words, and the thoughts and feelings they represent, "cross-flow" between them. However, what is actually the subject that is being talked about is made clear until the end of the TV commercial (Figures 13 and 14). It is then and there that the target concept of the metaphor, CHIENSE VIRTUE, is made explicit and the metaphorical mapping is completed. It is also at this point that the critical piece of the puzzle is in place, and the whole TV commercial begins to make a lot of sense as a metaphor realized in three modes: visual, aural, and verbal. That is a case of multimodal manifestation of a conceptual metaphor.

References

Forceville, C. (1996). *Pictorial Metaphor in Advertising*. London: Routledge.
Forceville, C. (2002). The identification of target and source in pictorial metaphors. *Journal of Pragmatics*, *34*, 1–14.
Forceville, C. (2005). Visual representations of the idealized cognitive model of anger in the Asterix album *La Zizanix*. *Journal of Pragmatics*, *37*, 69–88.
Forceville, C. (2006). Non-verbal and multimodal metaphor in a cognitivist framework: Agendas for research. In G. Kristiansen, M. Achard, R. Dirven, & F. Ruiz de Mendoza Ibáñez (Eds.), *Cognitive Linguistics: Current Applications and Future Perspectives* (pp. 379–402). Berlin: Mouton de Gruyter.
Gibbs, R. W. (1994). *The Poetics of Mind: Figurative Thought, Language, and Understanding*. Cambridge: Cambridge University Press.
Gibbs, R. W. (2006). *Embodiment and Cognitive Science*. Cambridge: Cambridge University Press.
Grady, J. (1997a). Foundation of meaning: Primary metaphors and primary scenes. Unpublished doctoral dissertation, Department of Linguistics, University of California at Berkeley.
Grady, J. (1997b). Theories are buildings revisited. *Cognitive Linguistics*, *8*, 267–290.
Grady, J. (2005). Primary metaphors as inputs to conceptual integration. *Journal of Pragmatics*, *37*, 1595–1614.
Grand Dictionary of Chinese Language. (2000). Shanghai: Grand Dictionary of Chinese Language Press. [《汉语大词典》(2000),上海:上海辞书出版社。]
Johnson, M. (1987). *The Body in the Mind: The Bodily Basis of Meaning, Imagination, and Reason*. Chicago: University of Chicago Press.
Kövecses, Z. (2002). *Metaphor: A Practical Introduction*. Oxford: Oxford University Press.
Kövecses, Z. (2005). *Metaphor in Culture: Universality and Variation*. Cambridge: Cambridge University Press.
Lakoff, G. (1987). *Women, Fire, and Dangerous Things: What Categories Reveal about the Mind*. Chicago: University of Chicago Press.
Lakoff, G., & Johnson, M. (1980). *Metaphor We Live By*. Chicago: University of Chicago Press.
Lakoff, G., & Johnson, M. (1999). *Philosophy in the Flesh: The Embodied Mind and its Challenge to Western Thought*. New York: Basic Books.
Yu, N. (1998). *The Contemporary Theory of Metaphor: A Perspective from Chinese*. Amsterdam: John Benjamins.
Yu, N. (2007a). Heart and cognition in ancient Chinese philosophy. *Journal of Cognition and Culture*, *7*, 27–47.
Yu, N. (2007b). The Chinese conceptualization of the heart and its cultural

context: Implications for second language learning. In F. Sharifian & G. B. Palmer (Eds.), *Applied Cultural Linguistics: Implications for Second Language Learning and Intercultural Communication* (pp. 65–85). Amsterdam: John Benjamins.

Yu, N. (2007c). Cultural identity and globalization: Multimodal metaphors in a Chinese educational advertisement. *China Media Research*, *3*, 25–32.

Zhang, Y. H., & Rose, K. (2001). *A Brief History of Qi*. Brookline, MA: Paradigm Publications.

21

Intercultural Communication Between Japanese and Thais Through Discrepancies in Images

Yuko TAKESHITA
Toyo Eiwa University, Japan

Abstract: In recent years, the relationship between Thailand and Japan has become closer and closer in several respects, such as economy and trade, tourism and cultural exchange. In addition, more and more young Thai people are studying Japanese in accordance with a greater number of Japanese companies conducting business in large cities such as Bangkok and Chiang Mai. Under such circumstances, the primary concern of this paper is to look for ways in which Japanese and Thais can communicate more effectively. The discussion is initially based on two kinds of questionnaires conducted in Bangkok — one for Thai students of the Japanese language and the other for Japanese business people and their spouses. The answers to these questionnaires illuminate the following:

- the image Thai people hold of Japan and Japanese people;
- the image Japanese people hold of Thailand and Thai people; and
- what Japanese think Thai people believe about Japan and Japanese people.

The data gathered from the questionnaires show some discrepancies in the mutual images for various reasons, e. g., inappropriate background information, insufficient interactions, and therefore, stereotyping. With the examination of those incongruous images and identification of possible reasons producing them, suggestions will be made so that this particular intercultural communication could be improved.

Introduction: The background

The study of Thai people through a questionnaire and interviews of Japanese business people was part of the study conducted by Honna and myself in Thailand on teaching Japanese as a foreign language of international communication (Honna & Takeshita 1996; Takeshita 2005; Takeshita 2006). The data presented here are re-examined to assist the focus of this paper.

The questionnaire for Japanese people was administered at another occasion by Takeshita in order to verify and objectify those personal comments obtained through interviews. Then the results were put together so that a comparison between Japanese and Thai people's images might be made.

The Thai subjects of the questionnaire — 34 male and 194 female students — are 228 young students of the Japanese language at Chulalongkorn University and at the Japan Foundation Bangkok Language

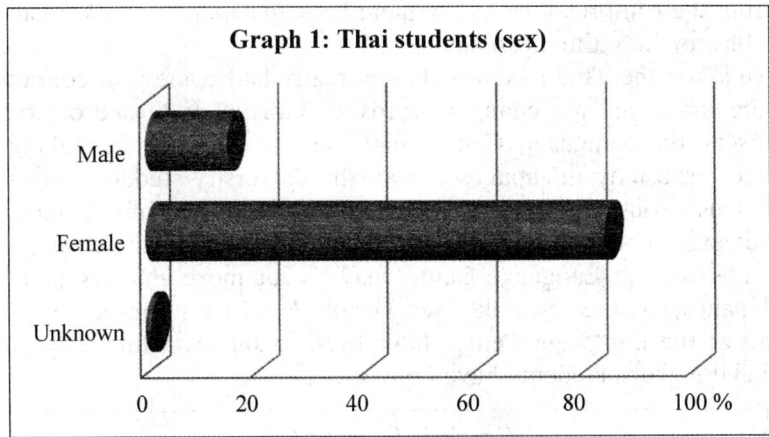

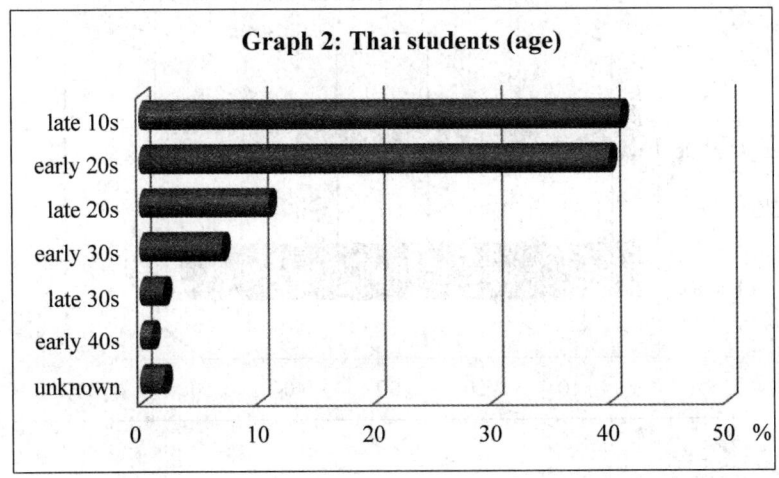

Center (See Graph 1 & Graph 2). By the time of the study, they had already been working or willing to work for Japanese companies in Bangkok. Their images of Japan and Japanese are important in that they have or will have close interactions with Japanese business people and their families in Thailand.

The Japanese interviewees are male representatives of 12 different Japanese companies of various sizes who are working with Thai people in Bangkok. Some of them are also among the subjects of the questionnaire described below.

The questionnaire for Japanese people was filled out by 67 business people and their spouses living in Bangkok — 34 males and 33 females (see Graphs 3 & 4). There are nearly equal percentages of men and women, more than 65% of the men are in their late 30s and early 40s, while almost 60% of the women in their 30s. Their lengths of stay in Thailand are not uniform (see Graph 5). These are people who are supposed to have the closest relationship with Thai people for a certain period of time and who will bring their impressions of Thailand back to Japan and talk about them in the future, i.e., the messengers.

We asked the Thai students if they really had come into contact with Japanese and actually exchanged words with them. It turned out that the students at the Language Center had more experience in talking with Japanese, especially in Japanese, than the university students (see Graph 6). It is also evident that the university students have a limited amount and range of experience because they are likely to meet Japanese on campus, while those at the Language Center have a lot more chances to interact with Japanese business people (see Graph 7). Fifty-four percent of the students at the Language Center have been to Japan, while only 25% of the Chulalongkorn students have done so.

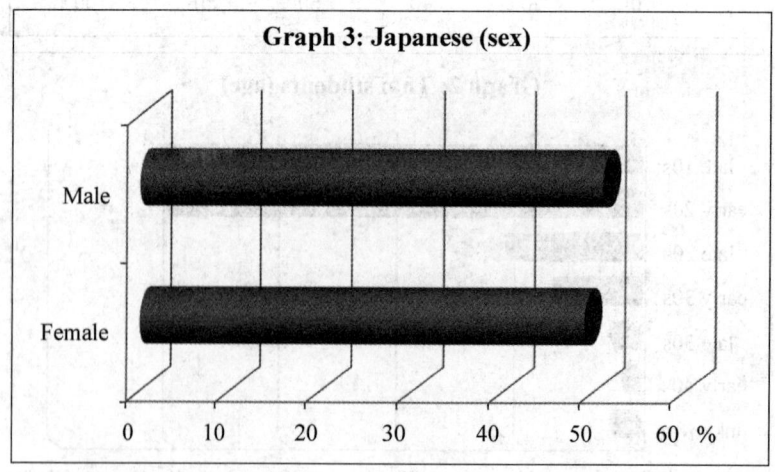

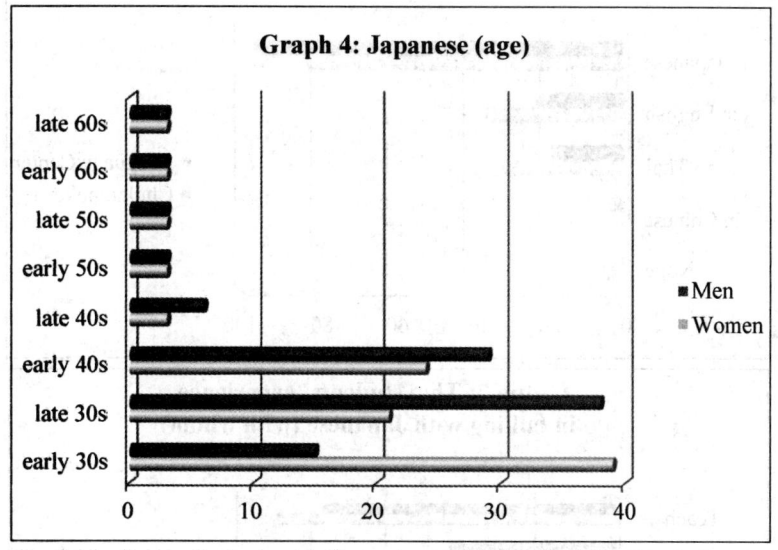

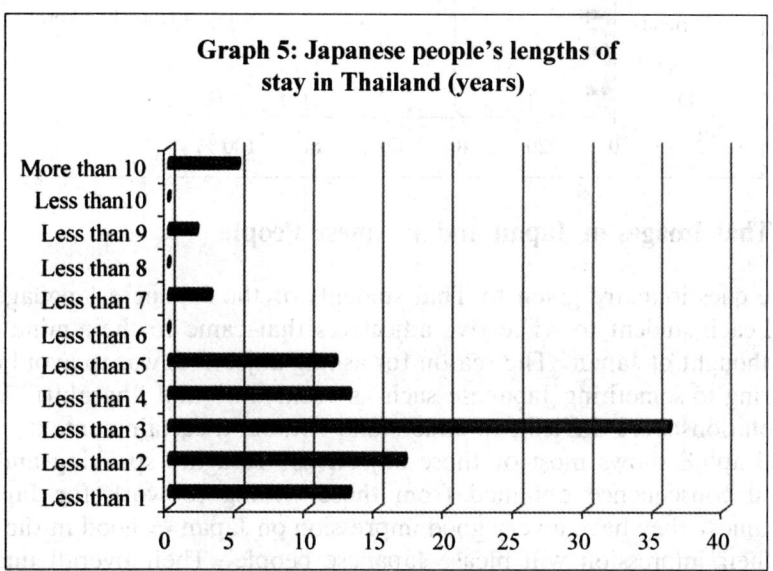

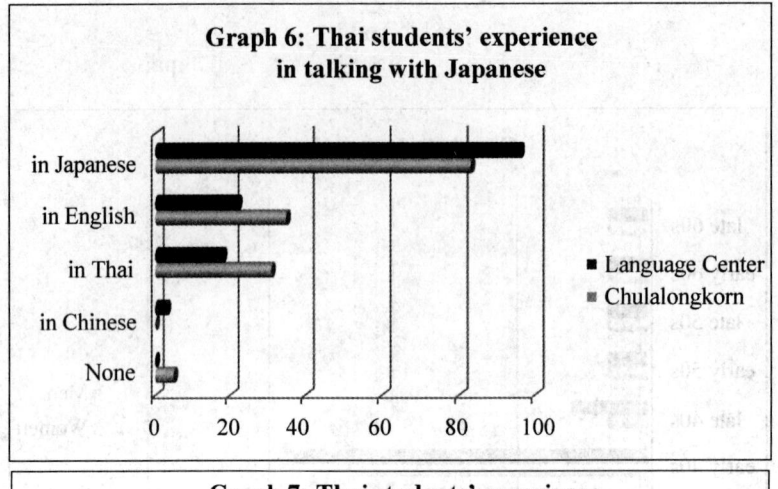

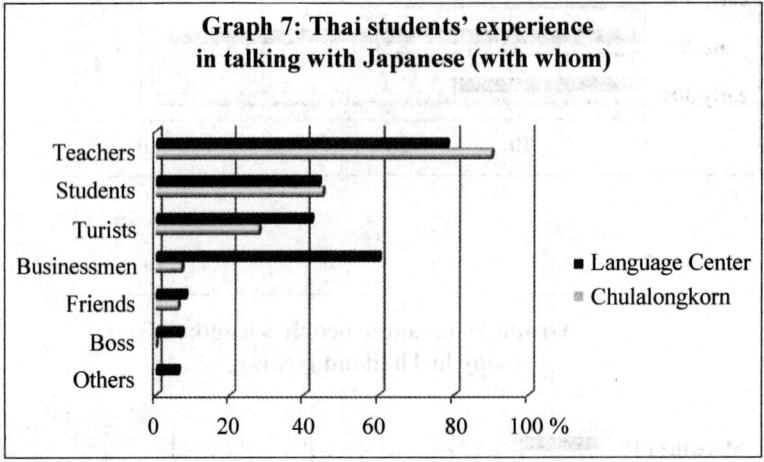

The Thai Images of Japan and Japanese People

In the questionnaire given to Thai students of the Japanese language, we asked each student to write five adjectives that came to their mind when they thought of Japan. The reason for asking adjectives was to avoid nouns referring to something Japanese such as "sukiyaki" and "harakiri" whose connotations were difficult to understand without a certain context.

Graph 8 shows most of those adjectives. Roughly speaking and as a natural consequence obtained from those willing to work for Japanese companies, they have a very good impression on Japan — good in the sense that their impression will please Japanese people. Their overall image is friendly and welcoming to a Japanese. To a Thai eye, the image of Japan may be summarized as the following: Japan is a clean, hygienic and beautiful country although the temperature is too low and the prices are two high; it is a small country but it has convenient and interesting things.

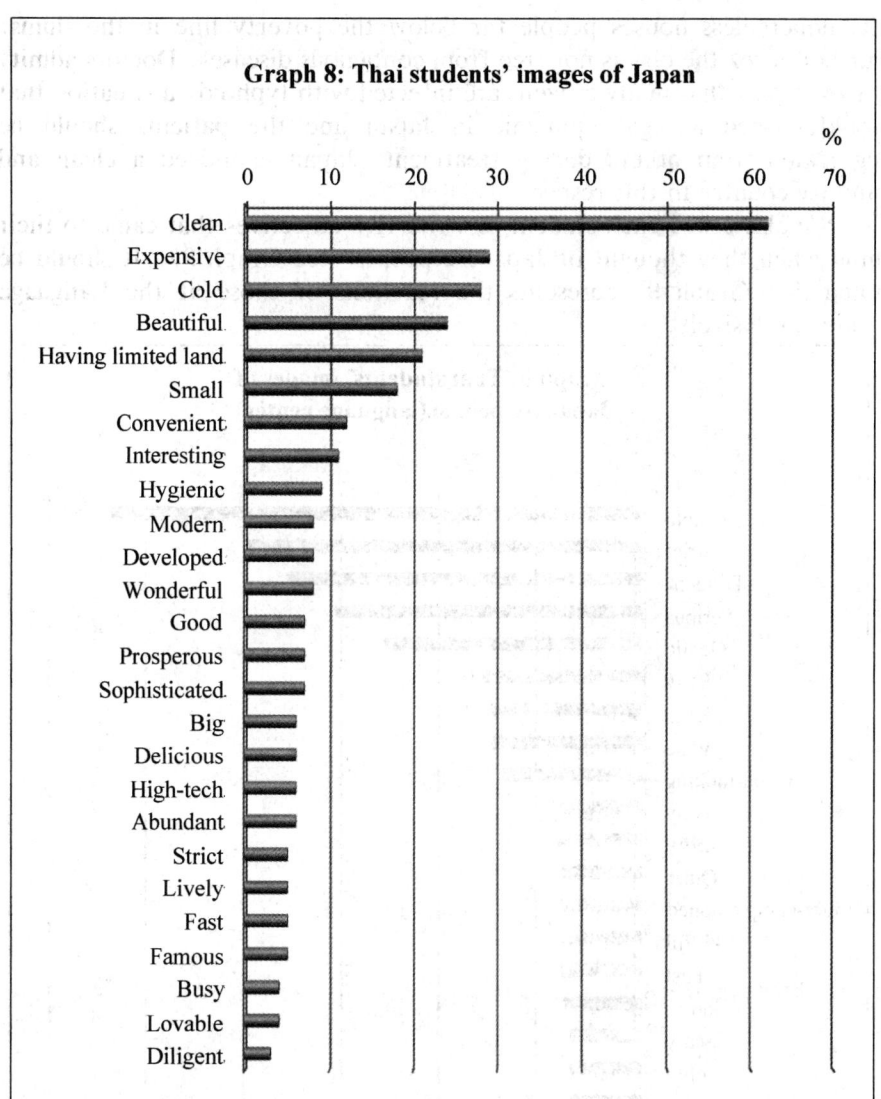

One can clearly see that lots of adjectives were presented as a result of making comparisons between Thailand and Japan from a Thai point of view. Specifically, the adjective "clean" was pointed out by more than 60% of the students. Why Japan seems to be a clean country to so many Thai students is quite understandable when we observe Bangkok from a hygienic point of view.

Thai people's efforts toward modernization of their capital city have not only led to constructions of magnificent skyscraping office buildings, brilliant-looking department stores and shopping malls, but to the world's most infamous traffic congestion and air pollution. It is also true that the city nonetheless houses people far below the poverty line in the slums. Furthermore, the city is not free from contagious diseases. Doctors admit, for example, that many citizens are infected with typhoid, a situation that would termed a legal epidemic in Japan and the patients should be segregated from others during treatment. Japan is indeed a clean and sanitary country in this respect.

We also asked each student to write five adjectives that came to their mind when they thought of Japanese people (see Graph 9). It should be noted that Graph 9 represents the reactions of those at the Language Center exclusively.

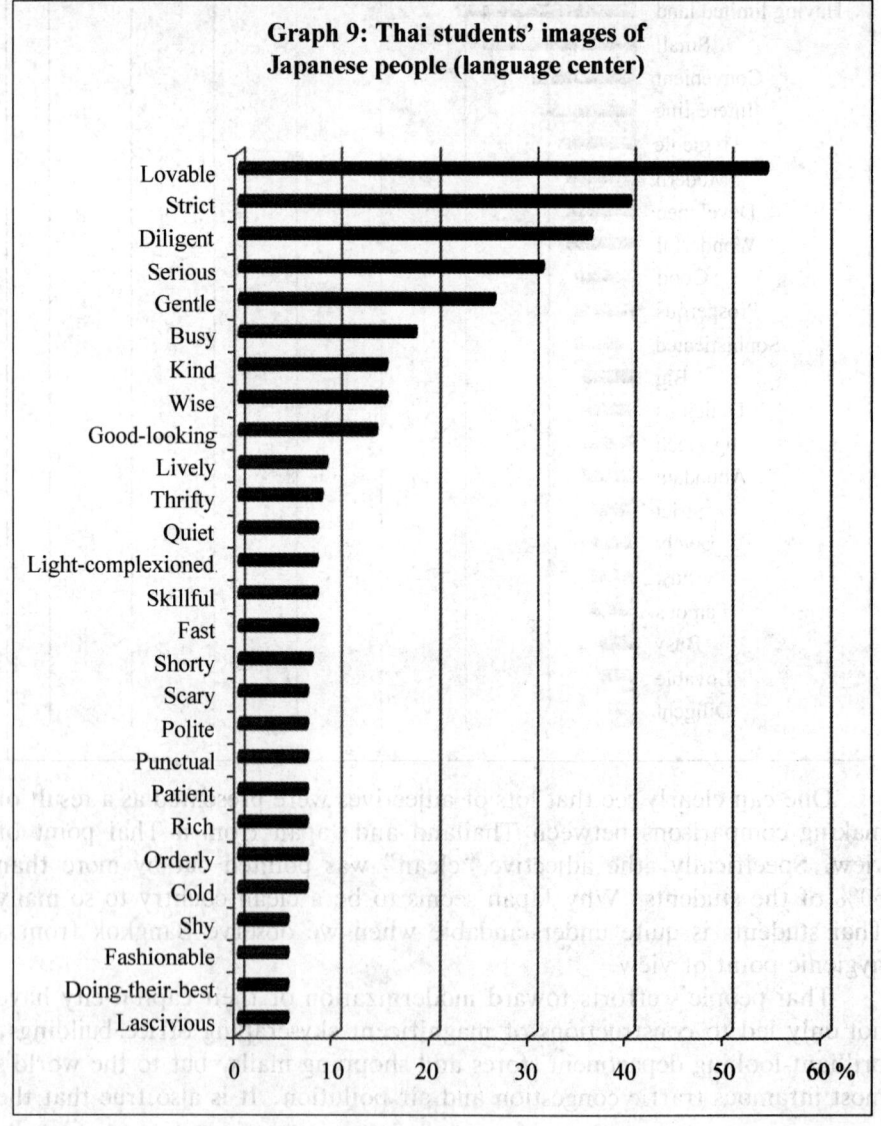

The speculation is that the students at the Language Center may have a more realistic view of Japanese than the college students since they are in closer contact with the Japanese business people. In fact, the data collected from the Chula students are somewhat different from those shown in Graph 9.

One example may be Japanese people's strictness. Forty percent of the students at the Language Center point out this quality, while only 25.7% of the Chula students do so. Perhaps, there is more strictness in business, especially in Japanese companies, while Japanese teachers try to create a relaxed atmosphere in the university classrooms to suit the Thai students' easy-going nature.

Another example concerns punctuality. Six percent of the students at the Language Center say Japanese are punctual, while only 1.8% of the Chula students do so. Thai punctuality is quite different from Japanese punctuality. Unless a Thai person has a chance to do something important with a Japanese for a certain period of time, he or she does not become conscious of punctuality as Japanese talk about it.

Generally speaking, the impression Japanese make on these students is not unfriendly. Adjectives that convey positive images, pleasing to Japanese, are listed at the top, such as lovable, diligent, gentle, kind, wise, good-looking and lively. Those with a negative image such as thrifty, scary, cold, lascivious, inscrutable and over-working have smaller percentages.

The word "lovable" is a translation of a Thai adjective "naa rak," a combination of *naa* (suitable for) and *rak* (to love). This word, also translated as cute, could be applied not only to people, both young and old, but also to animals, things, places and many more one could think of loving. It is possible to say that Mt. Fuji is *naa rak*.

Japanese People's Images of Thailand and Thai People

In a different questionnaire, Japanese people were also asked to write five adjectives to modify Thailand. Most of these results are shown in Graph 10. Some adjectives stand in direct opposition to those in Graph 8, such as hot versus cold, dirty and smelly versus clean and hygienic, and developing versus developed. Some adjectives in Graph 10 reflect the negative aspects of Thailand judged from a Japanese standard, such as their world-famous traffic jam, the unbridgeable gap between the rich and the poor, and the poorest corners and streets of Bangkok that are not well taken care of.

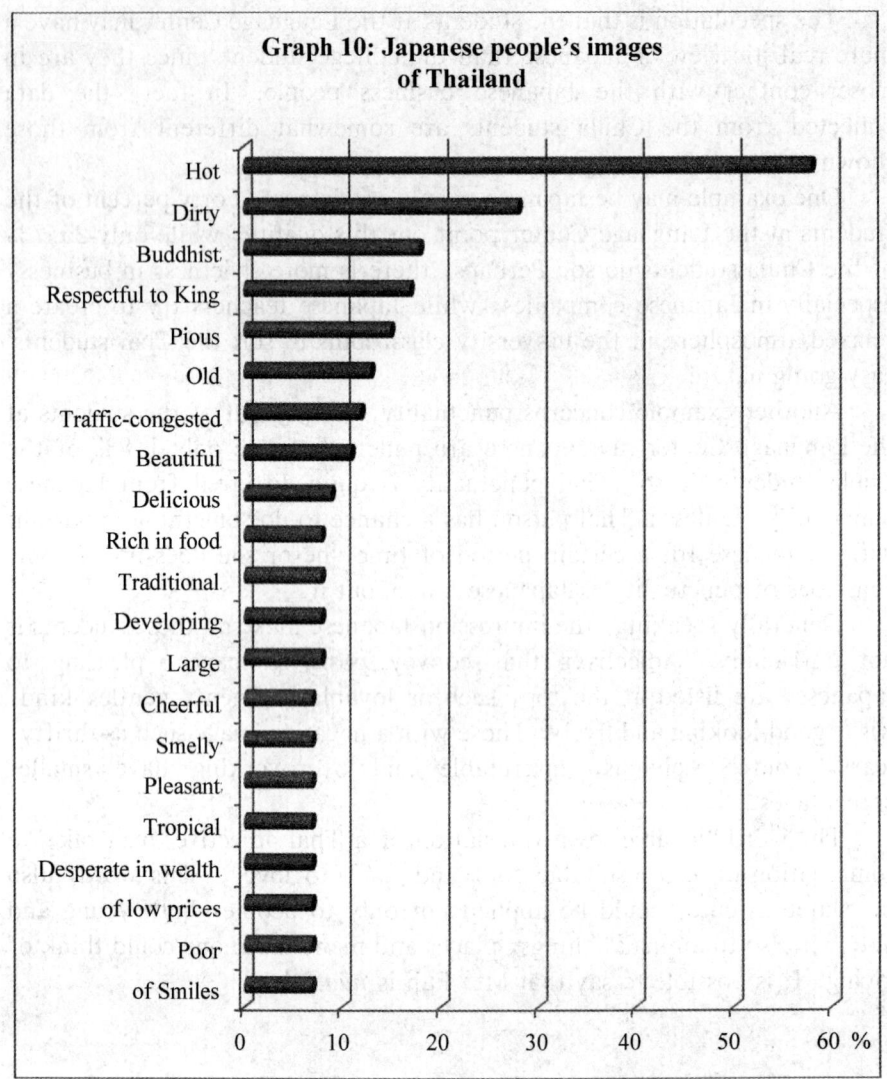

Graph 11 indicates Japanese people's images of Thai people. According to this graph, to Japanese people, Thai people appear to be pious probably because they visit the temple very often, but they are also irresponsible, saying "mai pen rai" all the time. "Mai pen rai" is a useful phrase for Thai people and it works in many ways, but here Japanese people most probably take it as "never mind" or "que sera sera" to ease one's pain or get rid of embarrassment in a difficult situation. In this context, Japanese consider Thai people as refusing to take the responsibility of what they have or haven't done such as mistakes and broken promises. Thai people appear to be shrewd and selfish because they refuse to face what seems to a Japanese to be a serious trouble again by saying "mai pen rai." They also appear to be gentle, cheerful, always smiling and easy-going, and they seem to live a very idle life, not being so diligent as Japanese.

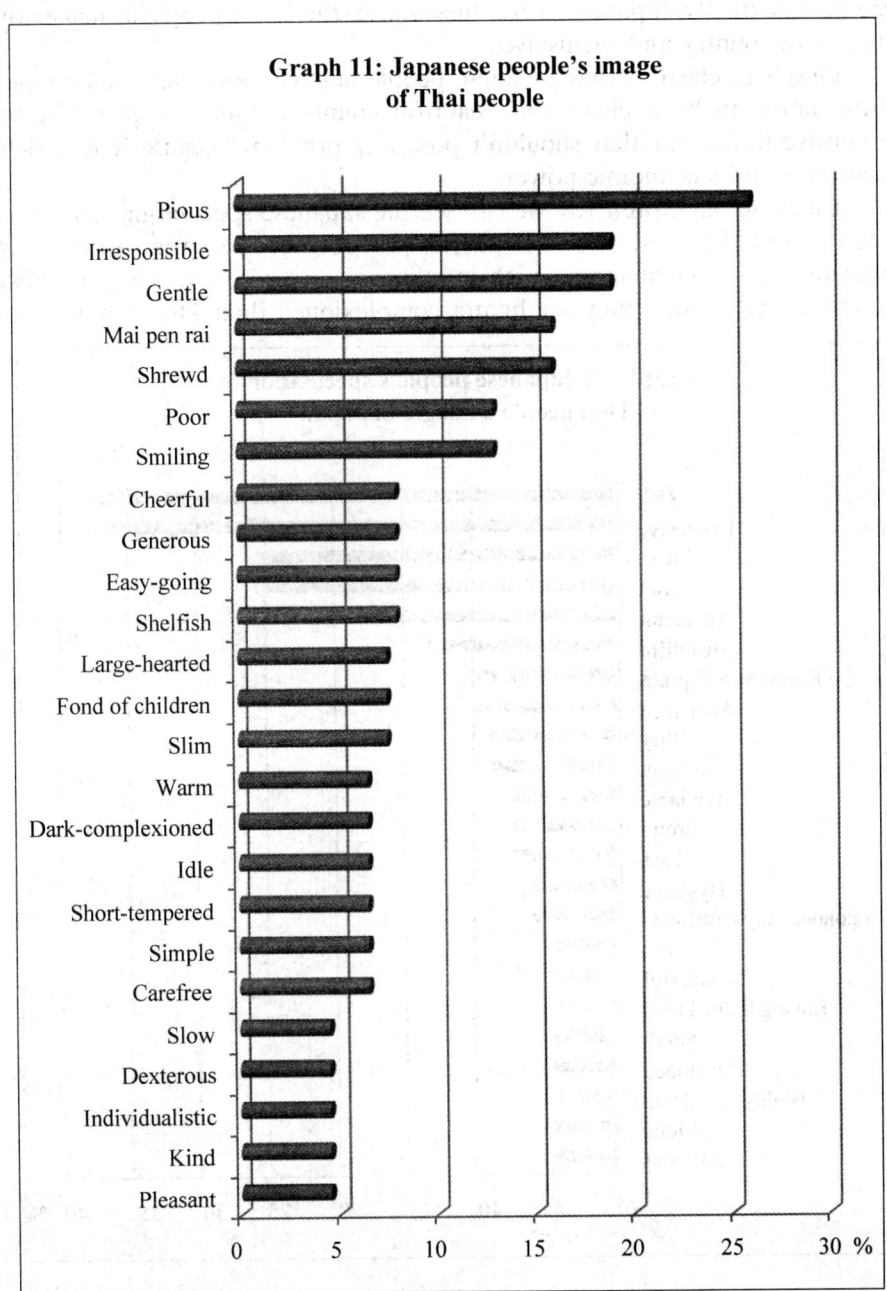

Graphs 12 and 13 are the results of having asked the Japanese people what they thought Thai people might answer if they were asked to give adjectives to modify Japan and Japanese. The intent of this question was to see how correctly Japanese were guessing at the Thai people's images of their own country and themselves.

Graph 12 clarifies that Japanese people believe most that Thai people think Japan to be a clean and beautiful country. Japan is abundant in expensive things but that shouldn't pose any problem because it is a rich country with its economic power.

Likewise, in Graph 13, we can see the Japanese speculation that Thai people think Japanese are rich people probably because they work in a diligent and serious manner, with intelligence and wisdom. They are also good-looking because they are lighter complexioned than Thai people.

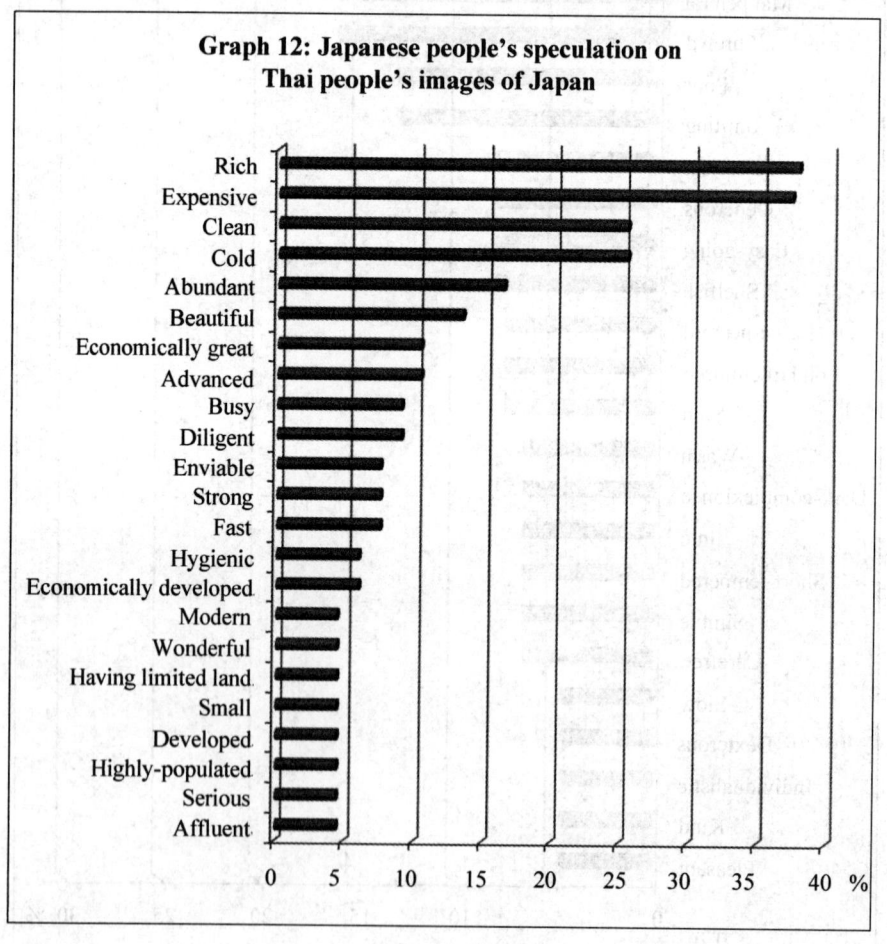

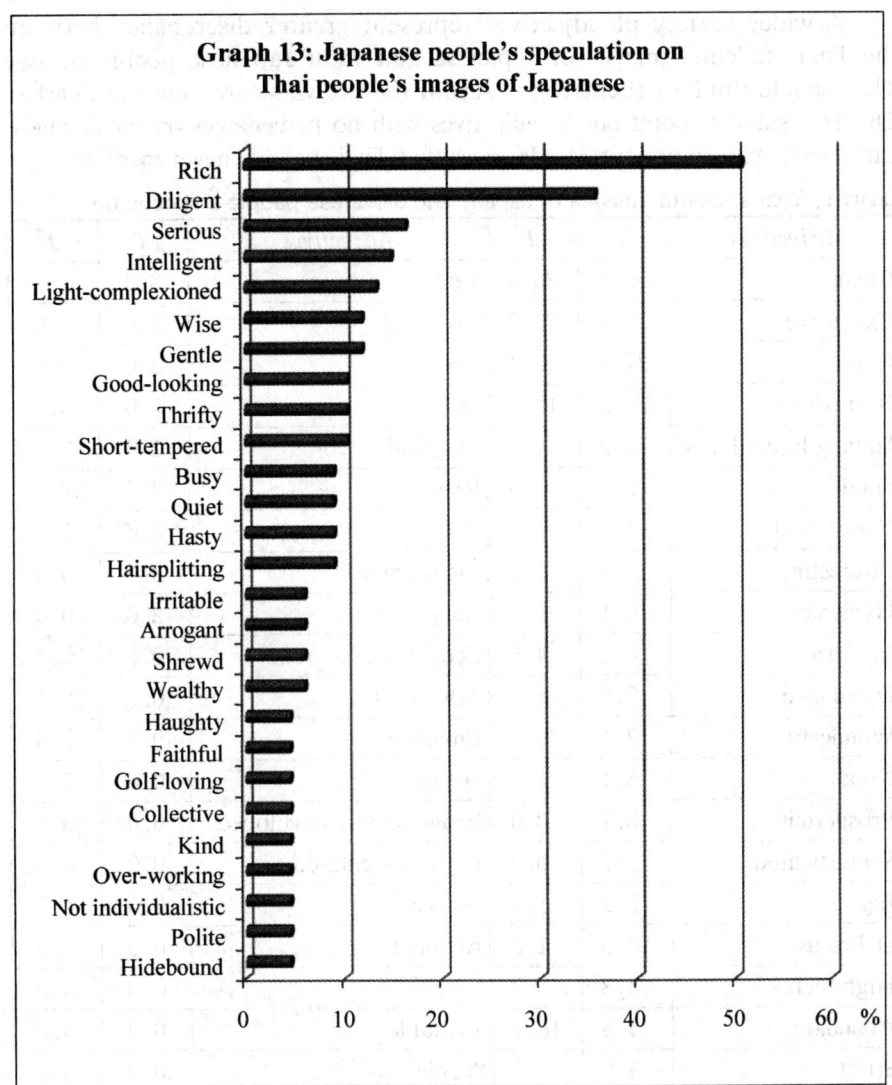

A Comparison of the Two Views

Naturally yet interestingly, the images Thai people hold of Japan and Japanese partially contradict the image Japanese people believe Thai people have. The Japanese people's guess and the actual reactions of the Thai students are presented in Chart 1 with the percentage of people who pointed out each adjective. The Thai students point out 7 adjectives that no Japanese think of while Japanese people have 18 adjectives on the list that no Thai pointed out.

A wider variety of adjectives represent greater discrepancy between the Thai students' images of Japanese and what Japanese people believe Thai people think of themselves. Again, the two views are shown in Chart 2. The Thai students point out 12 adjectives with no percentages on the Japanese part, and Japanese present 24 adjectives that Thai students never mention.

Chart 1: Thai students' images of Japan, and Japanese people's speculation

Adjectives	T	J	Adjectives	T	J
Clean	60.9	25.4	Safe	3.0	1.5
Expensive	28.7	37.3	Crowded	3.0	3.0
Cold	27.8	25.4	Cool	3.0	0.0
Beautiful	23.5	13.4	Old	3.0	0.0
Having limited land	20.9	4.5	Plentiful	2.6	3.0
Small	16.1	4.5	Rich	2.6	37.8
Convenient	11.7	1.5	Orderly	2.6	1.5
Interesting	10.9	3.0	Light-colored	2.6	0.0
Hygienic	9.1	6.0	Long	2.6	0.0
Modern	8.3	4.5	Economically great	0.0	10.4
Developed	7.8	4.5	Advanced	0.0	10.4
Wonderful	7.4	4.5	Enviable	0.0	7.5
Good	6.1	1.5	Strong	0.0	7.5
Prosperous	5.7	0.0	Economically developed	0.0	6.0
Sophisticated	5.7	0.0	Highly-populated	0.0	4.5
Big	5.2	1.5	Serious	0.0	4.5
Delicious	4.8	1.5	Affluent	0.0	4.5
High-tech	4.8	3.0	New	0.0	3.0
Abundant	4.8	16.4	Visitable	0.0	3.0
Strict	4.3	1.5	Scenic	0.0	3.0
Lively	4.3	0.0	Industrialized	0.0	3.0
Fast	4.3	7.5	Of Imperial Household	0.0	3.0
Famous	4.3	1.5	Scary	0.0	3.0
Busy	3.9	9.0	Of High-quality goods	0.0	3.0
Lovable	3.9	1.5	Near	0.0	3.0
Diligent	3.5	9.0	Of electric goods	0.0	3.0
Far	3.5	3.0	Of Tokyo	0.0	3.0

Note: T stands for Thai students, and J stands for Japanese people.

Chart 2: Thai students' images of Japanese, and Japanese people's speculation

Adjectives	T	J	Adjectives	T	J
Lovable	53.8	1.5	Hard-working	3.4	3.0
Strict	40.0	1.5	Earnest	3.4	1.5
Diligent	36.1	35.8	Lonely	2.6	0.0
Serious	30.8	16.4	Inscrutable	2.6	0.0
Gentle	25.6	11.9	Over-working	2.6	4.5
Busy	17.9	9.0	Intelligent	1.7	14.9
Kind	15.4	4.5	Short-tempered	0.0	10.4
Wise	15.4	11.9	Hasty	0.0	9.0
Good-looking	14.5	10.4	Hairsplitting	0.0	9.0
Lively	9.4	0.0	Irritable	0.0	6.0
Thrifty	8.5	10.4	Arrogant	0.0	6.0
Quiet	7.7	9.0	Shrewd	0.0	6.0
Light-complexioned	7.7	13.4	Wealthy	0.0	6.0
Skillful	7.7	1.5	Haughty	0.0	4.5
Fast	7.7	1.5	Faithful	0.0	4.5
Short	6.8	1.5	Golf-loving	0.0	4.5
Scary	6.0	1.5	Collective	0.0	4.5
Polite	6.0	4.5	Not individualistic	0.0	4.5
Punctual	6.0	1.5	Hidebound	0.0	4.5
Patient	6.0	1.5	Smiling	0.0	3.0
Rich	6.0	50.7	Bothersome	0.0	3.0
Orderly	6.0	0.0	Great	0.0	3.0
Cold	6.0	0.0	Tyrannical	0.0	3.0
Shy	4.3	0.0	Spoony	0.0	3.0
Fashionable	4.3	0.0	Anxious for buying	0.0	3.0
Doing-their-best	4.3	0.0	Inelastic	0.0	3.0
Lascivious	4.3	3.0	Family-minded	0.0	3.0
Calm	3.4	0.0	Nagging	0.0	3.0
Interesting	3.4	0.0	Restless	0.0	3.0
Smart in Action	3.4	0.0	Selfish	0.0	3.0
Small	3.4	0.0			

Note: T stands for Thai students, and J stands for Japanese people.

The adjectives for the image of Japan with most contrastive percentages between Thai and Japanese people are presented in Graph 14. Some adjectives such as "clean" and "having limited land" obtained high percentages from the Thai students while Japanese did not so much expect Thai people to think so. On the other hand, the adjective "rich" got a very high percentage from the Japanese while the Thai percentage was not worth mentioning. Generally speaking, Japanese people seem to be very much conscious of their country's economy, which is reflected in the high percentages of adjectives such as "rich," "abundant," and "economically great."

Graph 14: Contrastive adjectives (images of Japan)

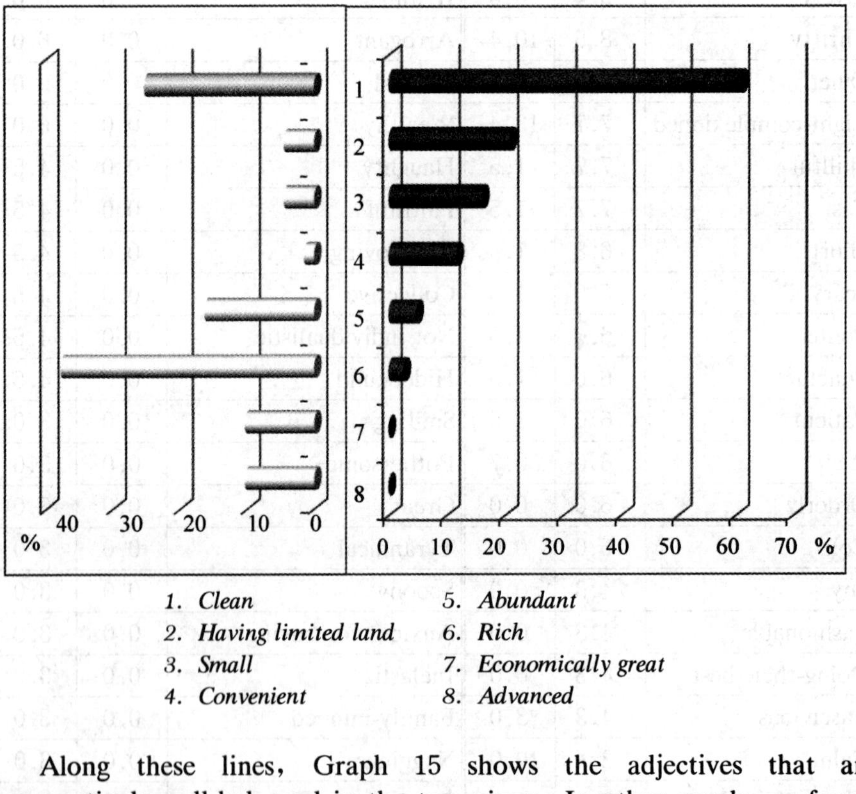

1. Clean
2. Having limited land
3. Small
4. Convenient
5. Abundant
6. Rich
7. Economically great
8. Advanced

Along these lines, Graph 15 shows the adjectives that are comparatively well-balanced in the two views. In other words, as far as these adjectives are concerned, Japanese people's grasp of their own image for the Thai students is to the point. The two prominent adjectives are "expensive," and "cold." Both of these adjectives represent rather obvious and observable contrastive aspects of the two countries.

Graph 15: Well-balanced adjectives (images of Japan)

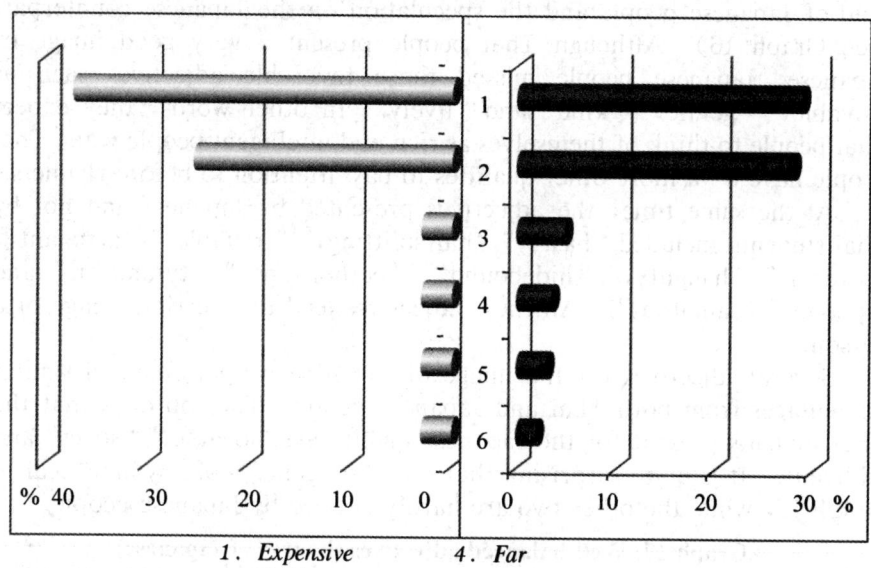

1. Expensive
2. Cold
3. High-tech
4. Far
5. Crowded
6. Plentiful

Graph 16: Contrastive adjectives (images of Japanese people)

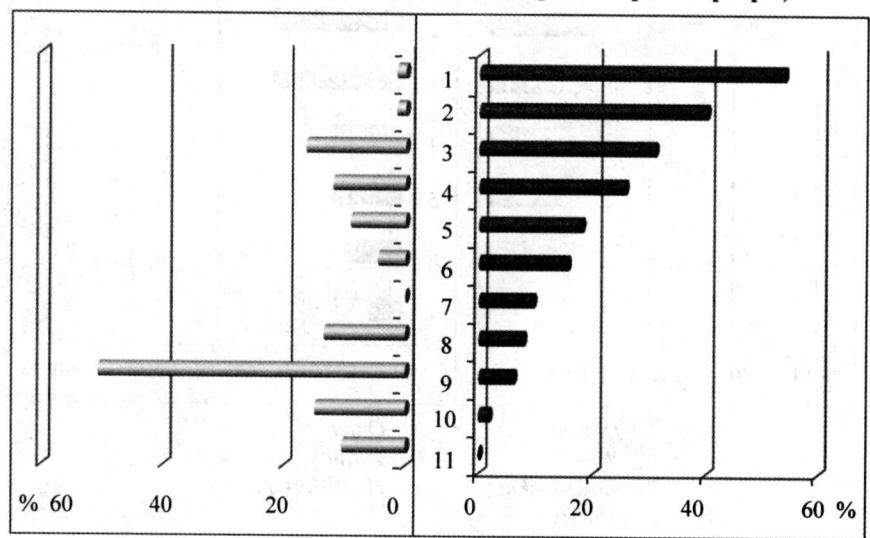

1. Lovable
2. Strict
3. Serious
4. Gentle
5. Busy
6. Kind
7. Lively
8. Light-complexioned
9. Rich
10. Intelligent
11. Short-tempered

A greater discrepancy is found between the actual image Thai people hold of Japanese people and the speculation on the Japanese counterpart (see Graph 16). Although Thai people present a very good image of Japanese, Japanese people missed those favorable adjectives such as "lovable," "gentle," "kind" and "lively." In other words, they expect Thai people to think of themselves as rich and intelligent people when Thai people have a lot more other qualities to pay attention to before richness.

At the same time, the adjectives presented by Japanese and not by Thai students included "hasty," "hairsplitting," "irritable," "arrogant," "shrewd," "haughty," "hidebound," "bothersome," "tyrannical" and "spooney" ("amorous"). All these adjectives lead to a terrible image of a person.

Several adjectives for the image of Japanese people obtained similar percentages from both Thai and Japanese people. The top ones that the Thai students present for the Japanese quality are "lovable," "strict" and "diligent." It is quite surprising that only "diligent" looks symmetrical in Graph 17, while the other two are hardly noticed by Japanese people.

Graph 17: Well-balanced adjectives (images of Japanese)

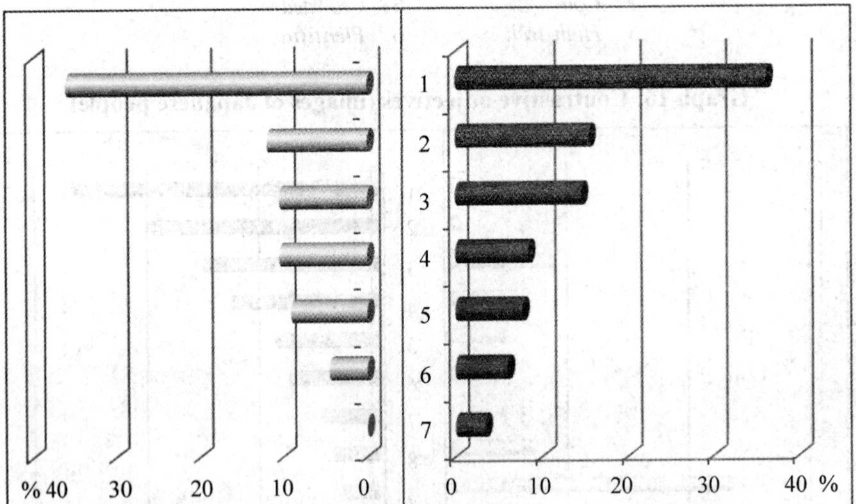

1. Diligent
2. Wise
3. Good-looking
4. Thrifty
5. Quiet
6. Polite
7. Hard-working

Conclusion

I did not expect the two kinds of reaction to look perfectly alike and symmetrical. There exist differences between the norms and criteria of the people judging each other, and one phenomenon can never be described in the same way from different cultural backgrounds. Also, there is a problem of translation. Approximately 70% of the Thai students' adjectives were translated from Thai into English by a Thai professor of English at Chulalongkorn University and 30% were written in Japanese by the students and translated by the author into English. All the Japanese people's adjectives were written by the respondents in Japanese and were translated into English by the author. The original meanings could be lost in such translation work, however carefully it might be done. Excluding these variables as much as possible, I would like to look for ways to help Japanese people to reflect upon themselves in a more meaningful way in Bangkok, and at the same time, to improve the images they have of Thai people in order for Japanese to establish a better relationship with Thai people.

The Japanese society in Bangkok is never small. Approximately 30,000 Japanese are said to be living in Thailand, a great majority residing in Bangkok. More than 1,000 companies are registered as members of the Japanese Chamber of Commerce and Industry in Bangkok (as of March, 1996), most of the 9,000 members of the Japanese Association in Thailand are the residents of the Bangkok area, and the Japanese School in Bangkok has an enrollment of 1,800 elementary and junior high students (as of July, 1996). There are also cram schools for these children to get them prepared for entrance exams back in Japan. A telephone communication network is well-established for all the members of the Japanese Association in Thailand.

Surprisingly, interviews with Japanese business people and their spouses revealed that their interactions with Thai people are quite limited. The business people may be working with their Thai colleagues in the office, but important things are discussed with a very few English-speaking Thai managers in English, who will give orders and directions to other Thai workers in Thai. After office hours and during weekends, hardly any personal relationship is maintained between Thai and Japanese people. Colleagues as they may be, they are not personal friends. Although those English-speaking Thai managers are efficient, the rest are considered to be lazy and irresponsible.

Most Japanese families employ a maid and a driver at home. This is partially because the Thai government encourages foreign residents to hire Thai workers to provide them with employment opportunities. Also, many Japanese companies forbid wives to drive in Bangkok for safety's sake. The mothers send their children to the Japanese School, and it is almost impossible to make Thai friends through their children's association.

On arriving in Bangkok, Japanese wives are eager to study Thai and soon make it a rule to spend several hours of the week at a language school for Thai lessons, but not many continue to the advanced level or until they can read and write in Thai. They soon find out that all they need is a handful of phrases to tell the maid to do things, tell the driver to go to places, place an order at a restaurant, and ask a vendor to give them a discount in town.

As some interviewees confessed, both Japanese men and women have formed their images of Thailand and Thai people most probably through observation, through what they see from their automobile windows on the streets, and through how their employees work at home. Many people lack actual exchanges of thoughts and shared experiences with Thai people.

It has already been mentioned above that the Thai students in this research are the people who will have the closest relationship with Japanese business people and their spouses staying in Bangkok. They might be so in the future, but as far as these Japanese people are concerned at this moment, it does not seem to be the case.

Many interviewees say Japanese and Thai people do not have a language in common. It has to be stressed, however, that they do have a language in common. Most Japanese businessmen in Bangkok are college graduates and probably all their wives have at least a high school diploma. That means they have studied English for a long time before arriving in Thailand. Even in countries where English is commonly spoken, Japanese are notorious for not speaking up in English when they do understand the language. The tendency seems to be even more prominent in Bangkok, partially because of the minute Japanese network. It should be lamented if the Japanese sense of economic superiority does not allow them to have a friendly and carefree relationship with the local people and prevents them from making use of English as a language for communication because they feel ashamed of making mistakes. Whatever the reasons may be, it is evident that the English language is not used effectively by either Japanese or Thai people. Thailand also has people who have studied English, such as the students in this research, and many of them are in Bangkok.

If these Japanese business people and their spouses stopped wasting their English proficiency, they could widen their field of activity by getting out of their own intimate circle. Then they are sure to begin to see different aspects of Thailand and Thai people. A Thai behavior will have a different meaning, a better meaning, if a person observing it actually experiences the Thai value behind it. Many Japanese have studied English and read about the Thai culture before coming to Bangkok. Once they are in the city, they observe objectively the behavioral patters and confirm that what they have known about the culture is true. Learning through personal interactions and experiences, however, will lead to real understanding and empathy, a condition which they have not yet achieved. When Japanese people who are lucky enough to have plenty of opportunities to learn a lot in Bangkok really take advantage of those opportunities, the graphs presented here should look different. For this process to take place, the English language is indispensable.

References

Honna, N. & Y. Takeshita. (1996). Teaching Japanese as an International Language in Asia — A Case Study in Thailand. In *kokusai komyunikeshon ni okeru gengo to bunka*. (Language and Culture Issues in International Communication) Monograph Series No. 6. Center for Research in the International Studies, Research Institute of Aoyama Gakuin University.

Takeshita, Y. (2005). Nihonjin to taijin no komyunikeshion: bankoku-ni okeru chosa-wo chushin-ni (Communication between Japanese and Thai People: The study of awareness in Bangkok). In Y. Takeshita & T. Ishikawa (Eds.), *tabunka-to jibunka: kokusai komyunikeshion-no jidai* (Multi-cultures and Our Own Cultures: The age of international communication) (pp. 56-75). Tokyo: Shinwasha.

Takeshita, Y. (2006). Intercultural communication between Thai and Japanese people: A survey in Bangkok. In *Intercultural Communication Studies: Special Issue, Volume XV: 3*, pp. 150-159.

Management of Conflict

22

Analyzing an Intercultural Conflict Case Study: Application of a Social Ecological Perspective

Ruifang ZHANG and Stella TING-TOOMEY[*]
California State University, Fullerton, USA

Abstract: Intercultural conflict is a multilayered and multi-contextual phenomenon. While past intercultural studies tend to use either a macro-level lens or a micro-level view to analyze intercultural conflict, this paper argues for the merits of using a social ecological perspective in analyzing a complex intercultural conflict situation. A real-life intercultural conflict case study, the "Anna Mae He Intercultural Conflict Story," will be used to illustrate the heuristic value of the social ecological model. The essay will end with a discussion of future theorizing directions of the social ecological framework.

Frustrations during intercultural conflict often arise because of our lack of necessary and sufficient knowledge to deal with culture-based conflict communication issues competently. Our cultural ignorance oftentimes compounds an already tense conflict situation. Intercultural conflict is defined in this chapter as the perceived or actual incompatibility of cultural values, situational norms, goals, face orientations, scarce resources, processes, and/or outcomes in a face-to-face (or mediated) context (Ting-Toomey & Oetzel, 2001). The greater the cultural distance between the

---

[*] Ruifang Zhang (M.A., 2009, California State University, Fullerton) is a master degree student. Stella Ting-Toomey (Ph.D., 1981, University of Washington) is a Professor in the Department of Human Communication Studies at California State University at Fullerton.

two conflict parties, the more likely the assessment of the conflict interaction process would be misconstrued. These cultural membership distances may include deep-level differences such as historical grievances, cultural worldviews, and beliefs. Concurrently, they may also include the mismatch of applying different normative expectations in a particular conflict episode.

This chapter is organized in four sections: First, the benefits of a social ecological perspective to explain a complex intercultural conflict case will be explored. Second, the core themes and concepts of the social ecological framework will be introduced. Third, primary social ecological theoretical concepts will be applied to explain a real-life intercultural conflict case, the "Anna Mae He Intercultural Conflict Story." Fourth, the chapter will end with a discussion on the future directions of research into intercultural conflict communication issues from the combined social ecological and face-negotiation lens.

Benefits of a Social Ecological Perspective: A Multilevel Theory

General Benefits of Multilevel Theorizing

There are a number of benefits of multilevel theorizing (see Slater, Snyder, & Hayes, 2006). Research or practice that focuses on any single level will, by definition, underestimates the effects of other contexts (Klein, Tosi, & Cannella, 1999; Stokols, 1996). The tendency in the intercultural conflict field is to focus on single case micro-level analyses or to bemoan the context-free nature of intercultural conflict quantitative studies. In addition, intercultural or international conflict experts either focus their research analysis on micro conflict processes (e.g., individual behaviors) or macro conflict processes (e.g., social structures and institutional dominance). In contrast, multilevel theorizing focuses on understanding themes and concepts at multiple levels as well as between different levels.

Multilevel theorizing fosters synthesis and synergy, creates links and loops where there were none before, and also illuminates reciprocal contextual influences. For example, in the study of intercultural conflict, Ting-Toomey and Oetzel (2001) developed a culture-sensitive situational model to explain the primary socialization factors, situational and relational boundary features, conflict communication process factors, and intercultural conflict competence dimensions to explain the macro-micro situational nature of explaining intercultural conflict. Situational and relational features are viewed as the mediating factors that link primary socialization factors and conflict process factors (Ting-Toomey, 2005). Oetzel, Arcos, Mabizela, Weinman, and Zhang (2006), using a multilevel theorizing process, analyzed the conflict patterns of the Muslim, Chinese, Colombian, and South African cultural worlds. They identified both the macro-level factors such as historical, spiritual, and political factors, and the micro-level factors such as facework meanings and harmony ideals, in shaping major conflict viewpoints in the different cultures.

Contextual Benefits of Multilevel Theorizing

A multilevel, contextual perspective in analyzing an intercultural conflict case provides the opportunity to understand (and possibly challenge) what are the deeply-held assumptions of a particular cultural conflict worldview or practice. A multilevel theorizing process may illustrate that a particular intercultural conflict case contains both consistencies and inconsistencies at multiple levels of analysis. Additionally, a multilevel perspective helps to illustrate the multitude of factors that shape system-level, community-level, workplace-level, and individual-level conflict interpretations within and across distinct levels.

More specifically, in utilizing a social ecological multilevel theoretical framework, there are four levels of research analytical units: macro, exo, meso, and micro-level analysis. The "macro-level" analysis refers to the larger sociocultural contexts, beliefs, values, ideologies, and worldviews that shape the individual outlooks and the various embedded systems under this broad umbrella. The term "exo-level" analysis refers to the larger environmental-level social webs or institutions with fairly established policies, norms, standards, and formal practices in place. These exo contexts (i.e., external environments) often have mediated and filtered (as versus direct) influence on the individual behaviors and reactions. On the other hand, the "meso-level" analysis refers to the immediate systems such as family unit, parent's workplace unit, or local church unit that have a direct impact on the individual's behaviors and the occurring interpersonal relationship dynamics. It also emphasizes the important interface or connections between the various systems (e.g., family stress influences workplace stress, and vice versa). Finally, the "micro-level" analysis refers to both the intrapersonal (i.e., personal and social identity-based issues, attributions, and emotions) and interpersonal-level features (e.g., peer group interactions, or face-to-face encounters) and the actual settings in which the individuals live out their daily lives. It also emphasizes the importance of how individuals act as active agents to construct meanings and interpretations of a given communication event (Brofenbenner, 1979; Oetzel, Ting-Toomey, & Rinderle, 2006). Brofenbenner (1979) viewed these four social ecological contexts as nested Russian dolls with reciprocal causal effects influencing each sphere. In addition to the macrosystem, exosystem, mesosystem, and microsystem of analysis, he later added a fifth context, the "chronosystem-level" of analysis — his level refers to the evolution phases, transitions, patterns, and consequences of developmental change over time.

Multilevel theorizing approaches such as the social ecological framework and the meso-level conceptual analysis have been implemented in other fields such as family systems (Brofenbrenner, 1977, 1979; Huston, 2000), organizational behavior (e.g., Klein, Tosi, & Cannella, 1999; Rousseau & House, 1994), and public health (e.g., Gregson, 2001; Williams & Williams-Morris 2000). More recently, organizational and interpersonal communication researchers (e.g., Myers & McPhee, 2006; Oetzel, Dhar, & Kirschbaum, 2007; Oetzel & Duran, 2004; Theiss & Solomon, 2006) have also begun to pay close attention to the importance of multilevel theorizing in understanding the complexity of human behavior on embedded contexts.

Social Ecological Framework: Core Themes and Concepts

The social ecological framework is an interdisciplinary approach that gained momentum in the mid 1960s and early 1970s to better address the influences of cultural and social contexts on human behavior and development (Brofenbrenner, 1977, 1979; Stokols, 1996). In family communication, for example, Ihinger-Tallman and Cooney (2005) used the social ecological framework to discuss the family system both as an institution and as a small group and to describe how the study of family should be understood within the nested historical, social class, and racial contexts. In the health care communication setting, for example, violent behaviors within intimate partner relationships in Native American communities were analyzed via macro, meso, and micro connective factors (Oetzel & Duran, 2004).

In the intercultural acculturation area, Kim (2001, 2005) used a macro-micro systems perspective to explain immigrants' adaptation and change processes in a new cultural milieu and emphasized the interdependent effects of multiple-level contextual factors. In the coordinated management of meaning theorizing process, Pearce (2005) used concepts such as "culture," "episode," "self," and "relationship" to connote the importance of macro-exo-micro level of understanding concerning intercultural meaning coordination process. Ting-Toomey and Takai (2006) identified several theoretical models that hold potential promise to explain macro-level and micro-level intergroup conflicts in embedded, layered contexts.

Social Ecological Perspective: Core Principles and Analytical Concepts

On a broad level, Stokols (1996) explains that the social ecological perspective consists of five core principles. First, communication outcomes are influenced by the cumulative effects of multiple physical, cultural, social, and temporal factors. Second, communication outcomes are also affected by individual attributes and specific situations. Third, social ecology incorporates concepts from systems theory, such as interdependence and homeostasis, and also to further understand the relationship between individuals and their broader contexts. Fourth, social ecology recognizes not only the interconnections among multiple settings, but also the interdependence of conditions within particular settings. Fifth, the social ecological perspective is interdisciplinary, involves multilevel domain analysis, and incorporates diverse methodologies. The key analytical concepts under the social ecological perspective are parallels and discontinuities, and cross-level effects.

Parallels and Discontinuities

In examining the reciprocal causation between the individual and the environment (e.g., intergroup conflict in a community setting), two specific types of relationships between and among levels of analysis can be probed: (a) parallels and discontinuities, and (b) cross-level effects (Klein et al., 1999; Rousseau & House, 1994). On the "parallels and discontinuities" relationship type, *parallel models* (also known as *isomorphic models*) posit that the relationship between and among variables (e.g., concepts such as apology and forgiveness) at one level (e.g., interpersonal reaction level) will be the same or similar at another level (e.g., the larger institutional / governmental reaction level) in terms of magnitude and direction. In contrast, when different types of relationships or reactions are found among concepts at different (or in opposite direction) levels, these are described as *discontinuities*.

Cross-level Effects

On the "*cross-level*" relationship type, studying intercultural conflict at any single level underestimates the fact that individuals, organizations, communities, and cultures are interconnected. Multilevel theorizing is influenced by the principles of interdependence and hierarchy from general systems theory. General systems theory emphasizes that different analytical levels are nested structures organized hierarchically. Given this assumption, three types of cross-level effects should be considered: (a) top-down effects, (b) bottom-up effects, and (c) interactive effects (Rousseau & House, 1994).

Top-down effects refer to how the larger cultural / institutional forces shape the intercultural conflict stance or practice — from the macro, the exo, the meso, to the micro level. From this top-down effect viewpoint, individual conflict ideologies and practices are shaped by the various layered structures in which people are nested hierarchically (e.g., does the larger cultural worldview or institutional level emphasize the communication phenomenon of apology or forgiveness and does the effect spill downward to the lower levels?). *Bottom-up effects* focus on how lower levels (e. g., individuals and interpersonal relationships) affect higher levels (e.g., workplace, institutional webs, and then culture). These types of effects are not as prevalent in the literature as are top-down, but they are no less important. *Interactive effects* involve simultaneous and mutual effects at more than one level. In some cases, the effects of one level (e.g., culture) moderate the outcomes at another level (e. g., family policies). Top-down or bottom-up effects differ from interactive effects in that the former assumes some sort of cumulative effect passing down (or up) from one level to the next in a systematic fashion, and that interactive effects assume simultaneous process impacts at multiple contextual levels.

Social Ecological Theory Application: The Anna Mae He Custody Case

Before we apply the social ecological framework step-by-step, let us examine the following real-life case study. A case study approach is used in this chapter because the use of a case study method can serve three important functions: (1) provide a context to translate a relevant theory to explain a complex communication phenomenon; (2) offer an opportunity to connect the practical utility of a dynamic theory to account for the layered complexities of a real-life social interaction situation, and (3) illuminate the contextual nature of conflict communication and the possible generation of practical strategies in addressing the problems (Braithwaite & Wood, 2000; Ellet, 2007). The factual, chronological history of the following Anna Mae He conflict case story is pieced together from the diverse sources listed in NOTE 1.

Anna Mae He: An Intercultural Conflict Case Story.

Anna Mae He, a baby girl, was at the center of a seven-year high-profile custody storm between her Chinese biological parents, ***Jack He*** and ***Casey Luo***, and her American foster parents, ***Jerry Baker*** and ***Louise Baker***. She was born January 28, 1999, in Memphis, Tennessee.

Shortly after Anna Mae He's birth in Memphis, Jack and Casey ran into legal and financial difficulties. Due to an unfounded sexual assault charge directed at Jack He by a fellow Chinese international student (Xiaojun Qi) at the University of Memphis, Jack He lost his graduate assistant job and graduate stipend at the university (he was ultimately found not guilty). Due to this, the entire family suddenly lost the financial support and the crucial health insurance for the baby girl. Anna Mae He had been born prematurely and incurred a medical bill of $12,000 at that point. The Chinese parents, Jack He and Casey Luo, were in desperate need of insurance help for Anna Mae He and they also worried about the daily care-taking of their baby girl. Via the recommendation of the Juvenile Court, they sought help from an adoption agency, the Mid-South Christian Service, and tried to find a foster family to take care of Anna Mae He temporarily.

Upon meeting Jerry and Louise Baker, the Chinese parents decided to entrust their baby girl with them. Mr. Baker was at that point employed by Pinnfund USA as a mortgage banker, and he earned approximately $435,000 annually and lived in a nice suburb with his wife, Louise. Jack He and Casey Luo felt they had met a kind couple, and they signed over a temporary 90-day custody order to this Memphis couple. The baby girl, Anna Mae He, henceforth, lived with her foster parents, the Bakers. Within the span of three months, the Bakers developed a strong attachment to the baby. And for the next eight years, Anna Mae was raised by the Bakers. She was brought up as an all-American girl, eating American foods, attending American school, and watching American TV programs. According to the description on ABC news (2008, February 7), "Anna thinks Hannah Montana is cool (but cannot tell you why); she skates on retractable roller skate shoes, and she plays Game Boy every now and then." Her best friend was the Baker's youngest daughter, Aimee, who was only 13 months younger than Anna Mae. They grew up as sisters during Anna Mae's first eight years.

During these years, many interactions between the Bakers and the Hes occurred, along with multiple court involvements. Back in the months of May and June, 1999, due to false sexual assault accusations against Jack He, the Chinese parents were in total distress and they started to renegotiate the custody terms with the Bakers and to extend foster care for Anna Mae He (A. M. H.). However, repeatedly, both Chinese parents emphasized the importance of not losing their parental rights over their infant daughter.

Meanwhile, the Bakers were actually not interested in being temporary foster parents to Anna Mae He — they wanted to adopt Anna Mae He formally as their own child, despite her parents' consistent objections. The Juvenile Court of Shelby County representative, Ms. Cloud, explained to Jack He and Casey Luo that "if the Bakers later refused to return custody of A. M. H. to them, they would have to go to court and let the judge decide whether they could have custody of A. M. H. returned to them." The Chinese mother, Casey Luo, emphatically expressed that she did not intend to place Ana Mae for adoption, but only desired to place A. M. H. in temporary custody with the Bakers until they got back on their feet financially. They then signed the Consent Order Awarding Custody of Anna Mae He to the Bakers.

On September 20, 1999, the University of Memphis decided to suspend Jack He from taking any further classes from the university. Jack thus lost his status as an international student and was subject to deportation. In November, 1999, Jack He asked Mr. Baker to return Anna Mae He back to their family. Mr. Baker told Jack He and Casey Luo that he would not return Ana Mae and also told Jack not to mention his request because Mrs. Baker was pregnant at the time. On May 3, 2000, Jack and Casey went to the Juvenile Court of Shelby County and signed a petition alleging a change in circumstances and seeking custody of Anna Mae He. On May 4, 2000, Jack He and Jerry Baker met at the Hes' apartment. Jack He told Jerry Baker that his wife, Casey Luo, was preparing to file the Petition to Modify Custody form and make changes to the Anna Mae's custody agreement. Jack He also told Jerry Baker that they wanted to send Anna Mae He back to China to live with their relatives until they settled their financial difficulties in America. Upon hearing the news, Jerry Baker became enormously upset and expressed that he would do everything possible to prevent the Chinese parents from sending Anna Mae He back to China. From the Baker's viewpoint, they thought they could offer Anna Mae a better and more comfortable life in Memphis. They filed a petition to adopt her, and to terminate the Hes' parental rights (ABC News, 2008, February 7). On June 28, 2000, the Juvenile Court denied the Petition to Modify Custody plea from Jack He and Casey Luo.

On January 28, 2001, it was Anna Mae He's second birthday. Jack He and Casey Luo wanted to take the child out for a family portrait. However, when they arrived at the Bakers' house, they were told that Anna Mae could not go because she was sick. The Hes then became upset and angry, started raising their voices and Casey Luo started screaming and crying. The Bakers asked them to leave; they refused. Then the police were summoned to remove them physically and told them not to return. The police issued a "no contact" order, stopping the Hes from any further contact, direct or indirect, with Anna Mae. As the Hes argued later in the court, they were afraid of being deported from the U.S., thus they dared not violate the "no contact" order from the police for the next many months.

On February 15, 2001, Jack He sent another petition to the Juvenile Court for custody of Anna Mae He and he also contacted the media and set forth the history of the case. In the same year, the Bakers petitioned the Chancery Court to adopt Anna Mae. They accused both Jack and Casey of "willful abandonment" of the child and declared that the couple had a "lack of financial ability." On February 7, 2002, the Chancery Court ordered the biological parents to surrender Anna Mae He's passport to the court and to pay a fee of $15,000 for the guardian *ad litem's* fees and costs for Jack He's DNA test and psychological evaluations. The Juvenile Court also further ordered that the Chinese parents should have no more direct contact with their daughter. In July of 2002, a Dr. Goldstein submitted a court report that claimed that the three-year-old Anna Mae He considered the Bakers as her psychological parents.

On September 23, 2003, Jack He and Casey Luo were allowed a brief visit with Anna Mae He. It had been two-and-a-half-years since they last saw Anna Mae. In 2004, Judge Robert Childers, a Tennessee circuit judge, terminated the Hes' legal parental rights to Anna Mae He on grounds of willful abandonment, despite the couple's persistent efforts to regain custody via numerous court appeals. At this point, Anna Mae He had turned five years old. She was raised to be a typical American girl — enjoying eating macaroni and cheese, playing with other American kids, and speaking only English. In the same year, the circuit court decision was affirmed by a majority in the Tennessee Court of Appeals. In October 2006, Jack He and Casey Luo subsequently appealed to the Tennessee Supreme Court. The Hes argued at the Tennessee Supreme Court that the trial court erred in terminating their parental rights. The Hes asked the High Court to rule on the custody issue directly — on how to interpret the word "temporary." In January 2007, the Tennessee Supreme Court, in a unanimous decision authored by Chief Justice William M. Barker, *finally* reversed the ruling by the state Court of Appeals and ordered that Anna Mae He be returned to her biological parents, Jack He and Casey Luo.

In February, 2008, Jack He, Casey Luo, and Anna Mae He returned to Changsha, Hunan Province of China, amidst the warm welcome of their families and extended families. Meanwhile, the eight-year-old Anna Mae He stood in bewilderment and curiosity, listening to all the foreign chatter, and absorbing the strange atmosphere of her ancestral homeland, China. Sadly, according to *China Daily* (6/1/2009), few months later, the Hes family was torn apart by the tough reality of re-entry and the endless disputes between the couple. In June, 2008, Casey Luo took the three children (Anna Mae He and her younger siblings, brother Andy and sister Avita) back to her hometown, Chongqing, and started a new life there.

Cultural adjustment has been quite difficult for Anna Mae He, who is clearly uncomfortable with the language barrier and the strange Chinese customs, norms, and different education systems. She speaks only English to her family members and keeps silent at the private bilingual school. She is now in the third grade. Her mother says she is trying to help Anna Mae He to understand that she is both American and Chinese. She wants Anna Mae He to learn to speak Chinese and to learn to love the country's history and beautiful landscapes. "But I don't want to force Anna Mae to do anything," she says. "If she doesn't want to speak Chinese or eat Chinese food, that's fine. I know it will take a long time for her to feel like a Chinese" (*China Daily*, www.chinadaily.com, 2009, June 1).

Social Ecological Macro-Level Analysis

This level of analysis focuses our analytical attention on the broad-level political ideologies, cultural worldviews, and societal expectancy norms that pave the way to some of the recurring intercultural conflict patterns. In other words, this analytical level focuses on the "big picture" political climate, cultural-level values, and habitual cultural practices that are valued or rejected in an intercultural conflict episode. Let us first analyze the political climate and backdrop of the Anna Mae He's intercultural conflict case study.

In trying to understand the layered, complex issues such as this custody battle, the importance of how the larger political environment shapes the behavioral choices in the conflict parties cannot be underestimated. In this custody battle case, the Bakers' lawyer repeatedly attacked Jack He's personal credibility and his "lying" behavior concerning his marriage to Casey Luo. However, if we move beyond the win-lose orientation of the lawsuit case, and are willing to use a social ecological macro lens to analyze the background of the custody battle case, it would not be too difficult for us to see the interaction effect between the macro environment and the individual's decision-making behavior. The macro context includes the particular historical time, the place, and the political environment that frame this conflict case history.

Back in the 1990s, the former Soviet Union had just collapsed. Even though this communist giant had died, the U.S. government back then still believed that the communist threat continued to exist. From this historical lens, the U.S. government strictly controlled the number of the visas for Chinese international students, and paid extra attention to the students' majors. Usually, the visa application took three to six months if the students' majors were chemistry, biology, and physics — the so-called "sensitive majors." Jack studied Economics in Arizona State University. Even though his major did not belong to any of those sensitive majors, he still had his own worries and stressors. In the 1990s international education climate, if Chinese international students did not have a full scholarship, there would be only a very slim chance for those students to obtain a visa. At that time, the visa was just for a one-time-effective period, which meant that whenever the Chinese students left the U.S. territory and wanted to return, they had to reapply for a visa. And, very often, an obstacle or a roadblock would arise when they went to the embassy for the second time, thus preventing them from reentering the U.S. So once these international students left China, they rarely returned to China until they completed their degrees in the U.S.

From this backdrop context, it is not difficult to understand why Jack He sought different "creative" strategies to enter the U.S. for his graduate studies. From this context, one can see that the macro system affects individual behaviors and vice versa. The macro contrastive political ideologies and the different cultural value systems between China and the United States influenced how the conflict characters behaved in the various conflict scenes. These macro features also asserted a strong top-down effect on how the subsequent court system, the university system, and the individuals assessed each other's intentions, viewpoints, and also further perpetuated each other's negative stereotypes. The Bakers thought Jack He did not have any personal credibility because he lied about his marriage to Casey Luo. In the chronicle of this intercultural conflict battle, Jack He actually married "again" in 2002. Due to this reason, the Bakers' lawyer claimed that Jack He was not the actual father of Anna Mae He (who was born in 1999). Jack He was even asked to take a DNA test to prove his fatherhood.

If we take the time to trace back the ecological family timeline of this particular conflict case story, Jack He actually first got married in 1994 to his first wife and, together, they applied to study at the Northern Illinois University. His first wife got the visa, whereas his application was rejected. His first wife went to America by herself alone that year. Next year, Jack He got the visa, but only an F2 visa as the dependent spouse. When he arrived in America, his first wife wanted a divorce from him and the divorce was granted. Four months later, Jack He was accepted by Arizona State University and received a partial scholarship. In 1997, he applied to the University of Memphis and was offered a full scholarship.

After Jack He moved to Memphis, he started to consider a second marriage. A friend from Chongqing sent him some pictures. He was attracted to the photo of Casey Luo. Even though they did not get a chance to meet each other face-to-face, they wrote frequent letters, emails, and soon fell in love with each other. Normally, Jack He would go back to China, meet with Casey, pursue the romantic relationship, and then get married. However, Jack had his own worries. At that time in the 1990s, it was difficult if not impossible to receive an international student visa and many international students were unable to return to America from China once they left the U.S. Jack He was aware of this and he chose a "creative" strategy to get Casey Luo to join him in the U.S. He went to the International Office and asked for an I-20 form (which identifies a dependent spouse of an international student), completed the form, and sent the form back to Casey. However, luck was not with them. Casey Luo's visa application (as a dependent of an international student) was rejected. Jack He then returned to China and went to the U.S. Embassy with Casey Luo. This time, his own visa application was refused too. The couple then went to a different Chinese city and reapplied. Finally, they both got the entry visas to the U.S.

They did not apply for the marriage certificate then because Casey had already used the I-20 form in her previous application as a dependent spouse. If they applied for a new marriage certificate then, the timing would not match. So the couple left China without formally getting married. The fact that they were not officially married at the time of Anna Mae's birth and the "tricky" method Jack He used to enter United States became the prime target of attack raised by the Bakers' lawyer. The opposing attorney's ferociousness included aggressive attacks on Jack He's personal credibility and trustworthiness problems, his lying behavior, and his lies to the U. S. government. Jack He counter-argued that he just wanted to get Casey Luo to enter the U.S. and be by his side. The Bakers' attorney even argued that Jack was not the real father of Anna Mae He and thus he had to take a DNA test to prove his fatherhood.

From the macro-historical level of top-down analysis, we can see how the political and cultural ideologies of the time spilled over to the filtered lenses and actions engaged in by the contrastive conflict parties. The Bakers could not imagine how difficult it was to receive an entry visa to the U. S. They believed that anyone who would use gimmicks and tricks to get into the United State lacked the minimum credibility and was not trustworthy. The Hes, facing many rejection experiences before in their visa applications in China, justified their "cheating act" as a no-choice last resort action in order to stay together in the U. S. for both love and professional reasons. These views, in turn, spilled over to the institutional, community, and the individual level's reactions and standpoints.

Next, let us analyze further how some of the cultural values and norms clashed in this particular intercultural conflict case story. In this custody battle, one of the primary intercultural conflict episodes was the conflict interaction scene at the Bakers' house on Anna Mae He's second birthday. Her Chinese parents, Jack He and Casey Luo, wanted to take their daughter out for a family picture. In China, especially for individuals born before the 1980s, taking a family portrait together is a very important Chinese family tradition. Taking a family picture together — especially at certain important occasions such as when a baby is 30 days old (in Chinese called "*mǎn yuè*," meaning the baby is one month old), 100 days old (in Chinese called "*bǎi tiān*," meaning the baby is now 100 days old), or when a parent turns 80 — has important cultural symbolic significance. Taking an official family portrait on an important birthday symbolizes the tradition of family cohesiveness and harmony (Gao & Ting-Toomey, 1998). Even now when many individuals can use digital cameras or cell phones to take daily pictures, still, many traditional Chinese families prefer to go to the studio for a formal family portrait. It is not the moment of taking the picture itself or owning a special high tech camera that matters here. It is the Chinese cultural worldview to "mark" the special family outing occasion — to be all dressed up and to have the "entire family under one roof" to take a proper picture together that symbolizes family continuity and longevity.

In this case, Jack He and Casey Luo not only wanted a family togetherness portrait, they wanted to be alone with Anna Mae. Due to the foster care situation, they did not see their daughter often and therefore, they treasured the limited time they could spend alone with their daughter. Family togetherness was what Jack He and Casey Luo had been craving and believed they deserved. But the American foster parents, Jerry and Louis Baker, refused to let them take Anna Mae out. If the Bakers had been offered — and were willing to listen to — an explanation of the significant Chinese cultural meaning of taking a family portrait together on a child's birthday, the intercultural confrontation scene would probably not have escalated so swiftly into runaway escalatory conflict spirals.

Social Ecological Exo-Level and Meso-Level Analysis

At the exo-level analysis, the interactive effect between people and their formal institutional environment is emphasized. While oftentimes, the institutional environment or policies may not directly impinge on the people's behaviors (e.g., governmental health care policies filter through various agencies and then impact the people's decisions), in the Anna Mae He's conflict case story, the courtroom's legal procedures and decisions actually do have a significant top-down impact on Jack He and Casey's family life. Additionally, the media and the community reactions also created a huge interactive impact effect on this intercultural conflict story and outcome. Thus, for this particular conflict case study, the exosystem analysis and mesosystem analysis are closely intertwined and the two units of analysis are combined here for further discussions and illustrations.

On the exo-level analysis, for example, the two key institutions that belong to this level of discussion and that have asserted tremendous impacts on Jack He and Casey Luo's custody battle case are the various courtroom legal rulings and the university formal policy concerning Jack He's status as an international student. At the university formal ruling level, Jack He was suspended from the University of Memphis because of the pending sexual assault court case mounted by a fellow international student. At the exo-level of courtroom analysis, for instance, the Tennessee state court decision was based on the assumption of who can meet the best interests of Anna Mae He. The court believed that instead of sending Anna Mae He back to China, keeping Anna Mae in the affluent Bakers' family met her best interests.

In court arguments, the Bakers used many rigid stereotypical evaluations concerning China (e.g., Chinese people mistreat girls, China is a remote place with a lot of pollution, etc.) to justify why it was in the best interest of Anna Mae He for her to stay in the United States instead of returning her back to her biological parents and to China. The Bakers' lawyer mentioned China's one-child policy, Chinese people's preference for boys, the way of cultivating family relations, which favored boys, and the weak socio-economic conditions of China as some of the key arguments that justified why the Bakers should be allowed formally to adopt Anna Mae He. The Chancery Court judge took in all these arguments and ruled that Anna Mae He's biological parents would not be fit parents to raise her. Those arguments, however, went far beyond the actual custody case and started to confuse national policies with the family's parental rights which were then further filtered through a biased, stereotypical lens concerning Chinese, or Chinese Americans (Wu, 2002).

Under the policy of protecting the right of Chinese citizens overseas, the Chinese Embassy also pointedly asked the American court for a clear justification of its legal decision. Furthermore, on the exosystem or "people's court opinion" level of analysis, the escalating attention mounted by the mainstream U.S. media (e.g., Good Morning America, ABC News, etc.) and the Internet also produced both sideways and top-down effects in changing the direction of the custody battle. The exo-level asserted tremendous influence in tipping the justice scale to a balance point between the two financially-strapped international students on the one side, and the well-to-do American couple on the other. Ultimately, the judge from the Tennessee local court had to resign due to the mounting pressure from the community for his unjustified legal court order. The active support and the strong appeals from legal scholars and cultural experts created a combined ripple effect on the exo-level and onward to the meso-level processes.

On the mesosystem level of analysis, supportive community actions definitely directly influenced the development of this epic custody battle. At this level, the meso-level context and its interaction effect with people who lived in the embedded contexts were emphasized. Many strangers from the immediate (and also far-flung) surrounding community chose to stand with the He family. Two Jewish lawyers provided them with free services, which were worth at least $500,000. After the media exposed this case, supporters established the "He Mei Fund" on the Internet and raised money for the Hes to pay for collecting evidence and legal investigation. After the local court forced the cancellation of the "He Mei Fund," those same supporters established the "Hes Get-together Fund" and supported the Hes till the end.

The person who was in charge of the "He Mei Fund" said, "We helped the Hes not because we thought the Hes did not do anything wrong. We helped the Hes because we wanted to create an equal stage for the Hes to be heard, to have equal conversation with the rich Bakers who had lawyers and who knew laws." Thus, the mesosystem level created tremendous movements on the sideway-direction level (i.e., in galvanizing the support of local community and individuals) and, simultaneously, created upward momentums on the exo-level (i.e., at the formal courtroom setting) and downward impacts on the micro-interpersonal level. With the overwhelming support of the surrounding community and the various Asian American advocacy groups, the united positive energy created a renewed sense of balance of power and justice between the two intercultural conflict factions. With the support of the mainstream media on their side, and together with the generation of adequate legal funds, the Hes family could finally assert their voice loudly and their case more persuasively and articulately. The back-and-forth courtroom dramas at the exo-level, the community activists on the meso-level, and the key players negotiating the various conflict episodes on the micro-level, all these levels reciprocally influenced each other and at multiple, synergistic directions.

In January, 2007, cycling back to the exo-level of analysis, the Tennessee Supreme Court, in a unanimous decision, finally ordered Anna Mae He to be returned to her biological parents. The Tennessee Supreme Court stated that: "Financial advantage and affluent surroundings simply may not be a consideration in determining a custody dispute between a parent and a non-parent. The evidence at trial showed that the parents have overcome many obstacles to achieve financial stability and are ably taking care of their other two children." So with top-down and bottom-up effects combined, each individual's behavior and the united force of each individual (and each social ecological level) brought about new momentums, changes, and the final decisive outcome for the Hes' family and also for the then seven-year old girl, Anna Mae He, the central innocent character of this conflict story.

Social Ecological Micro-Level Analysis

Micro-level analysis refers to both the intrapersonal and interpersonal levels of interpretations and meaning constructions concerning the conflict communication phenomenon. Three incidents in this case can illustrate micro-level intercultural-interpersonal encounter clashes. The first incident concerns language misunderstanding and cultural interpretation. At the time when the oral custody agreement was made between the two families, one attorney explained the possible consequences and risks of this oral custody agreement to Casey Luo, the mother of Anna Me He. The attorney said that this temporary custody "could" go for one year or it "could" go for 18 years. The misunderstanding possibly emerged due to ambiguity of the meaning of the word "could." The word "could" implied "different possibilities." The two families involved in the initial custody discussion appeared to have quite different interpretations concerning this particular word "could." These different interpretations significantly influenced what happened next.

In court, the Bakers said the Hes had agreed that they (Bakers) could raise A. M. H until she turned 18 years old. The Juvenile Court officer testified that Jack and Casey did not agree with the Bakers that they could raise A. M. H until she was 18 years old. But "18 years" was never ever explicitly written in the custody document (*People's Daily*, 人民网, 1/28/ 2005). One possible explanation for the Bakers' understanding was that the Hes were in agreement with this possible one 18 year duration custody plan. The Bakers concluded that since the lawyer actually explained to the Hes clearly that the custody "could" range from one to 18 years, then the Hes should know the precise meaning. However, since the lawyer's explanation used the subjunctive mood with the word "could," the Hes heard and interpreted the verbal phrase as a hypothetical scenario and not as actual lawful reality. Since the Bakers did not hear or perceive any explicit objections from the Hes, they believed that the lawyer and the translator had already explained everything in detail. They thought the time frame matter was settled.

Meanwhile, according to witnesses, Casey Luo was heard repeatedly mentioning the phrase, "temporary custody." From Casey Luo's cultural and Chinese language interpretations, when a parent places a child under someone else's custody, it implies a temporary time frame, and that she "could" actually get her baby girl back any time she wanted during this wide-open period. Indeed, the Juvenile Court officer testified that the mother, Casey Luo, was "fairly adamant that at some point she wanted her child back." The mother, Casey Luo, testified as follows: "I was told I can get my daughter back at any time. I asked him three or four times about that." Finally, the Juvenile Court interpreter, Pastor Kenny Yao, testified that the mother understood the custody agreement to be temporary and that it was for the purpose of "obtaining medical insurance for Anna Mae He."

As another Chinese cultural expert testified, there is a substantial difference between the concept "temporary custody" and the concept "adoption" in the Chinese language. While "temporary custody" means someone is helping out to take care of the baby while the parents are unable to do so, the word "adoption" means that "the parents are giving up their own rights and giving the parental rights to someone else." In the Chinese language, "temporary" means "not permanent," and "custody" means "taking care." This can explain why Casey Luo inquired repeatedly about whether the custody was temporary. This can also explain why Casey finally signed her name on the document-because she thought that she could get back her baby girl whenever she wanted without losing her parental rights during the custody time. Unfortunately, the Bakers did not interpret the word "custody" the same way as Casey Luo or Jack He did.

To the Bakers, the word "custody" refers to who has the legal decision-making authority in the life of a child. Decision-making authority usually is regarded in connection with major life issues such as religion, education, health and activities. In this case, the Bakers understood clearly what they could do within the law and what their legal rights were as temporary custodial parents. However, they went further to ask for a possible 1–18 years of custody, which was beyond Casey Luo's comprehension of the concept, "custody." In this case history, since English was Casey Luo's second language and she was not fluent in English, an English-Chinese translation process during each meeting was needed and, also, quite possibly created further cultural confusions. Once language translation was involved, there would be some loss in the meaning translation during the decoding and encoding process. Moreover, the involved conflict parties had their own distinctive sociocultural identities, educational backgrounds, individualized work experiences, different personal life scripts and, of course, their own conflict motivations and concerns. Those identities, backgrounds, experiences, conflict emotions, and personal concerns further colorized the conflict lenses and viewpoints of respective conflict parties in looking at the same conflict episode.

The second micro-level critical incident appeared at the time after the incident when Jack He and Casey Luo were removed from the Bakers house due to an incident at the Anna Mae He's second birthday. After that incident, the Hes did not appear at the Bakers' house for another four months. This became the Bakers' main argument in court — that both Jack He and Casey Luo had "willfully" abandoned their parental rights over Anna Mae He. Since the Bakers would not allow the Chinese parents to take Anna Mae He for a birthday family portrait, both Jack He and Casey Luo were irritated and raised their voices. Bakers then wanted them to exit the house. The conflict escalated from the "hidden" to the "obvious." Jack He protested loudly and repeatedly, "I won't leave." The Bakers had no idea why Jack and Casey sounded so aggressive over this small picture-taking event.

The Bakers subsequently called the police to remove Jack and Casey physically from their house. From Jack and Casey's testimony, they were warned not to return to the Bakers' house. However, the Bakers argued that the police just told them not to return to their house "that day." The Bakers actually first testified exactly with the same answer as Jack and Casey had provided. However, they changed their testimony later, claiming that the police only told the Hes not to come back "that day." During the trial, the police testified "possibly, yes" when asked whether he had said "that day." The trial court then said that the Hes had zero credibility. From Jack's and Casey's conflict lens, they interpreted the police warning as a direct legal instruction or legal order as "do not to return to the Bakers' house, or else ... " During that period, Jack He already had lost his legal standing or status as an international student in the U.S. Thus, he and his wife were extremely frightened that if they were caught by the police they would be deported immediately. That would then create a larger problematic situation including the notion that they might never see their daughter again or be reunited with Anna Mae as an intact family. Meanwhile, the Bakers argued that the "full four-month absence" is the legal limit for parents to lose their parental rights. Since Jack He and Casey Luo had not shown up for four months at the Bakers' house, this indicated that they willfully gave up their parental rights. It appears that Bakers took full advantage of Jack's and Casey's ignorance concerning the American legal system. In their testimony, Jack and Casey said "We do not have legal education. We did not know that the Tennessee statute had set number '4' as a limit." This incident also reflects the interconnection between the larger exo-level (i.e., police institution and cultural compliance issues) pressures and top-down impacts on the interpersonal conflict interaction incident on the micro level of understanding.

The third critical event concerns payment issues between the He family and the Baker family. The Bakers' lawyer accused Jack and Casey of willfully failing to support their daughter financially. The Court of Appeals said Jack and Casey did not pay the Bakers for providing foster care. In the Bakers' petition, they mentioned that when the Hes visited on December 22, 1999, they did not bring a gift for Anna Mae He. In actuality, after placing Anna Mae He with the Bakers, Jack and Casey visited their daughter one hour per week as instructed, and consistently bringing food and gifts to their daughter. The first 90 days of foster care service were supposed to be free. Earlier, the Bakers comforted Jack and Casey and reasoned that they were from a Christian family background and that they were all like brothers and sisters in a family, and that it was God's will for them to help out the He family. That was why the Bakers were introduced by Mid-South to the Hes and ultimately why they became the foster parents to Anna Me. Jack and Casey, however, still wanted to do their part and pay the Bakers, so they gave $300 in cash to the Bakers. However, the Bakers would not accept the money. At that time, Jack He worked at the school dorms from midnight to four o'clock in the morning and earned $5 per hour (*Lifeweek*, 三联生活周刊, www.lifeweek.com.cn, 2008, March 10). His monthly take-home was about $600. Mr. Baker was employed by Pinnfund USA as a mortgage banker from 1996 to 2001 and earned approximately $435,000 annually. Jack He's monthly earnings were just half of Mr. Baker's daily earnings. Jack He was in his darkest time, then, when he tried to hand over the $300 to the Bakers. Since the Bakers graciously refused the money, Jack was greatly touched and believed that he had met a generous and caring family in his life. He did not mention payment again because he thought the Bakers would refuse the money and interpreted it as a direct face insult. He did not realize that he should have continued to press the Bakers to take his payment for foster care for Anna Mae.

In the Supreme Court's final decision, the ruling boiled down to the following points: "Under the superior rights doctrine, a natural parent may only be deprived of custody of a child upon a showing of substantial harm to the child." This means that what determines a custodial dispute between the biological parents and foster parents should be based on whether there is substantial harm threatening a child's welfare. Additionally, the court document mentioned the following: "We note the testimony concerning the general conditions in China. This is not relevant to a finding for substantial harm. Financial advantage and affluent surroundings simply may not be a consideration in determining a custody dispute between a parent and a non-parent ... " Lastly, the ruling stated: "Given the lack of evidence of a threat of substantial harm to A. M. H. if she is returned to her parents, we conclude that physical custody of A. M. H. must be returned to the parents" (*Lifeweek*, www.lifeweek.com.cn, 2008, March 10). This three-paragraph decision was worded precisely and clearly. However, it took eight marathon years of back-and-forth wrangling between the Bakers and the Hes to arrive at this final judicial outcome. This lengthy process also reflects the eight precious years of a young girl's developmental family life script and the social ecological conditions that surround this special story.

Social Ecological Lens: Future Directions

Theorizing and Research Directions

As we can see, during the whole process of the custody battle there were many conflicts between the Chinese couple and the American couple. At each social ecological level, there were top-down effects due to cultural value misunderstandings (e.g., the birthday portrait incident), to bottom-up effects due to the persistent efforts of both Jack He and Casey Luo in fighting to reclaim their parental rights over Anna Mae He. There were also top-down effects coming from the meso-community level in generating public opinion and concrete legal fund support to help the Hes' continue their fight in the court system. There were also multiple reciprocal and interaction effects at the exo level in which the court system and the university system interacted together to create further blockades to the long drawn-out custody battle and also adding further fuel to accusations about the Hes' questionable personal credibility.

To reiterate, in utilizing the social ecological theoretical framework to analyze this complex child custody battle, it draws our attention to the importance of understanding the historical context, the larger political context, the cultural values' context, and the various institutional and community reactions to a real-life conflict situation. By applying some of the core principles and themes of the social ecological framework, the framework focuses our attention towards the "holistic picture" and the "layering, embedded contexts" that frame the various conflict decisions and outcomes. Core theoretical concepts such as top-down effects, bottom-up effects, and interaction effects (and even the new notion of the "sideway effects" between subsystems) help us to fill in the complex, interdependent nature of the links and loops in this intercultural case story. While the benefits of the social ecological perspective entail the systematic analysis of each level that asserts influence on the conflict case story, it is also critical to move the theoretical boundary even further to enhance the explanatory nature of this heuristic theoretical framework.

Theoretically, the social ecological theory may be enhanced used in conjunction with other intercultural-interpersonal communication theories such as expectancy violations theory (Burgoon & Ebesu Hubbard, 2005), coordinated management of meaning theory (Pearce, 2005), speech codes theory (Philipsen, Coutu, & Covarrubias, 2005), and/or conflict face-negotiation theory (Ting-Toomey, 2005). For example, in applying conflict face-negotiation theory to enhance the explanatory value of the social ecological lens, the following theoretical questions can be applied at each level of analysis. From the macro national culture lens, what were some specific Chinese and American cultural value dimensions that created further face threats along each macro, exo, meso, and micro level? How did the contrastive cultural and political ideologies between the two countries impact their assessments of fairness, justice, power, obligations, and rights' issues concerning their own conflict standpoint and from the standpoint of the little girl, Anna Mae He? How was face being repaired, maintained or compensated between the two families after the final verdict by the Supreme Court?

On the exo-level, how did the court system and the university system engage in mutual face support of each other to "ostracize" Jack He so that his international student status was in jeopardy? How did the various judges and lawyers present their self-face enhancement moves and other-face obliteration moves in the courtroom? What were some of the direct or indirect face threatening or face uplifting strategies that were evoked inside and outside the courtroom, or inside and outside the university system? What were some of the final turning point "face honoring" events that contributed to the ultimate validation of the actual "faces" and the actual "voices" of both Jack He and Casey Luo? On the meso-community reaction level, what facework balancing strategies were used to balance the "credibility face" of the Hes' family in conjunction with some of the obvious missteps (e.g., the early sexual assault charge filed by a fellow Chinese student towards Jack He although he was found not guilty later) that took place in their international lives? What facework strategies did the community and the He family use to rally the media for support and attention in what would otherwise be an under-reported child custody case?

On the micro-level, how did Jack He, Casey Luo, and the Bakers conduct their initial facework acquaintance process? How did they engage in strategic facework moves with each other as they became more polarized at each turn of the custody crisis? What role did the translators play in this marathon intercultural conflict case battle? What were their standpoints and perspectives in the various conflict face-negotiation sessions surrounded by lawyers, warring families, and community pressures? What would Anna Mae He's "authentic voice" sound like as she turns 18 and can choose between living in China or living in America? Thus, by utilizing the four levels of the social ecological perspective, the model allows us to ask more systematic researchable questions concerning a multi-contextual, intercultural conflict case. The social ecological perspective facilitates us to gain a fuller and more comprehensible understanding of a multilayered conflict case story.

Epilogue

This paper concludes with some background information about Anna Mae He and her life in China. How did Anna Me react upon hearing the judge's verdict? "Can we stay in America without going back to China?" "I'm used to staying here, I have so many friends here." "Do people treat girls harshly in China? Will they be hanged and punished by the ruler if they make mistakes?" "Do all the people in China ride bicycles? Do people have TV in China? Can I buy tennis shoes in China?" (news. QQ. com, 2008, March 27). Those were some of the initial questions Anna Mae He asked when she heard the judge's final verdict.

Just before Anna Mae He was about to leave the States, she celebrated her eighth birthday in the U.S. with her biological parents. The Hes also invited the Bakers to attend the birthday birthday celebration. Jack He and Casey Luo realized that instead of maintaining a long-lasting wall between the two families, it would be good for Anna Mae if she could continue to receive love and affection from both families, so that she would no longer feel torn or alienated by the conflicts between the two families. According to the ABC News (2008, February 7), Jack He commented: "You know, Anna loves the Bakers. And if I say something or do something negative about the Bakers, it means I'm holding [back] Anna. And I don't want to do that. We'll just move on and take care of the child." Jerry Baker chimed in: "What's happened in the past is in the past ... We're very grateful to the Hes for allowing us the opportunity to start a dialogue with them." He also concluded: "In the end, I truly do believe that you have two mothers that love the same child ... I truly do."

In February 2008, the He family finally returned to Hunan, Jack He's hometown in China. When they arrived at the train station, Jack felt totally lost because he had been away from his hometown for so long that nothing had remained the same. Suddenly, he heard someone called out his nickname from the crowd. It was his mother and his brother, sister, nephew, niece and all the neighbors. Anna Mae's aunt hugged her warmly and all the family members physically enveloped Anna Mae in the middle with teary affection. Anna Mae looked around at all these new Chinese relatives with surprise and curiosity.

The room was full of people, everyone smiled, and Anna Mae He smiled back. She asked her mother, "Is this grandparent's house?" Her grandpa heard the question and walked toward her and grabbed her hand, and told her, "Yes, you are now home." Anna Mae saw all the yummy snacks and fruits piled on the table; she grabbed an orange, peeled it, and placed one orange slice in her grandpa's mouth. Grandpa smiled with a deep contentment coming from his heart, and proceeded to savor the orange slice slowly and deliberately.

Note

Sources in The Anna Mae He's Story via *chronological order events*' placement:

People's Daily. 人民网。《中美两个家庭持续四年的战争：为了五岁的小贺梅》。(2005，January 28). Retrieved on April 10，2009，from http://www.people.com.cn/GB/jiaoyu/1055/3151525.html

ABC News. For the love of Anna Mae: Two families come together after custody battle, only to be torn apart. (2008，February 7). Retrieved on April 4，2008，from http://abcnews.go.com/TheLaw/story?id=4250114&page=1.

ABC News. Anna Mae Goes to China: Caught in a lengthy custody struggle, she starts new life with biological family. www.abcnews.com. (2008，February 11). Retrieved on April 2，2008，from http://abcnews.go.com/TheLaw/story?id=4269986&page=1

Life Week.《三联生活周刊》。贺梅案：一个家庭的7年诉讼纠葛(2008，March 10). Retrieved on April 10，2009，from http://www.lifeweek.com.cn/2008-03-10/0005320865.shtml

TSC State Opinions. Adoption of A. M. H. In the supreme court of Tennessee at Jackson, October 4，2006 session heard at Nashville. Retrieved on April 10，2008 from http://www.tsc.state.tn.us/OPINIONS/TSC/PDF/071/AMHOPN.pdf

Parental Rights News. Adoption of A. M. H., A Minor. In the Chancery Court of Tennessee for the Thirtieth Judicial District at Memphis. Retrieved on April 10，2008 from http://www.parentalrightsandjustice.com/upload/site/1/27/Childers_Final_Opinion.htm

Parental Rights News. Adoption of A. M. H., A Minor. In the supreme court of Tennessee at Jackson. Retrieved on April 10，2008 from http://www.parentalrightsandjustice.com/upload/site/1/79/jackhe_motion_for_determination.pdf

QQ News.《中美婴孩大战：贺梅回家不想回中国》。(2008，March 27). Retrieved on April 10，2008，from http://news.qq.com/a/20080327/002322.htm

The Fighting44.com. News. Update on Anna Mae He in China. (2008，December 1). Retrieved on December 12，2009，from http://www.thefighting44s.com/archives/2008/12/01/update-on-anna-mae-he-in-china/

China daily. Identity crisis after girl's custody battle. (2009，June 1). Retrieved on December 12，2009，from http://www.chinadaily.com.cn/china/2009-06/01/content_7958533.htm

References

ABC News. Anna Mae Goes to China: Caught in a lengthy custody struggle, she starts new life with biological family (2008, February 11). Retrieved on April 2, 2008, from http://abcnews.go.com/TheLaw/story?id=4269986&page=1

ABC News. For the love of Anna Mae: Two families come together after custody battle, only to be torn apart (2008, February 7). Retrieved on April 4, 2008, from http://abcnews.go.com/TheLaw/story? id=4250114&page=1

Braithwaite, D., & J. Wood. (2000). *Case Studies in Interpersonal Communication*. Belmont, CA: Wadsworth / Thomson Learning.

Brofenbrenner, U. (1977). Toward an experimental ecology of human development. *American Psychologist, 32*, 513–531.

Brofenbrenner, U. (1979). *The Ecology of Human Development*. Cambridge, MA: Harvard University.

Burgoon, J., & Ebesu Hubbard, A. (2005). Cross-cultural and intercultural applications of expectancy violations theory and interaction adaptation theory. In W. B. Gudykunst (Ed.), *Theorizing about Intercultural Communication* (pp. 149–171). Thousand Oaks, CA: Sage.

China Daily. Identity crisis after girl's custody battle (2009, June 1). Retrieved on December 12, 2009, from http://www.chinadaily.com.cn/china/2009-06/01/content_7958533.htm

Ellet, W. (2007). *The Case Study Handbook: How to Read, Discuss, and Write Persuasively about Cases*. Boston, MA: Harvard Business School Press.

Gao, G., & S. Ting-Toomey. (1998). *Communicating Effectively with the Chinese*. Thousand Oaks, CA: Sage.

Gregson, J. (2001). System, environment, and policy changes: Using the social-ecological model as a framework for evaluating nutrition education and social marketing programs with low-income audiences. *Journal of Nutrition Education, 33*, 4–15.

Huston, T. L. (2000). The social ecology of marriage and other intimate unions. *Journal of Marriage and the Family, 62*, 298–320.

Ihinger-Tallman, M., & T. Cooney. (2005). *Families in context: An introduction*. Los Angeles: Roxbury.

Kim Y. Y. (2001). *Becoming Intercultural: An Integrative Theory of Communication and Cross-cultural Adaptation*. Thousand Oaks, CA: Sage.

Kim, Y. Y. (2005). Adapting to a new culture: An integrative communication theory. In W. B. Gudykunst (Ed.), *Theorizing about Intercultural Communication* (pp. 375–400). Thousand Oaks, CA: Sage.

Klein, K. J., Tosi, H., & A. A. Cannella. (1999). Multilevel theory building: Benefits, barriers, and new developments. *Academy of Management Review, 24*, 243–248.

Life Week. 贺梅案:一个家庭的 7 年诉讼纠葛。《三联生活周刊》(2008, March 10). Retrieved on April 10, 2008, from http://www.lifeweek.com.cn/2008-03-10/0005320865.shtml

Myers, K., & R. McPhee. (2006). Influences on member assimilation in workgroups in high reliability organizations: A multilevel analysis. *Human Communication Research, 32*, 440–468.

Oetzel, J., S. Dahr., & K. Kirschbaum. (2007). Intercultural conflict from a multilevel perspective: Trends, possibilities, and future directions. *Journal of Intercultural Communication Research, 36*, 183–204.

Oetzel, J. G., & B. Duran. (2004). Intimate partner violence in American Indian and / or Alaska Native communities: A social ecological framework of determinants and interventions. *The American Indian and Alaska Native Mental Health Research: A Journal of the National Center, 11*(3), 49–68.

Oetzel, J., B. Arcos., P. Mabizela, A. M. Weinman, & Q. Zhang. (2006). Historical, political, and spiritual factors of conflict: Understanding conflict perspectives and communication in the Muslim world, China, Colombia, and South Africa. In J. Oetzel & S. Ting-Toomey (Eds.), *The Sage Handbook of Conflict Communication* (pp. 549–574). Thousand Oaks, CA: Sage.

Oetzel, J.G., S. Ting-Toomey, & S. Rinderle. (2006). Conflict communication in contexts: A social ecological perspective. In J. G. Oetzel & S. Ting-Toomey (Eds.). *The Sage Handbook of Conflict Communication* (pp. 727–739). Thousand Oaks, CA: Sage.

Parental Rights News. Adoption of A. M. H., A Minor. In the chancery court of Tennessee for the thirtieth judicial district at Memphis. Retrieved on April 10, 2008 from http://www. parentalrightsandjustice. com/upload/site/1/27/Childers_Final_Opinion. htm

Parental Rights News. Adoption of A. M. H., A Minor. In the supreme court of Tennessee at Jackson. Retrieved on April 10, 2008 from http://www. parentalrightsandjustice. com/upload/site/1/79/jackhe_motion_for_determination. pdf

Pearce, B. (2005). The coordinated management of meaning. In W. B. Gudykunst (Ed.), *Theorizing about InterculturalCommunication* (pp. 35–54). Thousand Oaks, CA: Sage.

People's Daily. 中美两个家庭持续四年的战争：为了五岁的小贺梅。《人民网》(2005, January 28). Retrieved on April 10, 2008, from http://www. people. com. cn/GB/jiaoyu/1055/3151525. html

Philipsen, G., L. Coutu, & P. Covarrubias. (2005). Speech codes theory: Revisions, and response to criticisms. In W. B. Gudykunst (Ed.), *Theorizing about Intercultural Communication* (pp. 55–68). Thousand Oaks, CA: Sage.

QQ News.《中美婴孩大战：贺梅回家不想回中国》。(2008, March 27). Retrieved on April 10, 2008, from http://news. qq. com/a/20080327/002322. htm

Rousseau, D. M., & R. J. House. (1994). Meso organizational behavior: Avoiding three fundamental biases. In C. L. Cooper & D. M. Rousseau (Eds). *Trends in Organizational Behavior* (Vol. 1, pp. 13–30). New York: John Wiley & Sons.

Slater, M., L. Snyder, & A. Hayes. (2006). Thinking and modeling at multiple levels: The potential contribution of multilevel modeling to communication theory and research. *Human Communication Research, 32*, 375–384.

Stokols, D. (1996). Translating social ecological theory into guidelines for community health promotion. *American Journal of Health Promotion, 10*, 282–298.

Tennessee State Opinions. Adoption of A. M. H. In the Supreme Court of Tennessee at Jackson, October 4, 2006 session heard at Nashville. Retrieved on April 10, 2008 from http://www. tsc. state. tn. us/OPINIONS/TSC/PDF/071/AMHOPN. pdf

The Fighting 44 News. Update on Anna Mae He in China (2008, December 1). Retrieved on December 12, 2009, from http://www. thefighting44s. com/archives/2008/12/01/update-on-anna-mae-he-in-china/

Theiss, J., & Solomon, D. (2006). Coupling longitudinal data and multilevel modeling to examine the antecedents and consequences of jealousy experiences in romantic relationships. *Human Communication Research, 32*, 469–503.

Ting-Toomey, S. (2005). The matrix of face: An updated face-negotiation theory. In W. B. Gudykunst (Ed.), *Theorizing about Intercultural Communication* (pp. 71–92). Thousand Oaks, CA: Sage.

Ting-Toomey, S., & J. Oetzel. (2001). *Managing Intercultural Conflict Effectively*. Thousand Oaks, CA: Sage.

Ting-Toomey, S. & S. Takai. (2006). Explaining intercultural conflict: Promising approaches and directions. In J. Oetzel & S. Ting-Toomey (Eds.), *The Sage Handbook of Conflict Communication* (pp. 691–723). Thousand Oaks, CA: Sage Publications.

Williams, D., & R. Williams-Morris. (2000). Racism and mental health: The African American experience. *Ethnicity & Health*, 5, 243–268.

Wu, F. H. (2002). *Yellow: Race in America Beyond Black and White*. New York: Basic Books.

23

Intercultural Sensitivity and Conflict Management Styles in Cross-Cultural Organizational Situations

Yu Tong
China Jiliang University

Chen Guo-Ming
University of Rhode Island, USA

Abstract: Increased cultural diversity in work places has aroused considerable attention to conflict management and intercultural sensitivity. However, few studies have investigated these two concepts together. The present study aims to bridge the gap in this line of research with an examination between intercultural sensitivity and conflict management styles in a hypothetical cross-cultural organizational situation. The results from 253 participants indicate that significantly positive and negative relationships exist among the dimensions of the two concepts. Limitations and directions for future research are discussed as well.

Introduction

With the rapid development of technology, increasing social mobility, globalization of economy, and the emergence of cultural diversity, intercultural human contact at both individual and organizational levels is increasing (Brislin & Yoshida, 1994; Chen, 2005). The wide-ranged expansion of human contacts on the one hand calls for people's sensitivity to cultural diversity; on the other hand, the expansion inevitably has caused and will continue to generate more conflicts in different situations. Conflict management and intercultural sensitivity have thus received considerable attention in the past decades (e.g., Blake & Mouton, 1964;

Chen & Starosta, 1997b; Morrill & Thomas, 1992; Rahim, 1983; Sternberg & Soriano, 1984; Triandis, 2006).

Conflict has been acknowledged as an important aspect of modern management (Wilson & Jerrell, 1981). Despite the negative effect of conflict, it can achieve productive outcomes, if managed effectively, such as improved relationships (Van De Vliert, 1997). more effective task completion (Amason & Schweiger, 1997; Jehn, 1997). and more creative problem solving and innovation (Janis, 1972). As the multicultural work force has become a reality due to business globalization and migration, cross-cultural conflicts caused more attention than usual in today's organizations both domestically and globally.

Increased cultural diversity in different settings calls for abilities to adapt to the unfamiliar environment and to learn to work and live productively with people from different cultural backgrounds, which highlights the ability of intercultural sensitivity (Chen & Starosta, 1997a). Research showed a high percentage of failed expatriate assignments because of expatriate employees' inability to adapt to the host culture's social and business environment (Black & Mendenhall, 1990; Copeland & Griggs, 1985; Mendenhall & Oddou, 1985). It was also found that high intercultural sensitivity was associated with high intercultural communication competence, such as cross-cultural adjustment, task effectiveness during overseas assignments, and healthy interpersonal relationships with culturally different individuals (Bhawuk & Brislin, 1992; Hammer, Bennett, & Wiseman, 2003; Kapoor, Konsky, & Drager, 2000).

Based on the importance of being effective in conflict management and sensitive to cultural differences, many organizations have promoted various training programs to improve both employees' cultural sensitivity and conflict management skills, aiming at reducing stress, enhancing relationships and improving job performance (Amason & Schweiger, 1997; Brislin & Yoshida, 1994; Jehn, 1997). It was hoped that with these training programs, employees can increase their awareness and understanding to cultural difference and effectively deal with culture-related work conflicts. However, few studies have investigated these two concepts as related. In order to bridge the gap in this line of research, the purpose of this study then was to examine the potential relationship between intercultural sensitivity and conflict management styles in a cross-cultural organizational context.

Literature Review

Conflict Management Styles

Numerous researchers have attempted to study people's behaviors in conflict situations, and to identify the most effective and most constructive approaches to deal with conflicts. Rahim and Bonoma (1979) categorized conflict styles into two basic dimensions: concern for self and concern for others. These two dimensions result in five distinct behavioral conflict management strategies: integrating, obliging, dominating, avoiding, and compromising.

Integrating refers to high concern for both self and others. This strategy involves efforts to reach an integrative solution meeting both parties' needs. Obliging represents low concern for self and high concern for others, which is associated with attempting to satisfy the needs of the other party while sacrificing one's own needs. Dominating refers to high concern for self and low concern for others. When using this style, an individual attempts to achieve one's own needs without considering the other's needs. Avoiding is a style in which one has low concern for both self and others. With avoidance, the problem has not been discussed or dealt with, thus fails to satisfy one's own needs as well as the other party's needs. Finally, compromising has moderate levels of concern for both self and others. This style involves searching for an intermediate position by each party giving in a little to reach a mutually acceptable decision. Compromisers partially meet each side's needs, but not all of them.

Ting-Toomey (1988) argued in her development of face-negotiation theory that face is an explanatory mechanism for conflict behavior in different cultural groups. The theory proposed three variables, including cultural, individual-level, and situational, that influence a person's selection of one set of face concerns over others. Subsequently, the selection of different sets of face concerns influences the use of various facework and conflict strategies in social encounters.

Ting-Toomey (2006) further indicated that "conflict style" is a culturally grounded concept, which shows that culture plays an influential role in an individual's preference of conflict styles. People in the same culture would understand and accept each other's approach in dealing with conflict much easier than those from different cultures. Studies have revealed that organizational problems increased in the culturally diverse workplace because of the workers' differences in cultural values, attitudes, and work styles (e.g., Chan & Goto, 2003; Leung & Chan, 1999; Sauceda, 2003).

In spite of strong support for cultural influence on conflict style preference, other studies as well presented inconsistent results. For example, Drake (1995) reported that when Americans and Taiwanese negotiated together inter-culturally, they did not necessarily adhere to conflict styles predicted by cultural variables. Instead, personality and situational concerns greatly affected their selection of conflict strategies. Thomas (1977) and Putnam and Wilson (1982) also contended that people make contingent rather than habitual responses in different conflict situations. However, other researchers argued against the contingency theory. As Sternberg and Soriano (1984) reported, individuals were quite consistent in their modes of conflict resolution, both within and across content domains. It was criticized that the emphasis of the situational influence on conflict style selection fails to acknowledge that not everybody is flexible enough to use the best style for a particular situation (Antonioni, 1998; Bell & Blakeney, 1977).

Personality is another important factor that may influence the choice of conflict styles. Terhune (1970) mentioned that participants who exhibit personality attributes such as aggressiveness, dominance, authoritarianism, and suspiciousness tended to escalate a conflict, while those who exhibit personality attributes such as egalitarianism, trust, and open-mindedness tended to mitigate conflict. Sternberg and Soriano (1984) also assessed that people's preferred conflict styles could be predicted from personality and intellectual factors.

The inconsistent results demonstrated that various factors might work together to influence a person's preference of conflict strategy. The selection of conflict management styles can be influenced by culture, personality, situation and some other factors. As culturally sensitive people are conscious to differences concerning these factors, they may also be more sensitive to intercultural conflicts than low sensitive people. As a result, people having different intercultural sensitivity levels may resort to different strategies in dealing with conflicts in intercultural communication. The multiple-faceted nature of conflict not only widens this line of research, but also leads to our consideration of the possible influence of a person's intercultural sensitivity on his / her communicative orientation towards conflicts.

Intercultural Sensitivity

Although research on intercultural sensitivity has been significantly increased in recent years, the concept still suffers from ambiguous conceptualization. For example, Chen (2007) and Chen and Starosta (1996) criticized that previous studies on intercultural sensitivity inappropriately mixed three related but separate concepts: intercultural sensitivity, intercultural awareness and intercultural communication competence.

According to Chen and Starosta (2000). intercultural communication competence is an umbrella concept that consists of a person's cognitive, affective, and behavioral abilities in the process of intercultural communication. Intercultural sensitivity is the affective aspect of intercultural communication competence, referring to "an individual's ability to develop a positive emotion towards understanding and appreciating cultural differences that promotes appropriate and effective behavior in intercultural communication" (Chen & Starosta, 1997a, p. 5).

Intercultural sensitivity is associated with a person's emotions toward intercultural encounters (Triandis, 1977). Chen and Starosta further concluded that an inter-culturally sensitive individual must possess six personal attributes: self-esteem; self-monitoring, open-mindedness, empathy, interaction involvement, and suspending judgment.

Self-esteem refers to a person's ability to express an optimistic outlook and confidence in intercultural interaction (Chen & Starosta, 1997a). The way an individual feels about oneself has a crucial influence on his / her communication with others. Kipnis (1976) and Tedeschi (1990) found that low self-esteem individuals have a higher tendency than high self-esteem individuals to resort to harsh strategies, such as coercion and legitimacy, in social interactions. In related research on self-confidence, Instone, Major, and Bunker (1983) reported that individuals who have high self-confidence are more likely to use influence attempts and less coercive strategies than those subjects who have low self-confidence.

Self-monitoring is a person's ability to consciously regulate behavior in response to situational constraints and to implement a conversationally competent behavior. High self-monitors have the ability to adjust their behavior to fit the situation. Self-monitoring has been considered to be relevant to organizational conflict. Caldwell and O'Reilly (1982) found that people high in self-monitoring will experience a lower incidence of interpersonal conflict than people low in self-monitoring. Baron (1989) also pointed out that high self-monitors reported higher preferences than low self-monitors for relatively conciliatory conflict resolution modes, such as collaboration and compromise.

Open-mindedness is a person's ability to openly and appropriately explain oneself and to accept other's explanations. Open-minded persons are more willing to consider and integrate another person's ideas than narrow-minded individuals. Researchers found that open-minded people may prefer adaptive and flexible approaches to conflict resolution with consideration of the opponent's views. For example, Moberg (2001) reported that open-minded persons tend to compromise and address conflict directly in conflict situations.

Empathy refers to a person's ability to project oneself into another person's point of view in order to adopt different roles as required by different situations. It is the ability of putting oneself in another person's shoes. According to Hakansson and Montgomery (2003). an empathic person is able to understand other persons' feelings and desires, sense others' emotions, and perceive similarity between self and others. As an empathic person has the ability to perceive and understand another person's situation, the empathizer can see the situation from a new angle, which certainly will play an important role when conflict exists.

Interaction involvement refers to a person's ability to perceive the topic and situation in order to initiate and terminate an intercultural interaction fluently and appropriately. Highly involved individuals are sensitive and attentive to self, other, and the circumstances, and, thus, can respond to the situation accordingly. High-involved persons are more effective at face-work than low-involved persons. On the other hand, according to Cegala (1981). low-involved individuals tend to feel withdrawn or distanced from interactions, because they often focus on "the world of inner, private experience" or are "preoccupied with other thoughts or goals" (p. 113).

Finally, suspending judgment refers to a person's ability to avoid rash judgment about the inputs of others and to foster a feeling of enjoyment of cultural differences. People tend to judge a person, object, or issue based on their present knowledge of the target, which, however, often leads to limited or biased judgment, especially when the important information of the target is missing (Anderson, 1981; Johnson, 1987). People who recognize the absence of relevant information when making judgments tend to make less extreme evaluations and are ready to alter a judgment as additional information becomes available (Jaccard & Wood, 1988; Yates, Jagacinski, & Faber, 1978). Generally speaking, a non-judgmental person will not be easily involved in preconceived beliefs and attitudes or be preoccupied with self and one's own culture.

The above literature review reveals a potential relationship between intercultural sensitivity and conflict management styles. It was then the purpose of this study to explore this possibility by examining the relationship among different dimensions of the two concepts. A hypothetical cross-cultural organizational situation was designed for the purpose of observation.

Method

Participants

Participants in this study were undergraduate students enrolled in an introductory communication course at a medium-sized northeastern university in the United States. A total of 253 students, 80 males and 173 females, were recruited from intact classes with their agreement to participate in the survey. These participants had diverse study fields and programs in the university. The average age for participants was 18.8 years.

Procedure

Survey method was adopted in the present study. Permissions were obtained from both course instructors and students. Students were told that participation was completely voluntary. An alternative assignment was offered to students who chose not to participate. All students in twelve sections, except one who was under 18 years of age, volunteered for participation. The survey was conducted during regular class meeting time.

Measures

Two instruments were used in this study. The 24-item Intercultural Sensitivity Scale (ISS) developed by Chen and Starosta (2000) was used to test participants' sensitivity levels. The scale was comprised of five factors: interaction engagement, respect for cultural differences, interaction confidence, interaction enjoyment, and interaction attentiveness. Interaction engagement is concerned with participants' feeling of participation in intercultural interaction; respect for cultural differences is related to participants' orientation towards or tolerance to their counterparts' culture and opinion; interaction confidence tests how confident participants felt in the intercultural contexts; interaction enjoyment deals with participants' reaction, positive or negative, towards intercultural communication; and interaction attentiveness is related to participants' effort to understand the ongoing process of intercultural communication. The overall scale and all the five factors had high internal consistency with .86 reliability coefficient separately. All 24 items were randomly ordered in this study.

In order to measure conflict management styles, a hypothetical scenario was developed. Participants were asked to finish questions of Rahim's Organizational Conflict Inventories II (ROCI-II) (1983) based on their possible responses to the specific conflict mentioned in the scenario.

The ROCI-II was slightly modified to fit the situation in this present study. Rahim's ROCI-II is an instrument to examine participants' behavioral orientation in conflict situations. ROCI-II consists of 28 Likert-type items and has been widely used to compare group conflict styles (van de Vliert & Kabanoff, 1990). Each style is a factor, which consists of four to seven items respectively. Participants were asked the extent to which they agreed or disagreed with each item, ranging from (1) strongly disagree to (5) strongly agree.

ROCI-II has demonstrated consistent and satisfactory coefficient values in past studies with Cronbach's alpha coefficient ranged from .77 to .86 for integrating; .68 to .83 for obliging; .75 to .79 for dominating; .72 to .86 for avoiding; and .67 to .78 for compromising (e.g., Gross & Guerrero, 2000; King & Miles, 1990; Weider-Hatfiend, 1988; Womack, 1988).

In this study, both scales showed satisfactory overall reliability coefficients, with .89 for intercultural sensitivity and .82 for conflict management style. All the five factors of the conflict management style scale had Cronbach's alpha coefficients of .80 and above. The integrating style had a .85 coefficient alpha; the obliging style .80; the dominating style .85; the avoiding style .81; and the compromising style .84. Three of the five factors of intercultural sensitivity demonstrated good reliability with the alpha coefficients of .79 for respect for cultural differences, .72 for interaction confidence, and .78 for interaction engagement. The alpha coefficients of .57 for interaction enjoyment and .48 for interaction attentiveness were lower than the satisfactory level. As the total number of items directly influences a factor's reliability, it may be the reason that these two dimensions only consist of three items each. However, interaction attentiveness, referring to a person's ability of sensing and perceiving messages in interactions (Chen & Starosta, 2000), is a very important dimension in the concept of intercultural sensitivity. Without efforts to understand the ongoing interaction, a person would not be able to further participate and enjoy the process of interaction. Therefore, the researcher decided to keep these two factors in this study.

Results

The primary research question for this study sought to find the relationship between dimensions of intercultural sensitivity and conflict management styles. In order to answer the research question, Pearson product-moment correlations were computed between the two concepts and their dimensions. The results are presented in Table 1.

Table 1 Pearson Correlation Coefficients for Variables

Variables	All	Integrate	Avoid	Dominate	Oblige	Compromise
All	.20*	.48*	-.25*	-.23*	.28*	.43*
Engage	.19*	.43*	-.23*	-.20*	.24*	.42*
Respect	.20*	.48*	-.16**	-.30*	.26*	.41*
Confidence	.13	.30*	-.21*	-.06	.20*	.18*
Enjoyment	.16**	.30*	-.17*	-.07	.18*	.28*
Attention	.01	.23*	-.23*	-.18*	.10	.25*

* $p<.01$; ** $p<.05$; N = 253

The results showed a significant, positive relationship between a person's intercultural sensitivity and conflict management styles ($r = .20$, $p<.01$). Most dimensions of the two concepts also exhibited significant relationships with each other, either positively or negatively.

Interaction engagement was significantly and positively related with integrating style, obligation style, and compromising, while significantly and negatively related with avoiding and dominating. Similarly, respect for cultural differences correlated significantly and positively with integrating, obliging, and compromising, but negatively with avoiding and dominating. Interaction confidence had significant, positive relationships with integrating, obliging, and compromising, and negative relationships with avoiding.

Interaction enjoyment reported similar results with interaction confidence. Interaction enjoyment was significantly and positively associated with integrating, obliging, and compromising, while negatively related with avoiding. However, both interaction confidence and enjoyment did not show significant relationships with dominating style. Finally, interaction attentiveness showed a significant, positive relationship with integrating and compromising, and a negative relationship with avoiding and dominating. But it did not report significant relationship with obliging style.

Discussion

This study investigated the relationship between intercultural sensitivity and conflict management styles. Overall, the results display moderate relationships between the two concepts and among respective dimensions. An individual's sensitivity to cultural differences is reflected as an important factor that influences one's preference of particular style for handling conflict. Although no previous study has simultaneously examined these two concepts together, these results are consistent with related studies on conflict management and some components of personal attributes. The results also provide clear support for the argument that individuals do have more or less preferred styles of managing conflict (Sternberg & Soriano, 1984).

The results suggest that the more sensitive people perceive themselves to be, the more likely they are to use integrating and compromising strategies to manage conflict, and the less likely that they are to use avoiding and dominating styles. The results are consistent with the characteristics of intercultural sensitivity and each style of handling conflict.

Burke (1970) suggested that integrating was related to the effective management of conflict, while dominating and avoiding were regarded as ineffective strategies of managing conflict. It is understandable that integrating is the ideal way to manage conflict because of the maximum degree to which the style meets each party's needs. It allows a person to work with his/her counterpart in the interaction and to behave in ways that seem to concern and support the counterpart. The use of integrating style can also produce "mutual commitment to solutions" and add to "the relationship climate of trust and openness" (Greeff & de Bruyne, 2000, p. 330).

In contrast, dominating seems to reflect a person's only concern about self, and avoiding shows a person's poor confidence of their effectiveness in dealing with intercultural communication. Although compromising asks both parties to give up some needs to meet a midway resolution, a compromising style is better than not resolving the problem or letting one party completely down. Therefore, compromising is also one of the favorite styles for sensitive persons in facing conflict situations. In other words, an inter-culturally sensitive person tries to get positive outcomes from intercultural interaction, both for self and others. The results strengthen Chen and Starosta's (2000) findings that inter-culturally sensitive persons are "more effective in intercultural interaction" (p.12).

Previous studies reported that an individual who has attributes of higher self-monitoring, greater open-mindedness, and more interaction involvement is usually more aware of personal and social differences, and is more concerned with self and other's face-work (e.g., Baron, 1989; Moberg, 2001). Thus, such individuals are more willing to adopt integrating and compromising conflict strategies because these are the two ways that can satisfy both interactants' faces, though different in satisfactory degree.

In addition, as inter-culturally sensitive persons are able to perceive various stimuli in their surroundings and to stand in other people's shoes, they are highly aware of what is going on in the interaction, and can accept the existence of the differences. They like to take the challenges of dealing with cultural differences, and have high self-confidence in managing cultural interactions. Therefore, such persons are not likely to ignore other persons' needs, to leave the problem, or to use harsh strategies that may result in more tensions. While dominating certainly lets the other party feel intimidated and threatened, avoiding can also let people feel frustrated and less satisfied.

On the contrary, people who measure low in intercultural sensitivity usually experience greater anxiety, more frustration with differences, and less confidence in handling intercultural communication (Cegala, 1984; Cegala et al., 1982). They focus more on their inner world, rather than on other people and the ongoing interaction. They greatly base their judgments of differences on their established perceptions, and usually tend to reject these differences. So, it is not surprising to see these people either try to use harsh strategies such as dominating because they view all the differences as attacking and respond accordingly, or tend to avoid the problem because they are unsure of themselves, and avoiding is another way to protect their values and beliefs unaffected.

The positive relationship that appeared between intercultural sensitivity and obliging strategy is interesting. Very few studies have indicated the relationship between personal attributes and an obliging style. Although an obliging style meets the other person's needs, it also sacrifices one's own needs. Since inter-culturally sensitive people are concerned with both self's needs and other's needs, it seems they shouldn't neglect their own needs to just satisfy the other party. This seemingly contradictory result can be explained partially by considering a mediating variable of willingness to engage in sacrifice, or perhaps one's tendency towards altruism. Inter-culturally sensitive persons may resort to an obliging style when they do not need to give up too much of their personal needs, but can remain a harmonious relationship if they do give up something to satisfy other interactants.

Another possible explanation is that, as inter-culturally sensitive persons are open to the difference, they are more willing to admit they "may be wrong or the issue is much more important to the other party", and thus, they are willing to "give up something with the hope of getting something in exchange from the other party when needed" (Rahim, 1985, p. 84).

In spite of the moderate relationships demonstrated among most dimensions, there are a few exceptions. No significant relationship between interaction confidence and a dominating strategy was shown. Previous studies reported controversial results on this issue as well. For example, Instone, Major, and Bunker (1983) found that people who have high self-confidence are more likely to use influence attempts than coercive styles. However, Schwarzwald and Koslowsky (1999) found that people who have low self-esteem tend to use less harsh strategies than people with high self-esteem.

In this study the structure of the sample might also be a plausible explanation of the result for the lack of significant relationship between interaction confidence and dominating. If a sample includes a large numbers of low self-confident persons who are anxious in facing conflict and prefer coercive styles to protect their fragile inner world, the results may show a strong relationship between confidence and harsh strategies. Or, if a sample consists of mostly low self-confident persons who are unsure of themselves and do not have enough courage to face or resolve the conflict, the results may demonstrate a significant relationship between confidence and less harsh strategies. It is possible that the sample in this study consists of similar amounts of the above two different types of people, which may neutralize the results and indicate no significant relationship in the two variables.

In addition, interaction enjoyment was not significantly associated with dominating style; nor did interaction attentiveness reflect any connection with obliging. As interaction enjoyment and attentiveness only have three items and report relatively low reliability, it might be the reason that affects the results.

Concluding Remarks

This study contributes to our understanding of the interplay between intercultural sensitivity and conflict management styles. It also demonstrates the complexity of the nature of conflict management. Various factors could influence a person's choice of conflict strategies, with intercultural sensitivity as one factor. More studies are needed to examine the two concepts.

The results of this study provide some potential implications for practitioners. The findings may encourage individuals to sense and perceive various stimuli in their surroundings and to adopt effective strategies when dealing with cultural differences. Organizations may begin to use intercultural sensitivity assessment to help make decisions, such as selecting employees for particular assignments, arranging team members to control conflicts in organizations, and designing training programs to create a better working environment and to improve productivity and effectiveness.

The results of this study may also contribute to the design and implementation of intercultural training programs. Generally speaking, intercultural training programs are aimed at helping trainees communicate more effectively, deal with the inevitable stresses accompanied with intercultural interaction, develop and maintain interpersonal relationships with people from different cultures, and accomplish various tasks in a new context or setting (Cushner & Landis, 1996). Gudykunst, Guzley, and Hammer (1996) further pointed out that intercultural training programs are to improve trainees' performance in specific intercultural situations. Brislin and Pedersen (1976) also suggested that cultural training, such as cultural awareness and sensitivity training "allow one to learn about himself [or herself] as preparation for interaction in any culture" (p. 6).

Despite the importance and the increasing interest in intercultural training programs, most such training is conducted without appropriate theory-driven guidance (Gudykunst, Guzley & Hammer, 1996). The present study may provide some knowledge in designing and evaluating a theory-based training program. Finally, the results could help individuals understand why and how their affective aspect towards cultural differences is associated with a preference for a particular conflict management style, and how to adjust their ability to adapt to new cultures.

The present study also has limitations, which may provide opportunities for future research. The first limitation relates to the low alpha values obtained for the two factors of intercultural sensitivity. As mentions above, interaction enjoyment and interaction attentiveness did not achieve satisfactory reliability in this study. This limitation may influence the results of this study.

Another possible limitation of this study includes the particular sample employed and the measurement of conflict style. The convenience sample from university students may provide different results compared with real organizational employees. The conflict style preference measured by self-report with responses to scenario rather than by involvement in the real situation, or by observation of actual behavior, may also limit these results, although such paper-and-pencil survey is a better way to control the process and measure differences.

Overall, the results of this study provide some valuable information for our understanding and application of intercultural sensitivity and conflict management styles. The present study endeavors to shed some light on the relationship between these two important areas of interpersonal communication and organizational effectiveness. More studies are encouraged to examine how and why a person's intercultural sensitivity tend to influence one's selection of specific styles of conflict management.

References

Amason, A. C., & Schweiger, D. M. (1997). The effects of conflict on strategic decision making effectiveness and organizational performance. In C. K. W. De Dreu & E. Van De Vliert (Eds.). *Using Conflict in Organizations* (pp. 208–222). Thousand Oaks, CA: Sage.

Anderson, N. H. (1981). *Foundations of Information Integration Theory*. New York: Academic Press.

Antonioni, D. (1998). Relationship between the big five personality factors and conflict managements styles. *International Journal of Conflict Management*, 9(4). 336-355.

Baron, R. A. (1989). Personality and organizational conflict: Effects of the type A behavior pattern and self-monitoring. *Organizational Behavior and Human Decision Processes*, 44, 281-296.

Bell, E. C., & Blakeney, R. N. (1977). Personality correlates of conflict resolution modes. *Human Relations*, 30, 849-857.

Bhawuk, D. P. S., & Brislin, R. (1992). The measurement of intercultural sensitivity using the concepts of individualism and collectivism. *International Journal of Intercultural Relations*, 16, 413-436.

Black, J. S., & Mendenhall, M. (1990). Cross-cultural training effectiveness: A review and theory framework for future research. *Academy of Management Review*, 15(1). 113-136.

Blake, R. R., & Mouton, J. S. (1964). *The managerial grid*. Houston, TX: Gulf.

Brislin, R. & Pedersen, P. (1976). *Cross-cultural orientation programs*. New York: Gardner.

Brislin, R., & Yoshida, T. (1994). *Intercultural communication training: An introduction*. Thousand Oaks, CA: Sage publications.

Burke, R. J. (1970). Methods of resolving superior-subordinate conflict: The constructive use of subordinate differences and disagreements. *Organizational Behavior and Human Performance*, 5, 393-411.

Caldwell, D. F., & O'Reilly, C. A. (1982). Boundary spanning and individual performance: The impact of self-monitoring. *Journal of Applied Psychology*, 67

(1). 124–127.
Cegala, D. J. (1981). Interaction involvement: A cognitive dimension of communicative competence. *Communication Education*, *30*, 109–121.
Cegala, D. J. (1984). Affective and cognitive manifestations of interaction involvement during unstructured and competitive interactions. *Communication Monographs*, *51*, 320–338.
Cegala, D. J., Savage, G. T., Brunner, C. C., & Conrad, A. B. (1982). An elaboration of the meaning of interaction involvement: Toward the development of a theoretical concept. *Communication Monographs*, *49*, 229–248.
Chan, D. K.-S., & Goto, S. G. (2003). Conflict resolutions in the culturally diverse workplace: Some data from Hong Kong employees. *Applied Psychology: An International Review*, *52*(3), 441–460.
Chen. G. M. (2005). A model of global communication competence. *China Media Research*, *1*, 3–11.
Chen, G. M. (2007). A review of the concept of intercultural effectiveness. In M. Hinner (Ed.). *The influence of Culture in the World of Business* (pp. 97–115). Germany: Peter Lang.
Chen, G. M., & Starosta, W. J. (1996). Intercultural communication competence: A synthesis. *Communication Yearbook*, *19*, 353–383.
Chen, G. M., & Starosta, W. J. (1997a). A review of the concept of intercultural sensitivity. *Human Communication*, *1*, 1–16.
Chen, G. M., & Starosta, W. J. (1997b). Chinese conflict management and resolution: Overview and implications. *Intercultural Communication Studies*, *1*, 1–16.
Chen, G. M., & Starosta, W. J. (2000). The development and validation of the intercultural communication sensitivity scale. Human Communication, *3*, 1–15.
Copeland, L., & Griggs, L. (1985). Going international. New York: Random House.
Cushner, K. & Landis, D. (1996). The intercultural sensitizer. In D. Landis & R. S. Bhagat (Eds.). *Handbook of Intercultural training* (pp. 185–202). Thousand Oaks, CA: Sage.
Drake, L. E. (1995). Negotiation styles in intercultural communication. *The International Journal of Conflict Management*, *6*(1), 72–90.
Greeff, A. P., & de Bruyne, T. (2000). Conflict management style and marital satisfaction. *Journal of Sex & Marital Therapy*, *26*(4), 321–334.
Gross, M. A., & Guerrero, L. K. (2000). Managing conflict appropriately and effectively: An application of the competence model to Rahim's organizational conflict styles. *The International Journal of Conflict Management*, *11*(3), 200–226.
Gudykunst, W. B., Guzley, R. M., & Hammer, M. R. (1996). Designing intercultural training. In D. Landis & R. S. Bhagat (Eds.). *Handbook of Intercultural training* (pp. 61–80). Thousand Oaks, CA: Sage.
Hakansson, J., & Montgomery, H. (2003). Empathy as an interpersonal phenomenon. *Journal of Social and Personal Relationships*, *20*(3), 267–284.
Hammer, M. R., Bennett, M. J., & Wiseman, R. (2003). Measuring intercultural sensitivity: The intercultural development inventory. *International Journal of Intercultural Relations*, *27*, 421–443.
Instone, D., Major, B., & Bunker, B. B. (1983). Gender, self confidence, and social influence strategies: An organizational simulation. *Journal of Personality and Social Psychology*, *44*, 322–333.
Jaccard, J., & Wood, G. (1988). The effects of incomplete information on the formation of attitudes toward behavioral alternatives. *Journal of Personality and*

Social Psychology, *54*, 580-591.

Janis, I. (1972). *Victims of groupthink*. Boston: Houghton Mifflin.

Jehn, K. A. (1997). Affective and cognitive conflict in work groups: Increasing performance through value-based intragroup conflict. In C. K. W. De Dreu & E. Van De Vliert (Eds.). *Using conflict in organizations* (pp. 208-222). Thousand Oaks, CA: Sage.

Johnson, R. D. (1987). Making judgment when information is missing: Inferences, biases, and framing effects. *Acta Psychologica*, *66*, 69-82.

Kapoor, S., Blue, J., Konsky, C., & Drager, M. (2000). Intercultural sensitivity: A comparison of American and Japanese value preference. *Intercultural Communication Studies*, *10*(2). 215-233.

King, W. C., & Miles, E. W. (1990). What we know-and don't know-about measuring conflict: An examination of the ROCI-II and the OCCI conflict instruments. *Management Communication Quarterly*, *4*, 222-243.

Kipnis, D. (1976). *The powerholders*. Chicago: University of Chicago Press.

Leung, K., & Chan, D. K. S. (1999). Conflict management across cultures. In J. Adamopoulos & Y. Kashima (Eds.). *Social psychology and cultural context: Essays in honor of Harry C. Triandis* (pp. 177-188). Thousand Oaks, California: Sage.

Mendenhall, M., & Oddou, G. (1985). The dimensions of expatriate acculturation: A review. *Academy of Management Review*, *10*(1), 39-47.

Moberg, P. J. (2001). Linking conflict strategy to the five-factor model: Theoretical and empirical foundations. *The International Journal of Conflict Management*, *12*(1). 47-68.

Morrill, C., & Thomas, C. K. (1992). Organizational conflict management as disputing process: The problem of social escalation. *Human Communication Research*, *18*, 400-425.

Putnam, L., & Wilson, C. (1982). Communication strategies in organizational conflicts: Reliability and validity of a measurement. In M. Burgoon (Ed.). *Communication yearbook 6* (pp. 629-652). Beverly Hills, CA: Sage.

Rahim, M. A. (1983). A measure of styles of handling interpersonal conflict. *The Academy of Management Journal*, *26*(2), 368-376.

Rahim, M. A. (1985). A strategy for managing conflict in complex organizations. *Human Relations*, *38*(1). 81-89.

Rahim, M. A., & Bonoma, T. V. (1979). Managing organizational conflict: A model for diagnosis and intervention. *Psychological Reports*, *44*, 1323-1344.

Sauceda, J. M. (2003). Managing intercultural conflict effectively. In L. A. Samovar & R. E. Porter (Eds.). *Intercultural Communication: A Reader* (pp. 385-405). Belmont, CA: Wadsworth.

Schwarzwald, J., & Koslowsky, M. (1999). Gender, self-esteem, and focus of interest in the use of power strategies by adolescents in conflict situations. *Journal of Social Issues*, *55*(1). 15-32.

Sternberg, E. J., & Soriano, L. J. (1984). Styles of conflict resolution. *Journal of Personality and Social Psychology*, *47*, 115-126.

Tedeschi, J. T. (1990). Self-presentation and social influence: An interactionist perspective. In M. J. Cody and M. L. McLaughlin (Eds.). *The Psychology of Tactical Communication* (pp. 301-323). Clevedon, England: Multilingual Matters.

Terhune, K. W. (1970). The effects of personality in cooperation and conflict. In P. Swingleb (Ed.). *The Structure of Conflict* (pp. 193-234). New York: Academic Press.

Thomas, K. W. (1977). Toward multi-dimensional values in teaching: The example of conflict behaviors. *Academy of Management Review*, *2*, 484-490.

Ting-Toomey, S. (1988). Intercultural conflict styles: A face-negotiation theory. In Y. Y. Kim & W. Gudykunst (Eds.). *Theories in Intercultural communication* (pp. 213–235). Newbury Park, CA: Sage.

Ting-Toomey, S. (2006). Managing intercultural conflict effectively. In L. A. Samovar, R. E. Porter & E. R. McDaniel (Eds.). *Intercultural Communication: A Reader* (pp. 366–377). Belmont, CA: Wadsworth.

Triandis, H. (1977). *Interpersonal Behavior*. Monterey, CA: Brooks/Cole.

Triandis, H. C. (2006). Culture and conflict. In L. A. Samovar, R. E. Porter & E. R. McDaniel (Eds.). *Intercultural Communication: A Reader* (pp. 22–31). Belmont, CA: Wadsworth.

Van De Vliert, E. (1990). Enhancing performance by conflict-stimulating intervention. In C. K. W. De Dreu & E. Van De Vliert (Eds.). *Using Conflict in Organizations* (pp. 208–222). Thousand Oaks, CA: Sage.

Weider-Hatfield, D. (1988). Assessing the Rahim organizational conflict inventory-II (ROCI-II). *Management Communication Quarterly*, 1, 350–366.

Wilson, J. A., & Jerrell, L. S. (1981). Conflict, malignant, beneficial or benign. *New Directions for Higher Education*, 38, 105–123.

Womack, D. F. (1988). A review of conflict instruments in organizational settings. *Management Communication Quarterly*, 1, 437–445.

Yates, J. F., Jagacinski, C. M., & Faber, M. D. (1978). Evaluation of partially described multi-attribute options. *Organizational Behavior and Human Performance*, 21, 240–251.

24

Dealing with Chinese Negotiating Partners: A Cross-Cultural Co-operation Strategy

Alexander THOMAS
Regensburg University, Germany

Abstract: International and global business requires more and more intercultural co-operations. Co-operations between Chinese and German partners in business, administration, education and politics are increasing. To fulfil the demands of productive and for all partners satisfying cooperation processes and qualified understanding of cultural specific orientations, goals, beliefs, intentions and motivation of both sides are necessary.

The article presents some realistic examples of business related Chinese-German interaction processes and explains why misunderstandings and cognitive discrepancies are coming up in the interpersonal interactions and how it is possible to develop cross-cultural competence on high level. It is discussed what methods of intercultural education and training are needed and be effective to develop cross-cultural competence, how the effectivity of intercultural training can be measured and in which state of interaction processes which type of training is most effective. It is discussed how important it is to undertake scientific research on analysing interaction processes between German and Chinese partners in different contexts, from business to education and teaching, in order to identify the specific cultural factors influencing the personal perception, assessment, attributions, intentions, motivations, emotions and behaviour of both of the partners. This material coming from the viewpoint of Chinese and from the viewpoint of German partners should than be an integrated part in the intercultural trainings to develop cross-cultural competence on that high level the cooperation between Chinese and German partners demands.

1. Introduction

The product manager of a large German pharmaceutical firm reports: "I only worked in Asia for three years before I was transferred to the USA. In Asia the unfamiliarity and strangeness comes over you on the very first day, you feel it like a hammer blow. It takes months before you begin to see behind everything that's different and spot some things here and there that are familiar. I experienced the reverse in the USA: many things at first appeared superficially foreign and strange, for instance the architecture of the cities, but not as strange as what I'd seen in Asia. I always had Germany in the back of my mind when I looked at the USA, and I wondered, sometimes with a feeling of hope, more often with a feeling of concern: When will it be like this back home? The question itself implies that the time is not too far off!

At first I got along very well with the people in the USA: 'They're people like you and me,' I thought. But the longer I was there, the more unfamiliar and alien they seemed to me in many ways. Today, from a distance, I would still say that the differences are overall much smaller than those between my East Asian partners and myself, but there were moments in the USA when I wasn't so sure, because so little went the way I expected it to. But there was also an important difference in my approach: in Asia I expected things to be different and then I found that we had some things in common; in America I expected the people to be the same and I encountered many things that were unfamiliar and alien."

Can Europeans understand the Chinese? The German translator of the book *The Character of the Chinese*, published by Arthur Smith in 1900, asked the same question and came to the following conclusions:

> "[Many people who have travelled to China continually emphasise] ... the enormous difficulties which Westerners have in trying to form an opinion about the character of the Chinese. They point out that, the longer one associates with this 'pigtailed' people and the more thorough one's knowledge of the language and customs of this distant land becomes, the more contradictory it all seems. Sir Robert Hart, the General director of the Chinese Customs service, who lived for more than four decades in the Middle Kingdom, expresses very much the same sentiments: 'China is a country that is very difficult to understand.' A few years ago I thought that I had managed to learn something about its affairs, and I tried to put my views down on paper. Today I seem like a complete beginner again. If I were asked now to write three or four pages about China, I really wouldn't know where to start. I've only learned one thing: in my country one usually hears: don't allow yourself to buckle, even if they break you trying! In China, in contrast, it's exactly the opposite: buckle if you must, but don't let them break you!"

So which difficulties can one encounter when trying to act effectively under culturally foreign conditions?

2. Requirements for Cross-cultural Management

Requirements for international management in connection with cross-cultural learning, understanding and action arise from three topic areas: one's own culture, the foreign culture and the interaction between these two.

1.1 One's Own Culture

Normally we assume that the way we behave is the way that everyone else in the world behaves. This assumption is rational and correct, because mostly we do not come into conflict with others, and get on relatively well together. When we find out that people in our environment do not behave as we do, or as we expect them to behave, it disturbs us and makes us curious about the reasons for their unusual or unexpected behaviour.

The way that we perceive the world, the way we judge it, and the way we try to influence it and influence the people with whom we come into contact, seem to us to be right and proper.

Other forms of perception, judgement and influence appear to be wrong, slightly odd, incomplete, primitive etc.

Our own ways of perceiving, judging, influencing and behaving have become habits in the course of our development. They are taken for granted, have become routine and are no longer regarded as anything special. At best, we only think about our behaviour or perhaps discuss it with those close to us when something goes wrong, when something does not happen quite as we expect and as we are used to.

In our everyday life we are no longer conscious of these habits; we have no need to be. That does not mean that we lack the ability to be conscious of them; indeed, in conflict situations one acquires an enhanced awareness of the way one perceives, judges and behaves. When however do habits which one takes for granted become a topic for reflection or discussion? Often only when we observe children, old people, disabled people, strangers or foreigners who deal with objects or people or behave in situations differently than we are used to. For all these groups we also have corresponding explanations: children are not yet able to behave 'normally', old people are no longer able to, the disabled cannot because of their specific disability and strangers or foreigners cannot behave appropriately because they do not belong to us, and they have not learned how to conduct themselves properly.

In view of this generalisation of the way we perceive the world one must make the following demand in relation to cross-cultural learning, understanding and behaviour:

We must learn to think about, discuss, recognise and understand the ways in which our perception, thought and behaviour is conditioned by our own culture.

1.2 The Foreign Culture

People from other cultures, with other cultural, religious and social traditions, with different values and legal or economic traditions have developed different ways to perceive, judge, feel and act. For many generations these people have grown up in different geographical, climatic, economic, political, social and intellectual-cultural conditions. They have developed alternative strategies for survival and different ways of solving problems than we have.

Perhaps many aspects of other cultures have developed in the same way as they have in our culture, but there can be no doubt that many other things are different (universalism v. cultural relativism). People who have been socialised in other cultures also assume that everyone else in the world behaves as they do, that their behaviour is correct and that it will produce the desired results.

We can draw specific demands from this in relation to cross-cultural learning, understanding and behaviour: We must learn to recognise the way in which foreign cultures determine perception, thought, judgement, feelings and actions. We must understand the ways in which foreign cultures approach problem solving and survival. And we must acknowledge that these approaches can be just as rational as our own.

1.3 Cross-Cultural Interaction

One can contemplate one's own thoughts and behaviour, as well as that of members of foreign cultures whom one has observed. And one can take note of all the different types of behaviour and compare them with interest, and yet one's own thoughts and behaviour may remain unaffected. The debate becomes however personally relevant as soon as the need arises to work with people from other cultures. In this case it is not sufficient to merely reflect on one's own behaviour and thoughts and to recognise those of the foreigner. The obligation or the intention to work together makes it necessary to <u>co-ordinate</u> the behavioural and thought patterns of <u>one's own culture and of the foreign culture</u> in the context of cross-cultural co-operation.

1.4 The Different Aspects of Cross-Cultural Co-operation

First, one must consider the extent to which one's own culture and the foreign culture are similar (cultural identity), the extent to which they differ from each other (cultural difference) and the degree to which the two can coexist (cultural compatibility) or are incompatible (cultural incompatibility).

One must also consider how one might alter one's own behavioural patterns and adapt to those of the foreign culture. How far can and should this adaptation to the foreign culture go? Not adapting and showing an unwillingness to adapt can cause direct conflict with the foreign culture. Such behaviour may be regarded by the members of the host culture as arrogant, snobbish, dominant and dismissive. Complete adaptation to a foreign culture can however become a caricature and descend into absurdity (e.g. the African who visits Hamburg harbour dressed in Lederhosen and Bavarian hat).

Second, it is also important to consider the ways in which the foreign partner could alter his behavioural patterns; to think about perhaps pointing out one's own aims and habits to him, so that he can recognise and acknowledge them and perhaps adapt himself to them. The foreigner is often forced directly or indirectly by the living conditions in the host country to adapt himself to its normal behavioural patterns.

Third, one must also look at the consequences, for the sojourner and for his partner in the host culture, of attempting to adapt cultural behaviour, i.e. whether the attempts are productive or destructive.

It is only under the most favourable of conditions that the individual can concern himself with all of these factors in relation to cross-cultural interaction. Exchanging thoughts and discussing experiences of foreign cultures with other sojourners is a helpful and common way of carrying out these analyses. When however the quality of cross-cultural co-operation has to be considerably higher, for instance in international management, it is all the more necessary to take academic findings from cross-cultural research into account when considering the above-mentioned factors and to use research from specific topic areas to set up and check the analyses.

There are therefore specific requirements when one is concerned with cross-cultural learning, understanding and action:

> One must understand which elements of one's own cultural orientation and that of the foreign partner are compatible (can agree) and look at the extent and direction to which the incompatible (conflicting) elements are changing. The compatible elements allow both sides to adapt themselves to the other's habits and customs. The elements that appear incompatible are usually resistant to attempts at compromise.

Compatible elements could be: rituals for meeting and communicating, organisation rules. Incompatible elements could be: taboo areas of religious origin or strongly connected with the culture's value system, human rights abuses.

In view of these points sojourners must develop the following:
— **Tolerance** for ambiguity (endurance and acceptance of unclear and contradictory situations and behavioural reactions)

— **Synergetic** forms of cross-cultural interaction
— **Respect** for foreign cultural approaches to life, survival and social co-operation.

3. Handling Sino-German Business Relations Effectively — Analysis of the problems and possible solutions

The specific demands of cross-cultural learning and understanding and of acting in a foreign cultural environment, particularly in connection with Sino-German business relations, can be more closely analysed by the following concrete example of interaction between the German and Chinese business partners.

Example I   The Sino-German Negotiating Problem

The manager of a German firm is on his fourth trip to China within a short time to negotiate contracts. The contracts are for joint-venture projects in the production and sale of electronic equipment. The talks have up until now been extremely amicable, the Chinese have been very interested in the German manager's suggestions and have asked many questions, and future meetings have been arranged.

The negotiations have however not really moved forward. Meanwhile the German representative began having severe problems with his own parent company. Time was short, and the talks did not appear to the firm's management to be having the desired results; displeasure was expressed at the "less than satisfactory" way in which the representative had handled the negotiations. The first jokes about the manager's "holidays abroad" did the rounds. Frustration and anger began to build up inside him. When a further round of negotiations lasting several days appeared to have failed to produce an agreement, the manager believed he had finally seen through the tactics of his Chinese partners. They just wanted to stall in order to squeeze the maximum amount of information out of him, which they could then use to play his firm off against the competition.

He was furious with his negotiation partners, and in addition to this stressed by the tiring week of negotiations and fatigued by the climatic conditions. He had pearls of sweat on his forehead, held his pen shakily and nervously, and suffered symptoms of stress.

In the end he reacted in a way that we here might describe as "telling someone where to get off" or "taking someone to the cleaner's". Quite unexpectedly, he yelled at his Chinese partners that he was no longer prepared to be stalled, that this "beating around the bush" must stop, that he wanted clarity and binding commitments and that his patience was at an end.

For the Chinese these complaints were made with a shocking directness and at a high volume. The Chinese negotiation partners became pale and silent. The negotiations were not brought to a conclusion.

After his return home the manager learned from his superiors that he would not be travelling to China again. The Chinese had expressed further interest in the planned joint venture in a letter, but without saying a word about the negotiations that he had led. The management said that the firm would have to more or less start from scratch again, and with a new representative.

This example demonstrates a series of typical difficulties presented by Sino-German negotiations, whose causes clearly lie in the different ways that perception, thought, feelings and behaviour are shaped by the two cultures.

Problem Analysis for Example I

(1) "Nothing is really moving forward"

The German manager expected that the offers made for the contracts and in the negotiations would be taken up, inquired about, replied to and that they would lead rapidly to a satisfactory conclusion. This should also happen within a time period which is not laid down, but which should be "within reason". Negotiations, according to the German notion of how they should proceed, follow a <u>linear concept</u> according to the pattern: start development — result. Proceeding to the result means continual progress; one's position should be constantly improved during the run of the talks (see Diagram 1).

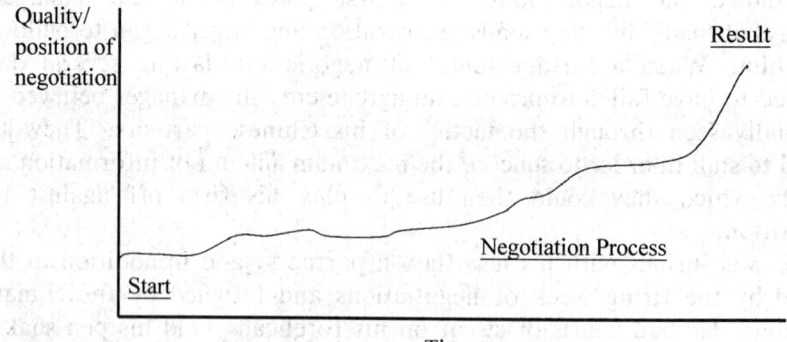

Diagram 1 The German pattern for a negotiating process

The Chinese in this example want to buy a product. For this to happen, all the people who will be directly or indirectly affected by the result of the negotiations have to get to know the product. The mutual exchange of information and the process of consultation requires a considerable amount of time. Lots of points are repeated, discussed again and again and looked at from different perspectives. The more important the product, and the more long-term the effects of a business deal, the more time is required by the negotiation process and the preparation for signing the contract.

According to Chinese notions of negotiation, the process follows a <u>cyclical pattern</u>: many stages of consultation and information and many discussions repeat themselves and encompass, during the course of the negotiations, ever larger groups of people, so that the results become more "watertight", more solid and stable and therefore generally of better quality (see Diagram 2).

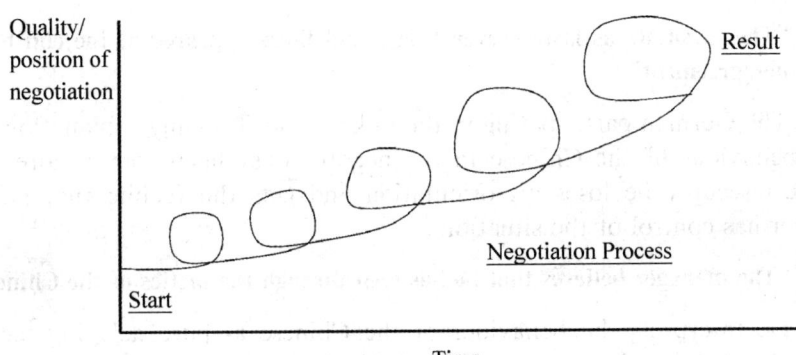

Diagram 2 The Chinese pattern for a negotiating process

(2) "Time was short, and the talks weren't going well"

Any process that becomes long and drawn out for no obvious reason is, from a German standpoint but also according to the principles of international management, unproductive and cost-intensive, does not therefore fit into usual patterns of management thinking and requires an explanation. Negotiations which are ineffective must be reflected upon, the causes of the ineffectiveness analysed and stated precisely. Either measures must to be taken to correct the problem, or the negotiations must be viewed as a failure. From the Chinese viewpoint, negotiations can be very productive, although, or perhaps precisely because they take a long period of time.

(3) "The negotiations do not appear to the management of the firm to be producing satisfactory results"

This is an old problem: the superiors and colleagues in the parent company, who are not familiar with the difficult and complex problems which their representatives are confronted with, or with the way that the Chinese handle negotiations, and who have no sensitivity or empathy, etc., become mistrustful about the way the negotiations are going. They also require an explanation for this abnormal course of events, which leads in this case to a person-specific causal attribution: the " less than satisfactory handling of the negotiations" by the representative.

(4) "The first jokes about the "holidays abroad" did the rounds"

Social pressure from one's colleagues and a certain ambivalence, with feelings varying between jealousy and admiration, have an adverse effect on the social position of a colleague working abroad for a firm. He does not receive any social support, but instead experiences an under-valuation of his work and reservedness.

(5) "The negotiations lasted several days and there appeared at the end to be no agreement"

The German participating in the talks cannot find any explanation for the behaviour of the Chinese in the negotiations, he becomes more and more insecure, he loses his orientation and gets the feeling that he no longer has control of the situation.

(6) "The manager believes that he has seen through the tactics of the Chinese"

He interprets the behaviour of the Chinese as pure delaying tactics intended to wear him down. He also believes that the Chinese want, through the continual stalling of the negotiations and by constantly starting discussions again from the beginning, to obtain information that they would not otherwise have access to and to use it to play him off against his competitors. This explanation of his Chinese negotiation partners' behaviour clears up everything that the German manager has up until now not been able to understand. He believes that he has found the real reason for the behaviour of the Chinese, he is then able to overcome his insecurity and gain a high degree of orientation and clarity of thought. What was unclear and contradictory has now become transparent and controllable.

Even though this interpretation of the behaviour of the Chinese negotiation partners is incorrect, because it does not have its roots in Chinese methods of thinking, behaving and negotiating, but rather corresponds to German cultural standards, it still has a high value for the German manager's orientation. He believes that he knows where he stands with respect to his partners and can adjust his behaviour accordingly. He does not have the culturally specific knowledge or the necessary sensitivity for culturally divergent behaviour to make a culturally adequate judgement about his Chinese partners. Nor does he have the ability to reflect upon the difficulties of interpreting Chinese behaviour on the basis of such cultural standards.

(7) **"He was also stressed by the tiring week of negotiations and fatigued by the climatic conditions"**

The unfamiliar living conditions and environment, including everything from climate and eating habits to social differences, exacerbated by the separation from family and friends, lead to physical and psychological stress, a factor which is commonly underestimated. Among the consequences are a narrowing of focus, fixation of thought, activation of stereotypes and prejudices against the members of the host culture, a general behavioural rigidity and an increase in tense, aggressive behaviour. Calmness and coolness disappear.

(8) **"He was furious with his negotiation partners and in the end he unexpectedly began yelling at them that he wasn't prepared to be stalled any more"**

Even if the Chinese delegation had recognised the physical and psychological stress that their German negotiation partner was enduring — which is rather improbable, because they were themselves totally occupied with their negotiation difficulties — they could not have understood or accepted the German manager's reaction. Someone who allows himself to lose control in such a way loses face in the eyes of the Chinese. He destroys co-operative harmony by embarrassing himself and his partners and he is therefore no longer a reliable or trustworthy partner for negotiation or co-operation. He loses his authority and his reputation.

The German manager, because of ignorance, a lack of tact and incorrect judgement about the reasons for the Chinese partners' behaviour (incorrect attributions), made the following mistakes:

(i) He did not take into consideration that in China, as in other East Asian countries all important decisions are discussed with all those who are to be affected, to see what degree of agreement can be reached. This mutual information exchange and consultation process requires a considerable length of time. A decision made in this way results is however very solid and not easily changed.

(ii) He failed to realise that it is precisely when decisions are of great importance and have far reaching consequences that, from the Chinese point of view, a correspondingly drawn-out negotiation process is required. It is also customary in bureaucratic command economies to take into consideration the wishes of the political and bureaucratic decision-makers, and there are also ponderous, prolonged procedures for making applications and receiving permission for projects. His partners could not have negotiated any faster, even had they wanted to.

(iii) Another point that he overlooked was that it is very unusual for the Chinese to resolve conflicts with others or problematic situations by openly and directly addressing the causes of the conflict or problem, in an attempt to bring clarity into the relationship and find a mutually satisfactory solution. The Chinese tend to overlook and ignore interpersonal conflicts and difficulties, or at most to address and settle them indirectly.

(iv) He also failed to recognise that it is not customary in China to display one's emotions in such an uncontrolled fashion, and to rebuke one's partners with whom one wants to negotiate further, especially when one may want at some point to work closely together with them. In China this leads inevitably to such a lasting loss of face that further cooperation with this specific German manager is impossible for the Chinese negotiation partners. Only when the person who has lost face is exchanged for a new negotiation partner can the negotiations be restarted and brought to a conclusion. This also applies, should a Chinese negotiator lose face.

In any event, the behaviour of the German manager, which is understandable from a German point of view, has not just cost a considerable sum and delayed the negotiations. There was also a large risk that the negotiations would fail altogether, producing no result and leading to a loss of the desired long-term economic advantages.

Example II   The Sino-German Banquet

After three weeks of strenuous negotiations, Mr. K., head of the German delegation of negotiators from a multinational concern, feels obliged to lay on a banquet for his Chinese partner. He makes detailed preparations, working with the hotel management to draw up the menu and specifying the seating plan with place cards. He is himself interested in sitting next to a Chinese engineer who particularly impressed him with his detailed technical knowledge, because he would like to speak with him. Half an hour before the start of the banquet, the Chinese interpreter arrives, checks the seating plan and alters it according to his own notion of a proper seating order. Mr. K. is quite taken aback, and feels as though he has been snubbed. Upon questioning the interpreter about this apparently high-handed action, he is simply told: "It is customary for us to do things this way".

Problem Analysis for Example II

In order to explain the situation from the Chinese point of view, one must see it on two separate levels, one being the importance of seating plans in reflecting social status, and the other being the treatment of the foreign guest (Mr. K.) by the Chinese host, represented by the interpreter.

(1) The importance of the seating order

According to Chinese cultural tradition, seating plans are not laid down to suit individual preferences, but according to a social hierarchy in which each guest has his proper place The existing social structure of a group, between groups and between individual representatives of groups must be reinforced for everyone by a visible representation of this structure at public and semi-public occasions through a corresponding seating plan. Disregarding this principle, which is important for creating and maintaining social harmony, leads to a loss of face for everyone who takes part in the public function. Firstly the host loses face because he has disregarded the social hierarchy of his guests. Then those placed below their rank in the social hierarchy lose face because they do not receive adequate recognition. And those placed above their rank lose face because they are placed in an inappropriately prominent position in the foreground and have to take seats which do not belong to them.

Since the interpreter wishes to spare Mr. K. this loss of face, he changes the seating plan, even at the risk of being reprimanded and criticised by Mr. K.

(2) The appropriate treatment of the foreign host by the Chinese guests

This aspect is taken into account by the Chinese interpreter, because he does not just have the task of sparing the host a loss of face, but rather also follows here the important Chinese cultural standard of hospitality. The relationship between guests and hosts should be as harmonious as possible and free from disturbances. The guests are therefore obliged to "... ease the burden of the host". In this situation the Chinese are the guests, represented above all by the interpreter, who has to make sure, if possible, that the host does not make any mistakes, so that the social relations between guest and host develop harmoniously and amicably.

Mr K., who wants to invite his Chinese guests to a banquet at the end of his stay in China, judges this occasion for social interaction in a way that serves the objectives that he has in mind and in accordance with his previous experience and practice with such social events. For Mr K. the banquet is a favourable opportunity to have a thorough discussion with the Chinese engineer whom he values so highly, in order to be able to convey this respect and to see if he could be won over as a trustworthy colleague for the future. He also wants to make sure that interesting and useful conversations take place during the banquet.

The German manager put his personal interests in the foreground and organises the banquet from his viewpoint alone. None of the Chinese guests would have any sympathy for this attitude, even if some of the Chinese guests had understood Mr K.'s desire to speak with of all people — the relatively unimportant Chinese engineer.

To organise the situation according to Mr. K. notions would not have been a celebratory farewell banquet for the Chinese guests, but rather a unique social disgrace for all concerned.

Both examples show that the difficulties for a German manager in dealing with Chinese partners can be traced back to the fact that he behaves in the way that he is used to behaving in Germany, and in a way that corresponds to his own patterns of thought and interpretation. There are in China however different rules and norms which govern the central requirements in both examples (effective leadership of negotiations and the organisation of a harmonious and social public occasion). Because both partners start from the assumption that everyone in the world, or at least Germans and Chinese, organise and judge both situations (the business negotiations and the banquet) in the same way they do, and because the Chinese possess no knowledge of the typical German principles of organisation and judgement and the German manager no knowledge of the corresponding Chinese rules, there is in the first case a serious conflict with far-reaching consequences. In the second example the conflict is only prevented by the rapid and "inconsiderate" intervention of the interpreter.

There is a potentially endless number of examples of this kind. In each case, the causes of problems in Sino-German business relations and of problems arising where Germans and Chinese live together are often seen as being caused by specific individuals and judged accordingly, although the cause of the misunderstandings and conflicts lies in the differing culture-specific patterns of orientation and behavioural habits.

4. Training to Develop Cross-Cultural Management Competence

Against the background of the above deliberations one may ask:

> Is there a way to prepare the personnel who work in China with qualifications so that culturally-determined communication and co-operation problems can be minimised?

This question can firstly be answered with some relatively simple observations:

(i) <u>Cross-cultural orientation training programmes</u> designed for a specific target group (e.g. managers) and for a particular target region (China) sensitise the trainees to the ways in which behaviour is determined by one's own culture and by the foreign culture. They can also produce an attitude of tolerance of and respect for foreign cultural behavioural characteristics among the participants, and enable them to apply what they have learned in negotiation and co-operation with Chinese partners.

(ii) <u>Coaching in situ</u> gives the subjects a deeper insight into the conditions for and the background of the apparently foreign behaviour of the Chinese (an insight into their orientation systems), an insight which is oriented towards everyday experiences in the Chinese host country. It is precisely when the trainee can contrast his own behavioural habits to the Chinese habits that he has observed and experienced that he can start to apply what he has learned in effective interaction with Chinese, even under stressful conditions.

In order to develop such programmes, it is necessary to carry out differential studies into the central cultural standards — the striking features of the specific cultural orientation system which actually lie behind the behaviour of the Chinese and Germans. Systematic analyses of those incidents between Germans and Chinese which are regarded as critical are extremely well suited to this task.

(iii) An evaluation of the real effectiveness of individual training measures prevents one having illusions about their effectiveness and points to possible solutions to problems.

In spite of the need for and the importance of cross-cultural training, which is constantly emphasised in speeches by politicians and economists, the interest in developing appropriate training measures and the willingness to invest in the corresponding basic and accompanying research is in Germany (particularly in contrast to the USA) noticeably lacking. There are certainly promising approaches for research and training, which have already been tried and tested in the USA, but which cannot be applied in Germany without further work, because of the different orientation systems. A critical examination of the methods and cultural adaptation is necessary because of German cultural traditions.

The following should illustrate the possibilities for qualifying management personnel in cross-cultural interaction, with particular reference to Sino-German co-operation.

4.1 The aims of the training programme

There are extensive catalogues which list the aims of cross-cultural training (Landis & Brislin 1981). Here one differentiates between general training on the one hand, which is related to the development of personality characteristics and personal and social skills, which facilitate acculturation and are intended to accelerate the adaptation to a foreign culture, and specific training on the other hand, which serves to develop skills which are needed under specific conditions at work, in the trainee's profession in general, in the learning process and in particular activities.

Cross-cultural training can therefore aim at the beginning just to sensitise trainees to foreign cultural thought patterns and behaviour, to promote a certain willingness to deal with partners from foreign cultures, and to encourage acceptance and tolerance of foreign lifestyles and working methods (Brislin 1986).

Culture-specific orientation training for a particular group of people travelling abroad, e.g. managers, language teachers or students, could in contrast also teach specific skills e.g. ways of solving typical problems experienced at work in China, a course in language teaching designed to deal with the habits and customs of American students, sex-specific role behaviour training as preparation for working in Japanese student groups etc. (Thomas 1988, 1993, Thomas & Sandner 1989).

Whereas cross-cultural training objectives which are too general and too obscure fail to properly meet the sojourner's need for concrete, tangible behavioural guidelines, a training programme which is in contrast too specific and geared to deal with particular aspects of behaviour is not suitable for qualifying trainees to adapt themselves flexibly to rapidly growing demands.

The following training objectives therefore attempt to strike a balance between the generalised and the specific, and are intended to give the trainees the skills they need to maximise their flexibility and their ability to generate positive transfer effects.

(i) Practical orientation training in those central cultural standards which are important for the host culture and which determine the behaviour of the native population in social interaction situations. The training is intended to offer help in solving work-related problems as well as everyday, practical difficulties encountered in the foreign culture.

(ii) Sensitisation to the way that the orientation of perception, thought and behaviour is shaped by foreign cultures.

(iii) Sensitisation to the way the trainee's own orientations are moulded by his own culture.

(iv) A cognitive reorientation in the regulation and control of the trainee's own behaviour and in the anticipation of foreign or strange behaviour, made possible by his wider knowledge of his own culture's orientation system and those of foreign cultures.

(v) Recognition of the way that members of the host culture usually judge (*attribute*) the determinants of behaviour in social interaction situations.

(vi) The development of the ability to recognise and anticipate those cross-culturally significant intersections during the individual's interaction with foreign partners which can be difficult to deal with and which often lead to cross-culturally based misunderstandings.

(vii) Learning to analyse the culture-specific causes of disruptions in cross-cultural communication and interaction, as well as of errors made in dealing with members of other cultures, so that the trainees can learn to avoid and cope with similar situations.

4.2 The phases of cross-cultural training

One can generally distinguish between three phases of cross-cultural training:

(1) Orientation training: Orientation training usually takes place in the native country of the trainee shortly before a period of work or study abroad and is intended to prepare him for the foreign culture, for the unfamiliar working and living conditions, and encompasses everything from regional studies to contrastive cultural training, which involves the contrast and comparative analysis of the thought patterns and behavioural habits of the trainee's native culture and of the foreign culture.

(2) Training "in situ": This form of training takes place during the sojourn in the host country and helps the trainee reappraise critical incidents and problems encountered in dealing with members of the host culture and with the working and living conditions. Cross-cultural training "in situ" can take the form of supervision or of different types of coaching.

(3) Reintegration training: Should problems be anticipated when a sojourner must return home and re-adjust himself to the local working and living conditions after a long stay abroad, reintegration training for his native country is useful in helping him to adapt. The training would take place shortly before or after the trainee returns home, would aim to ease his reintegration into his work and career and enable him to re-familiarise himself with the living conditions at home, which have come to seem somewhat strange after the long stay abroad.

4.3 The features of cross-cultural management training

The basic foundations and the central features of cross-cultural management training can be visually summarised as shown in Diagram 3.

In this diagram a clear distinction is made between the objective-organisational level and the facts on the one hand and the subjective-personal level and the interpretation of the facts on the other. The work assignments, working conditions and training objectives laid down by the organisation are subject to culture-specific influences. Moreover, this culture-specificity manifests itself particularly clearly in the way that work assignments, job demands and training objectives are subjectively interpreted and anticipated. There can be correspondences and similarities between the organisational level and the personal level, between the organisation-specific characteristics in the home culture and the target culture as well as in the individual values, convictions and attitudes of the German and his foreign partner. There can however also be differences which then lead to conflict situations.

Some of the generally important features of the training programme are shown in the lower half of the chart. One should note here that much diverse research and practical experience from the realm of management

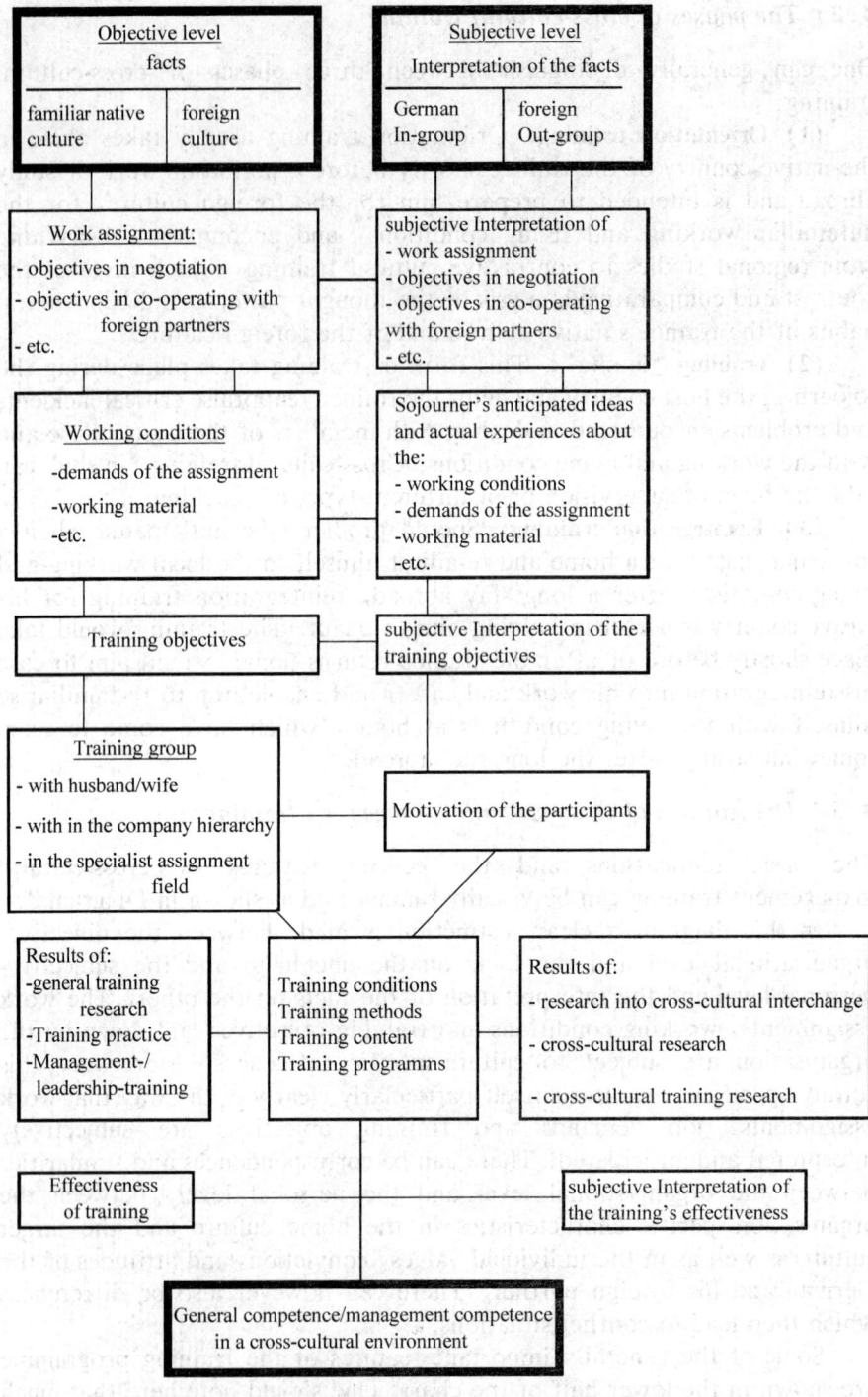

Diagram 3   Central features cross-cultural management training

and leadership training is also of fundamental significance for cross-culturally oriented management training. The relevant scientific knowledge must be obtained from different scientific disciplines, e.g. psychology, sociology, educational theory, anthropology, ethnology as well as from the area of comparative cultural sciences, jurisprudence and political science.

5. Training with the Culture Assimilator

Training with the culture assimilator is a primarily cognition-oriented form of training which is intended to develop the trainee's ability to recognise the patterns which lie behind the run of events in a foreign culture and the way these events are explained (isomorphic attribution), and to help him use these skills effectively in cross-cultural encounters. Culture assimilator training, developed by Fiedler, Mitchel and Triandis (1971), and Triandis (1984) is here based on insights obtained from social psychology and attribution research. From these findings it is proposed that social incidents and interactive processes become comprehensible, predictable and capable of being influenced when an individual has an accurate idea about why particular incidents and behavioural patterns in the social environment occur in the way they do and not differently (causal attribution) and about why his interaction partners follow certain objectives (final attribution).

The culture assimilator should help with the simulation of meaningful cross-cultural interaction. The trainee is presented with interaction situations in which conflict has arisen, which he should think through and possibly also re-enact in a role-play. He is here encouraged to understand and judge the behaviour of his interaction partners from different cultural viewpoints. The main difficulty in preparing material for the culture assimilator is identifying from the large variety of different examples the reasonably representative cross-cultural incidents, incidents which would also be familiar to the trainee and which enable him to obtain a deeper insight into the perception, thought and attribution patterns of his interaction partners in the host culture (see Diagram 4).

For each of the conflict situations described, the trainees are presented with different possible interpretations for the behaviour of the persons concerned, of which only one interpretation represents the correct answer from the viewpoint of the foreign culture. The other possible answers are incorrect interpretations based on an ignorance of cultural influences or on ethnocentrically-based errors. After choosing an explanation, the trainee is not only told whether his choice was correct or incorrect, but it is also explained to him why one alternative is correct from the view of the host culture, and why the others are not. This

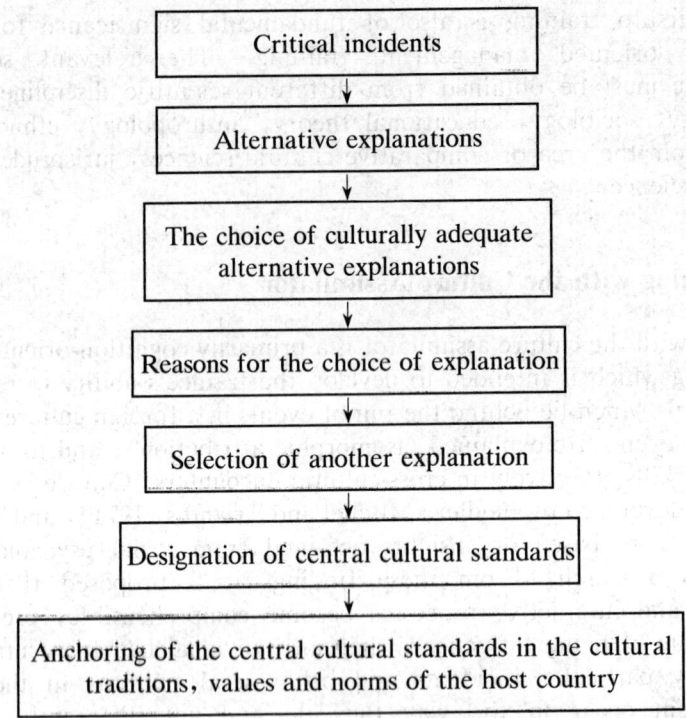

Diagram 4 Process of culture assimilator training

information should provide him with a comprehensible explanation for the suitability of his answer and help him build up a cultural frame of reference which enables him to deal with similar situations — at first during training and then in the host culture itself.

With the help of this feedback process, the central cultural standards of the host culture are imparted to the trainee and his attention is drawn to the significant differences between his own behaviour and that of his foreign interaction partners. To avoid teaching individual cultural standards in isolation, the embedding and anchoring of cultural standards in the values and norms of the host culture is continually pointed out during the course of the training.

Diagram 5 gives an overview of how the material for the culture assimilator is obtained.

Basic Research
Investigation of critical incidents
Establishment of relevant cultural standards
Structure of relationship between cultural standards

(to be continued)

Anchoring of cultural standards in cultural history
The degree to which cultural standards affect behaviour
Research into the application of the Culture Assimilator
Giving the trainee an understanding for the degree to which both sets of cultural standards affect behaviour
Informing the trainee about his own cultural standards and those of the foreign country
The application of foreign cultural standards in cross-cultural encounters
Evaluation of the degree to which foreign cultural standards affect behaviour
The development of cultural synergy

Diagram 5   The Development and Application of a Culture Assimilator

5.1   Research into the application of the Culture Assimilator

Culture assimilator training does not aim to develop concrete forms of behaviour, for example, "When you are sitting with Chinese partners at a negotiation table, you must always smile and direct your gaze towards the leader of the negotiating delegation." Instead the trainee learns, through typical, representative examples of "critical incidents", the forms of perception, judgement (attribution) and activity (intervention/organisation) which his foreign cultural partner takes for granted and regards as proper and correct. In other words, foreign cultural patterns of perception, thought and activity should be practised and learned with the help of this training.

A manager on an assignment abroad, equipped with these skills, should be able to achieve the following:

— Anticipate his foreign partner's behaviour more exactly and more reliably
— Put himself more easily in his partner's position (empathise), and be able to make isomorphic attributions
— Communicate his objectives and intentions more effectively to his partner
— Learn to respect the cultural values, norms and behavioural habits of his partner and communicate this respect
— Get to know his own culture-specific behavioural habits better through contrast with his foreign partner.

— Learn how to look for the advantages and disadvantages of both culture-specific approaches to dealing with challenges and solving problems, and learn how to evaluate their potential for cultural synergy.

The following is an example of a training unit from the "China culture and business assimilator" (Thomas & Sandner 1989).

(1) The critical incident in the cross-cultural encounter

"A delegation of German engineers, whose firm has been involved in a co-operation project with an engineering works in China for two years, travels to a recently established branch of the business, at the invitation of their Chinese partners, to survey the continuation of the project in the new factory. After a very warm reception, the German group is led proudly through the factory's three halls. The achievements of the Chinese workers are examined in a relaxed, friendly atmosphere. Mr. B., who can still remember well the tough negotiations over the co-operation contract, is very comfortable on his second visit to China. During the tour Mr. B. mentions this to the manager. He remarks casually, 'If only you'd made it so easy for us back then, you really had us in a corner.' The manager does not react, and finishes the conversation."

(2) The task for the trainees

"Mr. B. asks you why the mood of the Chinese manager worsened so quickly. Read through the incident carefully and then look at the following possible answers. Pick out the explanation which is in your view the correct one."

(3) The possible explanations given for the cause of the conflict

(A) The Chinese manager found it embarrassing to speak about a problem which, as far as he was concerned, had already been dealt with.
(B) The Chinese manager regarded the negotiations and the visit as two completely different matters which should remain separate.
(C) The Chinese manager found the German's impolite and unfriendly approach objectionable.
(D) The Chinese manager identifies himself very strongly with his company and did not want to discuss the subject.

(4) Comments on the explanations presented, made on the basis of and in relation to typical Chinese cultural standards for the orientation and regulation of behaviour

Possible answer (A):

"You have explained the situation correctly to Mr. B. After the

Chinese have completed the contract with the Germans, Mr. B. is naturally regarded as a friend. Earlier problems that had hindered the formation of this friendship are no longer talked about. And why should they be? There should be harmony between friends, harsh discussions are out of place.

Mr. B. certainly did not attach any significance to his words, but he put the Chinese manager in a terrible position because of his carelessness. The manager recognised that he was threatened with a loss of face, a humiliation that would be difficult to compensate for, and which he could only avoid by 'quitting the field'."

Possible answer (B):

"Well, your answer isn't wrong, even if you've not quite got to the heart of the matter.

It's true that a strong distinction is made in China between work, in other words here the negotiations, and the private sphere, which certainly includes polite visits such as this one. Although it's not very likely that ignorance of this fact alone would cause such a drastic reaction on the part of the Chinese, one can't rule such extreme cases out altogether.

I'll introduce you to similar situations during the course of the training, where you'll certainly be able to identify the more fundamental problems."

Possible answer (C):

"No, I don't think that was the reason. It's certainly true that the Chinese are extremely polite people, and that they react very sensitively to even the smallest violation of what is regarded as 'good manners'. But they are certainly not as over-sensitive and easily offended as your answer suggests. Don't be misled by a false view of the Chinese which suggests they must be treated with kid gloves. You should read through the incident again more carefully."

Possible answer (D):

"This answer is certainly incorrect. I think you've taken your western notions of loyalty and a sense of duty and applied them to the Chinese. Don't forget that we are dealing with a system that is certainly showing signs of wanting to embrace reform, but which is still fundamentally socialist. Morale at work in socialist systems is not high enough to lead to a strong identification with a company. You will have to look at this situation again."

(5) Comments on the anchoring of central cultural standards in cultural history

"The concept of saving face is a generic term which describes the way in which the Chinese are frequently seen to avoid embarrassing situations, to withdraw from interaction with others when critical problems arise. Even Chinese philosophers in the centuries before Christ (Mo-tsu and

Confucius) concerned themselves with the problem of how to avoid conflict with others. They taught that one should tolerate insults without feeling disgraced, so that one does not become involved in degrading fights or squabbles. Confucius emphasised that saving face contributes to inner as well as social harmony. It is for the Chinese the most elegant approach to human interaction and should above all serve to respect the feelings of the person to whom one is speaking. Saving face — one's own and that of others — is therefore an important principle for maintaining inner social harmony.

Avoid therefore, in encounters with the Chinese, situations which put your Chinese partner in a corner, which provoke him, or which are intended to invite certain reactions and therefore threaten him with loss of face. Be careful not to lose face yourself, and you will be respected."

5.2 Central cultural standards in the China business and culture assimilator

Research into the effects of central cultural standards on Sino-German management relations has produced the following list of Chinese cultural standards:

Central Chinese cultural standards
1. Saving face
2. Separation of work and private life
3. Fear of sanctions
4. Orientation towards hierarchical structures
5. Enjoyment of bargaining, haggling
6. Honouring of contracts
7. Friendships and politeness
8. Hospitality
9. National pride
10. Modesty and self-control

5.3 Central American and German cultural standards

Studies into German-American relations in the area of education have produced the following list of central American and German cultural standards (Müller & Thomas 1991 et al.):

Central German cultural standards (as seen by US-American managers)
1. Formalism
2. Orientation towards hierarchy and authority
3. Fulfilment of one's duty
4. Familiy-centredness
5. Differentiated approach to interpersonal accessibility / openness
6. Physical closeness
7. Direct style of interpersonal communication
8. Personal property
9. Traditional distinction between sex-roles
10. Forward-looking orientation
11. A functional approach to property
12. Ritualised encounters between sexes (dating)
13. Control of nature
14. Mobility

Central US-American cultural standards
1. Individualism
2. Equality of opportunity
3. Emphasis on action / "getting things done"
4. Emphasis on achievement
5. Interpersonal accessibility / openness
6. Personal reservedness
7. Social recognition
8. Calmness, coolness
9. Patriotism
10. Forward-looking orientation
11. A functional approach to property
12. Ritualised encounters between sexes (dating)
13. Control of nature
14. Mobility

6. Conclusion

For German training groups there is still a great lack of well-supported organisational psychology research, suited to developing material and concepts for management training to encourage cross-cultural learning and understanding. Anglo-American management research and comparative cultural studies have a long tradition and have contributed valuable findings which have helped in the development of corresponding training programmes. It is however not possible to apply their research data to German conditions without further work, precisely because of the culture-specific conditions under which they were obtained and the culture-specific orientation of the target groups for whom the training programmes were developed. There are a large number of commercially available training programmes, but their training material is usually based just on regional studies or put together from randomly collected impressionistic data. At best, colleagues with experience abroad report to junior members of staff in a firm on their observations and their own personal approach to dealing with foreign partners. Here stereotypes, prejudices and subjective explanations as well as individual strategies for solving conflicts are often accepted at face value and passed on to the next generation of managers without further analysis.

Particularly in view of the complexity demonstrated here of cross-cultural learning and understanding, and of acting in a cross-cultural context, these last few comments make it more than clear that systematic, targeted and practical research is necessary to produce relevant material for training programmes, if amateurism in the field of cross-cultural training is to be turned into professionalism.

References

Brislin, R. W. et al. (1986). *Intercultural Interactions. A Practical Guide*. Beverly Hills: Sage.

Fiedler, F. E., Mitchell, T. & Triandis, H. C. (1971). Culture assimilator. n approach to cross-cultural training. *Journal of Applied Psychology*, 55, 95–102.

Landis, D. & Brislin, R. W. (Eds.). (1983). *Handbook of Intercultural Training*. Vol. 1–3. New York: Pergamon Press.

Müller, H. & Thomas, A. (1991). *Kulturelles Orientierungstraining für die USA. SSIP-Bulletin*, Bd. 62. Saarbrücken: Breitenbach.

Thomas, A. (1988). Untersuchungen zur Entwicklung eines interkulturellen Handlungs trainings in der Managerausbildung. *Psychologische Beiträge*, Band 30, 147–165.

Thomas, A. & Sandner, R. (1989). *China Culture and Business Assimilator*. Regensburg: Unveröffentl. Trainingsmaterial.

Thomas, A. (1993). Psychologie interkulturellen Lernens und Handelns. In A.

Thomas (Hrsg.), *Kulturvergleichende Psychologie — Eine Einführung*. Göttingen: Hogrefe.

Triandis, H. C. (1984). A theoretical framework for the more effective construction of culture assimilators. *International Journal of Intercultural Relations*, 8, 301–310.

25

How to Avoid Language Conflict in Europe in the Third Millennium

Peter H. NELDE
KU Brussels, Belgium

Abstract: The European Union has sought to build as many unifying elements as possible within the European countries with their diverse languages, cultures and histories. Some conflicts that occur are rather predictable from the diverse backgrounds, but some newer types of problems have arisen that were not predictable. The following gives examples of those problems and suggests ways of handling them.

Russia and the European Union

Two examples of conflicts related to language and culture will show that conflicts do not always originate in historical, political and economical constellations of multilingual settings, but can also be self-generated in a multilingual community like the European, especially created to neutralize causes of conflict.

Example 1

In 1990, an eclectic list on the grievances of the former Soviet Union "nations", minorities / majorities, language communities led to the following list illustrating the divergent claim of language groups:

1.	Political independence	(Azerbeidjan / Armenia)
2.	Economic and cultural independence	(Belorussia)
3.	A change of status of the Republic	(Tartars)
4.	Rehabilitation of oppressed language groups	(Greeks, Germans, Turks)
5.	Autonomy	(Moldavia, Poles in Lithuania)
6.	Boundary change	(Armenians in Karabach, Tadjiks)
7.	More autonomous rights within their republic	(Jarkutsks)
8.	Interethnic exchanges	(Estonians back to Estonia, Estonian Russians back to Russia)
9.	Cultural associations	(Koreans, Tartars outside the Republic, Greeks in Georgia)

Example 2

At present the European Union deals with 72 language combinations — work for almost 3,000 translators and interpreters. Sometimes more than 700 interpreters are working the same day. French, English and German are the most important languages. Only tricks and an asymmetrical interpretation structure allow communication: for example, everyone speaks his own language, which will often be interpreted only into the major languages — a well organized tower of Babel.

By the way, is it really true that in the beginning of the EU the Danes regretted the competition of theoretically equal languages and suggested a reduction to English and French, simultaneously renouncing to use their own language? Rumors say that the congratulations sent by Great Britain and France to Copenhagen because of Danish wisdom and insight provoked a vehement Danish reaction. Accordingly, Danes expected the British to use French and the French to use English. No further comments have reached Brussels since.

That attempts have been made to avoid or overcome the resulting conflicts is shown by a series of plans which have been used in multilingual countries like Belgium, since Europe, with its language conflicts often dating from the nineteenth century, has obviously not prepared sufficiently for a multilingual (partial) European Union in the year 1995.

Ethnic Conflicts

Most contacts between ethnic groups do not occur in peaceful, harmoniously coexisting communities, but they are accompanied by varying degrees of tension, resentment and differences of opinion, all of which are characteristic of every competitive social structure. Under certain conditions, such generally accepted competitive tensions can degenerate into intense conflicts, in the worst case, ending in violence. The assumption of some sociologists that ethnic contact inevitably leads to conflict situations seems to be exaggerated, to say the least, given the fact that some ethnic groups do live peacefully together. The possibility of conflict erupting is, however, always present, since differences between groups create feelings of uncertainty of status. Sociologists who have dealt with contact problems between ethnic groups define conflict as contentions involving real or apparent scarcities, interests, and values, in which the goals of the opposing group must be attacked or at least neutralized to protect one's own interests (prestige, employment, political power, etc.) (Williams 1947). This type of conflict often appears as a conflict of values in which differing behavioral norms collide, since usually only one norm is accepted. Conflicts between ethnic groups, however, occur only very rarely as openly waged violent conflicts, and usually consist of a complex system of threats and sanctions in which threats constitute a key to understanding a conflict, especially if the interests and values of one group are endangered. Conflicts can arise relatively easily if — as is usually the case — interests and values have an emotional basis.

The magnitude and development of a conflict depends on a number of factors which are determined by the number of points of friction between two or more ethnic groups, the presence of equalizing or mitigating elements, and the degree of uncertainty of all the participants. Thus, a one-sided (monofactoral) conflict explanation or an explanation based on irrational prejudices will fail. Very different factors which influence each other and can reinforce and "escalate" each other, e. g. feelings of uncertainty and intimidation, and scares in areas of values and interests, can cause group conflict. Consequently, this group conflict is part of the social behavior in which different groups compete with each other, and should not be connoted only negatively, since in this way new — and possibly more peaceful — forms of coexistence can arise. On the other hand, tensions between ethnic groups brought about by feelings of intimidation can give rise to new conflicts at any time, conflicts which can be caused by a minority as well as by a majority group. As long as society continues to create new scares, because of its competitive orientation, the creation of new conflicts appears unavoidable.

Along with linguists and sociologists, political scientists also assume that language contact can cause political conflict. Language conflicts can be brought about by changes in the expansion of the social system when there is language contact between different language groups (Inglehart & Woodward 1967). Belgium and French Canada are examples of this. The reasons for this are the following: a dominant language group (French in Belgium, English in Canada) controls the crucial authority in the areas of administration, politics, and economy, and gives employment preference to those applicants who have command of the dominant language. The disadvantaged language group is then left with the choice of renouncing social ambition, assimilating, or resisting. While numerically weak or psychologically weakened language groups tend towards assimilation, in modern societies numerically stronger, more homogeneous language groups having traditional values, such as their own history and culture, prefer political resistance, the usual form of organized language conflict in this century. This type of conflict becomes especially clear when it occurs between population groups of differing socioeconomic structures (urban / rural, poor / wealthy, indigenous / immigrant) and the dominant group requires its own language as a condition for the integration of the rest of the population. Although in the case of French Canada, English appeared absolutely necessary as the means of communication in trade and business, nearly 80% of the francophone population spoke only French and thus was excluded from social elevation in the political / economic sector. The formation of a small French-speaking elite, whose only goal was political opposition to the dominant English, precipitated the latent, socially incited language conflict.

Most current language conflicts are the result of language separation accompanied by differing social status and one-sided preferential treatment of the dominant language on the part of the government: in these cases religious, social, economic or psychological scares and frustrations of the weaker group may be responsible for the language conflict. However, a critical factor in the expansion and intensification of such a conflict remains the impeding of social elevation to the point of blocking any social mobility of a disadvantaged or suppressed ethnic group (cf. the numerous language conflicts in multiethnic Austria-Hungary).

The climax of a political language conflict is reached when all conflict factors are combined in a single symbol or language, and quarrels and struggles in very different areas (politics, economics, administration, education) appear under the heading of language conflict. In such cases, politicians and economic leaders also operate on the assumption of language conflict, disregarding the actual underlying causes, and thereby inflame "from above" the conflict that arose "from below", with the result that language assumes much more importance than it had at the outset of the conflict. This language-oriented "surface structure" then obscures the more deeply rooted, suppressed "deep structure"(social and economic problems).

Conflicts in Multilingual Nations

Latent and manifest language conflicts can be described from different standpoints. Europe comprises about 70 to 80 languages, of which approximately 35 are spoken in the area of the European Union. In addition to a division into traditionally multilingual countries (those that are "administratively" multilingual), smaller divisions can be made according to language groups with a high predisposition to conflict because of their mobility or immobility, or according to the degree of heterogeneous population composition in densely populated urban areas that are highly industrialized.

Officially Multilingual Countries

The language conflicts of multilingual countries that developed historically are better known. These countries definitely include Great Britain, Ireland, Belgium, Luxemburg, Switzerland, Ex-Yugoslavia and since the late 1980's also the European part of the former Soviet Union. However, the conflict structures in these administratively multilingual countries are of completely different kinds. The Irish language conflict is closely linked to the inherent ideology of Irish which expressly restricts the spread of Irish as a native language. Irish, the mother tongue of a rural Catholic minority in a region (Konamara) with a high rate of unemployment, can only assert itself with great difficulty in urban centers where social advancement is important.

In the case of Belgium, whose language conflicts can also be explained as socioeconomic, the usual conflict description of a repressed minority is even less true. The oppression of the Flemish, which can be interpreted historically and which the respective literature always portrays as the oppression of a minority, in fact concerns a majority population so that the Flemish should actually be regarded as Europe's only repressed majority. In the case of Luxemburg, the explanation of the conflict is even more paradoxical than in Belgium. The trilingualism of the country can be regarded — in terms of language pedagogy — as a model for multilingualism in the Europe of the future. The dialect-like Luxemburg language of kindergarten is harmoniously succeeded by standard German taught from the first year of primary school on. French does not appear as native tongue until the second year of primary school. But the multilingualism of Luxemburg's schools can also be explained as an accumulation of deficits: The Luxemburgish language plays only a subordinate role as a written language; standard German is supplanted by French after only a few years of school; and French, only in rare cases the mother tongue of the student, is taught for reasons of language politics as a native and not as a foreign language from the second school year on, without students having the necessary prerequisites (Robert Bruch: "les classes des muets" = "classes of mutes"). For these reasons it can be presumed that most pupils have a triglossic deficit.

Conflicts in Switzerland, in contrast to Belgium, often have an indirect character and are frequently dealt with more academically than in other countries, although local newspapers by no means evade conflicts. Here, too, numerous oppositions and confrontations can be explained socio-economically, although a real portrayal of the conflicts would have to be based on much more complex relationships. The "Röstigraben" (the so-called "French Fries trench") between French- and German-speaking Swiss, the conflicts in bilingual cities like Freiburg and Biel, isolation from West Germans because of the increased use of spoken dialect (cf. the so-called "Basel-Lörrach effect"), and the Germanization of the last Rhaeto-Romance pockets in southeastern Switzerland show that even federated states cannot avoid language conflicts. Finally, the Balkan countries have shown once again how unresolved language conflicts and those that have seemingly quieted down can break out again because of the extreme socio-economic difference between north and south. A comparison of the official multilingual countries of Europe shows, in spite of a few common denominators, the broad span of characteristic conflicts among ethnolinguistic groups.

Autochthonous Minorities versus Allochthonous Minorities

Forms of multilingualism have been more diversified during the decades since World War II, or they have at least come to be evaluated differently. Originally the autochthonous minorities ("ethnic groups", "nationalities") who were residents of most European nations were the center of interest. But since the 1960s new, often socially defined minorities like migrants, guest workers, returning settlers from former colonies, refugees, emigrants, and transmigrants have moved into the foreground of the European context. All of these groups have brought about a new awareness among the majority population and by no means has this resulted in the native minorities being pushed into the background. Instead, they have been carried along by new currents like the so-called "renaissance of dialects and less common languages". A new regional consciousness oriented toward smaller units ("small is beautiful") has increasingly shifted the view of research, politics, culture and the public to minorities, whose significance in a culturally viable Europe, east and west, has been stressed.

The pressure from majority groups to standardize language, and the cultural and socioeconomic influences of the super-powers, which in turn threaten the majority groups themselves with loss of cultural independence, all put pressure on the smaller ethnic groups. These groups have no legal protection at all and are faced with the question whether or not it is desirable and possible to take measures to ensure the survival of their minority. For most of the smaller ethnic groups of Europe, this results in the usually undesirable and difficult choice of either conforming to the often economically stronger majority group and being further assimilated, or facing a conflict, the solution or outcome of which is completely unknown. In present-day Europe, with its increased tendency toward unification and international involvements, any language or culture contact between different ethnic-cultural groups seems to imply conflict. Since majority groups in their attitude toward linguistic or cultural minorities usually react considerably more negatively to allochthonous than to autochthonous minorities, the conflicts can be described without overlapping. The confrontations between the majority group or dominant groups and the autochthonous or allochthonous minority groups, i.e. the indigenous or the migrant groups, take place on different levels (social, political, economic, cultural), although the forms of discrimination are often similar.

In the Netherlands, Switzerland, and France, "autochthonous" and "allochthonous" are described and analyzed quite differently for methodological reasons. In Great Britain, however, sociolinguistic contacts are lacking between London linguists, examining the so-called "decolonized" languages, and the minority researchers in Scotland and Wales because of completely different conflict situations. No wonder there have been hardly any suggestions for solutions of the conflict which would try to neutralize the quite comparable language conflicts of the two groups.

Urbanization

Areas of linguistic concentration, like large cities, open another conflict perspective. The population explosion and increasing mobility in the 1980s have led to the disappearance of monolingual world cities in the last decade of this century. Much less obvious than in international metropolises is the conflict-laden multilingualism in European capitals. Here, too, the causes and occasions of conflict vary considerably, although many have their origin in the insufficient importance placed on minority languages. The following are a few random examples of such conflicts are the following:

- Dublin / Baile Atha Cliath: Irish as administrative language with a relatively small area of use is spoken almost exclusively as a second language, often learned with great effort;
- Helsinki / Helsingfors: The economically strong Swedish minority is bilingual, the Finnish majority mainly monolingual;
- Leeuwarden / Ljouwert: The Frisian minority, which has already weakened in terms of numbers compared to Dutch, is endangered more by a Frisian city dialect ("city Frisian") which is similar to Dutch, than by outside factors;

- Bruxelles / Brussel: First, the favoring of, or just the awarding of equal rights to, the numerical Flemish minority (smaller school classes, the same rights as the majority) has led to tensions. In addition, the threat of becoming an even smaller minority because of the presence of migrants provides more fuel for the conflict;
- Bratislava / Pressburg: In spite of successful Slovakification of a partly Hungarian, partly German population over the course of history, the introduction of the territorial principle finally slowed down the threatening Czechification in the 1970s. Now Slovakian independence and growing nationalism bring new pressures to bear on the minorities;
- Fribourg / Freiburg: The German minority, most of whom speak a local dialect, by doing so raise the threshold of language acquisition for majority speakers, whose learning motivation diminishes as a result;
- Bozen / Bolzano: The initial challenge to the Italians to further bilingualism, send more of their children to German schools and thereby emancipate the German minority, has now given way to the fear that too many bilingual Italians could harm the work market of the German minority;
- Pécs / Fünfkirchen: Repressive political measures so menaced the substance of the small German minority that the minority language has largely disappeared from public life.

These different situations of conflict, to which numerous other examples could easily be added, show that a single plan for solving such language problems would only meet with failure.

Language Conflict in Contact Linguistics

In contact linguistics, the term conflict remains ambiguous, at least when it is described generally as social conflict which can arise on the basis of a multilingual situation (Hartig 1980: 182). If we assume that conflict represents a counterpart to language contact and is interdependently connected with it, then both concepts can apply to individuals and to language communities. The notion appears to us essential here that neither contact nor conflict can occur between languages. They are conceivable only between speakers of languages. Oksaar (1980) correctly points out the ambiguity of the term language conflict in the sense of conflict between languages with reference to the personality of the speaker, as well as conflict by means of language(s), including processes external to the individual. Similarly, Haarmann (1980 II: 191) distinguishes between interlingual and interethnic language conflicts. Because of their conceptual interdependence, the paucity of research on language conflict equals that on the methodology of language contact research. Even among the founders of modern research in language contact, who publish simultaneously to those in the rapidly developing disciplines of sociolinguistics and language sociology, e.g. Weinreich (1953) and Fishman (1972), the term conflict rarely appears. While Weinreich views multilingualism (bilingualism) and the accompanying interference phenomena as the most important form of language contact, without including the conflicts between language communities on the basic of ethnic, religious, or cultural incompatibilities, Fishman (1972: 14) grants language conflict greater importance in connection with language planning. Haugen (1966) was the first to make conflict presentable in language contact research with his detailed analysis of Norwegian language development. Indeed, even linguists in officially multilingual countries (Switzerland, Belgium) resisted until the end of the 1970s treating conflict methodically as part of language contact research, since such an "ideologicalization" of language contact appeared to them as "too touchy" (Fishman 1980: XI). One reason for the late discovery of a term indispensable in today's contact research is to be found in the history of contact linguistics itself: in traditional language contact research (as well as in dialectology and research on linguistic change) the emphasis was always on closed groups, which were usually geographically homogeneous and could be described with relative ease socioeconomically, rather than on urban industrial societies. However, it is exactly in modern, urban society that conflicts result due to normative requirements of the more powerful, majority, group, which demands linguistic adaptation as a language contact alternative, and thus preprograms conflict with those speakers who are unwilling to adapt.

Despite the unsatisfactory research situation, which is essentially limited to empirical case studies in the area of research on language conflict, the following statements can be made about language conflict: (1) language conflict can occur wherever there is language contact, chiefly in multilingual communities, although Mattheier (1984: 200) has demonstrated that language conflicts can and do exist in so-called monolingual local communities; and (2) language conflicts arise from the confrontation of differing standards, values, and attitude structures, and strongly influence identity image, upbringing, education and group consciousness. Thus, conflict can be viewed as a form of contact, or, in terms of a model, as a complementary model to the language contact model.

Plans for Handling Conflict

The Territorial Principle and the Example of Belgium

In Europe, two principles of multilingualism were originally in opposition to each other: the individualist principle, mainly supported by the Romance side, by which every speaker is free to use his mother tongue or another language in all official and private domains, regardless of his place of residence; and the territorial principle, defended more by the Germanic side, which obliges the resident of a region, declared administratively to be monolingual, to use the respective territory-bound state language in official domains. Although the individualist principle prevailed up to the 1960s and led to extensive Frenchification of the country, today this principle can only be found in bilingual Brussels. In fact, the famous-notorious "liberté du père (!) de famille" ("liberty of the father of the family": free choice of one of the two national languages by the head of the family) was only abandoned in Brussels in the 1970s. Instead of a bilingual structure, Brussels today maintains two parallel, chiefly monolingual networks in official domains. The two largest sections of the country are either monolingual French or Dutch, in accordance with the territorial principle, except for a few communities on language borders and the German minority in eastern Belgium.

This application of the territorial principle met simultaneously with rejection and admiration in the world, since apparently the viability of a small multilingual nation was thereby maintained. No wonder the Canadian language legislation of Quebec (the so-called Law 101) was influenced by that of Belgium! The consequences for the individual speaker are considerable: whereas the chances of social advancement before introduction of this plan were unavoidably linked to the mastery of two languages (at least in the case of the Flemish and German populations), now life in many spheres can proceed mainly in one language, namely, the language of the respective territory.

De-emotionalization

With the introduction of the territorial principle, the Belgian lawmakers acted on the assumption that strict regulation in a few essential areas would leave room for the greatest possible freedom of language use in the unregulated areas. While in most multilingual countries the monolingualism required by the territorial principle applies to at least two domains (the educational system and public administration), Belgium adds the business domain with monolingualism in companies (language between employees and employers). Social tensions which result from language use according to social class (e.g., when managers use another language than union representatives) are thereby to be reduced. Parallel to language legislation, a plan for federalization and regionalization was developed that would prevent centralized language planning such as that practiced in France. Since such regionalized language planning was applied to only a few, albeit decisive, realms of life of the different language groups, liberality and tolerance are shown in the remaining domains as compensation, so to speak. Above all, in the area of quantitative evaluation of minorities, one of the most disputed and most often misused arguments of the respective opposition, Belgium has gone its own way and not followed the North American or Russian examples. The rights and duties of a majority or minority are thereby no longer dependent solely on the strength of numbers. On the contrary, if the relative size of an ethnolinguistic group is no longer the sole determining factor in language planning, the protection of a language community can proceed from the assumption that a numerical minority needs more help than the majority. The Belgian state has accordingly done away with language counts in the census and thereby surely contributed to considerable de-emotionalization.

Hypotheses on the Acquisition of Several Languages

In spite of many disadvantages, the Belgian model has proven itself in certain aspects. As an outgrowth of a conflict situation that has continued for decades, measures to avoid and neutralize conflict have been developed. The resulting de-emotionalization of the language dispute has led to individual language behavior that permits the acquisition of two additional languages corresponding to a free market economy. In this way, the multilingualism market, freed from numerous historical and social prejudices, stereotypes and emotions, has been able to adapt to levels of supply and demand. Today the Belgian multilingual situation can be characterized as especially liberal in relation to the three national languages (e.g. Dutch, French and German), as well as the most important foreign and neighboring languages (e.g. English, Spanish, Italian). To this must be added a purely economical argument: the function of the capital city as an international meeting place has furthered the willingness to learn other languages, insofar as the mastery of languages that meet demand obviously pays. Thus, the Belgian example shows that economically motivated language planning according to need is more successful in encouraging multilingual acquisition than a centralized language policy, which can seldom adjust to constantly changing language needs in a flexible way. In the interest of avoiding language conflicts in the context of multilingual acquisition, some results of West European experiences will now be presented as theses for discussion.

Multilingualism for Affluent Groups Only

There is no generally valid model of multilingualism that can be applied to all cultures, countries and circumstances. Situational and contextual elements are decisive for each respective multilingual acquisition plan.

Proponents of bilingualism often stress too hastily the temporary successes of multilingual education in so-called bilingual secondary schools. These are frequently elite schools (the European schools in Brussels, Kennedy High School in Berlin) at which the children of "privileged guest workers" (diplomats and representatives of multilingual corporations) or of the native upper class (affluent minorities) learn several languages. Because of repeated changes of location, these students recognize the uses of multilingualism more readily than their counterparts in monolingual secondary schools, where the same multilingual curriculum would probably meet with little success. In addition, in most cases there is the considerable higher expense of bilingual education, which not every school system and department of education are willing to finance. This serves as a warning against all forms of elite multilingualism, which would result if a "Eurocratic upper class" gains control of foreign language acquisition. Academics and the wealthy automatically have easier access to multilingualism for their children.

"Natural" Multilingualism

The trend toward artificial (guided) multilingualism corresponds to notions of fashion and prestige for many Europeans and North Americans, i.e., language communities of relatively high mobility. But this artificial multilingualism ignores the structural aid to learning, provided by the languages of the environment.

In secondary schools in eastern France, where many children understand and / or speak a German dialect at home, English since the beginning of the 1990s has become the first foreign language after the language of instruction (i.e., French). So the dialectal language structures for German that are already present remain unused, with the result that natively acquired proficiency goes to waste and is hardly used didactically in school. Luxemburg with its flexible translation solution ("from kindergarten dialect to standard language in school") provides a better example. It should be pointed out, however, that in European countries, with few exceptions (e.g. Hungary), the high prestige value of English endangers all multilingualism planning in schools. As is well-known, learning motivation in adolescents declines significantly in the acquisition of third and fourth languages. In the interest of avoiding conflict, the natural multilingualism that exists in all of the countries of Europe, except for Iceland and Portugal, rules out overly simplistic solutions for the future, such as "multilingualism = mother tongue + English."

Monolingualism Can Be Cured

Motivation and support for the acquisition of several languages is inadequate in most European nations. More than half of the world's population is already multilingual, and the trend is a growing one. That is why multilingual education portrays the norm and not the exception. In the spirit of the foregoing, every case of multilingualism should be tailor made for its language community. It should correspond to real economic need, and its strength should not be diluted with fashionable airs and ambitious but futile language planning.

The Prospects for the 21st Century

Since all European nations with few exceptions are indeed multilingual in an autochthonous as well as an allochthonous sense, it is regrettable that this enormous reservoir of potential facility for language acquisition has hardly been tapped.

Language is regarded as a symbol of conflict per se in many multilingual nations. A simple intensification of second language and multilingual instruction in schools in such conflict situations seems to me to be a waste of time and money. It did not work with the six-year minimum of obligatory Russian instruction in most former East Bloc countries, nor with the previously required six years of Dutch instruction in the Walloon part of Belgium. Language conflicts will stand a better chance of being neutralized by means of such measures as a de-emotionalizing of language, a kind of "symmetrical bilingualism" in the numerous language border areas of Europe, a decrease in prejudices and stereotypes effected by immersion in neighboring languages and cultures, and above all, increased attention to local and regional peculiarities (ecolinguistic factors) of the languages to be learned, than by state-wide educational language planning policies, curriculum regulations, the use of standard teaching textbooks that are distributed world-wide (e.g. Deutsch für alle), and teachers who lack motivation because they are insufficiently trained.

Past conflicts and possible new ones should in no case be suppressed or denied. Instead, they should be the starting point for a new approach, which would ready the linguistically unprepared Europe of 1994 or a conflict-conscious and linguistically more open, i.e. multilingual Europe of the future. Countries like Switzerland, as a non EU-country, and Belgium, as the probable EU center, play a pioneer role that should not be underestimated. If these officially multilingual countries are not able to transform language conflict and multilingual deficits into multilingualism that is marketable, tension- and conflict-free, and based on the educational system of the respective country, then to whom can this responsibility be entrusted? Preferably not to a "Eurocratic" administrative authority of some West European capital!

References

Fishman, J. A. (1972). *The sociology of language*. Rowley MA: Newbury.
Haarmann, H. (1980). *Multilingualismus I, II*. Tübingen, Germany: Narr.
Haugen, E. (1966). *Language conflict and language planning*. Cambridge MA: Harvard University Press.
Inglehart, R. F. & M. Woodward. (1967). Language conflicts and political community. In P. Giglioli (Ed.), *Language and Social Context*. New York NY: Penguin, 358–377.
Mattheier, K. A. (1984). Sprachkonflikte in einsprachigen Ortsgemeinschaften. In E. Oksaar (Ed.). *Spracherwerb — Sprachkontakt-Sprachkonflikt*. Berlin, Germany: de Gruyter, 197–204.
Oksaar, E. (1980). Mehrsprachigkeit, Sprachkontakt, Sprachkonflikt. In P. H. Nelde (Ed.), *Languages in contact and in conflict*. Wiesbaden, Germany: Steiner, 43–52.
Weinreich, U. (1953). *Languages in contact*. The Hague, Netherlands: Mouton.
Williams, R. M. (1947). The reduction of intergroup tension. *Social Science Research Council Bulletin 57*, 40–43.

26

Reporting on Sino-Japan Conflicts in *The New York Times*: A critical discourse analysis

CHEN Xiaoxiao
Beijing Foreign Studies University, China

Abstract: This paper is a critical discourse analysis of the news reports on Sino-Japan conflicts in *The New York Times* from April 1 to April 30, 2005. A critical discourse analysis is made to delineate the contrasting representations of China and Japan, locating some particular discursive strategies that harbor ideological inclinations. Findings indicate that *The New York Times* portrayed the Chinese government as aggressive, dominant and repressive and the Chinese as a frightening and violent group of people, so that China was made seem less victimized and sympathized in the reporting of Sino-Japan conflicts. In contrast, the Japanese government and its people were depicted as more rational and courteous, while their atrocities in World War II, their denial of history, and their military and political ambitions were played down or glossed over. In the concluding section, the author brings to light the underlying reasons for the ideologically framed news representations in *The New York Times*.

Introduction

Development in Sino-Japan relations is a frequent focus in American media, because ties between East Asia's two major powers — China neither a friend nor a foe of the US and Japan a staunch US ally — will do much to define America's future relations with Asia-Pacific region. Sino-Japan relations, however, have experienced twists and turns since the normalization of the bilateral ties in 1972. A downward spiral in Sino-

Japan relations came in August 1995, when Japanese conservatives protested against the Japanese Prime Minister Tomiichi Murayama's expression of his feelings of "profound mourning for all victims, both at home and abroad" of WWII (Japan). Thereafter, the situations appeared to go from bad to worse.

This paper is to examine how Sino-Japan conflicts were portrayed in *The New York Times* (hence abbreviated as the *NYT*) from January 1, 2001 to December 31, 2006. I will discuss and how Sino-Japan conflicts or disputes were represented in the news events and how China and Japan were depicted in their conflicts by the most prestigious American newspaper. This study will reveal how the American elites view China and Japan at the beginning of the 21st century and how the US positions itself in the triangular ties of the three big powers.

Trilateral Relations between China, the US and Japan

Sino-Japan relations are among the central factors in East Asian international politics. Some long-term disputes between China and Japan have led Sino-Japan relations toward increased strains and greater uncertainty. The troubled relationship between China and Japan is further complicated by these concerns:

Firstly, Sino-Japan relations are plagued by bitter argument over the World War II history. Chinese people are still plagued by memories of the atrocities committed by Japanese troops in World War II: the Nanjing Massacre, Japanese chemical weapons, experiments on human subjects in North China, Chinese "comfort women," Chinese labor etc. On the other hand, Japan has refused to recognize and apologize for its imperial past, for instance, by revising history textbooks in the public schools, which had already ignited strong anti-Japan protests in China in April, 2005. In addition, Koizumi regularly visited the Yasukuni Shrine, which commemorates Japan's war dead including 14 Class-A war criminals. Before that, Hashimoto's visit in 1996 had provoked general rage among Chinese people. Many argue that, by downplaying or even denying atrocities like the Nanjing Massacre and underscoring events like the atomic bombing of Hiroshima and Nagasaki, Japanese elites portray Japan falsely as the victim, rather than the victimizer, in World War II (Christensen, 1999, p.53).

Secondly, Taiwan will be a dangerous flash point in Sino-Japanese relations. Ties between Tokyo and Beijing could experience serious political tensions if Japan supports Taiwan's independence through steps such as allowing Lee Teng-hui to visit Japan or promoting Taiwan's international profile. A military confrontation between Taiwan and the mainland would pose perhaps the greatest foreseeable threat to Sino-Japan relations as well as to the US-Japan alliance. It is likely that Japan will threaten drastic actions, for some Japanese have posited that if China takes control of the region of Taiwan, China would be in a position to blockade sea lanes around Taiwan, which are critical for Japanese oil shipping, or would attempt to take over the Diaoyudao Islands (Wang, 2000, p. 361). Some Japanese politicians even remarked that Japan would assist the US forces if military conflicts took place between the US and China, which alarmed Chinese people (Inoguchi, 1996, p. 38; Zhang, 1997, p. 6). From a geopolitical perspective, Japan does not really favor Taiwan's unification with the Chinese mainland.

Thirdly, the equalization of power as China gains economic strength and Japan plays a bigger political and military role could intensify Sino-Japanese competition and rivalry. China is wary of Japan's military capability and desire to be a political power, for Japan has been increasing its defense budget and seeking military backing for its bid to become a political giant. The pace of Japanese technology development and weapons acquisition has also far exceeded that of China (Pollack, 1990, p. 718-719; Wu, 2000, p. 299). On the other hand, since Japan has long been accustomed to living with weaker neighbors, the prospect of China emerging as a strong power poses new challenges. Many Japanese politicians and media have stirred up an idea of China threat (Wu, 2000, p. 297).

Fourthly, Sino-Japan political strains are dampening bilateral trade, even though Sino-Japan economic and trade cooperation had been the most optimistic part of the bilateral ties. Trade between China and Japan is still growing, but there has been a slowdown in the growth rate. Sino-Japan trade accounted for 20 per cent of China's total overseas trade in 1994, but the figure dropped to 13 per cent in 2005. In 2004, South Korea surpassed Japan in terms of investment in China. Consequently, Conflicts and disputes are not rare in Sino-Japan trade relations.

Fifthly, in wartime the Japanese army openly violated international conventions by using chemical weapons, which caused severe casualties among Chinese soldiers and civilians. When Japan was defeated, large amounts of chemical weapons were buried and discarded on Chinese soil, with the purpose of covering up the evidence of their crimes. From 1989 to the present, China has been urging Japan to solve the issue. But until now Japan has failed to clear up and seal up these chemical weapons.

Sixthly, most of the lawsuits that were filed by Chinese victims of biological warfare, abandoned chemical weapons, the Nanjing massacre, the Pingdingshan massacre, etc., have been rejected by the Japanese government. The deep scars left by the war on the Chinese people remain unhealed. According to Sino-Japan Joint Communiqué in 1972, the Chinese Government decided to waive the claim of war reparations against the Japanese government. However, as for those realistic problems left over by the war of Japanese aggression against China, the Japanese side should take them into serious consideration and handle them properly.

Seventhly, the fire is added fuel by the 2002 Shenyang incident, in which five North Koreans who were dragged from the Japanese consulate in Shenyang on May 8 were permitted by Beijing to fly to the Philippines and on to South Korea on May 23. Japan accused Beijing of violating Japan's sovereignty and demanded an apology and the immediate return of the North Koreans to the Japanese consulate. China insisted that its officers had entered the consulate with the permission of a Japanese vice-consul in order to remove a potential "terrorist" threat to the Japanese staff.

Eighthly, dispute over natural gas or oil in disputed areas of the East China Sea strains Sino-Japan relations. Economic ties have grown tremendously between the two nations in recent years, but they remain in fierce regional competition. In early 2005 the East China Sea became a hotly-disputed area between China and Japan, for both were competing for the same undersea oil deposits. Two nations with hundreds of years of rivalry and a great need for oil with overlapping oil-field claims can create a highly volatile situation.

Ninthly, sovereignty of the Diaoyudao (which is called Senkaku by the Japanese) Islands is disputed. The Diaoyudao Islands, claimed by both China and Japan, are oil-rich and near key international shipping routes. According to China, Chinese historical records detailing the discovery and geographical feature of these islands date back to the year 1403. For several centuries they have been administered as part of Taiwan and have always been used exclusively by Chinese fishermen as an operational base. In 1874, Japan took Liu Chiu Islands from China by force. Diaoyudao, however, remained under the administration of Taiwan, a part of China. Taiwan (including Diaoyudao) was ceded to Japan in 1895 after the first Sino-Japanese War. After the Second World War, when U.S. troops were stationed on the Liu Chiu and Diaoyudao Archipelagoes, the KMT government which had received Taiwan did not immediately demand that the US give them sovereignty. Diaoyudao was returned to China at the end of World War II in 1945 based upon the 1943 agreement of the Big Three in Cairo. Japan, however, claims the islands as official Japanese territory in 1895. They insisted that, from 1885 on, the Japanese Government had made surveys of the Senkaku Islands through the agencies of Okinawa Prefecture and by way of other methods. According to their surveys, it was confirmed that the Senkaku Islands had been uninhabited and showed no trace of having been under the control of China.

Tenthly, Japan's developing and deploying advanced TMD (theater missile defense) is a source of tensions in Sino-Japan relations, because a US-Japan TMD could be part of a containment strategy aimed at China. Therefore, China could increase pressure on Japan not to go ahead with

TMD. On the other hand, if Japan fails to go ahead with the program, the US will doubt Japan's reliability as an ally in Asia-Pacific region.

Lastly, the US-Japan alliance could become a serious point of contention in Sino-Japan and Sino-American relations. American and Japanese efforts to redefine and strengthen the US-Japan alliance in response to the changing post-Cold War strategic environment have led Chinese civilian and military officials and think-tank experts to reevaluate the Washington-Tokyo security arrangement. Chinese become increasingly concerned if the alliance is aimed at "checking" or containing China (Christensen, 1999, p. 63). The situation will worsen if Tokyo colludes with the US to counter the rise of Chinese power and Beijing's assertion of its sovereignty over Taiwan and Diaoyudao and Nansha islands.

Undoubtedly, the interaction between China and Japan as well as their relations with the United States will be critical in determining the future of the Asia-Pacific region in the 21st century. Protracted tensions or conflicts between Beijing and Tokyo could destabilize the region and strain US bilateral ties with one or both countries. Efforts by the US to strengthen relations with one nation may strain ties with the other or between the two. This triangular dynamic is especially evident in China's reaction to steps taken by Washington to revitalize and reshape the US-Japan alliance for the post-War era and in Japan's uneasiness about improvements in Sino-American relations.

The trilateral relations among China, the US and Japan is complicated by Washington's asymmetrical ties with Japan and China. Japan is a long-standing and close American ally despite chronic differences over trade and other issues. The US had sought to strengthen and broaden the alliance, maintain Tokyo's confidence in the US commitment to Japan's security, and operate closely with the Japanese on regional security issues, including mutual concerns about China's rising power. On the other hand, the US has long-term strategic and security interests in maintaining good working relations with China, including obtaining Beijing's cooperation on key international issues such as arms control, proliferation, and stability on the Korean Peninsula.

Nevertheless, the revitalization of the US-Japan alliance — especially expansion of the scope of the alliance and enhancement of Japan's regional security role-are likely exacerbate tensions in China's ties with Japan as well as with the US.

Therefore, it can be inferred that the regional stability and prosperity in the early part of the 21st century will likely depend more on relations among China, Japan and the US than on any other factors including multilateral security arrangements. In fact, the US is closely related to the conflicts and disputes between these two regional powers. It will yield meaningful results to investigate how the US views Sino-Japan conflicts and how the US positions itself between China and Japan. In response to the above-discussed trilateral relations, I will examine the reporting of Sino-Japan conflicts by the *NYT* in the past six years. Specifically, this article attempts to answer these questions:

(1) What dominant themes in Sino-Japan conflicts are reported in the *NYT*?
(2) How are the national images of China and Japan represented in their conflicts by the *NYT* and why are they presented this way?
(3) How are the news reports of Sino-Japan conflicts affected by the underlying ideological positions of the *NYT*?

Based on the background information about the triangular relations among China, Japan and the United States, a critical discourse analysis of news coverage about Sino-Japan conflicts will yield a deeper understanding of news reporting in the *NYT*, and thus the above questions will be answered.

Research Methods

This study depends on 55 news reports on Sino-Japan conflicts in the *NYT* from January 1, 2001 to December 31, 2006. I sampled these news reports from the results (everything about China and Japan in *The NYT*) yielded by Lexis-Nexis news search. *The NYT* was selected because it is the most widely read newspaper among elites both within and outside of American government (Weiss, 1974, p.1), it carries higher volume of foreign news than other major US newspapers (Semmel, 1976, p.61), and it is often used as a source of event data by researchers (Hopple, 1982, p.73).

In this study, I will first turn to quantitative content analysis briefly to give a general description of the themes in Sino-Japan conflicts which were covered in the *NYT* from January 1, 2001 to November 30, 2006. I will then focus on critical discourse analysis in order to find out instances of ideological discourse in the news coverage concerned and to show how they are embedded in a much larger, but less transparent structure of power and ideological discourse in the trilateral relations among China, Japan and the US. Further, I will discuss the reasons China and Japan were portrayed that way in their conflicts by the *NYT*.

Quantitative content analysis, which has been a most popular research method in media studies, will only be touched upon in this article. This content analysis is based on a theme or topic analysis. As a result, the major themes in the coverage of Sino-Japan conflicts in the *NYT* will be revealed.

Critical discourse analysis (hence abbreviated as CDA), the focus of this study, is "a type of discourse analytical research that primarily studies the way social power abuse, dominance and inequality are enacted, reproduced and resisted by text and talk in the social and political context" (van Dijk, 2004, p.67).

CDA emerged in the late 1980s as a programmatic development in European discourse studies spearheaded by Norman Fairclough, Ruth Wodak, Teun van Dijk, and others. CDA stems from critical linguistics, a critical theory of language which sees the use of language as a form of social practice. Critical linguistics is a branch of discourse analysis that goes beyond the description of discourse to an explanation of how and why particular discourses are produced. Generally, CDA builds from three broad theoretical orientations. First, it derives from poststructuralism the view that texts have a constructive function in forming up and shaping human identities and actions. Second, it develops from Bourdieu's sociology the idea that actual textual practices and interactions with texts become "embodied" forms of "cultural capital" with exchanged value in particular social fields. Third, it draws from neo-Marxist cultural theory the view that these discourse are produced and used within political economies, and that they thus "produce and articulate broader ideological interests, social formations and movements within those fields" (Hall, 1996, p.156). What is crucial to CDA practices is the systemic-functional and social-semiotic linguistics of Michael Halliday, whose linguistic methodology offers clear and rigorous linguistic categories for analyzing the relationships between discourse and social meaning (Chouliaraki & Fairclough, 1999, p. 23). Next to Halliday's three metafunctions (ideational, interpersonal, textual meaning), systemic-functional analyses of transitivity, agency, nominalization, syntax, information flow, register and etc. have been adopted by CDA.

The purpose of CDA is to analyze "opaque as well as transparent structural relationships of dominance, discrimination, power and control as manifested in language" (Wodak, 1995, p.204). While most forms of discourse analysis intends to provide a better understanding of social-cultural aspects of texts, CDA aims to provide accounts of the production, internal structure, and overall organization of texts. One crucial difference is that CDA aims to provide a critical dimension in its theoretical and descriptive accounts of texts.

The word "critical" is a key theoretical concept in CDA that requires some explanation here. "Critical" indicates the need for analysts to decode the ideological implications of discourse that have become so naturalized over time that we begin to treat them as common, acceptable and natural features of discourse. That is, ideology has become common belief or even common sense. Adapting "critical" approach enables us to "elucidate such naturalizations, and make clear social determinations and effects of discourse which are characteristically opaque to participants" (Fairclough, 1985, p.739).

Ideology plays a vital role in CDA. According to Wodak (1996), "ideologies are particular ways of representing and constructing society which reproduce unequal relations of power, relations of domination and exploitation" (p. 18). Fairclough (1992) explains ideology as "an accumulated and naturalized orientation which is built into norms and conventions, as well as an ongoing work to naturalize and denaturalize such orientations in discursive events" (p. 89). For Widdowson (1990), "all discourses of theory, including those of linguistics, are ideologically loaded" (p. 39). Newspapers, which claim to be politically neutral and ideology-free, have to choose their discursive representations in line with their institutional policies which are ideological themselves because they are not nameless and neutral but have a history and a politics (Cameron, 1993, p.316).

In sum, the approach in this study is a critical, multidisciplinary approach to discourse analysis which focuses on issues of ideology, power, dominance, prejudice and hegemony, and the discursive processes of their enactment, reproduction, concealment and naturalization in news reporting.

The analysis of the newspaper discourse is done in three stages. A brief content analysis is first used in order to find out the major themes in the 55 news reports. Then a detailed characterization of the selected news reports is made, with a focus on some particular discursive strategies that are likely to harbor ideological meanings. I will concentrate on the 51 ideologically loaded reports, excluding the 4 relatively neutral news reports dated on November 13, 2004, April 20, 2005, April 23, 2005 and July 10, 2005. It is predicted that how the national images of China and Japan are portrayed in the news discourse will be revealed in this part. Finally, I will probe further into the working of the media industry, national interests of the US and the American ideological heritage in order to find out the reasons for the portrayals of China and Japan were depicted this way in the *NYT*.

Major Themes in the News Reports

The following table is about the major themes covered in the 55 news reports.

Themes	*Frequency*
anti-Japan protests in 2005	14
Yasukuni Shrine visits	8
mutual dislike / distrust	6

(to be continued)

Themes	Frequency
disputes about North Korean refugees	5
disputes over territory and recourses	4
Trade argument	4
Japan's apology	4
Taiwan issue	3
Japan's historical textbooks	2
military display	2
Japan's bid for UN seat	2
wartime Chinese laborers' lawsuit	1

Some topics are not only themes in some reports, but also recurring topics in other reports, including Japan's historical textbooks, shrine visits, Taiwan issue, and roles of the US. Compared with what is covered in Sino-Japan conflicts in the previous text, the news reporting of *NYT* includes all the major themes concerned. Particular stress (14 out of 55) is laid on Chinese people's anti-Japan protests in 2005, while only two are about Japan's revised historical textbooks and only one is about wartime Chinese laborers' lawsuit. Four reports focus on Japan's "apology" toward China and other Asian neighbors, even though Japan has never officially apologized to China until now. Five reports are given to Sino-Japan disputes about North Korean refugees. The frequent appearance of the third party — the US also implies that America has its own role to play in Sino-Japan conflicts. The following table is about the mention of the U.S. in the reports.

Theme of the Report	Date of the Report	Mention of the US
Military Display	September 11, 2005	16 times
Taiwan Issue	February 21, 2005	14 times
	February 6, 2006	twice
North Korean Refugees	May 10, 2002	7 times
Japan's Apology	October 4, 2006	5 times
Territory Dispute	July 10, 2005	4 times

(to be continued)

Theme of the Report	Date of the Report	Mention of the US
Anti-Japan Protests	April 15, 2005	4 times
	April 16, 2005	twice
	April 11, 2005	once
	April 18, 2005	once
Shrine Visits	June 24, 2006	twice
	August 5, 2006	twice
	August 15, 2006	3 times
Trade Argument	June 27, 2005	3 times
Japan's Bid for the UNSC Permanent Seat	April 1, 2005	3 times
Resources Dispute	November 3, 2004	twice
	April 14, 2005	once
Mutual Dislike	January 19, 2005	twice
	August 3, 2005	once
	October 9, 2006	once

From the above table, it can be inferred that the US is more or less involved in almost all Sino-Japan conflicts. Sino-Japan military rivalry is of great concern to the US because it will affect the US-Japan Alliance and the security pattern in Asia-Pacific region. Yasukuni Shrine visits and Taiwan remain sensitive issues in Sino-Japan relations and a focus of attention for the US in Asia. Chinese people's anti-Japan protests in 2005 had also drawn their attention because deteriorating bilateral ties between China and Japan will do harm to the interests of the US in Asia in the long run. Besides, the *NYT* had shown its concern for North Korean refugees' disputes and had highlighted Japan's expression of regrets or apology for its WWII atrocities. The voice of America could also be heard in Sino-Japan territory and resources disputes, trade argument, Japan's bid for the UNSC permanent seat and Sino-Japan mutual dislike or distrust.

Characterization of the Newspaper Discourse

The frequently used discourse strategies in the news reports under discussion are lexicalization, transitivity, thematization, passive voice, subjective commentary or judgment, vagueness, omission, information focus, rhetorical figures and quotation patterns. In the following text I hope to uncover the underlying meanings and motivations behind particular linguistic realizations by focusing on these discourse strategies.

Lexicalization refers to "choice of words that imply negative (or positive) evaluations" (van Dijk, 2004, p. 119). Deliberate choice of words often has a pejorative or laudatory effect as it reflects perceptions and judgments from the biased standpoint of certain cultural norms or social expectations.

In the news text on April 15, 2005, the headline goes as "China *Push*ing and *Script*ing Japan Protest." The use of two verbs "*push*" and "*script*" presents an image of China which is aggressive, impulsive and manipulating. In the report of April 16, 2005, the Chinese government was reported to "*tolerate*" and even "*help*" the anti-Japan protests. If "*tolerate*" sounds acceptable, "*help*" carries the personal judgment of the journalist who had a biased view of the Chinese government. In the headline of April 17, 2005 "Chinese Government *Permits* Protests Against Japan" and the headline of April 21, 2005 "By Playing At 'Rage,' China *Dramatizes* Its Rise," the Chinese government was reportedly supporting and taking advantage of the protests, which can be see in the attribution of "*allow*" to the Chinese government's attitude toward the protests in the report of April 23, 2005. In addition, a series of verbs are used when describing the protestors: "*rally*," "*attack*," "*overturn*" (cars), "*smash*" (storefronts). The use of such verbs as "*smash*" (its windows) and "*deface*" (its walls) is found in the report dated on April 21, 2005, while in the report of April 23, 2005 the two verbs "*threw*" (bottles) and "*vandalized*" (Japanese business) are used in the same vein. These verbs depict Chinese protestors as irrational and violent.

Japanese officials, however, was portrayed as rational, polite and eager to ease the conflicts in the headline of April 21, 2005: "Mollified by China's Move to End Protest, Japan Urges Talks" and the lead "Japanese officials *softened their tone* ... and *urged* its leaders to meet with Chinese leaders ... " In the same report, Prime Minister Junichiro Koizumi was reportedly "*responded favorably*" to calls by Chinese Foreign Minister, Li Zhaoxing. The adverb "*favorably*" corresponds with the tone in the headline and the lead. Thus a more positive and rational image of Japanese government is presented in contrast with the Chinese in the conflicts.

In June 26, 2001 report about the shrine visits, Chinese Prime Minister Tang Jiaxuan is reportedly "*barked* what sounded like an order to Japanese reporters." The attribution of this humiliating verb to the Chinese Prime Minister reflects the reporter's ideological intentions embedded in the news discourse.

In the reports about trade, China seemed to be domineering in the trade dispute on June 20, 2001, as seen in the lead "China has placed **high duties** on imported Japanese cars ... *in retaliation for* duties Japan put on ... ," while Japan appeared to be doing what it should do, as in "Japan raised tariffs on Chinese leeks ... *in an effort to* protect farmers from cheap imports." Besides, China was described as an aggressive partner who looked down upon Japan in the lead "... China's recent *slights* and *snubs* of Japan" (June 20, 2001).

In the reports on the disputes over North Korea refugees, the reporter used "*drag*" and "*wrest*" to describe what Chinese police officers did to the refugees on May 10, 2002. In the report one day later, more forceful or violent verbal phrases are applied to the Chinese policemen, as in "*knocking over* a 2-year-old girl, *wrestling* her mother *into submission* and *dragging away* her pregnant aunt."

The presentation of Chinese as aggressive or violent in the *NYT* can be also found in the August 9, 2004 report about China's soccer loss. After the use of such verbs as "*bellow*," "*yell*," and "*shout*," the writer termed the reaction of Chinese fans as "*insults* aimed at the Japanese team." The reporter showed his or her disapproval of Chinese fans when he wrote "The Japanese national anthem was drowned out by *sustained hisses and boos*." In the report on January 19, 2005, the mere mention of this incident goes "(Chinese fans) *aggressively harassed* Japanese fans." The use of these verbs, nouns and adverb tainted with personal feelings are powerful enough to manipulate the readers into turning against the Chinese side.

Transitivity, for Halliday (1985), specifies "the different types of processes that are recognized in the language and the structures by which they are expressed" (p. 101). It is a useful analytic tool that probes the way language represents reality in terms of how the primary or dominant agents are constructed, what they do to whom and with what consequences. To do a transitivity analysis it is necessary to identify every verb and its associated process. It is then of necessity to study the system of transitivity in the clause proposed by Halliday (1985, p. 117) in the following table:

Types of doing	*Examples*

Material
    Action
    Event
	The lion caught the tourist.
	The mayor resigned.

Behavioral	breathe, dream, sleep; smile, laugh

(to be continued)

Types of doing	Examples
Mental	
Perception	see, notice, stare at, etc.
Affection	like, dislike, hate, feel angry, etc.
Cognition	think, know, understand, interpret, et.
Verbal	John said he was hungry.
Relational	
Attribution	Sarah is wise.
Identification	Tom is the leader.
Existential	There was a storm.

Let's look at the report about the Sino-Japan protests on April 15, 2005. The second paragraph goes "Yet the police *herded* protesters into tight groups, *let* them take turns throwing rocks, then **told** them they had 'vented their anger' long enough and *bused* them back to campus." The police were depicted as "actors" and "sayers" who seemed to be puppeteering or manipulating the protesters by the use of the verbs of material type "*herded*," "*let*," "*bused*" and the verbal process "*told*." On April 24, 2005, Japanese Prime Minister Koizumi "*delivered* the most public apology in a decade over Japan's aggression in Asia, allowing the Chinese to accept the meeting with Mr. Koizumi." The use of the material verb "*deliver*" impresses the readers with an image of repentant Koizumi and "*allow*" puts China in a passive role in the reconciliation process. In trade, China was reported to be somewhat aggressive, as in the lead of the report on December 6, 2002: "China *is using* its new economic power to *outmaneuver* Japan" and the sentence "China *slapped* emergency tariffs on steel imports from Japan." The criticizing tone was sharp in the depiction of Chinese government which dealt with "a Japanese human rights advocate" in the North Korean refugees' dispute on November 8, 2002. In a news report of 79 words, five material verbs were used to describe what the Chinese police did to the Japanese:

> A Japanese human rights advocate expelled from China for working with North Korean refugees said the Chinese police had *held* him incommunicado for six days, *subjected* him to harsh interrogations lasting through several nights, and *forced* him to sleep handcuffed to a small chair. The man, Hiroshi Kato, 57, said the Chinese had *refused* to contact Japanese authorities about his detention and had *threatened* to hand him over secretly to North Korea.

Thematization looks at the organization of information within a clause. The positioning of a piece of information in a clause tells the kind of prominence or foregrounding the reporter wishes to attribute to it. Examining the reasons behind the motivation of organizing information in a certain way can therefore provide a glimpse into the ideological meaning embedded within a text.

In April 21, 2005 report about Sino-Japan protests, the reporter wrote "**Prime Minister Junichiro Koizumi responded favorably** to calls by the Chinese foreign minister, Li Zhaoxing, to protesters to stop the sometimes violent marches ... " The thematic foregrounding of Koizumi's response draws the reader' attention to the move on the part of Japan, while playing down the efforts made by China. In the May 25, 2005 report, when depicting the anger of Japanese, the reporter wrote "**In a land where courtesy is prized**, Japanese ministers made little effort to mask their anger at the abrupt departure on Monday of Wu Yi ... " By thematizing "**In a land where courtesy is prized**," the writer suggests that the sudden departure of Wu Yi was even intolerable to Japanese who were raised in a land of courtesy. Let's observe this sentence in the same report, "If **China's aim** is to discredit Mr. Koizumi and other conservative nationalists like Shinzo Abe, who is seen as a likely successor in 2006, she added, 'that will very likely backfire and help ensure that the strongly anti-China Shinzo Abe succeeds Koizumi.' " The foregrounding of "**China's aim**" shows that China itself should be responsible for the possible succession of Shinzo Abe. Therefore, China shouldn't shift the responsibility to Japan if it feels unhappy about the succession of Abe as prime minister.

In the disputes about territory on March 26, 2004, an expression goes "an island that **the Japanese call Uotsui-Jima, the largest of a chain known in Japan as the Senkaku Islands** and in China as the Diaoyu Islands." The thematization of Japan's naming of the islands reflects the writer's tilt for Japan in this issue. When talking about the mutual dependence of China and Japan on each other, a professor was quoted as saying "China needs Japan and Japan needs China." The subtle tilt in the positioning of the two pieces of information is not hard to be located. In the report about Japan's claim of China's military threat dated on December 23, 2005, a sentence goes "**Although Mr. Koizumi said he prayed for peace at the shrine**, most Asians regard it as a symbol of Japanese militarism." The thematic foregrounding of Koizumi's remarks underscores his glorified intentions of visiting the shrine.

The use of **passive voice** also manifests the ideological implications which seemed to be naturalized in the news discourse. In April 11, 2005 report, when talking about Japan's growing nationalism, two sentences read "Green Day ... will almost certainly **be renamed** 'showa day' soon to commemorate the birthday of the late emperor Hirohito, who led Japan during its conquest of Asia and who is a revered symbol of Japanese rightists ... " and "the previously named emperor's day **was changed** to green day in 1989." The agent or the doer who renamed "Green Day" and later changed the date for it is not told from the use of passive voice. Another typical use of passive voice is found in May 25, 2005 report, there is a sentence "anti-Chinese feelings *were inflamed* after a series of protests in China ... " The use of passive voice stresses that such "anti-Chinese feelings" didn't exist before, but was stirred up by anti-Japan protests in China. Generally, the application of passive voice to the actor or doer will put the agent in a subdued or even invisible role in something unpleasant the agent should be responsible for.

Subjective commentary or judgment, which is tinted with the reporter's voice and judgment, is undoubtedly the most conspicuous cases of ideological manipulation. Such examples can be mostly found in the reports about Sino-Japan protests.

For instance, in the lead of the April 21, 2005 report "by *playing* at 'rage,' China *dramatizes* its rise." the use of the two verbs "*play*" and "*dramatize*" connotes the writer's subjective judgment about the attitude of Chinese government toward the protests. Actually, this text is full of subjective commentary or judgment. Let's observe the following sentences:

(1) "... talk was dominated by Chinese 'feelings,' a word repeated over and over, *as if no other feelings counted*."
(2) "the events of the weekend here and their aftermath show that *this country has barely changed at all*."

In the first sentence, the writer apparently disapproved of Chinese "feelings." In the second sentence, the writer had jumped to the conclusion about China. Another instance of subjective commentary is found in April 25, 2005 report: "It was part of a broader curb on the anti-Japanese movement but *it also seemed the Communist Party had self-interest in mind*." What is notable is that no subjective commentary or judgment about Japan or Japanese authorities can be found in the news reports under analysis. Japan, a country which is ideologically closer to the US than China, will not easily fall prey to subjective evaluations in the American media.

Vagueness is a type of implicitness which mixes with the factual reporting of events. Vagueness about some information but not the other shows the reporter's ideological intentions. One telling example is the number of Chinese killed in the Nanking Massacre, which was reported as "*100,000 to 300,000*" in two news reports dated on April 11, 2005 and August 3, 2005. When talking about the causes for anti-Japan protests in China in the report on June 27, 2005, one of them was termed as dispute over "*narratives* in Japanese textbooks." The conspicuous vagueness about the disputable content in Japanese textbooks plays down the seriousness of the issue. On April 22, 2002, the reporter referred to the atrocities committed by the war criminals enshrined in Yasukuni as merely "their *role* in World War II.*"* Glossing over the hideous crimes committed by the war criminals reveals the reporter's intention to cover up something bad about the Japanese history. On October 19, 2005, Prime Minister Koizumi was reported to visit "the Yasukuni shrine, a ***nationalist*** war memorial." The vague use of "***nationalist***" shuts out the information about the nature of the shrine as the symbol of militarism in Japan in World War II.

Omission, in addition to vagueness, is another strategy that can be used to leave out some important information required in the news discourse. Omission, no matter whether it is done deliberately or unconsciously, reflects the reporter's bias against or in favor of one or the other party involved. Let's examine two examples. In April 21, 2005 report, a paragraph goes as follows:

> "China also claims never to have seized territory from a neighbor, but China attacked India by surprise in 1962 and the details of other campaigns, from Korea and Xinjiang in the north to Vietnam and Tibet in the country's south and west, are also absent from textbooks."

China here was depicted as an aggressive country invading its "neighbors" (among which, as a matter of fact, Xinjiang and Tibet are not neighbors, but unalienable parts of China), which was actually a reflection of the writer's prejudiced view against China. The true causes of these wars or conflicts were absent from the text, leaving gaps in the readers' knowledge of these events.

Nevertheless, in depicting the notorious Yasukuni Shrine, the report dated on April 22, 2002 reads "The Yasukuni Shrine is by far Japan's most controversial religious site, because of its dedication to the 2.5 million soldiers who fell in wars since the mid-1800's." The information about the soldiers enshrined, the wars they fought and the symbolic meaning of the shrine are missing from the text. It seems that the writer left out so important information just in order to gloss over the infamy of the shrine.

Information Focus is sometimes shifted by the writer in the middle or approaching the end of a text, so that the presumed focus fades as a result. This strategy can be cleverly used to divert the reader's attention from something the writer wants to play down to something else he or she intends to smuggle his or her own ideological connotations into. Consequently, the reader' evaluation or judgment about the event will be affected by the new focus. I have found that the reporters in the *NYT* tended to drag in some other issues when they reported the Sino-Japan protests. In the anti-Japan protests report of April 16, 2005, the reporter inserted a paragraph of quotation from "a leading campaigner for peasant rights and rural health care" who commented on nationalism as a "double-edged sword." This paragraph is a backup statement to the proposition in the previous paragraph "Unrest of any kind could open the door for people to rally against government corruption and land seizures, or to complain about economic inequality or political repression." Reading these arguments, the readers' attention will naturally be diverted to the domestic issues in China. As a result, the patriotic significance of anti-Japan protests will be reduced. In April 21, 2005 report, the reporter listed more information irrelevant to the focus of anti-Japan protests, such as "the Cultural Revolution," "the policies of Mao Zedong," "Chinese textbooks," "China's attack of India," and "campaigns from Korea and Xinjiang in the north to Vietnam and Tibet in the country's south and west." Moreover, these events or topics were ideologically framed or transformed when they were represented in the news discourse. China's image, undoubtedly, was demonized in these ideologically tainted expressions. In the anti-Japan protests report dated on April 25, 2005, "Falun Gong" emerged as the text approaches to its end. In the textbook argument on April 17, 2005, oddly, the reporter dragged in "the postwar Great Leap Forward" in China, which has nothing to do with the topic. In sum, there is a tendency in the *NYT* to make China seem less victimized and sympathized in reporting of Sino-Japan conflicts.

Rhetorical Figures is believed to be a bridge that enables us to cross the world of literal and factual meaning into the world of ideological persuasion. The most frequently used rhetorical figure in the news discourse under discussion is understatement. Let's examine some examples. In April 21, 2005 report about anti-Japan protests, Japanese textbooks were reportedly "*deemphasized* atrocities committed in China." But according to the report about the textbook dispute on April 17, 2005, Japan was reported to have avoided the issues of "comfort women" and "Chinese laborers" in the new textbooks. The word "*deemphasized*" is far from strong enough to cover the fact. In the Taiwan dispute report dated on February 21, 2005, the reporter said "the *mention* of Taiwan ... drew a firm response from China." Everybody knows that the word "*mention*" is surely an understatement for what the two allies (Japan and the US) had discussed about their major concern — Taiwan in their new joint security statement, while later in the same report, it was reported to be "a *short, cautious mention*." Thus what Japan and the US did say about Taiwan in their statement was further played down. In the February 6, 2006 report "Japanese *remarks* about Taiwan anger Beijing," the word "*remarks*" certainly an understatement because in the lead we read "Japan's prime minister *praised* his country's past rule over the island." Then the word "*praised*" does not suffice to depict the minister's glorifying their evil-doings in Taiwan. In the headline of August 13, 2003 report "Japan Apologizes to China for *Injuries* from Remnants of War," the word "*injuries*" is too weak to tell what Japan did to China in World War II. In the April 21, 2005 report, Japanese officials were said to "have apologized *numerous times* to China ... " It is a universal truth that Japan has never directly, publicly and sincerely apologized to China for their atrocities committed in World War II. Here *"numerous times"* does catch the readers by surprise. Apparently, the writer used this hyperbole to imply that China was demanding more than they should in spite of the countless apologies made by Japan. In short, the reporters in the *NYT* would turn to some rhetorical figures in order to restructure the readers' thinking, causing them to perceive the reality in an intended light.

Quotation patterns in the news discourses also reveal the newspaper's bias in favor of or prejudice against one or the other side in the conflicts. By giving voice to certain select people, quotation patterns serve to enhance the importance of those people, so that the readers are more likely to take in the intended ideological messages in the context. In contrast, those who are devoiced usually become the subjects of what others talk about, but are seldom given the opportunity to confirm or deny what others say of them. I have found that the *NYT* had a tendency to devoice China and the majority of its people when depicting the conflicts.

In April 11, 2005 report "Tokyo Protests Anti-Japan Rallies in China," three people were quoted: Japanese Foreign Minister Nobuta Machimura, Japanese Secretary General of Liberal Democratic Party Shinzo Abe, and South Korea's ambassador to the United Nations Kim Sam Hoon. What is noted is that approaching the end of the text Abe — the anti-China advocator — was quoted as saying "Japan is an outlet to vent that anger" and the following direct quotation from him furthers his point that anti-Japan protests were used by the Chinese to demonstrate their anger against the government. The patriotic feelings of Chinese were lost in such malicious remarks about the movement. In the April 17, 2005 report "Chinese Government Permits Protests against Japan," no voice from the Chinese government was heard. What could be heard were voices from the Japanese foreign ministry, and two unnamed Chinese who were quoted as saying that Chinese people were using the anti-Japan protests to demonstrate their anger against the government. That commentary fit in very well with what Japan and the US were propagandizing against the Chinese Communist Party. In the report on August 3, 2005 covering "ill will" between China and Japan, no voice from the Chinese government was heard, and the two "quoted" Chinese voices actually served to enhance the persuasion of the American ideological intentions in the context. One was saying that Chinese had "a victim's mentality" and Chinese didn't see "this much smaller country as being worthy of comparison with" China. The other was given six paragraphs to voice his opinion that anti-Japan mentality would resist as long as "an authoritarian government remains in place" and Chinese shouldn't criticize Yasukuni Shrine because "we have Mao Zedong's shrine in the middle of Beijing, which is our Yasukuni." These extremely opposite voices in China were used to justify whatever Japan had done to China and Chinese people.

Discussion and Conclusion

The questions that arise at this point are why the *NYT* presented Sino-Japan conflicts in such a way and why it tilted towards Japan from time to time but never toward China. To answer this question, we need to probe more deeply into the working of the media industry, national interests of the US and the American ideological heritage.

We can approach the question by first understanding the workings of the "political economy" (Jakubowicz et al, 1987, p. 17) of the media. Within this paradigm, the media is seen to operate under an economic imperative so that the ideas and values communicated through the media are "commodified" and exchanged for financial or material support by the owners and controllers of the media industry. As these media owners and controllers are inevitably influenced by Sino-Japan alliance, it accounts for the systematic exclusion of the voices from the Chinese government and the majority of its people. Hence, as we have seen earlier, mostly the Japanese or a few Chinese who opposed the government were given a voice in the news which was disadvantageous to China. The effect of using quotations, both direct and indirect, betrays a distinctively ideological purpose.

Moreover, patterns of foreign news coverage have been found to vary in association with a number of factors including "the apparent national interest of the United States" (Manheim, 1984, p. 644). As discussed in the previous text, the US-Japan alliance provides Washington the cornerstone of America's strategic position in Asia-Pacific region. That accounts for the frequent ideological inclination toward Japan in the news discourses of the *NYT*. The perception that the alliance checks the emergence of Japanese militarism has been shared by China and nearly all other regional states. If the US-Japan alliance goes too far to be a force containing Japan's militarism as it has been in the past, it will give rise to new fears and worries among the regional states. If the US and Japan are cooperating to thwart the emergence of China as a great and unified power, Beijing will take a range of countermeasures, including overt opposition to the US-Japan security Treaty and to the US forward military presence in Japan. That would be highly damaging to the national interests of the US. In this case, while the US maintains close cooperation with Japan, it occasionally remains relatively neutral in Sino-Japan conflicts, which is evidenced in the news coverage dated on November 13, 2004, April 20, 2005, April 23, 2005 and July 10, 2005.

Sino-US relations over the last century have been heavily affected by the ideological and cultural traditions of both sides. On the one hand, China wavers between seeking American support in China's economic development and diplomacy and fear and resentment of American cultural influence. On the other hand, anti-communism entered the US foreign policy thinking ever since the Russian revolution. The ideological aspect of difficulties in Sino-US relations is unlikely to disappear in the foreseeable future, for the bilateral ties are characterized by the impact of ideological traditions of both sides. In the following I will describe the ideological heritage on the American side, for one of the purposes of this paper is to find out why the US views China that way in the context of Sino-Japan conflicts.

According to American historian Michael H. Hunt (1987), there are three core ideas relevant to foreign affairs influencing the US' view of other nations, namely, quest for national greatness, racial hierarchy in attitudes toward other peoples and "limits of acceptable political and social change overseas" (p. 17-18). Quest for national greatness is a sense inherent with the birth of the US. The thinking elites believed that America was a place to build up an ideal republic according to the philosophical ideas, religious beliefs and moral values they had inherited from their homeland in Europe. The US, in their opinion, was born with the mandate to change the world in its own image. In its racial hierarchy, Asians of the yellow skin were put below Anglo-Saxon people. Americans were greatly concerned with their mandate to educate and change the inferior races besides conquering by force. Japan, which did best in learning from the West by the end of the 19th century, was regarded as "the good student" and China remains a promising student susceptible to change. This concept of racial hierarchy, to a certain degree, still exists implicitly among the Americans. Lastly, the American elites were somehow biased against radical revolutions in other countries even though they had gained independence by fighting against the British, because they wanted to maintain their overseas interests and they feared that those revolutions would impact the domestic social orders in the US. That could partly account for why the US has never truly befriended the New China established after the revolution of the Chinese Communist Party against the KMT.

These ideological traditions of the US are deeply embedded in the various aspects of its social life and foreign relations. Small wonder that China, which is led by the Communist Party, frequently falls prey to the demonization of American media, while Japan, which used to be a modest student of the West and a close ally of the US, is usually protected in portraying Sino-Japan conflicts in the *NYT*.

In summary, this study reveals that the dominant themes in the *NYT*'s reporting on Sino-Japan conflicts include China's anti-Japan protests in 2005, the Yasukuni Shrine visits, disputes over about Korean refugees, disputes over territory and resources, trade arguments and Taiwan issue, etc., etc.

This article has attempted to delineate the contrasting representations of China and Japan by analyzing a variety of discursive strategies, which portrayed Chinese government as aggressive, dominant and repressive and Chinese as a frightening and violent group of people, so that China was made less victimized and sympathized in the reporting of Sino-Japan conflicts. In contrast, the Japanese government and its people were depicted as more rational and courteous, while their atrocities in World War II, their denial of history, and their military and political ambitions were played down or glossed over in the news reports discussed. A further discussion, in the end, brings to light the underlying reasons for the ideologically framed news representations in the *NYT*. A critical analysis of news reporting, in this case, inevitably becomes a critique of those responsible for the ideological smuggling and persuasion.

It is hoped that this critical analysis of news reporting on Sino-Japan conflicts will, to some extent, contribute to the field of CDA and stimulate further research to be undertaken in areas beyond the newspaper or even media, namely, all areas of discourse that harbor ideological persuasion, so as to make transparent the processes that go into the construction of social inequality and ideological injustice.

References

Cameron, D. (1993). Style policy and style politics: a neglected aspect of the language of the news. *Media, Culture & Society, 15*, 315–330.
Chouliaraki, L. & N. Fairclough. (1999). *Discourse in Late Modernity: Rethinking Critical Discourse Analysis*. Edinburgh: Edinburgh University Press.
Christensen, T. J. (Spring 1999). China, The US-Japan alliance, and the security dilemma in East Asia. *International Security 23* (4), 49–80.
Fairclough, N. (1985). Critical and descriptive goals in discourse analysis. *Journal of Pragmatics*, 9, 739–763.
Fairclough, N. (1992). *Discourse and Social Change*. Cambridge: Polity.
Hall, S. (1996). The meaning of new times. *Critical Dialogues in Cultural Studies*. Eds. Morley D., Chen K. & Stuart Hall. London: Routledge.
Halliday, M. A. K. (1985). *An Introduction to Functional Grammar*. London: Edward Arnold.
Hopple, G. W. (1982). International news coverage in two elite newspapers. *Journal of Communication, 32*, 61–74.
Hunt, M. H. (1987). *Ideology and US Foreign Policy*. New Haven and London: Yale University.
Inoguchi, T. (Autumn 1996). The new security setup and Japan's options. *Japan Echo*, 38–39.
Jakubowicz, A. & Goodall, H. (1994). In (Eds.) *Racism, Ethnicity and the Media*. (pp. 14–27). Australia: Allen and Unwen.
Japan. The Ministry of Foreign Affairs. (15 August 1995). On the occasion of the 50th anniversary of the War's end (Translation). Tomiichi Murayama. June 6, 2007. <http://www.mofa.go.jp/announce/press/pm/murayama/9508.html>.
Manheim, J. B. (Sep., 1984). Changing national images: International public relations and media agenda setting. *The American Political Science Review, 78* (3), 641–657.
Semmel, A. K. (1976). Foreign news in four USA elite dailies: Some comparisons.

Journalism Quarterly, 53, 732–736.
Van Dijk, T. A. (2004). Principles of critical discourse analysis. In Michael (Ed.), *Critical Discourse Analysis: Critical Concepts in Linguistics, Vol. II.* (pp. 62–127). Toolan. New York: Routledge.
Wang, Q. K. (Autumn 2000). Taiwan in Japan's relations with China and the United States after the Cold War. *Pacific affairs 73* (3), 353–373.
Weiss, C. H. (1974). What American leaders read? *Public Opinion Quarterly, 38*, 1–22.
Widdowson, H. G. (1990). Discourses of enquiry and conditions of relevance. In J. Alatis (Ed.), *Georgetown University Round Table on Language and Linguistics.* (pp. 37–45). Washington, DC: Georgetown University Press.
Wodak, R. (1995). Critical linguistics and critical discourse analysis. In Verschueren J., Ostman J. O. and Blommaert J. (Eds.), *Handbook of Pragmatics* (pp. 201–232). Amsterdam: Benjamins.
Wodak, R. (1996). *Disorders of Discourse*. London: Longman.
Wu, X. (Mar.-Apr. 2000). The security dimension of Sino-Japanese relations: warily watching one another. *Asian Survey 40* (2), 296–310.
Zhang, G.. (19 August 1997). Japanese Cabinet Secretary talks wildly, claiming that Japan-US alliance cover Taiwan. *People's Daily 6*.

The Educational Context

27

Intercultural Dialogicality Between LC1 and LC2 in the EFL / ESL Classroom*

Song Li
Harbin Institute of Technology, China

Abstract: Drawing on M. Bakhtin's ideology of dialogism, the author argues that intercultural dialogicality is at the core of EFL /ESL teaching and learning and that the recognition of such dynamic forces in the English classroom is essential for successful learning and teaching of the target linguaculture. The EFL /ESL classroom is the meeting place where linguaculture 1 (LC1) and linguaculture 2 (LC2) are in constant dialogue with each other. It is from the interactions between their past experience in LC1 and LC2 and from the interaction between the Self and Other in both linguacultures that the learners develop their understanding of LC2 and (re)establish their identities in between the two, with LC1 functioning as resources in the process. Intercultural dialogicality is reality of the EFL /ESL classroom and intercultural interaction is to be taken both as the pedagogical ideology and the practical approach to engaged classroom teaching.

Introduction

The relationship between LC1(linguaculture 1) and LC2 (linguaculture 2) has been the concern of many language teachers and researchers. A

---

* This article was originally presented by the author at the 12th International Conference of Russia and the West: the Dialogue of Cultures, Moscow, Nov 28–30, 2007.

reflection on past efforts in theoretical and pedagogical explorations in second or foreign language teaching points at two observable trends: perception of the teaching / learning of the target language and culture as related to the native language and culture but handled as separate entities; 2) perception of the teaching / learning of the target language and culture as unrelated to the native language and culture. The first trend is characterized by the dominance of LC2 over LC1 while the second results in the rejection of learners' first language and culture in the classroom context.

In this article the author will challenge the treatment of language and culture as separate entities and the negligence of the potentials of LC1 by looking into the interactive relations between language and culture, and in particular the dialogicality between LC1 and LC2. Drawing on M. Bakhtin's ideology of dialogism (1981, 1986), the author argues that intercultural dialogicality is at the core of EFL/ESL teaching and learning, and the recognition of such dynamic forces in the English classroom is essential for successful learning and teaching of the target linguaculture. The author contends that the EFL/ESL classroom is the meeting place where LC1 and LC2 are in constant dialogue with each other. It is from the interactions between their past experience in LC1 and LC2 and from the interaction between the Self and Other in both linguacultures that the learners develop their understanding of LC2 and (re)establish their identities in between the two, with LC1 functioning as resources in the process. Intercultural dialogicality is reality of the EFL/ESL classroom and intercultural interaction is to be taken both as the pedagogical ideology and as the practical approach to classroom activities.

The research questions of the present study are: How are LC1 and LC2 related from a dialogical perspective? How do LC1 and LC2 interact in the EFL/ESL classroom context? And how do LC1 and LC2 work as resources for the learners' construction of their identities in the intercultural space between these two linguacultures? To answer these questions, the author will apply Bakhtin's theory of dialogism to EFL/ESL contexts and examine the intercultural interaction between LC1 and LC2. It will be concluded that intercultural dialogicality lies at the core of the EFL/ESL community of practice; intercultural dialogue is both the means and goals of EFL/ESL teaching and learning, through the process of which both LC1 and LC2 perceptions of both Self and Other can be enriched and developed.

Before a discussion of the above questions, a clarification of some terminologies seems imperative. Now it is widely agreed that language and culture can not be separated in foreign or second language teaching and learning; the teaching or learning of one presupposes the teaching or learning of the other. Agar (1994) demonstrates how language is bound up with culture by the special coinage of "languaculture". By languaculture is meant the unity of cultural perceptions, ideologies and modes of behavior through language. And in the same manner, Paul Friedrich uses another coined term "linguaculture" to suggest the inseparable relation between language and culture (as cited in Agar, 1994: 60). Other scholars have also used either of the two terms in the same sense (e.g. Fantini, 1997; Kramsch, 1993; Risager, 2004, 2005). Both terms embody the intrinsic link between language and culture. As it seems to be more easily manageable in pronunciation, the word "linguaculture" is adopted in this study to refer to the interlock between language and culture. And the abbreviated form LC is used for the word "linguaculture" for the sake of convenience.

It should be made clear that the use of this blended word does not mean a combination of language and culture nor does it indicate a simple addition of language to culture or culture to language in the language teaching curriculum. This term suggests a conceptual difference from the more widely adopted references of language and culture in separation. The selected term "linguaculture" presupposes an understanding of language and culture as an integrated entity, each is inseparable from the other and each is defined by the other. Language is culture and culture is mediated through language; there is no language outside culture and no culture outside language. Therefore, language should be treated as culture and within the cultural framework; culture is not and thus should not be treated as something additional to language as has been done in many EFL / ESL classrooms. For example, in China's English teaching materials, the cultural element of a linguistic form is often reduced to a footnote. The term "linguaculture" is used to suggest that language and culture are conditions to each other and must be treated as one organic entity in language teaching practice. The author believes that the English in EFL / ESL should be *English in culture and as culture*, and the substance of teaching and learning should be linguacultural literacy in English rather than English only as a self-contained language system. Such idea about English is the basic assumption for the present study.

LC1 in this study is used to refer to the linguaculture based on the learner's first language and culture, and LC2 to that based on the learner's target language and culture. More specifically, LC1 is the linguistic and cultural heritage pertaining to the first language of the learner. It covers linguaculture1 in two senses: LC1 represented in the learner's native language and LC1 represented in the learner's target language. In the case of ELT in China, LC1 is to be understood as Chinese linguaculture represented in both the Chinese language and the English language. In other words, to the present author, a Chinese learner of English is successful only when he / she has acquired the linguacultural literacy in English and is able to function in the English language in his / her own Chinese identity in intercultural contexts.

And considering that fact that both second and foreign language are an additional language to the first language and that the increasing use of

English as an international language in the globalized world has blurred the demarcation between English as a foreign or a second language, the distinction between EFL and ESL are ignored in the present study and the statements to be made about EFL are also assumed applicable to ESL situations.

Theoretical Grounding

Bakhtin's ideology of dialogism and dialogicality is the theoretical foundation for the present study. Dialogue in the Bakhtinian view goes far beyond the concretely situated verbal exchanges to encompass interaction of all kinds between people and their social, historical and physical contexts. The Bakhtinian dialogic view of language and culture offers profound insights into the relationships between the two and their roles in the construction of one's world.

For Bakhtin, language is in essence dialogic and social, as can be seen in the following quotation:

> Any word exists for the speaker in three aspects: as a neutral word of a language, belonging to nobody; as an *other's* word, which belongs to another person and is filled with echoes of the other's utterance, and, finally, *my* word, for, since I am dealing with it in a particular situation, with a particular speech plan, it is already imbued with my expression. ... Our speech, that is, all our utterances are ... filled with the words of others.
>
> (Bakhtin, 1986, pp. 88–89)

Thus, the language we have acquired or employ is the result of our interaction with others through their words or utterances, past or present, real or imagined. We make our own words out of the words of others. And there is no beginning nor ending to this interactive process between oneself and others:

> ... at any given moment of its historical existence, language is heteroglot from top to bottom: it represents the coexistence of socio-ideological contradictions between the present and the past, between different epochs of the past, between different socio-ideological groups in the present, between tendencies, schools, circles and so forth, all given a bodily form. These "languages" of heteroglossia intersect each other in a variety of ways, forming new socially typifying "languages".
>
> (Bakhtin, 1981, p. 282)

Dialogue, according to Bakhtin, is omnipresent and it is not only the way of language learning and use, but also the mode of human existence:

> Life by its very nature is dialogic. To live means to participate in dialogue: to ask questions, to heed, to respond, to agree, and so forth. In this

dialogue a person participates wholly and throughout his whole life: with his eyes, lips, hands, soul, spirit, with his whole body and deeds. He invests his entire self in discourse, and this discourse enters into the dialogic fabric of human life, into the world symposium.

(Bakhtin, 1981, p. 293)

It is through dialogic interactions that language is used and developed; and it is through dialogic interactions that the world is created and experienced with each person engaging in the ever flowing current of life imbued with and propelled by other voices, other texts, other ways of being and doing. In other words, a fundamental dialogicality is ubiquitous in human life: it is the way we relate to others, model our world and live our lives.

The ideology of dialogue is well expressed in the concept of "dialogicality", which can be understood in two senses: one is the concretely situated interaction between two participants, and another a more abstract notion for any interactive process that happens between subjects in particular social, historical and physical contexts. Dialogicality involves, on the one hand, the manner in which "one speaker's concrete utterances come into contact with, or 'interanimate', the utterances of another" (Wertsch, 1991, p. 54) and on the other hand, it can denote the human ability "to take part in interactions with others and with sociocultural contexts as well as physical environments" (Linell, 2007, p. 618). Dialogue or dialogicality is both the means and end for human communication and therefore it is both the process and the product of human development.

Breaking away from the formalist view of language, Bakhtin's ideology of dialogue offers profound insights into the nature of language, language use and human development. Its more important contribution, however, is in its philosophical guidance which offers a world view to approach language, culture and learning from a new perspective (Hall et al, 2005). Bakhtinian dialogism and dialogicality emphasize the cultural and interpersonal dimensions of utterances or language in use and examines discourses that are formed by multiple voices and contexts. Therefore, it is particularly relevant for the EFL / ESL classroom where dialogue takes place along different dimensions. Explicitly, dialogue occurs between the teacher and the learner, one learner and other learners, learners and teachers with the immediate texts and contexts of the classroom setting. Implicitly, interactions also take place inside the leaner's own self where the past experience, present state of existence and future imaginings all come into play. The EFL/ESL classroom is also a site of interaction where the learner experiences the linguistic and cultural diversities between LC1 and LC2 in multiple voices for the (re)construction of meaning and identity. It is at the intersection of LC1 and LC2 that intercultural dialogicality finds its place.

Dialogic Relationship between LC1 & LC2

By intercultural dialogicality the author means the dynamic interactive nature and process in between LC1 and LC2; or the dialogical property or quality that exists and functions in the intercultural contexts where people of diverse cultural backgrounds engage in meaning making actions. Intercultural dialogicality distinguishes itself from dialogicality in the more general sense in that the participants are of diverse cultural backgrounds and therefore bring into the dialogue different worldviews and approaches to their life problems, including the use of language. Intercultural dialogicality is thus more hetereglossic, multi-voiced and contested. In the following section, the author will discuss how intercultural dialogicality takes place in the EFL/ESL classroom.

Bakhtin's dialogic philosophy captures the dynamics in EFL/ESL learning and teaching. Dialogicality permeates the whole process of the teaching and learning practice. It lies in the interaction between teacher and learner, learner and learner, teacher and teacher, teacher/learner and their social and physical contexts, the historical and the situational. The multi-faceted interaction between LC1 and LC2 occurs when two diverse linguacultural systems contest and negotiate with each other in the learners and teachers' endeavor to (re)construct their cognitive schemata as well as their identities in between the two.

On each of the above planes, and amongst the heteroglossic languages in the classroom, two voices stand out as most powerful: that of the Self in LC1 of the learner and local teacher and that of the Other in LC2 as represented by the target linguaculture discourses and the widely employed "native-speaker" foreign teachers. When the Self in LC1 meets with the Other in LC2, the learners' established images of Self and Other will be challenged and so are their taken-for-granted discursive use of the language in discourses where they claim their identities and perform their different social roles and tasks. In the same contact with LC2, however, the foreign or second language learner does not discard his LC1 but relies on it as a frame of reference for sense making about new linguistic forms and all that embedded in them. Therefore, the interaction between LC1 and LC2 involves a two-way process of dialogues; LC1 and LC2 influence each other and both function as dynamic impetuses for the changes in the learner in his/her experience of the foreign or second language learning.

Impact of LC1 on LC2

The intrinsic link between language and culture in second language learning is undeniable and so is the impact of LC1 on LC2. For years, the connection between L1 and L2 in second or foreign language learning has provoked much controversy among researchers. H. H. Stern (1983) generalized these diverse views into two kinds: the Restructuring Hypothesis and the Creative Construction Hypothesis. The Restructuring Hypothesis holds that "a second language learner develops his second language by a process of restructuring his first language" while the Creative Construction Hypothesis contends that "the second language growth is independent of a particular first language and develops rather in the manner in which a child 'creates' his first language" (Stern, 1983, p. 396).

Based on the Bakhtinian philosophy of dialogicality as the mode of the world and way of human existence, the present author finds the Creative Construction Hypothesis runs completely against the nature of human learning and development. Although man is blessed with the innate ability or mechanism to acquire and use language, and L1 and L2 learning may have parallels in the process, the very term L2 makes a distinction of the two in that it presupposes the learner's previous experience and the effect of that experience with L1 learning on the learner. The Constructive Hypothesis fails to see the cognitive impact of the learners' existing knowledge and competence in LC1 and all that he has internalized about the world in LC1.

In contrast, the Restructuring Hypothesis fully recognizes the learner's dependence of L1 in L2 learning and the main manifestation of such impact is in the much-discussed phenomenon of language transfer in the second or foreign language learning. Language transfer is cross-linguistic influence "resulting from similarities and differences between the target language and any other language that has been previously (and perhaps imperfectly) acquired" (Odlin, 2001, p. 28). The similarities between L1 and L2 are believed to facilitate the learners in their development of target language knowledge and skills, and thus lead to positive transfer. In contrast, the differences between L1 and L2 will interfere or hinder the learners' command of the knowledge and skills of the target language, and may lead to negative transfer in the learning process. Transfer is observed to occur on different levels of language and language use, from phonetic sounds to semantic, syntactical and discourse structures and styles, from linguistic features to nonstructural factors and sociocultural behaviors (Odlin, 2001).

To further Stern's generalization of controversies over the L1 and L2 connection, the present author divides the Restructuring Hypothesis into two sub-categories: the Constructive Hypothesis and Destructive Hypothesis. By the Constructive Hypothesis, the author means that the learner's previously established knowledge and experience with LC1 facilitates him or her in the learning of a new language. In contrast, the Destructive Hypothesis sees LC1 as related to LC2 learning but functions as a hindrance or destructive factor rather than a facilitator in the process. The Constructive Hypothesis and Destructive Hypothesis are parallel to positive transfer and negative transfer respectively but they emphasis more on the working of LC1 in LC2 learning. Both the constructive and destructive functions of LC1 evidence the interaction or dialogue between LC1 and LC2. Constructive or deconstructive, the active role that LC1 plays in LC2 learning process is an undeniable fact and therefore must be given serious consideration by second or foreign language teachers.

What the author wishes to pinpoint here is that the constructive power of LC1 has not been fully and widely recognized by the EFL/ESL community. Although there are researches on positive transfer of L1 and the importance of L1 in L2 learning and teaching and there seems to be increasing interest in this direction, much more attention has been given to the negative influence of L1 on L2, C1 on C2, resulting in an unduly effort by language teachers to reduce or even eliminate LC1 in the EFL/ESL classroom. In a keyword search of "language transfer" by the author at the time of working on the present study in an online database (CNKI) for academic journals, it is found out that almost one third of the 949 feedback articles between 1998–2007 focused on their concern for negative transfer while only about 200 of them have positive transfer listed as keywords. It is high time that language teachers emancipated themselves from such excessive concern over negative transfer and started to pay due attention to the dialogic nature of second or foreign language learning because LC1 has much more to contribute to second or foreign language teaching and learning than the language teachers have assumed.

The impact of LC1 on LC2 in EFL/ESL can be observed from two perspectives: the social cultural and the cognitive.

Socioculturally, language is developed and used within different contexts by diverse social groups. The English language has evolved into the most widely used lingua franca in the world but also with many regional variations. The variety of Englishes around the world and the number increase in the outer and expanding circles in Kachru's concentric categorization of English speakers (1982) speak loudly for the impact of LC1 on LC2 in addition to other social, economic and geographical influences from each region. L1 linguistic forms and structures together with the sociocultural meanings embedded in them are resources for the formation of new terms, new expressions and styles in discourse. The marked LC1 features in the new English variations in turn serve to distinguish one English-speaking group from another or one variety from another (Crystal, 1997). This is because language is one of the most distinctive markers of its speakers' identities; the linguistic and sociolinguistic features in a person's speech or writing carry with them, among other things, rich information about his/her socio-cultural identities such as ethnicity, social status, and cultural background, etc. In a discussion of the role of Chinese linguaculture in ELT in China, Song (2005) points out the significance of LC1 in the dialogic process of EFL/ESL. Song argues that, in the case of ELT context in China, Chinese linguaculture is part of Chinese English learners' identity constructs and it constitutes an important part of the learners' intercultural communicative competence. According to Song & Fu (2004) and Song (2006), intercultural communicative competence is essentially the ability to negotiate meanings and identities with the cultural Other and it involves one's communicative competence in both LC1 and LC2 (see Figure 1 below).

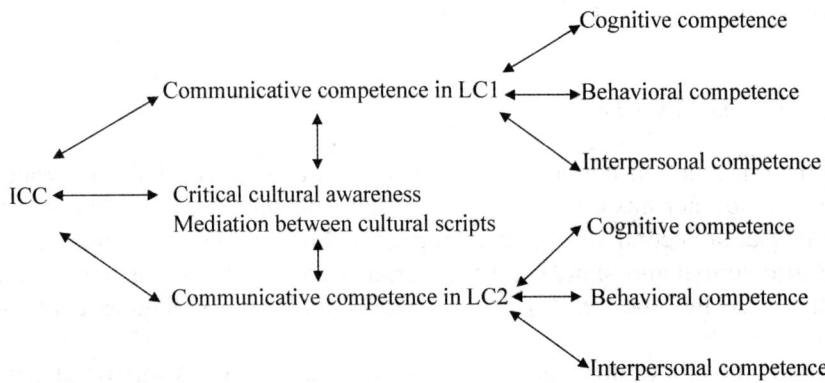

Figure 1   Components of Intercultural Communicative Competence
(adapted from Song & Fu, 2004 and Song, 2006)

In the above model, intercultural communicative competence develops along the intersection where LC1 and LC2 interaction takes place and where learners are expected to learn to cross boundaries.

From the cognitive perspective, LC1 establishes a framework of reference for LC2 learning. Learning is a cognitive process and cognitive learning is based on schemata or mental structures by which the learner organizes his / her perceived environment. Studies by educational psychologists have proved that schematic structures of cognitive development change by the process of assimilation and association, and that learning is expected to occur when the learner can relate new knowledge to what he / she already knows (e.g. Ausubel, 1968; Novak, 1993). In EFL/ESL learning context, the learning of LC2 also goes under the same process of assimilation and association. The learner does not enter the classroom with an empty mind but with a cognitive schema established in his / her earlier experiences in LC1 and some limited experience with LC2 depending on the history of his / her learning.

Song (2005) contends that LC1 acts as impetus for ELT as it forms the basis of the learners' conceptual constructs and if handled appropriately, it can reduce the cognitive load of the learner and activate the learners' existent schemata, turning all their past experience and prior knowledge into resources in their construction of new meanings.

The cognitive psychologists' view that pre-established cognitive structures are essential to the learning of new concepts and knowledge unveils the intercultural dialogicality between LC1 and LC2 in ELT. Throughout the English learning process, the dialogicality between LC1 and LC2 engages the learner in constructing and reconstructing of meaning and identities in between the Self in LC1 and the Other in LC2, between the old self as product of LC1 and the emerging new self as outcome of the interaction with LC2. Here Bakhtin's dialogism once again finds its evidence in the EFL/ESL classroom.

Impact of LC2 on LC1

The interaction between LC1 and LC2 is a two-way dialogic process. What the learner has established in himself/herself in LC1 influences the learning of a second or foreign language. Meanwhile, the contact with LC2 also contributes significantly to what becomes of the learner in terms of the way he/she relates to the world and others linguistically and socioculturally.

The immediate influence of LC2 on the learner is its mirror effect of the learner's LC1 makings. It is in experiencing the differences of the Other in LC2 that the learner comes to a fuller awareness and realization of his/her own ways of being and doing in LC1. This process of getting to know the Self takes place in two ways: 1) in contrasting the Self and the Other, and 2) in perceiving the Self in the eyes of the Other. As culture and language are acquired mostly beyond our consciousness, we tend to take for granted our everyday way of life, including our use of L1. Only when different life styles and different ways of language use come into our view or consciousness do we realize that our life patterns and language use may have been regulated by different rules. In learning a foreign or second language, our cultural makings or cultural identities are thus brought to our conscious awareness in our contact with the Other through LC2. A Chinese student may have never realized what it means to him/her to be a friend and how he/she has been friends with other Chinese until when he/she sensed that his/her American friends have kept a distance from him/her for they would not share everything with him/her and would not spend as much time with him/her as the Chinese friends do and that they seemed to have no intention to invite him/her to eat out after he/she had treated them to dinner twice already. Interestingly the way of friend-making in China is learned consciously for the first time in the learner's interaction with the American friend.

The Other's views of us also have an effect on our perception of ourselves. We may not realize that we have particular qualities or manners until we learn about our own image "reflected" in the eyes of the Other. Foreigners' travelogues often reveal how we look like to the rest of the world even though their descriptions may be inaccurate as their views of us are filtered through their own cultural lens. Overseas Chinese students are made to believe that they are indeed very hardworking because their Western teachers have repeatedly praised them for this. Korean students may be surprised when being told by their fellow international students and teachers that they are very courteous while they are almost equally often blamed for not behaving properly in terms of social manners by their parents back home. Kramsch (1993) summarizes the impact of C1 and C2 on foreign language learners' perception of cultural reality and cultural imagination with the following figure.

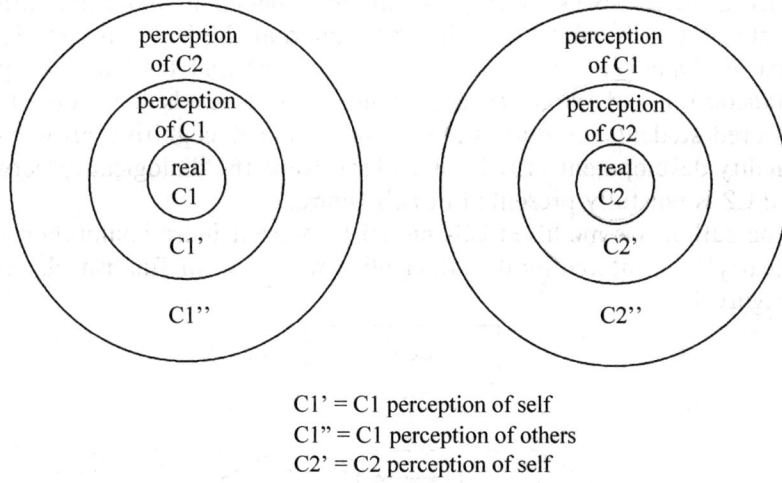

C1' = C1 perception of self
C1" = C1 perception of others
C2' = C2 perception of self
C2" = C2 perception of others

Figure 2 Interactions between C1 and C2
(from Kramsch, 1993, p. 208; title by the author)

As indicated in the above figure, our perception of Self and Other comes from both C1 and C2. This also holds true for the interaction between LC1 and LC2 in EFL/ESL learning if we take the language element as constitutive and constructive in the frame of reference we use to form cultural reality and perceptions. We may as well substitute all the C1 and C2 in the figure with LC1 and LC2 and their variants respectively. In the English classroom, the learners' understanding of the Self and Other also develops along these four dimensions: LC1 perception of Self, LC1 perception of Other, LC2 perception of Self and LC2 perception of Other. A self-perspective and an other-perspective work together in the formation of our perceptions of the Self and the cultural Other.

Li Ying (2004) applies Kramsch theory of cultural reality and cultural imagination to ELT in China and proposes an empowerment-oriented model for pedagogical practice. She demonstrates the interaction between C1 and C2 in Figure 3.

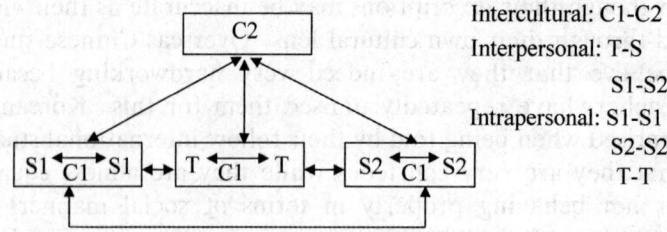

Figure 3 Interaction between C1 and C2 in ELT (Li Ying, 2004)

The dialogic interaction in an EFL / ESL classroom, as Li points out, happens at three levels: intrapersonal, interpersonal and intercultural. This coincides with what the author has stated at the beginning section of the article. Dialogues at the three levels co-exist and tend to take place simultaneously, and dialogues occurring at these levels have effectively empowered students in that students have gained cognitive growth and personality development (Li, 2004). However, the dialogicality between C1 and C2 is not fully presented in Li's figure.

The author has modified Li's model to present more comprehensively and clearly how intercultural dialogicality works in an English classroom (see Figure 4).

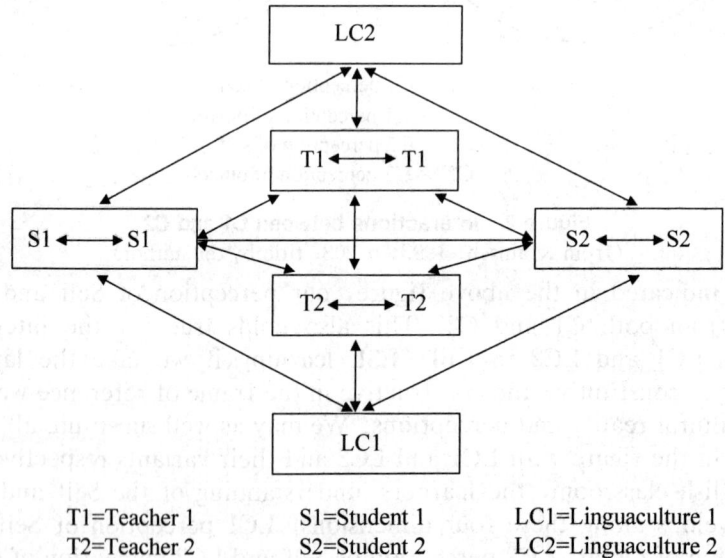

T1=Teacher 1   S1=Student 1   LC1=Linguaculture 1
T2=Teacher 2   S2=Student 2   LC2=Linguaculture 2

Figure 4 Intercultural Dialogicality in EFL /ESL Classroom

In the above model, English language teaching and learning is depicted as a dialogic process that engages the teacher and the learner in active interactions with each other and within themselves. Through the dialogues at different levels and between different interactants, both the teacher and the learner strive to work out new understandings of themselves and others, and in such process they use the resources in both LC1 and LC2 to construct meanings and identities. Within the EFL / ESL context, intercultural dialogicality happens at every level and in every stage of the teaching / learning process, externally (interpersonally) between teachers and learners, internally (intrapersonally) in their own minds, and cross-culturally between LC1 and LC2.

Then what becomes of the learners as the result of the interaction between LC1 and LC2 and in particular with their LC1 meanings and identities being challenged by LC2? Viewed from a dialogistic perspective, the learners not only adjust their self-perceptions according to the Other's perception of them, but also tend to redefine the world, people and their behavior patterns when coming into contact with alternative approaches and choices in their encounter with the Other while learning another language. Learning LC2 "is not an evolutionary improvement on what precedes it; rather, new knowledge enters adversarial relationships with older, more established ones, challenging their position in the power play of understandings, and in such confrontations new insights can be provoked" (Kramsch, 1993, p. 238). Since EFL / ESL learning is an interactive process, the learner will no longer be his / her old self. Instead, new outlooks and new understandings are developed in the dialogues with the Other through LC2 and in the reflections on LC1 during the process. In this sense, learning another language is also a process of personal growth. The interaction between LC1 and LC2 leads to personal growth rather than a personal split into two personalities in two linguacultures. Gao Yihong (2001) illustrates this personnel growth with the formula $1 + 1 > 2$, meaning the learning of a foreign language does not produce a double-identity person nor replace one cultural identity with another as indicated with another formula "$1 - 1 = 1$"; instead, the learner becomes enlightened and intellectually more mature than before with more choices at his / her disposal in making decisions.

Through the interactions at intrapersonal, interpersonal and intercultural levels, a "middle landscape" is taking shape in the learner's mind, who finds himself / herself in searching of a third place in between LC1 and LC2 (Kramsch, 1993; Byram, 1997). The learning of English as a foreign or second language places the learner at the very intersection between different voices, different frames of reference and different behavioral choices. This intersection or dialogic interaction of cultures creates the opportunity for the third culture or third place. By developing a third place, Kramsch refers not to some actual event but "a state of mind" that is constantly working out ways of situating himself / herself in between alternative ways of doing and being through the target language he / she has learned while still retains his / her own voice in using the target language with the cultural Other.

At the age of globalization and multiculturalization, with English becoming an international language, the development of a third place is highly important in EFL / ESL teaching and learning. Song & Fu (2004) proposes a framework for an intercultural communicative approach to English teaching. Viewed from Bakhtinian philosophy of dialogism, the interaction between the constituents in the model is made even more evident.

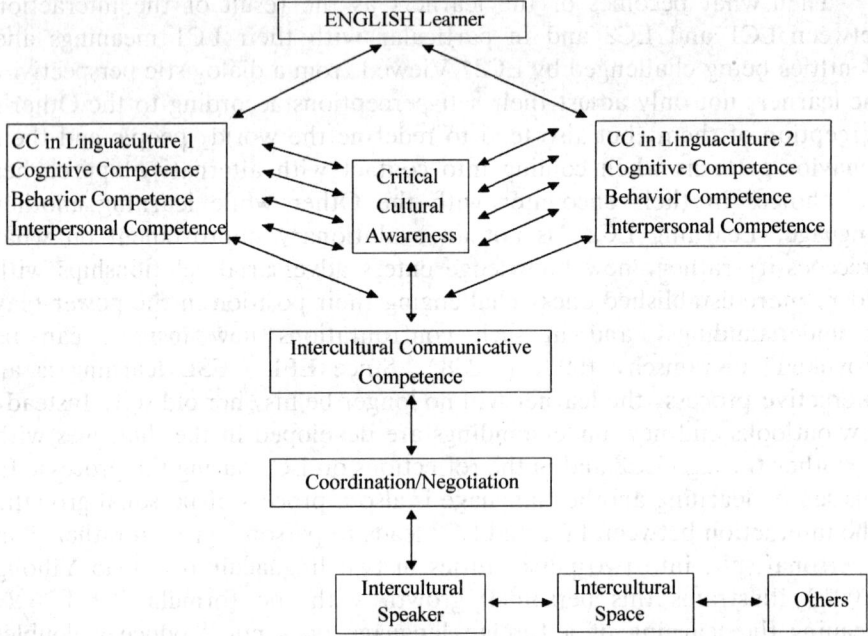

Figure 5　Framework for the Development of Intercultural Communicative Competence in ELT (Song & Fu, 2004)

As shown in Figure 5, ENGLISH[①] teaching or learning is an interactive process between the learner and the cultural Other. In this process, the learner will have to develop communicative competence (CC) in both native and target languages and a high cross-cultural awareness so as to be able to make critical judgments and appropriate choices of behaviors in specific contexts through coordination and negotiation with other people, both native and non-native alike, and between other ways of being and doing. The intercultural approach sets the goal of EFL / ESL teaching and learning towards producing competent intercultural speakers who are able to transcend cultural boundaries and build up an

---

① The capitalization of the word English is used in the figure to indicate the status of English as an international language, stressing its heteroglossic nature.

intercultural space with others.

Concluding Remarks

This paper has examined the interaction between LC1 and LC2 from Bakhtin's dialogic perspective. It is argued that the EFL/ESL classroom is saturated with intercultural dialogicality at the intrapersonal, interpersonal and intercultural levels and intercultural dialogicality functions in important ways towards the learners' perception and redefinition of the Self and the cultural Other. Perceiving intercultural dialogicality as reality of the EFL/ESL classroom offers rich implications for teaching and learning English as a foreign or second language. Dialogic approach is strongly recommended for EFL and ESL classroom. Both LC1 and LC2 need to be embraced as resources for intercultural language learning. This understanding calls for a more rational and more balanced treatment of LC1 and LC2 resources in classroom teaching. In addition, the dynamics of intercultural dialogicality for meaningful learning should be emphasized. To facilitate intercultural language teaching/learning in the EFL/ESL classroom, dialogical interactions should be designed whenever and wherever possible in the classroom. Dialogues at all levels can be organized and examined for more effective teaching/learning.

To conclude, intercultural dialogue is reality, process and outcome of English language teaching/learning, and there is much to be desired from an intercultural dialogic approach in the EFL/ESL classroom. That points to the direction of future research and pedagogical efforts.

References

Agar, M. (1994). *Language Shock: Understanding the Culture of Conversation*. New York: Morrow and Foreign Language Learning. Mahwah, NJ: Lawrence Erlbaum.
Ausubel, D. P. (1968). *Educational Psychology: A Cognitive View*. New York: Holt, Reinhard and Winston.
Bakhtin, M. (1981) *The Dialogic Imagination*. Austin: University of Texas Press
Bakhtin, M. (1986). *Speech Genres and Other Late Essays* (Eds). C. Emerson & M. Holquist. Austin: University of Texas Press
Bazerman, C. (2005) An essay on pedagogy by Mikhail M. Bakhtin. *Written Communication*. Vol 22; 333
Byram, M. (1997). *Teaching and Assessing Intercultural Communicative Competence*. Toronto: Multilingual Matters
Crystal, D. (1997). *English as a Global Language*. Cambridge: Cambridge University Press.
Fantini, A. (1997) Language: its cultural and intercultural dimensions. In A. Fantini (Ed.). *New Ways of Teaching Culture* (pp. 3-15). Alexandria, VA: TESOL Publications.

Gao, Y. H. (2001). *Foreign Language Learning: 1 + 1 > 2*. Beijing: Peking University Press

Hall, J. K., Vitanova, G. & Marchenkova, L. (Eds.) (2005). *Dialogue with Bakhtin on Second and Foreign Language Learning: New Perspectives*. Mahwah, NJ and London: Lawrence Erlbaum Associates

Kachru, B. (Ed.) (1982). *The Other Tongue — English across Cultures*. Urbana: U of Illinois Press.

Kramsch, C. (1993). *Context and Culture in Language Education*. Oxford: Oxford University Press.

Li, Y. (2004). *Teaching Culture in the Context of Traditional Culture of Learning*, MA Thesis, Anhui University

Linell, P. (2007). Dialogicality in languages, minds and brains: Is there a convergence between dialogism and neuro-biology? *Language Sciences*, *29*, 605–620

Novak, J. D. (1993). How do we learn our lesson?: Taking students through the process. *Science Teacher*, *60*(3), 50–55.

Odlin, T. (2001). *Language Transfer: Cross-linguistic Influence in Language Learning*. Shanghai: Foreign Language Education Press.

Risager, K. (2004) A social and cultural view of language. In H. L. Hansen (Ed.). *Disciplines and Interdisciplinarity* (pp. 21–34). Copenhagen: Museum Tusculanum Press.

Risager, K. (2005). Languaculture as a key concept in language and culture teaching. In B. Preisler et al. (Eds.). *The Consequences of Mobility: Linguistic and Sociocultural Contact Zones*. Retrieved Sept. 20, 2005, from www.ruc.dk/cuid/publikationer/publikationer/mobility/mobility2/Risager/.

Song, L. & Fu, L. (2004). Intercultural communicative language teaching: Rethinking the communicative approach to ELT in China. *EA Journal*, *22*(1), 20–42.

Song, L. (2005). Role of Chinese Linguaculture in ELT in China, paper presentation at the 3rd Asia TEFL Conference, Beijing.

Song, L. (2006). Exploration of intercultural communicative competence. Paper presented at the Annual Conference of International Association of Intercultural Communication Studies, Trinity University, San Antonio. August 2–4, 2006.

Stern H. (1983). *Fundamental Concepts of Language Teaching*. Oxford: Oxford University Press.

Wertsch, J. V. (1991). *Voices of the Mind: A Sociocultural Approach to Mediated Action*. Cambridge, MA: Harvard University Press.

28

Covert Culture in the Foreign Language Classroom: Confronting Contrast in Target and Base Mindsets*

Eleanor H. JORDEN
Cornell University-Emerita, USA

Abstract: Every successful foreign language class enables the students to understand and function better in an increasingly diverse and interdependent world. In addition, every foreign language classroom provides a laboratory for the study of the diversity of cultures. There is always the contrast between the base language and base culture of the students and the target language and target culture being studied. In the classroom the target language and culture may be present in a variety of forms, some of which are rarely recognized. In particular, teaching materials written entirely by target native speakers often overlook the difference in learning styles that are used by students from a different culture. A study of the learning style of American students, contrasted with the traditional teaching style of Japanese, provides an interesting study of diversity and accommodation.

A number of years ago, as I was lecturing on Japanese structure to a group of American college students, I had an occasion to analyze a complex Japanese verb form. Following my usual procedures, I wrote the form on the board and proceeded to divide it into its component, meaningful parts, explaining — as I drew lines to mark the morph boundaries — what each

---

* This article is included as a commemoration of Eleanor Jorden (1920–2009), a recognized international scholar, a prolific author and an influential educator and expert on Japanese language and pedagogy. She was awarded four Honorary Doctorates and she received Japan's prestigious Order of the Precious Crown in 1985.

contributed to the overall meaning. On this particular day, our class had a visitor from Japan who was observing our Japanese program. I still remember the comment he made when we met following the session. He pointed to the analyzed form on the board and said, with a smile, "As you drew those lines, I felt as if I were being violated!"

In recent years I have had occasion to think back to this story frequently. As serious, cutting edge research on Japanese language pedagogy has gradually placed an ever stronger emphasis on the importance of culture in foreign language learning, we have now reached the point where we speak of language *in* culture rather than language *and* culture, and we define foreign language learning as learning to perform a foreign culture. However, 'culture' in this context does not refer to the consciously learned, aesthetic culture of art, music, literature, and the like, or to consciously learned, informational culture, which deals with facts about the culture, but rather to behavioral culture, which the native speaker acquires outside of consciousness, as one acquires a native language in the process of being socialized within a society. Unless we understand the cultural framework within which the Japanese interact, we cannot hope to speak or write appropriately, or listen or read with anything approaching full understanding.

Understandably, this cultural emphasis is concentrated specifically on the target 'language in culture' (hereafter 'LinC') — i.e., the foreign language being studied, in the framework of the acquired culture. But every foreign language class brings together two languages and two cultures①— i.e., the base LinC (= the native LinC of the learners) as well as the target LinC. While some level of the same target LinC is the goal of all instruction in that LinC everywhere, the base LinC exerts a tremendous influence on how that target is achieved. In an American classroom, particularly at the more elementary levels, the English language as the base language is constantly functioning as a sieve through which the base native strains the foreign language: "No plurals in Japanese? How do they manage?" "Many different equivalents for 'I'? Weird!" On the cultural level, the reactions are similar. One's native LinC is the norm, and for the beginning learner, all deviations from it seem surprising. But even when learners have progressed to the point where they expect and accept differences, their base will continue to exert a strong influence, and the more the instructor understands and acknowledges that base, the more effectively instruction will proceed.

However, such challenges to learning are all related to the target

---

① Many groups of learners include representatives of more than one LinC. However, since this study is dealing with learners studying in the U.S., we can presume that most non-American learners in such groups have some experience with American LinC and can function with it as the base, even if it is not ideal for them.

LinC, the deliverable of the foreign language class. The topic I am interested in examining is the culture of the classroom itself — the culture of the delivery system used in bringing the target to the base — using Japanese as the sample LinC. My specific concern is the learning situation that involves native American, adult learners, who represent the base, taught by a native Japanese instructor who has undergone no training in teaching Japanese to Americans or whose training in pedagogy has been based on principles of traditional, native Japanese language pedagogy. In other words, both the deliverable and the delivery system in such situations relate to the target. Unless native Japanese instructors have studied and adopted the widely accepted principles of American pedagogy, which identify the learners and how they learn as the focus of instruction, it can be assumed that their native mindset will prevail as the basis for their instruction, resulting in a methodology that is markedly different.

For almost twenty years, I have been involved in a program that trains Japanese, newly arrived from Japan, to teach Japanese in American colleges and universities. Originally an integral part of the program *Exchange: Japan*, it prepared the participants to discharge their teaching responsibilities in exchange for which they received tuition, room and board, and a small stipend as they pursued a master's degree in a field of their own choosing. The program's originator and director arranged all the college/university placements; and it was he who invited me to prepare a curriculum for the teacher training program and assume the role of academic director. After sixteen years of successful operation, during which a surprising number of participants later changed their field of specialization to Japanese language pedagogy and pursued advanced degrees, *Exchange: Japan* came to an end and was reorganized under a new administration. Now called the Alliance for Language and Educational Exchange (ALLEX), it continues the work of *Exchange: Japan*, including the teacher training program, its basic curriculum, and its faculty.

It might seem unusual to bring native Japanese to the United States to learn how to teach their native language, but the program director realized that traditional Japanese pedagogical training would not prepare them adequately to move into American academic institutions to teach Japanese, in most cases as the only Japanese instructor, without mentors or advisors, and at the same time to fulfill requirements for a graduate degree program. Clearly the participants would need a program that emphasized orientation to American culture, covering all the areas that would touch on their lives. Since the training program aimed at preparing Japanese specifically to teach their language to Americans, it would be important to learn American instructional style, so different from that of Japan in its emphasis on how students learn as the guide to how teachers should teach.

The nine-week, full-time-intensive curriculum originally developed was an expansion and enrichment of the one I had originally devised for a four-week, teacher training workshop offered at Cornell University for a number of years. A key element of the new program was the inclusion of a beginners' class in Japanese language, which provided a model for observation when taught by master instructors and served as an experimental lab when taught by the trainees. The textbook[1] used in these classes was the one the trainees were expected to use in their own programs later. It had been written by a team consisting of a native Japanese linguist, who, as a specialist in student-focused, Japanese language pedagogy, wrote all the Japanese material, and a native American linguist, who handled the linguistic and cultural analysis, presented in English from the point of view of the American learner.

The teacher trainees over the years all exhibited similar reactions to the textbook and to the program in general. During the first 2–3 weeks, they would demonstrate confusion, shock, and, in some cases, even incipient hostility to some features of the methodology. At the same time, they would register amazement at the rapid progress being made by the American learners whose classes they were observing, analyzing, and beginning to teach. This period would be followed by a gradual understanding of this approach that had so surprised them earlier, with a final realization of its overall effectiveness in teaching Japanese to Americans. As they gave their teaching demonstrations to the class of learners, their gradual conversion would become apparent.

Obviously a conversion resulting from only nine weeks of instruction needed further nurturing, in the form of guidance and reinforcement. After moving on to the colleges where they would be teaching Japanese for two years, the trainees were encouraged to transmit, by e-mail to the training program faculty, any questions or problems that arose. Once each year the entire class would re-convene for a two-day, intensive, refresher seminar, during which questions and problems of general interest — as well as success stories — were shared and discussed. In particular, guidance was offered on how to incorporate cultural sensitivity and newly learned teaching techniques into programs based on more traditional textbooks. Each year, at the end of their teaching assignment, those trainees who had decided to change careers and remain in the field would either take positions immediately as Japanese lecturers in American colleges or would enter graduate programs in Japanese pedagogy for further study. Of course there were those who, either by choice or by the requirements of their position, gradually reverted to a more traditional way of teaching Japanese but it is safe to say that even they were permanently affected by their contact with this new way of viewing language pedagogy.

At the conclusion of the first training program offered under the new ALLEX administration in 2005, I asked the trainees to submit their

---

[1] Jorden with Noda (1987), *Japanese: The Spoken Language*, Part 1.

personal reactions to the student-focused textbook they had been using. Any temptation to think that it hadn't mattered very much was quickly dispelled as I read the replies. One of the most analytical claimed that everything in the book was so completely new to him that it seemed like a textbook based on a language other than Japanese. He described the structural analysis and notes as "so elaborate and logical" as to prevent him from having either doubts or questions. He also pointed out the marked contrast with native Japanese grammar, resulting in his viewing his native language in a totally new way. In his words, the textbook had become not only a teaching tool but also a volume to study.

The comments of the participants were striking in the clear indication of their awareness that there was indeed a fundamental difference in an approach to foreign language teaching that focused on how the learner learned. Many mentioned the detailed, carefully ordered analysis of the structure of Japanese that included even the description and marking of accent and intonation. It was pointed out that there was pedagogical value in the careful control over the introduction of new patterns without any loss of authenticity. Several mentioned opposition to the use of romanization, which lessened when they realized both the way in which it was being used (i.e., not as an orthography but as a pedagogical representation that served to remind the learners of what they had heard during class hours) and also its usefulness in the analysis of inflected forms. There were repeated references to the rapid progress made by the learners, including their use of complex structures much earlier in their training than the trainees would have expected. But most significant to me were the comments that showed an awareness of a cultural connection — a realization that culture was the driving force in many of the differences in approach. For many of the trainees it was a shock to realize that Japanese was systematic and could be explained. The Japanese "*feel* what is right and wrong," was the explanation of one trainee, who had never before thought there might be a different way to view a language. For another trainee, it came down to "the logical and systematic approach to language rooted in the Western tradition."

When we examine elementary Japanese language textbooks, prepared by native Japanese using a traditional, native Japanese approach and used in many American colleges, we find clear evidence for the original expectations of the trainees. The native avoidance of romanization in the language classroom leads to the introduction, from the very beginning, of the complex native orthography, which uses totally unfamiliar symbols. This precludes any marking of accent or intonation; in fact there is little indication of truly serious concern for developing accurate pronunciation. The exclusive use of the native orthography also complicates the analysis of inflected forms: with 'American ears,' the American hears the sequence /n-o-m-u/ as consisting of four sounds and can analyze sound by sound, but 'Japanese ears' hear *no-mu* and cannot separate out the final *-u*, which is actually the signal of the imperfective. The implications of this complicate the entire analysis of inflected forms.① And the dominance of vocabulary and topics of conversation over structure becomes clear as new patterns are introduced according to their occurrence in script-driven dialogues, thus accounting for the trainees' amazement at the newly encountered emphasis on system and on structurally based ordering, which determines the choice of topics of conversation.

On a conscious level, native Japanese who teach their language to foreigners following traditional methods can be expected to rely heavily on their own language learning experience for guidance. This fact has been noted over the years. All Japanese consciously begin the arduous task of learning how to read and write as soon as they enter school. It might seem reasonable then to introduce the writing system immediately in courses for foreigners, particularly since mastery of the native orthography requires an inordinate amount of time and effort. The difference that is overlooked is the fact that the Japanese child who is beginning school is already fluent in the spoken language. Thanks to recent research, we now know the importance of spoken language competence to reading and writing and are even more aware of the vast difference between the beginning foreigner and the Japanese child entering school.

Native Japanese are also apt to rely on their own foreign language learning experience, which in most cases was the study of English, with strong emphasis on a grammar-translation approach and considerably less concern for authentic spoken English. In fact, this approach was further impetus for emphasizing written language over spoken. This explains the limited concern for accurate pronunciation noted above and the comment of at least one trainee who was surprised and pleased to find truly authentic spoken language included in the learner-focused textbook.

However, what has been surprisingly ignored in studies of language pedagogy is the influence over classroom instruction exerted by the instructor's unconsciously acquired, behavioral culture. I call this type of classroom culture 'covert,' because with all attention focused on the learning of the target LinC; it remains undercover, totally outside of consideration and outside of consciousness. When the instructor is a native Japanese whose pedagogy follows the traditional target model, we have an interesting contrast in mindsets between the native Japanese instructor and native American learners. What can we expect? Throughout a class session, whether modeling the target language, conversing, explaining, analyzing, correcting, praising, or criticizing, an instructor is communicating with the learners and communication is culture-based.

---

① In some cases, a traditional Japanese pedagogue who otherwise uses native orthography exclusively may revert to romanization for this kind of analysis.

According to Hall (1983), communication is 10% verbal and 90% behavioral, the latter being the core culture that drives members of a society. We can certainly assume that neither instructors nor learners leave their unconsciously acquired culture at the door when they enter the classroom. Thus the instruction, delivered in accordance with a Japanese mindset, is interpreted by the American learner according to a very different set of American cultural assumptions.

Most basic to this discussion of differences between Japanese and Americans is the question of their attitudes toward language in general. For Westerners, language is clearly the most precise means of communicating available to mankind and precision in language use is a positive goal of verbal behavior. Rambling, ambiguous speech and writing are avoided by the careful American speaker / writer, who hunts for just the right word and exactly the clearest way to present an argument. But language for the Japanese is very different indeed. It is assumed that language is ambiguous; in fact vagueness and ambiguity are in no sense negative qualities and polite language is regularly more indirect. Actually, for the Japanese, perfect communication between individuals transcends language, occurring through *isin-densin*, unspoken, mutual understanding transmitted by way of the belly, the seat of the emotions for the Japanese. During a research project on Japanese attitudes toward language that I conducted with Professor Mari Noda in Tokyo, we collected reactions to recordings of Americans speaking Japanese. When the competence of one speaker received particularly high praise, the interviewee was asked if he thought this American was capable of any further improvement. He replied, "Oh, no! The next step would be *isin-densin*, and only the Japanese can communicate that way."

In his discussion of Japanese culture, Hall (1983:95) points out that "the pull of Japanese culture as a whole is to the heart and not to the mind, whereas in the West it is the opposite." Of course when the subject is mathematics or any of the physical sciences, the Japanese mind is in control and precision becomes crucial, but language for them is a different domain. The Japanese visitor who observed my dissection of an inflected form as personal violation was watching the methodology of science imposed on a non-scientific entity that was very close to his heart. I was performing linear analysis on an item that should have been viewed as a single unit. Even entire sentences should not be dissected but should be understood holistically.

We can hardly be surprised at the reactions of the trainees to a curriculum for Japanese that stressed the language as a system that could and should be subjected to rigorous analysis if it is to be understood by American students. With 'simple before complex' and 'frequently used before rarely used,' as basic principles, an order for the introduction of grammatical patterns is determined that perfectly meshes with an

American learner's mindset. This contrasts strongly with the random ordering, determined by occurrence in script-driven texts, expected by the trainees.

Imagine, too, the reaction of the trainees to the use of romanization as a teaching tool. The emotional connection the Japanese have with their writing system is indeed 'heart': their language is the orthography and the orthography is the language. Although Japanese regularly use romanization to input their language into computers, this is a purely mechanical use that transforms the material into 'real' Japanese, i.e., Japanese in its native orthography. A Japanese linguist who has long lived and taught in the United States once remarked, "I hate romanization, but I am Japanese and my students are not. For them it is useful." In the course of their program, the trainees, too, gradually began to understand its value as a learning tool for the learners, even if it remained emotionally unappealing to them.

In his division of cultures into high-context and low-context, Hall (1983) classifies Japanese as a clear example of the former and American as an example of the latter. The result is very different communication styles. The meaning of every occurrence of language depends on the context in which it occurs. Thus we say that a word means what it means in the sentence, the sentence means what it means in the discourse, and the discourse means what it means in the culture. For the high-context Japanese, the cultural context plays so important a part that much is assumed to be understood and goes unstated. For the low-context American, who prefers to have all the conditions of the discourse spelled out in detail, the Japanese seem vague and imprecise. Frequent breakdowns in communication and misunderstandings are the result.

This has widespread influence on language pedagogy. Japanese, considered to be a truly foreign language native to a truly foreign culture in American language circles, is extremely different from any Indo-European language and culture. This obviously means that low-context American learners require extensive, detailed explanations if they are to understand the intricacies of this LinC that is so foreign to them. In the explanatory material of a textbook, linguistic terms must be precisely defined and English translations and equivalents must be accurate and consistent. However, the high-context, traditional Japanese instructor is unconsciously making different assumptions. Grammatical explanations can be very brief and are best linked to English patterns, in spite of significant differences in meaning and use. Lengthy lists of vocabulary in isolation need no further explanation than English glosses to become part of a learner's target language repertoire. Familiar English grammatical terminology can be used without explanation or definition, on the mistaken assumption that everyone knows what these terms signify in Japanese on the basis of their use in English. Actually, in the America of today, many young learners have little knowledge as to what words like 'adverb;'

'subject,' and 'object' mean even in English, further adding to the confusion. Most surprising is the omission of any reference to what is probably the most distinctive feature of Japanese, namely the fact that there are no stylistically neutral utterances in the language. Also missing are discussions of hierarchy or of in-group / out-group identification, so basic to the culture and so crucial to the determination of stylistically appropriate language use.

All communication reflects an unconscious assessment of information shared by the participants, which in turn informs the speaker / writer as to what needs to be expressed and what can be assumed to be understood. Too much information is insulting but too little interferes with comprehension. In a cross-cultural setting, these assessments become significantly more difficult since so many are culture-based. In a foreign language teaching setting, a traditionally oriented target native presents analyses and explanations of the target language in a style and to a degree assumed to be appropriate. However, the base native is operating under a different cultural system, and when that target-based system is 'truly foreign,' confusion and misunderstanding may result. Consider the American learners who are introduced very early in their course to *ikimasita* simply as the equivalent of '[he] went.' Their American culture-based assumption is that this word can of course be used in speaking to anybody about anybody. The Japanese instructor knows that this is only one of many ways to say '[he] went,' all of which reflect the relationship between the discourse participants and involve hierarchical and in-group / out-group distinctions. Since it would be pedagogically unthinkable to teach all these equivalents immediately to a beginning learner, the decision is made, without any explanation, to use the alternate considered most generally appropriate for foreign adults with limited Japanese competence. This is a clear example of mis-communication. Of course the Japanese instructor has made the appropriate selection and of course beginners should not be taught the many different ways of expressing 'went' at the beginning of their course. However, a word to them about the overall system and where *ikimasita* fits in that system would prevent consternation and re-learning later, when they learn the reality and realize their frequent errors that could have been avoided.

Another area of frequent miscommunication relates to authenticity, which, for American learners, is a positive concept. They assume they should encounter the target language just as it actually occurs in a given context. They also assume that the Japanese material in any textbook written by native Japanese is authentic — that is, a sample of accurate Japanese language. However, the Japanese make different assumptions. Bearing in mind their conviction that their language is difficult for Americans to learn and their desire to be considerate to these foreigners who, after all, are making the effort to try to master it, they often alter the language in an attempt to make it easier. There are frequent examples of sequences that are indeed Japanese, but not the Japanese that would occur in the given context. In many cases the changes make the Japanese closer to English. An example is the overt expression of the subject of a sentence in contexts where it would regularly occur in English, but definitely not in Japanese. Another example is the practice of choosing lesson topics on the basis of subject matter, regardless of the structural implications. Thus, we often find introductions chosen as the most appropriate topic for a first lesson. As a result, the authors are required either to write authentic material that includes many structural patterns too difficult for Lesson 1, or to write stiff, overly simplified, unnatural Japanese. They usually choose the latter. Authenticity is also abandoned in many suggestions for supplementary practice in which students are encouraged to produce conversations or written material far beyond their capability. As the pedagogical linguist Hector Hammerly (1973) once pointed out, practice does not make perfect; it makes permanent. The more learners practice 'funny' Japanese, the longer it will persist.

Of course it may be that many features of the language are considered so unique to Japanese that, as in the case of *isin-densin*, American learners are assumed to be unable to handle them. Rather than introducing concepts that are totally foreign, it is perhaps thought to be more considerate to the learner simply to use just one style throughout an elementary course without any explanation, even in contexts where it lacks authenticity. A conviction, held by many Japanese, is that the Japanese language in *every* respect is uniquely difficult and all but impossible for American learners to truly master. This conviction accounts for the surprise expressed so often by the trainees, that the learners they were observing progressed so rapidly and actually were beginning to use complex grammatical patterns with understanding and growing assurance.

Learners learn what they are taught and as they are taught, but with an influential underpinning of their own, native LinC. Most American learners conform uncritically to the approach used by their Japanese instructors, assuming that this is *the* way this truly foreign language is learned. In general it is only those American learners with more background in language learning or linguistics who may challenge their instructors with more probing questions. However this unquestioned acceptance ends when learners transfer to another program and are exposed to a different methodology. At this point, the American learner becomes aware of the importance of pedagogy and compares the outcomes of each approach. Listening to the comments of such learners can be a learning experience for the instructors.

As the importance of acquired, behavioral culture in foreign language learning becomes increasingly evident, there is need to expand related research beyond consideration of the target LinC itself and examine the culture of the classroom. Instructors are no less representatives of their culture when they are instructing. Research into traditional Japanese-style courses and learner-focused courses that compares every phase of instruction, from curriculum design, goals, participating instructors, and classroom activities to student reactions and outcomes, would be extremely informative. In the past fifty years, we have learned a great deal about the importance of language in culture, as opposed to language alone, in Japanese language pedagogy. It is now time to begin the serious study of 'pedagogy in culture.'

References

Hall, E. T. (1983). *The dance of life: The other dimension of time*. Garden City, NY: Anchor Press/Doubleday.

Hammerly, H. (1973). The correction of pronunciation errors. *The Modern Language Journal*. Vol. 57, No. 3.

Jorden, E. H. with M. Noda (1987). *Japanese: The spoken language*, Part 1. New Haven, CN: Yale University Press.

29

An Analysis of Language Use and Topic Management in Business Decision-making Meeting*

Bertha DU-BABCOCK
City University of Hong Kong, China

Abstract: This paper builds on and contrasts with the earlier published framework of Du-Babcock (1999), by analyzing the topic management patterns and turn-taking behaviors of ten additional groups of Hong Kong bilingual Chinese in their first- and second-language decision-making meetings. While eight of the ten additional groups matched Du-Babcock's earlier findings, two groups did not follow the original findings and offered new reasons for such a result. This paper discusses why the topic management patterns and turn-taking behaviors emerged as they did across these ten groups. The paper also suggests implications for international business communication practices and future research.

It has become increasingly common in international business contexts for bilinguals at varying second-language competency levels to exchange messages and make group decisions in their first and second languages. Since these bilinguals have actual or potential prominence in international business communication situations, ascertaining (a) whether and how they communicate in their topic management strategy and turn-taking behavior,

---

* This article is partly based on a research study (Project no. 9030827) funded by the City University of Hong Kong. The generosity and kind support of the University Research Committee are gratefully acknowledged.

and (b) whether and how they make decisions in the same or different ways in their first and second languages is of significant and practical importance.

A large and rapidly growing segment of these bilinguals speak English as a second or foreign language. This is because English has emerged as the world's prominent linking language (Crystal, 1997; Kameda, 1996) — a genuinely global language (Gilsdorf, 2002, p. 366), in international business communication, and individuals from around the world are learning English in order to fulfill this linking role. Of 75 percent of English-speaking individuals who are second-language users, Chinese bilinguals (including overseas Chinese around the world) constitute the largest and the most rapidly growing segment of "the global English picture" (Crystal, 1997; Kachru, 1992). This phenomenon suggests that English-language speakers of varying competency have the potential to directly communicate with and relay messages to native- or non-native English speakers in international business contexts.

Given the uniqueness of the language environment of Hong Kong (see, for example, Du-Babcock, 1999), bilingual Chinese live in a collective culture (Hofstede, 1991) and speak Cantonese (a high-context language) in general and English (a low-context language) with native-English speakers and non-Cantonese speakers in business conversations. As Cantonese and English are spoken concurrently in the workplace, Hong Kong bilingual Chinese cannot help but monitor and unconsciously compare first- and second-language messages when they switch between these two codes. Given its prominence as an international financial center and its pattern of multiple and simultaneous language use, Hong Kong is an ideal research site for a comparison of the first- and second-language business communication practices of Chinese bilinguals.

The present study extends Du-Babcock's (1999) study and re-examines the business communication behavior of ten additional groups of Hong Kong bilingual Chinese as they interacted in first- and second-language decision-making meetings. In her study, Du-Babcock provided an in-depth analysis of a decision-making meeting by a group where she examined how the strategic topics were managed throughout the meetings. To enhance its applicability, this extension of the study reports on the analysis of ten additional groups' meetings which were previously collected. For consistency, I adopted the same method of codifying turn-taking and topic management. It is hoped that the extension of Du-Babcock's (1999) study not only provides the breadth of issues to be generalized, but also examines factors that are likely to affect those groups that are deviating from the previous findings.

Literature Review

This section builds on the literature review and discussion sections of Du-Babcock's (1999) study in which she describes how the cultural and language environment impacts on communication practices in Hong Kong and why different communication practices might be expected in other language environments where Chinese dialects are not the dominant communication medium (see Du-Babcock, 1999, p. 548). In Hong Kong, second-language communication exists side-by-side with first-language communication, and bilingual Cantonese switch between languages according to the needs of a particular communication situation. As a result, bilinguals with less than native-like second-language competency see a discrepancy in their first- and second-language communication abilities (especially the ability to accurately and confidently decode messages). Nevertheless, the uniqueness of the bilingual language environment allows individuals to verify and check the accuracy and completeness of second-language messages through follow-up and associated first-language conversations, as other Cantonese speakers are almost always present and available in dominant Cantonese-speaking communication environment.

Du-Babcock's (1999) study offered alternative theoretical explanations for the differing turn-taking behavior and topic management strategies that Cantonese bilinguals might follow in their first- and second-language decision-making meetings. The study concluded that the language and cultural context affects not only communication behavior of Hong Kong bilinguals in their inter-connected first-and second-language meetings, but also their topic management strategies. The language proficiency-based explanation argued that it was first- and second-language proficiency differentials that triggered the various communication behaviors of these Cantonese bilinguals. Prior research (see, for example, Bilbow, 1996; Du-Babcock, 1999; Du-Babcock, Babcock, Ng, & Lai, 1995) has established that language proficiency is positively related to communication effectiveness and participation rates in second-language communication environment. The results of Du-Babcock's (1999) study concurred that individuals with higher second-language proficiency participated at a higher rate in second-language meetings than did individuals with a lower second-language proficiency ($r = .37$, $p < .05$). Du-Babcock's (1999) results also showed that although low-second language proficient individuals might have contributed fewer ideas, they were still able to participate and contribute ideas to their designated functional areas at meetings. That is, the constraint of second-language proficiency might have prohibited groups from discussing the issues interactively, yet the "narrow band" approach allowed the group members to supply specialized information related to their functional areas (e.g., financial, production, and marketing) without hindrance from any deficiency in second-language proficiency.

Based on the literature reviewed, two sets of research questions are now put forward. The first set of research question focuses on whether bilingual individuals exhibit similar turn-taking behavior in that they not only exhibit different communication behavior, but also perceive first-and second-language meetings differently. The second set of research question investigates whether and how second-language proficiency affects the communication behavior of Hong Kong bilinguals in four identified variables.

Research Question 1: Do Hong Kong bilingual Chinese exhibit different communication behavior in interconnected first-language and second-language decision-making meetings?

Research Question 2A: Does second-language proficiency correlate with the communication behavior of Chinese bilinguals in four identified variables?

Research Question 2B: Do individuals with higher second-language proficiency exhibit different communication behavior than individuals with lower second-language proficiency?

The second explanation of Du-Babcock's (1999) study for differing topic management strategies draws on the notion that language communicators choose can influence and change message content. The linguistic relativity principle (sometimes also referred to as the Sapir-Whorf Hypothesis) addresses this issue by theorizing about the relationship between the language people speak and its thought pattern (see also Hunt & Agnolix, 1991). According to this principle, speakers of different languages necessarily construe the world differently and are locked into the world view given to them by the languages they use. As a result, the languages that speakers know and use will structure their understanding of the world, and in many ways the language people speak is a guide to the language in which they think (Hunt & Agnolix, 1991, p. 377). The linguistic relativity principle applies especially to bilinguals, as they switch between languages and so adjust their perceptual and thinking processes to fit the language they are using and introduce different content into their first- and second-language messages (see also Kay & Kempton, 1984; Matsumoto, 1994; Wierzbicka, 1985).

The linguistic relativity principle continues to generate as much controversy as it did when first formulated over a half a century ago. Current studies offer at least partial support of its validity despite its having been dismissed by experts from various disciplines (Davies, Sowden,

Jerrett, Jerrette, & Corbett, 1998; Lee, 1996, 1997). I would argue that the linguistic relativity principle offers a plausible, but not proven, theoretical basis for inferring that the language communicators choose to use does affect the message content in international business communication. Research studies on international business communication that could either prove or disprove this controversial principle are lacking.

Kaplan's (1966, 1987) spiral-linear thinking patterns and Ma's (1993) Taoist thinking pattern model relate the language causation notion to Asian and Western cultures. This line of research suggests that Asians (e.g., Chinese, Japanese, Koreans) think and make decisions in circular or spiral patterns, while Westerners (Americans and Europeans) think and make decisions in sequential or linear patterns. Du-Babcock (1999) suggests that Chinese (and other Asians) may adapt to Western thought and decision patterns when interacting in a Western language (e.g., English), but retain Chinese thought patterns when communicating in their native language (e.g., Cantonese).

While Whorf's (1956) linguistic relativity claims the idea that culture, through language, affects the way people think, Kaplan's (1966, 1987) spiral-linear thinking pattern and Ma's (1993) Taoist thinking model can be said to supplement the Whorf hypothesis. Consistent with Kaplan's model that individuals from Asian or high-context cultural societies are inclined to reveal a spiral or circular thought pattern, whereas individuals of Western cultural societies tend to follow linear thinking pattern, Du-Babcock's (1999) empirical-based study concluded that Chinese bilinguals may consistently adapt to Western style of thinking patterns when using low-context language, yet retain Eastern spiral or circular thinking patterns when using high-context language. Based on the relevant literature review, Research Question 3 focuses on whether bilingual communicators adopt similar topic management strategies, as reported by Du-Babcock (1999).

Research Question 3A: Do all Chinese bilinguals adopt culture-specific topic management strategies and, in the process, use different topic management strategies in their interconnected first- and second-language meetings?

Research Question 3B: Can topic management patterns identified by Du-Babcock (1999) be applied to all Chinese small-group decision-making groups? That is, do all groups follow spiral or circular thinking patterns in their first language (Cantonese) meetings and linear or sequential patterns in their second-language (English) meetings?

Method

Research Participants

Sixty-one (N = 61) individuals enrolled in two sessions of a strategic management course at a Hong Kong tertiary institution were chosen to participate in the study. A total of ten Hong Kong bilingual Chinese groups (consisting of 5 to 7 persons per group) were then formed and competed in a computerized business strategy simulation. Although random assignment was not possible, the participants were comparable in the subject matter covered during the simulations.

Although levels of second-language proficiency varied among group members (ranging between 3 and 6 on a 7-point Likert scale), all group members possessed adequate vocabulary and interactive listening skills for business-related communication in English. The work experience of these simulation participants also varied from part-time summer employment to full-time low-level managerial positions as well as mid-level regional managers in both government and private firms. Sixty percent (60%) of participants had five to 15 years of work experience. Typical employers included the Hong Kong Housing Authority, American Standard, Hong Kong Bank, and various small-to medium-size Chinese firms. There were 41 male and 20 female participants.

Procedures

The simulation used in the study is a computer-based replication of a manufacturing industry that produces and sells consumer durable goods (Cotter & Fritzsche, 1991). The simulation participants assumed the role of the top management of individual companies in an industry. Although not formally required by the simulation exercise, the groups designated functional roles for individual members, such as president, finance, marketing, human resources, and sales managers.

The simulation provided the setting for the development of realistic business dialogs and required the competing teams to hold a series of meetings to develop and execute corporate strategies in the following eight areas: price and advertising; salespeople; finance; product models; research and development; production scheduling; plant construction and expansion; and sales (Cotter & Fritzsche, 1991, pp. 11-26). Because of the interactive nature of the computer model underlying the simulation, a decision made by one firm influenced not only the financial and competitive position of that company but also that of its competitors.

All the group decision-making meetings were held and videotaped in videotaping studios equipped with professional facilities. To enable comparison of first- and second-language communication, the groups made decisions using English (designated as a second language) and Cantonese (first language). The meetings held in English were transcribed verbatim in English, and the meetings in Cantonese were transcribed in colloquial Cantonese.

To ensure consistency for comparison, the English and Cantonese transcripts of the current data set were coded and classified in the same way as Du-Babcock's (1999) study in terms of turn-taking behavior and topic management. To conduct comparative analysis between these ten additional groups, similarities and differences in the use of Cantonese and English were defined by (a) the length of speaking time by individual group members and (b) the number of turns taken by individuals. Speaking time was calculated by using a stopwatch to measure the exact length of each conversational turn. All of a speaker's times for these turns were then added together to obtain the total individual speaking time for a meeting.

The topic analyses of the ten additional groups focused on the turn-taking behavior and topic management in both their first-language and second-language meetings. The analyses of turn-taking behavior and topic management followed the specific technique developed by Du-Babcock (1999) whereby the meeting dialogs were initially arranged by turns for both first- and second-language meetings. The utterances of each turn were then related to one of the eight possible decision topic areas prescribed in the strategic management discussions, or a ninth category for background or non-related conversation. Once the dialogs were categorized by decision area, the turns were assigned numerical numbers starting at Turn 1 and continuing through to the end of the dialog. Then, each decision area was plotted to show its frequency in the dialogs in both the first- and second-language meetings.

Results and Interpretations

In this section, I describe findings for the three research questions that focus on whether the current study exhibited similar or different turn-taking behavior and topic management strategies as reported in Du-Babcock's (1999) study.

Research Question 1 asked whether Hong Kong bilingual Chinese exhibited different communication behaviors in interconnected first-and second-language decision-making meetings. To answer Research Question 1, paired sample t-test was performed and the results (see Table 1) show that the mean score of the speaking time in English meetings was slightly shorter than that of Cantonese meetings (402.71 seconds and 433.22

seconds, respectively), and that the average number of turn-takings in the Cantonese meetings was more than that in English meetings (32.93 turns and 23.69 turns, respectively). In addition, the length of speaking time per turn was one-quarter shorter in Cantonese, as compared to English (17 seconds and 13 seconds per turn, respectively). The results also showed that individuals felt they were more influential ($t = 2.36$, $p<.05$) and more information was exchanged ($t = 5.45$; $p<.001$) in Cantonese meetings than in English meetings.

Table 1 Mean Scores of the Four Identified Variables in English and Cantonese Meetings

Variables	English	Cantonese	Mean Difference
Amount of speaking time (second)	402.71	433.22	30.51
Turn-taking (number)	23.69	32.93	9.24
Felt degree of influence	4.31	4.75	-.44[b]
Felt degree of information change	4.13	5.06	-.93[a]

Keys:
[a] The mean difference between the two meetings is significant at $<.001$
[b] The mean difference between the two meetings is significant at $<.05$

Research Question 2 examines the effect of second-language proficiency on a bilingual's communication behavior. Research Question 2A asked whether communication behavior of Hong Kong bilinguals correlates with their second-language proficiency. Research Question 2B asked whether bilinguals with higher second-language proficiency participated at higher rates, with corresponding higher perceptions of influence and information exchange.

To answer Research Question 2A, Pearson Correlation Coefficients were performed. Results showed that there was a significant relationship between second-language proficiency and the amount of English used during the meetings ($r = .315$, $p<.05$) and the perceptions regarding the amount of information exchanged in the second-language meetings ($r = .298$, $p<.05$). Weak correlations were found between second-language proficiency and the number of turns taken, and felt degree of influence (see Table 2). Although second-language proficiency did not strongly affect the way individuals perceived their felt degree of influence, individuals who perceived that more information was exchanged in the second-language meetings also felt they were more influential in the outcome of the meetings ($r = .295$, $p<.05$). The results also showed that individuals who participated at higher rates took more turns ($r = .696$, $p<.01$) in the second-language meetings.

Table 2 A Comparison of Pearson Correlation Coefficient among the Four Identified Variables

Variables	L2P	TIME	TURNTK	INF	EXC
Second-Language Proficiency (L2P)	1	.315*	.125	.161	.298*
Amount of speaking time (TIME)	.315*	1	.696**	.005	.146
Turn taking (TURNTK)	.125	.696**	1	.086	-.106
Influence (INF)	.161	.005	.086	1	.295*
Information exchange (EXC)	.298*	.146	-.106	.295*	1

Keys: L2P = Second-language Proficiency; TURNTK = Turn-taking; INF = Degree of Influence; EXC = Information Exchange
* significant at $p<.05$; ** significant at $p<.01$.

In sum, the findings show that (a) individuals who self-reported higher second-language proficiency perceived that more information was exchanged, (b) individuals who perceived themselves influential also felt more information was exchanged, and (c) individuals who participated at a higher rate in speaking time also took more turns in the English meetings.

To cross check the effect of the second-language proficiency on the four identified variables, analysis of variance (ANOVA) was also performed to examine whether there were differences among individuals with low, intermediate, and high second-language proficiency. Based on a 7-point Likert scale, individuals who self-reported their second-language proficiency at 3 were classified as low, and those who self-reported at 4 were considered intermediate. Individuals who scored 5 and above were classified as high second-language proficiency speakers. The self-reported second-language proficiency levels were also cross-checked with the overall impression from the videotapes. Table 3 compares mean scores and mean differences of the four identified variables among three groups. The results show that mean scores of individuals who possessed intermediate level of second-language proficiency are generally higher than those who possessed low second-language proficiency; similar results were recorded for the mean score differences between individuals with high and intermediate levels of second-language proficiencies. These results show that individuals with high second-language proficiency participated at a higher rate than individuals with low second-language proficiencies at a .05 significant level with regard to the amount of speaking time. No significant difference was found between intermediate and low second-language proficiency individuals, nor between intermediate and high second-language proficiency individuals.

Table 3: A Comparison of Mean Scores of the Four Identified Variables among Three Groups

Variables	Mean Scores			Mean Differences			
	L	M	H	M-L	H-L	H-M	L
Amount of speaking time (seconds)	204.44	365.74	497.55	161.29	293.10*	131.81	204.44
Turn taking (number)	17.11	23.79	25.23	6.68	8.12	1.44	17.11
Felt degree of influence	4.25	4.26	4.53	.01	.28	.27	4.25
Felt degree of information exchange	3.50	3.95	4.50	.45	1.00	.55	3.50

Keys: L = Low second-language proficiency;
M = Intermediate second-language proficiency;
H = High second-language proficiency.
* significant at p<.05

These findings also reveal that individuals who possessed higher second-language proficiency and participated at higher rate, may not necessarily take more turns in the English meetings. Results of such a conflicting finding may be due to the method used in measuring turn-takings, since the number of turns taken was based on the turns taken by each individual irrespective of the length of time spent on each turn. Also, as noted by Du-Babcock (1999), it is likely that individuals who had lower second-language proficiency were "followers" and tended to devote their turns to confirming and following the lead of the higher second-language proficiency participants.

To further examine whether individuals with low second-language proficiency were inclined to devote their turns to confirming or showing involvement and agreement in their second-language decision-making meetings, the frequency of back channels was counted. Back channel is behavior where a participant responds or reacts to a previous statement made by the speaker at that time (see, for example, Goodwin & Goodwin, 1992; Kendon, 1990). As back channels are usually short, some researchers do not consider them to be complete utterances. Studies by Goodwin and Goodwin (1992), and by Kendon (1990) suggest that non-verbal back channels (e.g., eye gaze, head nodding, facial movement) are essential in social interaction; however, in this study, only verbal back channels were measured. Prototypical back channels commonly used in this study included such utterances as "yes", "OK", "U-hmm", "2.35 per unit, right?"

To quantify the verbal back channel behavior, the frequency of back channels was computed against the total number of turns taken by each individual, to obtain a percentage. The mean scores of the verbal back channels among three groups were then compared. The results showed that the mean scores of back channels used by low second-language proficiency groups (16.4%) were more than those of intermediate groups (11.5%) or high (10.9%) second-language proficiency groups. This result may explain why lower second-language proficiency individuals can still maintain an almost equivalent number of turn-takings, irrespective of any possible second-language deficiency constraints.

In sum, the results of the current study are consistent with Du-Babcock's study (1999) in that (a) Hong Kong bilinguals exhibited different communication behaviors in their interconnected first-and second-language proficiency with regard to the four identified variables, and that (b) bilinguals with higher second-language proficiency who participated at a higher rate in the English decision-making meetings perceived that more information was exchanged than individuals with lower second-language proficiency. In addition, the study also confirms Du-Babcock's speculation that lower second-language proficiency individuals are more likely than those with intermediate or high second-language proficiency to use verbal back channels to show their involvement and to cross-check or re-confirm the issues discussed.

Research Question 3 asked whether bilinguals would adopt culture-specific topic management strategies between high-context Cantonese and low-context English language meetings. For consistency, this extended study adopted the same method of topic analysis categorization that focused on turn-taking behavior and patterns of communication interaction during first-language and second-language meetings.

The results show that eight of the ten groups followed the same patterns of topic management as reported in Du-Babcock's (1999) study. These eight groups consistently displayed different topic management practices, in which a circular or spiral pattern occurred in Cantonese meetings and a linear or sequential pattern occurred in English meetings. In the Cantonese meetings, circular or spiral topic management discussions were organized around major topics, with Finance, Expansion, and Salespeople being the most representative. In the English meetings, topics were sequentially discussed. Figure 1 presents the contrasting patterns of topic management in Cantonese and English meetings for a typical replicating group.

To illustrate these contrasting patterns, the analysis looked at the overriding difference and the dimensions that define this difference. In the Cantonese meeting, finance was discussed four times (in Turns 69–90, 107–112, 149–152, 160–174). The topic first arose in Turn 69 and ended in Turn 174 (see Figure 1). A group decision was made on the fourth occasion (Turn 174). In contrast, finance was discussed only twice (in Turns 59–68, 98–99) during the English meetings, with the initial interaction occurring in Turns 59 to 68 and a group decision being announced in Turns 98 and 99.

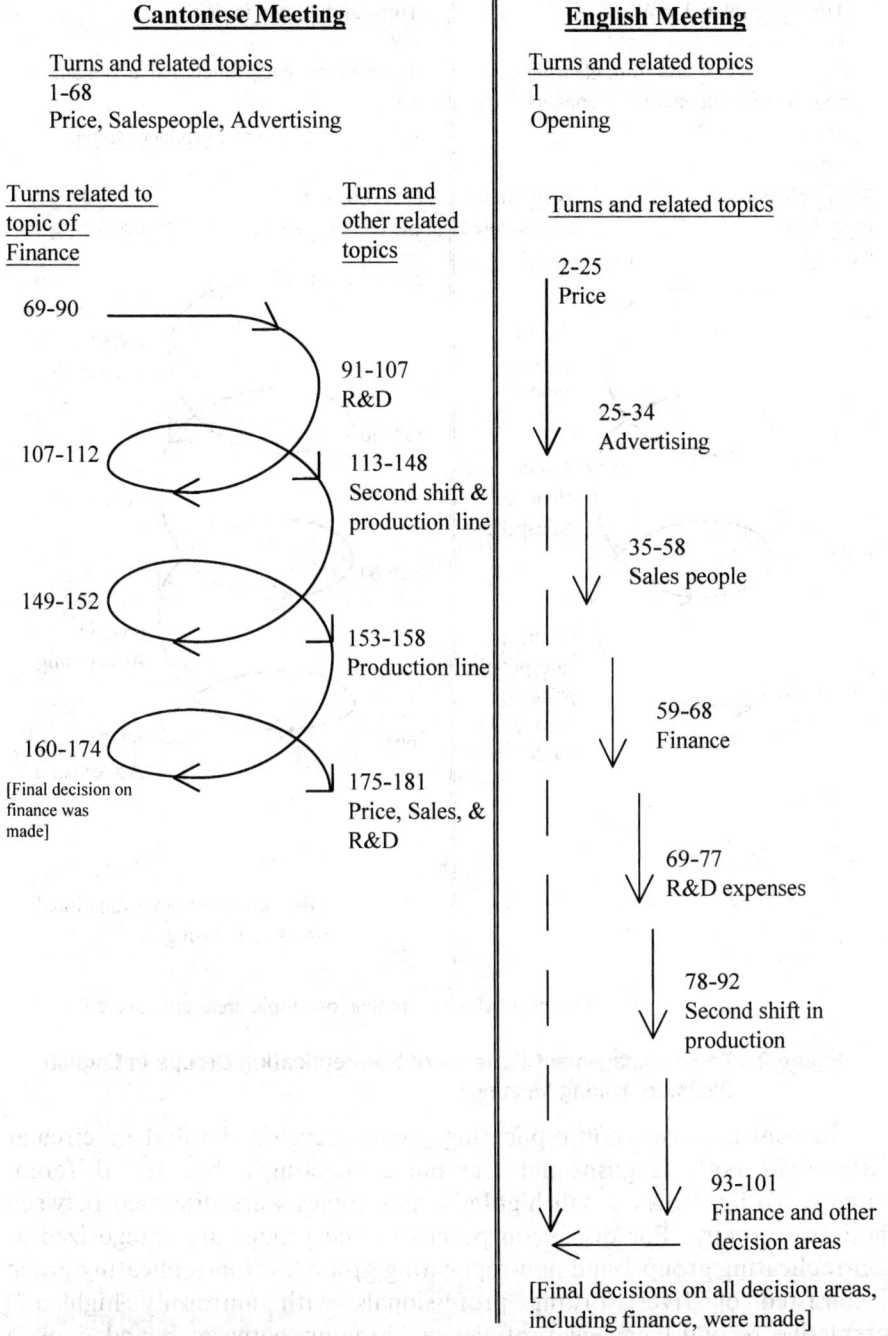

Figure 1 A Comparison of Topic Management Patterns among Replicating Groups

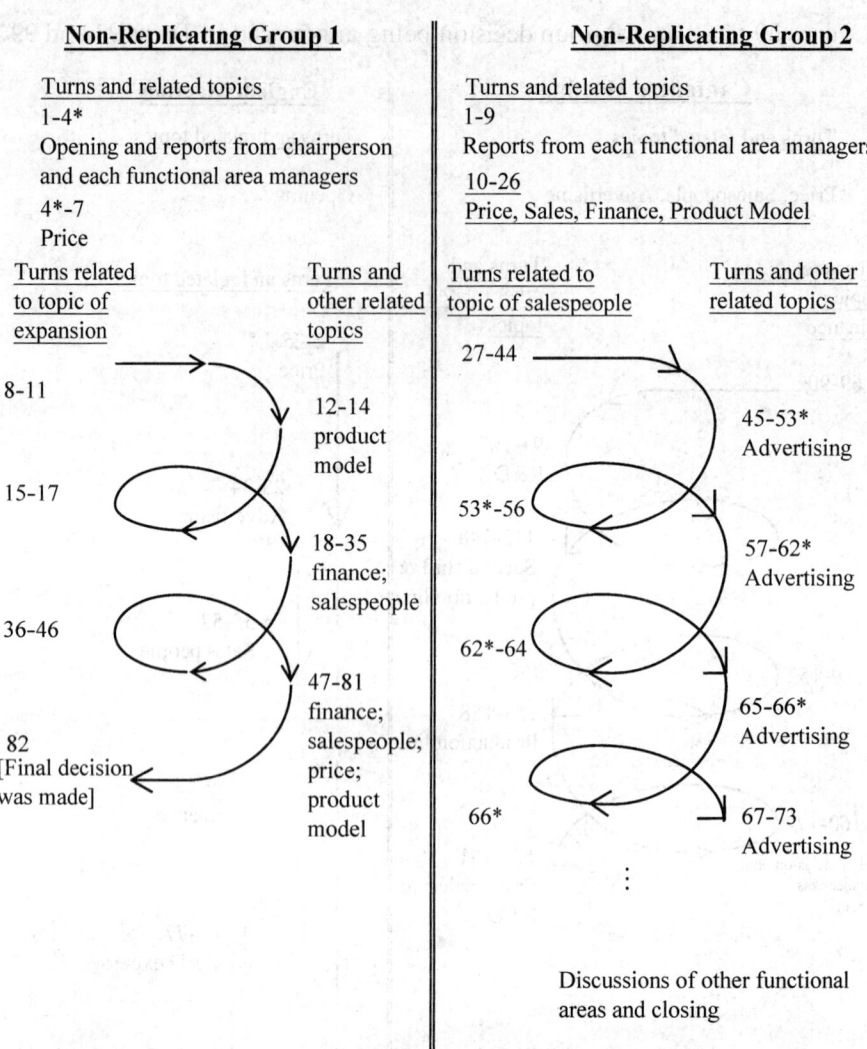

Figure 2 Topic Management Patterns of Non-replicating Groups in English Decision-making Meetings

In contrast, two non-replicating groups developed spiral or circular patterns in both English and Cantonese meetings, but for different reasons. To illustrate, I will highlight how topics were discussed between these two groups. For discussion purposes, the groups are categorized as non-replicating group 1 and non-replicating group 2. Non-replicating group 1 consisted of five working professionals with uniformly high and interactive second-language proficiency, ranging between 5 and 6 on a 7-point Likert scale. From examination of the meeting transcripts, the topic analysis of this group shows that the spiral topic management pattern reflected an interactive analysis of how the eight decision areas mutually influenced one another in terms of achieving optimal performance. It is believed that the structured and simulated computerized decision-makings created a framework for these work professionals to make decisions. Taken together, their work experience and adequate second-language of proficiency facilitated their discussions, as they had adequate vocabulary to communicate interactively in well-defined topic areas of communication in second-language meetings.

The meetings in English best illustrate how the non-replicating group 1 members adopted and displayed a spiral or circular pattern. In the meeting, the chairperson focused the first seven turns (7 out of 85 of the total turns) on soliciting contributions from all the functional managers, to report on the results of the company competitiveness in the industry from previous quarter's printouts, and to suggest a reaction to the market in the current quarter. After the group members had grasped the overall market situation, discussions were centered around three major areas: pricing, expansion, and salespeople. The remaining five topic areas were discussed only when they were related to these three major areas. For example, the topic area of "product expansion" was discussed three times (turns 8–11; 15–17; 36–46) and reconfirmed in Turn 82. Figure 2 shows how the topic area of "product expansion" was discussed and dealt with in the meeting. The topic was first discussed briefly from turns 8 to 11 and from 15 to 17, elaborated on in detail from turns 36 to 46, and the decision finalized or reconfirmed in turn 82. During the discussion, other related topics such as product model (turns 12 to 14), finance (turns 18 to 22), and salespeople (turns 25 to 35), were also introduced.

The video and transcript showed that the group members actively participated not only in their own responsible functional area but also in other functional areas where they thought the topic areas discussed were relevant to their own. As a result of the highly interactive and balanced second-language proficiency of the group members, the pattern of topic management was spiral or circular.

In contrast, the non-replicating group 2 consisted of seven members with wide and varying second-language proficiency (ranging between 4 and 6). Due to its large size, the group lacked cohesiveness and developed "free riders" who either missed meetings or came to the meetings unprepared. For example, one group member missed three, and another two members missed two out of the four taped meetings and consequently were not familiar with the previous discussions and decisions. To place themselves in context, these three individuals sought relevant information from other group members, resulting in their presence being disruptive and their uneven presence limiting the development of an effective communication environment. In one incident, two members, who had missed prior informal meetings, asked other group members to bring them up-to-date (summarizing prior discussions) so they could participate in the present meeting. It was likely that this irregular attendance of group members and uneven preparation created the conditions for such a random and chaotic spiral topic management practice in the second-language meetings. The video and English meeting transcript show that the spiral or circular topic management pattern exhibited by the group represented a repeat or rehash of previous meeting discussions, and a random, potentially chaotic discussion process.

To illustrate this group's interactions, I will use two topic areas, salespeople and advertising, as examples. From turns 27 to 44, the discussion was centered on salespeople issues and the decision was semi-made at turn 44 (see Figure 2); while advertising was discussed three times in turns 44 to 53; turns 57 to 62; and turns 65 to 73. In looking at the discussion of the advertising issue, the two unprepared group members interrupted the group discussion twice (turns 53 to 56 and 62 to 64) to seek information and confirm the discussion of salespeople on issues for which a decision was already semi-made in turn 44. If the interrupted turns (53 to 56; 62 to 64) made by the two unproductive members are ignored, the interaction pattern becomes linear, with the topic of salespeople discussed between turns 24 and 44, and advertising between turns 45 and 73. Thus, the spiral or circular interaction pattern of the English meeting was only introduced by unprepared group members who needed to check and confirm previously discussed issues.

Discussion

In this section, I discuss the research findings, limitations, and implications of the study. I use the current findings as a foundation and build on them to compare and contrast the generalizability of Du-Babcock's framework (1999) on turn-taking behaviors and topic management strategies. I then propose recommendations for facilitating international business communication research and practice on communication encounters, where Asian bilinguals or high-context communicators participate in an intercultural decision-making meeting.

Findings

Generally speaking, the findings of the current study are consistent with those reported in Du-Babcock's (1999) study. The findings show that the length of speaking time among individuals in Cantonese meetings was slightly longer than in the English meetings, and there were more turn-takings in the Cantonese meetings than in the English meetings. The findings also indicate that the Cantonese discussions were more interactive and the speaking time per turn was about one-quarter shorter than in the English meetings. As for the felt degree of influence and information exchange, the results showed that bilinguals felt that they were slightly more influential and that more information was exchanged when making decisions in their first language (Cantonese) as compared to their second language (English).

In terms of the second-language proficiency, the findings showed that the second-language proficiency positively correlates with the amount of speaking time and the felt degree of information exchange, and tangibly correlates with turn-taking and felt degree of influence. Although the differences of the amount of speaking time and turn taking behavior were not significant between individuals with low and intermediate levels, and between intermediate and high second-language proficiency, individuals with high second-language proficiencies outperformed the low and intermediate second-language proficiency individuals in all four identified variables.

The new data provided in this extension of study requires a partial reinterpretation of Du-Babcock's (1999) explanation of the factors and conditions that stimulate sequential or linear topic management patterns in second-language meetings. In her analysis, Du-Babcock implicitly assumed that she had identified a universal pattern that would apply to all bilinguals in the Hong Kong language and cultural environment. Her conclusions do hold for a sizeable majority of the bilingual groups (8 of 10 groups) but also adds some clarifying detail. In particular, while reinforcing Du-Babcock's proposed framework, the extension of study further identifies reasons why two non-replicating groups unexpectedly carried out circular or spiral topic management patterns in both English and Cantonese meetings. In the following, I will provide plausible explanations for these overall results.

The communication behavior of the bilinguals can only be understood in the light of how group communication fits into the Hong Kong language and cultural environment. In the Hong Kong multiple-language environment, bilinguals have immediate or quick access (in most instances) to first-language messages and information. The bilinguals in the study perceived that first-language communication carried more, if not equivalent, information and influence, so they naturally preferred to communicate as much as possible in their first language, Cantonese. Thus, in a multiple language environment such as Hong Kong when one language (Cantonese in this case) is dominant, messages in the dominant language carry more weight or value than equivalent second-language communication.

The bilinguals in eight groups developed a differentiating approach to managing first- and second-language meetings. In their scheduled second-language meetings, group members sequentially exchanged information but did not make decisions, as these decisions were made mostly in their out-of-meeting first-language discussions. The English meeting was conducted in such a way that the members reported their respective functional areas one after the other, without integration of in-depth analysis among all the related areas; as a result, a linear and sequential topic management pattern was derived.

When required to communicate in English in scheduled second-language meetings, the group members adopted a linear or sequential pattern of information exchange. This linear or sequential pattern of topic management, however, did not meet the information processing requirements of the integrated decision-making task. This was because, being less confident in communicating in their second language and seeking to balance their communication behavior, the Hong Kong bilingual Chinese were motivated to supplement their second-language communication with additional informal out-of-meeting first-language communication. Adding the out-of-meeting first-language communication to the scheduled in-meeting second-language discussions allowed lower proficiency members to compensate for their second-language deficiencies. Consequently, these meeting attendees would explore the difficult issues in their first-language meetings, and so avoid the relative discomfort of interactive second-language exchange. As such, the bilinguals exchanged information in an orderly and organized way during the scheduled second-language meetings, and better prepared themselves to interactively analyze and make complex decisions in the out-of-meeting first-language discussions. Due to the time lapse between videotaped meetings and input of their decisions on the computer, these bilinguals knew that they were not compelled to make decisions in their second-language meetings, so they understandably chose to analyze and make decisions in their first language where they had higher language proficiency.

The second factor that possibly contributes to spiral-linear topic management patterns in the English meetings is the composition of second-language proficiency of the group members. In the non-replicating group 1, the group possessed one characteristic that differentiated it from the other groups in that all of the members had high and balanced second-language proficiencies. This meant that the members engaged in interactive analysis and decision making, and did not have to conduct supplemental informal out-of-meeting first-language discussions. Both the Cantonese and English meetings therefore represented completed communication tasks.

In comparison, although the non-replicating group 2 also developed circular or spiral topic management patterns, these patterns represented a disorganized and inefficient information exchange rather than an integrated analysis of interconnected variables. The topic management pattern could have been linear or sequential, but became spiral because the discussions were interrupted a few times by members who were previously absent requesting to be filled in on earlier decisions. Thus, if their disruptive turns are removed, the sequence of topic management becomes linear.

In sum, two of the ten groups in this extended study continued the spiral or circular patterns when interacting in a Western language (English) and did not develop linear or sequential topic management patterns in their second-language meetings. This result suggests that speaking in English did not by itself, or independently, introduce a "so-called" Western linear pattern into their second-language meetings. Consequently, the results of the present study support the language proficiency argument and cast doubt on language use theory in that the bilinguals in both the non-replicating groups 1 and 2, who had interactive proficiency and related confidence in second-language communication or who had to participate in disorganized conversations, used circular or spiral topic management practices regardless of the language used.

Limitations

As an extension study, I attempted to follow the same research design as in Du-Babcock's (1999) study, and use the same coding system to codify topic management patterns. The out-of-meeting first-language could not be controlled due to the time lapse between videotaped meeting discussion and data input for market competition. This could be the drawback of the research design. However, it reflects a common phenomenon in Hong Kong's second-language communication environment; that is, whenever time or condition allows, Hong Kong bilingual Chinese hold out-of-meeting first-language meeting or prepare scripts and act them out during required second-language meetings.

The communication task represented in the current study necessitated the use of an all-channel, interactive communication pattern for effective decision making. Engaging in strategic management discussions, the interlocutors in all ten groups were required to share information from their respective functional areas in order to reach optimal decisions and to meet the information-processing requirements of the complex task. To avoid sub-optimization, or the acceptance of lower-than-optimal performance in an organizational unit (see Simon, 1976), the group members had to interactively integrate functional inputs and make decisions that contributed to the profitability of the entire firm, not just adopt decisions that would improve results in their respective areas of interest. Circular or spiral topic management patterns were displayed in the English meetings for only two groups; consequently, with a sample size of two, the analysis of why the respective topic management patterns arose in these groups can only be suggestive.

Lastly, the composition of the groups does not permit the

measurement of intercultural communication that would have accrued if non-Cantonese individuals had been included in the groups. Whether and how Cantonese speakers would have interacted similarly or differently with individuals from other cultural backgrounds remains speculative and an issue for future research.

Implications

Against the background of the findings and limitations of the current data, I recommend that future research investigate and more precisely define how Chinese (as well as individuals from other high-context cultural societies) of varying second-language competencies communicate in a language environment where English or another low-context language is a dominant language. These studies could better define how to structure a communication environment to solicit the involvement of second-language speakers with intermediate second-language proficiency in intercultural group meetings. As such, these studies could be structured to investigate how bilinguals from high-context cultural societies (e.g., Japan, China's Taiwan and Hong Kong) communicate in a language environment where English (or another international business language) is the dominant mode of communication (see Babcock & Du-Babcock, 2001) and where they do not have ready access to other native speakers.

The current study provides possible markers for improving both the quantity and quality of intercultural communication in which bilinguals with varying second-language proficiency participate in international business communication. When bilinguals with intermediate second-language proficiency participate in an intercultural group meeting requiring interactive decision making, the challenge is to create a communication structure where their communication potential can be more fully utilized.

This study clarifies when and why bilinguals (in this Hong Kong bilingual Chinese case) communicate differently in their first- and second-language meetings in a language environment where they have ready and easy access to other Cantonese first-language speakers. All ten additional groups in the current study were composed of members who had sufficient second-language competency to present topics prepared in advance in their second language, but only one group had members whose language proficiency and confidence allowed them to interactively discuss and make decisions entirely in their second-language. It is hoped that the analysis and guidelines proposed in this article can guide international business communication practice and future research.

References

Babcock, R., & B. Du-Babcock. (2001). Language-based communication zones in international business communication. *The Journal of Business Communication, 38*, 372–412.

Bilbow, G. (1996). Managing *impressions in the multicultural workplace*. Unpublished doctoral dissertation, City University of Hong Kong, Hong Kong.

Cotter, R., & D. Fritzsche. (1991). *The Business Policy Game: Player's Manual* (3rd ed.). Englewood Cliffs, NJ: Prentice Hall.

Crystal, D. (1997). *English as a Global Language*. Cambridge: University Press.

Davies, R. L., P. T, Sowden, D. T. Jerrett, T. Jerret, & G. C. Corbett. (1998). A cross-cultural study of English and Setswana speakers on a colour triads task: A test of the Sapir-Whorf hypothesis. *British Journal of Psychology, 89*, 1–15.

Du-Babcock, B. (1999). Topic management and turn taking in professional communication: First- versus second-language strategies. *Management Communication Quarterly, 12*, 544–574.

Du-Babcock, B., R. Babcock, P. Ng, & R. Lai. (1995). A comparison of the use of L1 and L2 in small-group business decision-making meetings. *Research Monograph No. 6*. Hong Kong: City University of Hong Kong, Department of English.

Gilsdorf, J. (2002). Standard Englishes and world Englishes: Living with a polymorph business language. *The Journal of Business Communication, 39*, 364–378.

Goodwin, C., & M. Goodwin. (1992). Assessment and the construction of context. In A. Duranti & C. Goodwin (Eds.), *Rethinking context: Language as an Interactive Phenomenon* (pp. 151–189). Cambridge: Cambridge University Press.

Hofstede, G. (1991). *Cultures and Organization: Software of the Mind-Intercultural Cooperation and its Importance for Survival*. Maidenhead, Berkshire: McGraw-Hill (UK).

Hunt, E., & F. Agnoli. (1991). The Whorfian hypothesis: A cognitive psychology perspective. *Psychological Review, 98*, 377–389.

Kachru, B. (1992). Teaching world Englishes. In B. Kachru (Ed.), *The OtherTongue* (2nd ed.), pp. 355–365. Urbana & Chicago, IL: University of Illinois Press.

Kameda, N. (1996). *Business Communication toward Transnationalism: The Significance of Cross-Cultural Business English and its Role*. Tokyo: Kindaibungeishai.

Kaplan, R. (1966). Cultural thought patterns in inter-cultural education. *Language Learning, 16*(1/2), 1–20.

Kaplan, P. (1987). Cultural thought pattern revisited. In U. Connor, & R. Kaplan (Eds.). *Writing Across Languages : Analysis of L2 text (9–21)*. Reading, MA: Addison-Wesley.

Kay, P., & W. Kempton. (1984). What is the Sapir-Whorf hypothesis? *American Anthropologist, 86*, 65–89.

Kendon, A. (1990). *Conducting Interaction: Patterns of Behavior in Focused Encounters*. Cambridge: Cambridge University Press.

Lee, P. (1996). *The Whorf Theory Complex: A Critical Reconstruction*. Amsterdam: John Benjamins.

Lee, P. (1997). Language in thinking and learning: Pedagogy and the new Whorfian framework. *Harvard Educational Review, 67*, 430–471.

Ma, R. (1993, February). Taoist thinking pattern as reflected in communication. Paper presented at the Annual Meeting of the Western States Communication Association, Albuquerque, New Mexico.

Matsumoto, D. (1994). *People: Psychology from a Cultural Perspective*. Pacific Grove, CA: Brooks/Cole Publication.

Simon, H. (1976). *Administrative Behavior: A Study of Decision-Making Processes*

in Administrative Organization. (3rd ed.). New York: Free Press.
Whorf, B. (1956). *Language, Thought, and Reality*. Cambridge, MA: MIT.
Wierzbicka, A. (1985). A semantic metalanguage for a cross-cultural comparison of speech acts and speech genres. *Language in Society, 14*, 491–514.

Appendix

Exhibit 1: Cross-Cultural Business Communication Module Design

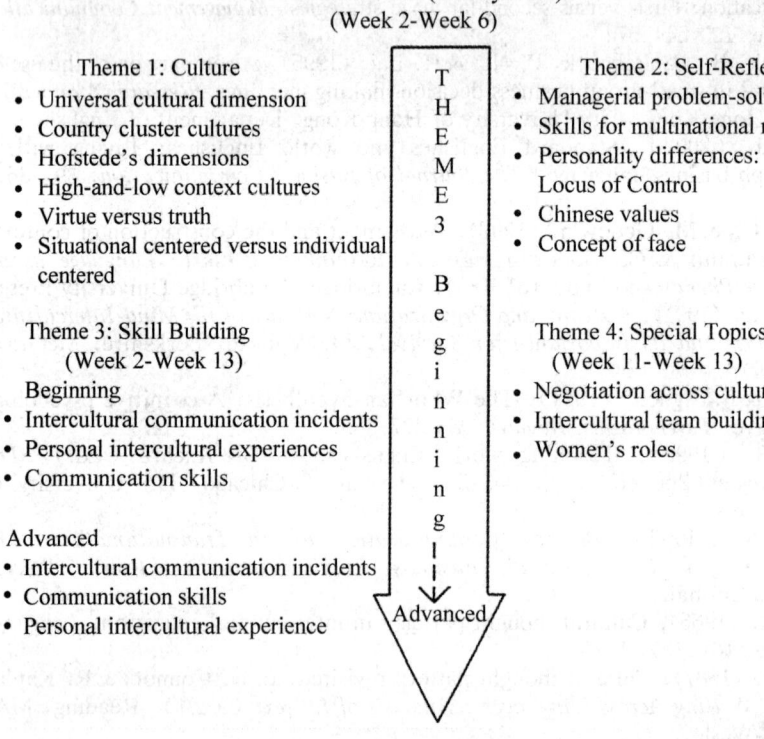

Themes 1 & 2 (Theory Base)
(Week 2-Week 6)

Theme 1: Culture
- Universal cultural dimension
- Country cluster cultures
- Hofstede's dimensions
- High-and-low context cultures
- Virtue versus truth
- Situational centered versus individual centered

Theme 2: Self-Reflection
- Managerial problem-solving styles
- Skills for multinational managers
- Personality differences: Locus of Control
- Chinese values
- Concept of face

Theme 3: Skill Building
 (Week 2-Week 13)
Beginning
- Intercultural communication incidents
- Personal intercultural experiences
- Communication skills

Advanced
- Intercultural communication incidents
- Communication skills
- Personal intercultural experience

Theme 4: Special Topics
 (Week 11-Week 13)
- Negotiation across cultures
- Intercultural team building
- Women's roles

30

Do They Tell Stories Differently? Discourse Marker Use by Chinese Native Speakers and Nonnative Speakers

LI Xiaoshi
Michigan State University, USA

JIA Xuerui
Harbin Institute of Technology, China

Abstract: Based on Schiffrin's definition of discourse markers and her discourse model, this study investigates and compares discourse marker use in elicited narratives by Chinese native speakers and learners of Chinese as a foreign language. The quantitative analysis demonstrates that native speakers produce discourse markers more frequently than learners. The results also show that extra-curricular exposure to the target language environment and interactions with native speakers promote the use of appropriate discourse markers. A qualitative analysis was conducted to investigate the meanings and functions of the most-frequently-used markers by both groups. Pedagogical implications for Chinese as a second / foreign language and L2 instruction in general are discussed, including the integration of the functions and meanings of discourse markers into L2 instruction.

Introduction

Achieving speech fluency and coherence in a target language is an important yet difficult task for second / foreign language (L2) learners. Studies have shown that discourse marker (DM) use is a significant feature of oral discourse and colloquial speech (Brinton, 1996; Schiffrin, 1987, 2001) as well as an integral part of sociolinguistic and stylistic variation (E. Andersen, Brizuela, DuPuy, & Gonnerman, 1995, 1999; Stubbe & Holmes, 1995). Consequently, for second language learners, mastery of appropriate discourse marker use is an important and integral aspect of sociolinguistic and communicative competence. This paper presents the results of a study on the differences of discourse marker use by Chinese[①] native speakers and learners of Chinese as a foreign language (CFL). The paper outlines, compares, and contrasts the different meanings and functions of the DMs used by these two groups of speakers while exploring the pedagogical dimensions of discourse marker use and sociolinguistic competence.

In the following sections, we first provide a definition of discourse markers while sketching the theoretical framework that forms the basis of my analysis. Following, we review and situate the present study in relation to the relevant literature on DM use in oral narratives as well as in Chinese. Next, we present a quantitative analysis of DM use by Chinese native speakers and CFL learners. The following qualitative analysis presents the meanings and functions of the most frequently used DMs in native speaker and learner speech. We conclude by summarizing the major findings of the present study, relating them to previous work, and discussing the implications of this research for CFL and L2 classroom teaching.

Discourse Markers and Theoretical Framework

One of the most influential and systematic studies on DM use is by Schiffrin (1987). She defines DMs as "sequentially dependent elements which bracket units of talk" (p. 31). Schiffrin further offers a tentative guideline of the conditions that allow an expression to be used as a discourse marker. For expressions to function as DMs, they must: 1) be syntactically detachable; 2) commonly used in initial position of an utterance; 3) have a range of prosodic contours; and 4) operate at multiple levels and planes of discourse. Common English discourse markers include *well*, *like*, *I mean*, *so*, among others.

Based on her analysis of English DMs in unstructured interviews, Schiffrin (1987) proposes a model of discourse coherence consisting of five separate planes of analysis. *Ideational Structure* reflects different semantic relationships among ideas (or propositions) within the discourse, including cohesive, topic, and functional relations. *Exchange Structure* reflects the dynamics of conversational interchange and indicates the sequence of conversational roles and how turn changes interrelate. *Action Structure* indicates how different speakers' speech acts are sequenced and determined, reflecting participant identity, social factors, and actions. *Participation Framework* indicates the different ways in which speakers

---

① In the current study, *Chinese* refers to Mandarin Chinese.

relate to each other, as well as how they relate to the discourse. *Information State* reflects the ongoing organization and management of participants' knowledge and meta-knowledge, as well as their interactional relationship.

Schiffrin also differentiates DMs in terms of planes of use: primary planes and secondary planes. She argues that *all* markers "have uses in more than one component of discourse (either separately or simultaneously)" (p. 316). She further claims that the linguistic properties and semantic meanings of the markers contribute to the overall communicative effect. She proposes that DMs have core meanings that "do not fluctuate from use to use; rather, what changes is the discourse slot in which they appear" (p. 318). Moreover, in regards to DM meaning and use, Schiffrin (1987) suggests that "if an expression used as a marker does have meaning, its primary use in discourse will be in the organization of referential meanings at a textual level - and that if a marker does not have meaning, its primary use will be elsewhere ... as an expression loses its semantic meaning, it is freer to function in non-ideational realms of discourse" (p. 319).

Based on a distributional and interpretive analysis of specific DMs, Schiffrin (1987) additionally claims that markers, because of their indexical properties, are important indicators of discourse coherence. She argues that discourse markers "provide contextual coordinates for utterances: they index an utterance to the local contexts in which utterances are produced and in which they are to be interpreted" (p. 326). The local contexts include the planes of discourse, interlocutors, and prior and/or upcoming discourse. As contextual coordinates, DMs contribute to coherence. She argues that "since coherence is the result of integration among different components of talk, any device which simultaneously locates an utterance within several emerging contexts of discourse automatically has an integrative function" (p. 330). In essence, DMs serve an integrative function in discourse by indexing an utterance to local contexts and thus contributing to discourse coherence.

Other researchers refer to discourse markers as pragmatic markers (G. Andersen, 2001; Fraser, 1990; Park, 2003) or discourse particles (Hansen, 1998; Schourup, 1985; Vanderkooi, 2000), suggesting both the range of linguistic approaches adopted and the multiplicity of functions which DMs are found to perform (Jucker & Ziv, 1998). In this paper, I adopt the Schiffrin's (1987, 2001) definition of discourse marker because I employ her model as the theoretical framework.

Literature Review

Discourse Markers in Oral Narratives

Some studies have shown that discourse markers play differential functions in narratives compared to conversations. Norrick (2001), for example, argues that DMs have special organizational functions in oral narratives. These arise because of the unique structural and sequential conventions of oral narratives which are quite different from the turn-by-turn exchange in spoken conversation. Norrick demonstrates that although *well* and *but* function differently in regular conversations, they have similar function in narrative context. In natural conversations, *well* functions as a hesitation device and *but* indicates contrast or cancels some feature of the previous discourse. In oral narratives, however, both markers can lose their primary semantic sense and function instead to introduce the expository section or mark the transitions to the following sections of the story.

Koike (1996), through the analysis of personal experience narrations of eight Spanish speakers, contends that when expressions function as DMs in oral narratives, they can take on special functions and meanings. Investigating the Spanish time adverbial *ya* (already; now; soon; at times), Koike found that in narrative discourse *ya* can function as a discourse marker by highlighting different elements in a sentence and conveying emotional emphasis. In addition to indicating temporal and aspectual information, the multifunctionality of *ya* makes it a useful device for narrators by enabling them to convey an emotional element in storytelling as well as organize narrative content. Koike further claims that the multi-functional ability of the adverbial marker assists the listener in processing information, which in turn, contributes to the overall success of the oral narrative.

Adopting a theory based on framing and verse / stanza analysis (Gee, 1985, 1989; Hymes, 1981, 1982), Minami (1998) investigated Japanese speakers' use of politeness markers (e.g. formal / informal verb-ending forms) and psychological complements (e.g. *omou* (think), *ki ga suru* (feel)) in narrative discourse. Verses / stanzas are defined as thematic groups of lines or idea units, the shift of which usually involve a thematic change such as character, event, location, or time. Minami demonstrates that politeness markers and psychological complements have special functions in Japanese narratives. The use of formal and informal verb-ending forms indicates the perspective (internal or external) that the narrator cognitively takes while narrating. Formal verb styles indicate the external positioning of the narrator in relation to the event being told; informal styles suggest an internal perspective that reduces the distance between narrator and event. Psychological complements, on the other hand, index politeness by softening the illocutionary force of the message or speech act.

The aforementioned studies provide ample evidence of how well-developed narrative study is in the broader realm of discourse analysis. Also, a great variety of narrative texts have been examined. These include oral narratives such as conversational narratives (Koike, 1996; Labov,

1972; Norrick, 2001), retold stories (Norrick, 1998), and memory recall stories or elicited narratives (Chafe, 1980; Stromqvist & Verhoeven, 2004). Differing types of narratives result in differing types of DM use. Moreover, since it has been found that some DMs have particular functions in different types of contexts (Koike, 1996; Minami, 1998), any study that compares DM use between two or more groups should place controls so that the same type of DMs are elicited. One solution to this dilemma can be achieved by eliciting specific narratives. This method has been successfully used by Chafe (1980) and Stromqvist and Verhoeven (2004), though they did not use their elicited narratives to explore group differences in DM use. They used a specially designed silent video, *The Pear Stories* (Chafe, 1980), to collect linguistic data from around the world by asking the participants to retell the story and investigate the differences in language use by different groups of speakers.

Discourse Markers in Chinese

Research in Chinese discourse marker use is rather scarce. Miracle (1989, 1991) was among the first scholars to systematically investigate Chinese discourse markers. He applied Schiffrin's (1987) discourse marker framework to the analysis of DM use in Chinese conversations. His corpus consisted of the following: regular conversations by native Chinese speakers (university students) in a variety of settings in Taipei, Taiwan; recordings of university classroom interactions; and recordings of local television talk shows on current social issues. The DMs examined in his studies include 好 *hǎo* (good; yes), 但是 *dànshì* (however), 可是 *kěshì* (but), 不过 *búguò* (but; however), and 那(么) *nà(me)* (so; and then). He demonstrates these markers all carry a "core" meaning derived from their syntactic usage. For example, 好 *hǎo* (good; yes) functions as a marker of closure and transition — one which is closely related to its use in resultative verb compounds such as in 我已经买好票了 (*Wǒ yǐjīng mǎihǎo piào le*; I already bought the tickets) indicating successful completion of an action. The semantic notion of contrast was found to be basic to the use of 但是 *dànshì* (however), 可是 *kěshì* (but), and 不过 *bùguò* (but; however) as DMs. The marker 那(么) *nà(me)* (so; and then) maintains a core function of marking continuation, which is also basic to the use of 那(么) *nà(me)* as a sentence connective.

Adopting Halliday and Hasan's (1976) tripartite model consisting of ideational, textual, and interactional levels, Wang and Tsai (2005) examined 好 *hǎo* (good; yes) in natural Chinese conversations as well as in radio interviews and call-ins. They demonstrate that on the ideational level, 好 *hǎo* can function as an adjective such as 这本书很好 (*Zhè běn shū hěnhǎo*; This book is very good) or a degree adverb as in 我好冷哦 (*Wǒ hǎolěng òu*; I am very cold). On the textual level, 好 *hǎo* marks the closure of the previous discourse and indicates the transition to the following topics / activities. On the interactional level, 好 *hǎo* conveys positive evaluation or agreement / acceptance with the preceding move made by another interlocutor and at the same time indicates that the speaker is ready for a new exchange or the next stage of discourse.

The studies by Miracle (1989, 1991) and Wang and Tsai (2005) were carried out in the region of Taiwan. The Chinese spoken by the people of Taiwan bears different syntactic and lexical-semantic features from that spoken by the Chinese Mainlanders, the focus of the present study.

Discourse Markers by Non-native Speakers

As previously mentioned, studies on non-native speaker discourse marker use are rare. Even rarer, are those on Chinese language acquisition. Hays (1992), employing Schiffrin's (1987) discourse model, examined the use of DMs in English interviews by a group of Japanese native speakers. The results of the study showed that most speakers demonstrated ability to use "*and*", "*but*", and "*so*", which Hays attributes to the crucial nature of these markers in developing ideas as well as the fact that they are usually explicitly taught. Hays also found that these learners very often omit discourse markers in places where English native speakers normally use them. It was also found that discourse markers on ideational plane are generally acquired before markers on other planes of discourse. Finally, Hays suggests L2 learners might rely on native language markers as an interlanguage strategy to help in establishing coherence in their L2 spoken discourse.

Lee's (2004) quantitative study examined the acquisition of English DMs by Korean immigrants. The variables he looked at were gender and immigrant generation. The findings showed that women do not use DMs more often than men. As to the effect of immigration generation, it was found that 1.5-generation speakers use discourse markers the most, suggesting acquired yet overgeneralized discourse marker use. Lee attributes this to the intense pressure of linguistic and cultural assimilation. Importantly, it was also found that *all* of the speakers showed limited range of DM preferences. Lee further claims that L2 learners were clearly shown to be aware of using DMs in their speech and were able to acquire their patterns of use.

Another interesting study by Sankoff and colleagues (1997) examined discourse markers used by Anglophone speakers of Montreal French in both their L1 (English) and L2 (French). They found that these speakers used DMs in their native language about twice as frequently as in their second language. They also found a degree of individual DM variability such that different speakers maintained different marker preferences. Finally, the frequency of discourse marker use was found to correlate with speakers' knowledge of French grammar and more native-like control of DM use in L2 indicating heightened success in second language learning.

Summary of the Literature Review and Justification for the Current Study

In summary, the role of DMs in natural conversations has attracted considerable attention from linguists working with English discourse (Fraser, 1990; Schiffrin, 1987, 2001; Schourup, 1985). The field is well established and has produced a large body of work that has shown that DMs are a systematic and important element of fluent, meaningful, and coherent speech. Considering its importance however, there have been few studies on DMs in Chinese (Chen & Weiyun, 2001; Miracle, 1989, 1991; Wang & Tsai, 2005), and even fewer in Chinese oral narrative contexts. Moreover, most DM studies have focused on native speaker usage, and only a limited number of studies have examined discourse marker use by nonnative speakers. Since DM use is generally agreed to be a necessary feature of oral discourse and important for colloquial speech (Brinton, 1996; Sankoff et al., 1997; Schiffrin, 1987, 2001), the ability to use and appropriately apply DMs is undoubtedly an important aspect of sociolinguistic and intercultural communicative competence. As Svartvik (1980) stated, "If a foreign language learner says five sheeps or he goed, he can be corrected by practically every native speaker. If, on the other hand, he omits a well, the likely reaction will be that he is dogmatic, impolite, boring, awkward to talk to etc, but a native speaker cannot pinpoint an 'error'" (p. 171). If L2 speakers want to sound like native speakers and become more assimilated into L2 culture, they need to acquire how "things are said" and be able to use the "conventional expressions" such as DMs (de Klerk, 2005). This type of competence is especially critical in the upper-levels of language proficiency. However, discourse marker use is usually not included in L2 formal classroom instruction (Hellerman & Andrea, 2007). Consequently, learners are expected to acquire DMs through real-life contacts with native speakers and those who would like to be acculturated to L2 culture are expected to use DMs more.
. The present study examines the differences of DM use by Chinese native speakers and CFL learners in narrative contexts, which will provide some insights for the acquisition of communicative competence and CFL learning / instruction. The research questions explored are the following:

1) What DMs are used by Chinese native speakers and CFL learners in elicited narratives?
2) What are the differences of DM use between Chinese native speakers and CFL learners in elicited narratives?
3) What are the meanings and functions of the most frequently used DMs by Chinese native speakers and CFL learners?

Method

The data used in this study comes from two sources. One is data collected from a group of nine advanced-level CFL learners (from third- and fourth-year Chinese classes) at a university in the U.S. southwest. Three of the participants were Chinese heritage learners and six were American students. Seven out of nine of them had previously studied or traveled in China (from five days to 21 months). Only two of participants, Topher① and Sophie, had never been to China. Since the focus of the study is to look at the use of discourse markers in narratives, I adopted Chafe's video, *The Pear Stories* (Chafe, 1980), as the elicitation device. *The Pear Stories* is a six-minute long story video designed by Chafe and his colleagues with only images and no language tracks. They used the video to collect linguistic samples around the world in order to examine the differences in language use. The learners in this study were shown the video and asked to retell the story. The second set of data was similarly collected from a group of nine native Chinese speaking college students at a Chinese university in mainland China. Thus a balance was struck between the groups in terms of age and education level. The procedures of the study were approved by IRB for human subject protection and all the participants were recruited on a voluntary basis. All of the narratives were audio taped and then transcribed in standard *Hanyu Pinyin* orthography and Chinese characters by the author.

Table 1 Participant Information

	NS / NNS	*Age*	*Gender*	*Year in U.S. / CHS Level*	*Experience in China*	*Heritage Learner*
Xin	NS	18	Female	Freshman		
Nan	NS	18	Female	Freshman		
Emma	NS	18	Female	Freshman		
Wujing	NS	19	Male	Freshman		
Qiao	NS	19	Male	Freshman		
Slavy	NS	18	Male	Freshman		
RD	NS	20	Male	Freshman		
Liu	NS	18	Male	Freshman		

(to be continued)

---

① Student names are pseudonyms chosen by students themselves.

	NS / NNS	Age	Gender	Year in U.S. / CHS Level	Experience in China	Heritage Learner
Zhao	NS	19	Male	Freshman		
Topher	NNS	21	Male	3rd year	None	No
Amy	NNS	20	Female	3rd year	10 months	Yes
Cheryl	NNS	21	Female	3rd year	5 days	Yes
Sophie	NNS	21	Female	3rd year	None	No
Wen	NNS	20	Female	3rd year	3 years	No
Marie	NNS	22	Female	4th year	6 months	No
Chen	NNS	21	Female	4th year	2 months	Yes
Lee	NNS	22	Female	4th year	21 months	No
Renee	NNS	23	Female	4th year	2 months	No

Note: NS = native speaker; NNS = non-native speaker

Quantitative Analysis and Results

In order to investigate which discourse markers are used by the two groups of speakers, all of the DMs used in the narratives were identified according to Schiffrin's (1987) DM criteria: syntactic detachability, common utterance-initial position, various prosodic contours, and multi-level discourse function. Excluding pause fillers such as "*uh*" or "*um*", a total of eight different DMs were used by the native speakers: 然后 *ránhòu* (then), 那个 *nèige* (that), 就是 *jiùshì* (that is), 结果 *jiéguǒ* (result), 好像 *hǎoxiàng* (like), 所以 *suǒyǐ* (so), and 后来 *hòulái* (then; later), and 但是 *dànshì* (but). Eight partially differing DMs were used by the Chinese learners: 然后 *ránhòu* (then), 那个 *nèige* (that), 结果 *jiéguǒ* (result), 好像 *hǎoxiàng* (like), 所以 *suǒyǐ* (so), 后来 *hòulái* (then; later), 但是 *dànshì* (but), and the English "*and then.*"

Quantitative analysis of the discourse markers showed that native speakers used them much more frequently than the CFL learners. Not surprisingly, the nine native speakers produced longer narratives with nearly twice as many words as the learners (6676 vs. 3350). Native speakers produced four times as many

DMs as the learners (331 vs. 83) and native speakers used DMs twice as frequently as the learners (4.96% vs. 2.48%)①.

Choice in discourse markers also varied by group. Preliminary analysis (Figure 1) shows that the most frequently used DMs by native speakers are 然后 *ránhòu* (then) (160 times) and 那个 *nèige* (that) (114 times). For learners, the two most frequent DMs are also 然后 *ránhòu* (then) (32 times) and 那个 *nèige* (that) (18 times). T-test result ($p<.05$, $t = 2.67$, $df = 7.42$) indicated that the use of 然后 *ránhòu* (then) is significantly different between the two groups, with native speakers using it more than CFL learners. Although the use of 那个 *nèige* (that) by the two groups is not significantly different ($p>.05$, $t = 4.89$, $df = 1.31$), the distribution result (Table 2) showed that native speakers use them more often than learners and only two learners used 那个 *nèige* (that) as a discourse marker. Learners used 结果 *jiéguǒ* (result) just once, while native speakers used it ten times. Interestingly, the English discourse marker "*and then*" occurred in learners' productions 11 times.

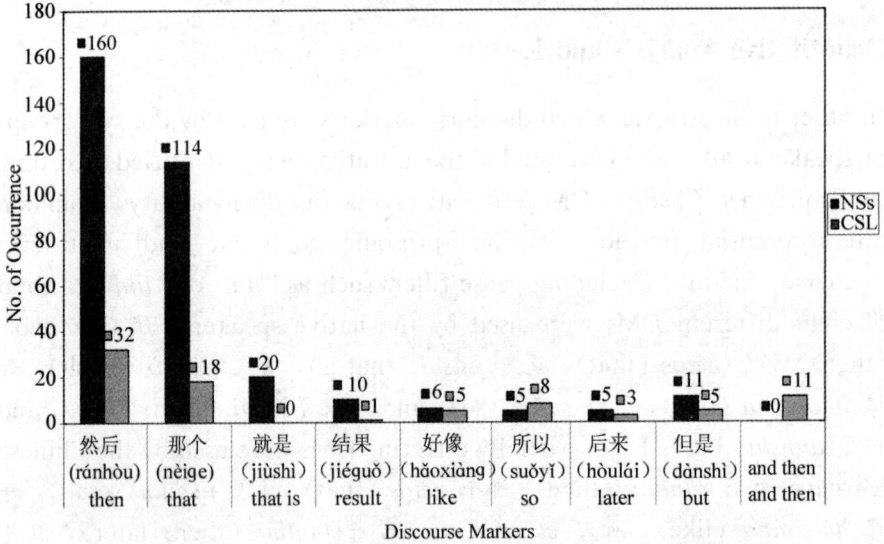

Figure 1　DM use by Chinese Native Speakers and CFL learners (No. of occurrence)

---

① Frequency = total number of DMs / total number of words

Mirroring the findings of Lee (2004) and Sankoff et al. (1997), further analysis of individual DM use (Table 2) found that each speaker maintained their own preference for specific markers.

Table 2 DM use by Individual Speakers

Name	然后 ránhòu then	那个 nèige that	就是 jiùshì that is	所以 suǒyǐ So	结果 jiéguǒ Result	好像 hǎoxiàng like	后来 hòulái later	但是 dànshì but	and then	Total
NSs										
Xin	28	25	1	1			1			56
Nan	4	4								8
Emma	23	10	1					2		36
Wujing	1	8	3	2				3		17
Qiao	10	6	5	1	9		1			32
Slavy		11	8				2	1		22
RD	10	12		1		3	1	3		30
Liu	35	27				2				64
Zhao	49	11	2		1	1		2		17
NNSs										
Topher										0
Sophie	1									1
Cheryl	2					1		1		4
Renee	6									6
Wen	2	2				1	1	1		7
Chen	4			3						7
Lee	3			2					2	7
Marie	10			1						11
Amy	4	16		2	1	3	2	1	11	40

Two extremes of DM use were also noted among the learners. One learner, Amy, accounted for almost 50% (40 out of 83) of all the learner DMs. Of the 18 occurrences of 那个 *nèige* (that), Amy produced 16 of them; she also produced three of the five 好像 *hǎoxiàng* (like). Moreover, all 11 occurrences of "*and then*" were produced by this one person. On the other extreme we find Topher, who did not use a single discourse marker across his entire narrative. If we exclude Amy and reexamine the distribution (Figure 2), we find the most frequently used DMs by learners are 然后 *ránhòu* (then) (33.73%) and 所以 *suǒyǐ* (so) (7.23%). This partially differs from native speakers, who used 然后 *ránhòu* (then) (48%) and 那个 *nèige* (that) (34.44%) most frequently.

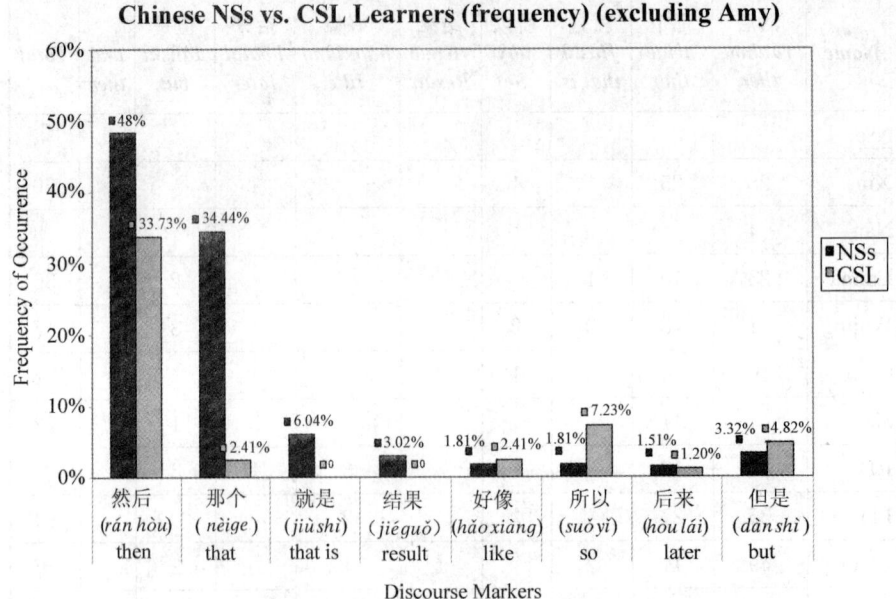

Figure 2　DM use by Chinese Native Speakers and CFL learners (Excluding Amy) (Frequency)

Functions and Meanings of Discourse Markers

Schiffrin's (1987) discourse model based on the five planes of analysis — Exchange Structure, Action Structure, Ideational Structure, Participation Framework, and Information State — is adopted in analyzing the meanings and functions of the more frequent discourse markers used by native speakers (然后 *ránhòu* and 那个 *nèige*) and learners (然后 *ránhòu* and 所以 *suǒyǐ*). This is followed by an analysis of the interesting case of the English discourse marker "*and then*".

Chinese Native Speakers

然后 **ránhòu** (**then**). The frequent use of 然后 *ránhòu* by native speakers is due to the sequentiality of narrative discourse — the sequence of events and the temporal decisions made by the narrator. Linguistically, the core meaning of 然后 *ránhòu* is "then" and it primarily functions on an ideational level by indicating temporally cohesive relationships among propositions within the discourse. In essence, it means "what happens next", as the following example illustrates.

Example 1: Xin narrates how the little boy in the video accidentally hit a rock in the road and fell off his bicycle, she said:

(他)不小心绊到了一个石头上,然后车子就倒了。

(*tā*) *bùxiǎoxīn bàndào le yígè shítou shàng*, **ránhòu** *chēzi jiù dǎole*.

(He) ran into a rock accidentally, **then** the bicycle fell.

Sometimes, however, the core meaning may fluctuate and 然后 *ránhòu* can mean, in narrative contexts, almost anything involving the concept of "next" or "then", such as "what I can say next", "what I want to say next", "what I can think of next", "what else", and "what is shown next in the video". At other times, however, the core meaning may be lost entirely and the expression becomes semantically bleached. In so doing, 然后 *ránhòu* acquires even more linguistic freedom allowing it to serve in non-ideational realms of discourse. For instance, it can function as a verbal filler and hesitation device, providing the narrator with linguistic planning time. A closer look at the following excerpts illustrates this.

Example 2: When RD started his narration, he inserted his own comments.

最开始的时候出现了一个比较胖的人。戴着草帽。他是在收梨。嗯,收获梨子。然后,(停顿),但是,我看他,在收梨子时候不是很认真。

Zuì kāishǐ de shíhòu chūxiàn le yīgè rén. Dài zhe cǎomào tā shì zài shōulí. En, shōuhuò lízi. **Ránhòu**, (pause), *dànshì, wǒ kàn tā, zài shōulízi shíhòu búshì hěn rènzhēn.*

At the very beginning, a pretty fat person appears, with a straw hat. He is collecting pears, um, harvesting pears. **Then**, (pause), but, I think he is not collecting pears in a very careful manner.

Example 3: When Liu was telling what the farmer in the video was doing, he said:

他好像摘梨子,然后,嗯,在一个梯子上面进行劳动,

Tā hǎoxiàng zhāi lízi, **ránhòu**, *en, zài yígè tīzi shàngmiàn jìnxíng láodòng.*

He is like picking pears, **then**, um, working on a ladder.

In Example 2, 然后 *ránhòu* can be interpreted as "what happens next" and the DM, 但是 *dànshì* (but), steers the discourse in another direction, towards the narrator's personal commentary. 然后 *ránhòu* also functions as a hesitation device by providing the narrator time to plan content and organize the response. In Example 3, 然后 *ránhòu* can be interpreted in two ways. It can mean "what is next" indicating the narrator realizes there is something more he wants to say about the man picking pears. In order to do so, he uses a filled pause "um" to redirect the hearer to further information about the man. It can also be used as a hesitation device. In both of these cases, 然后 *ránhòu* functions simultaneously on several planes of discourse. The primary plane is on the level of Ideational Structure where it directs the hearer to the context of what happens next. The secondary and tertiary planes are Action Structure and Information State because, as the discourse progresses, the narrator changes directions and thus adopts 然后 *ránhòu* as a hesitation device. In this context, 然后 *ránhòu* functions to manage the narrator's own, as well as the hearer's, information state in regards to the progression of the narrative — what the hearer expects him to say next, and what he does say next. At the same time, 然后 *ránhòu* marks certain actions, such as hesitation, searching for words, and planning content. In these two examples, 然后 *ránhòu* indexes adjacent utterances only to the speaker in that it is the speaker who controls the direction and orientation of the discourse. The following example illustrates the multiple functions of 然后 *ránhòu*.

Example 4: Zhao describes the scene of the man picking pears.

Z: 他的那个装束很有一点墨西哥人的味道。然后戴了一个那个,那种小帽子。这个故事发生在墨西哥吧?
L[①]: 我不知道。
Z: 然后,然后,这儿戴了一个小围巾,然后,在这儿,在腰部的位置,系了一个,白色的一个,那个,像围裙似的。然后,它是用来装梨的。

Z: *Tā de nèige zhuāngshù hěnyǒu yīdiǎn mòxīgērén de wèidào.* ***Ránhòu*** *dàile yígè nèige, nèizhǒng xiǎomàozi. Zhège gùshì fāshēng zài mòxīgē ba?*
L: *Wǒ bùzhīdào.*
Z: ***Ránhòu****, **ránhòu**, zhè'er dài le yīgè xiǎowéijīn, **ránhòu**, zài zhèr, zài yāobù de wèizhì, jìle yīge, báisè de yígè, nèige, xiàng wéiqún shìde.* ***Ránhòu****, tā shì yòng lái zhuānglí.*

Z: His clothes have much of a Mexican flavor. **Then**, (he) wears a, that, that kind of little hat. Did this story happen in Mexico?
L: I don't know.
Z: **then**, **then**, here he wears a small scarf, **then**, here, around waist, (he) wears a, white, that, like apron, **then**, it is used to hold pears.

In Example 4, when the narrator starts to explain why he thinks the man's clothes look Mexican, the first token of 然后 *ránhòu* functions as an act of clarification. The fourth and fifth occurrences of 然后 *ránhòu* can be interpreted as "and". In this context, they contribute to the cohesive relationship between ideas or propositions which lack a temporally sequential relationship. Thus, in these three contexts, 然后 *ránhòu* functions primarily on an ideational level while maintaining functionality

---

① L is the interviewer who is the author.

on the actional level by indicating the narrator's act of clarification. However, these markers also function on an informational level by enabling the narrator to manage informational flow between interlocutors. Thus, these three cases of 然后 *ránhòu* function as contextual coordinates by allowing the speaker to clarify and manage propositions. At the same time, they also contribute to discourse coherence by functioning as cohesive devices connecting propositions within the narrative.

Differently, the second and third instances of 然后 *ránhòu* mark conversational exchange and enable the transition back to the topic of the story. In this context, they function primarily on an ideational plane indicating cohesiveness and topic relationships between ideas and propositions. However, as with discourse markers in general, these two instances maintain functionality on several planes simultaneously. They function on planes of Exchange Structure and Participation Frame by marking speaker change and indexing conversational structure. On the level of Action Structure, they function to signal the narrator's acceptance of the hearer's response. On the level of Information State, the narrator uses the discourse markers to organize narration and manage information between interlocutors. As contextual coordinates, the markers index adjacent utterances to both the hearer and the speaker, as well as to prior and the upcoming discourse. Table 3 summarizes the meanings and functions of 然后 *ránhòu* (then) across the planes of discourse.

Table 3 Meanings and Functions of 然后 ránhòu (then)

Primary plane of discourse	
Ideational Structure	Indicating temporal relationship between propositions / ideas
Secondary planes of discourse	
Action Structure	A device for hesitation, word searching, content organization, clarification, and acceptance of the previous discourse.
Information State	Managing the interlocutors' information state regarding what is going to be done next, what is expected next, and what really happens next.
Exchange Structure	Indicating speaker change
Participation Framework	Marking conversational structure

那个 **nèige (that)**. For the native speakers 那个 *nèige* was another frequently used discourse marker. Its frequency in the narratives can be explained, at least in part, by the need of speakers to refer to people and things. In modern Chinese, 那个 *nèige* primarily functions as a demonstrative meaning "that". As the following example illustrates, this primary semantic sense is maintained during its use as a DM,.

Example 5: RD describes the scene where the man realizes he is missing a basket of pears.

那个摘梨的那个人发现一个筐空了。
Nèige zhāilí de **nèige** rén fāxiàn yīgè kuāng kōng le.
That, that man who is picking pears found that one basket was empty.

It is on the ideational level, that the discourse marker 那个 *nèige* primarily functions. Here, it contributes to the relationship among ideas through its referential meaning. Anything shown in the video can be referred to as "that" — 那个果子 *nèige guǒzi* (that pear), 那个小孩 *nèige xiǎohái* (that boy), and 那个车子 *nèige chēzi* (that bicycle) among others. In addition, 那个 *nèige* is also used to emphasize information. However, the core meaning of demonstrative can fluctuate or even be lost, which allows 那个 *nèige* to function, similar to 然后 *ránhòu*, as a hesitation device.

Example 6: Liu describes the scene in which a man and goat pass by the three baskets of pears.

(他们)从,那个,三个筐的,边上走过去了。
(*Tāmen*) *cóng*, **nèige**, *sāngè kuāng de*, *biānshàng zǒuguòqù le*.
They walked by, **that**, three baskets.

In the above example, 那个 *nèige* functions primarily on the level of Ideational Structure by maintaining discourse cohesiveness and topic relationships among ideas. Secondarily, it functions on the level of Action Structure by signaling and emphasizing the information in the relevant discourse. On the level of Information State it functions by assisting the hearer process information and by helping the narrator organize discourse and manage information exchange. As a contextual coordinate, 那个 *nèige* indexes adjacent utterances and enables both the speaker and hearer to organize information. It also indexes the utterances to prior and upcoming discourse by connecting shared information with the new ideas.

Table 4 summarizes the meanings and functions of 那个 *nèige* (that).

Table 4   Meanings and Functions of 那个 **nèige** (that)

Primary plane of discourse	
Ideational Structure	Indicating topic relationship between propositions/ideas through its referential meaning
Secondary planes of discourse	
Action Structure	A device for hesitation, signaling, emphasizing the action
Information State	Helping the narrator for speech organization and information exchange and assisting the hearer for information processing

CFL Learners

然后 ránhòu (then) and 所以 suǒyǐ (so). 然后 *Ránhòu* and 所以 *suǒyǐ* are the most frequently used discourse markers by learners of Chinese.

The meanings and functions of 然后 *ránhòu* as used by the learners are similar to those of native speakers. The sole exception to this being that it is rarely used as a hesitation device. For this purpose, Chinese learners often rely on the English markers "*uh*" and "*um*" when hesitating and word searching.

The core meaning of 所以 *suǒyǐ* signals a cause-effect relationship between ideas and propositions. However, 所以 *suǒyǐ* can sometimes function similarly to 然后 *ránhòu* by indicating a sequential relationship between phrases. Example 7 illustrates this.

Example 7: Chen explains how the group of three boys returns the hat to the little boy.

C: 他骑车,可是他忘了他的, hat?
L: 帽子。
C: 帽子。
L: Uhuh.
C: 啊,所以别的孩子叫,叫他。"你别忘了你的帽子。"所以他,啊,给他他的,他的帽子。

C: tā qíchē. Kěshì tā wàng le tā de, hat?
L: màozi.
C: màozi.
L: Uhuh.
C: Uh, **suǒyǐ** bié de háizi jiào, jiào tā, "nǐ bié wàng le nǐ de màozi." **Suǒyǐ** tā, uh, gěi tā tā de, tā de màozi.

C: He rode a bike. But he forgot his hat?
L: hat.
C: hat.
L: Uhuh.
C: Um, **so** other kids called him, "Don't forget your hat." **So**, he, um, gave him his, his hat.

In this example, the first token of 所以 *suǒyǐ* indicates a causal relationship between utterances. The second occurrence of 所以 *suǒyǐ* is interpreted as *then*, and indicates a temporal relationship between propositions. Primarily functioning on an ideational level, 所以 *suǒyǐ* indicates a cohesive relationship between ideas. On the levels of Exchange Structure and Participation Frame (the first 所以 *suǒyǐ* in Example 7), it functions by signaling turn / speaker change and topic shift. On the informational level, 所以 *suǒyǐ* helps the interlocutors connect prior information with upcoming information. As a contextual coordinate，所以 *suǒyǐ* indexes adjacent utterances to both the hearer and the speaker, but also to both prior and subsequent discourse. Table 5 is a summary of the meanings and functions of 所以 *suǒyǐ* (so).

Table 5 Meanings and Functions of 所以 suǒyǐ (so)

Primary plane of discourse	
Ideational Structure	Indicating a cause-effect or sequential relationship between propositions / ideas
Secondary planes of discourse	
Exchange Structure	Indicating turn / speaker change
Participation Framework	Marking topic shift
Information State	Helping the interlocutors to connect prior with upcoming information

And then. As previously mentioned, English discourse markers often crop up in the speech of CFL learners. In particular, we found that Amy, who speaks fluent Chinese, consistently uses the English DM, *and then* in both conversation and narrative. She uses *and then* so frequently in fact, that according to Myers-Scotton's (1992) definition, this expression qualifies as a loan word rather than a code-switch. Because her parents are from Hong Kong, has traveled there on several occasions to visit relatives. As people from Hong Kong are frequent code switchers (Wright & Kelly-Holmes, 1997), this may be playing a role in Amy's frequent usage. The meaning and function of *and then* in Amy's speech are similar to those of 然后 *ránhòu*, previously discussed.

An obvious question that emerges is whether the English DM *and then* is replacing the translation equivalent 然后 *ránhòu*? The answer is no. Amy knows 然后 *ránhòu* and uses it frequently as well.

Example 8: Amy describes the three boys leaving after helping the little boy pick up the pears.

    And then, 然后,他们,他们,捡完以后就走了。
    ***And then**, ránhòu, tāmen, tāmen, jiǎn wán yǐhòu jiù zǒu le*.
    And then, then, they left after they picked up (the pears).

This finding suggests that L2 learners might use features of their L1 as a strategy to achieve discourse fluency and coherence. As cited earlier, a similar finding by Hays (1992) showed that Japanese learners of English often rely on Japanese markers in their L2 speech in order to manage conversational flow and improve discourse coherence.

Discussion

Variation was found in both native speakers' and learners' discourse marker preferences. Frequent use of 然后 *ránhòu* and 那个 *nèige* by NSs was partially due to the conformation of their core meanings with the nature of narrative structure and organization. Because these expressions can serve multiple discourse functions, they are convenient for native speaker use. Learners' most frequently used discourse markers were 然后 *ránhòu* (then) and 所以 *suǒyǐ* (so). My speculation for the reason is that these two expressions are formally introduced in CFL classes as connectives, functioning respectively as a time adverbial and as an indicator of a phrasal cause-effect relationship. Thus, first of all, these expressions become part of a learners' repertoire, and also, the core meanings of these two markers go well with the sequential nature of narrative context. This notion echoes a study by Hays (1992), who found that English markers explicitly taught in second language classrooms (e.g., *and*, *but*, and *so*) are used more frequently than other markers. Moreover, "*then*" and "*so*" can function as discourse markers in English (Schiffrin, 2001), thus facilitating positive transfer to Chinese DM use. On the other hand however, 那个 *nèige*, one of the two most frequent markers for native speakers, formally functions as a demonstrative in Chinese and is often introduced as such in CFL classes. Seldom is it, or other expressions such as 就是 *jiùshì* (that is), 结果 *jiéguǒ* (result), and 好像 *hǎoxiàng* (like), formally taught as a discourse markers and thus students might be unaware it can be used to mark discourse. Therefore, this bears pedagogical implications for CFL and L2 instruction including explicit instruction in the polyfunctional nature of discourse markers. A good way to do this is to introduce the expressions with authentic examples from native speaker speech. Another technique that is worth trying is to let learners listen to and then analyze native speakers' speech. The purpose of including discourse markers in L2 instruction is to develop learners' awareness of how native speakers use them and then their ability to make informed choices in authentic situations. The study also found that learners sometimes adopt linguistic features in their native language as a strategy to achieve fluency and discourse coherence. In this study, Amy used the English marker "*and then*" many times in her narration. Similarly, Hays (1992) found that Japanese learners of English very often use Japanese marker *n* to assure information flow. Sankoff et al. (1997) also showed that Anglophone French speakers often adopt English discourse markers in their French speech. These findings suggest that learners actively use both language resources in order to achieve their communicative purposes and establish discourse coherence.

It was also found that there was considerable variability in DM use and frequency at the level of the individual. Specifically, recall the two extreme cases of Amy and Topher. My interpretation of this is based on extracurricular exposure to a native Chinese environments and increased opportunities to interact with native Chinese speakers. Amy though born in the U.S., had traveled to China on numerous occasions. Moreover, in the home environment, she often talks to her mother in Chinese. On the other hand, Topher has never visited a Chinese speaking-country, nor has he interacted with native speakers outside classroom. As noted by Sankoff et al. (1997, p.193), because discourse markers are "not subject to explicit instruction, they are likely to be an accurate indicator of the extent to which a speaker is integrated into the local speech community. That is, only L2 speakers with a high degree of contact with native speakers will master the use of discourse markers." Other studies (Mougeon, Rehner, & Nadasdi, 2004; Rehner, Mougeon, & Nadasdi, 2003) have also shown that learners who have more extracurricular exposure to the target language — such as experience in the target language environment and contact with native speakers and media — tend to produce significantly more target-like variants than those who have had less exposure. This suggests that extracurricular exposure to the target language environment and interaction with native speakers are significant factors in the development of sociolinguistic and intercultural communicative competence. It therefore seems reasonable that creating more opportunities for L2 learners to experience the target language environment and interact with native speakers should be a significant component of second language instruction. Study abroad and language partner programs are both good venues to provide ample opportunities for learners to interact with native speakers and thus develop their communicative competence.

Conclusion

Because discourse markers play such an important role in colloquial speech and sociolinguistic/communicative competence, the acquisition of DMs is an important task facing second language learners. This study examined the similarities and differences between DM use by Chinese native speakers and Chinese language learners. Schiffrin's (1987) framework was found effective to accomplish the task. Results found a large 2:1 difference in discourse marker frequency between native and nonnative groups. Moreover, it was found that the two groups use partially different DMs in their narratives. The functions and meanings of the DMs are summarized in Table 6.

Table 6 Functions and Meaning of DMs

	Core Meaning	Primary Plane of D.	Secondary Plane of D.	Participation Coordinates	Textual Coordinates
然后 (ránhòu) / and then	then	Ideational Structure	Exchange Structure; Participation Framework; Action Structure; Information State	speaker speaker/hearer	prior/ upcoming
那个 (nèige)	that	Ideational Structure	Action Structure; Information State	speaker/hearer	prior/ upcoming
所以 (suǒyǐ)	so	Ideational Structure	Exchange Structure; Participation Framework; Information State	speaker/hearer	prior/ upcoming

Notes: D = Discourse

As any other study, this study has limitations. First, only English-speaking learners of Chinese were investigated. As one of the findings in this study indicates, learners' native language might have an effect on their discourse marker use. Therefore, in order to gain more understanding of how learners of Chinese use discourse markers, studies that examine learners with different native languages are needed. Second, only DM use in narratives was examined. Speakers might use discourse markers differently in different situations and contexts. Consequently, future research studies are needed along the line of Chinese discourse marker use by learners with different native language backgrounds in order to see the influence of L1 on discourse marker use in L2 and also in natural conversations to see how discourse markers are used in different speech contexts.

References

Andersen, E., Brizuela, M., DuPuy, B., & Gonnerman, L. (1995). The acquisition of discourse markers as sociolinguistic variables: A crosslinguistic comparison. Paper presented at the Twenty-Seventh Annual Child Language Research Forum 27, Center for the Study of Language and Information, Stanford.

Andersen, E., Brizuela, M., DuPuy, B., & Gonnerman, L. (1999). Cross-linguistic evidence for the early acquisition of discourse markers as register variables. *Journal of Pragmatics*, 31(10), 1339–1351.

Andersen, G. (2001). *Pragmatic Markers and Sociolinguistic Variation: A Relevance-Theoretic Approach to the Language of Adolescents*. Amsterdam / Philadelphia: John Benjamins.

Brinton, L. J. (1996). *Pragmatic Markers in English: Grammaticalization and discourse functions*. New York: Mouton de Gruyter.

Chafe, W. L. (1980). *The Pear Stories: Cognitive, Cultural, and Linguistic Aspects of Narrative Production*. Norwood, NJ: Ablex.

Chen, Y. H., & Weiyun, A. (2001). *Dui bu dui* as a pragmatic marker: Evidence

from Chinese classroom discourse. *Journal of Pragmatics*, *33*(9), 1441-1465.
de Klerk, V. (2005). Procedural meanings of well in a corpus of Xhosa English. *Journal of Pragmatics*, *37*, 1183-1205.
Fraser, B. (1990). An approach to discourse markers. *Journal of Pragmatics*, *14*, 383-395.
Gee, J. P. (1985). The narrativization of experience in the oral style. *Journal of Education*, *167*, 9-35.
Gee, J. P. (1989). Two styles of narrative construction and their linguistic and educational implications. *Discourse Processes*, *12*, 287-307.
Halliday, M. A. K., & Hasan, R. (1976). *Cohesion in English*. London: Longman.
Hansen, M.-B. (1998). *The Function of Discourse Particles: A Study with Special Reference to Spoken Standard French*. Amsterdam/Philadelphia: John Benjamins.
Hays, P. R. (1992). Discourse markers and L2 acquisition. *Papers in Applied Linguistics: SLRF 1992 Proceedings*, 24-34.
Hellerman, J., & Andrea, V. (2007). Language which is not taught: The discourse marker use of beginning adult learners of English. *Journal of Pragmatics*, *39*, 157-179.
Hymes, D. (1981). *"In vain I tried to tell you": Studies in Native American Ethnopoetics*. Philadelphia, Pennsylvania: University of Pennsylvania Press.
Hymes, D. (1982). Narrative form as a "grammar" of experience: Native Americans and a glimpse of English. *Journal of Education*, *2*, 121-142.
Jucker, A. H., & Ziv, Y. (1998). *Discourse Markers: Descriptions and Theory*: John Benjamins.
Koike, D. A. (1996). Functions of the adverbial ya in Spanish narrative discourse. *Journal of Pragmatics*, *25*, 267-279.
Labov, W. (1972). The transformation of experience in narrative syntax. In *Language in the Inner City* (pp. 354-396). Philadelphia: University of Pennsylvania Press.
Lee, H. (2004). Discourse marker use in native and non-native English speakers. In Moder & Martinovic-Zic (Eds.), *Discourse across Languages and Cultures* (pp. 116-127): John Benjamins.
Minami, M. (1998). Politeness markers and psychological complements: Wrapping-up devices in Japanese oral personal narratives. *Narrative Inquiry*, *8*(2), 351-371.
Miracle, W. C. (1989). Hao: A Chinese discourse marker. *Papers from the Annual Regional Meeting of the Chicago Linguistic Society*, *25*(2), 213-227.
Miracle, W. C. (1991). Discourse markers in Mandarin Chinese. Unpublished PhD Dissertation. The Ohio State University.
Mougeon, R., Rehner, K., & Nadasdi, T. (2004). The learning of spoken French variation by immersion students from Toronto, Canada. *Journal of Sociolinguistics*, *8*(3), 408-432.
Myers-Scotton, C. (1992). Comparing code-switching and borrowing. *Journal of Multilingual and Multicultural Development*, *13*(1-2), 351-371.
Norrick, N. R. (1998). Retelling stories in spontaneous conversation. *Discourse Processes*, *25*(1), 75-97.
Norrick, N. R. (2001). Discourse markers in oral narrative. *Journal of Pragmatics*, *33*, 849-878.
Park, J.-R. (2003). A study of selected Korean pragmatic markers: Synchronic and diachronic perspectives. Unpublished PhD Dissertation. University of Hawaii.
Rehner, K., Mougeon, R., & Nadasdi, T. (2003). The learning of sociolinguistic variation by advanced FSL learners: The case of nous versus on in immersion French. *Studies in Second Language Acquisition*, *25*, 127-156.

Sankoff, G., Thibault, P., Nagy, N., Blondeau, H., Fonollosa, M. O., & Gagnon, L. (1997). Variation in the use of discourse markers in a language contact situation. *Language Variation and Change*, 9(2), 191–217.
Schiffrin, D. (1987). *Discourse Markers*: Cambridge University Press.
Schiffrin, D. (2001). Discourse markers: Language, meaning, and context. In D. Schiffrin, D. Tannen & H. E. Hamilton (Eds.), *The Handbook of Discourse Analysis* (pp. 54–75). Malden, Massachusetts: Blackwell Publishers.
Schourup, L. (1985). *Common Discourse Particles in English Conversation: Like, well, y'know*. New York: Garland Publishing, Inc.
Stromqvist, S., & Verhoeven, L. (2004). *Relating Events in Narrative Vol. 2: Typological and Contextual Perspectives*. Mahwah, NJ and London: Lawrence Erlbaum.
Stubbe, M., & Holmes, J. (1995). 'You know', 'eh' and other 'exasperating expressions': An analysis of social and stylistic variation in the use of pragmatic devices in a sample of New Zealand English. *Language and Communication*, 15(1), 63–88.
Svartvik, J. (1980). Well in conversation. In S. Greenbaum, G. Leech & J. Svartvik (Eds.), *Studies in English Linguistics for Randolph Quirk* (pp. 167–177). London: Longman.
Vanderkooi, D. R. (2000). Cohesion and salience in Niellim narrative: A look at discourse particles and participant reference. Unpublished Master's Thesis. The University of Texas at Arlington.
Wang, Y.-F., & Tsai, P.-H. (2005). Hao in spoken Chinese discourse: Relevance and coherence. *Language Sciences*, 27, 215–243.
Wright, S., & Kelly-Holmes, H. (1997). *One Country, Two Systems, Three Languages: A survey of changing language use in Hong Kong*. Clevedon, England/Philadelphia: Multilingual Matters.

31

Intercultural Communication Education and Foreign Language Education: Shared Precedents, Procedures, and Prospects

Warren B. ROBY
Washington State University, USA

Abstract: Intercultural Communication, although a field in its own right, has always drawn from other disciplines such as interpersonal communication, cultural anthropology, and social psychology for an understanding of culture and for suggestions on how to teach it (Dodd, 1987). This paper will introduce Intercultural Communication Educators (ICEs) to another discipline which has an important interest in teaching culture: foreign language education. The first section will demonstrate that Foreign Language Educators (FLEs) have a rich tradition of reflection about the place of culture in the language curriculum. The next section will enumerate the techniques which FLEs have used to teach culture, including some recent efforts to use audiovisual and computer technology. These first two portions will reveal that ICEs and FLEs unwittingly have much in common as regards understanding and teaching culture. The paper will conclude with a list of FLEs' current foci of interest about aspects of culture which may provide a basis for conscious cooperation with ICEs.

Historical Sketch

According to Kelly (1969), the teaching of culture has always been an "unstated aim" of foreign language teaching (378). It appears that language educators have always taken for granted that in the course of teaching a foreign language, that language's culture must be treated. This follows logically from the observation that language is at once a vehicle, product, and producer of culture (Galisson, 1984). However, Kelly notes that certain schools of language teaching have given overt attention to culture. He singles out the Direct Methodists of the nineteenth century in this regard. He also notes the importance given to culture in the US military's language programs during the Second World War.

The 1950s saw an amplification of the role of culture in language teaching. The Modern Language Association convened an interdisciplinary seminar in the summer of 1953 at the University of Michigan to examine the relationship between language and culture. This group published a report in the December, 1953 issue of the Association's Publications (volume 68, pages 1196–1218). This report did much, as evidenced by many citations (e.g. Nostrand, 1956; Brooks, 1968; Rivers, 1968) to bring culture into the consciousness of foreign language teaching professionals. The dominant attitude of the day was expressed by the eminent Charles Fries:

> To deal with the culture and life of a people is *not just an adjunct* of a practical language course, something alien and apart from its main purpose, to be added or not as time and convenience may allow, but an *essential feature of every stage of language learning*. (Fries, 1955, p. 14)

In the 1960s and 70s many conferences, workshops, and publications were devoted to the issue. Notable among these were the Northeast Conference on the Teaching of Foreign Languages (1960, 1972, and 1976), numerous publications by Howard Lee Nostrand and his *Emergent Model of a SocioCultural System* (1978), Lado's (1964) and Rivers' (1968) chapters on culture in their respective methodology textbooks, full-length treatments such as Seelye's (1974), Lafayette's (1975 & 1978), and the collection edited by Luce and Smith (1979). This last volume was published by Newbury House, which specializes in foreign language pedagogy. However, the contributors were from a wide variety of disciplines. A major theme of the book was "cross-cultural literacy" and the editors noted that diverse groups such as the Joint National Committee for Languages, the Society for Intercultural Education, Training and Research, and the International Communication Association and others were engaged in "professional dialogue" on the topic (p. 8).

In the 1970s one of the best discussions of the role of culture in language teaching was provided by Nelson Brooks (1975), who certainly ranks as one of the authorities in the field. One of Brooks' major contributions was to clarify just what is meant by the word culture. He differentiated between "culture as *everything* in human life, and culture as the *best* of everything in human life" (p. 20). Brooks calls the first sense Culture BBV: belief, behavior, and values. The second sense is Culture

MLA: Music, Letters, and Arts. This distinction is sometimes referred to as culture and Culture, or more commonly, as culture and civilization. The intercultural educator who chooses to read what language educators have written about culture will soon note that these two notions of culture are not always kept discrete. This is certainly the case among French writers (Mounin, 1984).

The decade of 1980s was a period of much interest in culture. It contained continuations of earlier efforts, such as Seelye's updating of his work in 1984 and the anthology edited by Valdes (1986). The latter began with an excerpt on language and thought from the 1911 *Handbook of American Indian Languages* by Franz Boas and grouped writings from the 50s, 60s, and 70s with recent articles. The second edition of Luce and Smith's *Toward internationalism: Readings in cross-cultural communication* appeared in 1986 and The Northeast Conference maintained its tradition of periodically focusing on culture in its 1988 meeting (Singerman, 1988). Brown accorded much importance to culture, specifically culture shock and acculturation, in his methodology textbook (1980 & 1987).

Gail Robinson's *Cross-cultural Understanding* (1985) merits special attention. She sought to extend what she termed the "behaviorist and functionalist" approach to culture, taken by the likes of Nostrand and Seelye, with a "cognitive and symbolic" (pp. 8–12) perspective. She felt that to focus only on observable behaviors and the purported functions of those behaviors was inadequate. She said consideration must be given to what is "inside" the minds of the members of a culture. This is the notion of culture as world view; ethnography is the method she recommends for studying it. Robinson also drew from symbolic anthropology: "culture ... is a dynamic system — an ongoing, dialectic process, giving rise to symbols which may be viewed historically" (p. 11). These symbols are conceptualizations and communications of meaning. Finally, Robinson raised to the fore of culture teaching a concern for its sociopolitical implications: she listed "justice and kindness" (p. 1) as goals of work. The societal and global benefits of cross-cultural understanding were appreciated by the participants in the MLA's 1953 seminar and by later writers, but many FLEs appear to have been involved in culture teaching primarily out of a motivation to do full justice to the culture's language. Robinson's social priority is shared by some who have already written about culture in the current decade (Ramirez & Hall, 1990).

In 1987 a major contribution to the FLE tradition of reflection on culture was made by Louise Damen in her 400-page *Culture learning: The fifth dimension in the language classroom*. She provided the FLE community with a readable and applicable survey of the fields of linguistics, anthropology, and sociology, psychology, and communication. This was not the original contribution of her book: many FLEs have training in these fields (especially linguistics and anthropology), and are thus aware of what can be garnered from them. It is Damen's inclusion of intercultural communication which is of special note.

Damen sketched the history of intercultural communication. She highlighted the World War II effort, the publication of Edward T. Hall's *The Silent Language* in 1959, and the founding of the Peace Corps. She stressed its eclecticism. In fact, she viewed it as a "filter" for the five disciplines listed above:

> The addition of the intercultural filter through which theoretical concepts and theories from a variety of disciplines and professional practice pass brings added dimension to both theory and practice. (p. 28)

Damen specifically maintained that FLEs can benefit in their practice by using the filter of intercultural communication as they draw from other fields. She included specific suggestions for the classroom implementation of the insights gleaned. She also maintained that "there is a need for professionals in the field of intercultural communication to understand the particular circumstances, problems, and variables at work in the multicultural language classroom" (p. xvi). Damen has thus called for dialogue, and by her book has prepared her FLE colleagues for it; this article, on a much more modest scale, is attempting to similarly prepare the ICE community.

The preceding outline introduces ICEs to the main currents of thought about culture and the principle shapers of that thought within the FLE community. Another summary of this history can be found in Morain (1983). The ways in which FLEs put their thoughts into practice will now be exhibited.

How Foreign Language Educators Teach Culture

Foreign language educators handle the teaching of culture in three ways: through culture and civilization courses, through textbooks, and through classroom activities. The first and second of these ways will be dealt with only briefly because, for reasons which will be given, there is less opportunity for transfer to the inter-cultural class.

At the university level, every foreign language department offers courses which have the words "culture, civilization, or society" in their titles. These courses focus on a specific language group, for example, French, German, or Spanish, and stress the divergences from American culture. For this reason the syllabi from such courses are probably of little benefit to intercultural educators who must treat many cultures at a time. Textbooks are likewise discounted because of their bidirectional rather than multidirectional nature. However, those books, such as *Poco a poco* (published by Heinle & Heinle), which provide cultural information in sidebars and in English, can perhaps be mined for vignettes.

Classroom activities are the third way in which culture is taught in foreign language courses. The room itself is important:

> Every foreign language classroom should be a "cultural island," alive with colorful posters and pictures. ... A bulletin board is useful for posting current events, advertisements, comic strips, cartoons, and other items of interest ... A map of the foreign country and a wall calendar on which students could mark the foreign holidays also belong in every foreign language classroom (Hendon, 1980, p. 197).

If, in the following discussion, the reader encounters techniques which seem familiar, he or she is cautioned not to dismiss them for lack of originality. Rather, the reader should reflect that no method or technique has an existence apart from the context in which it is employed.

> ... a technique, like all behavior, is not some*thing*. It is not a static, formalized object or condition. Rather, it is an instance, a realization of potential, the particular manifestation of our ability to select, from a bundle of options, that piece of behavior which we believe will work, given our formal training, our experience, and the prevailing conditions (Clark, 1984, p. 583).

Intercultural educators should seek out their colleagues in foreign languages so that they can compare notes on the implementation of the techniques which they both employ.

Seelye's books (1974 & 1984) are the most complete sources of classroom suggestions for culture teaching in the foreign language teaching community. They set the pattern for later writers (notably Lafayette, 1978 and Damen, 1987) and have much visibility because they are published in conjunction with a major professional organization, the American Council on the Teaching of Foreign Languages (ACTFL). All of the techniques which Seelye lists are tied to his seven goals of cultural instruction (see Appendix).

Seelye gives much space to the Cultural Assimilator, a technique which he notes was developed by social psychologists (Fiedler, Mitchell, & Triandis) and which is an example of a technique which intercultural educators share. This prominence is justified because it is "the approach to training that has been subjected to the most and to the best research" (Brislin, *et al.*, 1986, p. 25). Lafayette (1978) also includes the Cultural Assimilator, and further follows Seelye in commending Minidrama. This technique goes a step beyond the critical incident technique of the Cultural Assimilator. In Minidrama the students stage a problem so as to be emotionally, not only intellectually, involved in its resolution. A goal is for the participants to realize that "this could happen to me too" (Seelye, 1974, p. 92). Skits involve dialogue, a hoary practice in foreign language teaching which gives students speaking practice, so they are using the language while learning the culture.

Seelye and Lafayette both list the Cultural Capsule. Seelye attributes its origin to a foreign language teacher, Darrel Taylor, who collaborated with an anthropologist, John Sorenson. A Culture Capsule is a brief oral or written explanation, prepared by a teacher or a student, of one minimal difference between two cultures. It is normally accompanied by photos or other realia. Seelye gives an example of a "French Bread" capsule which involves an activity: the students taste what they have been studying! After the presentation and activity, the students answer content-related questions. This last activity is not to be considered optional if one follows the contention of Lafayette that culture, because it is important enough to be taught, merits to be tested as well.

Culture Clusters are three or four Capsules combined into a simulation or skit. This is analogous to tying together critical incidents into a mini-drama as was mentioned above. The assumption is also the same: the students will learn best by being involved in creating a cultural situation. The procedure is as follows. Each capsule is presented on a separate day. The culmination is the skit in which the teacher acts as the narrator who guides the students' action and speech. Seelye's example of a Culture Cluster is a family meal in France. The first cluster has to do with setting the table, the second concerns table etiquette, and the third is a presentation of the role of meals in French family life.

Seelye lists several other techniques under the rubric of "Asking the Right Questions." His goal is to get the students to be observers of culture, and from their observations to generate hypotheses and "hazard productive guesses" (p. 124). Seelye advocates using "the exotic as springboard":

> Culturally contrastive patterns can best be exploited for their motivating interest by using them as *points of entry* (emphasis added) into the target culture. Once inside, the student should be helped to discover that even seemingly bizarre behavior makes perfect sense once it is seen within the context of the rest of the culture (p. 121).

This discovery and open-ended approach of Seelye's is congenial with Robinson's later emphasis on the dynamism inherent in cultures and on the necessity of viewing cultures from the inside.

The food examples which Seelye used to illustrate Culture Capsules and Clusters are contained within Robinson's eight multi-sensory modes of culture transmission: (1) emotion, (2) sound, (3) space, (4) time, (5) body movement and dance, (6) touch, (7) taste, foods and food sharing, and (8) aesthetics and visual adornment. She prefaced her suggestions of using these modes in teaching culture by acknowledging that "experimental education" is often looked on askance in higher education. She chose to "risk pointing out the obvious to underscore the academic soundness of using different sensory modes in transmitting cultural learnings" (p. 27).

Robinson's advocacy of multisensory means to teach culture provides a transition to the consideration of the use of technology.

Teaching Culture with Technology

To augment their classroom activity, FLEs have many commercial resources available to them, and there are promising ones in development.

Culture Capsules are available on audiocassette from the Audio Forum in Guillford, Connecticut. Tapes are available for major culture/language groups such as Chinese, French, German, Italian, Japanese, and Spanish. All are in English and may be considered "crash courses" in culture for eventual travelers. The ICE could perhaps extract portions, such as the treatments of greetings, to illustrate points of contrast between American culture and these others.

Video is being used increasingly in foreign language teaching. It is often justified because of the ability of the visual medium to present language in its cultural context. A notable example is the popular *French in Action* series which was produced with major support from the Annenberg/CPB project. Since 1982 the Project for International Communications Studies at the University of Iowa has been collecting "authentic" video material; that is, commercials, newscasts, documentaries, sitcoms, etc. which were not produced for the purpose of language teaching. Enough material to fill 16 videodiscs has been amassed and interactive software has been developed to allow learners to explore it. Other universities are putting together interactive video materials thanks in part to support from IBM (Horwitz, 1991). For the Apple environment there is *A la rencontre de Philippe* developed by the Athena Project at MIT and *In the French Body* and *In the German Body* from the University of Massachusetts at Boston. The latter programs are unique in their focus on proxemics.

Computers are being used increasingly to teach foreign languages. Many software packages attempt to teach cultural points as well as features of the language (see LaReau & Vockell, 1989, for examples). One promising computer application is telecommunications. Hammadou (1991) has conducted preliminary research with students using France's videotext network called *Télétel* (also known as *Minitel*). This popular network has attracted the attention of mass communication researchers in this country (Miller, 1986) because of its impact on French society. When students access such a network, they are doing what millions of French people do everyday. This supports the claim of Hammadou and others (Challe, 1989) that telecommunications is a way to transmit "up-to-date cultural information" (Hammadou, 1991, p. 7). Telecommunications can also facilitate the common practice of having "pen pals" in a foreign country. Both the American Association of Teachers of French and the American

Council on the Teaching of Foreign Languages have conducted workshops to train teachers to use *Minitel*.

The evolution of dictionaries, vital tools for language learners and teachers alike, is another promising development. Lado (1964) foresaw a role for dictionaries in culture teaching:

> A very comprehensive dictionary collecting ... words and phrases and including also idioms, proverbs, names of heroes, well-known legends and stories, heroic deeds, beliefs, etc., would be in fact an excellent index to a culture. Such a collection coupled with a systematic analysis of the structure of a culture would constitute a most complete codification of its content (pp. 23-24).

There has also been recent interest in increasing the dictionary's treatment of culture as a means of elucidating vocabulary, especially "fixed expressions" ... which "can be culturally opaque or transparent depending on the degree of cultural knowledge a learner needs to draw upon for purposes of decoding" (Bool & Carter, 1989, p. 174). To do so would require extensive notes, but space is not an issue with computer-based dictionaries, many of which are appearing (Wooldridge, 1991). It may be that Lado's vision of a comprehensive treatment of culture will become a reality in expanded, electronic versions of conventional dictionaries rather than in new works. Wyatt (1989) foresees a great boon to reading coming from such online annotation: it could delineate the "culturally determined schema" (p. 68) in online passages.

Conclusions

FLEs and ICEs belong to different paradigms (Thomas Kuhn's sense): we are in different departments, we read different journals, and we belong to different professional associations. Yet we have a common interest in the teaching of culture, and as this paper has shown, we use some of the same classroom techniques in our work, and we tap some of the same sources for theoretical insights (e.g. cultural anthropology and social psychology). Moreover, we are quite likely to bump into each other in the library because many of the books in our two fields are at the beginning of the Ps in the Library of Congress system! Thus, it would appear that there is much basis for a professional dialogue. Many FLEs who have written about culture (Nostrand, 1956; Edgerton, 1972; Robinson, 1985; Damen, 1987) have stressed the need for interdisciplinary cooperation, so ICEs who approach their FLE colleagues will most likely get a friendly response.

At a minimum we can swap classroom experiences. At a higher level there is room for cooperation in attempting to better understand the function of fixed expressions, which were mentioned in the previous section. Language teachers are grappling with how to properly teach stock idioms and other "frozen patterns used to direct the flow of conversation and often, additionally, to mark the speaker's attitude to an interlocutor or to earlier remarks" (Cowie, 1989, p. 204). FLEs can provide their ICE colleagues with many examples of these. The latter can perhaps apply the theoretical base and terminology of interpersonal communication to help the FLE better understand the function of such expressions and what they reveal about a culture. Fixed expressions relating to requests and apologies are already the focus of crossdisciplinary inquiry (Blum-Kulka, House, & Kasper, 1989).

A common focus on language by FLEs and ICEs is natural. Some language items are epitomes, crystallizations of the values of a culture (e.g., *amae*, *sempai*, and *kohai* in Japanese) (Doi, 1973; Nakane, 1970) This is the "they have a word for it" phenomenon. We demonstrate respect for other cultures by attempting to understand them through their own terms. It will be a good learning experience for our students to wrestle with the difficulty of translating foreign expressions (Kohls, 1979). Moreover, by focusing on language, we will return to our common roots. Edward T. Hall, who has been influential in both FLE and ICE circles, said in his seminal *The Silent Language* that he, as a researcher of culture, wanted to emulate the "dramatic progress ... of linguistic science" (p. 61) and make it possible to "teach each cultural situation in much the same way that language is taught" (p. 50).

Final Note

The author is a member of the FLE community who has been greatly helped in his work by insights emanating from the ICE community. This paper is his humble contribution to the dialogue between the two communities which Damen has espoused:

> It is time to build two-way, multi-lane bridges of interchange so that professionals in intercultural communication and in second or foreign language learning may combine forces to their mutual benefit and to the ultimate advantage of their students. Together they may profitably explore the multifaceted concepts of language and culture and their roles in human interaction. Their combined efforts should enhance research and practice in both fields. (p. xvii)

References

Blum-Kulka, S., J. House & G. Kasper. (1989). Investigating cross-cultural pragmatics: an introductory overview. In S. Blum-Kulka, J. House, & G. Kasper (Eds.) *Cross-cultural Pragmatics: Requests and Apologies* (pp. 1–34). Norwood, NJ: Ablex.

Bool, H. & R. Carter. (1989). Vocabulary, culture, and the dictionary. In M. L.

Tickoo (Ed.) *Learner's Dictionaries: State of the Art* (pp. 172–181). Singapore: SEAMEO Regional Language Centre.

Brislin, R. W., K. Cushner, C. Cherrie & M. Yong. (1986). *Intercultural Interactions: A Practical Guide*. Beverly Hills: Sage.

Brooks, N. (1968). Teaching culture in the foreign language classroom. *Foreign Language Annals, 1*, 204–217.

Brooks, N. (1975). The analysis of foreign and familiar cultures. In R. C. Lafayette (Ed.) *The Culture Revolution in Foreign Language Teaching* (pp. 19–31). Skokie, Ill: National Textbook Company.

Brown, H. D. (1980). *Principles of Language Learning and Teaching*. Englewood Cliffs, NJ: Prentice Hall. Second edition appeared in 1987.

Challe, O. (1989) Le minitel: la télématique à la Française. *The French Review, 62*, 843–856.

Clarke, M. A. (1984). On the nature of technique: What do we owe the gurus? *TESOL Quarterly, 18*, 577–594.

Cowie, A. P. (1989). Pedagogical description of language: Lexis. *Annual Review of Applied Linguistics, 10*, 196–209.

Damen, L. (1987). *Culture Learning: The Fifth Dimension in the Language Classroom*. Reading, MA: Addison-Wesley.

Dodd, C. H. (1987). *Dynamics of Intercultural Communication*. Dubuque, IA: Wm. C. Brown.

Doi, T. (1973). *The Anatomy of Dependence*. New York: Kodansha.

Edgerton, M. F. (1972). Preface. In J. W. Dodge (Ed.) *Other Words, Other Worlds: Language-in-culture* (pp. 10–11). Montpelier, VT: Northeast Conference on the Teaching of Foreign Languages.

Fiedler, F. E., T. Mitchell, and H. C. Triandis, (1971) The Culture assimilator: An approach to cross-cultural training. *Journal of Applied Psychology, 55*, 95–102.

Fries, C. C. (1955). American linguistics and the teaching of English. *Language Learning, 6*, 1–22.

Galisson, R. (1984). Pour un dictionnaire des mots de la culture populaire. *Le Français Dans Le Monde, 24*, 57–63.

Hall, E. T. (1959). *The Silent Language*. Garden City, NY: Doubleday.

Hammadou, J. (1991). Student interaction with Minitel telecommunications. *IALL Journal, 24*, 7–18.

Hendon, U. S. (1980). Introducing culture in the high school foreign language class. *Foreign Language Annals, 13*, 191–198.

Horwitz, D. S. (1991). Merging technologies. *Didactic Review, 3*, 4–5.

Kelly, L. G. (1969). *25 Centuries of Language Teaching*. Rowley, MA: Newbury House.

Kohls, L. R. (1979). *Survival Kit for Overseas Living*. Chicago: Intercultural Press.

Lado, R. (1964). *Language teaching: A scientific approach*. New York: MaGraw-Hill.

Lafayette, R. C. (1975). *The Culture Revolution in Foreign Language Teaching*. Skokie, Ill: National Textbook Company.

Lafayette, R. C. (1978). *Teaching Culture: Strategies and Techniques*. Arlington, VA: Center for Applied Linguistics.

LaReau, P. & Vockell, E. (1989). *The Computer in the Foreign Language Curriculum*. Santa Cruz: Mitchell.

Luce, L. F. & E. C. Smith (1979). *Toward Internationalism: Readings in Cross-cultural Communication*. Cambridge, MA: Newbury House. 2nd ed. 1986.

Miller, J. (1986). France confronts the new media: Issues in national communications and cultural policy. In S. Thomas (ed.) *Communication and Culture: Language, Performance, Technology, and Media: Selected Proceedings from the Sixth International Conference on Culture and Communication* (pp. 325–341). Norwood, NJ: Ablex.

Morain, G. (1983). Commitment to the teaching of foreign cultures. *Modern Language Journal, 67*, 403–412.

Mounin, G. (1984). Sens et place de la civilisation dans l'enseignement des langues. *Le français dans le monde, 24*, 34–36.

Nakane, C. (1970). *Japanese Society*. Berkeley: University of California Press.

Nostrand, H. L. (1956). On teaching a foreign culture. *Modern Language Journal, 40*, 297–301.

Nostrand, H. L. (1978). The 'emergent model' applied to contemporary France. *Contemporary French Civilization, 2*, 277–294.

Ramirez, A. G. & J. K. Hall. (1990). Language and culture in secondary level Spanish textbooks. *Modern Language Journal, 74*, 48–65.

Rivers, W. (1968). *Teaching Foreign Languages*. Chicago: University of Chicago Press.

Robinson, G. L. N. (1985). *Crosscultural Understanding*. New York: Pergamon Press.

Seelye, H. N. (1974). *Teaching Culture: Strategies for Foreign Language Educators*. Skokie, Ill: National Textbook Company. [Updated in 1984]

Singerman, A. J. (1988). *Toward a New Integration of Language and Culture*. Middlebury, VT: Northeast Conference on the teaching of foreign languages

Valdes, J. M. (1986). *Culture Bound: Bridging the Cultural Gap in Language Teaching*. Cambridge: Cambridge University Press.

Wooldridge, R. (1991). List of electronic dictionaries. *ACH Newsletter, 13*, 1; 4.

Wyatt, D. H. (1989). Computers and reading skills: the medium and the message. In M. C. Pennington (Ed.) *Teaching languages with computers: The state of the art* (pp. 63–78). La Jolla, CA: Athelstan.

Appendix

H. Ned Seelye's seven goals of cultural instruction (1974, pp. 39–45)

1. **The sense, or Functionality, of Culturally Conditioned Behavior:**
   The student should demonstrate an understanding that people act the way they do because they are using options the society allows for satisfying basic physical and psychological needs.

2. **Integration of Language and Social Variables:**
   The student should demonstrate an understanding that such social variables as age, sex, social class, and place of residence affect the way people speak and behave.

3. **Conventional Behavior in Common Situations:**
   The student should indicate an ability to demonstrate how people conventionally act in the most common mundane and crisis situations in the target culture.

4. **Cultural Connotations of Words and Phrases:**
   The student should indicate an awareness that culturally conditioned images are associated with even the most common target words and phrases.

5. **Evaluating Statements about a Society:**
   The student should demonstrate the ability to evaluate the relative strength of a generality concerning the target culture in terms of the amount of evidence substantiating the statement.

6. **Researching Another Culture:**
   The student should show that he has developed the skills needed to locate and organize information about the target culture from the library, the mass media, people, and personal observation.

7. **Attitudes toward Other Cultures:**
   The student should demonstrate intellectual curiosity about the target culture and empathy toward its people.

后　　记

　　几年前,为纪念中国跨文化交际学会(CAFIC)与美国的国际跨文化交际学会(ICICS)多年的密切合作,笔者向上海外语教育出版社建议出版一套近年来国内外学者跨东西方文化交际研究的文集。这一构想得到了出版社领导的首肯,也得到了当时国际学会主席美国三一大学 Bates Hoffer 博士和著名学者日本青山学院大学 Nobuyuki Honna 教授的积极响应。从获悉文集出版的构思伊始,一些中外学者就给予了有力支持。之后的两年中,文集编辑组成立,中外几位编者协同商议,选定各篇文字,形成了《跨文化交际:东西方对话》这部中外同仁的研究成果汇编。

　　本文集收录了 31 篇论文,作者分别来自美国、日本、德国、俄罗斯、英国、中国等多个国家以及我国香港特别行政区,入编的论文多数是近年来发表在国际跨文化交际学会会刊《跨文化交际研究》(*Intercultural Communication Studies*)的论文,几乎涵盖了 21 世纪初该领域研究的方方面面。

　　北京外国语大学胡文仲教授在调查研究的基础上,对我国跨文化交际领域近年来的研究做了较为全面的总结,不仅肯定了我国此领域研究取得的进步,而且指出无论在内容还是方法上,我国学者的研究都在与国际主流研究日益靠近。美国三一大学 L. Brooks Hill 博士提出了新的理论框架,并预测了研究的发展趋势;路易斯维尔大学 Robert N. St. Clair 博士对当前研究的热门话题"文化空间"(或称"第三文化",即不同文化相互跨越彼此边界,相互兼容之动态现象)进行了精辟的论析。德国雷根斯堡大学 Alexander Thomas 博士和美国罗德岛大学陈国明教授分别探讨的德国人在与中国伙伴商业谈判中如何协商对话与不同组织结构文化之冲突的管理研究,有很高的理论和实践价值。香港城市大学 Ron Scollon 博士和香港浸会大学陈凌博士关于社会身份、话语认同以及文化认同等当前热点话题的新思维是该领域研究的一个突破。Nobuyuki Honna 教授从社会语言学的视角,指出英语是亚洲通用语,而且具有文化多元性;他主张把英语当作具有多元文化性的通用语开展教学,这是很有前瞻性的创意。哈尔滨工业大学贾玉新教授也从社会语言学的视角探讨了语言使用的多样性和相对性,提出了一个语用学研究的跨文化视角。Bates Hoffer 教授关于非言语行为的实证研究,也为我们开辟了一个新的视域。本文集还涉及跨文化研究与外语教学的关系,北京外国语大学孙有中教授对教育家杜威博士的理论讨论,对跨文化研究和教学颇有启迪;哈尔滨工业大学宋莉教授关于跨文化交际能力与教学的论述,很有新意,对教学无疑有指导意义。可见,中外专家学者对跨文化交际研究从不同角度进行了多方面的探讨,较充分地反映出中外学者们的真知灼见,展现了东西方文化交流对话的结晶。

当然,在编写本文集的过程中也有一些遗憾,诸如美国加州州立大学富勒顿分校教授 William B. Gudykunst 博士、俄克拉荷马大学教授 Young Yun Kim 博士等国际著名学者以及我们的朋友、成就斐然的上海外国语大学跨文化研究中心教授 Steve Kulich(顾力行)博士的文章,出于种种原因均未能收入。对此,我们谨向他们以及他们的读者深表歉意。

令人备受鼓舞的是,我国跨文化交际研究的事业方兴未艾,越来越多的青年学人不断加盟到这一队伍之中。人们已经意识到,在"地球村"概念越来越真实的21世纪,"跨文化交际能力"既是构建跨文化身份与全球和谐社会的精气神所在,也是保障这一社会活动的终极资本;年青一代肩负着跨越文化边界、超越自我、超越对立,并最终实现人类社会和谐大同的责任和义务。

同时,我们必须意识到,跨文化交际研究仍然任重而道远,尤其在建构具有中华民族特色、有助于弘扬中华文明的研究理论方面,仍可大有作为。我国博大精深的文化传统是21世纪构建和谐社会的重要源泉,是培养具有跨文化交际能力之"跨文化人"的基石。笔者十分欣赏当代儒家代表杜维明先生关于儒家人文精神的概述:儒家人文精神不是一般道德意义上的人,而是由人的感性、觉情之美学、道德规约之伦理以及信仰的宗教价值组成的人文精神[1]。笔者坚信,倡导儒家"仁者与天地万物为一体"之"人类宇宙"的世界观,是我们建构具有自己文化特色的跨文化交际理论的非常有价值的思想源泉。实际上,如果缺乏对儒家人文精神的深刻认识,并把其当作宝贵资源,任何跨文化交际理论都可能有失完整。倡导"万物并育而不相害,道并行而不相悖"的最高理想的儒家思想,是对以"启蒙心态"为核心的"人类中心"世界观之缺失及其对人类社会和大自然造成严重后果的反思和批判,这已为现代以及当下很多中外学者所意识到。

笔者深信,东西方对话需要"互为主观"、"互相参照"[2],需要以他人为镜反观自身,从而使我们重新发现自身文化价值,同时促进不同文化间的相互学习与合作。笔者还认为,具有文化多元化的全球化心态,是"跨文化人"身份建

---

[1] 见北京大学高等人文研究院院长、美国哈佛大学教授、哈佛—燕京学社社长杜维明教授的《儒家传统与文明对话》(河北人民出版社)2006年版第11页。
[2] 见汤一介先生《新轴心时代与中国文化的建构》(江西人民出版社)2006年版第2页。

构的基本条件,也是儒家"人类宇宙"世界观①视野下无止境的"学习成为[完备]人"的过程中不可或缺的阶段;跨文化身份是自我品格在质和量方面的变化和提升,它不是对国民身份的取代,而是自我与家庭、社会以及国家认同的延伸、扩展和丰富。笔者相信,培养具有现代意识的"一体之仁"的跨文化人应成为未来的跨文化交际研究的重要目标和途径。

借此机会,我们谨对上海外语教育出版社的大力支持表示诚挚的谢意,策划编辑梁晓莉女士给了我们很多具体的指导,文字编辑李健儿先生给我们提了许多宝贵的建设性意见,我们一并表示深深的感谢。

贾玉新
2013 年 10 月 5 日

---

① 见杜维明论文《连接东方与西方》(Joining the East and West),载《哈佛国际评论》(*Harvard International Review*)1998 年刊第 48 页。